anglistik & englischunterricht

English Via Various Media

Hans-Jürgen Diller · Erwin Otto
Gerd Stratmann (Hrsg.)

anglistik & englischunterricht

Band 62

English Via Various Media

UNIVERSITÄTSVERLAG C. WINTER
HEIDELBERG

English Via Various Media

Frau Anne-Marie Simon-Vandenbergen
ist mitverantwortliche Gastherausgeberin für Sektion I News Paper

UNIVERSITÄTSVERLAG C. WINTER
HEIDELBERG

Die Deutsche Bibliothek – CIP-Einheitsaufnahme

Anglistik & Englischunterricht: A & E. – Heidelberg: Winter.
Früher Schriftenreihe
ISSN 0014-2328
Bd. 62. English Via Various Media. – 1999

English Via Various Media / [Hrsg.: Hans-Jürgen Diller ...] – Heidelberg: Winter, 1999
(Anglistik & Englischunterricht; Bd. 62)
ISBN 3-8253-0884-7

Herausgeber:
Prof. Dr. Hans-Jürgen Diller
Dr. Erwin Otto · Prof. Dr. Gerd Stratmann

Redaktionsassistentin: Sandra Graßhoff

ISBN 3-8253-0884-7
ISSN 0344-8266

Anschrift der Redaktion:
Sandra Graßhoff, Ruhr-Universität Bochum, Englisches Seminar
Universitätsstraße 150 · 44801 Bochum

Imprimé en Allemagne. Printed in Germany
Satz: OLD-Satz digital, Neckarsteinach
Druck: Strauss Offsetdruck, Mörlenbach

Inhalt

III. Film

IV. ... notabene: the book

Rubrik

Hans-Jürgen Diller, Bochum

Introduction

The title of this volume may strike readers as somewhat arch. It has a history which ought to be explained. The present volume of *a&e* was originally planned as two. The first was to be filled with a selection of the proceedings of the Section "Newspapers in English", which met at the Fourth Conference of the European Society for the Study of English (Debrecen, Hungary, 5-9 September, 1997). Since "Newspapers in English" is a topic that in spite of its undoubted importance has only a fairly restricted number of researchers nationally, a European range of contributors seemed the ideal solution. It was this idea that prompted Anne-Marie Simon-Vandenbergen (Ghent) and myself to jointly convene a section at Debrecen, and the Euro-wide response justified our expectations. The section was one of the largest in Debrecen, even though we had to disappoint a number of intending participants. We are proud of the often innovative and distinguished contributions that we have been able to recruit for this volume, and we remember with gratitude the stimulating discussions we enjoyed at the conference. We also have to thank my fellow-editors of *a&e* for an opportunity to publish the papers comparatively soon after the conference.

The second volume planned for 1998, on "Media Old and New in Teaching and Research", was intended as a counterpoint to the first. In contrast to the printed newspaper, its emphasis was to be on the electronic media and their role in teaching as well as in research and the practical work of the translator. While working on the two volumes we became increasingly aware that both would be ready for publication at about the same time and that the borderline between the newspaper and the electronic media has in fact become much fuzzier than we had realized at the beginning (cf. the contributions by Hundt, Rademann and Sand, below). So we felt that it would be preferable to publish all the papers between two covers.

I. Newspapers in English

The topic of the conference section was nothing more specific than "Newspapers in English", and there was no plan to emphasize teaching over research. Nevertheless, there soon appeared at least two pervasive strands running through the papers which provided an unsought unity. The first strand is a surprisingly strong interest in historical problems, which suggests that newspapers, which are increasingly becoming available in computer-readable form, may develop into a major source for a new social history of English. The other strand shows in an equally astonishing number of analyses that are indebted, strictly or loosely, to approaches familiar from literary studies. The rift that we have all learnt to deplore (and accept) as dividing our discipline may not be so final after all. Equally heartening was the recurrent experience of the chance, but also the challenge, that newspaper texts present to the teaching of the language in its various contexts.

Friedrich **Ungerer** (Rostock) takes an entirely fresh look at newspapers. While it has long been the done thing for linguists to refer to the inner diversity of "Newspaper English", that diversity itself has rarely been the focus of their attention. With his concept of "text ensemble" Ungerer seems to be the first to take seriously the truism that a newspaper is more than just an unordered accumulation of texts. He describes in detail the methodology that enables him to describe what we might call the "rich harmony" or "monotony", as the case may be, of four text ensembles. Although he modestly calls his contribution a "first step", one important result is visible even now: that the "quality papers" with their comparatively low circulations are considerably more diverse than the mass-circulation "populars". This discovery might commend the broadsheets to those who would like to teach a wide range of text types and communicative purposes.

Ungerer's paper has grown out of a long-term project on the history of "Newspaper English" which is also researched by Kristina **Schneider** (Rostock). Her paper, which describes the principles that have guided the design of the Rostock corpus, stresses above all the need for socio-stylistic stratification. It appears that "popular journalism", which for most of us was born with Alfred Harmsworth's (later Lord Northcliffe's) *Daily Mail* in 1896, is a much older phenomenon. If that view gains acceptance, the social history of English is going to look rather different indeed.

Another historical study, with a narrower focus, is presented by Rolf **Herwig** (Jena), who uses the CD-ROM "Changing Times" (a historical cross-section of more than 200 years of *The Times*) for a diachronic study of English war reportage. The rise, development and perhaps disappearance of newspaper text types is yet another way in which the study of newspaper English can enhance our understanding of the language's history.

A short span of time is covered in the papers by Mike **Reynolds** & Giovanna **Cascio** (Sheffield) and Marianne **Hundt** (Freiburg). Reynolds/Cascio again assume a low-level focus, pursuing the spread of contractions in one provincial and two national dailies through various genres over two decades. Both genre and "audience design" are shown to contribute to the observed trend. A continuation of this study on a year-to-year basis would be of the greatest interest as it might show both continuities and discontinuities in the development, thus linking the style of the paper to its economic fortunes.

Hundt reports on the importance of press texts in the framework of a larger project. At Freiburg they are "cloning" the now classic one-million-word computer corpora of 1960s English, the Brown Corpus of written (printed) Standard American English and the London-Oslo/Bergen Corpus of its British counterpart (see also Sand below, Section II). "Frown" and "FLOB" replicate as exactly as possible the composition of these corpora in 1990s English in order to study micro-historical language changes. The press sections were among the first to be completed, which offers a fine opportunity for detailed study of the press as a channel of American influence on British English. Hundt also gives careful thought to the sort of information that may be reliably gathered from copora of this size. For many recent changes, such as the spread of contractions, *help* + infinitive, or the *'s*-genitive, an American origin seems likely. These findings ought to affect the notion of correctness on which we base the teaching of English and, more specifically, the marking of our students' essays.

While the historical papers belong to linguistics *sensu stricto*, many of the synchronic papers in this section show an interesting kinship with literary studies. This is most impressive in the article by Mick **Short,** Elena **Semino** and Martin **Wynne** (Lancaster), who analyse the presentation of speech in newspaper reports. The approach extends and adapts a concept for the analysis of *Erlebte Rede* ("Free Indirect Speech") and similar phenomena which was first proposed by Mick Short and Geoffrey Leech in *Style in Fiction* (London and New York: Longman, 1981). The discovery in journalism of language uses that are conventionally regarded as literary is a fascinating and intriguing process. Although few literary scholars are likely to hang on to the Russian Formalists' notion of a separate "language of literature", our teaching practice still draws a pretty thick borderline between *literarische Texte* and *Gebrauchstexte.* Concrete, specific observations like those by Short and his team may help us to see the difference less dogmatically and the borderline as less impenetrable. And the influences may not even be in only one direction: conventionally we see literature as adapting, "aestheticizing" or "autonomizing" the language of other fields. But here it seems quite possible that the techniques of fiction are now influencing journalism. There is massive food for thought here.

Similarly, Karsten **Pedersen** (Copenhagen) applies the Bakhtinian concept of polyphony to the study of newspaper texts. Like Short and his associates, he reminds us that the "facts" reported by the media are largely speeches, which makes the audibility of one "voice" through another a necessity. His paper is an engaging example of European cross-fertilization: on the one hand, he is fully aware that the Anglo-Saxon linguistic tradition is ill equipped to study subjectivity, on the other he is committed to that tradition in his close study of telling details. Modal auxiliaries, the conjunction *but* and the choice of speech-act verbs function as the *locus* of polyphony and multi-layered subjectivity.

While Pedersen emphasizes the audibility of one voice through another, Geert **Jacobs** (Antwerp) reveals the all-too-frequent use of press releases, whose intended effect is, rather, the drowning of one voice in another. Press releases are handed out by public relations experts to ensure their clients a desirable image in the media. Often welcomed by overworked reporters as a help in their story-writing, the releases are also a temptation for them to abdicate their responsibilities of mediating and evaluating. Their effect is hard to assess, but the sameness of the "hard" news sections of many papers gives a hint of their pervasive presence. Press releases are hard to come by, but Jacobs is able to give us one example, which shows how even the minute details of pronouns and other deictics are being pre-fabricated.

Michael **White** (Madrid) uses the story of the conflict between the British government and the Bundesbank in 1992 to illustrate the usefulness, even indispensibility, of the concept of metaphor in the analysis of news texts. The question whether a metaphor is a journalistic ornament or a linguistic necessity has to be decided in each case individually. Here, too, a study of newspapers along with literary texts may be rewarding. Newspapers may even be the best material to demonstrate the by now generally accepted omnipresence of metaphor in "ordinary", "non-literary" language use.

Torben **Vestergaard's** (Aalborg) paper deals with a grammatical structure which should be particularly interesting to German readers because it seems to be far less common in their language than in English. The "Free Adjunct", especially the adjunct participle, has a wide range of meanings; Vestergaard indicates ways of distinguishing and decoding them. Moreover, he discusses at some length the reasons for its popularity in journalism, its usefulness in factual writing, but also the traps it lays for the hurried writer.

Evelina **Graur** (Suceava) investigates the interface between editorial matter and advertising, demonstrating the linguistic consequences of editorial responsibility even for advertising copy. Where the rest of this section takes the delimitation, though not the characterization, of newspaper English for granted, Graur reminds us that even this sub-language has its fuzzy edges.

II. Electronic tools and texts

Although Tobias **Rademann's** (Bochum) paper was also read at Debrecen, it has been included in Section II of this volume, since it discusses newspapers in the shape of electronic tools. With an increasing number of schools going "ans Netz", the reading of on-line newspapers written in English from all over the world (as opposed to just Britain) adds a new, global dimension to *Landeskunde* which deserves to be brought to the attention of teachers, students and pupils. But the pitfalls are many. Above all, intending users must be warned that an electronic paper may not necessarily be an exact replica of its printed version. On the other hand, the opportunities of information retrieval and combination which the new medium offers are so enormous that it would be frivolous to disregard them. There cannot be many places where preparation for the 21st century is as urgent as here.

The use of the Internet in teaching is also the subject of Helmut **Brammerts'** paper. He draws on experience gathered in several years of international cooperation to report on progress in an "autonomous learning" project known as the "Tandem" project, which links students from several continents. The advantages of the new learning method can hardly be overestimated, if it is regarded as a supplement rather than a substitute for more conventional "heteronomous", teacher-guided language learning. Basically, the "tandem partner" is but an adaptation of the pen-friend of the nineteen-fifties or even the inter-war years to the technology of the nineteen-nineties. But anyone who has experienced the ease and speed of email correspondence will appreciate that the new medium generates a spontaneity of expression which was seldom reached in the old ink-and-paper letter. But Brammerts is careful to show how much organizational detail and how much caretaking behind the scenes is necessary to enable the autonomy of the new learning method. The practical tips in his article, including WWW addresses, will be welcome to teachers planning similar tandems. The goal of the Tandem project is above all to create language fluency and confidence; it is less oriented towards traditional, rigorously defined, item-based learning objectives.

These latter are the concern of Helmuth **Küffner** (FernUniversität Hagen) and Dieter **Wessels** (Bochum), who report on the use of the computer in self-training and distance-teaching. Küffner illustrates with a few examples, taken from various ESP courses, how the right mix between new and conventional media has to be organized in the case of distance teaching, which he defines as "guided self-teaching". He is careful to stress at the outset that the "personal medium" (traditionally known as the teacher) is by no means made redundant in distance teaching. Wessels, the author of a computer course for Business English, offers a critical survey of a large number of marketable courses which should convey a first picture to intending users.

In a second article, Tobias **Rademann** (Bochum) demonstrates with a few simple examples how electronic sources can be used in translation classes or rather in the homework for such classes. Netsurfing and browsing provide not only an unprecedented quantity of texts, the search engines and routines that are available today make it easy to find translation equivalents for phrases of quite recent origin. One of his most telling examples is perhaps a headline from the *Frankfurter Allgemeine* which finds its exact equivalent in the same day's *Washington Post.*

The remaining papers in this section are chiefly concerned with computer corpora and data bases as research tools. But Andrea **Sand's** (Freiburg) account could also interest teachers, at university as well as school level. She gives a succinct survey of the still short history of corpora compilation with copious references to both printed and electronic sources, including websites. This rapidly expanding form of language documentation has become highly complex, but also increasingly user-friendly; specialized corpora also attend to the needs of FL teaching. Above all, the size and the sophisticated tagging of the BNC permit searches which open new horizons for sociolinguistics and discourse analysis. For instance, too much research on gender language was previously based on anecdotal and unrepresentative evidence. Now a few keystrokes tell us that women do indeed use an adjective like *lovely* much more frequently than men. When compared with the 100 million words of the British National Corpus (1.3 Gigabytes) or a newspaper on CD-ROM (ca. 450 Megabytes) the early corpora with about 1 million words and 11-12 Megabytes look diminutive, but they still have their merits, some of which were pointed out in connection with Hundt (Section I). The sheer size of BNC-scale corpora makes proofreading impossible; the consequences, if not discovered by chance, can only be guessed.

The by now numerous CD-ROM versions of newspapers offered year by year by Chadwyck-Healey are of course not designed with the linguist's interests in mind. That means that, for instance, function words like *and* or *you* are treated as 'stop words' and are irretrievable by the software provided with the CDs. They are trivial to the ordinary user but intensely interesting to the linguist, who has to spend much time and ingenuity to obtain them.

The use of the computer and of computer-readable text is not the exclusive privilege of the linguists and stylometricians. But while linguists can still, to some extent, construct their own corpora (even the BNC is the product of a consortium of scholars and a commercial publisher) the data required by literary scholars is so vast that they have to rely entirely on the products provided by publishers. Again the leader in the market is Chadwyck-Healey. Fritz-Wilhelm **Neumann** (Erfurt) and Ewald **Mengel** & Carmen **Müller** (Bayreuth) discuss the Full-Text English Poetry Database, Neumann the CD-ROM version, Mengel & Müller the online version. Both also deal briefly with Gutenberg and other non-commercial providers who make a large number of literary texts available without charge, but also without claiming standards of philological accuracy. Neumann has a useful reference which enables readers to gain access to these providers; he also stresses the usefulness of programming skills in the humanitities. According to one voice, Gutenberg is content to offer texts which are "99.9% correct in the eyes of the general reader". (It should be remembered, however, that the FTEPD is also based on older editions that are out of copyright.) Starting with a succinct description of the nature of the FTEPD and of such basic information-retrieval concepts as pattern matching, clusters, and adjacency, Neumann shows how the new technology may enable scholars "to redescribe the broad river of literary history" and to "comprehend the system of literature as a larger entity and not as the individual achievement of a few prominent poets", but he also illustrates with a few telling examples how the results of a computer search, giving a more solid foundation to our general concepts of literary traditions, can enhance our close reading of individual texts.

Mengel & Müller's main emphasis is on LION (LIterature ONline), the Internet version of Chadwyck-Healey's full-text literary databases. After a brief discussion of the numerous tools provided by LION (and not omitting the, for many, prohibitive prices of most of LION's sub-corpora) they describe two applications which illustrate the usefulness of the full-text databases, which in their totality comprise more than 210,000 individual works, from short poems to entire novels. While Neumann is more interested in the "system(s)" of literature (more specifically, poetry) and in intertextuality, Mengel & Müller concentrate on the reflection of "the real world" in literature, for instance on the literary representation of female self-confidence or the impact of science on poetry. These questions, too, can be answered with reference to a breadth of data that has hitherto been inconceivable. The limitation to élite literature (*Höhenkammliteratur*), inconsequentially vilified in the 'sixties and 'seventies, now stands a real chance of being overcome on a methodologically sound basis. That hope presupposes, however, that the researcher is capable of phrasing his or her questions in a way that the computer can "understand". It is not going to do your thinking for you. Both Neumann and Mengel & Müller are concerned with illustrating the format of "computer-understandable" questions that can serve as a reasonable approximation of the researcher's own questions. And the differences between their questions make it clear how essential it is for researchers to have a clear preliminary understanding of the problem they want to investigate. Both articles, by the way, contain references.

The "his or her" in the preceding paragraph was not just a polite bow to political correctness. It seems reasonable to expect that literary gender studies will be among the chief beneficiaries of the electronic literary databases. For long periods, and for obvious political reasons, women have been more represented among the Other Ranks than among the officers of the literary batallions. Their voices are certain to become more audible in the new medium. A particularly interesting example of the insights that are now possible is afforded by Susanne **Schmid** (FU Berlin). In a study of Alpine imagery in eighteenth and nineteenth-century poetry she demonstrates that certain views lately advanced by feminist critics will have to be revised in the face of the broader evidence that she is able to present.

III and IV: Film and Book

Unlike Sections I and II, Sections III and IV are directly concerned with subjects with well-established classroom uses. Section III, unfortunately, is less comprehensive than was originally intended. We regret above all the absence of survey articles on filmed drama and documentary films which we had hoped to include. But we are happy to offer a case study of a filmed novel and particularly one of an early and very special documentary film.

Against the background of a by now vast literature on "novel into film", Jens P. **Becker** (Kiel), illustrates the peculiarities of both media in his exemplary analysis of the transposition of L. P. Hartley's *The Go-Between* by Joseph Losey, not ignoring the characteristic and idiosyncratic losses which the novel underwent in the production of this cult film, which has been described as "an unusually close transcription of a novel in cinematic terms". Losey, who likes to cooperate closely with the novelists whose works he puts on the screen, is seen by Becker as a representative of "eine Art Retro-Kino" which tries to counterpoint the lavish but unimaginative "Kostümfilm".

Ingo **Neubert** (Reutlingen) gives a very full account of *The Chair*, together with a short reference to resources for the analysis of documentaries. But his main concern is the aesthetic and political problematic of the documentary film. *The Chair*, shot in 1962 in 'Direct Cinema' technique, documents lawyer Donald Moore's struggle to avert the execution of his client, Paul Crump. Neubert makes it abundantly clear that, even though it shows events that really happened to a real lawyer and a real prisoner, the film is the director's composition rather than a chunk of reality in the raw. Whereas the shots were taken while the outcome of the struggle was still uncertain, the 'cutting' of the film, the piecing-together of the scenes, had to take place after the event. While the actors and the camera crew don't know the end, the viewers do.

If it is true that the computer won't do your thinking for you, it is equally true that the camera won't do your imagining for you. And since it does do your selecting for you, it will actually limit your imagination. The new media, including film, can easily become a danger if the imaginations that come under their influence are not properly trained or, to use an old-fashioned moral expression, educated.

Since our most traditional medium, the book, has ways of exercising our imagination that are still unrivalled and also indispensible, the editors felt that one article in this volume should be exclusively devoted to it. Bärbel **Mosner** (Bochum) points out that many of the "medial" qualities of the book – easy to pick up, easy to put down, self-determined reception speed, no technology beyond a pencil – continue to be genuine advantages when it comes to internalizing and remembering the wherefore of the medium, i.e. its "message". With proper training, reading offers more possibilities of mental interaction than do the reception processes involving the other media. But while the training in other media is mainly concerned with "skills", which have to develop with changing technologies, reader training is concerned with habits and attitudes which, once developed, have to be maintained and even cultivated. A truly humane use of the new media has to keep its roots in these habits.

By way of conclusion, it is a pleasant duty to thank those who have helped to bring this volume into existence, especially the contributors and Professor Anne-Marie Simon-Vandenbergen (Rijksuniversiteit Gent) as co-editor for Section I. Special thanks are due to Sandra Graßhoff, Stephan Pieper, Christiane Owczarski and Christiane Rumpenhorst of the Englisches Seminar der Ruhr-Universität Bochum who did the proofreading and prepared printable files on the computer. To thank our fellow editors Manfred Beyer and Joachim Kornelius is a sadder duty, since it also means to say good-bye to them in that capacity. Their decision to resign is deeply regretted even though we must respect their reasons. Joachim Kornelius was an editor of *a&e* from its very inception in 1977. There are no words to adequately express what the journal owes to his energy and initiative.

Friedrich Ungerer, Rostock

Newspapers as Text Ensembles

1. Introduction

To approach the main issue of this paper, the concept of text ensemble, in a comparatively straightforward manner we need not dwell on the notion of text as a linguistic unit, but may be satisfied with the naive idea that in the context of newspapers a text is typically a newspaper article – typically, because diagram-like presentations like the weather report, crosswords and other more marginal text types cannot be excluded. Linguistic scruples should be further allayed if we consider that this definition of the newspaper article as the basic text unit is not contradicted by major linguistic text conceptions, e.g. de Beaugrande and Dressler's (1981) standards of textuality. Problems might arise for the description of advertisements, and this is one of the reasons why they will be excluded from our discussion.

Leafing through a couple of newspapers it is clear that they comprise quite a large number of texts. In fact, an average British newspaper contains about 100 editorial texts of more than 10 lines, and quite often the number of texts is much larger. This inevitably raises the question of how the articles of a newspaper fit together, according to what principles they are distributed across the paper, or more generally, how the newspaper is composed as a single whole – if it is.

To tackle these questions the paper will start with a short review of the most obvious organising principle, the classification based on topical sections (such as politics, business or sports) and then go on to discuss alternative organising principles, in particular the notion of network and – my favoured choice – the notion of text ensemble. This will lead to a closer look at the criteria available for the description of text ensembles and the way in which they may be approached. Since the discussion of the individual cases would be too cumbersome, a statistical analysis will be proposed. Data collection and analysis will be exemplified by a pilot project which is based on a sample of four newspapers. The last two sections of this paper will try to coordinate the findings of the pilot analysis, look at possible applications and suggest some improvements and extensions.

2. Newspaper articles and newspaper sections

Classifications according to topics appear to be the most natural ones. In the context of newspapers a topical taxonomy will be a first choice as well, but as it emerges from closer analysis, this soon comes into conflict with competing classifications. Compare Figure 1, which assembles the section headings of three of the newspapers that have been analysed in the pilot project – the fourth newspaper selected for analysis, the *Sun*, does not carry any section headings.

The Guardian (international ed., 4 June 1997)	*The Express* (4 June 1997)	*USA Today* (European ed., 4 June 1997)
News	News	The Nation
Britain	Comment	The World
World news	Feature	Washington
Comment and analysis	World news	Life
Obituaries	Diary	Science
Finance Guardian	Entertainment Express	Editorial Page
Sport news	Your health	Weather Page
	City	Sports
G 2	Education & training	Money
Title Story	The last word	
Wheen's World	Sport (pull-out section)	
Inside Story		
Arts		
Notes & Queries		
Society		
Weather		
TV & radio		

Figure 1: Section headings in three newspapers (The Guardian, The Express, USA Today)

As a short glance at the table shows, the headings do contain topical sections, such as 'world politics' ('world news') and 'national politics' (called 'Britain' in the *Guardian* and 'The Nation' in *USA Today*). Topical sections also include business (labelled 'Finance Guardian', 'City' in the *Express* and 'Money' in *USA Today*) as well as 'science', 'art', 'education and training', 'health', 'weather' and 'sports', and there will be more topical sections if one looks at several issues of the newspapers because some of them are not a daily feature. In addition, there are section headings that are topical only in a rather vague sense; compare 'Society' in the *Guardian* (which covers environmental problems), 'Life' (in *USA Today*), or – the most extreme case – a section called 'The Last Word' (in the *Express*);

this section not only runs to 10 pages, but also assembles such diverse topics as Why-is-it? questions, a personal column, the horoscope, letters to the editor, crosswords and, finally, TV and radio programmes.

Yet cutting across topical distinctions is another typology, the distinction between text types, in particular between 'news' and 'comment' (called 'Editorial Page' in *USA Today*). Other categories used by the newspapers are 'Title Story' and 'Inside Story' (in the *Guardian*), as well as 'Diary' (in the *Express*), the latter definitely a clearer indication of a personal column (Diller 1993:7f) than 'Wheen's World' in the *Guardian.*

What is perhaps more interesting than the competition between categories is the fact that none of the three newspapers adheres slavishly to their self-imposed section structure. Political sections contain business news, business sections contain personal news, the 'Washington' section of *USA Today* includes gossip about the President's favourite songs, not to mention the *Express* where the topical mix is even more widespread. Similarly, commentaries are not restricted to the respective sections, but appear among political news, business news, and, of course, in personal columns and letters to the editor. Some of this confusion is unavoidable because there are articles that seem to permit multiple classification, yet in other cases a more convincing classification than the one provided by the newspapers seems possible. Is this disregard of section structure simply to be put down to negligence or to the pressures of day-to-day journalism? Or does it reflect the journalists' underlying conviction that sections may be good as an organising principle of editorial work or as a rough guide for the reader, but do not really capture the essential ties that hold the newspaper together? Indeed, one might argue that the individual articles are not just united by a classification dominated by one or two major criteria (such as 'topic' and 'text type'), but that they are in fact linked by a host of different ties, which establish a kind of interdependence between the texts. Following a fashionable trend in the neighbouring field of sociolinguistics and other scientific disciplines, this interdependence could be understood in terms of networking, and consequently, a newspaper would have to be regarded as a network of texts.

3. Text networks and text ensembles

Applying the notion of network to a selection of newspaper texts and proceeding in a rather informal way, one might arrive at the diagram contained in Figure 2.

The diagram is based on a selection of texts from the *Express* of June 4, 1997. Since the articles are identified by their headlines, preference has been given to texts whose headlines are more or less self-explanatory.

Explanations:
Articles are represented by boxes and identified by their headlines,
the numbers refer to their position in the newspaper.
Links between the articles are indicated by connecting lines,
bold lines indicate multiple links

Figure 2: Excerpt from the text network of The Express *of June 4, 1997*

Complex as it may appear at first sight, the diagram does in fact represent an extreme simplification of a text network. The only variables used are 'text type', 'topic' and, in addition, 'style', which is evaluated as 'neutral', 'involved' or 'sarcastic' – all these labels will reappear in the systematic discussion of the variables in section 4 below. In a more realistic network representation many other variables would have to be considered as well, and the number of links between the individual articles would increase to such an extent that it would be impossible to accommodate them in a two-dimensional diagram.

What the diagram shows nevertheless is that the interdependence between the articles is based on different variables, yielding not only the expected correlations between hard news, commentaries and letters to the editor (e.g. E 1, E 24 and E 98, all of them concerned with business), but also revealing quite unexpected links, as between E 10 and E 146 (both interview-type articles, one on jobs for single mothers, the other on the

Tour de France) or highlighting more technical links, as between E 67 (*City file*) and E 140 (*Sports in brief*) for instance, both of them diagram-like service elements. In addition, the figure gives a glimpse of the all-pervasive phenomenon of multiple links between texts by showing a few examples of dual and triple links. These links are indicated in the diagram by bold lines and the respective labelling; yet a satisfactory representation is again not possible in a two-dimensional diagram, but instead calls for statistical treatment.

Summarizing, one could say that, if properly handled, the notion of text network seems better suited to capture the interdependence of texts in a newspaper than an overarching classification based either on topics or on text types. However, there is one thing that the concept of a text network does not really convey, and this is why I prefer the related notion of text ensemble. Originally used as an adverb meaning 'together', the notion of ensemble is nowadays most naturally envisaged as an ensemble of musical instruments or musicians. Other uses concern sets like coat, scarf and hat or architectural ensembles, e.g. buildings of a certain period. Comparing the meaning of *ensemble* with the concept of network, both can be said to express that certain elements are connected with each other. Yet while a network only suggests that there is a link as opposed to having no link at all, the notion of ensemble seems to go further by emphasizing that each link does in fact contribute to the common effect produced by the ensemble. Another important aspect is that although both networks and ensembles are basically non-hierarchical, the notion of ensemble seems better suited to integrate some hierarchical aspects. Architectural ensembles may include a church or a palace which is more prominent than the other buildings, and in a musical ensemble the first violin tends to play the leading part more often than other instruments or musicians.

Since linguistic analysis should perhaps not completely rely on metaphors, powerful as they may be, the following list assembles some statements which try to capture the intermediate position claimed for the text ensembles between a strictly hierarchical system of texts and their accidental agglomeration. Taken together these statements may serve as a preliminary definition of what a text ensemble should be like:

(1) Text ensembles consist of the texts collected in a suitable self-contained unit (newspaper issues, magazines, brochures, books, certain radio and television programmes)
(2) The member texts can be described within a framework of interdependent variables (e.g. 'text type', 'topic', 'style'), using suitable categories or values (e.g. 'interview', 'politics', 'involved style')
(3) Some of the variables may be dominant compared with others, but there is no strict multilevel hierarchy of variables.

(4) Some member texts may be completely homogeneous, i.e. they may share the same values for all the variables, but in order to establish a text ensemble, there must also be member texts which differ with regard to some of the values.

How can we prove that this notion of text ensemble is a viable concept for newspapers? The first statement does not seem to need any scientific proof. As for the other statements, the first step will be to establish a reliable set of variables for the evaluation of the member texts, i.e. the individual newspaper articles. The second step will be to process the data statistically and this will be done by calculating the contingency coefficients and by applying cluster analysis. Contingency coefficients should provide information about the interdependence of the variables involved (statements 2 and 3), while cluster analysis can be used to assess the degree of homogeneity or diversity between the articles (statement 4). Apart from these general aspects, the statistical analysis should also be helpful in deciding to what extent individual newspapers deviate from the overall results and how this may contribute to their characteristic profile.

4. Criteria for the description of text ensembles

As texts have to do with communication, an obvious and linguistically attested source of variables for text ensembles are the parameters of the communicative event as developed by Hymes (Saville-Troike 1989: 138), a catalogue that has already been applied to newspaper texts by Kniffka (1980: 35). Yet considering that Kniffka's intentions were somewhat different, a new attempt has been made to adapt Hymes' criteria to the investigation of newspaper text ensembles, paying attention to the conditions just mentioned, and incorporating some experiences from the pilot analysis. The result is presented in Figure 3.

Since the list of source categories (left-hand column) was primarily designed for conversational events, there are several criteria which are irrelevant in a newspaper context, for instance 'rules of interaction' and 'act sequence'. The setting (i.e. time and place) in which the paper is produced or read is also of little interest. As for the variable 'message form', it is fixed as 'written medium' and can be neglected unless it is claimed for the evaluation of visual aspects such as layout and the use of colour. If, in addition, we integrate the variable 'norms of interpretation' into the hearer-oriented variables, we find that all the other source variables have their equivalents in the box, among them 'text type' and 'topic', which we have already identified as the major criteria of pigeonhole classifications.

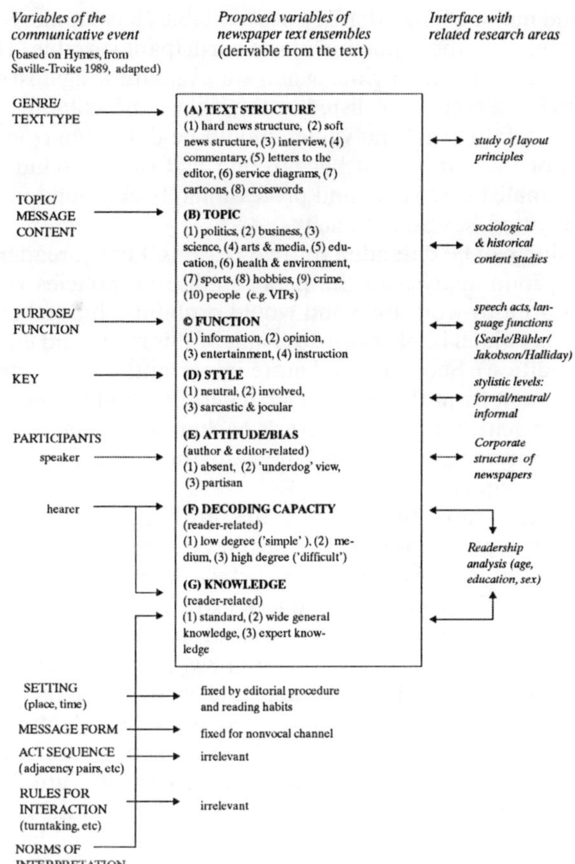

Figure 3: Variables of the speech event and variables for newspaper text ensembles

In adapting the communicative variables for newspaper purposes two kinds of changes have been made on the level of variables. One of them was to disentangle complex categories at the expense of their richness. This is particularly true of the first variable, the 'text type'. As exemplified by the term 'hard news structure', only the structural aspects, the so-called inverted pyramid structure of presenting the most important element first (Lüger 1995: 94ff), has been retained. The content-related aspects of the hard news concept have been shifted to the topic variable and its functional aspects to the function variable. The label 'text type' will therefore be replaced by 'text structure' in the following.

The second major change that Hymes' variables have undergone in our adaptation concerns the reduction of the participant variable. The reason for this change becomes obvious when we evaluate it against the background of the research areas listed in the right-hand column. Following our second condition that the values should be derivable from the text, major parts of the participant background had to be excluded, among them the journalist's personal and professional background or the reader's age, education, sex and ethnicity.

This decision can be defended for two reasons. Firstly, readership analysis and in-group analysis of the paper's editorial policies would have added an enormous work load and would prohibit a limited application of the analysis (which is, of course, the aim of this study and embodied in the third condition). Secondly, and more importantly, by selecting the attitude component from the speaker's background and the decoding and knowledge capacities from the hearer's background it seems possible to capture the decisive variables which regulate the interaction between the text and its participants.

Apart from indicating the variables, the box has also been used for the presentation of the categories (or values) used in the pilot project below. As for the text structure variable, its structural interpretation has already been mentioned. The fact that 'hard news structure' is linked to the 'inverted pyramid' suggests using 'soft news structure' for descriptive texts that do not show the peculiarities of hard news structure, without paying attention to the content. The category 'interview' is related to the predominance of the direct speech elements, whether the full interview structure is present or not; 'commentary' is characterized by its argumentative structure; 'service diagrams', 'cartoons' and 'crossword' are determined by their ratio of pictorial elements and diagram-type arrangement.

Skipping over the values of the topic and function variables, which are more or less self-explanatory, the next set of categories that may need some explanation are the values of the variable 'style'. Here the choice of categories is not only influenced by Hymes' original notion of 'key' (Saville-Troike 1989: 141f), but also by other authors who have found the category 'involved' useful in characterizing 'personal' journalistic style;[1] by contrast the stylistic standard distinction of formal, neutral and colloquial style seems less relevant.

The last variable that deserves some comment is the variable 'attitude' (or 'bias'). The original idea was to use the categories traditionally applied to English newspapers, i.e. 'conservative', 'liberal' and 'labour'. Yet going through just a handful of newspaper articles showed that a party-political perspective is not really visible in most cases. Where such a view is expressed, it makes more sense to contrast it with a non-party-political stance without distinguishing any further between political leanings; this is why the category 'partisan' was chosen. What seemed helpful was to introduce another distinction, the one between a neutral view (labelled '(bias) absent' to distinguish it from the style value 'neutral'), and an 'underdog view', as the second category was provisionally called. It stands for the perspective of ordinary citizens towards government decisions, their attitude towards big business, their sympathy for people like themselves, etc. To give just one example, if a report on the bankruptcy of a large company focuses on the economic and political consequences, it will be rated as 'neutral' ('bias absent'). If the report on the same subject puts emphasis on the loss of jobs involved and the problems of the dismissed employees it will be evaluated as 'underdog view'. Obviously, there are links with the style category 'involved', but there does not seem to be a total overlap.

Returning to more general aspects, the selection of variables and values contained in the box of Figure 3 does not only lend itself to an intuitive, holistic evaluation, but can to a considerable extent be supported by accepted linguistic procedures. To point out just a few examples, values of text structure can be analysed according to van Dijk's (1988: 55) or Bell's (1990: 171) schemata or Toulmin's argument structure (Lüger 1995: 127f); 'function' can be related to illocutionary indicators, involved and sarcastic style can be pinned to certain linguistic triggers (Biber 1988: 102; Ungerer 1997: 313ff). Finally, 'decoding capacity' can be understood in terms of phrasal and syntactic complexity (Jucker 1992: chs. 4-9). All these investigations would, of course, require comprehensive studies, which go far beyond the scope of this paper.

As for the intuitive evaluation, it should be carried out by a panel of at least six judges to comply with accepted standards of empirical psychology and to reduce the subjectiveness of the assessment. Yet even this goal was beyond the possibilities of the present study. What was feasible as a first step was a pilot project based on the author's own intuitive assessment, and this will be described in the following section.

5. The pilot project

5.1. Data collection and other preliminaries

The pilot project is based on the analysis of four newspapers: The International Edition of the *Guardian,* the *Daily Express, USA Today* European Edition, all of them published on June 4, 1997, and the *Sun* of June 9, 1997. Altogether 441 editorial texts of more than ten lines were analysed (shorter items were neglected, surely a somewhat problematic decision). The texts of each newspaper were numbered and evaluated for the seven variables contained in the box of Figure 3, using the values listed there and avoiding dual assignments even where they would have been desirable. The values were collected in tables produced by *Excel*; they were represented by short labels, which were later translated into numbers for statistical processing – see Figure 4 for a short specimen. The result was a data file of nominal values comprising about 3000 data.

Guardian data

	A	B	C	D	E	F	G
1	hns	cri	inf	neut	und	med	wide
2	hns	cri	inf	neut	und	med	stan
3	hns	pol	inf	inv	und	med	wide
4	hns	art	inf	neut	abs	med	exp
5	com	pol	ent	part	sarc	diff	wide

Explanations
Capital letters refer to the box in figure 3
Letter combinations refer to first few letters of values in this box

Exceptions
hns: hard news structure
sns: soft news structure

Numbers refer to numbers given to articles in each newspaper

Figure 4: Specimen of the data file for variables and values

This collection of data was then subjected to statistical analysis of two kinds, the calculation of contingency coefficients and a reduced form of cluster analysis.[2] Where necessary the analysis was supported by frequency counts. The statistics programme used was the SPSS for Windows.

5.2. Contingency coefficients I: general observations

One of the reasons why the analysis in terms of contingency values was chosen was that it can be safely applied to our data, which consist of nominal values, i.e. non-ranking values like 'hard news structure', 'soft news structure', 'interview' and 'commentary'. Contingency coefficients are based on so-called cross tables of frequency counts and used to express the statistical interdependence between pairs of variables, even – and this is important – where no causal relationship exists between these variables. The method can be applied to any two of our variables, e.g. 'text structure' and 'topic area' or 'text structure' and 'decoding capacity'. The degree of interdependence is represented on a scale between zero for variables that do not co-vary at all and 1 for variables which co-occur in every case. The coefficients were calculated for all combinations possible between the seven variables used in the data. The procedure was carried out for the complete data and for each of the four newspapers; the overall analysis was expected to provide a yardstick against which the results for the individual papers could be evaluated. Figure 5 contains selected results of the analysis.

	text str.	topic	function	style	attitude	decoding	knowledge
text str.							
topic	0.721 (0.772)						
function	0.743 (0.743)	0.648 (0.613) U--					
style	0.612 (0.610)	0.422 (0.450) G+ E+ U-	0.518 (0.502) S-				
attitude	0.502 (0.543) S+	0.528 (0.570) E+ S+	0.368 (0.386)	0.479 (0.501)			
decoding	0.314 (0.401) G++ E+	0.394 (0.439) G+ U+ S-	0.184 (0.264)	0.199 (0.242) U+	0.266 (0.228)		
knowl.	0.257 (0.379) E+ S++	0.476 (0.513) G+ S-	0.183 (0.229)	0.199. (0.259) U+	0.354 (0.342) G- S+	0.581 (0.461) G- S--	
	text str.	topic	function	style	attitude	decoding	knowledge

Explanations:

plain numbers:	calculated for total
numbers in brackets:	average of calculations for the four newspapers
(+) and (-)	deviation of more than 0.1 from average value
(++) and (--)	deviation of more than 0.2 from average value
G = *Guardian*	E = *Express*
U = *USA Today*	S = *Sun*

Figure 5: Contingency coefficient analysis

The coefficients listed in Figure 5 refer to the complete data, the 441 articles analysed. The numbers in brackets give the average values of the coefficients calculated for the individual newspapers. Although this is not the normal procedure, they have been added to indicate the distortion caused by the fact that the *Express* contained 147 articles while the other papers only consisted of about 100 articles each. Neglecting the letters below the digits for the moment, let us first attempt a general evaluation of the results.

If we look at the diagram, we find that the conception of the newspaper as text ensemble is confirmed in several ways. About half the coefficients are higher than 0.4, which may be assumed to indicate a quite satisfactory statistical co-variation between the variables involved (though no causal relationship!). Not surprisingly, the variables which co-vary best are 'text structure' and 'topic area', and the interdependence with the variable 'function' is also strong. This explains why, for practical purposes, these three variables are often combined in 'mixed' terms like 'hard news' (combining the inverted pyramid structure, politics and information) and 'soft news', (combining an alternative text structure, the topic 'people' and function 'entertainment'). Yet since there is no total overlap between the variables (which would be indicated by a coefficient of 1), our view that these variables should be regarded as independent, though statistically interdependent, is fully supported. What is also confirmed is the leading role played by the variables 'text structure' and 'topic', a dominance we have claimed for the newspaper text ensemble.

The next variable, 'style', indicates a good degree of co-variation with the variable 'text structure', but a lower one with 'topic'. Turning to the participant variables, the author and editor-related variable 'attitude' still shows an acceptable degree of interdependence with 'text structure' and 'topic', but less so with the variable 'function', while the links with the reader-related variables 'decoding capacity' and 'knowledge' yield lower coefficients, though there is still some co-variation to be observed (otherwise the coefficients would approach zero).

However, it would be wrong to assume that these variables and other variables affected by lower contingency coefficients (such as the variable 'function') are unimportant for the constitution of newspaper text ensembles. What the relatively low coefficients tell us is simply that these variables often do not change when other variables assume different values. The reason for this is not difficult to find when we look at the way the values of these variables are distributed in terms of frequency. Compare Figure 6, which shows that the variables 'function', 'decoding capacity' and 'knowledge' all have one dominant value (63.3 %, 68.0 % and 69.6 % respectively) while the other values have lower or even negligible percentages. This severely reduces the chance that the salient value can be replaced by another value of the same variable and implicitly restricts co-variation.

Summing up at this first stage of the statistical analysis, we may say that the interdependence of the seven variables is confirmed, though in varying degrees. While relatively high coefficients are observed for the combination of the two 'lead' variables, 'text structure' and 'topic', some of the other combinations yield lower coefficients. But since we do not have any experience of the degree of co-variation typical of newspaper text en-

	A text struct.	B topic	C function	D style	E attitude	F decoding	G knowl.
1	37.6%	14.1%	**63.3%**	56.0%	38.5%	**68.0%**	**69.6%**
2	18.1%	9.3%	18.8%	32.9%	56.7%	30.4%	28.8%
3	5.9%	1.9%	15.4%	11.1%	4.8%	1.6%	1.6%
4	14.1%	7.9%	2.5%				
5	5.4%	2.9%					
6	11.3%	8.4%					
7	4.5%	27.2%					
8	2.9%	3.9%					
9		6.6%					
10		17.9%					

Total number of objects: 441

For explanation of labels and the number code of values see figure 3

Figure 6: Frequency count of variable values for all texts

sembles, these results can only be regarded as a first reference point for further investigations. The same applies to the fact that 11 (or almost 12) coefficients (out of a total of 21) rise above the level of 0.4. Yet however 'dense' or 'loose' the typical newspaper text ensemble will finally turn out to be, the proposed combination of variables seems to work, though it is, of course, open to further improvement.

5.3. Contingency coefficients II: deviation of individual newspapers

Apart from endorsing the notion of text ensemble in general, contingency coefficients can also tell us something about the individual newspapers investigated. For this we need not look at the individual tables of coefficients compiled for each of the newspapers. For ease of handling, the significant deviations have been integrated in Figure 5, where they are indicated by combinations of letters and +/- signs, which have been added to some of the digits (where no letter/sign combinations are added, all newspapers are close to the average values). As explained in more detail in the figure, letters refer to newspapers while plus and minus signs indicate the direction of the deviation. On the whole, minus signs (which indicate lower coefficients) are due to an extreme dominance of one value for the respective variable, and this restricts co-variation with other variables, as explained above.

An example are the negative deviations for the function/topic and style/topic coefficients for *USA Today*. The low function/topic coefficient (a mere 0.398 compared with the overall value of 0.648) seems to be caused by the one-sided distribution of the values for the variable 'function'. Here the value 'information' has a 89.5 % share, the value 'opinion' accounts for the remaining 10.5 %, while the two other values ('entertainment' and 'instruction') are not represented at all. For the style/topic coefficient the situation is less extreme, but again the values for the variable 'style' are shared between two values (the value 'neutral' commands a 67.4 % share, the rest is accounted for by the value 'involved', the value 'sarcastic' is not represented).

Higher-than-average coefficients for individual newspapers (which are indicated by plus signs) are less easily explained. One pattern seems to be a combination of two variables with fairly evenly distributed values, a set-up that permits a relatively high degree of co-variation. An example is the decoding/text structure coefficient for the *Guardian*, which at 0.533 deviates remarkably from the average of 0.314. Here the decoding variable has an exceptionally strong middle value (53.7 %), the two other values are 38.0 % for 'simple decoding' and 9.3 % for 'difficult decoding', the latter also a comparatively high value. These values interact with a text structure variable of which half the values have frequencies between 9 % and 40 %, signifying a fairly even distribution as well. If these percentages do not sound impressive, one should remember that they only establish the *Guardian's* decoding/text structure coefficient in the range of 0.5, a comfortable middle position (which is, however, far above the average for this coefficient, as we have seen). Similar observations might be made about the style/topic coefficient, calculated for the *Guardian* at 0.567, which is also well above the 'average' of 0.422.

Skipping further details and generalising from the example discussed, we might say that positive deviation, as just exemplified for the *Guardian* in one case (and there are other cases), can indeed be seen as a positive sign pointing to a versatile editorial policy. If papers assemble a number of minus signs as *USA Today* does with regard to the variables 'function', 'style' and (almost) for 'attitude', this might reflect a more rigid, one-sided, news-oriented editorial policy (and this is the impression one gets when naively comparing this newspaper with the *Guardian* or the *Express.*)

What remains a puzzling case is the *Sun*. Its data is characterized by some extremely one-sided frequencies, a 96 % share for 'simple decoding' and a 94 % percentage for 'standard knowledge'. These values may be partly due to the author's prejudice and thus be put down as an example of circularity (see below – final section). However, these extreme cases yield quite contradictory results, a remarkable positive deviation for the knowledge/text structure coefficient but a negative one for a number of other combinations involving the decoding and knowledge variables. Another interesting feature is the *Sun's* attitude/text structure coefficient, which is characterized by a complete dominance of the 'underdog view' value for the variable 'attitude'; the variable 'text structure' is represented by a range of 5 values which score in the narrow range between 11 % and 33 %. This particular mixture produces the highest coefficient of all newspapers for this combination, i.e. 0.671, closely followed by the *Sun's* coefficient for the attitude/topic combination, which reaches 0.650. Although there may be a simple explanation for this special concoction of values, it is tempting to speculate whether it perhaps reflects the special recipe of the *Sun* and may reveal more about it than the popular surface characterization that the paper aims at entertainment rather than information, that it focuses on crime and human interest stories, which are presented in a highly involved style.

Discussing the deviations one should not overlook the agreement with regard to the dominant variables (i.e.'text structure', 'topic area' and also 'function'), which show high scores for all newspapers. This indicates that all of them can still be safely placed in a common concept of text ensemble.

5.4. Cluster analysis

Very simply, cluster analysis provides an analysis in terms of closeness or distance. Unlike the calculation of contingency coefficients it is not concerned with the co-variation of variables, but with the closeness of the objects themselves. Transferred to the domain of newspapers, this means that the cluster analysis does not compare the variables 'text structure' or 'topic' or 'function', but evaluates the closeness or distance of the individual newspaper texts, i.e. the degree of homogeneity addressed in the last statement of our definition in section 3. This is done by examining how many of its variable values each article shares with other texts in the paper. The technical problem is that the hierarchical cluster analysis is designed for ordinal values, i.e. ranks, rather than nominal values, which are non-ranking. If we re-examine our data from this perspective, we find that the values used for the variables 'style', 'attitude', 'decoding capacity' and 'knowledge' can perhaps be understood as ranks. Yet this is not possible for the first three variables 'text structure', 'topic' and 'function', which assemble quite diverse values that cannot be ranked – think of the various kinds of text structures or topics. In other words, our data only agree with the input conditions of cluster analysis to a certain extent. However, we can still make use of cluster analysis if we keep these restrictions in mind when assessing the results.

Clusters are calculated on the basis of yet another coefficient, the agglomeration or similarity coefficient, which is measured on an open-ended scale starting with zero. A zero similarity coefficient indicates that two objects (i.e. newspaper texts) share all the values of their variables; the similarity coefficient '1' indicates that a pair of articles differs in one value in the sense that one object has the neighbouring value (e.g. that the stylistic level is not neutral, but involved). Higher coefficients are achieved if a pair differs with regard to more values and/or if the differing values for the same variable are more distant from each other, for instance if one object has a value ranked 1 and the other object a value ranked 3 or 5 or 7. This is where the non-ranking sets of values for the variables 'text structure' and 'topic' and 'function' may distort the result in our newspaper context, but we will avoid this problem area by focusing on the lower coefficients where these differences can be neglected.

One way to show the results of the clustering is by listing the pairs and their similarity coefficients in an agglomeration schedule, which ranks the articles starting with zero coefficients. These schedules were compiled for each of the four newspapers. Since they take up about 10 pages in all, the main results have been extracted from the schedules and collected in a table (see Figure 7, Table A). The table contains the number of texts assigned to each integer similarity coefficient (e.g. to 0, 1, 2, etc); the respective percentages have been added to eliminate the distortions due to the differing number of texts per newspaper. The percentages in the column marked '0' refer to the number of articles that share all their variable values, those listed in the next column refer to articles differing in one value, and so on.

Interpreting these results, we find that they endorse the claim contained in statement 4 of our definition of the text ensemble that some member texts may be completely homogeneous in terms of variable values, if – and this is confirmed by figure 7A – other member texts differ with regard to some of the values.

This granted, it is still interesting to see how the share of completely or almost homogeneous texts varies between the individual newspapers. Compare table 7 B, which shows a marked difference between the *Guardian* on the one hand and *USA Today* and the *Sun* on the other, while the *Express* holds a middle position. If the *Guardian* has only a 24 % share of completely homogeneous texts and a much larger percentage of texts which are close, but not completely homogeneous, this promises a more varied kind of text ensemble. Thus the cluster analysis of the *Guardian* nicely confirms the analysis of the positive deviations shown by the contingency coefficients for this newspaper.

By contrast, *USA Today* and the *Sun* have a much larger share of homogeneous texts, pointing to a less varied type of text ensemble. Since the cluster analysis only registers similarities quantitatively, it does not provide a reason for these differences. Yet remembering the deviations reg-

Table A

	0-	1-	2-	3-	4-	5-	6-	7-	8-	9-	10-
Guardian	26	31	11	9	9	4	2	3	2	-	11
(108= 100%)	24%	29%	10%	8%	8%	4%	2%	3%	2%	0%	10%
Express	56	39	15	7	5	5	2	1	3	2	12
(147 = 100%)	38%	27%	10%	5%	3%	3%	1%	1%	2%	1%	8%
USA Today	36	21	10	5	4	-	-	1	2	1	5
(86=100%)	42%	26%	12%	6%	5%	0%	0%	1%	2%	1%	6%
Sun	49	21	5	7	1	4	-	1	3	-	8
(100=100%)	49%	22%	5%	7%	1%	4%	0%	1%	3%	0%	8%

Table B

	1st column	1st-2nd column	1st-3rd column	1st-5th column
	0-	0-1	0-2	0-4
Guardian	24%	53%	63%	79%
Express	38%	65%	75%	83%
USA Today	42%	68%	80%	91%
Sun	49%	71%	76%	84%

Figure 7: Cluster analysis: agglomeration schedule

istered for *USA Today* and the *Sun* in the contingency analysis, it becomes clear that the homogeneity is of a different nature for each of the two papers. While *USA Today* has many articles that combine variable values like 'hard news structure', 'politics', 'information', 'neutral style' and 'neutral attitude', the homogeneity of the *Sun* rests on chains like 'entertainment' – 'people' – 'involved style' – 'simple decoding' – 'standard knowledge' (the variable 'text structure' is more diverse for this newspaper and therefore not included in the chain). Obviously, these chains are something that can be more successfully handled by the cluster analysis than by means of contingency coefficients. This is one indication that both types of statistical analysis tend to complement each other.

6. Newspaper ensembles: an integrated view and its applications

If we try to characterize the relationship between cluster analysis and the interpretation of contingency coefficients, we find that the two methods are related in the same way in which statement 4 of our definition (restricted homogeneity) is related to statements 2 and 3 (interdependence of variables, with room for dominating ones). While the cluster analysis is concerned with the closeness or distance between the newspaper articles when evaluated against the variables, the contingency coefficients reflect the distribution of certain variable values. Figure 8 tries to capture this relationship in an informal way and without any claim to statistical validity.

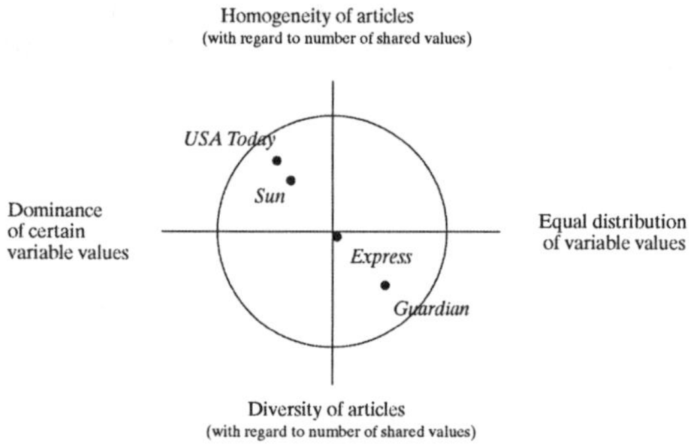

Figure 8: Homogeneity and distribution of values in newspaper ensembles

The circle in the figure delimits the area in which newspaper text ensembles can be placed, the dots indicate (but without statistical validity!) the different positions taken up by the individual newspapers with regard to the coordinates used. Roughly, *USA Today* and the *Sun* are characterized by a high degree of homogeneous articles (though of different kinds for each of the papers) and a remarkable dominance of certain variable values. By contrast, the *Guardian* has a larger percentage of less homogeneous articles and shows a more equal distribution of values for a number of variables; the *Express,* finally, holds a kind of middle position in every respect.

However, it would be wrong to interpret this diagram in the sense that the *Express* is a better newspaper than the other newspapers because it represents a more perfect text ensemble. *USA Today*, the *Sun* and the *Guardian* may be regarded as equally 'good' text ensembles if, for instance, their special combination of variable values is more in line with the envisaged readership. In other words, the evaluation as text ensemble contributes only one set of data to the assessment of a paper and must therefore be complemented by elements such as sociological readership profiles. Yet as far as the text-related data are concerned, the proposed analysis promises to provide more comprehensive data and more reliable results than the judgments of editors and publishers. In addition, our analysis can also be used to check if a chosen editorial overall concept is actually observed throughout the paper. This again seems to permit an assessment which may be superior to the intuition of editors, who often push the unifying aspects while leaving diversity, which is an essential ingredient of the text ensemble, to look after itself.

7. Final remarks

Since the investigation here was a pilot study there is much room for improvement, as the suggestions below show. They will be followed by a few more general considerations which aim to place the notion of text ensemble in a more general context.

7.1. Extending the sample

There can be no doubt that the sample should be extended beyond the four newspapers examined in the pilot study. The first step would be to analyse a weekly set for each of the newspapers; this would eliminate the distortion caused by the fact that certain sections of the papers are not produced on a daily basis but only once a week. Even more attractive would be the inclusion of more 'marginal' papers, for instance more partisan papers, censored papers in dictatorial regimes and papers with a non-Anglo-Saxon cultural background; extending the scope even further one might, of course, include newspapers from other historical periods right back to the beginnings of newspaper journalism. No doubt, it would be most interesting to see how the composition of these newspapers would be reflected in the statistical analysis and how this would change our conception of text ensembles by changing the standards for our variables and perhaps adding totally new variables.

7.2. Improving the evaluation of the data

As already suggested, the ideal solution would be to extract the values for the variables from the text itself by quantitative, and largely computerized, procedures. What can be achieved more easily is the establishment of a panel of 'judges', i.e. having the newspapers evaluated against the variables by several people and comparing the results. This would provide more representative data and at least reduce the circularity inherent in the pilot study.

One specific problem that has been more or less neglected so far is the length of the articles (except for the 10-line threshold for texts practised in the pilot study) and the space they take up in the newspaper. Again the most satisfactory solution would be a word count or character count which could be based on the computerized versions of current and recent newspapers available on CD ROM or the internet. The difficulty is that these electronic versions are sometimes incomplete and neglect the aspect of space, the size of the headlines, the layout in general (Kniffka's phenotypical features; see Kniffka 1980: 35), although these aspects are as important as the actual length of the texts. An interim solution would again be the assessment by judges, based on a set of agreed values.

7.3. Transferring the notion of text ensemble to other genres

It would be unnatural to assume that the notion of text ensemble is restricted to newspapers. But where should one look for other likely candidates? There are certainly various kinds of 'text collections' that come to mind: magazines of various kinds, theatre programmes with accompanying articles, college prospectuses, perhaps also dictionaries and encyclopaedias, conference publications, Festschriften and almanacs. All these candidates are characterized by a mixture of texts, one of the conditions for qualifying as text ensembles, but quite a number of them are more readily subordinated to a dominant variable than newspapers, for instance time, location, topic or purpose. In other words, the hierarchical feature may be stronger than it is with newspapers, but this should not keep us from investigating these collections from the perspective of the text ensemble. This could be done in comparison with the hierarchical model of text conglomerates developed by Görlach (1991) and exemplified by the text type 'book', which may consist of preface, dedication, table of contents, bibliography, annotations and, of course, the text proper.

Returning to the text ensemble, the last and perhaps most interesting aspect is whether this notion can be transferred to fictional texts. Venturing a final statement, one might claim that works of fiction are not to be regarded as text ensembles per se, but may well make use of the notion of text ensemble as a construction principle. A classical example would be the comparison between a collection of personal letters (which may be regarded as a text ensemble) and the way letters are used in an epistolary novel from the 18th century, where the self-supporting balance of the text ensemble is subsumed under an overarching aesthetic concept. Needless to say, late twentieth century literature offers many more, but also much more complex examples.

Notes

1 The term 'involvement' was introduced by Biber (1988: 104ff), who used it to characterize the interactional aspects of spontaneous conversation and contrasted it with the detachment of informational texts, in which he included press texts. However, taking a more differentiated view of journalistic texts, Diller (1993: 13f) and Ghadessy (1988: 22) have since used the term 'involved' to denote subjective stylistic aspects of personal columns and sports commentaries respectively, among them 2nd person reference to readers and the use of emphatics, amplifiers and hedges, and this interpretation is taken up in the proposed classification.

2 The statistical analysis was only made possible by the cooperation of Prof. U. Kück, University of Rostock, without whose patient assistance the analysis would not have been possible.

Bibliography

Beaugrande, Robert de & Wolfgang Dressler: *Introduction to Text Linguistics.* 2nd ed. London, 1981.

Bell, Allan: *The Language of News Media.* Oxford, 1991.

Dijk, Teun van: *News as Discourse.* Hillsdale, N.J., 1988.

Diller, Hans-Jürgen: "Introduction: British Columnists – why study them, and how?" – In Hans-Jürgen Diller et al. (Eds.): *Practical Stylistics. British Columnists.* (anglistik & englischunterricht 51), Heidelberg, 1993, pp. 7-27.

Ghadessy, Moshen: "The Language of Written Sports Commentary – a Description". – In Moshen Ghadessy (Ed.): *Registers of Written English.* London, 1988, pp. 17-51.

Görlach, Manfred: "Text Types and the Linguistic History of Modern English". – In Claus Uhlig & R. Zimmermann (Eds.): *Anglistentag 1990 Marburg. Proceedings.* Tübingen, 1991, pp. 142-153.

Jucker, Andreas H.: *Social Stylistics: Syntactic Variation in British Newspapers.* Berlin, 1992.

Kniffka, Hannes: *Soziolinguistik und empirische Textanalyse. Schlagzeilen- und Leadformulierung in amerikanischen Tageszeitungen.* Tübingen, 1980.

Lüger, Heinz-Helmut: *Pressesprache.* 2nd ed. Tübingen, 1995.

Saville-Troike, Muriel: *The Ethnography of Communication.* 2nd ed. Oxford, 1989.

Ungerer, Friedrich: "Emotions and Emotional Language in English and German News Stories". – In Susanne Niemeier & René Dirven (Eds.): *The Language of Emotions.* Amsterdam, 1997, pp. 307-328.

Mick Short, Martin Wynne and Elena Semino, Lancaster

Reading Reports: Discourse Presentation in a Corpus of Narratives, with Special Reference to News Reports

1. Introduction

This paper reports on an ongoing corpus-based project examining speech, thought and writing presentation (ST&WP) in British C20 written texts. The corpus presently comprises extracts from fictional prose, newspaper reports and (auto)biographies but this paper focuses mainly on the newspaper data. The usefulness of a corpus approach in the study of discourse presentation in newspapers has recently been demonstrated by Waugh's discussion of a corpus of articles from *Le Monde* in "Reported Speech in Journalistic Discourse".

Below, we (a) describe how our corpus has been constructed, (b) describe the model of ST&WP analysis used in tagging the corpus, and how, in particular, our model was modified to cope sensibly with newspaper data, (c) discuss some preliminary statistical findings concerning the newspaper data, and (d) examine in detail one particular news story (about OUP's publication of a 'politically correct' Bible in the USA), to show how the corpus can be used for more qualitative and comparative forms of analysis related to ST&WP. If other scholars are interested in making use of our corpus, we are prepared, after discussion, to make it available as a research resource.

So far, there have been two main phases to the project. The first phase[1] involved the balanced collection of 40 samples of approximately 2,000 words each from novels and newspapers, 20 from each text-type (a total of 88,631 words). The newspaper data was taken exclusively from news reports because news reports, like novels and (auto)biographies, are narratives. This allows us to compare discourse (re)presentation in narrative discourse across the three different genres, or text-types. Each text-type was subdivided into two sub-sets. 10 of the novel-set were from popular fiction and the other 10 were from serious fiction. The newspaper data was similarly subdivided into a broadsheet and a tabloid section, with 10 samples from each. The tabloids excerpted are *The News of the World, The Sun, The Daily Star, The Daily Mirror, The Daily Express,* and *Today.* The broadsheets are *The Independent, The Independent on Sunday, The Guardian, The Daily Telegraph,* and *The Times.* The excerpted issues appeared on 4-5 and 11-12 December, 1994. Selection was limited to two 2-day periods, so that accounts of the same news items in different newspapers could be collected, allowing for textual comparison (see section 5 below).

After they had been converted to an electronic format, the texts comprising the corpus were then hand-tagged for speech, thought and writing presentation, using Leech and Short's *Style in Fiction* speech and thought presentation model as a starting point. Our corpus-based approach thus differs from some other newspaper corpora, e.g. Waugh, "Reported Speech in Journalistic Discourse", which was not electronic and not systematically tagged. Our rather specialised corpus also differs from the major large electronic linguistic corpora (e.g. the British National Corpus), which are much more general in terms of the text-types sampled and are grammatically (and to some extent semantically) tagged, using automated software. During the process of tagging our corpus, a series of additions, subtractions and modifications to the original Leech and Short model have been made, some of which (those important for the discussion of newspaper reporting) will be outlined below. So far, three reports on this first phase of the project have been published, Short *et al.*, ("Using a Corpus ..."), Semino *et al.*, ("Using a Computer ...") and another is Wynne *et al.*, ("A Corpus-based Investigation ..."). These works contain details of the sampling methods and the tagging methodology, which are not reproduced here for space reasons. This paper will refer to some of the findings presented in Semino *et al.*, "Using a Computer ...", but will also look at some areas not covered by this work. In particular, it will compare the statistical results of the first and second phases of the project, concentrating on the newspaper data, and examine in detail the report of an individual news story in the different newspapers.

The second phase of the project[2] has involved extending the corpus (a) by doubling the size of the text-type categories outlined above and (b) by adding a further text-type: (auto)biography, of the same size as the others, and which has also been subdivided into a popular and a serious section. The collection techniques were the same as for the first stage of the project, with the newspaper data coming from two 2-day periods (28-29 April and 12-13 May) in 1996. The corpus now contains 258,348 words of contemporary British English, divided into three main genres, namely prose fiction (87,709 words), newspaper news reports (83,603 words), and biography and autobiography (87,036 words).[3] The word-number discrepancies among the three major sub-sets arise because we decided that it made more sense to collect samples which formed a coherent 'sub-whole', rather than to collect exactly 2,000 words from each text. The whole corpus constructed to date has now been tagged, and we are currently checking the tagging, and putting the finishing touches to the corpus. For more detail on the construction of the corpus and its annotation, see Wynne *et al.*, "A Corpus-based Investigation ...".

2. *Categories and Sub-categories*

The Leech and Short speech and thought presentation scale was originally developed to try to account for speech and thought presentation in the novel, where the narrator is the reporter of the speech and some character is assumed to have been the speaker of the original utterance. However, in fiction, unlike speech presentation in the real world, the novelist makes everything up. As a consequence, there is no separately perceivable anterior discourse event, and the reader has normally to assume that there is an exact match between Direct Speech (DS) or Free Direct Speech (FDS) strings and the wording of the anterior speech event. In news report, on the other hand, real people were involved in the anterior speech event and the newspaper reporter tells us what they said. As a consequence, there is the logical possibility, in spite of their assumed *verbatim* character, of DS strings not being exactly the same as the original, even though they claim to be, perhaps because of (i) errors or (ii) minor adjustments as a consequence of the need to integrate the speech reported into the reporting context (see Slembrouck, "The Parliamentary Hansard ..."). And it is even possible for presentations to be manipulated unreasonably by the reporter, perhaps for ideological reasons, thus misrepresenting, consciously or unconsciously, what was originally said.

As a result of observing phenomena like those just mentioned, a number of speech presentation theorists have, of late, wanted to suggest that the faithfulness criteria traditionally associated with DS, and which have been used to distinguish it from other forms (e.g. IS) should be abandoned, and with it the other, less full, faithfulness claims associated with the other categories on the speech presentation scale (Fludernik, *The Fictions of Language* ..., Sternberg, "Proteus in Quotation-land ...", Tannen, *Talking Voices* ...). As a consequence, choices of presentation category would be decoupled from the anterior discourse situation, and would only be associated with presentational rhetoric in the posterior, reporting situation. But we have recently suggested (Semino *et al.*, "Using a Computer ...") that the addition of the NV category provides the final piece of the presentation jigsaw in the faithfulness model (NV = Narrator's Representation of Voice, see section 3.5 of this paper); and we will argue in detail elsewhere (Wynne *et al.*, "Faithfulness Revisited ...") that examples of non-verbatim DS are not sufficient to abandon entirely the more traditional account of speech presentation, and that a more complex, pragmatically-based model which systematically distinguishes speech, thought and writing presentation is needed to account properly for the meanings and effects of the different forms of discourse presentation (see also Short *et al.*, "A (Free Direct) Reply ..."). Although we will not rehearse those arguments here, our qualitative analysis of the '"PC" Bible' newspaper articles in 5 below will be relevant to that argument, as we will show in section 6.

In addition to the straightforward narration of events, actions and states (N), the Leech and Short model has the categories listed below. Here we merely list the categories, as they will be familiar to many. Appendix 1 contains a list of categories and exemplifications from our newspaper data for those who are not familiar with the model:

[Narration (N)]
Narrator's Representation of Speech Act (NRSA)
Indirect Speech (IS)
Free Indirect Speech (FIS)
Direct Speech (DS)
Free Direct Speech (FDS)

With FDS and DS there is little or no apparent narratorial intervention in what is presented. As readers, we feel that we are being presented with the original utterance *verbatim*. Then, as we move along the scale towards the other end, the 'interference' of the narrator becomes stronger and stronger. With IS, the assumption is normally that the propositional content of what the original speaker said is represented, but using the words and structures of the reporter, not the original speaker. FIS is a 'half-way house' between the DS and IS forms, and NRSA is even more reduced than IS, giving only the speech act value of the utterance, perhaps with some indication of the topic.

3. Modifications to the Categories

In the course of tagging the corpus, we have found the need to change the categorisations in a number of ways. We will not present detailed arguments in favour of these changes here, as they are the subject of Semino *et al.*, "Using a Computer ...". However, it will be helpful to summarise the changes and give examples in order to help the reader follow the statistical comparisons which are the subject of section 4.

3.1. Collapsing the DS and FDS Categories

Short, "Speech Presentation, the Novel and the Press", suggested that DS and FDS were not really separate major speech presentation categories, but that FDS was a minor variant of the major category, DS. This was because, unlike the other speech presentation categories, FDS had no distinct faithfulness claim attached to it. Basically, the *verbatim* claim of DS was as faithful as one could get. The process of tagging the corpus has confirmed this view. In terms of their definitions, DS-FDS ambiguities are rife in our codings, and we feel that the divisions we have made in terms of DS and FDS have been fairly arbitrary. In the tables presented in 4 below, we have presented the DS and FDS codings separately, for completeness, but our discussion links them together.

3.2. Narrator's Representation of Speech (NRS)

When coding, we had a difficulty over what to do about reporting and reported clauses in DS and IS. Traditionally, the whole sentence, reporting clause plus reported clause, has been referred to as IS or DS. But technically the reported clause is the DS or IS string, the reporting clause being the reporter's link between that report and the discourse in which the report is embedded. As a consequence, we tagged each reporting clause as NRS (Narrator's Report of Speech). Hence, the example below would have the italicised portion tagged as NRS and the emboldened portion as IS:

> *Chechenia vowed* **that Russian troops would leave in coffins**.
> (*The Times*, Russian tanks roll towards rebel capital)

3.3. Embedded Quotation Phenomena (q)

One particular aspect of newspaper reporting which made us want to alter our codings, is that in news reports, unlike fictional prose, the text-type for which the Leech and Short model was developed, small stretches of direct quotation which would be unhelpfully tagged as DS often occur within stretches of more indirect speech report. This kind of phenomenon is related to what others, commenting on fictional prose, have called 'slipping' or 'coloured narration' (see McHale, "Free Indirect Discourse ..."). Consider the following example:

> He said the Bosnian situation was "a disastrous, humiliating affair".
> (*Daily Express*, Major faces Clinton snub on Bosnia)

If no quotation marks were present, this extract would clearly be NRS plus IS, and we felt that the presence of the quotation marks was not sufficient to change the basic IS categorisation of the reported clause. The argument that it is a mixture of IS and DS, resulting in an overall FIS tag, for example, would not seem to do justice to the phenomenon, as the 'flip-flop' interpretative effect would not be properly accounted for (see also Fludernik,

The Fictions of Language ..., pp. 377-8). For this reason, we decided to categorise it, and others like it, as NRS plus IS, but to add the letter 'q' (quotation) to the IS tag. Using the 'q' tag in this way allowed us to ask the computer to call up examples of 'q' across the whole corpus, and so observe the patterns associated with the 'q' phenomenon (which, we soon saw, occurred in a wide range of speech and writing presentation categories). The 'q' forms of speech presentation allow the news reporter to foreground brief selected parts of what is, overall, a relatively indirect representation of the original with a few directly quoted words from the anterior discourse. Such a strategy achieves vividness and precision without sacrificing the journalistic need for brevity. This kind of quotation phenomenon can even be found in the Narration (N) part of our newspaper data:

> The changes have been made by Oxford University Press in a bid to take the "oppression" out of Christianity.
> (*Daily Express*, For God's sake stop rewriting our Bible)

What might at first sight look like a 'scare quote' is clearly, when read in context, a one-word quotation (see Appendix 2 for the full text of the article).

3.4. Narrator's Representation of Speech Act, with Topic (NRSAP)

Technically, the 'q' phenomena described above amount to instances of a sub-category within a number of the major speech presentation categories. The two examples discussed in 3.3. above are ISq and Nq respectively. Another sub-categorisation forced on us by the news report data in our corpus related specifically to the Narrator's Representation of Speech Act (NRSA) category. In the novel, instances of NRSA are usually brief, and the addition of information about the topic of the speech act concerned is fairly unimportant. When the narrator in Joyce's 'The Dead' tells us that 'Mr Darcy told them the history of his cold', the speech of Mr Darcy is being backgrounded (though not without some irony), because it is not important to the main development of the story. But when we look at newspaper data, we find that the specification of the topic can be very extensive indeed:

> They complained to their local councillors: about the noise, the loss of Happy Mount park, the fact that Crinkley Bottom's garish entrance arch all but eclipsed the motto on the original park gates ...
> (*The Independent on Sunday*, Bare ladies' protest puts end to Crinkley Bottom)

The row which occurred when Lancaster City Council decided to turn the Morecambe seaside resort's Happy Mount park into a 'Crinkley Bottom' theme park, inspired by the entertainer Noel Edmonds, proved irresistible to the British national press, and the fact that the relevant part of Morecambe is called 'Bare' was also the source of much happy punning, as can be seen in the above extract's headline. But, more relevant to our concerns, this particular article included this 33-word NRSA. This kind of NRSA, with extensive topic specification, is very common in our newspaper data, and we decided to give it a special designation, NRSAP, where 'P' stands for topic (we could not use 'T' as we wanted to restrict its acronymic use to stand for 'Thought' in thought presentation tags).

3.5. Narrator's Representation of Voice (NV)

Across our data, including the newspaper part of the corpus, we came across examples of speech presentation which were even more minimal than the briefest NRSA, and which we decided to code separately. Here, the only faithfulness claim being made by the reporter is that speech occurred between the participants specified. Not even the speech act (let alone the propositional content or the actual words used) is specified, as in the emboldened part of the quotation below:

> **We spoke to vice madam Michaela Hamilton from Bullwell, Notts,** who arranged girls for a Hudson orgy at the Sanam curry house in Stoke. (*The News of the World*, Hudson fixed sex orgies as his charity fund collapsed)

Examples like these are often used to introduce a sub-part of a news report where extensive quotation is likely to occur, as happens for obviously salacious purposes in this extract (Hudson is an ex-England soccer star).[4]

3.6. Narrator's Representation of Internal States (NI/NIi)

In the novel, in particular in third-person narration, where the narrator has privileged access to the minds of characters, it is common to find the narration of an internal state (NI) of a character which is not a representation of some specific thought. For example, in chapter 7 of Jane Austen's *Emma*, when Emma's friend, Harriet, has just received a letter from Mr Martin proposing marriage, Harriet asks Emma to read the letter and we are told that 'Emma was not sorry to be pressed.' In theory, one would not expect to find such cases in news report, except perhaps where some person tells of their own feelings or state of mind. But actually they are quite common:

> As the Cabinet split deepens, Tory MPs pushing for a referendum are worried Mr Blair will steal a march on Mr Major.
> (*Daily Express*, Portillo piles on Euro pressure)

Here we are told about the state of mind of Tory MPs, something which the writer has no direct access to. He presumably *infers* the mind state of the group as a consequence of talking to them and observing their behaviour. To distinguish this kind of thing from the privileged access to internal mind states found in fictional narration, we coded examples like the above as NIi (*inferred* internal state). Note that NIi can cover not just the feelings of individuals but also very large groups (although, it would seem that, through a kind of reverse synecdoche, 'Britain' really refers to (a sub-part of) the British government in the quotation below):

> Britain is reluctant to withdraw after two years of gruelling effort to relieve civilian suffering and prevent the war spreading.
> (*Daily Express*, Major faces Clinton snub on Bosnia)

4. Statistical Comparisons

In our tagging there are (a) three different discourse presentation scales (speech, thought, writing), (b) some sub-categories of major categories (e.g. IS vs. ISq), and (c) separate tags for different sorts of ambiguities (so, an ambiguity between IS and FIS would be coded as IS-FIS). As a consequence, there are well over 100 different tags in our tagged corpus. The table in Appendix 3 represents the top 20 tags in statistical terms. That is, they are the 20 most frequent tags in the corpus as a whole. From the nineteenth most frequent tag, and below, the tag-incidence figure is below 1% of the tags for any of the six major text-type sub-categories of the corpus. This table is based on frequency of tags. It does not indicate how many words of text are devoted to each category. However, the information we presented in Short *et al.*, "Using a Corpus ...", concerning the first phase of the project, with the 88,631-word sample, indicated that the differences between proportions of category instances and proportions of words used were very slight. We are not yet in a position to provide accurate word-count information. We hope to be able to provide this information in the near future, but do not expect the comparative frequencies to vary significantly in percentage terms from the category-instance figures we provide here. In the table presented in Appendix 3, there are two columns for the whole corpus and for each of the six sub-parts of the corpus. For each pair of columns, the first is the raw score of category tags and the second expresses that raw score as a percentage of the tags in the relevant sub-part of the corpus.

4.1. N, NRS, NRT and NRW

Unsurprisingly, the most frequent category in the corpus as a whole is N, the tag for stretches of narrative action and description. This is followed by NRS, which again is unsurprising, given that most DS and IS strings, and some FIS strings, will be accompanied by NRS. What is more interesting, though, is that for both the broadsheet and popular newspapers, the NRS category is more frequent than N (broadsheets: 24.80 %:18.81 %; tabloids: 25.42 %:23.51 %). These figures are a measure of how much news report is, in fact, *speech* report, particularly for the broadsheet newspapers. The thought presentation equivalent of this category, NRT, is the ninth most frequent category. But the overall corpus percentage for NRT is 1.96 % as against 17.73 % for NRS, and the newspaper figures for NRT are the lowest across the text-types, with the figures for fiction texts easily beating the combined figures of the newspaper and (auto)biography texts. For the writing equivalent, NRW (the thirteenth most frequent tag: 1.10 %) newspapers come between the other two text-types.

If we restrict ourselves to the top eight categories overall (i.e. categories constituting 2 % or above of the whole corpus), we can see that apart from narration (N), and internal narration (NI), all of the other categories are *speech* presentation categories. Hence speech presentation wins out significantly in quantitative terms compared with thought and writing presentation.

4.2. IS, (F)DS and NRSA(P)

Within the reported clauses of reported speech, DS is the highest speech presentation category, and if our argument concerning the wisdom of collapsing the DS and FDS categories together into one (see 3.1 above) is taken into account, the dominance of DS would be all the greater. NRSAP is a subset of the NRSA category, and so those two scores should also be added together.

In our report on the first phase of the corpus in Short *et al.*, "Using a Corpus ...", we pointed out that:

> 'For 'high' literature, popular fiction and the tabloids the quantitative norm is clearly at the DS/FDS end of the scale. However, this is not true of the broadsheets. Most broadsheet presentation falls into IS (14.5 %) and NRSA (13.8 %). Together they account for 27.3 % of the words in the broadsheets.... NRSA and IS are also the least 'dramatic' of the speech presentation forms and so correspond best with the serious and balanced image that the broadsheets cherish. NRSA and IS, with their summarizing function, are also well represented in the tabloids, accounting for 16.38 % of words. However, the tabloids prioritize the more direct end of the scale. Combined, FDS and DS account for 26.25 % of the words in the tabloids. This compares with 12.67 % of the words in the broadsheets for the same categories. This predominance of DS in the tabloids is presumably the result of a wish to present news stories in a vivid, dramatic and striking manner.
> (Short *et al.* "Using a Corpus ...", 128-9)

To compare the larger newspaper corpus in these respects with the above remarks about the smaller one, below we present a table giving the scores for combined DS and FDS, IS, and the combined scores for NRSA and NRSAP (which were not distinguished at the earlier tagging stage):

	DS + FDS		*IS*		*NRSA(P)*	
Text type	*Tags*	*Words*	*Tags*	*Words*	*Tags*	*Words*
Broadsheets	11.54 %	16.06 %	14.36 %	13.10 %	12.78 %	10.99 %
Tabloids	17.63 %	27.47 %	10.11 %	8.02 %	11.41 %	9.04 %

There are some very similar statistics here to those reported in Short *et al.*, "Using a Corpus ...", confirming the earlier claims. The combined IS and NRSA wordscore for the broadsheets is now a little lower (24.09 % compared with 27.30 %), and the equivalent tabloid score is now slightly higher (17.06 % compared with 16.38 %), but the broadsheet figure is still considerably higher than the tabloid score. The broadsheet DS + FDS scores are rather higher (16.06 % compared with 12.67 %), but the equivalent tabloid scores are much the same (27.47 % compared with 26.25 %). Nonetheless, the broadsheet/tabloid differences are still quite large, and in terms of the percentage of tags, IS alone still outweighs DS + FDS in the broadsheets, whereas for the tabloids the figures are reversed. Interestingly, the figures for the serious and popular (auto)biographies, which have many similar functions, reflect the same kind of reversal pattern, even more clearly:

	DS + FDS		*IS*		*NRSA(P)*	
Text type	*Tags*	*Words*	*Tags*	*Words*	*Tags*	*Words*
Serious (auto)biography	5.26 %	5.28 %	7.62 %	6.80 %	10.60 %	7.19 %
Popular (auto)biography	18.25 %	21.19 %	4.39 %	2.90 %	6.70 %	3.69 %

4.3. NI and NIi

If we look at NI and NIi, we can see how the incidence of these categories varies in relation to the major functions of the various text-types. Unlike fictional prose, more or less all the newspaper NI-data is of the kind which must have been inferred through what someone else said or did, and so was coded as NIi. In other words, there is virtually no 'directly perceived' NI in news reports. Below we present a table which compares the incidence of NIi and 'directly perceived' NI tags:

Text-type	*NIi tags*	*'Directly perceived' NI tags*
Serious fiction	27 (1.04 %)	194 (7.48 %)
Popular fiction	31 (1.06 %)	175 (5.99 %)
Serious (auto)biography	247 (8.96 %)	91 (3.30 %)
Popular (auto)biography	193 (7.19 %)	88 (3.28 %)
Serious newspaper	118 (4.34 %)	0 (0 %)
Popular newspaper	85 (3.24 %)	1 (0.04 %)

The 'directly perceived' NI tag-scores for serious and popular fiction are proportionally the largest, reflecting the importance of privileged narration for fiction. The (auto)biography section has the highest NIi scores, and although these texts are clearly not fictional, we also see figures of 3.30 % and 3.28 % respectively for 'directly perceived' NI in the serious and popular sections of the sample. It is highly likely that the incidence of 'directly perceived' NI in this section of the corpus relates to the privileged-narrator access of autobiography, but we have not yet looked at comparisons between biography and autobiography, and so cannot confirm this empirically.

One might expect that the fiction texts would score zero for NIi. But in fact the serious fiction set has 2.04 %, and the popular fiction set 1.44 %, of tags in this category, presumably as a result of first-person narrators and other characters making internal narration inferences about other characters. However, an astonishing 8.96 % of the serious (auto)biography tags are NIi tags, and the equivalent figure for the popular section is 7.19 %. Inference concerning the internal states of others is thus 2-3 times greater in (auto)biography than news report. These varying patterns across the different parts of the corpus clearly begin to give us a sense of the statistical character of text-type variation with respect to discourse presentation.

4.4. The Quotation Phenomenon: 'q'

In Appendix 4 we give figures concerning the distribution of the 'q' phenomenon in our data.[5] Altogether in our corpus we have 28 coding types which involve 'q', representing 2.98 % of total tags. However, a little over half of these codings only have 1 or 2 instances across the whole corpus. Hence, in Appendix 4, we give the top 11 'q' codings, representing 5 tags or above across the entire corpus. Of the 17 'q' codings not represented in the table, only 3, all single instances, are from the newspaper part of the corpus, and so almost all of the relevant newspaper tags are represented in the table in Appendix 4.

Some reasonably obvious general patterns appear. First of all, 'q' tags are spread across all three discourse presentation scales (but with relatively few, predictably, for thought presentation). Secondly, the 'q' phenomenon can be found reasonably well represented in all six of our text-types. Thirdly, three of the most common tag-types concern writing presentation. NRWAPq is the fourth most frequent 'q' category, IWq is sixth and FIWq is eighth. NRWAPq occurs in all text-types, and IWq occurs in all text-types except popular news report. As would be expected, the 'q' tags cluster towards the indirect end of the three discourse presentation scales. Overleaf is a table indicating the frequency of 'q' for the speech presentation tags at the indirect end of the continuum.

We would not expect to find the quotation phenomenon in NV, as this category only refers to clauses like 'they talked to one another'. Similarly, it is predictable that, once we have a distinction between NRSA and NRSAP, all of the 'q' instances will be in the NRSAP category, as the quotation will be a sufficient condition to specify the topic of talk. If we recalculate the percentage of tags with 'q' so that it does not include NRSA and NV, the total percentage of 'q' tags as a proportion of NRSAP, IS and FIS tags is 12.89 %, giving an indication of its importance in these categories in news report.

In the newspaper data, NRSAPq, ISq and Nq are well-represented in both the serious and popular sections, but a pattern does begin to emerge

Category	*Total tags*	*'q' tags*	*%*
NV	377	0	0.00
NRSA without P	389	0	0.00
NRSAP	959	132	13.76
IS	1095	128	11.69
FIS	165	26	15.76
Total	2985	286	9.58

with respect to writing presentation, which is consistently more common in the broadsheets, something which would correspond with the images and attitudes which the two newspaper types represent. Writing representation is also common in the (auto)biographies, but with no obvious discriminatory patterns between the high and low sections of that part of the corpus.

5. Qualitative Analysis of News Reports of the '"PC" Bible' Story

We will now discuss, mainly in qualitative terms, the news story which we alluded to in section 1, concerning OUP's publication of a 'politically correct' Bible in the USA in 1994. As we said earlier, we collected news stories from newspapers over a 2-day period in order to allow textual comparison across the newspaper corpus. Appendix 2 gives (in untagged form, for ease of reading) the texts of the six newspapers in which the story appeared, four of which are tabloids (*The Daily Express*, *The Daily Mirror, Today,* and *The Sun*), and two broadsheets (*The Times* and *The Daily Telegraph*).

5.1. The Headlines and Related Matters

All six newspapers take the same general 'line' on the story, concentrating on the opposition to the new text and ridiculing it directly or indirectly. This common 'line' can be easily seen by comparing the headlines (the differing representations below reflect the upper/lower case choices made in the different papers, but print size and style is not reflected):

For God's sake stop rewriting our Bible (*Daily Express*)
God is a Mother in Bible rethink (*Daily Mirror*)
PC BIBLE 'IS AN INSULT' (*Today*)

STORM AS TRENDIES CENSOR THE BIBLE (*The Sun*)
Word is made PC for him-her (*The Times*)
Bishops pour scorn on non-sexist Bible (*The Daily Telegraph*)

The Daily Mirror and *The Times* concentrate in their headlines on the changes to the Bible, but in very different ways. *The Times* headline is clearly ironic, signalling an ironic (and thus critical) flavour for the article as a whole. The *Mirror* is more straightforwardly antipathetic, as seen in 'God is a Mother ...'. In other contexts, this statement might be seen as positive, but given the general concern of the tabloids to preserve the traditional, it is unlikely to be positive here. From the correspondence across various quotations in the set of articles, it is also clear that this part of the *Mirror* headline is factually inaccurate. There is considerable allusion (even in the *Mirror* article itself) to God being referred to in a 'gender-neutral' way, as 'Father-Mother' (6 references), and Jesus Christ being referred to as 'the Human One' (6 references).

Of the remaining four headlines, three concentrate on the verbal opposition to the changes, using heavily emotional language ('storm', 'insult', 'censor'). But perhaps the most interesting is the headline from the *Daily Express*, which is ambiguous. Is 'For God's sake stop rewriting our Bible', with its rather obvious play on the referential and exclamatory uses of the word 'God', (a) a plea/exhortation on the part of the *Express* editorial team or (b) a Free Direct report of a similar speech act uttered by someone else (probably one of those interviewed?) who is opposed to the new Bible? It is impossible to know; and if it is quotation without quotation marks, it is unattributed, and not referred to again in the main body of the article. This makes sure that the headline will not constitute a libel problem. The ambiguity is also rhetorically helpful for the newspaper, as it shuttles interpretatively between two construals: (a) the uttering of a remark by the newspaper on behalf of its readers which many of them would have liked to make and (b) the evocation of such a statement being uttered by an authority figure (most likely a member of the Church of England establishment). Interestingly, *The Telegraph*'s headline makes specific reference to such authority figures, and like those who buy the *Express*, readers of the other two 'verbal opposition' headlines are likely to infer, correctly or not, that 'storm' and 'insult' relate to the views of religious establishment figures. The *Sun* headline also makes reference to 'trendies' who have ordered/performed the rewriting, and it is perhaps no accident that the two newspapers most likely to have taken a more sympathetic line, *The Guardian* and *The Independent*, did not report the story at all.

Today's headline is an example of Nq, but the quotation is unverifiable as the source is not revealed in the headline, and does not reappear in the main body of the article. This points up a particular problem in assessing whether direct quotation in news report is accurate or not. In this case there is no way of determining the matter without consulting the reporter who wrote the article and the person claimed to have made the remark. And in any case, without a tape-recording it would be impossible to resolve a difference of view between the individuals concerned. This problem also applies to attributed quotation of speech; and even for writing report, most of the time readers will not have access to an original to enable checking, or the time and inclination to do so, even if they do have such access. We originally chose to examine this set of articles not just for their intrinsic interest, but also because we thought we could verify the quotations from the 'PC' Bible. But even this has not been possible. OUP have not published the book in the UK, and so far we have been unsuccessful in getting hold of a copy of the American publication.

Thus, although in principle discourse report in newspapers is verifiable, for most readers the situation is much as it is when reading novels, even when, as in this case, a good deal of the discourse report is writing report. You only have the text in front of you to go on. Hence there will be a tendency to assume that direct quotations are accurate *verbatim* reports, that IS is accurate with respect to propositional content, but not necessarily employing the words and structures used to utter that content, and so on. Interestingly, however, as we will show below, even when the original discourse is inaccessible, it is possible for the researcher to get nearer the truth in some cases, by correlating what is said across the different articles.

5.2. The Main Body of the Articles

As we might expect from the headlines, the overall structure of each of the six stories involves a mix of (a) reporting offending phrases from the new Bible, (b) reporting opposition to the new edition and (c) making critical commentary in either a direct or indirect form. The report of the opposition to the new Bible is perhaps most interesting for its source variation. There are vague references to what was said by unattributable 'church leaders', 'churchmen' etc. (a total of 6 references) and the OUP's 'panel of expert readers' (1). In addition, the six articles quote, or report more indirectly, the antithetical comments of 9 different clerics, only one of which (the Archdeacon of York, George Austin) is referred to in more than one article (*The Express* and *The Times*). Hence there is no way of being able to ascertain the accuracy of the reports from 'triangulation' across the different reports. As a consequence, the remainder of this analysis will concentrate on 'triangulating' the reports of what appears in the new Bible and the, unacknowledged, OUP press release. In effect, then, much of the articles appear to be *writing report*, because of their reliance on this unacknowledged written source.

The single word 'oppression' occurs, isolated within quotation marks, in three of the articles. Twice it occurs in an Nq structure and once in ISq. Here is the Nq example from the *Express:*

> The changes have been made by Oxford University Press in a bid to take the "oppression" out of Christianity.

If an example like the above was read in isolation, it would be difficult to know whether the quoted word was real quotation, or an example of 'scare quotes'. But when it turns up as part of an Nq or ISq structure in three different articles, where in each case OUP is said to be trying to take the 'oppression' out of either the Bible or Christianity more generally, it would appear that the word is being quoted, either from a preface to the edition of the Bible, or, more likely, from an OUP press release. After all, (i) the reporters are hardly likely to have had the time to read the new edition of the Bible, looking for things to comment on (and as we shall see below, what they quote is very similar), and (ii) OUP have a vested interest in inducing interest in the edition through its notoriety.

The use of the 'q' structure in three of the six articles is interesting because there is no real need for the quotation marks, and yet three of the writers apparently feel the need to use them. Similar, but more extensive, patterns can be seen in the use of other words and phrases. Reference to the removal of bias against the left-handed is referred to in all six articles, which point out that references to God's right hand have been replaced by 'mighty hand'. In all six articles, 'mighty hand' is in quotation marks, and five of the articles immediately precede 'mighty hand' with 'God', either inside or outside the quotation marks. The one exception is the *Times*, which uses 'his-her "mighty hand"' for obvious ironic purposes. Jesus Christ is quoted as being referred to as 'the Human One' in the *Sun* and the *Telegraph*, and the same phrase is also used (but not in quotation marks) in all of the other articles. God is quoted as being referred to as 'Father-Mother' in the *Sun* and the *Telegraph*, and the term also occurs in every article except that from the *Express*. It even occurs in the *Mirror*, in spite of the fact that it partially contradicts the article's own headline 'God is a Mother in Bible rethink' (which thus looks like an example of sloppy writing by the sub-editor responsible for the headline). The one exception to the 'Father-Mother rule' for these articles is the *Express*, which reports, apparently inaccurately, the reference to God as 'Mother':

> ... congregations will be asked to thank Our Mother who art in Heaven.

Given the ambiguity of the *Express* headline, it looks as if this newspaper is sacrificing reporting accuracy to rhetorical effects which will appeal to its readership.[6] 'Thanks to Our Mother in Heaven' also appears, along with two other 'offending phrases' on the front cover of a representation of the 'Holy Bible' next to the article, and there is a photograph of 'AGAINST: Archdeacon Austin' next to the headline. So the *Express* is clearly making more of the story than the other papers, of which only the *Times* has a picture, of Tyndale, on whose translation the much-loved 1611 Authorised Version of the Bible was based, and who, the *Times* reporter gleefully declares, 'will be spinning in his grave'.

6. Conclusions

The discussion in section 5 is reminiscent of work in Critical Discourse Analysis, of course, and our corpus is of potential interest for those wanting to compare different treatments of the same news item. But what are we to make of all of this for ST&WP theory? Clearly the *Express* is fiddling the evidence a bit in the '"PC" Bible' story. However, finding some people who do not always abide by discoursal rules is not an automatic argument for throwing the rules away, and, in any case, as far as we can see, even the *Express* reporter does not illicitly use overtly DS strings. Moreover, it is clear that the other articles are all accurately quoting the phrases explored in detail in 5.2 above. Of course, using direct quotation is useful rhetorically as a foregrounding device in the reporting context. But given the correspondences across the articles, it would appear that the writers are, by and large, still governed by an impulse to report DS strings accurately, in spite of the recent claims of some theorists (e.g. Sternberg, "Proteus in Quotation-land ...", Tannen, *Talking Voices ...* and Fludernik, *The Fictions of Language ...*, but for opposing views, see Toolan, "Review of M. Fludernik ..." and Short *et al.*, "A (Free Direct) Reply ..."). Moreover, this story is in a relatively unimportant 'fun' area for most of the newspapers, appearing anywhere between pages 5 and 13, where we might expect reporting attitudes towards accuracy rules to be more relaxed than in more prominent articles.

More careful consideration will need to be given to a wide range of reporting contexts and the various media of representation before firm conclusions can properly be reached concerning faithfulness in discourse report. Before a complete theory of discourse representation can be attained, factors like whether the reporting discourse is spoken or written, and whether the reported strings are speech, thought or writing will have to be taken into account, as well as pragmatic factors like legal considerations, the importance of the words being reported, and so on. We hope to expand on this in Wynne *et al.*, "Faithfulness Revisited ...".

The use of tagged electronic corpora of the sort we have developed will be one of the ways in which more accurate and detailed assessments can be arrived at. They allow researchers more easily to observe patterns across large amounts of data, and thus (a) check existing theories and (b) discover new aspects of textual organisation which need explanation. But as we hope to have shown in section 5 above, our corpus does not just afford an opportunity to observe patterns and trends across discourse types, but can also be used for interesting qualitative comparative analysis of related texts. There is plenty more to be said, even about the six short news reports discussed in section 5 above, but we hope to have indicated the ways in which scholars interested in news-text analysis can use a corpus-based approach in interesting ways.

Notes

1 We are grateful for the pump-priming grant for this initial phase of the project which we received from the Faculty of Social Sciences, Lancaster University.

2 We would like to express our thanks to the Humanities Research Board of the British Academy for supporting this project in 1996/7 with a Larger Research Grant (M-AN2314/APN/3489), and to Lancaster University's Committee for Research for a further grant to complete the work on this second phase of the project.

3 The word-counts, although apparently precise, are in fact approximate, and are probably slight over-estimates. We are checking word counts at the moment, and, in any case, there is always some ambiguity over how to count words (e.g. are hyphenated sequences to be counted as one word or more?). We do not expect the final figures to change significantly, however.

4 This might be an interesting issue with respect to cross-cultural studies of newspaper discourse. In the discussion following his presentation at the conference where this paper was also presented (the 1997 ESSE conference in Debrecen, Hungary), Hannes Kniffka indicated informally that in the English language newspapers from Saudi Arabia which he had studied, NV could well occur with reasonable regularity without being used to introduce further details of the discourse referred to.

5 Waugh, "Reported Speech in Journalistic Discourse", has also commented on the presence of what she calls 'combined direct/indirect speech' in *Le Monde.* Clark and Gerrig, in "Quotations as Demonstrations", use the term 'incorporated quotations' for stretches of direct speech embedded within indirect speech.

6 References to the language of the Bible being changed to avoid racism, and in particular suggestions that the Jews killed Christ are also made, but more patchily across the articles, and in a rather wide variety of presentation forms. As the patterns with respect to these items are not very clear, we have not commented

on them extensively here, but it looks as if these areas are being deemed by a number of the reporters as not being so salient for their readers as some of the others, or perhaps as areas to be positively avoided.

Bibliography

Clark, H. H. & R. J. Gerrig: "Quotations as Demonstrations", *Language* 66, 1990, 764-805.

Fludernik, M.: *The Fictions of Language and the Languages of Fiction*. London: Routledge, 1993.

Leech, G. N. & M. H. Short: *Style in Fiction*. London: Longman, 1981.

McHale, B.: "Free Indirect Discourse: A Survey of Recent Accounts", *PTL* 3, 1978, 249-87.

Semino, E., M. Short & J. Culpepper: "Using a Computer Corpus to Test a Model of Speech and Thought Presentation", *Poetics* 25, 1997, 17-43.

Short, M.: "Speech Presentation, the Novel and the Press". – In W. van Peer (Ed.): *The Taming of The Text*, London: Routledge, 1988, pp. 61-81.

Short, M., E. Semino & J. Culpepper: "Using a Corpus for Stylistics Research: Speech and Thought Presentation". – In J. Thomas & M. Short (Eds.): *Using Corpora in Language Research*. London: Longman, 1996, pp. 110-31.

Short, M., E. Semino & M. Wynne: "A (Free Direct) Reply to Paul Simpson's Discourse", *Journal of Literary Semantics*, XXVI, 3, 1997, 219-28.

Slembrouck, S.: "The Parliamentary Hansard 'Verbatim' Report: The Written Construction of Spoken Discourse", *Language and Literature* 1, 2, 1992, 101-119.

Sternberg, M.: "Proteus in Quotation-land: Mimesis and the Forms of Reported Discourse", *Poetics Today* 3, 2, 1982, 107-56.

Tannen, D.: *Talking Voices: Repetition, Dialogue, and Imagery in Conversational Discourse.* Cambridge University Press: Cambridge, 1989.

Toolan, M.: "Review of M. Fludernik, *The Fictions of Language and the Languages of Fiction*", *Language and Literature*, 3, 3, 1994, 223-8.

Waugh, L.: "Reported Speech in Journalistic Discourse: The Relation of Function and Text", *Text* 15, 1, 1995, 129-73.

Wynne, M., M. Short & E. Semino: "A Corpus-based Investigation of Speech, Thought and Writing Presentation in English Narrative Texts". – In A. Renouf (Ed.): *Explorations in Corpuslinguistics*, Amsterdam: Rodopi, 1998, pp. 231-45.

Wynne, M., M. Short & E. Semino: "Faithfulness Revisited: A Pragmatic Approach to the Theory of Discourse Presentation" (working title), in preparation.

APPENDIX 1: DISCOURSE PRESENTATION CATEGORIES

Below, the speech presentation categories are presented in order from the most free/most faithful type of presentation (FDS) to the most minimal (NV). The presentation category referred to within each quotation is italicised Examples are also given of simple Narration (N), the 'q' category and the Narrator's Representation of Internal states (NIi), as these categories are also referred to in this paper. It should be noted that we work with three parallel scales, which we systematically distinguish, speech, thought and writing. The thought and writing presentation scales each have a set of categories parallel to those of the speech presentation scale, and strictly, NIi belongs to the thought presentation scale. However, the point about NIi in non fictional writing is that the internal states represented are not reported as a result of some sort of privileged mind-access (as is often the case in fictional narration), but on the basis of external, mainly verbal behaviour. This category thus connects the speech presentation and the thought presentation scales in newspaper reporting.

The speech report scale

FDS

I was knee deep in mud, bullets and hippos...
(*News of the World*, I was knee deep in mud, bullets and hippos...)

DS

Lynn says: "*When I met his plane at Heathrow I was shocked by how he looked. He's lost at least a stone and a half he's wasted away.*"
(*News of the World*, I was knee deep in mud, bullets and hippos...)

FIS

Shadow Home Secretary Jack Straw called for the Queen to be stripped of most of her powers and the number of working Royals cut to around six.
The monarchy would be run more along the lines of Scandinavian countries with its most popular member, the Queen Mother, probably left out.
(*Daily Express*, Don't destroy our monarchy)

IS

A government spokesman in Moscow said *the troops would pause before entering Grozny.*
(*The Independent.* Russians pit huge forces against rebels)

NRSA

Most were receiving calls from readers *who were attempting to inform on their friends or neighbours*
(*The Independent*, Lottery winner joins the elite)

NRSAP

Russian liberals, including some of Mr Yeltsin's closest former allies such as the former prime minister, Yegor Gaidar, have denounced military action as a threat not only to lives in Chechnya but to Russia's fledgling democracy.
(*The Independent*, Russians pit huge forces against rebels)

NV

Speaking outside the Royal Mews, scouser Gordon still had on his official uniform under a scruffy coat
(*News of the World*, Everyone got off their heads and started feeling randy)

NRS

This is the 'reporting clause' in what is normally known as DS and IS, though it can also occur in some other strings (for example, FIS in some cases). Examples would be the non-underlined portions of the DS and IS examples quoted above.

Other Categories Referred to in This Paper

'q'

[Technically the quotation phenomenon, q, can occur within any of the speech presentation categories except DS and FDS (for obvious reasons) and NRSA (see section 3.4 for discussion). It can even occur within N. The example below contains ISq.]
He said Sheene and Austrian pal Berger *"totally co-operated"* when questioned in March.
(*The Sun*, Barry Sheene in sex quiz)

NIi

As the Cabinet split deepens, *Tory MPs pushing for a referendum are worried Mr Blair will steal a march on Mr Major.*
(*Daily Express*, Portillo piles on Euro pressure)

Daily Express, 5/12/94, Author: Paul Fuller

For God's sake stop rewriting our Bible

New scriptures may be PC but they're not gospel truth

ANGRY churchmen have condemned a politically-correct Bible which has rewritten the scriptures to avoid giving offence.

It attempts to do away with alleged sexism, racism and even bias against left-handed people.

Traditionalists have accused the authors of heresy and claim they are making a mockery of the Bible message.

"We are not at liberty to change the word of God just to be politically correct," said the Rev. Tony Higton. "If you are going to tear some pages out of the Bible and rewrite others where will it finish?

"You end up with something that would ultimately be a different religion." The most obvious change is the removal of God's male identity.

Crippled

Jesus becomes the Human One instead of the Son of Man and congregations will be asked to thank Our Mother who art in Heaven.

The authors have gone out of their way to avoid any suggestion of anti-Semitism.

Jews as a race are no longer held responsible for crucifying Christ.

Out go references which class people specifically as blind or crippled. Even bias against left-handed people is banished.

The authors have removed verses which talk of "God's right hand" and replaced them with references to "God's mighty hand".

The changes have been made by Oxford University Press in a bid to take the "oppression" out of Christianity.

The new Bible is to be published in America in February and last night its opponents in the Church of England vowed to fight publication here.

Mr Higton, of Hawkwell church near Rochford Essex, said: "The Bible was originally written in Hebrew and Greek and we do need accurate translation. I actually prefer the word Mankind to Humanity.

"But to go as far as removing bias against left-handed people is ridiculous.

"If we allow these changes we are making human opinions more important than God's word-and that is dangerously close to saying human beings are more important than God."

The Archdeacon of York, the Venerable George Austin, said: "The traditional language of the Bible is part of its majesty.

"It's ludicrous to invent language in this way. It will mean nothing to ordinary parishioners."

Nigel Lynn, editor of OUP's bible section, admitted: "I'm sure some people will take great exception to it.

"But it's controversial whichever way you go. Others would say the only controversial thing is not doing this."

Daily Mirror, 5/12/94, Author: Don Mackay

God is a Mother in Bible rethink

AN UNHOLY row broke out yesterday over a new politically-correct Bible. God the Father has become our Father-Mother in Heaven. Jesus is no longer the Son of Man but the Human One.

Any references to women's servitude to men have been scrapped.

So, too, have lines equating darkness with evil, in case they could be classed as racist.

In Thessalonians, the "Jews who killed both the Lord Jesus and the prophets" has been altered to "those who killed."

Remarks about disabled people are also taboo.

Even God's "right hand" has become "mighty hand" in the new Good Book, published by the Oxford University Press but aimed at the politically sensitive American market.

Nonsense

The publishers, who are said to be considering a British launch, too, claim to have removed "oppression" from the Bible.

But retired canon of Oxford's Christ Church John Fletcher – who was on the OUP's advice panel – said: "It's nonsense.

"This Mother-Father thing is mad."

And the Church of England is sticking by its authorised versions of the King James and the New English bibles.

Spokesman Steven Jenkins said yesterday: "The Synod debated possible changes in the Bible last July and decided to stand by its traditional terms of references for God.

"But the reading of the Bible, and which one, is a personal thing."

Today, 5/12/94

PC BIBLE 'IS AN INSULT'

AN UNHOLY row has blown up over the first politically-correct version of the Bible. The new-look Good Book has cut out references which could offend women, Jews, black people, the disabled and left-handed.

Church leaders say it "crucifies" Christianity. The new Bible, produced by Oxford University Press, calls God the Father-Mother and Jesus the Human One. General Synod member Rev John Broadhurst said: "The Bible has been received from the past and only nutcases would be offended by it."

OUP spokesman Andrew Potter said the Bible was being published in America and they were waiting for reaction before deciding if there is a market in Britain.

The Sun, 5/12/94

STORM AS TRENDIES CENSOR THE BIBLE

CHURCH leaders yesterday blasted a politically-correct bible which calls God "Father-Mother" to avoid offending women.

The new book – rewritten to exclude any racist, sexist or "unfeeling" language – also calls Jesus "the Human One" instead of Son of Man.

References to the Jews crucifying Christ have been axed. And the expression "God's right hand" is changed to "God's mighty hand" to pacify left-handed folk.

The new Bible, produced in America by Oxford University Press, may be published in Britain next year.

Last night, Archdeacon of Oxford, the Venerable Frank Weston said: "One has to be sensitive, but extreme solutions of this kind are silly."

The Times, 5/12/94, Author: Alan Hamilton

Word is made PC for him-her

THE time has come to pray to God the Father-Mother and Jesus the Human One for the soul of William Tyndale.

Tyndale, upon whose 16th-century translation of the Bible much of the majesty of the Authorised Version is based, will be spinning in his grave at news that yet another travesty of the world's best-selling book is about to be launched in the name of political correctness. Sexism and racism have no place in the new version being prepared by the Oxford University Press for the American market. God ceases to be male and becomes a hyphenated bisexual, while the Son of Man, who cannot possibly be said to have been killed by the Jews, becomes the Human One. Even the left-handed are spared offence: God's right hand becomes his-her "mighty hand".

The new OUP Bible is not the first to tinker with the Word of God in pursuit of current fashion. A children's illustrated Bible issued earlier this year by the British publisher Dorling Kindersley could not bring itself to describe Mary as a virgin, but referred to her instead as "a girl, and not married", thus undermining one of the basic tenets of Christian belief. It also illustrated the archangel Gabriel with no wings.

Although the British approach to the Christian religion is generally regarded as more traditionalist than the American, even the General Synod of the Church of England has been divided on whether to update the scriptures.

Conservatives such as the Ven George Austin, Archdeacon of York, believe in the majesty of the Authorised Version and do not believe that de-sexing the Father and Son means much to the average parishioner. Liberals take the view that there have been new English translations at regular intervals for the past 300 years and there is no reason to stop.

The OUP's panel of expert readers that vets its new Bible editions has been far from enthusiastic about the impending PC version, describing it as "nonsense". The publishers however, have an eye to a new market, although they will not say at this stage whether the new version will be unleashed on poor William Tyndale's home country.

The Daily Telegraph, 5/12/94, Author: Victoria Combe

Bishops pour scorn on non-sexist Bible

PROMINENT Churchmen yesterday scorned plans to publish a politically-correct Bible which refers to Jesus as "The Human One" instead of the "Son of Man" and God as "Father-Mother".

The non-sexist non-racist version of the Bible, which includes only the Psalms and Gospels, is being published by Oxford University Press in America in February and is being considered for publication in Britain.

The Rev John Fenton, a retired canon of Christ Church, Oxford, and an OUP adviser, has told them the book is "silly" and should not be published here.

"It is all ridiculous," said Mr Fenton, father of James Fenton, the poet. "The Bible is a book from the ancient world and it is a mistake to think you can update it to appear as if it was written yesterday."

The amended Bible strives to take the "oppression" out of Christianity by removing language which is deemed insensitive to women, the disabled and left-handed people. Verses which refer to the "right hand" of God have been changed to the "mighty hand".

In an effort to be 'gender-inclusive', the text has also been cleansed of male pronouns in reference to God and the term "Father-Mother" employed.

Any verses which describe evil as darkness have been removed on grounds of racism and where possible the Jews become "people" of non-specific race.

The Rt Rev Nigel McCulloch, Bishop of Wakefield dismissed the new Bible as an "unhelpful" novelty which was being used by the publishers as a moneyspinner.

The Rt Rev John Taylor, Bishop of St Albans, said he feared the new Bible reflected a "worrying trend" in political correctness which threatens to "emasculate Christianity."

The politically correct movement has not had much success in the Church of England. But in America, feminist theology is thriving.

APPENDIX 3: THE 20 MOST FREQUENT TAGS IN THE CORPUS

	whole corpus		*serious biography*		*serious fiction*		*serious news*		*popular biography*		*popular fiction*		*popular news*	
Total	16299	100.00 %	2756	100.00 %	2595	100.00 %	2722	100.00 %	2685	100.00 %	2921	100.00 %	2620	100.00 %
N	3584	21.99 %	677	24.56 %	586	22.58 %	512	18.81 %	603	22.46 %	590	20.20 %	616	23.51 %
NRS	2889	17.73 %	338	12.26 %	325	12.52 %	675	24.80 %	454	16.91 %	431	14.76 %	666	25.42 %
DS	2055	12.61 %	121	4.39 %	348	13.41 %	286	10.51 %	410	15.27 %	487	16.67 %	403	15.38 %
NRSA	1348	8.27 %	292	10.60 %	125	4.82 %	348	12.78 %	180	6.70 %	104	3.56 %	299	11.41 %
NI	1250	7.67 %	338	12.26 %	221	8.52 %	118	4.34 %	281	10.47 %	206	7.05 %	86	3.28 %
IS	1095	6.72 %	210	7.62 %	48	1.85 %	391	14.36 %	118	4.39 %	63	2.16 %	265	10.11 %
FDS	919	5.64 %	24	0.87 %	277	10.67 %	28	1.03 %	80	2.98 %	451	15.44 %	59	2.25 %
NV	377	2.31 %	78	2.83 %	45	1.73 %	80	2.94 %	66	2.46 %	60	2.05 %	48	1.83 %
NRT	319	1.96 %	49	1.78 %	80	3.08 %	20	0.73 %	64	2.38 %	92	3.15 %	14	0.53 %
FIT	276	1.69 %	29	1.05 %	114	4.39 %	0	0.00 %	16	0.60 %	117	4.01 %	0	0.00 %
IT	211	1.29 %	41	1.49 %	44	1.70 %	19	0.70 %	43	1.60 %	55	1.88 %	9	0.34 %
NRWA	199	1.22 %	89	3.23 %	18	0.69 %	18	0.66 %	43	1.60 %	8	0.27 %	23	0.88 %
NRW	180	1.10 %	72	2.61 %	12	0.46 %	30	1.10 %	43	1.60 %	7	0.24 %	16	0.61 %
FIS	165	1.01 %	47	1.71 %	35	1.35 %	26	0.96 %	20	0.74 %	19	0.65 %	18	0.69 %
IS-FIS	133	0.82 %	22	0.80 %	11	0.42 %	44	1.62 %	16	0.60 %	21	0.72 %	19	0.73 %
NRTA	120	0.74 %	23	0.83 %	34	1.31 %	7	0.26 %	22	0.82 %	31	1.06 %	3	0.11 %
N-FIT	117	0.72 %	7	0.25 %	47	1.81 %	0	0.00 %	17	0.63 %	44	1.51 %	2	0.08 %
DW	107	0.66 %	60	2.18 %	6	0.23 %	11	0.40 %	16	0.60 %	5	0.17 %	9	0.34 %
N-NRSA	90	0.55 %	26	0.94 %	12	0.46 %	14	0.51 %	25	0.93 %	8	0.27 %	5	0.19 %
IW	73	0.45 %	19	0.69 %	4	0.15 %	17	0.62 %	25	0.93 %	2	0.07 %	6	0.23 %

APPENDIX 4: THE 11 MOST FREQUENT 'q' TAGS IN THE CORPUS

	whole corpus		*serious (auto)biography*		*serious fiction*		*serious news*		*popular (auto)biography*		*popular fiction*		*popular news*	
Total	485	100.00 %	126	100.00 %	30	100.00 %	167	100.00 %	50	100.00 %	16	100.00 %	96	100.00 %
NRSAPq	132	27.22 %	23	18.25 %	10	33.33 %	47	28.14 %	13	26.00 %	5	31.25 %	34	35.42 %
ISq	128	26.39 %	25	19.84 %	0	0.00 %	63	37.72 %	4	8.00 %	4	25.00 %	32	33.33 %
Nq	75	15.46 %	20	15.87 %	9	30.00 %	20	11.98 %	8	16.00 %	2	12.50 %	16	16.67 %
NRWAPq	33	6.80 %	17	13.49 %	2	6.67 %	4	2.40 %	8	16.00 %	1	6.25 %	1	1.04 %
FISq	26	5.36 %	9	7.14 %	2	6.67 %	10	5.99 %	1	2.00 %	0	0.00 %	4	4.17 %
IWq	24	4.95 %	9	7.14 %	1	3.33 %	6	3.59 %	7	14.00 %	1	6.25 %	0	0.00 %
ISq-FISq	15	3.09 %	2	1.59 %	1	3.33 %	8	4.79 %	0	0.00 %	0	0.00 %	4	4.17 %
FIWq	10	2.06 %	5	3.97 %	0	0.00 %	4	2.40 %	1	2.00 %	0	0.00 %	0	0.00 %
Nq-NIq	8	1.65 %	4	3.17 %	0	0.00 %	1	0.60 %	2	4.00 %	0	0.00 %	1	1.04 %
NIq	5	1.03 %	1	0.79 %	1	3.33 %	2	1.20 %	1	2.00 %	0	0.00 %	0	0.00 %
Nq-FISq	5	1.03 %	1	0.79 %	0	0.00 %	2	1.20 %	0	0.00 %	1	6.25 %	1	1.04 %

Karsten Pedersen, Copenhagen

Modality, polyphony and linguistics in political newspaper texts

Towards a unification of the description of different linguistic phenomena

The following article is a sketch of a first attempt at a uniform mode of description to address subjectivity in newspaper discourse. In order to be able to show how quite disparate parts of speech work together to give an overall impression of Sender's presence in a text, I have drawn on French polyphony theory for a vocabulary with which it is possible to address Sender's relation to different expressions in texts. I selected three areas of interest, namely: the reporting of speech, conjunctions, and verbal modality. These areas of interest were selected because of their disparity and of their functions in newspaper texts.

The collection of political newspaper texts on which my research is based, originates from four Californian broadsheet newspapers *The Christian Science Monitor* (CSM), *The Sacramento Bee* (SB), *The Peninsula Times Tribune* (TT) *and San Jose Mercury News* (SJM)) and was compiled during the last part of the 1992 Presidential election campaign in the USA.

Immediately below I will sketch the semantics and the functions of the three areas. Note that the descriptions are quite superficial and therefore fail to do justice to the vast areas of research that they deal with.

Reported speech/speech act description

Basically the reporting of speech is letting (part of) another Sender's utterance into one's own utterance. This can be done in a host of different ways on a scale ranging from indirect speech (Sender's reformulation of an instance of reported speech (RS)) to direct speech (which is normally known as quotation) (Waugh 1995:148). In newspaper texts the use of reported speech functions mainly as Sender's alibi for the reported text's existence in the real world; a way of saying that this is what was really said, but it also functions as Sender's way of modalising the contents of the instance of reported speech as well as commenting upon the status of the original Sender of the reported text.

Conjunctions

When I talk of conjunctions in this article I refer to adversative contrastive conjunctions of which *but* is the prototypical representative. So when I talk of *but* I refer to what is also known as denial *but* (cf. e.g. Blakemore 1987). In Pedersen (1: 1997, 74-90) and (2: 1998) I propose a polyphonic analysis of the structure signalled by the adversative contrastive conjunctions rather than an analysis of the conjunctions themselves. Central to the analysis of this structure is the fact that *but* links two contrasting utterances both of which are deemed true. One of the utterances is regarded to be the more salient of the two, whereby the other is stamped "not salient in the actual instance". The function of adversative contrastive conjunctions in newspaper texts is an argumentative one and therefore they can be seen as part of the argumentation of the text. The modality of the adversative conjunctive constructions lies in marking the two utterances linked by the conjunctions as "salient" and "not salient", respectively.

Verbal modality

In this article verbal modality covers only the modal auxiliary verbs in English, in connection with which we can isolate two central modalities: probability of realisation (*can/could*, *may/might*, *will/would, shall*) and desirability (*must*, *should*). The polyphonic analysis of the modals (Pedersen 1997: 91-106) is based on the insights in Klinge (1994). The function of verbal modality in newspaper texts is to let the Sender comment upon future events based on reported events.

Three different areas under the same heading: Modality

The modal aspect of the description of the three areas of interest mentioned above is rooted in the fact that modality has scope over propositions. In the present paper modality is regarded as Sender's comment on a proposition. In connection with the conjunctions, Sender comments on the salience of propositions; in connection with reported speech, Sender comments on the trustworthiness of the Sender of the reported text or on the contents of the reported text; and in connection with the modals, Sender comments on the probability for realisation/the desirability of the proposition in question.

The polyphonic metaphor

The Anglo-American linguistic tradition does not make available a methodology or a set of terms to address what could be called inherent linguistic subjectivity (but cf. Lyons 1995:341). As a result of this the various approaches to media language lack a vocabulary to address the language of subjectivity. This has led e.g. Bell to say that Fowler's critical linguistics (Fowler 1991; Fowler et al. 1979) ultimately supports conspiracy theories (Bell 1991:214). In Pedersen (1997) I try to show how language-inherent subjectivity can be described using traditional Anglo-American insights viewed through polyphonic glasses. Below follows a brief introduction to the French polyphony theory. A more comprehensive description of polyphony theory is found in Nølke (1989a and 1993a)[1]. Polyphony theory deals with the identification of different voices in texts and with the relation that these voices can be shown to contract with different discourse individuals. Discourse individuals are entities such as Sender, Receiver etc. The most prevalent discourse individual is the Sender (in the sense that Sender controls what is said), and in this article I want to focus on Sender's relation with various utterances[2] identified in the text. Polyphony theory is interested in what is said 'according to the utterance'. The phrasing "according to the utterance" emphasises the fact that the theory deals with what happens in the language system (*langue*). A discourse individual can be said to be committed to an utterance, to present an utterance, and to be non-committed to an utterance. We can see presentation as a reflection of the maxim of quality (that one normally says only that which one believes to be true). So merely stating something amounts to a kind of commitment by default.

The example below is the prototypical polyphonic example:

(1) The wall isn't white.[3]

Here we can identify two different utterances; an implicit utterance that claims that the wall is white (or at least one that gives us (1) as a natural response) and an explicit utterance (1) that claims that the wall is not white. The Sender is non-committed to the former and committed to the latter. The identification of the implicit utterance is rooted in the notion that (1) is uttered as a response to an idea, an utterance or the like to the effect expressed in the implicit utterance.

Below I will briefly comment on the polyphonic description of the three areas of interest in this article.

The description of newspaper texts

As mentioned earlier, this article is far from exhaustive in the sense that it says all there is to say about speech act describing verbs, adversative conjunctions, or the modal auxiliary verbs in English; neither does it claim to be exhaustive in the sense that it deals with all relevant aspects of newspaper discourse. What it does claim, however, is that it introduces the first steps towards a typology of implicit subjectivity in political news reports and in political news analyses. The present paper is the presentation of a mode of newspaper analysis that takes as its point of departure the notion that language is inherently subjective. Therefore the approach exploits the polyphonic metaphor in combination with more traditional linguistic approaches. This combination is the main difference between the approach presented here and the approaches presented in Fowler *et al.* (1979) and Fowler (1991).

In the following I will first show how the three areas of interest can be described in a uniform vocabulary taking the immediate context into consideration.

Qualification of speech acts

In this section I will show how speech act describing verbs can be seen as a reflection of Sender's evaluation of the instances of RS they introduce and how the context can influence the reading of an RS. Speech acts can be qualified by the use of speech act verbs and adverbials both dealing with how the Sender of the reported text said what was said; moreover they can be qualified by context (context validation). Speech act verbs all share the same core viz., *SAY*. The difference between the verbs lies in the interpretation or qualification of the speech acts that they introduce. Such a qualification can be positive, negative, or neutral and at the same time characterise the speech act introduced. The two examples below illustrate the importance of the context. In these cases, the marginal speech act describing verbs' characterisations of the speech act introduced can be supported or let down by context, or, if the verb is only marginally interpretative, the context can control the reading of the text. In the two examples below the context in (2) supports a positive reading of the text (*RASP* is hardly interpretative), and in (3) the context supports the negative connotations of the verb and thereby supports a somewhat sinister (Republican) reading of the text.

(2) "I have nearly lost my voice trying to give you a voice," Clinton RASPED at Detroit's metropolitan airport. "If you will be my voice

tomorrow, I'll be yours for four years." Smiling democratic officeholders and candidates accompanied Clinton and his wife, Hillary, on every platform, and democratic national chairman Ron Brown flew along. The Clinton campaign also dished out two election-eve commercials and a half-hour televised program, all infused with a message of optimism. "Something's happening out there," one advertisement said. "A feeling call it hope that our country can move in a new direction." (SJM, Nov. 3).

(3) "You'll see another Michigan Miracle," CROWED Qayle. But Republican realists gripe that Bush blew his chances in Michigan and the rest of the industrial battleground. "He started campaigning far too late," said Metcalfe. "He didn't take the economy seriously until it hit him in the face." "Too much family values stuff," said radio man Collins. "The convention was a lost chance." "He blew it by not using his Desert Storm popularity to make domestic changes," said Tanter, the Republican rebel. "There are no Reagan Democrats now only Clinton Republicans." Bush trails by 12 points in the latest Michigan polls. But from the Third Base bar ("your last stop before home") to glossy Battle Creek suburbs, you hear anxiety deeper than poll numbers. "When we went for Reagan in '80, it was time for a change," said Dennis Trantune, who moved here from Merion PA. "Now there's the same feeling." Everyone agrees Bush came alive in the last TV slugfest. "He got his pound of flesh," said local Republican chairman Mark Behnke (SJM, Oct. 27).

RASP and *CROW* are both non-factive.[4] Clearly *CROW* has more negative connotations than *RASP*, but that is not where the main difference between (2) and (3) is seen. The main difference is the context (in these cases the text following the RS). Adverbials have the capability of doing basically the same job as the speech act verbs. This will be especially clear in connection with *SAY*, whereas the combination of adverbials and marginal speech act describing verbs makes it possible for the Sender to further positively or negatively qualify an RS. An argumentative clash between speech act verb and adverbial is unlikely (but not impossible), for that would mean that the Sender disagrees with herself.

Verbal qualification

Although speech act reporting may take many different forms, one feature remains common to all instances of speech act reporting. And that is the fact that the introduction of an RS is tantamount to disclaiming responsibility for the utterance of the RS. Unless otherwise indicated the

Sender of the reporting text presents the RS. Thus, in the cases where we are dealing with commitment or non-commitment, it will be marked in the context or by the use of a verb that clearly signals that the RS is true or untrue (without some kind of qualification, none of the speech act describing verbs in my corpus have the latter capacity). The prototypical speech act verb *SAY* is hardly interpretative at all. So *SAY* hardly qualifies the speech acts it refers to. This is what we see in (4):

(4) Clinton has dropped from about 50% toward 40, and we have the President back up to a 6 or 7 point difference," Mr. Black SAYS (CSM, Nov. 2).

Therefore we will have to look beyond *SAY* in order to find interpretative speech act describing verbs. Some of these are barely interpretative, but more so than *SAY*. In (5) below we see how *OBSERVE* is used as a speech act describing verb:

(5) Shirley OBSERVES that voters, unlike pundits, aren't quick to write off an incumbent President. "Voters take this election more seriously than we realize, and that is why there is hope for Bush," he SAYS. They know the e[c]onomy is in trouble. Yet they also know that Bush is a decent man. But is Clinton? (CSM, Nov. 2).

OBSERVE is a factive verb. That means that according to the utterance the Sender of the reporting text in (5) commits herself to the truth of the RS introduced by *OBSERVE*. Thereby we have a contrast between *OBSERVE* and *SAY* which is also used in the text, but which is not factive. We could also say that the Sender merely used *OBSERVE* for stylistic purposes and that he did not mean to commit himself to the truth of any of the instances of RS in (6). In that sense *OBSERVE* is just a stylistic variant of *SAY*. Sender's reasons for the choice, however, do not alter the lexical meaning of the verbs used, and therefore a choice that the journalist intended to be insignificant nonetheless does carry a meaning. *TELL* is a non-factive verb and that means that unless otherwise indicated *TELL* signals that the Sender of the reporting text is merely presenting the RS. This is seen in (6) below:

(6) Bush TOLD NBC that he knows many Americans feel things "haven't gone too great on the economy" and that there is an impulse "to have it out on George Bush" (TT, Oct. 27).

Still, there is a feeling among linguists that *TELL* is somewhat more strongly committed to the truth of the speech act it introduces than *SAY* is (cf. the discussion in Tsohatzidis 1993).[5] Again, even if this is the case it does not prevent an actual choice of *TELL* over *SAY* from being stylistically determined. Newswriters may prefer *TELL* plus indirect object over *SAY TO* plus indirect object because it is marginally shorter. This suspicion is strengthened by the fact that the construction *SAY TO* does not occur in my corpus,[6] and by the context immediately following (6):

(7) He [Bush] SAID he was confident voters would recognize signs of [economic] improvement as well as his accomplishments in foreign policy (TT, Oct. 27).

On the other hand, the fact that *TELL* precedes *SAY* lends an extra emphasis to the contrast between the two verbs. What this means is that the Sender of the reporting text seems to support Bush's notion that many Americans feel the bad economy has damaged him, but does not support the notion that since there are signs of economic growth we will see a reversal of the public image of Bush. Thereby Bush (in (7)), "many Americans", and (through *TELL*) the Sender of the reporting text all support

a) bad economy = low support for Bush;

and on the other hand Bush is on his own when he supports

b) good economy = high support for Bush.

This notion is confirmed by the adversative conjunctive structure of which (7) is a part:

(8) He [Bush] SAID he was confident voters would recognize signs of improvement [in the economy] as well as his accomplishments in foreign policy. However, in two new tracking polls Clinton's lead over Bush widened slightly to 11 percent. (TT, Oct. 27).

So, we will have to accept the notion of verbs as meaning-carrying even if we accept the idea of a stylistically motivated choice of speech act describing verb, as well as the fact that a choice did take place and that this choice is in perfect harmony with context as well as with textual structures. No matter why any Sender chose any verb, the choice affects the overall 'message' of the text.

In conclusion, there are some features worth mentioning. First of all, there is the problem of deciding whether a speech act describing verb is merely an instance of variation or whether it really does have a semantic impact on the utterance. What I said above is in fact a combination of the two: that stylistic variation changes the meaning of the utterance.

Adverbial qualification

If we accept the notion that *SAY* does not contain any interpretative qualities, the Sender of the reporting text will have to do something in order to provide RS with interpretations signalling her (non-)commitment to the RS in question. And this is where the adverbials come in. They can be used to express (non-)commitment, and they can be used to express modes of utterances ('chanted derisively', 'said triumphantly', etc.). The latter is by far the most common use of adverbials. Especially in connection with relatively neutral speech act describing verbs such as *SAY,* the Sender of the reporting text can use adverbials to express her stance in phrases like 'said truthfully', 'noted correctly', etc. This is what we see in (9) below:

(9) Yet just how well this outspoken and often irascible fellow would do remained the big imponderable in the election – it turned "the end game of this campaign," as New York Times reporter Robin Toner APTLY PUT IT, "into a very delicate affair." (CSM, Nov. 3).

By using the adverbial APTLY the Sender of the reporting text says that Robin Toner's formulation is to the point, and thereby correct. This means that by using APTLY, the Sender of the reporting text supports what Robin Toner says, and commits himself to the utterance expressed by the quotation.

Conjunctive structures

The standard analysis of adversative conjunctive structures is the same whatever the actual grammatical structure of the utterance under scrutiny. This makes the analysis a relatively straightforward matter in which $utterance_1$ is identified as an utterance which the Sender presents, and $utterance_2$ is identified as one to which the Sender commits herself. There are a number of factors to take into consideration in connection with adversative conjunctive constructions. Conjunctions can be further qualified by the use of adverbials, speech act describing verbs, and other kinds of lexical or sentential qualifications. Such qualifications can alter the actual analysis of a conjunction in an actual utterance so that the Sender of the reporting text's pattern of commitment differs from that of a standard analysis. What this suggests is that here, too, we will have to make the original standard analysis for adversative conjunctive constructions context-sensitive in the sense that we must discuss what different kinds of qualification do to the analyses.

First let us take a look at a relatively unproblematic utterance:

(10) ALTHOUGH[7] the President still trails Arkansas Gov. Bill Clinton, the election has taken on a new air of uncertainty (CSM, Nov. 2).

Here we have two utterances that originate from the Sender of the reporting text: one that says that the President trails and another one that says that the campaign has taken on an air of uncertainty. What makes this a prototypical example of adversative conjunctive constructions is the fact that the Sender of the reporting text presents $utterance_1$ and commits himself to $utterance_2$, and thereby he claims that the fact of $utterance_2$ is more important than the fact of $utterance_1$. According to the utterance what is denied in (10) is a generally held view, which is not realised in this case. In (11) we see how the Sender of the reporting text can structurally support an RS:

(11) ALTHOUGH his lead remains strong in public opinion surveys, Clinton said he was not taking anything for granted (TT, Oct. 24).

If we merely analysed $utterance_2$ the way it was proposed above, we would have to say that the Sender of the reporting text presents the RS because of the use of the speech act describing verb *SAY* (and that analysis is naturally still valid for the isolated phrase "Clinton said he was not taking anything for granted"). The reason why this is not the case in (11) is the use of the adversative conjunctive construction. Because of the structure, the Sender of the reporting text is able to give Clinton's utterance an emphasis that it does not receive from *SAY*. Therefore the structure signals the Sender's commitment to the RS. Naturally it is also possible for the Sender of the reporting text to place an RS as $utterance_1$, thus signalling non-commitment to the RS. This is what can be seen in (12):

(12) He [Bush] said he was confident voters would recognize signs of improvement as well as his accomplishments in foreign policy. HOWEVER, in two new tracking polls Clinton's lead over Bush widened slightly to 11 points (TT, Oct. 27).

Here Bush's utterance (contained in $utterance_1$) is accepted as true and at the same time deemed 'not as salient as the information in $utterance_2$'.

We see here that the adversative conjunctive construction makes it possible for the Sender to dismiss part of the utterance as unimportant, not by signalling non-commitment to it but by signalling commitment to another part of the utterance. This is what is always the case in these constructions, but when the Sender uses a quotation and thereby disclaims responsibility for the RS, he adds to the structurally determined relations between the Sender of the reporting text and what is said in the utterance. Naturally both utterances in such a structure can be quotations. If they come from the same reported Sender, it will be the Sender of the reporting text's way of showing that what the Sender of the reported text said is contradictory, or that she[8] changed her mind. If the quotations come from different reported senders, the reporting Sender can use RS to show that the two reported senders have opposing or incompatible views. In both cases the structure makes the Sender of the reporting text select the RS in utterance$_2$ over the RS in utterance$_1$. In (13) we see how the Sender of the reporting text selects an RS belonging to one reported Sender over an RS belonging to another reported Sender:

(13) Before publishing the latest charges, the magazine attempted to find evidence verifying the charges, "often without success," according to a statement released by the publisher. EVEN SO, analyst Chagall says the Flowers [Clinton's alleged lover] article could bring further tightening of the race, possibly by pushing some Clinton voters over to Perot (CSM, Nov. 2).

In spite of their difference the two instances of RS (in isolation) would receive an identical analysis (Sender's presentation of each of the RS). As it turns out, according to the utterance the publisher's words count less than the words of the (election) analyst because of the salience of the second utterance in the construction. Also according to the utterance, what the publisher says would normally lead to the implication that the effect of the claims will be weakened, but that this turns out not to be the case (because of *even so*). Thus, by means of the structure the Sender of the reporting text selects part of the utterance assigned to one reported Sender over part of the utterance assigned to another reported Sender and commits herself to the former. The Sender of the reporting text can use a host of different qualifiers when she wants to qualify an RS. Naturally this is also true when RS enters into an adversative conjunctive structure. As long as the negative evaluation belongs with utterance$_1$ and the positive evaluation belongs with utterance$_2$ nothing revolutionary happens to the standard analysis of the structure. We can see that in (14):

(14) According to conventional wisdom, Texas billionaire Ross Perot has hurt Bush by pulling away Republican support. BUT "if these voters return to Bush, which I think is the most likely change for them to make, the race in California might be closer than political analysts now say," said Steven Chaffee, a professor in the department at Stanford University (TT, Oct. 25).

The writer of the article from which this extract is taken seems to know that adversative conjunctive constructions deal with what happens "contrary to expectation" (cf. Halliday and Hasan 1976:242-3). This is what is reflected in the opening phrase "According to conventional wisdom".

The structural fact of utterance_2 as more salient than utterance_1 is further emphasised by the qualification of the evaluative utterance "a professor in the department at Stanford University" which lends authoritativeness to the RS expressed in the second utterance. Thereby the structural salience of the utterance is further emphasised by the qualification of the RS. Remembering the standard analysis of the adversative conjunctive construction and thereby knowing that the Sender of the reporting text always regards utterance_2 as superior to utterance_1, we will have to say that in connection with (14) above we see a structural emphasis on the RS, and a structural/contextual qualification of *SAY*. What this means is that by using an RS as utterance_1 the Sender of the reporting text stresses the distance between herself and the RS, whereas by using an RS as utterance_2, she commits herself to the RS, and thereby signals its importance.

Verbal modality

Among other things, modality can express the probability with which the proposition of a modalised utterance is realised. E.g. *will* has only a little or even no modality left[9]. On the other hand e.g. *may* has a relatively high degree of modality. Perkins (1983:106-10) suggests that the difference between present tense and past tense modals is a modal difference where the past tense is thought to add some extra conditionality to the semantics of the verbs. This means that the present tense modals are not as modal as their past tense counterparts. And it lies in this formulation that the past tense modals place the propositions that they modalise further from realisation than do the present tense modals. That said, we must remember that no matter how far away from realisation a proposition is thought to be, a modalised utterance is and remains the expression of the probability with which a given proposition is realised. The initial claim of an utterance is a) the proposition and b) the conditions for the realisation of the proposition. All that the modals can do is qualify that claim. Thereby we say that the mentioning of a proposition is a preliminary claim of the existence of the proposition.

So when we deal with modalised utterances, these utterances present us with the statement that it is possible that the proposition is realised, and a statement that signals Sender's idea of how close to realisation the proposition is. Below I will show how it is possible to see verbal modality in terms of prediction/probability and desirability of realisation.

Desirability

In order to highlight Sender's role in the evaluation of the proposition being modalised, I prefer to talk of 'desirability' rather than 'obligation'. And there are two modals that express obligation, *must* and *should,* where the former is the least modal. In addition *should* is connected with some kind of action. This can be reflected in the analysis in the phrasing 'to bring about' (Klinge 1994:74). In (15) below we see how the Sender finds it desirable that the proposition modalised by *must* be realised. And since *must* is the modal used the Sender signals a relatively strong desire for the realisation of the proposition:

(15) If we are to promote and rely on co-operation, we MUST be ready to pay our fair share in support of these institutions and help reposition them to manage new missions and new challenges (CSM, Sept. 30).

With *should* the Sender signals a somewhat weaker desire for the proposition to be realised. This is illustrated in (16):

(16) Even though it seems highly unlikely (at this writing [sic] Perot doesn't seem likely to win electoral votes in any state), no writer SHOULD omit the possibility that he might pull off the upset of all time and win (CSM, Nov. 3).

The reason why *should* is used in (16) is that the actions that have to be taken in order to realise the proposition are actions that are not in Sender's control.[10] When *must* is used, the notion of action is absent, whereas the notion of realisation of the proposition is stronger. Where *should* signals incertitude because of Sender's lack of control over the actions, *must* signals certainty for the very same reason; there is an air of inevitability over *must.* And therefore the main difference between *must* and *should* lies not in the desirability of someone bringing about the realisation of the proposition, but in the probability of realisation of the proposition.

Prediction/probability of realisation

"A speaker/writer must always indicate or imply a commitment to the truth or otherwise of any proposition s/he utters, or to a prediction of the degree of likelihood of an event described taking place or having taken place" (Fowler 1991:85).

First, the notion of truth is not really well-chosen. Not that it is not a factor, but since we must suppose that the Sender regards the proposition to be true unless otherwise informed (cf. the maxim of quality), it does not seem appropriate to deal with truth as a heading. Instead I propose that we talk of speculations or predictions in the sense that what this kind of modality does to a sentence is to qualify the strength of the prediction of the proposition. This means that we can try to list the degree of probability of realisation signalled by the different modals. This, in fact, has already been done for the relation between *must* and *should* above. And this distinction mirrors Perkins's distinction between primary and secondary modals, where primary means closer to realisation (most probable), and secondary means further away from realisation (least probable) because of the notion that the secondary modals are more conditional than their primary counterparts. A prototypical example of a primary modal utterance is seen in (17):

(17) It is safe to predict that Perot WILL finish with at least 25 percent of the vote in the Southwestern states (SJM, Nov. 3).

The relatively low conditionality of the subordinate clause in (17), signalled by *will*, is emphasised by the present tense of the entire utterance as expressed by "It is safe to predict". Therefore what is signalled is the Sender's conviction that the proposition of (17) is very close to realisation (or Sender's commitment to the proposition). In order to underline the fact that the use of a present tense modal does not mean that the Sender regards the proposition of the utterance as fulfilled we can take a look at (18) below.

(18) COULD President Bush finish third? As they head into the final week of a disappointing campaign, Republicans MAY now have to think the unthinkable (SJM, Nov. 3).

According to the utterance, the proposition 'Bush finish third' has a relatively low degree of probability. This is not the case with the proposition 'Republicans think the unthinkable' for by mentioning the former, the Sender created a context in which the latter can be regarded as relatively probable and this is what is reflected by the use of the present tense modal *may*. The fact, however, that none of the propositions are actually realised at the time of speaking makes it possible to regard both propositions as relatively improbable as reflected in (18a):

(18a) COULD President Bush finish third? As they head into the final week of a disappointing campaign, Republicans MIGHT now have to think the unthinkable.

The difference between *may* and *might* is minimal (cf. Coates 1983:154). On the other hand, the difference between them and thereby the difference between (18) and (18a) lies in their distance from realisation. What is modalised by *might* in (18a) is slightly more removed from realisation than what is modalised by *may* in (18). Below we see a number of modalised utterances most of them from The *Peninsula Times Tribune* of October 2:

(19) Perot WON'T win the election. He WON'T win a single state, but he WILL royally mess things up for the others (TT, Oct. 22).
(20) Perot's vote WILL have little significance as a percentage of the total vote. It WILL be surprising if it surpasses 10 percent nationwide. Within particular states, the Perot vote WILL be critical. He probably WILL hold the balance of power in Texas and Florida, with a combined electoral vote of 57. One way or another. There goes the old ball game (TT, Oct. 22).
(21) At their worst, these ads' imitation of authenticity CAN breed a new level of cynicism (TT, Oct. 22).
(22) Governor Thompson insists that neither candidate CAN win without Wisconsin, and their schedules over the final weekend indicated that they agree (CSM, Nov. 2).
(23) The game MAY appear to be over but there's still a joker in the deck (TT, Oct. 22).
(24) His candidacy CLEARLY cost Carter the 14 electoral votes of Massachusetts and MAY have deprived Carter of 15 electoral votes from Connecticut, Maine and Vermont (TT, Oct. 22).
(25) In that guess, I MAY be quite wrong (TT, Oct. 22).

will is used to make predictions with few qualifications (e.g. PROBABLY in (20)). *can* is used in constructions with qualifications that work as kinds of conditions that must be fulfilled before the proposition is realised. When *may* is used, there is somewhat more doubt as to the probability of the realisation of the proposition than in connection with *will* and *can*. Thereby *may* becomes the most modal of the present tense modals. In support of this Coates (1985:152-5) mentions that *may* seems to have very much in common with *might*. An especially good example of the modality (conditionality) of *may* is seen in (24) where *may* is contrasted to the adverb CLEARLY. Thereby *may* receives the reading 'not clearly'.

What we have seen here is that there is no doubt that the extracts above reflect the Sender's wish to express events or actions whose realisation are regarded as possible and that are not realised at the time of speaking. At the same time the modals express different degrees of probability of realisation of the proposition in question.

In connection with the past tense modals, *might* (which is the morphological past tense of *may*) is the least modal. This is reflected in Coates's (1985:153-4) notion of *might* and *may* competing to occupy the same semantic space.

(26) Even though it seems highly unlikely (at this writing [sic] Perot doesn't seem likely to win electoral votes in any state), no writer SHOULD omit the possibility that he MIGHT pull off the upset of all time and win. That WOULD keep the pundits busy for years, explaining how they called it wrong! (CSM, Nov. 3).

We see that in (26) the Sender has the possibility of choosing *may* over *might* because of the present tense of the opening of (26). The reason for selecting *might* therefore is significant and reflects the notion of *might* as signalling the proposition as slightly further removed from realisation than signalled by *may*. In (27) below we see how the Sender uses *could* to signal the low possibility of the proposition being realised.

(27) This year the joker COULD control the losing hand (TT Oct. 22).

(28) below is parallel to (27) in the sense that the context makes it possible for the Sender to view the proposition ('many of Perot's backers decide they waste their vote by supporting him and opt for either Mr. Clinton or President Bush') as relatively probable.

(28) That Perot achievement WILL hold, it seems to me, even if many of Perot's backers decide today they WOULD waste their votes by supporting him and opt for either Mr. Clinton or President Bush (CSM, Nov. 3).

Contextually, because of the present tense verbs, the indications are that the second modal verb, *would*, could easily be exchanged for a present tense modal. The reason why this does not happen, then, seems to be because the Sender wants to signal his belief that the probability of the realisation of the proposition is relatively low.

Just like RS and adversative conjunctive constructions the modals can receive contextual qualification[11], also modals can be qualified by adverbials and by evaluative phrases. This means that in context, the presence of other modals (verbal qualification), adverbials, and evaluative phrases influence the analysis of the modalised proposition of the utterance in question.

The modals can directly influence each other and thereby serve as qualifying contexts for each other. This is what we saw in (28) above, where the mutual influence of the modals lies in the relation of the tenses: the present tense of *will* contrasted with the past tense of *would* highlights (and thereby emphasises) the probability of realisation of the two propositions. This means that what the Sender signals is a very firm belief that the proposition modalised by *will* is realised and a belief that it is not quite as certain that the proposition modalised by *would* is realised.

We find the same kind of interplay between modals and other verbs.[12] We see that in (29 [=part of (13)]):

(29) Even so, analyst Chagall SAYS the Flowers [Clinton's alleged lover] article COULD bring further tightening of the race, possibly by pushing some Clinton voters over to Perot (CSM, Nov. 2).

It is clear that the present tense of *SAY* could easily serve as a context in which the modal verb was also in the present tense. This would give us (29a):

(29a) Even so, analyst Chagall SAYS the Flowers [Clinton's alleged lover] article CAN bring further tightening of the race, possibly by pushing some Clinton voters over to Perot.

In (29a) the possibility introduced is considered to be relatively close to realisation whereas in (29) we see a possibility which is considered to be relatively far from realisation. What we see in (30) is that the reverse situation of (29) and (29a) can also be true:

(30 [=18]) COULD President Bush finish third? As they head into the final week of a disappointing campaign, republicans MAY now have to think the unthinkable (SJM, Nov. 3).

In (30) the initial question, which is in the past tense, serves as the context for using the present tense in connection with the proposition modalised by *may*. This emphasises the notion that the presentation of even a remote possibility (as e.g. signalled by *could*) is nonetheless first and foremost a display of a possible state of affairs, so even the presentation of a remote possibility can serve as the conditioning context for a relatively probable possibility.

Adverbial and evaluative qualification

In the case of the modals, adverbials can be used to minimise or maximise the degree of probability with which a modalised proposition is realised. In other words, an evaluative utterance or an adverbial (or a combination of both for that matter) can strengthen or weaken the degree of modality expressed by a modal verb. In (31) we see adverbial qualification:

(31 [=20]) Perot's vote WILL have little significance as a percentage of the total vote. It WILL be surprising if it surpasses 10 percent nationwide. Within particular states, the Perot vote WILL be critical. He probably WILL hold the balance of power in Texas and Florida, with a combined electoral vote of 57. One way or another. There goes the old ball game (TT, Oct. 22).

WILL signals a high degree of probability regarding the realisation of the proposition. Therefore PROBABLY weakens the certainty that the proposition will be realised. So in this case the modality of the utterance is increased.

(32) IT IS SAFE TO PREDICT that Perot WILL finish with at least 25 percent of the vote in the Southwestern states (SJM, Nov. 3).

Here the phrase "It is safe to predict" further minimises the proposition's distance from realisation and thus emphasises Sender's conviction that the proposition is realised. Thereby *will* in (32) loses even more of its modality.

Also modals that signal low probability of realisation of the proposition are qualified by adverbials and evaluative utterances. This is what we see in (33), which starts with an evaluative phrase:

(33) THE CHARGES ARE JUST WEIRD. Why WOULD tricksters smear Perot's daughter and not Perot? (SJM, Nov. 3).

By characterising the charges as weird, Sender has already signalled his non-commitment to the proposition of the question that follows. And so the non-commitment is emphasised by the use of a modal that signals a low degree of probability.

This means that the modals specify the probability of realisation of the proposition they modalise and that they influence each other and enter into relationships with adverbs and utterances to emphasise or limit the degree of modality.

We have seen how the notion of tense plays a part in the interpretation of modality. Also we have seen that in political newspaper discourse two kinds of modality are put into use (desirability and prediction/speculation). All in all 'degree of probability' is the key phrase here, for modality is Sender's possibility to present a proposition and subjectively comment on the degree of probability with which that proposition is thought to be realised.

Conclusion

In conclusion we can say that the polyphonic metaphor makes it possible to talk of subjectivity in newspaper discourse in a terminology that goes beyond traditional Anglo-American categories without losing the insights of the tradition. This is not to say that polyphony theory does so unproblematically; e.g. although it is clear that polyphony theory is able to deal with the qualification/evaluation of RS, my paper does not at all address the difference between the possibility for the Sender of the reporting text to relate to the reported text or to the Sender of the reported text. Nonetheless it is evident that the speech act verb chosen represents a modalisation of the RS or the Sender of the RS and that this modalisation must have an impact on the reception of the RS. The adversative conjunctive structures impose quite a complex modality, because here we face the modalisation of two interrelated propositions. Both propositions are deemed true, but one of them is deemed more salient than the other. So the conjoined propositions are modalised as 'true and important' and 'true and not so important' by the use of conjunctions.

In connection with the modals, the description offered above differs from Klinge's (1994) analysis only in the sense that it illustrates the notion that modality imposed on propositions originates from a (more or less well-defined) Sender.

Polyphony theory lets us talk technically/linguistically of subjectivity. The Anglo-American tradition does not provide a vocabulary to address linguistic subjectivity (cf. Lyons 1995 Ch. 10). This means that newspaper analysis can take the step from dealing with distortion of news to the identification of subjectivity in newspaper texts as a reflection of Sender's existence in the world.

In order to do this, the approach sketched above needs complementation integrating context into the analysis. The polyphonic metaphor (and my quasi-polyphonic terminology) makes this complementation possible, and that must be the next task at hand.

Notes

1 Note that the terminology that I use in this article is not identical to the terminology normally used in polyphony theory as seen in e.g. Nølke 1993a.
2 In my terminology I operate with discourse individuals and their relations to utterances that may be implicit as well as explicit (cf. the analysis of (1)).
3 As pointed out by Klinge in a personal discussion, this example is deceptively illustrative. We must suppose that there is a reason behind any utterance and that reason might very well serve as a voice. Thus "The wall is white" is just as polyphonic as "The wall isn't white". So the polyphony does not hinge on the negation but is inherent in language.
4 Kiparsky & Kiparsky (1971) define factive verbs as verbs whose complements the Sender regards as true and even though the concept is not unproblematic (cf. Pedersen 1997:47-53) the distinction between factive and non-factive verbs is quite illustrative. In my terminology the Sender is committed to the complement of a factive verb and presents the complements of non-factive verbs.
5 What I am saying here is that even if a Sender wants to objectify the introduction of RS in his text, he might reveal his subjectivity by the choice between *say* and *tell*. But it also works the other way round: Sender might be taken to express something that he did not want to, because of Receiver's conception of the verb chosen. Geis (1987, esp. chapters 5 and 6) makes this point in connection with verbs that are only rarely used as introductory verbs, such as e.g. *trumpet* or *seethe*. I think, however, that this might also apply to central speech-act describing verbs whose lexical meanings are very similar.
6 Only in constructions with an infinitive adjunct where *to* is the infinitive marker does the combination *SAY TO* occur in my corpus.
7 BUT is the prototypical representative for the class of adversative conjunctions in that it can unproblematically be classified as a coordinating conjunction (cf. Bache and Davidsen-Nielsen 1997:174).
8 I use the personal pronoun 'she' to refer to Sender and Receiver in general and the appropriate pronoun (mostly 'he' since most of the journalists are male) to refer to the physical, real-world Senders and Receivers.
9 Naturally this does not mean that *WILL* cannot enter into constructions of a relatively high degree of modality. It only means that prototypically *will* is not very modal.
10 Note that when the actions have to be taken by the Sender, the proposition has a negative implication: "I should lose weight" (negative implication: "but I won't").
11 Cf. also Coates's notion of modal harmony in Coates (1983:45).
12 Probably this is valid for the relation between verbs in general, but it falls outside the scope of this article to deal with that.

Bibliography

Azar, M.: "Concession Relations", *Text* 17, 3, 1997, 301-316.
Bache, Carl & Niels Davidsen-Nielsen: *Mastering English: An Advanced Grammar for Native and Non-native Speakers*. Berlin and New York, 1997.

Ballmer, Thomas & Waltraud Brennenstuhl: *Speech act classification: a study of the lexical analysis of English speech action verbs*, Berlin, 1980.
Bell, A: *The Language of News Media*. London and Cambridge (Mass.), 1991.
Blakemore, D: *Semantic Constraints on Relevance*. Oxford, 1987.
---: *Understanding Utterances*. Blackwell, Oxford, 1992.
Coates, J: *The Semantics of the Modal Auxiliaries*. London, 1985.
van Dijk, T. A.: *Prejudice in Discourse*. Amsterdam, 1984.
---: *News Analysis. Case Studies in International and National News*. Hillsdale, NJ, 1987.
---: *News as Discourse*. Hillsdale, NJ, 1988.
---: *Elite Discourse and Racism*. Dewberry Park, 1993.
---: *Discourse studies: a multidisciplinary introduction*. London, 1997.
Ducrot, O.: *Dire et ne pas dire*. Paris, 1972.
---: *Le dire et le dit*. Paris, 1984.
Fairclough, N.: *Critical discourse analysis*. London, 1995a.
---: *Media discourse*. London, 1995b.
Fowler, R.: *Language in the News; Discourse and Ideology in the Press*. London & New York, 1991.
Fowler, R., B. Hodge, G. Kress, T. Trew: *Language and control*. London, 1979.
Geis, M. L.: *The Language of Politics*. New York, 1987.
Gruber, H.: "Evaluation devices in newspaper reports", *Journal of Pragmatics* 19, 1993, 469-486.
Halliday, M. & R. Hasan: *Cohesion in English*. London, 1976.
Janssen, T. A. J. M. & W. van der Wurff (Eds.): *Reported speech: forms and functions of the verb*. Amsterdam, 1996.
Kiparsky, P. & C. Kiparsky: "Fact". – In D. Steinberg & L. Jakobovits (Eds.): *Semantics*, CUP, Cambridge, 1971.
Klinge, A.: "The Impact of Context on Modal Meaning in English and Danish", *Nordic Journal of Linguistics*, 19, 1996, 35-54.
---: "On the linguistic interpretation of contractual modalities", *Journal of Pragmatics* 23, 649-675, 1995.
---: *Legal Discourse and Modality: An Investigation of Semantic and Pragmatic Aspects in Insurance Policies*. Copenhagen, 1994.
Lyons, J.: *Linguistic semantics*. Cambridge, 1995.
Nølke, H.: *Polyfoni: En sprogteoretisk indføring*. Copenhagen, 1989a.
---: "Modality and Polyphony; A Study of Some French Adverbials", *Travaux du Cercle Linguistique de Copenhague* 23, 1989b, 45-63.
---: *Linguistique Modulaire: de la forme au sens*. Aarhus, 1993a.
---: *Le Regard du locuteur. Pour une linguistique des traces enonciative*. Paris, 1993b.
Palmer, F. R.: *Modality and the English Modals*. Longman, London and New York, 1990.
Pedersen, K: *The analysis of newspaper texts*. Unpublished Ph.D. thesis. Copenhagen, 1997.
---: "The Analysis of *but*". Unpublished ms. Copenhagen, 1998.
Perkins, M. R.: *Modal Expressions in English*. London, 1983.
Rieber, S.: "Conventional implicatures as tacit performatives", *Linguistics and Philosophy* 20, 1997, 50-72.
Searle, J. R.: *Expression and Meaning: Studies in the Theory of Speech Acts*. Cambridge, 1989, (1979).

Sperber, D. & D. Wilson: *Relevance.* Oxford, 1986.
Sweetser, E. E.: *From etymology to pragmatics.* Cambridge, 1995, (1990).
Quirk, R., S. Greenbaum, G. Leech, J. Svartvik: *A Comprehensive Grammar of the English Language.* London & New York, 1985.
Tsohatzidis, S. L.: "Speaking of truth-telling: The view from wh-complements", *Journal of Pragmatics* 19, 1993, 271-279.
Verschueren, J.: *On Speech Act Verbs.* Amsterdam, 1980.
Vestergaard, T.: *Engelsk Grammatik.* Copenhagen, 1985.
Waugh, L. R.: "Reported Speech in journalistic discourse: The relation of function and text", *Text* 15, 1, 1995, 129-173.

Torben Vestergaard, Aalborg

Free Adjuncts in newspaper discourse

1. Introduction

The events reported in newspapers should of course be both new and true, but they should also appear to be true. In this paper we shall be concerned with how a particular syntactic construction is put to use in newspaper discourse in such a way as to help confer the appearance of truth upon the claims made in the news report. The construction in question is the one termed "free adjunct" by Zandvoort (1961) and Kortmann (1991), and "supplementive clause" by Quirk et al. (1972, 1985), i.e. constructions exemplified by the underlined sequences of the following examples:

(1) *Born in 1869*, Pfitzner was a contemporary of Richard Strauss... (97,27)[1]
(2) [...] the cockroach, *albeit groggy*, crawled out. (96,25)
(3) By the end the Scots were in tatters, *having succumbed to a short sharp tryfest.* (97,31)

For present purposes we will define the object of analysis as subjectless non-finite or verbless adverbial clauses. It is a construction which seems to be widely used in all the Romance languages, whereas in the Germanic languages it occurs much more sporadically, except for English, where it appears to be both as generally used as in e.g. French, and, interestingly, to be used in the same genres, such as for instance brochures, and for the same discoursal purposes.[2]

After a preliminary discussion of the realizations of the construction I shall turn to a characterization of its semantic relations to the matrix clause in which it occurs and to its application in newspaper discourse. In particular, I shall argue that the discoursal function of a fairly large group of instances, which have previously been labelled "accompanying circumstances", "exemplification", etc., is best captured if we adopt an argumentation theoretical point of view. Finally, I shall discuss possible reasons for the construction's popularity in newspaper discourse.

2. Delimitation

2.1. Free adjuncts and other adverbial clauses

Zandvoort (1961: 35) talks about a free adjunct when a participial, infinitival or nominal construction a) is equivalent to an adverbial clause, and b) "there is a clear break between the participle [...] and the rest of the sentence [...]", and judging from his cross-references on p. 210, his definition covers not only infinitival constructions playing the role of Greenbaum's (1969) conjuncts and style disjuncts (*to begin with*, *to be frank*) but also clear cases of infinitival purpose constructions. Quirk et al. (1972:760 and 1985:1123-1127) are more restrictive in their definition of the phenomenon, which they refer to as "subjectless supplementive clauses", only admitting participial or verbless clauses. I shall follow Quirk et al. in excluding clauses, of whatever form, functioning as disjuncts and conjuncts.

I agree with Zandvoort, 1961:36, Quirk et al. 1972:760, Kortmann, 1991, that non-finite clauses with overt subject, so-called absolute clauses such as (4), also exemplify the construction:

(4) Daniel's view of the symphony was boldly drawn [...], *the bucolic rhythms of the scherzo lurching like a juggernaut* [...]. (96,27)

I shall nevertheless exclude them from consideration here, mainly because their textual frequency is so low that, within the scope of the present study, it has proved impossible for me to collect a sample big enough to allow reasonably well-founded conclusions.

The decision by Quirk et al. not to include infinitival purpose clauses among their supplementive clauses seems to be based exclusively on semantic considerations, for whereas one of the intriguing characteristics of other supplementive clauses/free adjuncts is their semantic indeterminacy, their "chameleon-like semantic quality of adapting to context" (Quirk et al. 1972:760), purpose clauses are both semantically quite determinate and syntactically easy to isolate: they can be opened by the connector *in order to* (Thompson, 1985:57).

2.2. Free Adjuncts vs. postmodifying clauses

As examples (1) – (3) show, free adjuncts can occur in three positions: initial, medial (i.e. immediately following the subject of the main clause) and final. Clauses in medial and final position create problems of demarcation, however, as the structures in question may also function as postmodifying elements in the Noun Phrase ("reduced relative clauses"). Thus in the following example, either interpretation would make sense:

(5) Frannie, *intelligent, articulate,* is increasingly stressed. (96,29)

(Cf. "Frannie, *who is* intelligent and articulate,..." or "Frannie, *though* intelligent and articulate,..." or "Frannie, intelligent and articulate *as she is*,..."). In such cases, the principle I have followed, inspired by Quirk et al., 1972, has been to exclude all cases where the sequence in question could follow its putative Head in a sentence where *only* the postmodifier interpretation would be possible. Thus, on the strength of (5'), (5) is considered adverbial rather than postmodifying:

(5')*Yesterday Al had an argument with Frannie, *intelligent, articulate.*

The following example, (6), on the other hand, must be considered structurally ambiguous, and it is only because the context shows that the "logical subject" of *speaking* is *Ifshin* rather than *McCain*, that it can be classified as postmodifying and thus excluded:

(6) It was in 1970 [...] that the navy pilot John McCain first came across Ifshin, *speaking on Hanoi radio about American war crimes against North Vietnam.* (96,6)

Note further that insertion of *who was* before *speaking* would result in a grammatical sentence.

3. *Internal structure of free adjuncts*

3.1 Realizations

As is well known, free adjuncts can be realized by non-finite clauses with the verb in the present or past participle:

(7) *Risking confrontation with the unions,* Mr Brown insisted there would be no "blank cheques" for public sector workers. (97,9)
(8) *Built by a Finn after the war,* it [the cottage] is constructed of the land [...] (97,25)

In addition, verbless clauses with an Adjective Phrase, a Noun Phrase or a Prepositional Phrase as their main lexical element are possible:

(9) *Futile and anti-climactic,* [...] Evita's life after death remains the great Argentine story of our time. (97,28)

(10) *Apparently an ordinary Essex town*, [Braintree] is thought to lie in a pocket of the paranormal. (96, 29)

(11) Now he has chosen to be the token Republican in a Democratic administration whose policies he questions [...], *in harness with military professionals yet to be appointed [...]* (97,6)

Finally, though quite rare, adverbial infinitival clauses which are neither purpose clauses, on the one hand, nor conjuncts or disjuncts (cf. above, 2.1), on the other, do occur:

(12) England [...] went down to defeat by New Zealand A by 90 runs here last Sunday *to become the first touring side to lose a first-class game in New Zealand...since the rookies of Sri Lanka in 1983.* (97,30)

In terms of textual frequency, present participial clauses account for well over half of the examples, followed by past participial clauses, adjectival clauses, nominal clauses, infinitival clauses, and finally verbless clauses with a prepositional phrase as their main constituent, cf. table 1. As table 1 also shows, the overwhelming majority of examples occur in final or initial position (54 and 38 per cent respectively), whereas less than 10 per cent occur in medial position.

Table 1. Frequency of realizations

	I	M	F	
NP	10		3	13
PP	2		2	4
AP	8	4	2	14
ing	29	4	80	113
ed	18	4	3	25
to			5	5
	67	12	95	174

3.2. Syntactic link with matrix clause

In the vast majority of cases the understood subject of the subjectless adverbial clause is felt to be identical with the subject of the main clause, as in all examples cited until now. Where no such link exists, the non-finite clause is felt to be "dangling":

(13) *Famed for their diuretic properties*, medieval apothecaries called them [dandelions] *dens lionis* [ital.], the lion's tooth [...]. (96,24)

There is, however, a series of borderline cases, where there is less than total identity between the subjects of the dependent and the main clause. In the first place, the implied subject of the dependent clause, though not identical with, may be at least somehow retrievable from the subject of the main clause:

(14) *A wizard of deadpan wit*, Lewis's celebrated books on Indochina and the Italian Mafia catalogue with anthropological exactitude the weirdest rites and rituals. (96,29)
(15) *Forced to prowl round the outside of the garden squares where the very expensive cars were parked*, my mood darkened. (96,24)

"Dangling" clauses, as well as the more or less acceptable types exemplified in 14-15, are relatively rare. There is however a fairly frequent type of non-identity of subjects which seems to be absolutely normal and unremarkable. In this type, the link between main clause and dependent clause is provided, not by the implied subject of the dependent clause being more or less identical with that of the main clause, but by the subject of the dependent clause being the *entire main clause*, or at least a proposition contained therein. As Halliday (1994:229) puts it, the "domain" of the dependent clause may be "some larger segment of the primary clause, up to the whole clause":

(16) Spain's new conservative prime minister, José María Aznar, was sworn in at the week-end, *bringing the first change in government in almost 14 years.* (96,3)

In this example, it is not Mr Aznar who brought the first change in government in Spain, but his having been sworn in. As further examples of this type, consider the following:

(17) Hong Kong has lost 30 per cent of its British population in just nine months, *abruptly reversing what had been an end-of-empire gold rush.* (97,1)
(18) [...] the House of Commons emptied after an unruly Prime Minister's question-time, *leaving only a few MPs to debate the newly published North report on parades and marches.* (97,12)

In my data the "Matrix-Clause-as-Subject" type accounts for 12 of the 174 instances. In all but two examples (viz. 41, 43 below) it is realized by present participial clauses, and the participial clause is invariably in final position (cf. further below, 4.2).

The adjunct clause may be headed by a conjunction indicating its exact semantic relation to the sentence as a whole:

(19) [...] the Serbian leadership had violated the constitution *by* annulling opposition victories in local elections [...] (97,3)
(20) *Though* odds-on favourite before the tournament began, he was dissatisfied with his form throughout [...] (96,32)
(21) *while* pretending to decentralise [...], Tory administrations have in fact presided over an extraordinary and unprecedented concentration of might [...] (96,29)

The existence of such cases would seem to contradict Thompson & Longacre's claim that free adjuncts, which they refer to as "absolutive clauses", carry "no explicit signal of the relationship between the main and subordinate clause;" (1985:201). But they would in general seem to be right when they state (ibid:203) that free adjuncts are used "when there is no need to specify more than that the clauses are related." Or, as I hope to show in what follows: semantic indeterminacy is in fact an outstanding characteristic of free adjuncts, but this is an effect of their form and position, which in a great many cases make it possible to leave the nature of the semantic link between the matrix clause and the dependent clause unspecified.

4. Semantic relations

My main concern in this part of the paper will be to take a closer look at the somewhat vague terms "attendant circumstances", "accompanying circumstances", "contingencies" in order to see what is achieved communicatively by hitching two propositions together but leaving the exact nature of the link between them vague. Before I go on to do so, however, let me remark that there is in fact a very large group of free adjuncts where the link between matrix and adverbial clause is not vague (though it may very well be indeterminate, cf. below). This group falls into two clear sub-groups, temporal and causal, and is thus roughly co-extensive with the "more informative" end of the scale of relations established by Kortmann (1991:119 ff.[3]).

4.1. Temporal adjuncts

Temporal relations can be relations of anteriority, simultaneity or posteriority, or "time before" – "same time" – "time after". In my data, there are 44 instances of temporal free adjuncts, the majority of which denote time before (19) or same time (19), with only 6 denoting time after:

(22) Newcastle simply could not keep up the pace. *Having established their 12-point lead*, they then dropped 21 out of the next 45. (96,30)
(23) *Speaking in Bonn*, Mr Zyuganov said: [...]. (96,1)
(24) [...] a car pulled up at the Franks' hiding place in Amsterdam, *disgorging an SS sergeant* [...] (97,28)

4.2. Causal adjuncts

Under the term "causal", I subsume various relations between two propositions which all share the property that the one, the Precedent (p), is a conceptual/logical pre-condition for the second, the Consequent (q). Pairs like cause-effect, reason-consequence, means-end are thus all considered causal. So, too, are cases where the cause-effect relationship is hypothetical, as in conditional clauses, as well as cases where a "cause", hypothetical or real, does not have the expected effect, as in concessive and adversative clauses. Below, I illustrate the main types where the relation between adjunct and main clause is considered "causal". First, in (25-28), the adjunct is Antecedent and the matrix clause Consequent:

(25) *A complex and intriguing man who once wanted to be a Latin teacher, and who hikes for pleasure*, Cohen does not quite fit in either political party... (97,6)
(26) The NLD won 32 per cent of the seats in the new parliament. *Stunned*, the junta responded by arresting 3,000 NLD workers [...] (96,22)
(27) When they found they had gone too far in beating Biko, Kruger tried to take the heat off *by claiming Biko had died after a hunger strike*. (97,12)
(28) *Though odds-on favourite before the tournament began*, he was dissatisfied with his form throughout but mentally he remained unparalleled. (96,32)

Causal and temporal relations share the feature of directionality (hence the "*post hoc ergo propter hoc*" fallacy), and in some cases it is hard to determine whether the adjunct is causal or temporal; or rather: it would be a mistake to insist on an either-or interpretation, as the construction is capable of expressing both relations at one and the same time:

(29) Mr Yeltsin is still trailing by six points in the opinion polls, *having made up much lost ground*. (96,1)

Is he trailing six points behind *after*, *because of* or *in spite of* having made up much lost ground? Since it is impossible to decide which, but on the other hand, the relationship between matrix clause and adjunct is not open to just any interpretation, I regard the relationship between matrix and adverbial in such cases as "indeterminate" rather than "vague" (cf. also Kortmann 1991:113).

As we saw above, temporal relations expressed by free adjuncts are overwhelmingly relations of anteriority or simultaneity, and only rarely posteriority. The tendency for the dependent clause to express the Antecedent recurs among the causal relations, although not to the same extent, 44 of the "cause" clauses being Antecedents and as many as 17 Consequents, illustrated in (30)-(31):

(30) The US economy surged in the final three months of last year, *making 1996 the second best year for growth since the late 1980s.* (97,19)

(31) [Dandelions] spangle grass vergers, *irreverently jostling carefully planted daffodils.* (96,24)

Although over a third of all cause clauses are Consequents, it is worth noting that half of them, 8 out of 17, are of the "main clause as subject" type exemplified in 30. As mentioned, this type invariably follows the main clause, and this lack of mobility throws some doubt on its adverbial status.

4.3. "Accompanying circumstances"

As a first step towards an explicitation of the concept "accompanying circumstances", I would like to ask what is achieved communicatively by using the free adjunct construction at all? For it will be apparent that in very many cases the information contained in the free adjunct might just as well have been given in a non-restrictive relative clause, or perhaps even in a co-ordinated main clause (cf. Quirk et al. 1972:762)[4]

(32) *Born 88 years ago in the terminal London suburb of Enfield*, Lewis himself now lives outside Braintree in a parsonage. (96,29)

(32')Lewis himself, *who* was born 88 years ago..., now lives outside Braintree...

(33) *Written in 1969 or 1970,* the manuscript circulated in samizdat and was published abroad before becoming a cult classic in the final years of the Soviet Union. (97,29)

(33')The manuscript was written in 1969... *and* circulated in samizdat...

There are two features that distinguish the original versions and the rearranged versions of (32) and (33): first, in the originals the relevant sequences are non-finite, and second, they occur in initial position. I shall address each in turn.

The *finite* element specifies the point of reference of the proposition in relation to the speech event, and thereby makes it something that can be argued about, doubted, contradicted, etc. (Halliday 1994: 70). In particular, the finite element makes it possible for the proposition to be affirmed or denied; i.e. it specifies the proposition for "polarity", as Halliday (1994: 75) puts it. Material presented in non-finite rather than finite form is thus taken out of polarity, that is, it is being offered as not under discussion. This status as something indisputable is further enhanced by placing the material in *initial* position, the position which, in unmarked cases, is reserved for "given" information, i.e. information that is presented as recoverable (Halliday 1994:298). Although in actual fact, the information conveyed in the adjunct clauses in (32) and (33) is definitely neither known to the reader nor recoverable from context, it is nevertheless being presented in the position in which this kind of information normally occurs, and in this way it is "backgrounded" (Hopper & Thompson, 1980).

As is well known, backgrounded information in the sense of "given" information in initial position can have the function of serving as the textual link between the information supplied in the preceding sentences and the new information to be supplied in what follows (Givón, 1984; Thompson, 1985; Thompson & Longacre, 1985; Ramsay, 1987). But information that is regarded as both indisputably true and as known to speaker and hearer alike also has another important function in discourse: it can be used to back up propositions about which there might be disagreement or doubt with knowledge which, for present purposes at least, is regarded as beyond doubt. When we call upon known information to do this job for us, we are engaging in *reasoning* or *argumentation*, a process whereby we try to derive new knowledge from old (cf. Toulmin, 1958; Perelman & Olbrechts-Tytecha, 1969). It is this property of free adjuncts that makes them suitable fillers of the antecedent role in causal relations (cf. above), but we see the same property at work also in examples where the role played by the free adjunct would normally be classified as "specification", "circumstance" or "addition" (cf. Kortmann, 1991: 122-124). As an example of this use of the construction, consider the following:

(34) *At 38*, Hoddle will be the youngest England manager and the least experienced [...] (96, 30)[5]

In this example, the function of the free adjunct is clearly to provide evidence (Data, in Toulmin's terms) for the assessment (Claim) made in the matrix clause, and interestingly, whereas the information given in the free adjunct is factual, i.e. information about which there can in principle be absolute certainty, one of the two claims in the matrix clause is an evaluation, i.e. a claim about which there can never be absolute certainty (for the distinction between factual and evaluative claims see Atelsek, 1981).

An example like (34) is exceptional in that the relation between the factual proposition of the adjunct and the evaluative proposition of the matrix clause is simple and logical: the evidence offered in the adjunct is directly relevant to the claim made in the matrix clause. But in the majority of cases the relation between the fact (Datum) and the prediction/evaluation (Claim) is tenuous (35-36):

(35) *Cast in bronze or modelled in plaster or Sculpmetal (a clay-like medium with a metallic finish)* they [the sculptures] are made in such a way that they generate a deep ambiguity concerning their status. (96,26)

(36) *Written in 1969 or 1970,* the manuscript circulated in samizdat and was published abroad before becoming a cult classic in the final years of the Soviet Union. (97,29)

There are all in all 8 cases where, although antecedent and consequent express a factual and an evaluative proposition, respectively, there is no necessary logical connection between them. In addition there are 4 cases cast in the same mould, but in which both propositions are factual without there being any logical link between them whatsoever; (1), (8) and (33) above as well as the following example are instances of this type:

(37) *Born in Hungary in 1951*, Schiff can earn over $8,000 a performance [...] (97,26)

In the great majority of cases, 27, in which the adjunct provides factual evidence for an evaluative Claim made in the matrix clause, however, the order is reversed, so that the antecedent follows the consequent:

(38) The only discordant note was struck [...] when Asako forgot her husband's name during her speech, *calling him Hiroshi instead of Satoshi.* (96,25)[6]

(39) Politically, he was even sharper, *accusing the Clinton White House of having "a smell of Watergate [...]"* (97, 6)

And in a common variant of this type, the consequent contains an interpretation based on the factual proposition of the antecedent:

(40) China rebuked the United States for issuing annual reports critical of Beijing's human right records, *saying they interfered in China's internal affairs.* (97,3)

As I have argued, the use of free adjuncts as suppliers of factual background to evaluations and interpretations is what we should expect. But as Matthiesen & Thompson remind us, discoursal and syntactic categories are not co-terminous (1988:276), and as there are cases where the free adjunct expresses the consequent rather than the antecedent in a causal relationship (cf. above 4.2), so there are cases where it is the adjunct that expresses interpretation/evaluation, and the matrix clause that provides the factual background:

(41) But the public voted the Iranian Gabbeh as its most popular film – *a tribute to its discernment since the film, though beautiful, has little obvious narrative [...]* (97,26)

(42) Hong Kong has lost 30 per cent of its British population in just nine months, *abruptly reversing what had been an end-of-empire gold rush.* (97,1)

In neither of these examples is there any doubt that the ostensibly backgrounded adjunct clauses contain interpretive comments on the information supplied in the matrix clause. There are, however, also cases where it is easier to comprehend the adjunct clause as background although, conceptually, it undoubtedly contains evaluations of the factual information of the matrix clause:

(43) *Most bizarre of all,* one of last week's rows was over the single European currency [...] (97,9)

This example, from a parliamentary report, follows a couple of paragraphs in which Parliament's propensity for bizarre behaviour in the pre-election months has been amply documented.

5. *Newspaper discourse*

In her study of the English "detached participial clause", a subtype of free adjuncts as defined in this paper, Thompson, 1983: 46, notes that the construction is particularly suitable for, and particularly frequent in, "a discourse whose purpose is to describe events rather than to state temporal or logical relationships between them," and moreover "discourse that attempts to describe by creating an image." This discourse she dubs "depictive", a discourse type which, judging from her examples, seems to be a subtype of narrative discourse. Although in a technical sense, newspaper discourse must undoubtedly be considered narrative both on text-internal and text-external grounds (cf. Bell, 1991; Hartley, 1982), it obviously differs from Thompson's depictive discourse in that it is certainly also concerned with establishing temporal and logical relationships between the events it narrates. This tallies well with Kortmann's finding (1991:141) that in terms of its use of free adjuncts, newspaper discourse occupies a position midway between fiction and science.

However, news discourse is not just concerned with relating events; it is also, and more importantly, concerned with relating events in such a way that they will be seen to be true. An account of an event is the more likely to have the appearance of truth if exact, quantitative information about it is available, and for this reason such events are more likely to hit the media than those about which less exact information is available. This is the news value which Galtung & Ruge (1973) term "facticity", and it is this value that is behind journalism's obsession with exact figures of all kinds, even participants' age, regardless of their relevance to the story being narrated. There is one type of free adjunct which lends itself admirably to supplying the kind of fact that journalism is so fond of, viz. the one discussed above under the cover term "accompanying circumstance". With a total of 41 examples, this type, accounting for just under one fourth of the examples, is the largest single type in my corpus. And I would like to suggest that the reason for its popularity is precisely its capability of providing factual background information to the more salient information central to the story.

As I argued earlier on in this paper (above § 4.3), the general form of free adjuncts renders them particularly suitable carriers of information that can be seen as "antecedent" in relation to the information provided by their main clauses, whether that relation is temporal, causal or evidential. This is borne out by the data corpus: out of a total of 174 examples 109 expressed an antecedent role, and only 30 a consequent role, with simultaneity accounting for 19 of the remaining 35 instances. This means that whenever we come across a free adjunct, the default option will be to give it some sort of antecedent interpretation. In some cases the antecedent interpretation is soundly based in the conceptual relationship between the two propositions, as in (34, 38, 39, 40) above, or in the following example:

(44) Last week he held out an olive branch to his defeated opponent, Mr Basayev, *calling him a "comrade in arms"*. (67,4)

In examples like these, the adjunct does two things: it provides the factual background or justification for the interpretation expressed as an evaluative claim in the matrix clause, and at the same time, it adds narrative detail. In other examples, as we have seen, the logic is less than watertight, consider (35) and (36) above. And in others still, such as (37), repeated here in full, there is absolutely no logical/conceptual link between the two propositions:

(37) *Born in Hungary in 1951*, Schiff can earn over $8,000 a performance, and half the year travelling the global concert circuit pays for flats in London and Florence, plus New Year jaunts up the Nile. (97,26)

From a normative point of view it would be tempting to say that this is an abuse of the construction since all that is achieved by using it is that two pieces of information are hitched together, whose only internal connection is that they are information about the same entity. But although many of us might agree with such proscriptive pronouncements, we would also have to admit that they do not bring us any closer to an explanation of the construction's popularity in newspaper discourse. To explore that question, let us first note that the sentence contains the following propositions:

a. Schiff was born in Hungary in 1951.
b. Schiff can earn over $8,000 a performance.
c. Schiff travels the global concert circuit half the year.
d. This pays for flats in London and Florence plus New Year jaunts up the Nile.

All the information offered is factual information,[7] but it is not factual information of the same kind. For whereas the fact conveyed in (a) – the non-finite adjunct clause – is absolutely unremarkable (after all, everybody was born somewhere and sometime), the facts related in the finite part of the sentence are all of the more spectacular kind, which is the reason for relating them, of course. In addition, the facts about place and date of birth are probably easier to check than e.g. questions concerning his fees. What this means is that the adjunct clause in such cases serves to provide the neutral background of facticity in which the more sensational information given in the rest of the sentence is anchored. Finally, in this case, there may also be pragmatic implicature at work, in that the information of (b) – (d) somehow appears surprising seen against the background of the information of (a). Thus, the very lack of noteworthiness of the proposition conveyed by the adjunct clause in itself contributes to making the information of the matrix sentence all the more noteworthy and hence tellable.[8]

6. Conclusion

As we have seen, causal and temporal free adjuncts account for over half – 105 out of 174 – of the occurrences of free adjuncts in my, admittedly small, data corpus. In addition, less than a tenth of the examples – 15 – express the relations of "manner", "explicitation" or "evaluation" (cf. 41-42). This leaves us with a total of 54 cases, just under a third, which provide the main focus of interest for this paper. These are the cases which are traditionally thrown into the ragbag of "accompanying circumstances".[9] As I have tried to show, an argument theoretical approach may throw new light on some of these instances, in that they can be seen as providing the factual evidence upon which the evaluative claims of the matrix clause is based, or, in a weaker form, the factual basis in which the evaluative claims are anchored. Finally we have seen four instances, viz (1), (18), (33) and (37), where both the adjunct clause and the matrix clause express factual propositions, but where at least the facts presented in the adjunct clause are facts of the less colourful type, such as date and place of birth, so that the adjunct can still be seen as acting as a kind of background to the matrix clause, conceptually as well as syntactically – as the "framework within in which the [rest] of the clause complex can be interpreted" as Fries (1995:58) puts it.[10] On the background of those cases it was argued that one reason for the popularity of the free adjunct construction in newspaper discourse is that it helps establish the basis of facticity for the more spectacular claims which are the *raison d'être* for the news story.

However, these final four examples, together with (13) and (32), belong in the category of examples referred to in section 4.3. in which the conceptual relationship between matrix clause and adjunct is merely additive, and where the information given in the adjunct clause might just as well have been given in a co-ordinated main clause. This subtype of "accompanying circumstance", which might be dubbed "co-ordinative adjunct",[11] all in all comprises 10 cases. In addition to the above I cite the following two (note that [46] contains two coordinated adjunct clauses):

(45) *Part of a huge cargo of cultural contraband*, they [the antiques] had arrived at the Lok Mak Chau border post in the middle of the night [...]. (96,25)

(46) *Running north-south and known as the Hundred Foot Washes*, the dykes helped convert the East-Anglian Fens, once one of Europe's largest wetlands, into some of the most productive agricultural land in Britain. (97,24)

In these cases, then, the material in the adjunct clause is presented as syntactically backgrounded in relation to the rest of the sentence without this back-grounding being justified at the conceptual level, and we might thus wonder why the writer did not simply choose to present his material in two co-ordinated clauses if this is the clearest reflection of the inherent relationship. There are various, not at all incompatible, explanations. In the first place, the construction is a way of cramming "as much information into as few words and sentences as possible" (Fries 1995: 58). Second, note that the shared element between the adjunct and the matrix clause (the subject, except in [13], where the adjunct is "dangling") in all the examples cited has a form that indicates previous mention: it is either a definite NP, a personal pronoun or a last name without title or first name. In fact, the referent of the subject is in all cases the topic of the section in question, and by choosing an alternative to the co-ordinated construction, the writers thus avoid opening too many sentences with the same noun or pronoun. Finally, since in the great majority of cases, the adjunct construction indicates some conceptual link between adjunct and matrix clause other than mere addition, the use of the construction will give the text a deliberative flavour that is absent in a co-ordination, which simply lists facts. In addition to signalling facticity, the adjunct construction can thus also be employed to indicate connectedness.

Notes

1 Quotations are from two issues of the *Guardian Weekly*, viz 12.05.1996 and 09.02.1997. References are by year and page number.

2 In French linguistics the construction is often referred to as *attribut indirect*, see e.g. Prebensen 1973. For its use in French company brochures, see Nielsen 1996.

3 Kortmann's scale ranges from "concessive" and "contrast" at the most informative end to "accompanying circumstance" and "addition" at the least informative end. The logic behind it is that it requires more knowledge to interpret the relation between two propositions as one of "adverbial modification" rather than simply as "side-by-side-information".

4 The problem of the relationship between the adjunct and the matrix clause is also dealt with in Quirk et al. 1985: 1123-1127, but in lesser detail and less succinctly.

5 It might be objected that in this example the adjunct simply expresses cause. This is not so, however; Hoddle's age is adduced, not as the direct cause of his becoming the youngest manager, but as the writer's justification for making the claim. In a real causal relation, the cause in itself triggers off the effect: [...] last autumn Barmby would have found the net with his eyes closed. But now, *off balance*, he put the ball well wide. (96,30)

6 From a causal as well as from a temporal point of view, the adjunct clause in (38) is the antecedent of the matrix clause, since forgetting someone's name both causes and precedes misnaming him. But argumentatively, the roles are reversed, for since *forgetting* is an internal event, we cannot legitimately claim that people have forgotten something unless we have external evidence, and in this example, that evidence is offered in the adjunct clause, which is accordingly the antecedent.

7 This is in fact not quite true. Strictly speaking the facts of (b), (c) and (d) are that (b) he can earn over $ 8,000 a performance, and (c) he spends half the year travelling the concert circuit, and (d) that he owns flats in London and Florence etc. But the claim that he can afford (d) *because of* (b) and (c) is not a factual claim, as causal judgments can never be factual.

8 I owe this observation to Mick Short. It is worth noting, however, that the juxtaposition of adjunct and matrix clause does not always give rise to pragmatic implicatures of this type.

9 Kortmann (1991: 121ff) further subdivides this class into exemplification, specification, accompanying circumstance and addition.

10 Fries regards adjuncts, and all subordinate clauses in thematic position, as the theme of the clause complex. As the question of thematicity is irrelevant in the context of this paper, I have not gone into that question here.

11 I am grateful to Hans-Jürgen Diller for this suggestion.

Bibliography

Atelsek, J.: "An anatomy of opinions". *Language in Society* 10, 1981, 217-225.

Bell, A.: *The Language of News Media*. Oxford: Blackwell, 1991.

Fries, P. H.: "Patterns of information in initial position in English". – In P.H. Fries & M. Gregory (Eds.): *Discourse in Society: Systemic Functional Perspectives. Meaning and choice in Language: Studies for Michael Halliday.* Norwood: Ablex, 1995.

Galtung, J. & M. Ruge: "Structuring and selecting news". – In S. Cohen & J. Young (Eds.): *The Manufacture of News.* London: Constable, 1973, pp. 62-73.

Givón, T.: *Syntax. A Functional-Typological Introduction.* Amsterdam 1984.

Golkova, E.: "On the English infinitive of purpose in functional sentence perspective". *Brno Studies in English* 7, 1968, 119-128.

Greenbaum, S.: *Studies in English Adverbial Usage.* London: Longman, 1969.

Halliday, M. A. K.: *An Introduction to Functional Grammar.* London: Edward Arnold, 1994 (1st ed. 1985).

Hartley, J.: *Understanding News.* London: Routledge, 1982.

Hopper, P. J. & S. Thompson: "Transitivity in grammar and discourse". *Language* 56, 1980, 251-299.

Kortmann, B.: *Free Adjuncts and Absolutes in English. Problems of Control and Interpretation.* London and New York: Routledge, 1991.

Matthiesen, C. & S. A. Thompson: "The structure of discourse and 'subordination'". – In J. Haiman & S. A. Thompson (Eds.): *Clause Combining in Grammar and Discourse.* Amsterdam: John Benjamins, 1988, pp. 275-317.

Nielsen, A. E.: *Argumentationsstrategier i franske præsentationsbrochurer. Fra det sproglige til det retoriske niveau.* Ph.D. thesis. The Aarhus School of Business. Aarhus, 1996.

Perelman, C. & L. Olbrechts-Tyteca: *The New Rhetoric. A Treatise on Argumentation.* Notre Dame: University of NotreDame Press, 1969. (French original: *La nouvelle rhétorique: traité de l'argumentation*, 1958).

Prebensen, H.: "Apposition, attribut indirect et complement de circonstance en francais moderne." *Actes du 5me congrès des romanistes scandinaves.* Turku: Turkun Yliopisto, 1973, 149-159.

Quirk, R. et al.: *A Grammar of Contemporary English*. London: Longman, 1972.
---: *A Comprehensive Grammar of the English Language*. London: Longman, 1985.
Ramsay, V.: "The functional distribution of preposed and postposed "if" and "when" clauses in written discourse". – In R. S. Tomlin (Ed.): *Coherence and Grounding in Discourse.* Amsterdam: John Benjamins, 1987, pp. 383-408.
Thompson, S. A.: "Grammar and discourse: the English detached participial clause" – In F. Klein-Andreu (Ed.): *Discourse Perspectives on Syntax*. New York: Academic Press, 1983, pp. 43-65.
---: "Grammar and written discourse: Initial vs. final purpose clauses in English." *Text 5,* 1985, 55-84.
Thompson, S. A. & R. E. Longacre: "Adverbial Clauses" – In T. Shopen (Ed.): *Language Typology and Syntactic Description. Vol. II: Complex Constructions.* Cambridge: Cambridge University Press, 1985, pp. 171-234.
Toulmin, S.: *The Uses of Argument.* Cambridge: Cambridge University Press, 1958.
Zandvoort, R. W.: *A Handbook of English Grammar*[2]. London: Longman, 1961.

Michael White, Madrid

The Bundesbank and the making of an Economic Press Story

1. Introduction

1.1. Contextual events

In September 1992, the European Monetary System (EMU) suffered the most serious crisis of its history. For our purposes, a telegraphic outline[1] of the main components of the crisis will suffice to provide the contextual framework within which we can see how the press handles such an issue:

- Over the summer of 1992 and particularly as September arrived, the trading situation on the foreign exchange markets was such that the status quo of currency parities within the Exchange Rate Mechanism (ERM) was felt to be unsustainable.
- At this stage, currencies tended to be grouped together as strong, with the D-Mark as hallmark, or weak, particularly the Lira and Sterling followed by the Peseta, Escudo and Punt and to a certain extent the Franc.
- The authorities of weaker currency countries desperately sought to ward off the threat of realignment.
- At this juncture the key to a satisfactory outcome was clearly seen to lie with the Bundesbank. However, sharply conflicting interests were involved here:
  1) On the one hand, the Bundesbank has a statutory obligation to protect the value of the German currency, and at this time the central bank authorities, wrestling with the Herculean problems deriving from German re-unification and monetary union, were forced to run high interest rates to counteract inflation and attract funds.
  2) On the other hand, Britain, finding itself in the depth of recession, urgently needed to reduce interest rates but could not do so without jeopardising its ERM parity unless a corresponding cut was made in German rates. Many other European countries found themselves in a similar dilemma.
- At a vital meeting of the Finance ministers of the EU held at Bath, U.K., the remaining members of the EU made a concerted effort to persuade the German authorities to reduce interest rates and thereby aid recession-hit countries and defuse the tension mounting on the markets.

- This demand put the Bundesbank President in a very awkward position:
  1) On the one hand, he and the bank he represented were being called upon to act as a de facto European Central Bank and take steps demanded by the EU as a whole.
  2) On the other hand, those steps ran counter to what he and the Bundesbank council deemed German monetary performance demanded. Moreover, the Bundesbank President is the president of a democratic Council made up of (at that time) 18 members[2] with different loyalties and where the President's vote counts as that of any other member.
- The Bath meeting ended with an agreement that the Bundesbank would reduce interest rates and that Italy would devalue the Lira.
- On the following Monday the Bundesbank Council decided on an interest rate cut of a mere ¼ %. This was so slight as to threaten to produce an altogether contrary to desired effect on the market. Next day, when an interview by Mr Schlesinger gave the impression that further devaluations, especially in the case of Sterling, were needed, a full-scale crisis broke, leading to the exit from the Exchange Rate Mechanism (ERM) and drastic loss in exchange value of the Lira and Sterling, followed by successive realignments of other currencies within the EMS.
- In the wake of this dénouement, British authorities and, to some extent, the British press laid the blame on Germany and the Bundesbank as primarily responsible for the crisis. The Bundesbank authorities flatly denied the charge. While abroad they were considered the outright victors of the crisis, they had also to contend with criticism at home for having failed to carry out their statutory mandate.

1.2. The handling of events by the press

Now, I have just narrated the events which made up the currency crisis in the most "congruent" (Halliday 1994: 342) style possible.[3] Basically, this is the case because typical actors – the Bundesbank president, the British, German or European financial authorities – are the agents of typical processes – holding meetings, negotiating with and persuading counterparts to take certain measures, in short the doing of diverse things. Furthermore, this is in line with the claim that economics is the result of decisions taken by rational agents (see Henderson 1982: 149 and Gerard 1993: 61). However, if I turn to the press coverage of the crisis, this is precisely the kind of discourse that is rarely forthcoming. In fact, my very narration itself is a result of a conscious effort to raise rational actors who in the press coverage of the issue are embedded, disguised or entailed in a morass of metonymy and metaphor. How this comes about and its effect on the discourse produced will now be the object of study.

One of the essential tenets of cognitive linguistics (which is the theoretic framework informing my analysis) is that thought is metaphoric and that consequently our conceptualisation makes natural and constant recourse to metonymy and metaphor in its processes. Two immediate consequences follow: firstly, the fact that the use of metaphor and metonymy is to a very large degree highly conventional and secondly that it is so conventional as to go unnoticed in ordinary use or naturally occurring discourse (Gibbs 1994: 22; Lakoff & Johnson 1980; Lakoff & Turner 1989). For instance, if we came across a press heading such as the following:

- Parent warns child on traffic dangers –

the sentence would be found to meet all semantic criteria for good construction. The predicate "warn" will imply a human agent and a human recipient, here provided by "parent" and "child" respectively. If, however, the heading we come across reads as follows –

1) Bundesbank warns Bonn on federal debt (FT1:1-H)[4] –

it is quite obvious that different linguistic processes are operating. The agent in this case is an institution – the Bundesbank –, the recipient, a city – Bonn. Yet the sentence is not only meaningful but is as automatically understood to be so as the former one. This is possible because of the conventionalised processes at work: the metonymic processes whereby a location may stand for an institution seated at that location and an institution may stand for the people who run that institution. The first effect here is a referential one producing a great economy of wording: I don't have to spell out something to the effect of "The German Executive Authorities" or "The current political party governing Germany" (see Boers & Demecheleer 1994: 684-5). But further metaphorical processes are at work: the institution, the Bundesbank, and the German Executive Power or Government are being personified and, what is more, quite specific personality traits emerge through the predicate or accompanying co-text. The Bundesbank, for instance, is not just "informing" Bonn or "asking" Bonn a question but "warning" Bonn. To grasp the full implications involved here, let us recall our "cognate" example:

- Parent warns child on traffic dangers

This sentence is not only satisfying semantically, it also conforms highly with expectations. If, however, I introduce the following switch:

- Child warns parent on traffic dangers

expectations, certainly prototypical expectations, are tampered with since the warning agent somehow or other is expected to wield some form of ascendancy over the warned. Thus

1) Bundesbank warns Bonn on federal debt (FT1:1-H) –

very decidedly carries certain implications and not others. In fact, it carries a wealth of these, for example:

- The Bundesbank is in a position which commands a certain authority: it can warn.
- If the Bundesbank warns, it probably has a stricter outlook on and a sharper awareness of the potential danger of the question at issue than the recipient of its warning.
- Bonn has a certain degree of responsibility for the existence of federal debt.
- Bonn is either unaware, or at least less aware than the Bundesbank of the potential danger of this debt.
- There is a certain degree of independence between the two institutions.

This initial example puts us on the track of how journalists cope with such issues as the activity taking place within an institution. The most conventional of devices such as elementary forms of metonymy can, by means of their accompanying predicates or co-text, convey highly sophisticated meanings simply and effectively. This is very evident in the case of the overriding device of personifying the Bundesbank, which on the macro level provides a framework enabling them to construct discourse concerning the bank and on the micro level it provides a vast supply of choices from which the concrete attributes are mustered. It is these which give the specific interpretational direction that journalists wish to bring to bear in their explanation of the nature of the Bundesbank and of its activities. Let us now see how this claim is borne out empirically, striving at each moment to consider the respective devices used in connection with an as fair as possible interpretation of the meaning of the events and processes unfolding.

Chronologically, we can distinguish two periods: before and after the crisis. While the same rhetorical devices operate in both periods, differences of perception, expectation and attitude clearly justify this division and enable us to relate more effectively the use of these devices to the conveyance of meaning.

2. Prior to the Crisis

During the lead-up to the crisis, the conviction that the Bundesbank was the decisive piece in the evolution of exchange rates and the sheer difficulty of getting its authorities to accede to an interest rate cut, forces press discussion of the whole issue of the crisis to try, in the first place, to come to terms with and explain the nature of this institution. That task is by no means as simple as it might appear. We shall now analyse the way the press handles it under four headings:

(i) the make-up of the Bundesbank,
(ii) the Bundesbank as guardian of German currency values,
(iii) the Bundesbank wielding power,
(iv) the Bundesbank and other institutional authorities.

2.1. The make-up of the Bundesbank

In connection with example 1) above, we have already seen the conventional metonymy of an institution representing the people who run that institution. But a major issue[5] lies embedded in the whole process: are those individuals who run an institution referentially co-terminous with that institution or are we to distinguish individuals – no matter how high-ranking – from the institution itself and hence also distinguish between individual and institutional acts and pronouncements. Looking at the actual case at hand the mainstream journalistic way of dealing with the Bundesbank is through personification, but when we pursue the referential range of that personification we find extreme flexibility. In effect, "the Bundesbank" for journalists refers indifferently to at least the following three cases:

(i) The agent of the formal decisions taken by the collective council,
(ii) The president and individual council members in their diverse pronouncements,
(iii) The agent of a conception of the macro-economic scenario deemed by journalistic analysis to constitute Bundesbank policy and which in turn is likely to entail significant market repercussions (e.g.: "The Bundesbank thinks/objected to/is sceptical of..." etc.).

Thus when we look at the make-up of the Bundesbank, as appearing in the press, case i) presents no problems. Case ii) deserves considerable attention and what is highlighted is that the considerable differences between council members can give rise to widely diverging opinions. Again, personification of the institution is the vehicle by which such meanings are put across:

2) Many voices go into *a Bundesbank utterance.*[6] (FT 11:3-H)
3) ... the Bank *makes its views known* to the outside world in a bewildering multiplicity of ways. This is primarily because of *its pluralistic way of making decisions.* (FT11:3-L)

4) When in recent weeks, *a variety of Bundesbank's views* ricochet onto the foreign exchange markets from several different angles, the Central bank can *stand accused* of inconsistency. (FT11:3)

These examples clearly highlight the pluralistic composition of the Bundesbank council and certain consequences ensuing from this fact. Secondly, however, at the very outset of our discussion, we can see that, even here where our concern is to come to grips with the make-up of the Bank, the very language used underlines the power of the Bundesbank since the entailment of the expression "*a variety of Bundesbank's views ricochet* onto the foreign exchange markets *from several different angles*" shows the potentially devastating effects which the mere views or opinions of the bank or rather its council members might have.[7]

Case iii), on the other hand, means journalists are pushing the referential range of "the Bundesbank" to a flexibility bordering on looseness, which can give rise to considerable controversy with Bundesbank officials being forced on stage to deny journalistic inferences attributing to the Bank ideas, conceptions or potential steps which the Bank is adamant to disown. In this respect, journalists could well stand accused of shortcomings in rigour and of appropriation of a role which is not theirs but, nevertheless, this aspect of journalistic procedure is essential in endowing journalists that leeway which makes for penetrating analysis and insight, and this certainly is something demanded of the profession. In this sense, the practice seems justified and it is likewise mainstream for journalism to discover, detect or deduce institutional policy or thinking which the institution in question strives hard to conceal and indeed deny.

2.2. The Bundesbank as guardian of German currency value

While the Bundesbank's statutory mandate to defend the value of German currency may just be a statement of fact, the personality attributes which are raised by the press when dealing with the issue – sheer determination, tenacity, and resolution to withstand contrary tendencies – highlight an aspect of the Bundesbank which shows that in carrying out its mandate it is behaving in a way that is both characteristic of a certain personality and at the same time conferring that personality on the institution. As a result, the idea that the Bundesbank is the kind of person that acts with a singleness of purpose which makes it inexpugnable comes across:

5) Reimut Jochimsem, a council member, said ... the *Bundesbank had to pursue tight monetary policies* because of strong growth in money supply. (FT3: 15)

6) The Bundesbank's *do-or-die war on German inflation* is continuing to dominate management of the European exchange-rate mechanism. (T5: 13-E-L)
7) The Bundesbank *would be watching closely* the further development of the economy. (FT7: 2)
8) The Bundesbank *will not be deflected from its policy* of pursuing firm monetary targets by outside criticism or failure to meet these in the short term, Mr. Issing, a director of the German Central Bank, said yesterday. (FT11: 3)
9) The Bundesbank *objected to profligate spending* by the governments, to above-inflation wage rises and, most recently, to interest rate subsidies for eastern Germany... (T11: 21)

2.3. The power-wielding nature of the Bundesbank

The foregoing characteristics set the scene for a logical corollary of this conception of the Bundesbank, namely, that it is the agent of authority and wields power. We have already analysed the implications of "warn"; to this are added predicates consonant with that analysis, such as other countries being at the mercy of the Bundesbank, or this institution in the domineering role where it can be seen as sceptical of others or of conducting and leading processes:

1) *Bundesbank warns Bonn* on federal debt. (FT1: 1-H)
10) If the French vote in favour of the Maastricht treaty, the EC's leaders may not summon up the courage to examine their respective currency values with a view to realignment. They would thus abandon all hope of using exchange-rate adjustment as a tool of revival and leave their economic and political fates *at the mercy of the Bundesbank*. (T5: 13-E)
11) The Bundesbank *has always been sceptical* about whether Britain would accept the anti-inflationary discipline inherent in the system [i.e. EMS]. (FT11: 3)
12) The Bundesbank *finds itself in the unenviable position of having to conduct* an independent monetary policy against the background of an economic policy that *it despises* and which *it tried hard but unsuccessfully to prevent.* (T11: 21)
13) The Bundesbank *leads the system, it leads the intervention* ... (T11: 21)

All these characteristics are setting up and reinforcing a scenario whereby the economic institution, the Bundesbank, is being endowed with very clearly defined personality traits, and it is important to point out that these are not necessarily co-terminous with the real personality traits of the members of the Bundesbank executive council. Rather, these traits are supplying the vehicle by which journalists are conveying their abstract conception of the fundamental philosophy underlying the policy and proven practice of the Bundesbank institution over the years. Thus, at this stage in time, dominated by the threat of an impending currency crisis, the picture of the nature of the Bundesbank which comes across in the press is highly coherent because the type of interaction it is seen to engage in is highly consonant with the type of personality with which it is endowed. Let us now go on to see empirical evidence of this interaction in the development of the negotiations under relevant headings.

2.4. Interaction between the Bundesbank and other institutional authorities

Having established that the Bundesbank comes across in the press as occupying a towering economic position, it is not surprising that we find the entities or people interacting with it presented in dependent roles: those of supplicant, for instance, or that of having to combine forces to try to influence Bundesbank decisions. Secondly, having also presented the Bundesbank as by nature a stolid upholder of its principles, neither is it surprising to find the other parties' attempts to bring about a change in the bank's policy being described in terms of such dynamically intense verbs as 'urge' or 'force'. Furthermore, all these factors are clear instances of making 'sense of phenomena in the world in human terms' (Lakoff and Johnson 1980: 34) and of providing 'structure for understanding' (Lakoff and Turner 1989: 53). Witness the empirical evidence for this claim in the following sub-sections:

2.4.1. Bundesbank as object of pleas

14) Mr. Gordon Brown ... called on the UK *to urge* the Bundesbank to signal an interest rate cut when it met on Thursday. (FT 1: 1)
15) Gordon Brown ... urged Mr. Lamont ... *to press* the German Bundesbank to signal its readiness for a cut in interest rates. (T1: 14)
16) Speaking on Saturday after nine hours of hard bargaining, including *concerted pressure* on Germany to cut interest rates, Mr. Lamont said he hoped that the Bundesbank's promise would contribute to stability on exchange markets. (FT7: 1)

2.4.2. The Bundesbank as capable of ignoring external requests or pressure

17) Although the Bundesbank *is notoriously impervious to political pressure* even from the German government, the shadow Chancellor believes that pressures for an interest rate cut are increasing. (T 1: 14)
18) He [Mr. Issing] *denied* the Bundesbank *was operating too rigid a policy* based on *"sticking blindly"* to monetary targets. (FT11: 3)
19 [=8]) The Bundesbank *will not be deflected* from its policy of pursuing firm monetary targets *by outside criticism* or failure to meet these in the short term, Mr. Issing, a director of the German Central Bank, said yesterday. (FT11: 3)
20) The Bundesbank *is equally opposed*, however, to creating the impression that it is allowing pressure from foreign finance ministers to dictate its anti-inflationary monetary policies. (FT11: 3)

2.4.3. Reactions towards impasse

The intensity of the interaction implied by the opposition of 'urge', 'press' and 'concerted pressure' on the one hand, and 'notoriously impervious' and 'will not be deflected' on the other, once more underlines the conflict dimension and creates the impression of an impasse. The supposed lack of co-operation on the part of the Bundesbank is interpreted by the British press as opposition to the European Monetary System as a whole and, as easily happens in impasse scenarios where negotiation and argumentation cannot move forward, recourse is often made by one side or the other to more highly charged attitudinal attacks on, or criticism of, their counterparts. Hence, the British endeavour to lay responsibility on Germany for the situation is linguistically aided and abetted by the very powerful negative charge associated with a crime schema:

21) But if the EMS does suffer a breakdown in the next few weeks, the Bundesbank *can hardly claim to have been nowhere near the scene.* (FT11: 3)

The manner in which the Bundesbank is anticipated as probably rejecting such allegations likewise rests not on abstract argument but on the communicative strength of a metaphor. This is brought about by a similar personification of the EMS and the use of the very conventional metonymy for subjection – being brought to one's knees. At the same time there is an effective attempt to counteract the negative attitudinal import of the accusations and to clear the personified Bundesbank's name of any sinister conniving – "not hatching a conspiracy".

22) The Central bank *is not hatching a conspiracy to bring the EMS to its knees*. (FT11: 3)

Finally, the ultimate in configuring the Bundesbank's supposed imperviousness is the metaphorical association of policy and action with the sheer inanimateness of the actual Bundesbank building. In other words, the personification dimension of the Bundesbank, so powerful in the whole issue in the press, is here eliminated and what is censurable is precisely the lack of personal attributes.

23) The Bundesbank slab-like headquarters on the outskirts of Frankfurt gives the German central bank *the look of a monolith*. (FT11: 3)

2.4.4. Interest rate cut as a Bundesbank concession

Given the picture of the Bundesbank we have been outlining above, it is not surprising that when the interest rate cut comes, it is presented as a concession by a powerful agent. Again, personification is at the root of the getting across of meaning from the use of possessives to giving the Bundesbank a mind and heart together with their metonymical qualities:

24) Bundesbank *allows flicker of hope* (FT7: 2-H)
25) The *Bundesbank's pledge* does not exclude the possibility of other nations having to raise interest rates in the event of external shocks… (FT7: 2)
26) It was "the first time the Bundesbank *had committed itself* openly and publicly not to raise rates". (FT7: 2)
27) The Bundesbank *is no longer in a frame of mind* to raise rates. (FT7: 2-Q)
28) His [i.e. that of Mr. Schlesinger] willingness to agree to the "no increase" statement marked something of *a change of heart at the top of the Bundesbank*. (FT7: 2)

3. Aftermath of the Crisis

3.1. Causal inquiry

The cataclysmic collapse of sterling on Wednesday 16th September 1992 – Black Wednesday – despite massive Bank of England intervention and unprecedented interest rate rises[8] also ushered in a complete change of perspective. The previous atmosphere of negotiation and, albeit not bereft of tension, mutual co-operation disappears and the attempt to come to terms with the aetiology of events now gives rise to overt conflict as the British authorities openly blame their German counterparts for the dénouement. The resulting scenario is analogous to that described by Shapiro, van den Broek and Fletcher (1995) with respect to the role of motivational factors in causal assignation in another great financial crisis, Black Monday.[9] These authors claim:

> [...] causal attributions are also known to be highly selective and directionally biased, especially when people attempt to justify their beliefs or try to persuade others to reach a particular conclusion. [...] An explanation is selective if it reports only some of an event's relevant antecedent conditions, and it is biased if an alternative explanation may also be supported by the available evidence. (Shapiro, van den Broek and Fletcher 1995:59)

In fact, selectivity and bias is perhaps inherent to argumentation in conflict situations. Secondly, in such a situation, conflicting parties are forced to pull out all the stops in their effort to convince and to outdo contrary arguments. My interest here will be to show how, in this extreme situation, the different parties and, to a certain extent, the press systematically recurred to metaphor to support their side of argument. In the first place, the quest for causal factors leads the press and British financial authorities to a reappraisal of the events preceding 'Black Wednesday', that is, the events dealt with above in section 2. I shall deal with this reappraisal under different headings as follows:

3.2. The Bath Meeting of Financial authorities as an anti-climax

We saw in section 2 how this meeting was hailed as a historic development in European co-operation where the Bundesbank was seen to be acting in the wider interests of the whole Union. Such claims or expectations were, however, shattered by the events of Black Wednesday. Now in retrospect, the idea that is singled out is that the remaining European authorities carried their pressure on the German authorities too far and this idea comes across through the forceful use of the conflict metaphor:

29) He [i.e. Mr. Lamont] had *secured from the mighty Bundesbank* a promise not to raise interest rates. (FT19/20 :2)
30) Perhaps the turning point came earlier this month during the informal meeting of finance ministers in Bath when Mr. Helmut Schlesinger, Bundesbank president, and Mr. Theo Waigel, Germany's finance min-

ister, *were ambushed* by their 11 counterparts and urged to lower interest rates to help a general European economic recovery. (FT18: 8)

31) "It was *a bloodbath*", says one participant. (FT18: 8)

32) This private *arm-twisting* may explain, first, the Bundesbank's grudging cut of a ¼ percentage point in the Lombard rate… (FT18: 8)

Clearly, here the communicative force derives from the conventional metaphors ARGUMENT IS WAR and PSYCHOLOGICAL FORCE IS PHYSICAL FORCE. Secondly, this is abetted by the reiterative personification of the Bundesbank which is not only the agent of the action of cutting interest rates but also the bearer of such a specific human attribute as acting in a grudging manner. The independence of the Bundesbank is underlined by the same device of personification and with so conventional a term as "bow", nevertheless laden with semantic and semiotic import, putting forward that notion of independence in such an uncompromising way.

33) The Bundesbank *bowed to no man*, least of all a politician. (FT19/20: 2)

34) But characteristically, the *Bundesbank's reply* was that *it cut interest rates to please itself*, and promptly trimmed a measly quarter of a percent off the Lombard rate. (T19: 21)

At the level of events then, the press shows a certain comprehension for the Bundesbank position. Nevertheless, the inadequacy of the minimum interest rate cut finally acceded to by the central bank to produce the desired effect on the market forum, was held to be one of the essential factors triggering the dramatic events of September 16th and the selective attribution of causes in this respect easily leads British representatives to blame the German authorities.

3.3. British Blame on the Bundesbank

In the first place, there is the realisation that while the dominating influence of Germany conditions the policies of other countries, the primary concern of the Bundesbank is with those policies warranted within the country and exclusively due to internal German variables and which, at this juncture, happen to have very detrimental effects in the rest of Europe. Once more the personification of the Bundesbank is poignant in getting these points across – particularly graphic is the presentation of the Bundesbank as a person holding 99 % of the votes. Other personal behaviour attributes show the Bundesbank as wanting "the best of both worlds" and as taking decisions which automatically affect other countries to the latter's disadvantage. In the context, these attributes are easily read as connoting an abuse of power on the part of the Bundesbank.

35) "At the present time I see no benefit in going back into the EMS – *one man has 99 per cent of the votes and that man resides in Germany*" (David Rough, group director of investments, Legal & General). (FT18: 4)
36) The Bundesbank *wants to have the best of both worlds* – it wants the system to be flexible enough *to allow it to run its own monetary policy*, but not so flexible as to lead to competitive devaluations which would be harmful for German exporters. (FT18: 3)
37) Through its stern efforts to bring down German inflation during the past two years the Bundesbank *has effectively exported* deflation to other ERM members. (FT18: 3)
38) As a result of the financial pressures in Germany caused by German unification, *members of the ERM will continue to pay a price for the privilege of allowing the Bundesbank to decide their monetary policies.* (FT18: 3)

While other countries may not like those policies, they must nevertheless concede, albeit grudgingly at times, that such questions are strictly a matter of German sovereignty. What the British authorities cannot accept, however, are statements made by Bundesbank officials and leakages of information from central bank sources which they considered to have been devastating on an unstable market and thus playing a crucial role in the collapse of sterling. If "critics follow a scent like hounds"[10], journalists do so all the more. Thus, it is ironic that in such a complex and technical issue as currency exchange values one of the most singly crucial causal events in triggering the 1992 currency crisis was deemed to be the mere implications of certain words pronounced by Mr. Schlesinger in a press interview. As British journalists home in on this factor as a causal element, metaphor is once more to the forefront carrying censure via such attitudinal terms as "loose talk", "whispering campaigns" "collapse" or "undermine" and highlighting the dramatic effects in "blood-letting".

39) *A thunderous silence* was the reaction of the Bundesbank itself, an ironic answer to the charge from Downing Street that top German officials had precipitated the currency *collapse* with their *loose talk*.(FT18: 2)
40) ... British officials, who had spelt out a series of occasions on which the Bundesbank's alleged *"whispering campaign"* had undermined the pound ... (FT18: 2)

41) Twice in a matter of days, *the mighty central bank has been forced to issue agonised denials* of statements attributed to it, on each occasion too late *to prevent a blood-letting* on the currency markets. (FT17: 19)

More subtle and much more dramatic censure is carried via the war metaphor:

42) ... within the space of just over a week, the Bundesbank has helped orchestrate two important *coups.* (FT18: 3)
43) ... the charges in London of *Bundesbank sabotage* forcing the devaluation of sterling. (FT18: 18)
44) Britain cannot blame the Bundesbank for its economic problems. But under the rules of the European Monetary System, it is entitled to assistance, rather than to *sniping.* (FT17: 18-E)
45) Treasury officials claim the Bundesbank *plotted to force sterling* to devalue so it would not have to bail Britain out. (S17: 2)

"Coups", "sabotage" or "sniping" and "plotting" are not just any or another aspect of war. Rather, they are perhaps standardly associated with the most disreputable manner of carrying out warfare and obviously this aspect of reprobation towards German behaviour is forcefully carried over. Once again, this seems to be bearing out the point made above, where in conflict situations the drive towards forceful argumentation (that is, argumentation which not only carries a point but also impedes or pre-empts counter-arguments) draws heavily on metaphor for its purposes. It is in this context too that the associative or connotative dimension of language is exploited to the full as in the case of the censurable type of warfare (see examples 42-45 above).

3.4. Conflict in Anglo-German relations

The immediate conflict with the Bundesbank obviously spilled over into Anglo-German relations in general and once more the conventional metaphors for anger and conflict deriving from the domains of heat and war provide the conceptual framework for the relevant meanings with "basic level terms" (see Lakoff 1987: 31-40 and Ungerer & Schmid 1996: 66-78) from the war schema proliferating: "guns", "target", "fire", "attack":

46) *British guns target Germany.* (FT17: 2-H)
47) Major *turns his fire on Bonn* for ERM chaos. (FT19/20: 1-H)
48) Mr. Kohl ... responded with *a furious attack* on Mr. Lamont. (FT19/20: 1)

As well as the war schema, *The Sun* takes advantage of the homophonous similarity of the German chancellor's surname with that of coal to raise a humorous instance of the prototypical metaphor for conveying anger, namely heat (See Kövecses 1986, Lakoff 1987: 380-415), and this metaphor is then followed up in the ensuing lead.

49) Major *heaps Kohls of fire.* (S19: 2-H)[11]
50) Britain's *war of words* with Germany *hotted up* last night as premier John Major publicly blamed the Bundesbank for Britain's monetary crisis. (S19: 2)

The effect of such confrontation takes its toll on the relations between both countries and the resultant situation of animosity at the level of nations is put forward through the prototypical way of metaphorically capturing differences and disappointments in interpersonal relations, namely bitterness, here predicated of Britain.

51) *Britain's bitterness* over Germans mounts. (ST20: 1-H)
40) ... the *bitterness* of British officials who had spelt out a series of occasions on which the Bundesbank's alleged "whispering campaign" had undermined the pound ... (FT18: 2)

The interesting question from our vantage point will be to see how Germany rejects such British allegations and, in keeping with the evidence hitherto presented, once again, here we find the use of metaphor to be sustained. For instance, recalling Shapiro, Van den Broek and Fletcher's point (quoted above in section 3.1) regarding selectivity and directional bias in causal attribution, it is obvious that in German circles British claims will be found wanting on precisely those premises of selectivity and directional bias, and hence German representation of events sets out to expose this failing. The point is that they manage to achieve this not by any abstract argument or by adducing financial figures, but by the use of the conventional metaphors of "scapegoat" and "whipping boy", both of which are lexicalised in German as well as in English[12]. Moreover, the moral involved here is further spelled out through the use of the mundane idiom of "putting one's own house in order" prior to placing blame elsewhere.

52) Indeed the instant reaction to the bitterness of British officials ... was to talk of "the very natural desire of the British government to find a *scapegoat.*"(FT18: 20)
53) One bank official said anonymously later, however: "The hunt for a *scapegoa*t is in fact something which always happens in times of crisis,

although everyone would do better to put their own house in order first." (T18: 4-Q)

54) "...of course we understand that one needs a *whipping boy* at such a moment, and it is easy to look abroad to find one". (T. Waigel, German Finance Minister) (FT18: 2-Q)

The Times, which had been highly critical of Britain's handling of the crisis harbours a similar opinion and gets it forcefully across by the use of another biblical metaphor, namely the 'figleaves' which Adam and Eve "sewed together" to cover their nakedness, newly discovered after the eating of the apple (Gen. 3.7). Thus, showering blame on Germany is shown to be a decoy or cover-up for embarrassing responsibility within the government.

55) There were strong suggestions yesterday that the latest position was no more than a *figleaf* to cover the government's embarrassment at having to abandon the central plank of its economic policy. (T18: 2)

3.5. Re-appraisal of the Bundesbank in the wake of the crisis

The Bundesbank is considered the outright victor of the crisis and this fact triggers off the enquiry as to how this bank can be capable of such feats. Again here, at every stage, metaphor plays a crucial role which we may single out under the following headings.

3.5.1. Bundesbank's achievement in the field of monetary stability

Metaphors from the domains of sports, marriage and war are tapped in highlighting the formidable success of Bundesbank policy in promoting and safeguarding monetary stability (in this respect see Marsh, 1992):

56) To complain of "fault lines" in the ERM as if nobody had ever noticed that the Bundesbank is the *pivotal* central bank and Germany the *main player* is peculiar. (FT22: 18-E)

57) *Wedded to* price stability, it has always kept money tight, when this objective has been threatened. (FT23: 2)

58) The Bundesbank's anti-inflation *track record* makes it a model for many nations. (FT23: 16)

59) ... the Bundesbank is *not about to abandon its targets lightly.* (FT23: 2)

3.5.2. The Stature of the Bundesbank

The domain of sport and the pillars of the traditional state, namely military and ecclesiastical hierarchy, highlight the extraordinary power of the Bundesbank:

60 [=56]) To complain of "fault lines" in the ERM as if nobody had ever noticed that the Bundesbank is the *pivotal* central bank and Germany the *main player* is peculiar. (FT22: 18-E)

61) When he speaks, a German central banker combines *the moral authority of a high-priest with the fire-power of a general.* (FT23: 16)

3.5.3. Dependence of other countries on the Bundesbank

All the foregoing features configure a scenario where the Bundesbank is seen as a strong, powerful and dominating entity and where this power and dominion derives from strict orthodox financial policies which have been doggedly maintained despite their demanding costs. As opposed to this the other European countries are weaker because their policies, over time, are not comparable with those of the Bundesbank. As a result, their attempt to benefit from the Bundesbank-like stability without the sustained effort warranted by such a policy is shown up as a chimera. These ideas are masterfully captured by the metonymic expression for dependence – "in the hands of" – by the journey metaphor – "hitch a ride … on the coat tails" as if the power of the Bundesbank were quasi magical – and by the stereotype (a news value in itself, see Bell 1991: 157) of the proverbial strictness of the German governess.

62) In the *leaner and tougher* ERM, the members most likely to keep their places are those which, virtually without condition, place control over their monetary affairs in *the Bundesbank's hands.* (FT18: 3)

63) Countries … which hoped *to hitch a ride to price stability on the Bundesbank's coat tails* have suffered *a bumpier journey* than they imagined. (FT17: 18-E).

64) John Major thinks the ERM is a model of deflationary virtue. Hiring a *strict German governess* has cured the continentals of wicked devaluation habits and will do the same for Britain. (T14:19)

4. Conclusion

We have seen in this study mechanisms by which an economic issue is turned into a press story. The first remarkable conclusion is that, curiously, plain statements of detailed economic facts are quite sparse indeed. Rather, a wealth of metaphoric processes form the staple of how journalism gets its meaning across. A question raised by colleagues at Debrecen is the following: could all this array of metaphors have been done without? The short answer is: it wasn't and it isn't.[13] But of course the question deserves more than a facetious reply; in point of fact it is the most crucial of questions. In section 1.1 above, I set out to summarise the contextual events being dealt with by the press but, in conscious contrast to that media, my objective was to do so prescinding with metaphor as far as possible. Nevertheless, as pointed out to me at the Debrecen conference by Geert Jacobs, my account was still quite indebted to metaphor and value stances in my text were by no means absent. This of itself is indicative of how difficult it would be to do without metaphor – what we would in all probability achieve would be either a difference of degree in metaphor use or a substitution of one metaphor or set of metaphorical expressions for others.

Secondly, what are we to say of the actual metaphors used by the press and set out above? My claim is that on a basis of the evidence adduced, it can be maintained that these processes are both structural and communicative devices – not that there is a clear boundary between both, as a matter of fact they clearly overlap and interrelate. By structural, I mean that they provide a framework by which the currency crisis is conceptualised and within which discourse is constructed. By communicative, I mean the greater or lesser felicity of the individual choices in so far as communicative force within the general structural framework is concerned. The competitive nature of journalism as well as it being a mass media ensure that communicativeness is a primary target. As the use of rhetorical devices is basically geared towards communicative ends ((see van Dijk (1988) and de Beaugrande (1991)), we must conclude that the very proliferation of metaphor as we have seen in this analysis is in itself proof of the communicative potential of this device.

Thirdly, the metaphoric framework by which meaning was got across clearly plays a role in the overall configuration of the resulting discourse. The network of lexical and semantic interrelatedness set up by the reiteration of metaphoric expressions cannot but contribute to the cohesion and cohesiveness of the text as a whole, a point I have dealt with elsewhere (White 1997).

Fourthly, my questioner at Debrecen, Torben Vestergaard, raised the issue as to the innocence or otherwise of the metaphors appearing in my analysis. If all discourse can carry and indeed conceal ideological positionings[14], metaphor, which typically highlights one/some aspects of phenomena and downplays or altogether hides others, could potentially provide a very powerful weapon for ideological manipulation. In light of metaphor´s rootedness in conventional reasoning, this view has much to commend it: metaphor seems "naturally convincing" and is extremely difficult to argue against (see Lakoff 1992, Lakoff and Turner 1989). Thus, it is not surprising to find a proliferation of metaphor use in contexts where persuasion is at a premium – political partisan discourse, for instance, or publicity (see Forceville 1995). In the array of metaphoric expressions presented in this article, there is little doubt, but there are cases where their force alone is particularly persuasive and it would be extremely difficult to counteract the message entailed. For instance, if the currency crisis is conceptualised as war and in that war the Bundesbank is held up to be orchestrating coups or practising plotting, sniping and sabotage, the position of the bank is certainly infinitely less defensible than it would be if it were referred to as being caught up in self-defence which would be considered highly legitimate. I have already mentioned that stereotype (which we have seen tapped for metaphorical purposes) is considered by Bell (1994: 157) to be in itself a newsvalue – that is, the closer a news item conforms to stereotype, the higher its chances are of getting into print. While stereotype is not to be written off completely as a valid component in argumentation (see Lee et al., 1995), nevertheless, it should demand a critical perspective on the part of informed participants.[15] In short, then, with respect to this question as to the innocence or otherwise of metaphor, it would seem that the critical approach warranted by all discourse could be called upon to incorporate an extra effort in the presence of metaphor use.

Finally, by mode of post script, I would like to make the following comment. It is not uncommon to come across the idea that institutions are impersonal entities, impervious to and indeed crushing the individual. The fact is, as we have seen above in the case of the Bundesbank, that our mode *par excellence* of deciphering the activity carried on by that institution is through personification and this could be a manner of putting the person back into the institution and a reminder that the activity carried on within such entities is the result of choices and decisions by rational agents who are ultimately responsible and to be held responsible for all acts.

Acknowledgements

I am grateful for the very helpful comments of the organisers and colleagues of the panel at ESSE 4, Debrecen, at which an earlier version of this article was presented. Credit is given to individual contributors on specific points, but I would also like to extend my gratitude to all who, within and outside sessions, offered me their comments which have been to great avail for me. Needless to say, final responsibility rests with myself.

I am also grateful to my Institution, Escuela Universitaria de Ciencias Empresariales, Universidad Complutense de Madrid, for funding my presence at Debrecen.

Notes

1 Obviously a fuller account would demand greater qualification of the ensuing statements, some of which may even be questionable, but they do, I feel, provide a suitable starting point for the present analysis.

2 In 1992 the Bundesbank Council consisted of 18 members: 11 representatives of the *Landeszentralbanken*, each representing one of the Federal States of the former West Germany, plus 7 central council members (see Marsh 1992: 61-65).

3 Halliday´s "congruent" is roughly equivalent to "literal". The perspective, however, is reversed. When we talk about the "literal" meaning of an expression, our point of departure is the expression, our "point of arrival" the meaning. But in situations like the one discussed here, we start with a "meaning" (an extra-linguistic state of affairs) and arrive at a way of putting it into words (an "expression") which, in Halliday´s terminology, can be either "congruent" or "metaphorical".

4 See explanation for quote references of examples in the Bibliography section.

5 I wish to acknowledge my indebtedness to H-J. Diller for having raised this point and for his lengthy and stimulating correspondence on the issue. Nevertheless, all limitations in my final appraisal are my own responsibility.

6 The part of examples considered to be operating metaphorically or more exactly the metaphorical expressions I wish to draw attention to in the different examples given are emphasised by the use of italics and in all cases indicate my own emphasis.

7 I'm grateful to my questioner at Debrecen, Torben Vestergaard, for amongst other things, spelling out the implications of this example.

8 To grasp the full import of this rise, let us recall that interest rate increase patterns very typically are ¼ or ½ percentage point. At mid morning the British Authorities brought in a full 2 % increase and as this was not effective introduced a further increase of 3 %. As interest rates had been at 10 % a rise of 5 % meant a staggering overall hike of 50 % in a matter of hours.

9 Monday, 19th October 1987 when stock markets, especially Wall Street, fell dramatically.

10 This phrase, quoted in Villacañas (1994: 188) comes from the work of George Moore early in the century.

11 The origin of the phrase is, of course, biblical: Proverbs 25.22.

12 "Scapegoat" is derived from the Bible (Lev. xvi): "that one of two goats that was chosen by lot to be sent alive into the wilderness, the sins of the people having been symbolically laid upon it, ..." A whipping-boy is a "boy educated together with a young prince or royal personage, and flogged in his stead when he committed a fault that was considered to deserve flogging". *The Shorter Oxford Dictionary on Historical Principles (*1933/1973).

13 By this I mean that the standard journalistic practice is to take advantage of such metaphor use.

14 In this respect, although I wouldn't subscribe to all their tenets, Critical Linguistics has a great deal to tell us (see Fowler et al. 1979, Fowler 1991, Kress & Trew 1979, Hall et al. 1980, Fairclough 1995).

15 For instance, even from the evidence put forward above, there seems to be a stereotype building up by which the Bundesbank is characterised as being utterly inflexible, impervious to other considerations and taking decisions merely according to its own interests and regardless of the costs to all other parties. Now while we are not to disdain the information implied by this stereotype, it, nevertheless, calls for considerable critical nuances for as Marsh (1992: 168-193) has pointed out, the Bundesbank in actual fact is a master at managing to reconcile its own position with the diverse variables of economic reality and the positions of the different authorities involved in economic policy and decisions.

Bibliography

Sources:
The Financial Times, September 1992
The Times, September 1992
The Sunday Times, September 1992
The Sun, September 1992

Citations follow the following code: FT = *Financial Times*, T = *Times*, ST= *Sunday Times*, S = *Sun*. The following figure refers to the date issue for the month of September 1992 and this in turn is followed by a semicolon plus another figure which is the corresponding page reference. Where examples are actual headings, this is indicated by -H following the page entry. For example: FT9: 1-H = This is a reference to page one of the *Financial Times* for the 9th September 1992 and the quotation is a heading or S25: 2 will mean a quotation from page 2 of *The Sun* for September the 25th 1992.

Bell, Allan: *The Language of News Media,* Oxford, Blackwell, 1991.

Boers, F. & Demecheleer, M.: "Travellers, patients and warriors in English, Dutch and French economic discourse", *Revue Belge de Philologie et d'Histoire*, 1995, Vol. 73, 671 91

Beaugrande, R. de: *Linguistic Theory: The Discourse of Fundamental Works*, London: Longman, 1991.

Fairclough, N: *Media Discourse*, London, Edward Arnold, 1995.

Forceville, Charles: *Pictorial Metaphor in Adverstising*, London: Routledge, 1996.

Fowler, Roger: *Language in the News: Discourse and Ideology in the Press,* London: Routledge, 1991.

Fowler, Roger, B. Hodge, Gunther Kress & Tony Trew: *Language and Control,* London: Routledge & Kegan Paul, 1979.

Gerrard, Bill: "The significance of interpretation in Economics". – In Willie Henderson, Tony Dudley-Evans & Roger Backhouse (Eds.): *Economics & Language*, London: Routledge, 1993, pp. 51-63.

Gibbs, Raymond W. Jr.: *The Poetics of Mind: Figurative Thought, Language and Understanding*, Cambridge: Cambridge Univ. Press, 1994.

Hall, S., D. Hobson, A. Lowe & P. Willis (Eds.): *Culture, Media and Language*, London: Hutchinson, 1980.
Halliday, Michael A.K: *An Introduction to Functional Grammar*, 2nd ed., London: Arnold, 1994.
Henderson, Willie: "Metaphor in Economics", *Economics*, 1982, 147-153.
Jucker, A.: "News Actor Labelling in British Newspapers", *Text*, Vol.16, No 3, 1996, 373-390.
Kövecses, Zoltan: *Metaphors of Anger, Pride and Love*, Amsterdam: John Benjamins, 1986.
Kress, Gunther & Tony Trew: *Language as Ideology*, London: Routledge & Kegan Paul, 1979.
Lakoff, George: *Women, Fire and Dangerous Things: What Categories reveal about the Mind*, Chicago: University of Chicago Press, 1987.
---: "Metaphor and War. The Metaphor System used to justify War in the Gulf". – In M. Pütz (Ed.): *Thirty Years of Linguistic Evolution. Studies in Honour of René Dirven on the Occasion of his Sixtieth Birhtday.* Amsterdam: John Benjamins, 1992.
Lakoff, George & Mark Johnson: *Metaphors We Live By*, Chicago: University of Chicago Press, 1980.
Lakoff, George & Mark Turner: *More than Cool Reason. A field guide to Poetic Metaphor*, Chicago: Univ. of Chicago Press, 1989.
Lee, Yueh-Ting, Lee J. Jussim & Clark R. McCauley: *Stereotype Accuracy: Toward Appreciating Group Differences*, American Psychological Association, Hyattsville, 1995.
Marsh, David: *The Bundesbank, the Bank that Rules Europe*, London: William Heinemann, 1992
Shapiro, B.P., P. van den Broek & C. R. Fletcher: "Using Story-Based Causal Diagrams to Analyze Disagreements about Complex Events", *Discourse Processes*, Vol. 20, 1995, 51-77.
Ungerer, Friedrich & Hans-Jörg Schmid: *An Introduction to Cognitive Linguistics*, London: Longman, 1996.
van Dijk, Teun A.: *News as Discourse*, Hillsdale, NJ: Lawrence Erlbaum, 1988.
Villacañas, Beatriz: "The Tenant of Wildfell Hall: The Revolt of the "Gentlest" Brontë", *Revista Canaria de Estudios Inglesas*, Vol.29, 1994, 187-196.
White, Michael: "The Use of Metaphor in Reporting Financial Market Transactions", *Cuadernos de Filologìa Inglesa*. Univ. de Murcia, Vol. 6, 2, 1997, 233-245.

Geert Jacobs, Antwerp

Newspapers and press releases

1. Introduction

In this article I shall try to show that the study of newspaper language cannot be complete without taking into account the role that press releases play in today's media business. Press releases are short, often one-page, written texts that journalists receive from all sorts of organizations, including, most prominently, business corporations and political parties. By their very nature, press releases do not compete for journalists' attention *per se*; instead, they are meant to be transmitted by them, as accurately as possible, preferably even verbatim, in their own news reporting.

First, I shall explain why it is necessary to study the impact of press releases on what is published in the newspapers. In a lot of previous research it has been taken for granted that it is the journalists who 'make' the news. I shall now argue that the news is also often 'managed' for them and I shall present a case study to illustrate how press releases in particular may shed new light on newspaper language. Crucially, in examining such news management practices, it is not enough to adopt the traditional critical approach and restrict the analysis to an exploration of how newspapers are based on press releases. I shall argue that a complementary perspective is needed, one that allows researchers to examine how writers of press releases in turn actively anticipate the requirements of newspaper reporting. That is why, at the end of this article, I shall draw from the same case study to provide preliminary evidence of how press releases are – what I would like to call – 'preformulated'.

2. Newsmaking and news management

Newsgathering is a misleading term because it presupposes that the news is out there, waiting to be talked about by journalists. Instead, it has now been generally accepted that it is the journalists who have to *make* the news by talking about it.[1] It is interesting to note in this respect that the impact of journalists on the news seems to have gradually increased over the years. While newspapers are reported to have their origin in the early seventeenth century, for example, it was not until the

1860s that journalists began to actively make news by interviewing public figures (cf. Schudson 1978). Even more strikingly, in the early days of radio broadcasting, the BBC – with a total newsroom staff of only four (!) – regularly announced that 'there was no news that night' (Bell 1991). Today this is unthinkable: there is always news unless a strike makes us do without.

It should be clear that this notion of newsmaking lies at the heart of the study of newspaper language. To look at the style of tabloid headlines is one way of exploring journalists' newsmaking activities. Among the most influential approaches to the topic of media discourse is that of critical linguistics, critical discourse analysis and social semiotics. Here it is argued that if the news is not a set of events but the journalists' reactions to them, then it is certainly not a set of *random* reactions, if only because the journalists' professional activities are determined by a variety of social structures and relations (Fowler & Kress 1979: 185, Fairclough 1989: 23; Hartley 1982). To give just one example, a number of recent studies in the field have amply shown that today's newspaper language reflects economic pressures to win bigger audiences and to raise increased advertising revenue. At the same time, it should be borne in mind that newspapers are not just influenced by the journalists' interpersonal context; they also serve as social agents in their own right, shaping public opinion, setting people's agendas.

In the terminology of one of the leading figures of this critical movement, viz. Gunther Kress, the media perform at least two functions (1983): an ideological function, i.e. making sense of the world in accordance with the social structures that they are determined by, as well as a political function, i.e. making sense of the world *for others* through creatively reproducing these social structures. Kress adds that the world may present itself in two ways to journalists: not just in the form of 'physical' events, which journalists can then classify in accordance with their own ideological positions, but also – and even much more frequently – in the form of events that have already been assimilated (by others) into an ideological schema. Events of the latter type belong to the domain of so-called news *management* and I would suggest that they include issuing press releases:[2] since the news plays such an important political role, apparently a lot of groups, or even individuals, have a stake in trying to furnish the media with their own (version of the) news. News management allows them to play a pro-active role, i.e. to take the initiative with the news rather than to wait for the journalists' inquiries. The newsmakers' agenda-setting is anticipated by that of the news managers. The result is that journalists cannot reclassify the events; they are forced to more or less literally present the classification that others have imposed on the events.[3]

The far-reaching impact of news management can be guessed at from the following sample of one day's international newspaper headlines (*The Times*, 29 November 1994):

Norwegian PM warns of tough times ahead
Balladur calls for a more flexible Union
Yeltsin issues ultimatum to Chechnya
China urged to deal with high inflation
UN threatens to recall its forces from Bosnia
"Major has issued death sentence"

These headlines seem to confirm L.V. Sigal's claim that "most news is not what has happened, but what someone says has happened" (1973: 69; 1986). This 'someone' clearly does not refer to the newsmaking journalist, but to the news managing politician, business organization, etc. As Allan Bell (1991) confirms: "[n]ews is what people say more than what people do. Much – maybe most – of what journalists report is talk not action: announcements, opinions, reactions, appeals, promises, criticisms" (53).[4] Of course, press releases should have been added to Bell's list and in the following section I shall provide an illustration of their impact on news reporting.

3. Case: Edwina Currie's talk show performance

The case that I shall briefly present here deals with the story of a talk show led by Clive James and produced by London Weekend Television back in 1987.[5] In it Edwina Currie – who was then Britain's Junior Health Minister – made a number of saucy comments on Prime Minister Thatcher's love life when she was an undergraduate at Oxford University. In particular, talking about an old Oxford University ruling that students' beds had to be moved out of their rooms during the daytime and put in the corridors, Currie suggested that when Mr Denis Thatcher came round, he and the future Prime Minister could '*do it on the floor*'. Needless to say that this sparked off a major row in Westminster. One fellow Conservative MP even called on Currie to 'consider her position'. Here are some of the tabloid headlines about the incident:

Oh, Edwina what a thing to say about Mrs Thatcher's love life! (*Daily Mirror*)

EDWINA FLOORS 'EM
CURRIE ON THE CARPET (*Star*)

> Edwina tugs covers off the love life at Maggie's old college (*Daily Express*)

Certainly, the case provides interesting data for analysing newspaper language. One striking feature is the use of direct quotes from the talk show; in fact, all newspapers (even the so-called quality newspapers *The Daily Telegraph* and *The Independent*) present a more or less literal rendering of the crucial exchange between talk show host Clive James (CJ) and Edwina Currie (EC):

> CJ: Did you have to put your bed in the corridor during the day?
> EC: They had that rule I think in Margaret Thatcher's day. [...]
> CJ: You mean when Denis came to call ...
> EC: She could do it on the floor.

In contrast with the media's consensus about the exact wording of the exchange, even repeated listening to the recording of the talk show does not make it at all clear what Edwina Currie really said. In particular, it is difficult to decide if it was '*She* could do it on the floor', '*They* could do it on the floor' or '*One* could do it on the floor'. Indeed, Currie later defended herself by saying that she had been talking "in entirely general terms" and that she had "said nothing about the Prime Minister in this context" (*The Independent*).

I would now like to argue that this sketchy treatment of how the newspapers reported the incident would be incomplete – and indeed misleading – if we failed to take into account the news management efforts that were at the basis of the reporting. The interesting thing about this case – and indeed the reason why I turned to it in the first place – is that the row was sparked off before the programme was shown on TV. The prerecorded talk show was to be broadcast on Saturday night 20 June, but all the newspapers already carried the story on Saturday morning without having seen the show. Their reporting was based on a London Weekend Television press release that had been issued the day before, on Friday 19 June (see the appendix). More specifically, this means that in this particular case it would be wrong to point to the use of direct quoting or to the doubtful reformulation of Edwina Currie's original words as typical features of newspaper reporting. Actually, they were both in the London Weekend Television press release and the newspapers just copied them. Even some of the headlines – including the *Star*'s 'EDWINA FLOORS 'EM' – were anticipated – 'preformulated' I shall call it later in this article (cf. also Jacobs 1999) – by the headline of the press release:

> THATCHER FLOORED BY CURRIE

And if the *Mirror* and *Express* articles start with what we would all agree is a typically tabloid reference to "outspoken Junior Health minister Edwina Currie" – Jucker (1992) calls this a 'noun phrase name apposition' – , again we have to add that exactly the same opening can be found in the press release that those newspapers started from.

Certainly, I do not want to suggest that direct quotes, witty headlines, and noun phrase name appositions are no typical features of newspaper – esp. popular newspaper – reporting. On the contrary, I shall suggest later on in this article that writers of press releases actively anticipate the requirements of newspaper reporting; in this way, the present analysis actually serves to reconfirm direct quotes, witty headlines, and noun phrase name appositions as typical features of newspaper reporting. However, what I do want to show with this example is that newspaper language does not stand on its own and, in particular, that its relation to the language of press releases should be considered a fruitful area for further inquiry. I have argued elsewhere that press releases can be considered so-called projected discourse because they are meant to be copied as newspaper articles (Jacobs 1999), but the question could now be raised if newspaper articles themselves are not – to some extent at least – projected by press releases.

I would like to make a further point here. The above case does not only illustrate the impact of press releases on news reporting. Even more drastically, it also shows how press releases can become news events in their own right. The whole story might well have failed to make it into the newspapers altogether if it had not been publicized in a press release. Significantly, in her defence, Currie focused attention on the London Weekend Television press release, and she claimed that it offered a misrepresentation of her words. As a result, she announced that she would be protesting to the television station. London Weekend Television, for its part, stood by the version of events as they were described in the press release, and a spokeswoman said that the quotes 'were verbatim'. It should also be noted that the Tory MP who demanded Currie's resignation, viz. Richard Holt of Langbaurgh, had not seen the show. It looks as if for him the TV station's press release had acquired the political power of a speech in the House of Commons. At the same time, it needs to be pointed out that the impact of press releases on the media can easily be overlooked, even in this specific case, where news management practices are perhaps at their most blatant: as it is, both the *Daily Mirror* and the *Daily Telegraph* articles did not even mention the London Weekend Television press release that was at the heart of the controversy.

4. A critical view of the news

The kind of news management I briefly illustrated in the above case study is of course only the tip of the iceberg. In today's world of sound bites at carefully rehearsed press conferences and of photo opportunities led by omnipotent spin doctors, it may actually seem as if the journalists' news-making role is limited to selecting newsworthy stories from the mass of P.R. prefabrications that is offered to them. Apparently, the only thing journalists have to do is recycle, simply repeat what was talked about before. In other words, they are no more than 'gatekeepers'. This observation has led Teun van Dijk, for example, to look at journalists' newsmaking as "source text management"; he claims that

> to a certain extent, the press will be a mouthpiece of the organizations that provide the necessary input texts. The assumed freedom of the press consists in the possibility to voice interests of conflicting organizations, to make rigorous selections in the mass of offered text data on the basis of news value criteria, to pay limited or biased interest to non-institutional events (e.g., protest demonstrations, squatters, strikes), and to transform the input data (1988: 129).

From one perspective Van Dijk's view is even too optimistic since it has been shown that the media fail to make these 'rigorous selections'. CNN's live reporting of the 1991 Gulf War was a case in point. At first sight it seemed to represent probably the closest we ever got to the ideal of objective reporting, i.e. the naive realism of 'showing history as it happens'. On closer scrutiny, though, the TV coverage of the Gulf War was the summit of news management: since they depended completely on the military who provided them with information and who proofread journalists' news copy, the US media were giving a totally one-sided picture of what was happening (cf. Taels & Vanheeswijck 1995). Even more drastically, Van Ginneken (1996) reports that dozens of CIA agents have worked as journalists with all major US news organizations since World War II.

The impact of press releases, too, seems to leave very little room for optimism. By their very nature, they represent the views of the organizations that issued them. Hess (1989), for example, talking about US government agencies, recognizes that press releases "are an agency's opportunity to order information in a manner that the agency considers most advantageous to its mission" (47). Unfortunately, instead of blowing the whistle, the media are very often guilty of 'whistle-*swallowing*'.[6] Allan Bell, who is a journalist as well as a linguist, reports that "[a] story which is marginal in news terms but written and available may be selected ahead of a much more newsworthy story which has to be researched and written from the ground up" (1991: 59). As early as 1924 Nelson Crawford, in *The Ethics of Journalism*, notes reporters' habits of giving most space to those who furnished them with "typed copies of speeches, ready-prepared interviews, and similar material" (quoted in Schudson 1978: 138). Apparently, news is first and foremost a "practical activity geared to deadlines" (Tuchman 1978: 82): often journalists simply do not have the time to check if the press release is correct. And, as Gandy (1982) says about TV broadcasting, "[t]he absence of a satellite link in a foreign capital reduces the probability that news film from that nation will appear on the network news, just as budgetary limitations determine that a full crew will not be assigned to cover a demonstration at the local school board, especially if that meeting is scheduled to begin at 4 P.M." (57). Clearly, the use of press releases – as well as the functioning of newspapers in general – should also be viewed in economic terms as they form part of a time-saving as well as cost-reducing routinization of news production.

Herman & Chomsky (1988) go one step further: they provide what is probably one of the most elaborate accounts of how the media, far from manufacturing the news, actually 'manufacture consent', i.e. they mobilize support for dominant special interest groups, simply because they depend on information provided by them. Thus, instead of "enabling the public to assert meaningful control over the political process by providing them with the information needed for the intelligent discharge of political responsibilities", the effect of the media is "to inculcate and defend the economic, social, and political agenda of privileged groups that dominate the domestic society and the state" (298).[7] In Herman & Chomsky's so-called propaganda model the use of press releases is one of those 'filters' which – along with the size, ownership and profit orientation of the mass media – help dominant social forces to "fix the premises of discourse and interpretation, and the definition of what is newsworthy in the first place" (2).

Clearly, such news management practices have remained unexplored for too long. It is only recently that this – perhaps rather dim – view of the news has come to inspire research into media discourse. Here we can situate Fairclough's critical linguistic effort to provide discursive evidence that the (British) media operate as a means for the expression of the power of dominant groups, as in the following extract from a newspaper article:

> Quarry load-shedding problem
>
> UNSHEETED lorries from Middlebarrow Quarry were still causing problems by shedding stones on their journey through Warton village, members of the parish council heard at their September meeting.
> The council's observations have been sent to the quarry management and members are hoping to see an improvement. (1989: 50)

Here, according to Fairclough, the unspecified causality through passives and nominalization allows the journalist to avoid mentioning elites as the cause of the problem.

More generally, in pointing to newsmaking and news management practices and denouncing the complicity of the press, critical researchers in particular have started to draw attention to a crucial influence in the social conditioning of the news. They rightly understand the news to be the product of bureaucratically functioning media, which in turn serve as mouthpieces of today's dominant social forces.

5. A different perspective

But there is more. In an interesting review of critical theory, Peter Bruck argues that critical researchers frequently fail to see that there may be at least some room for alternatives, i.e. that the media are not invariably, seamlessly reproducing the dominant ideology. He suggests that they show "discursive openings, inconsistencies, and contradictions" (1989: 113). To find these, Bruck continues, researchers should pay attention to how the media reprocess the discourses of others:

> we need to make the analytical separation between the discourses the media produce and the discourse they use as material to build on, process, and deliver. We need to be interested in the structures of transformation. We cannot ignore – as most content analysis does – the discursive components from which reports are constructed (117).

Of course, this is not to say that, so far, no research has focused on the media's reprocessing activities. On the contrary, as Astroff & Nyberg (1992) confirm, some of the most useful studies within the critical literature are those that "have faced the need to untangle the relationship between various meaning-making institutions in society" (6). Norman Fairclough, for example, has drawn attention to how the British Labour Party leader Michael Foot cautiously criticized Ken Livingstone from the Greater London Council

> In general I do think that one factor that influenced the election was some of the affairs that have happened at the Greater London Council.

and how his words were then transformed into the fierce monosyllabic tabloid newspaper headline

> Foot blasts red Ken over poll trouncing (1992: 161).

Clearly, the idea that the media act as 'secondary definers', selecting and interpreting the information supplied by 'primary definers', is not new and, as I showed above, critical research actually played a major role in unravelling the newsmaking and news management processes from this perspective. What Bruck seems to suggest, however, is that, if structures of transformation have been taken into account, then the analysis has been bent too much in one direction and that – in the words of Hall, Critcher & Jefferson (1978) – this may have obscured some of the 'strategies of negotiation' that are at the heart of the news.

Surely, too little research has so far focused on the language of news management in general and on that of press releases in particular as objects of analysis in their own right.[8] Dealing with the US media coverage of the U2 incident in 1960, when an American spy plane was shot down over Soviet territory, Jef Verschueren (1985) looks at how political discourse is rendered in news reporting, but points to an interesting area for further research when he indicates that those who give a speech or issue a public statement are usually very much aware that journalists are listening and that therefore they will finetune their language with a view to future media coverage. Similarly, Fairclough too realizes that the statements of sources and press releases are not just reproduced by the media, but that sources also "design their statements and press releases to harmonize with discourses favoured by the media" (1995: 98). After having drawn attention to the impact of press releases on newspaper reporting, it is the following question that this article aims to put forward: viz. how the language of press releases is designed – 'preformulated' – for the media, and how this may shed light on the negotiated character of the news. After all, as Gandy (1982) puts it:

> Whereas the journalist selects from an array of sources and events on the basis of perceived utility in producing news that will meet organizational requirements, sources select from an even larger array of techniques on the basis of their perceived effectiveness in being covered, reported, and transmitted in the right form, at the right time, and in the right channel (14).

From the White House conventions of quoting US presidents (Sigal 1973: 107-114; Keane 1991: 102) to the use of embargoes, news managers can, to some extent at least, control how newsmakers retell the news. Reception may also be explicitly co-ordinated by some or other textual aspect of the message itself. John B. Thompson (1995) refers to the use of prerecorded laughter sequences in comic TV shows, for example, and to the fact that as early as the 16th and 17th centuries books were composed with a view to being read aloud, i.e. they were produced with the aim of being re-embedded in contexts of face-to-face interaction. It is such design features that should be looked at in press releases.

I would like to argue that the exclusive focus on the journalists' newsmaking may not just be misleading and that news management practices should be taken into account (as I have shown with the reporting about Edwina Currie's talk show performance); looking at the media only also serves to obscure a number of highly interesting strategies of symbolic construction in the very sources of the *media*ting texts that are traditionally used as the primary materials for studying the news. In the final section of this article I would like to very briefly consider one such strategy of symbolic construction, one way in which press releases are preformulated for news reporting.

6. Tonight, tomorrow night?

Let's take another look at the following extract from the London Weekend Television press release about the Currie interview:

> (London Weekend Television, London: 19 June 1987)
> Speaking on LWT's *The Late Clive James* show tonight (Saturday, 20 June 1987) at 10.30 pm, Mrs Currie – who went to Oxford after the Prime Minister – says that when she and Mrs Thatcher were at Oxford, few other women studied there, and house rules were very strict.

As I explained above, this press release was issued on 19 June. The TV show that it talks about was probably recorded some time before that. Still, 'tonight' does not refer to that moment of recording or to 19 June. As is spelled out between brackets, it refers to the day of broadcasting, viz. 20 June. This is interesting because what, from the point of view of the writer of the press release, is 'tomorrow night' is actually referred to as 'tonight'. In other words, the writer of the press release takes the perspective of the journalists, who will write about Edwina Currie's TV performance in the newspapers of the day of the broadcasting, i.e. 20 June. In doing so, he or she provides the journalists with a piece of text that they can simply copy in their own reporting. It is for this and many other examples of the complex 'point of view operation' (Brown & Levinson 1987) in press releases that I have proposed the term 'preformulation' and I would like to argue here that they deserve far more research attention.

The general drift of this article should be clear by now. I have not just wanted to draw attention to the impact of news management on what we get to read in the press and see on TV (in particular the impact of press releases on the language of newspapers); I have also argued that no analysis of media discourse can afford to ignore the specific strategies of symbolic construction used to manage the news.

Notes

1 For a detailed account of the notion of newsmaking see the British sociologist John B. Thompson's theory of 'mediazation' in *Ideology and Modern Culture* (1990) and *The Media and Modernity* (1995).
2 The term 'news management' was first used by James Reston in 1955 in his testimony before a US congressional committee on government information. Michael Schudson (1978) – with awkward precision – situates the start of news management at the Paris 1919 peace conference. As far as press releases are concerned, Cook (1989) says that while in the 1880s US presidents still thought granting interviews improper, members of Congress were "willing subjects. Many dropped by Newspaper Row, that section of 14th Street between Pennsylvania Avenue and F Street where most bureaus were located, and others went so far as to interview themselves, the first appearance of what are now known as press releases". In Cook's view, Representative Benjamin Butler was the first to send in such "lengthy self-prepared opinions" (20). Note that Cook (1989) and Bell (1991), among others, use the term 'newsmakers' for what I call 'news managers'.
3 Cf. Erving Goffman on 'getting the first word in' (1974: 257).
4 Again, John B. Thompson's theory proves useful here (cf. also Jacobs 1996 for a summary of some of Thompson's ideas on the topic).
5 I would like to thank Stef Slembrouck, who introduced me to the data presented below.
6 Peltu coined the term when he denounced the media for not alerting the audience to public hazards (1988: 16).
7 Tuchman (1978) sees the newsmaking business as an ally of various legitimated news managing institutions (e.g. because ministers have more access to the media).
8 That there has not been enough empirical research to address this question is clear from the disagreement about the simple question whether or not press releases get copied verbatim. Cook (1989), in a span of a couple of pages, mentions one source that "hundreds of press releases are sent to the media by members of Congress, and hundreds are run verbatim or with insignificant changes" (103) and another source that "[a] very small percentage of press releases ever gets reprinted, and relatively few form the basis for stories. In fact so few releases are used, one might ask whether their production is a waste of time" (108). Romano (1986) says that the practice of reprinting press releases was rather common in the past, but that current journalistic practice demands otherwise, except in matters of culture and entertainment. Bell (1991) points out that it is not unusual for press releases to get 'published' (largely) untouched. No empirical evidence is presented, though. Working on a small corpus of press releases issued by major Belgian business organizations, Bernaers (1995), finally, reports that no press releases got quoted verbatim.

Bibliography

Astroff, R. J. & A. K. Nyberg: "Discursive hierarchies and the construction of crisis in the news: a case study." *Discourse & Society* 3, 1992, 5-23.

Bell, A.: *The Language of News Media.* Oxford, 1991.

Bernaers, B.: "Van persbericht tot kranteartikel". Unpub. Ms, University of Antwerp, 1995.

Brown, P. & S. C. Levinson: *Politeness: some universals.* Cambridge, 1987.

Bruck, P. A.: "Strategies for peace, strategies for news research". *Journal of Communication*, 39, 1989, 108-129.

Cook, T. E.: *Making Laws and Making News: media strategies in the U.S. House of Representatives.* Washington, D.C., 1989.

Fairclough, N.: *Language and Power.* Harlow, 1989.

---: *Discourse and Social Change.* Cambridge, 1992.

---: *Media Discourse.* London, 1995.

Fowler, R. & G. Kress: "Critical linguistics". – In R. Fowler, B. Hodge, G. Kress & T. Trew (Eds.): *Language and Control.* London, 1979, pp. 185-213.

Gandy, O. H., Jr.: *Beyond Agenda Setting: information subsidies and public policy.* Norwood, NJ, 1982.

Goffman, E.: *Frame Analysis: an essay on the organization of experience.* New York, 1974.

Hall, S., C. Critcher & T. Jefferson (Eds.): *Policing the Crisis: mugging, the state, and law and order.* London, 1978.

Hartley, J.: *Understanding News.* London, 1982.

Herman, E. S. & N. Chomsky: *Manufacturing Consent: the political economy of the mass media.* New York, 1988.

Hess, S.: *Live from Capitol Hill: studies of Congress and the media.* Washington, D.C., 1989.

Jacobs, G.: "The telling and retelling of press releases: a look at frame-analytical theory and a single-case analysis". Paper presented at the conference on frame and perspective in discourse, University of Groningen, 1996.

---: *Preformulating the News: an analysis of the metapragmatics of press releases.* Amsterdam and Philadelphia, 1999.

Jucker, A. H.: *Social Stylistics: syntactic variation in British newspapers.* Berlin/New York, 1992.

Keane, J.: *The Media and Democracy.* Cambridge, 1991.

Kress, G.: "Linguistic processes and the mediation of 'reality': the politics of newspaper language". *International Journal of the Sociology of Language* 40, 1983, 43-57.

Peltu, M.: "Media reporting of risk information: uncertainties and the future". – In H. Jungermann, R. Kasperson & P. Wiedemann (Eds.): *Themes and Tasks of Risk Communication.* Jülich, 1988.

Romano, C.: "The grisly truth about bare facts". – In R. K. Manoff & M. Schudson (Eds.): *Reading the News.* New York, 1986, pp. 38-78.

Schudson, M.: *Discovering the News: a social history of American newspapers.* New York, 1978.

Sigal, L. V.: *Reporters and Officials: the organization and politics of newsmaking.* Lexington, MA, 1973.

---: "Sources make the News". – In R. K. Manoff & M. Schudson (Eds.): *Reading the News.* New York, 1986, pp. 9-37.
Taels, J. & G. Vanheeswijck: "De Golfoorlog en het televisiejournaal". Unpub. Ms, University of Antwerp, 1995.
Thompson, J. B.: *Ideology and Modern Culture: critical social theory in the era of mass communication.* Cambridge, 1990.
---: *The Media and Modernity: a social theory of the media.* Cambridge, 1995.
Tuchman, G.: *Making News: a study in the construction of reality.* New York, 1978.
Van Dijk, T. A.: *News as Discourse.* Hillsdale, N.J., 1988.
Van Ginneken, J.: *De Schepping van de Wereld in het Nieuws: de 101 vertekeningen die elk 1 procent verschil maken.* Houten, 1996.
Verschueren, J.: *International News Reporting: metapragmatic metaphors and the U2.* Amsterdam, 1985.

Appendix

Thatcher floored by Currie

Outspoken Junior Health Minister Edwina Currie has suggested that Margaret and Dennis Thatcher's courtship might have taken place on the floor of her Oxford University room…

Speaking on LWT's *The Late Clive James* show tonight (Saturday, 20 June 1987) at 10.30 pm, Mrs Currie – who went to Oxford after the Prime Minister – says that when she and Mrs Thatcher were at Oxford, few other women studied there, and house rules were very strict.

She says: 'There was a rule that you couldn't have more than two men in your room at any one time – why two men was alright I don't know. One of the other rules was that we had to put beds in the corridor during the day. It was alright to invite a man for tea, but the bed had to come out into the corridor.'

At this point, Clive James asks what might have happened when Dennis came to call on Mrs Thatcher, to which Mrs Currie replies: '… she could do it on the floor…'

The controversial Tory also also [sic] enlarged on her outrageous statement that making a speech is a bit like having an orgasm.

She tells her host: 'Being with you has the same sort of effect, Clive!'

19 June 1987

Evelina Graur, Suceava

Ads and Accompanying Discourses

The press-advert brotherhood

Newspapers have always offered advertising a place in their pages. Before turning into the most seductive and expensive branch of marketing, advertising gathered its forces from the press. The earliest newspapers – often referred to as newsheets or mercuries – were essentially means for communicating notices of events such as the departures and arrivals of ships, store openings, engagements and marriages. They also carried information on prices, lists of imports and exports, ads for lost horses and runaway slaves, patent medicines and miraculous cures. On the whole, these varied notices and announcements are the richest and most faithful reflection any society ever made of its whole range of activities. Indeed, long before turning into a sophisticated profession or public service, advertising *was* news in itself.

As if in token of "gratitude", advertising soon freed the press from direct political control, its revenue becoming a vital ingredient in the make-up and survival of newspapers. Consequently, when a copy ad (*Newsweek*, 27 January 1997) reads

> Without advertising, the cost of *Newsweek* would be news in itself.

and underneath

> Did you know that every ad in *Newsweek* helps pay for the rest of its essential pages? In fact, *Newsweek* would cost you more than double without advertising. A price that would be something to read about. Advertising. That's the way it works.

the ad obviously fulfils a "noble" purpose: that of bringing back to memory "the legend of the advertiser as the midwife of press freedom."[1]

But with the advent of more sophisticated technology, advertising has moved into new media: the telephone, radio, cable and satellite TV, computer networks. Advertisers' choices of substances for their ads have proved ingenious and innovative: ads for services are relayed by telephone (especially when lines are busy and connections cannot be made right away), magazines carry talking micro-chips or cosmetic samples;

there are ads for milk chocolate written on the side of cows grazing in the field, ads for detergent, newspapers or computer companies on buses and trams; there are ads on T-shirts, vapour trails and fireworks patterns in the sky. Although such variety and inventiveness succeeded in making ads leave the periphery of receivers' attention and fixing products or services more firmly in readers' memory, they cannot compensate for ads' unsolicited intrusiveness upon our lives. So when a copy ad (*Newsweek,* 28 October 1996) reads

> When advertising does its job, millions of people keep theirs.

and underneath

> Good advertising doesn't just inform. It sells. It helps move product [sic] and keep business in business. Every time an ad arouses a consumer's interest enough to result in a purchase, it keeps a company going strong. And it helps secure the jobs of the people who work there. Advertising. That's the way it works.

it is obvious that its discoursive content merely accounts for advertising's **constant, supportive**, yet often **unwelcome** encroachment on our lives. Ads seldom apologise to us for taking away some of our precious time because they belong to a "commercial arena permeated by competitive consumption."[2]

All advertisers' decisions reflect this competitive consumption context. Firstly, they are interested in placing their ads in those media where they can reach as many potential customers as possible at the lowest costs. Secondly, they favour those media whose audience has a rather high purchasing power. These basic requirements account for the fact that advertisers are not interested in passive readers or viewers, but active ones, capable of buying the advertised products, and whom I would call reader-consumers.

But the spirit of competition characterises media themselves. Nowadays television has become the most time-consuming medium, being in visible competition with the radio which, "in general, became *par excellence* the medium used while doing something else, mainly housework, preparing and eating meals and getting up or ready for bed" (emphasis Seymour-Ure).[3] The considerable reduction of the time spent by people *just listening* to the radio has not yet been matched by a considerable reduction in the newspaper reading time. As Seymour-Ure remarks, "TV' s main effect was to change the way in which people used their papers, more than to reduce their use."[4] Many people watch TV and read a newspaper at the same time. Moreover, once provided with the latest news on TV, people usually want to look for further details in a newspaper. On the other hand, newspapers themselves have moved towards TV by including entertainment sections and by turning TV itself into a consistent feature in its own right. When advertisers have to decide which medium to choose, they are likely to consider these aspects too.

Newspapers – a tolerant host for advertising

There are people who buy a newspaper only because they want to find out what is on TV, or buy a new house or simply because they want to compare a newspaper account of, say, a football match with their own impressions. Some of these desires may not be fulfilled unless people buy the whole newspaper in which they might find *something else* to attract their attention. Although commercial television has become the leading advertising medium for mass consumer products, newspapers seem to have remained a **loyal, effective** and **tolerant** host for advertisers.

Consider, for example, the following caption of a shampoo ad published on a whole inside page of *The Sunday Times,* 19 September 1993:

> What the TV ads don't tell you about shampoos.

The main point made by the copy ad which follows is that commercials do not have enough time to say "worthwhile things" and cannot afford to pay for longer spots in order to tell the story of proper hair care by using the same three ingredients: the pretty girl, the hair-tossing shot and the promise to leave your hair perfect. The copy ad ends with the following lines:

> If shampoo makers advertised in the press, they could have large spaces in which to tell their stories.
> They could reach their intended audience more accurately and more often.
> They could have high quality colour to show hair and product off to the best advantage. All of this for a fraction of the cost going on TV.
> Why don't they? Perhaps because they believe that, deep down, you value a glossy image more than useful information.
> Do you? Why not write and tell us what you think?*

Using the press properly is an art. If advertisers learn the art, both they and you will benefit.

USE THE
POWER
OF THE
PRESS

Unlike other ads which publish a response coupon in order to ease readers' path towards consumerism, the present ad uses an asterisk to indicate that it is possible for people to enter into dialogue with the Newspaper Publishers Association, responsible for the placement of the ad. Nevertheless, the oddest thing in this final section of the ad is the slogo USE THE POWER OF THE PRESS which has been chosen to function as logo too. One may therefore wonder whether this ad is an indicator of the existence and availability of shampoos on the market.

In spite of the familiar advertising format of the discourse, there is no shampoo brand being advertised. The picture of a bottle placed in the middle of the page does not bear any brand-name and the plural noun "shampoos" in the caption is not typical of the advertising practice which usually requires clear identification of the product or service that is being advertised. And yet *there is* a product whose image readers are invited to build: **the source of information** and **the solicitor of opinion,** namely the press.

We may conclude that this ad, disguised as a shampoo ad, is an index of the existence and availability of both **press** and **press advertising**, the latter viewed not as a class of 'advertising' but as one of 'press'. To put it differently, the producer and the commodity coincide: the press is selling itself to us. The exophoric reference of the pronoun "you" in the copy ad is straightforward: "you" means the addressee in various hypostases: press readers, shampoo consumers, and advertisers. The press is thus loyal to all its audience members, satisfies most of their tastes and needs, and tolerates diversity.

Speaking about loyalty and tolerance, we would like to bring some more insight into an earlier statement, namely that newspapers have remained a loyal, effective and tolerant host for advertising.

Let us consider first the familiar small-print columns of classifieds. On the one hand, they may be regarded as a category of press advertising scattered throughout the newspaper or occupying the very last pages. On the other hand, they may be taken to represent a primary form of press which shipwrecked in the fragmentariness of life and showed no intention whatsoever of indulging in commentaries and interpretations of reality. This paradoxical nature of classifieds reveals itself through people's various ways of reading newspapers. Two of them are worth mentioning in this respect. First, there are people who begin with the classified section of the newspaper and end their reading session with the first pages (we do not include here those who, out of purchasing interest, read *only* the classifieds). Such readers scan and skim the ads as if they were **warming up** for an extensive type of reading. Second, there are others who, after exhausting their main points of interest, choose to linger a *little longer* over the ads pages as if they were trying to put the finishing touches to their newly acquired knowledge of the world. From a behavioural perspective, such readings embody the readers' tacit recognition of a newspaper as a whole. Whenever it reaches the reader, it is the result of "a whole series of selections as to what items shall be printed, in what position they shall be printed, how much space each shall occupy, what emphasis each shall have. There are no objective standards here. There are conventions."[5]

The ads in the classified section are **lineage, semi-display** and **display ads.** They exist according to a **format convention**. Yet, when notices to readers coexist with classifieds, there is clear evidence of a **tolerance convention**:

> Readers are advised to seek appropriate professional advice before sending any money or entering into any commitments. *The European* cannot be held responsible for loss or damages incurred as a result of responding to advertisements. (*The European,* 15-21 May 1997, Business section, page 28)

> Newsweek International and their representatives cannot be held responsible for loss or damages incurred as a result of transactions with individuals or companies advertising in our magazine. We recommend readers to make the necessary enquiries before sending any monies or entering into any agreement with advertisers. (*Newsweek,*10 June 1996)

Mention should be made that the announcement in *Newsweek* is published twice on both sides of the same page. The second time there is only one display-ad for instant cash machines that separates it from the same magazine's invitation to advertise in *Newsweek Executive Classified.* Since the reduced space of classifieds does not allow advertisers to make detailed claims about the effectiveness of their products or services, newspapers feel it is their duty to warn people about the possibility of being taken in. What is interesting, though, in the above mentioned examples is that the relationship between readers and newspaper/magazine publishers may be differently constructed. For *The European*, whose notice begins with a passive construction in which the noun "readers" is in subject position, it is clear that the *receiver* of *advice* is more important than the *advisor.* Readers need appropriate professional advice so that their conversion into customers may be a smooth one. The second sentence re-establishes the balance by placing the publication in subject position and its readers in agent position. As a result of readers' response to advertisements, however, the agent's status is more one of *consumer* than of *reader*. *The European* has thus chosen to warn the 'reader' in the consumer first and then the 'consumer' in the reader. *Newsweek* preserves itself in subject position in both sentences, and places readers in agent and object positions. It seems that the magazine felt that its duty was more towards the '*consumer*' in the reader than the '*reader*' in the consumer.

Newspapers have accepted the reality of potentially misleading ads and, while not offering real protection to reader-consumers, activate their frame of recognition and self-protection. Such a notice – if any – could not have identified the deception in the "chic-looking ad in Oct. 14 issue of the New Yorker [which] invited readers to call 'Paul's furs' for a free video, showing a 'lively collection of fox, mink, and racoon'. If the fur-friendly did call, they heard Paul McCartney's voice (unidentified) requesting their mailing information. But those who ordered got a shock: the video was actually a plea from PETA (People for the Ethical Treatment of Animals). Instead of warm coats, it showed the cold-blooded slaughter of fur-bearing animals".[6] The response that the paper gave when it was asked to account for the deception is testimony to our belief that the ad's intention to mislead readers[7] is a problem to be solved by readers themselves. In our opinion, the advertiser obviously took advantage of the capacity to be ambiguous in product presentation and did offer a "lively collection of fox, mink and racoon". That it was different from what readers hoped it to be is "caveat emptor"!

Consequently, such notices placed by newspapers are nothing but avowed efforts of **negotiating** readers' status as *consumers.*

Building authority

The newspaper-advert brotherhood may prove to be less tense when ads borrow newspaper headlines and leading paragraphs in building the image of a product or service. The image of an effective and caring AXA Equity & Law Society is built by prefacing its claims with the caption **Five terrible things that will never happen to you** which is followed by a picture of five newspaper cuttings, each bearing the headline and the news item itself:

(1)
STRUCK BY COCKTAIL STICK
A SURREY BUSINESSMAN was recovering last night from emergency surgery to remove a cocktail stick which he had swallowed at his office party last December.
Raymond Barrow, 29, of Guildford, was admitted to hospital after complaining of chest pains. Surgeons finally removed the stick, which

had not shown up under X rays, from an artery wall. "It was a close thing" admitted the senior surgeon.

(2)

CAT NIP TURNS NASTY

ONE YEAR AFTER being bitten by a stray cat she had adopted, Mrs Hazel Whittingstone, a teacher of Chiddingford was being treated in the emergency ward of Chelmsford hospital for a rare infection caused by the bite. It will be several weeks before she will be back in the classroom, say doctors.

(3)

Tree catapults gardener 30 feet

A STORM-DAMAGED TREE hurled a gardener into the air when he attempted to saw through the topmost branches.

Joseph Stebbings, aged 41, of The Bungalow, East Bergholt, had been working on the fallen tree when it sprang back, tossing him into a neighbour's garden 30 feet away. He suffered multiple injuries and a hospital spokesman said it would be several months before Mr Stebbings would be fit to work again.

(4)

Falling dog kills three

A DOG, which fell from the 13th floor of a Birmingham tower, caused the deaths of three people in a freak chain reaction.

The first victim, Edith Cary, 72, was killed when the dog fell on her head. The next victim was Kenneth Dyer, 46, who was hit by a bus as he ran to help the injured pensioner. Finally, the shock proved too much for a passer-by who witnessed the event and collapsed with a heart attack. He died in the ambulance on the way to hospital.

(5)

Mystery pineapple hurler

POLICE are investigating an incident in which a man was struck on the head by a pineapple which detectives believe was thrown from a moving car.

The advertiser admits that some of the details actually provided by newspapers were changed "so as not to cause offence". The careful selection of newspaper material in terms of spot news was crucial in devising a reason ad, capable of suggesting strong motives why people should be prepared for almost anything. Unlike other ads which **blur** the boundaries between them and their accompanying discourses (ads printed in the format of news, for example) in an attempt to invest themselves "with some of the authority of the accompanying discourses"[8], the ad under discussion **exploits** these boundaries in order to build its **own authority**.

Another example of building authority, though from another perspective, is provided by an ad for Beefeater Dry Gin. The ad exploits the information contained in the leading paragraph of a newspaper article entitled **Why a G & T may never taste the same again:**

> IT'S ENOUGH to make Britain's G & T brigade leap on to the wagon. Under the cover of Euro bureaucracy, Gordon's is cutting the strength of its gin – but not the price.

The newspaper cutting portrayed in the top half of the ad, above the caption and the copy ad, bears the date *Friday, 15 May 1992-3*. This illustrates the advertiser's wish to stress on the truthfulness of the source and construct the product's image on the **ruined reputation** of a competing similar product. In other words, the ad uses **the power of the press** in order to inform readers on the **new** "world's finest London dry gin".[9]

In the case of some ads, **choice** is the underlying pattern on which they function. Some newspapers publish, next to the crosswords section, the name of a product that could be won by those who manage to find the right answer to a cryptic puzzle contained in a tiny box below the product name. *The Independent on Sunday*, 27 September 1992, publishes such an ad for Zenith Swiss Watches and its cryptic puzzle writes *Belzebub in Review Section.* That means that the answer must be looked for in the review section, then written down in the tiny box and sent to the newspaper. Consequently, the ad is twice parasitic: first on the newspaper's review section where the correct answer lies, second on the crosswords format. There is only one correct answer to be accepted in the box and finally rewarded with "a Swiss-made gold-plated-strap Zenith watch". The novelty achieved by this type of ad is that it is not enough for readers to **want** the product: they have to **earn** it.

Ads – masters of newspaper pages

Advertising imposes its own needs on newspapers, structuring the latter into distinct categories and sections. As Negrine points out, "editorial space is, in practice, the space left over after advertising has taken its share in the newspaper".[10]

Over the past couple of years British Airways has advertised extensively in *The Sunday Times* and has been in competition with Virgin Atlantic and Kuoni Travel Agency over the bottom of the front page. However, its ads have been also printed on inside pages and sometimes more than one page was needed to carry the company's message. For instance, *The Sunday Times* of 18 September 1994 published three entirely blank pages.

The first one carried the caption **Prepare to boldly go where no European business traveller has gone before**, while the last one simply read **In space**. The ad obviously assumes and exploits knowledge of "Star Trek", a well-known science-fiction serial. Every new adventure of the people on the *Enterprise* was a new journey into the unknown, another search for new forms of life and civilisations, a constant desire "to boldly go where no one has gone before". The concept of space is used in the copy ad to attract readers' attention to much more down-to-earth, though essential matters in our life:

> NEW CLUB EUROPE. MORE SPACE IN THE AIRPORT (CHECK-IN BY PHONE AND SPEED THROUGH FAST TRACK). MORE SPACE IN THE LOUNGES (14 ACROSS EUROPE, AND COUNTING). MORE SPACE IN THE PLANE (INTRODUCING CLUB EUROPE'S BIGGEST EVER SEAT).

Speaking about comfortable seats in air planes, it has recently occurred to us that they are frequently advertised with direct reference to newspapers. An ad for Air Portugal reads:

> **With our Navigator £ 399 fare, it's not only the papers that are free**
> Business flights have a plentiful supply of "Broadsheets". Trouble is you get "Tabloid" room to read it in. With our Middle Seat Free* offer you've now got the room to stretch yourself, and your mind out, room to enjoy the comforts of Navigator class and contemplate the fine Portuguese food and wines [… .] (*The Sunday Times,* 16 October 1994)

The term "broadsheets" in the copy ad is both anaphoric, referring to the papers that are free on the plane, and cataphoric, referring forwards to the "Middle Seat Free offer". Stylistically, "broadsheet" and "tabloid" become metaphors for *comfort* and *discomfort* respectively.

Interestingly, if one goes on to the next page of the same newspaper that publishes the above mentioned ad, he/she will find another one for British Airways. The ad occupies the bottom of a double page and reads:

> If you were reading this in your Club Europe seat you wouldn't be nudging your neighbour.

Though individualised by the well-known slogo "The world's favourite airline", the ad echoes the previous one for Air Portugal. The demonstrative "this" does not simply refer to a broadsheet among hundreds and thousands of such papers, but to the very broadsheet actually printing the ad.

Adverts have gradually developed such a strong sense of belonging to the newspaper page that "certain stories, e.g. travel, motoring, fashion, only exist because of their ability to bring advertising with them".[11] Moreover, some ads have already adopted the continuation pattern of newspaper articles and intend to create suspense. For instance, an ad for Renault 19 begins on page 10 of *The Sunday Times*, 28 February 1993 and reads:

Chariot for sale?! I'm off to page 20

The ad continues as indicated on page 20 with the following phrase:

Time to get rid of these old wheels!

Blank spaces running short or very small-printed text have been extensively used lately because people are likely to look for reasons why particular areas haven't been extensively covered by text or pictures. But there are ads which go beyond the visual aspect and exploit their **own printed substance.** For example, of all the ads for Rolex we have come across so far, the following one seems to **speak** through its own substance and communicate a sense of allegiance to the newspaper page:

If you want to wind your Rolex, turn the page.
It was Rolex who invented and patented the perpetual rotor for the very first successful self-winding wrist chronometer. Today, this clever little device still reacts to the slightest movement of the wearer's wrist. OK, now you can turn over. (*The International Herald Tribune,* 23-24 November 1996)

It is a pity, however, that the functional aspect of *turning pages* remains confined within the boundaries of the ad and is not overtly sustained by the layout of the whole page. Thus, four out of the six articles that make page 3 (on which the ad is printed) are continued from page 1 and end on page 3, but neither of the remaining two requires the turning of the page. If people want to read *more*, they need to turn the page. But the turning of pages or the winding of a Rolex depends entirely on reader-consumers' needs, desires and moods.

Conclusions

The medium in which an ad appears is an important parameter in defining categories of ad. Newspapers still prove effective in packaging readers for the benefit of advertisers and their financial dependence on ads make them tolerant hosts for "restless" ads. Many adverts take advantage of newspapers: they usually afford to have longer copy and demand more reflection from readers who are *supposed* to have more time to scrutinize them; they blur or exploit the boundaries of accompanying discourses in order to build their own authority; they attempt to fit in with their hosts in every possible way.

Notes

1 Curran and Seaton: *Power Without Responsiblity,* 1991, p. 8.
2 Cook: *The Discourse of Advertising,* 1994, p. 230.
3 Seymour-Ure: *The British Press,* 1991, p. 147.
4 idem 3, p. 148.
5 idem 1, p. 137.
6 *Newsweek,* 28 October, 1996.
7 At the opposite pole of honesty and truthfulness there are advertisers who believe that their claims of 'fact' need more substantiation than usual. Levi Strauss, for example, decided to promote Dockers brand pants by placing an actual pair of $55 khakis under plastic shields in Manhattan bus shelters. Their ads have been interpreted by city officials as an invitation to stealing and the firm was asked to remove the pants. However, Levi Strauss was of a totally different opinion: the stir that might have been created by a theft was meant to indicate that the product was successful and that people wanted it badly. The company even prepared for an eventual theft by placing an outline of the pants underneath the trousers themselves along with the following message: "Apparently they were very nice pants".
8 idem 2, p. 31.
9 "The World's Finest London Dry Gin" is the slogo for Gordon's bottle not Beefeater and is therefore ironically meant.
10 Negrine: *Politics,* 1991, p. 80.
11 idem 10, p. 80.

Bibliography

Bell, Allan: *The Language of News Media.* Oxford: Blackwell, 1993.
Belsey, Andrew & Ruth Chadwick (Eds.): *Ethical Issues in Journalism and the Media.* London: Routledge, 1994.
Blakemore, Diane: *Understanding Utterances.* Cambridge, Massachusetts: Blackwell, 1995.
Brown, Gillian & George Yule: *Discourse Analysis.* Cambridge: Cambridge University Press, 1989.
Caldas-Coulthard, Carmen Rosa & Malcolm Coulthard: *Texts and Practices.* London: Routledge, 1996.
Coulthard, Malcolm: *An Introduction to Discourse Analysis.* London: Longman, 1996.

Cook, Guy: *The Discourse of Advertising.* London: Routledge, 1994.
Curran, James & Jean Seaton: *Power Without Responsibility.* (4th ed.), London: Routledge, 1991.
Duranti, Alessandro & Charles Goodwin (Eds.): *Rethinking Context.* Cambridge: Cambridge University Press, 1994.
Dyer, Gillian: *Advertising as Communication.* London: Routledge, 1993.
Fairclough, Norman: *Language and Power.* London: Longman, 1995.
Fowler, Roger: *Language in the News.* London: Routledge, 1992.
Giglioli, Pier Paolo (Ed.): *Language and Social Context.* London: Penguin Books, 1990.
Hodge, Robert & Gunther Kress: *Language as Ideology.* London: Routledge, 1993.
Levinson, Stephen C.: *Pragmatics.* Cambridge: Cambridge University Press, 1991.
McCarthy, Michael: *Discourse Analysis for Language Teachers.* Cambridge: Cambridge University Press, 1994.
Mey, Jacob L.: *Pragmatics. An Introduction.* Cambridge, Massachusetts: Blackwell, 1996.
Negrine, Ralph: *Politics and the Mass Media in Britain.* (3rd ed.). London: Routledge, 1991.
Nunan, David: *Introducing Discourse Analysis.* London: Penguin Books, 1993.
Schiffrin, Deborah: *Approaches to Discourse.* Oxford: Blackwell, 1994.
Seymour-Ure, Colin: *The British Press and Broadcasting since 1945.* Oxford: Basil Blackwell, 1991.
Simpson, Paul: *Language Ideology and Point of View.* London: Routledge, 1994.
Toolan, Michael: "What is critical discourse analysis and why are people saying such terrible things about it?", *Language and Literature* 6, 2, 1997, 83-103.

Marianne Hundt, Freiburg

The Press Sections of Standard One-Million-Word Corpora

1. Introduction

In 1991, at about the same time when the first newspaper corpora on CD-ROM became available, a group of students at Freiburg University were engaged in what at first sight must appear as an almost anachronistic activity: They were keying in extracts of roughly 2,000 words from British newspapers. The sampling model was the press section of the LOB corpus (see Sand/Siemund 1992). 1992 saw the beginning of a new Brown corpus. The ultimate aim was to compile parallel one-million-word corpora of the early 1990s that matched the original LOB and Brown corpora as closely as possible, and that would provide linguists with an empirical basis to study language change in progress (see Mair, 1997). An additional attraction of the new LOB and Brown corpora – FLOB and Frown – is that they provide more suitable databases for a comparison with the Indian, Australian and New Zealand corpora (samples representing language use of the late 1980s) than the original LOB and Brown.

In the initial stages of the project, the press sections were used to test the feasibility of the corpus-based approach to language change: Would a span of thirty years prove sufficient to investigate ongoing change? In what follows, I will present a choice selection of previous results, mixed in with some new data and topped off with statistical tests whenever these were felt to add some spice to the discussion.

2. Testing hypotheses on language change

On some questions, the press sections of one million-word corpora obviously do not provide enough data. Examples would be phenomena at the interface between grammar and the lexicon, such as expanded predicates. Algeo (1995: 214) found only 199 and 245 core expanded predicates in the complete Brown and LOB corpora, respectively. Among the suspected grammatical changes in Barber (1964: 130-144), though, some are likely to occur frequently enough for an investigation based on small newspaper corpora to offer sufficient and interesting data. Three examples of successful research using the press sections only of Brown, LOB, Frown and FLOB will illustrate this.

2.1. *The spread of the s-genitive to non-human nouns*

An early empirical study on the spread of the *s*-genitive is Ainsworth (1992). For BrE, she sampled editorials from *The Times* (August 1920 and August 1990).[1] Her results confirm Barber's hypothesis: The *s*-genitive with non-human nouns had increased from only 9 instances in 1920 to 117 in 1990. *Of*-genitives, on the other hand, had decreased from 152 in 1920 to 124 in 1990.[2] The question whether these results merely reflect the house-style of *The Times* or whether they are indicative of a general trend in BrE cannot be answered on the basis of such a small and stylistically homogeneous sample. Examples where the house-styles of individual papers have a bearing on the results are discussed in section five of this paper. In the case of the *s*-genitive, however, Siemund's comparison of LOBpress and FLOBpress (1995: 360-364) shows that the spread of the *s*-genitive to non-human nouns holds for a more varied selection of British newspapers. Notably in the category 'other nouns', they have more than doubled from 38 in 1961 to 79 in 1991. This change proves significant in a chi-square test ($p \leq 0.001$). A comparison with the press sections of Brown and Frown shows that American journalistic prose is more advanced in this ongoing change than BrE: In the category 'other nouns', the figures have increased from 74 in 1961 to 145 in 1992 (see Hundt, 1997: 138).

Ainsworth's case study showed that the increase in *s*-genitives could not have been caused by a general growth in the number of genitive constructions. The increase in *s*-genitives goes hand in hand with a decrease in *of*-genitives. For British newspapers, this has been confirmed in a study by Raab-Fischer (1995). Table 1 lists the raw frequencies of *s*- and *of*-genitives,[3] relative frequencies (in brackets) and the results of a chi-square test.[4]

As noted above, AmE is more advanced in the growing use of *s*-genitives with 'other nouns'. A comparison with additional nonfictional material[5] has shown that in AmE, the change has spread to other genres. So far, this does not seem to be the case in BrE (Hundt, 1997: 138f.). This finding confirms previous results: Jahr (1981) found the highest frequencies of *s*-genitives in the press sections of Brown and LOB. Two lessons are to be learnt from this case study: First, newspapers are a good source for the study of ongoing change because journalese appears to be more open to innovations than other expository writing; second, we have to be extremely careful with generalisations of results obtained from newspaper data precisely because they are not representative of trends in written English as a whole.

Table 1: S-genitives and of-genitives in British newspapers

	LOBpress		FLOBpress		significance
	s-genitives	*of*-genitives	*s*-genitives	*of*-genitives	
personal names	443 (71.3 %)	178 (28.7 %)	692 (80.3 %)	170 (19.7 %)	p≤0.001
personal nouns	259 (34.9 %)	483 (65.1 %)	245 (40.5 %)	360 (59.5 %)	p≤0.001
collective nouns	175 (24.9 %)	528 (75.1 %)	311 (44.9 %)	381 (55.1 %)	p≤0.001
geographical & locative nouns	159 (25.0 %)	478 (75.0 %)	286 (46.4 %)	331 (53.6 %)	p≤0.001
temporal nouns	80 (34.9 %)	149 (65.1 %)	120 (45.5 %)	144 (54.5 %)	p≤0.05
other nouns	38 (1.8 %)	2059 (98.2 %)	79 (3.8 %)	1984 (96.2 %)	p≤0.001

2.2. Contractions

Krug (1994, 1996) has used LOBpress, FLOBpress, Brownpress and Frownpress to test the hypothesis that contractions have increased in the written medium. Contractions are treated at length in the paper by Reynolds/Cascio. I will therefore focus on the following methodological question: Do the press sections of standard one-million-word corpora allow us to ask different or other questions on the use of contractions than those we could base on the analysis of newspapers on CD-ROM? From there I will go on to present data on regional differences in the spread of contractions.

It is obvious that rare sensationalist spellings like *wanna, gonna* or *gimme* are among those phenomena that cannot be studied on the basis of small balanced samples. Other contractions, notably *'s, n't, 'll* and *'d*, do occur frequently enough, though. One of the main advantages of the press sections is that the ratio of contracted forms can be established by relating them to the number of strings which could, in theory, have been contracted but were not. This type of analysis is not possible with data from newspapers on CD-ROM. Uncontracted auxiliaries and the particle *not* are among the stopwords that cannot be searched with the software included with, for example, *The Guardian* on CD-ROM.[6] But even if they could be searched, the amount of data that such a search would yield would be far too much for easy analysis.

The following table summarizes data from Krug's appendix 2 (1994:142-145). The figures include only those cases where variation between contracted and uncontracted strings is possible (i.e. *ain't* was excluded).[7] The figures for uncontracted strings are given in brackets. Percentages indicate contraction ratios.

Table 2: Contraction ratios in British and American newspapers

	LOBpress	FLOBpress	Brownpress	Frownpress
not-contractions	162 (635) 20.3 %	266 (529) 33.5 %	210 (480) 30.4 %	543 (392) 58.1 %
be[8]-/*has*-contractions	93 (1274) 6.8 %	329 (1125) 22.6 %	166 (867) 16.1 %	630 (689) 47.8 %
will/shall-contractions	16 (200) 7.4 %	45 (202) 18.2 %	40 (170) 19.0 %	57 (115) 33.1 %
have/had and *would/ should*-contractions	25 (648) 3.7 %	74 (556) 11.7 %	38 (502) 7.0 %	97 (479) 16.8 %

The contraction ratios – and not the absolute frequencies of contracted forms – allow us to conclude that contractions have become more widespread in journalese over the last thirty years. The problems with contractions in newspapers on CD-ROM is that we are not only unable to establish contraction ratios but that we cannot even safely assume that an increase in the number of contractions has not been caused by a difference in corpus size. The only information we usually have on the size of CD-ROM corpora is in terms of mega-bytes, not in terms of the number of words. But even if we had a reliable way of estimating the number of words in a newspaper on CD-ROM, we would still face the problem that an increase in the raw frequencies of contracted forms could have been caused by other factors. Written English may simply have become more 'verby' over the last thirty years, i.e. the number of both finite and non-finite verbs may have increased. This hypothesis can only be tested once FLOB and Frown have been tagged, but it would fit in well with other observations that indicate a growing colloquialisation of the more agile written genres, such as journalese (cf. Mair, 1997; Mair/Hundt, 1997 and Hundt/Mair, forthcoming). An increase in the use of contractions might therefore simply be linked to an increase in the number of finite verbs. Contraction ratios, however, show that not only the overall frequency but also the relative frequency of contractions has increased over the last thirty years.

The choice between contracted and uncontracted forms is a clearly defined syntactic variable.[9] The data obtained from the press sections of one-million-word corpora can therefore be subjected to statistical procedures like the chi-square test. This allows us to separate free variation from significant differences between samples. In the case of contractions, the differences between LOBpress and FLOBpress on the one hand and those between Brownpress and Frownpress on the other prove significant. In addition to the diachronic development, regional differences between British and American newspapers also prove significant: The growing use of contractions is more advanced in American journalese (see Table 1 in the Appendix). These findings, in turn, can serve to relate other national varieties to AmE and BrE. Table 3 summarizes the results of searches in the press sections of the Wellington Corpus of New Zealand English (WCNZE) and the Australian Corpus (ACE).[10]

Table 3: Contractions in New Zealand and Australian newspapers

	WCNZEpress	ACEpress
not-contractions	297 (649) 31.4 %	299 (521) 36.5 %
be-/has-contractions	406 (985) 29.2 %	362 (959) 27.4 %
will/shall-contractions	40 (178) 18.3 %	40 (178) 18.3 %
have/had and *would/ should*-contractions	80 (534) 13.0 %	80 (554) 12.6 %

Apart from the *be-/has*-contractions, New Zealand and Australian journalese show no significant differences from BrE journalistic prose (see Table 1 in the Appendix). The differences between the New Zealand and Australian press sections on the one hand and Frownpress on the other prove significant.[11] We can thus conclude that in the growing use of contractions in journalistic prose, AmE is more innovative than other national varieties of English. Whether contractions have increased in other genres as well remains to be verified on the basis of the completed FLOB and Frown corpora.

2.3. Phrasal verbs

An increase in the number of multi-word verbs is among the suspected changes mentioned by Barber (1964: 140). While expanded predicates are not frequent enough for an analysis based on the press sections only, a search of phrasal verbs does yield a sufficient amount of data. Since a comprehensive study of phrasal verbs in the press sections of LOB, Brown and their 1990s counterparts would merit a study in its own right,

Siemund (1995: 358-360) and Skandera (1995: 52-56) focus on phrasal verbs with *up*. Their results confirm Barber's hypothesis. A greater variety of phrasal verbs is used more frequently in the 1990s press sections than thirty years earlier. The figures in Table 4 include both phrasal verbs like *make up sthg.* and phrasal-prepositional verbs like *make up for sthg.*[12]

Table 4: Phrasal verbs in the press sections of LOB, FLOB, Brown and Frown

	Types	Tokens	Type-Token Ratio
LOBpress	79	241	32.8
FLOBpress	107	272	39.3
Brownpress	104	246	42.3
Frownpress	126	288	43.8

The increasing use of phrasal verbs in newspapers, like the increase in contractions, fits the trend towards a more colloquial journalistic style. Siemund (1995: 358) also points out that purists like to attribute this change in BrE to the influence of AmE. Skandera (1995: 55), who only compared the overall frequency of phrasal verbs with *up* in BrE and AmE, found no striking differences. A look at the type-token ratios, however, indicates that at least in terms of the range of different phrasal verbs, AmE might be more advanced than BrE. However, only the difference between LOB and Brown proved statistically significant in a z-test;[13] the difference between FLOB and Frown is below the level of statistical significance. While this means that BrE has caught up with AmE in the range of different phrasal verbs with *up* it does not necessarily mean that AmE has directly influenced BrE. A more detailed analysis of phrasal verbs in the press sections will have to show whether phrasal verbs with *up* are typical of a general trend in journalistic prose and whether BrE, generally, has caught up with AmE in this area of ongoing change.

3. *Combining small samples with databases on CD-ROM*

For some hypotheses about ongoing language change, the press sections of standard one-million-word corpora provide just about enough evidence for verification. But even if the data from small, balanced samples do not enable the linguist to cover the area exhaustively, they will often provide enough material to formulate new hypotheses. For analytical fine-tuning, additional examples can be gathered from newspapers on CD-ROM or other suitable corpora. Two case studies will illustrate the procedure.

3.1. Incipient grammaticalisation of help

Mair (1995) uses the press sections of Brown, LOB and FLOB to investigate changes in the complementation patterns of the verb *help*. Previous research commented on semantic differences as well as stylistic and regional stratification (ibid.: 261-263): *Help* with the bare infinitive was considered colloquial and an Americanism. Earlier corpus-based studies seemed to have confirmed that it was used more frequently in AmE than in BrE (ibid.: 261). A comparison with the more recent FLOB data, however, shows that *help* + bare infinitive has gained ground in BrE over the last thirty years. This has not eliminated the regional difference. Evidence from the press section of Frown shows that AmE is still more advanced in this ongoing change (see Table 5).

Table 5: Complementation patterns of the verb help *in the press sections of LOB, Brown and their 1990s counterparts*[14]

	LOBpress	FLOBpress	Brownpress	Frownpress
help + bare infinitive	4	21	9	36
help + object + bare infinitive	1	8	10	21
help + *to*-infinitive	14	6	5	7
help + object + *to*-infinitive	3	7	4	2
bare infinitive : *to*-infinitive	5 : 17	29 : 13	19 : 9	57 : 9
total	22	42	28	66

In the qualitative analysis of his data, Mair observes that a new pattern is emerging: *Help* + bare infinitive has increased especially after inanimate NPs, a context in which it occurs only once in LOBpress. The following examples are from Mair (1995: 264ff.):

(1) No doubt legislation could fix a suitable scale of fines to help finance National Defence [...] (LOB B27 6f.)
(2) A plan to help 60,000 jobless youngsters find work each year will be rejected by the TUC conference today. (FLOB A06 245f.)
(3) The theatre's emergency Phoenix fund will help back the cost of some repairs. (FLOB A34 96f.)
(4) This [additional money] is used to help pay the clergy and bills like heating and lighting. (FLOB A40 49f.)
(5) But it [authoritarian kitsch in downtown Baghdad] helps us understand how and why a tyrant manages to pluck victory – his own survival – from the jaws of military catastrophe. (FLOB B15 140ff.)

Furthermore, *help* + bare infinitive is used with a function similar to a preposition: "A 'plan to help youngsters find jobs' is nothing more specific than a 'plan *for* them to find jobs'; and money used to 'help pay' for something is just money used *for* paying something" (ibid.: 265). The increase in frequency as well as the semantic changes are taken to be indicative of incipient grammaticalisation. Mair (1995: 267) concludes "[...] that the rigorous and systematic comparison of matching databases has its uses." Additional data on *help* (followed by *understand* and *pay*) were sampled from a quality daily (*The Guardian*, 1991) on CD-ROM. They confirm that

(a) the bare infinitive is most frequent when *help* itself is realised as a *to*-infinitive (ibid.: 268)
(b) the construction with the bare infinitive has lost its formal ring formerly associated with it in BrE (ibid.: 268) and
(c) examples with the bare infinitive often show semantic bleaching and grammaticalisation, even in cases where the helpers are active agents (ibid.: 269).

Additional evidence for the hypothesis that BrE has been catching up with AmE in the use of bare infinitives after *help* can be obtained from the BNC. A search for all patterns of *help* followed by *edit* in the spoken demographic sample yields 126 bare infinitives and 66 *to*-infinitives (Mair, 1997b). The fact that data from spontaneous spoken conversations do not produce markedly different proportions of bare infinitives and *to*-infinitives is a further proof that the bare infinitive has lost its former stylistic connotation.

3.2. Dispelling a myth: The alleged decline of whom

The documentation in *Webster's Dictionary of English Usage* (1989: 957-959) is ample proof that the 'correct' use of *who* and *whom* has attracted comments from prescriptivists for well over two hundred years. Sapir (1921: 166-74) is an early descriptive source forecasting the eventual disappearance of inflected *whom*. According to Quirk et. al. (1985: 367), *whom* is replaced by *who, that* or zero relative pronoun mainly in informal texts. This stylistic marking of the uninflected form would fit the trend towards a more colloquial written style if *whom* were used less frequently in the press language of the 1990s. It therefore comes as a slight surprise that this is not the case: *Whom* has not decreased in either American or British newspapers over the last thirty years. In LOBpress and Brownpress, *whom* occurs 37 and 26 times, respectively. Their 1990s counterparts, FLOBpress and Frownpress, yield 41 and 32 occurrences of *whom* (see Siemund, 1995: 371 and Skandera, 1995: 40). Furthermore, the qualitative analysis of the FLOB and Frown data shows that the case distinction between *who* and *whom* is still observed in British and American newspapers of the 1990s. Of the 552 occurrences of *who* in FLOBpress, only one could have been replaced by *whom* (Siemund, 1995: 371). The figures from Frownpress are only marginally higher: Eight of the 643 instances of *who* disregarded the case distinction (Skandera, 1995: 40f.).

A first conclusion we can draw from this case-study is that complaints do not necessarily indicate change in progress.[15] They may simply be indicative of a strong prescriptive influence. Complaints about the loss of case distinctions in *wh*-pronouns are likely to be based on the few instances where the rules are violated. These are then blown out of all proportion because the more numerous cases that are in accordance with the rule remain unnoticed. Corpus-linguistic evidence can thus be useful in re-establishing a sense of proportion.

The persistence of *whom* is a curious exception to the trend towards a more colloquial style in newspapers. It would have been interesting to discover in how far this exception has to be attributed to prescriptivism. Unfortunately, none of the British publishers of newspapers who were asked to provide information on their house-styles were willing to do so. One editor replied that "[...] this is not information that we like to give out." Evidence from two fairly informal sections of the British corpora, however, confirm that *whom* is probably not decreasing significantly in written texts in general. LOB's section E (hobbies) yields only two instances of *whom* compared to seven in the same section of FLOB. Section K (general fiction) of LOB and FLOB each contain 10 occurrences of *whom*.

Further indication of fairly stable variation can be found in a comparison of several years of *The Guardian* on CD-ROM. The overall number of stories in which *whom* is used does not support the hypothesis that the inflected pronoun is losing ground (see Table 6). The qualitative analysis of sets of 100 randomly sampled occurrences of *whom* also hints at stable variation rather than ongoing change.

Table 6: Whom *in* The Guardian

	total number of stories	interrogative pronoun	direct object	prepositional object (no PP stranding)
Guardian 1990	3052	0	23	77
Guardian 1991	3015	2	27	71
Guardian 1992	3457	0	27	73
Guardian 1993	3355	0	29	71

As an interrogative pronoun, the use of *whom* is absolutely marginal. For the function of *whom* as a relative pronoun, my data confirm Bauer's (1994: 76) finding that "*whom* is used virtually exclusively where there is relativization on obliques with no preposition stranding." The results also fit in with those obtained by Schneider (1992a and 1992b). In Early Modern English, uninflected *who* first encroached on the domain of *whom* in interrogative clauses and as a prepositional complement if the preposition was stranded (1992a: 448). These are precisely the contexts in which *whom* is rare in present-day English. A comparison of data from LOB and Brown shows that "an immediately preceding preposition categorically demands case marking" (Schneider, 1992b: 235). Relative clauses without preposition stranding are therefore a stronghold of the inflected pronoun. This is also borne out by an analysis of spoken data from the BNC:[16] 188 (69.8%) of the 269 occurrences of *whom* are preceded by a preposition. Uninflected *who* does occur in this context, as the following examples illustrate:[17]

(6) Share a room with who? (KBM, 1722)
(7) You don't like listening to who? (HUV, 1347)
(8) You vote for who you want. (KDX, 75)
(9) Fair on who? (KBW, 3398)

However, this does not indicate that the uninflected pronoun is replacing *whom* in this context. Note that three of the examples given above are interrogatives – a clause-type which does not favour the use of *whom*. Out of 16 examples of *to* followed by oblique *who*, 14 were questions. There is further indication that the inflected pronoun is still more frequent immediately after a preposition: 27 occurrences of *with whom* compare with only 12 instances of *with who* in the spoken sections of the BNC.[18]

On the other hand, the BNC data also show that the inflected pronoun has a formal connotation: Of the 269 instances of *whom* in the spoken texts, only 21 (7.8%) are from spontaneous conversations. There is thus clear evidence that in informal spoken language, *whom* is avoided. This, in turn, may explain why some linguists have predicted that *whom* was slowly disappearing.

4. Newspapers on CD-ROM and the problem of house-styles

The corpus linguist who uses individual newspapers on CD-ROM as the main source of data has to interpret these against the background of recent socio-linguist studies. One of them is Jucker (1992), who demonstrates that certain aspects in the use of noun phrases in British newspapers are socially stratified. Some differences in usage patterns between up-market, mid-market and tabloid newspapers can be attributed to the phenomenon that Bell (1991) has labelled 'audience design'.

The first example that illustrates the problem of house-styles can be found in Siemund (1995: 368f.). He compares the results on concord with the noun *government* from Bauer (1994: 64) – based on a corpus of editorials from *The Times* only – with data from LOBpress: Usage patterns found in Bauer's *Times* corpus turn out to be conservative when compared with the more balanced LOB sample. The following table is from Siemund (1995: 369).

Table 7: Concord with government *in* The Times *corpus (Bauer 1994) and LOB-press:*

	British government		Non-British government	
	Singular	Plural	Singular	Plural
The Times Corpus (1960)	0	23	8	0
LOBpress (1961)	61	3	27	2

An obvious application for databases on CD-ROM are all phenomena at the interface between grammar and the lexicon. Lovejoy (1995: 58f.), for instance, discusses the reliability of data from CD-ROMs for a study of regional differences in noun-preposition collocations. His conclusion is that "[...] the newspaper databases were better sources than originally expected" (ibid.: 59), but he also points out that the main problem was the difference in style and content of the papers he compared (*The Guardian* for BrE and the *Miami Herald* for AmE). Stylistic differences between individual papers occasionally turned out to be a problem in my study of the relation between NZE, BrE and AmE (Hundt, 1998). As one variable, I investigated complementation patterns of the verb *appeal*. Like Lovejoy, I used *The Guardian* and the *Miami Herald* as samples representing British and American usage. Because New Zealand newspapers are not yet generally available on CD-ROM, New Zealand data had to be sampled locally. I had access to a machine-readable database of two dailies published in Wellington – *The Dominion* and the *Evening Post*. The American and British newspapers confirmed previous observations on regional differences, i.e. a preference for *appeal against* in BrE and *appeal* without a preposition in AmE: In the *Miami Herald* from 1992, there was not a single instance of *appeal* with the preposition. In *The Guardian* (1991), on the other hand, 99 of the 100 sampled instances of *appeal* were followed by *against*. The evidence from the *Dominion/Evening Post* at first seemed to suggest that usage in NZE was divided between the British and American variants:

There were 89 cases of *appeal against* and 80 cases of *appeal* without the preposition. Once the data were listed separately for the two newspapers it became apparent that the variable is stylistically stratified within NZE:

Table 8: Complementation patterns of appeal *in two New Zealand newspapers*

	appeal against	*appeal*
The Dominion	63	11
Evening Post	26	69

Further evidence, that the divided usage in the two papers was not accidental, could be found in the on-line style sheets of the two papers: The style-guide of the *Dominion* explicitly proscribed the American variant, while that of the *Evening Post* did not recommend a particular complementation pattern.

Another popular area for the investigation of differences between national varieties of English are spelling conventions. Peters/Fee (1989) use them as one example to illustrate that a specific mix of AmE and BrE variants can develop into a new national standard. Typical examples from the field of orthography are the variation between *-our* and *-or*-spellings, *-ise* and *-ize* or the variable omission of <e> in words like *judg(e)ment* and *acknowledg(e)ment.* That there are also regional differences in the spelling conventions for <%> is less well known. The BrE variant is *per cent* (two words) whereas AmE generally has *percent* (one word). The press section of the New Zealand corpus contains 208 instances of this orthographic variable. Of these, 173 (83.2%) illustrate the British and 35 (16.8%) the American variant. One possible conclusion would be that, on the whole, NZE is more British in its spelling of *per cent.* Again, a look at the house-styles of different newspapers shows that in this case, variation within NZE is likely to have been caused by prescriptive forces: The on-line style-sheet of the *Dominion*, for instance, prescribes the spelling as two words while the journalists of the *Evening Post* are recommended to use the 'American' variant.

How do we avoid the skewing effect that different house-styles may have on the results of data obtained from papers on CD-ROM? The obvious solution is to use a set of stylistically varied newspapers.

5. Skewed results from a balanced sample

One of the hypotheses gained from Barber (1964: 134) is that – due to the gradual loss of the distinction between *shall* and *will* – the overall frequency of *shall* in the 1990s corpora is expected to have decreased. One aspect that contributes to the levelling of the distinction is the growing use of contracted forms (see section 2). A comparison of the press sections of Brown and LOB with their 1990s counterparts, however, at first sight seems to indicate that BrE might be lagging behind AmE in the gradual loss of *shall*:

Table 9: Shall *and* will *in the press sections of standard one-million-word corpora*[19]

	LOBpress	FLOBpress	Brownpress	Frownpress
shall	27	20	26	8
will	625	668	681	596

While the overall frequency of *shall* in FLOBpress has not markedly decreased from that in LOBpress, there has been a shift in the distribution of this auxiliary (Siemund, 1993: 29f.): In LOBpress, there are 14 occurrences in category A (reportage), 9 in B (editorials) and 4 in C (reviews). Siemund points out that this reflects the size of the three categories.[20] In FLOBpress, on the other hand, *shall* is no longer evenly spread over the three text categories. 16 of the 20 occurrences are from section B (ibid.). Interestingly, of the 26 instances of *shall* in Brownpress, 19 are to be found in the editorial section, as are 5 out of the 8 in Frownpress.

The results from FLOBpress show another skewing effect: Of the 16 occurrences of *shall* in the editorial section, 10 are from only two texts. The first is an example where the formal and conservative character of *shall* goes hand in hand with the content of the editorial. In the second extract, this formal connotation of *shall* is one of the stylistic features contributing to the irony of the text (cf. Siemund, 1993: 39):

> A new Europe will not change those of us who have pride in our heritage. We *shall* still fly the Union flag and have our own National Anthem. 'Land of Hope and Glory' at the last night of the Proms will still bring a lump to the throat.
> So will those immortal words "They grow not old, as we that are left grow old. Age *shall* not weary them, nor the years condemn. At the going down of the sun, and in the morning, we *shall* remember them." We *shall* still remember that they gave their lives to ensure that some of the Europeans whom we are now joining by negotiation, did not conquer us by force.
> We *shall* find ourselves ever closer bound to our European partners. If it avoids another 1914 and 1939, for that alone, it will have all been worthwhile.
> (FLOB B26 195-207)

> But Royton was here when Oldham was nobbut two wigwams and a saloon, and we, the true sons of Aethelfrith, whose kin goes back to Cerdic, *shall* still be here when Oldham has shrivelled up small enough to fit into one of its jackboots.
> All our people forced to live in Oldham *shall* come home to a green, working-class Royton again. We *shall* have a Tory council to repair our houses after the first complaint. There will be a 50-year waiting-list for outsiders wishing to move in.
> (FLOB B23 154-161)

Data from the provisional nonfictional corpora support that the results from FLOBpress are skewed: *Shall* has decreased from 50 in LOB- to 17 in FLOBNonfictional and from 41 in Brown- to 21 in FrownNonfictional. The completed FLOB and Frown corpora are therefore expected to yield more directly comparable figures than those obtained from the press sections only.

6. Discovering unsuspected change?

Apart from testing existing hypotheses on language change, the systematic comparison of word frequencies in parallel corpora might also help to discover previously unsuspected language change. A possible candidate for such a change could be *after*: It has increased from 218 occurrences in LOBpress to 326 in FLOBpress (Siemund, 1993:75), a change that proves highly significant ($p \leq 0.001$) in a chi-square test. Figures from the American corpora are not quite as high, but *after* has increased from 225 in Brownpress to 270 in Frownpress, a development that proves significant at the 5 % level.[21] The difference between LOBpress and Brownpress is not significant whereas that between FLOBpress and Frownpress is ($p \leq 0.05$). If what we have discovered is a genuine linguistic change, it is likely to be more advanced in British journalistic writing. However, an analysis of the contexts in which *after* is used (see Table 10) does not point at a possible pattern that can account for the increase.

Table 10: Functions of after[22]

	finite clause	non-finite clause	NP[23]	other[24]
LOBpress	30	26	138	24
FLOBpress	79	62	162	23
Brownpress	57	30	114	24
Frownpress	60	48	134	28

Siemund (1993:77f.) suspected that a growing use of *after* in finite clauses with the simple past instead of the past perfect could be one possible cause. The past perfect in finite clauses introduced by *after* has decreased from 13 in LOBpress to only four in FLOBpress. This hypothesis does not find any support in the data from the American corpora (see Skandera, 1995: 50). One possible step from here would be to investigate the relation of *after* to other prepositions and conjunctions to find out whether *after* is spreading at the expense of other possible function words. Instead, I did a search in the provisional nonfictional subcorpora. The results suggest that *after* might not be spreading at all: The figures have decreased slightly from 205 in the nonfictional LOB subcorpus to 194 in FLOB, a change that is unlikely to be significant. The results from the American nonfictional subcorpora show even less variation: The search yielded 172 occurrences from Brown and 174 from Frown.

So far, we have not discovered any unsuspected change from the press sections of one-million-word corpora simply by comparing word frequencies. What we can learn from the example of *after* is that (a) statistically significant differences in word frequencies do not necessarily imply that what we have discovered is also linguistically relevant[25] and that (b) results obtained from the press sections have to be tested against data from more varied samples, i.e. a comparison of LOB and Brown with the completed FLOB and Frown corpora.

7. Conclusion

Our experience with the press sections of standard one-million-word corpora has confirmed the "received wisdom" of corpus linguistics that "[...] small corpora [...] are adequate for grammatical purposes, since the frequency of occurrence of so-called grammatical or function words is quite high" (Sinclair, 1991: 100). The *of*-genitive exemplifies that the press sections contain almost too much information on some patterns. The sole reason why the frequency of *of*-genitives in Frownpress, WCNZEpress and ACEpress has not been established yet is that it would involve the manual analysis of a total of 15,607 occurrences of this function word. So far, the only searches that can be done in the new LOB and Brown corpora are word-based searches. This puts an obvious limit to the range of hypotheses on language change that could be tested with the press subcorpora. Part-of-speech tagging will enable linguists to verify, for instance, whether English has become more 'verby' over the last thirty years or to investigate whether the number of passive constructions has decreased. These developments would tie in with other observations indicating that recent changes tend not to have affected grammatical rules but are indicative of a shift in stylistic preferences.

In terms of corpus-size, other phenomena are examples of what Bauer (1994: 50f.) has called “Murphy’s Law” in corpus linguistics, i.e. that a corpus never seems to be the right size for the object under investigation. A case in point is the variation between *who* and *whom*: The press sections provide sufficient evidence on *who* to conclude that it is not frequently used in contexts that call for case marking. The data on *whom*, however, is not conclusive. There are too few instances to reveal the contextual patterning of *whom* that larger samples show. For borderline cases like this, additional material can be sampled from corpora on CD-ROM. Furthermore, with low frequencies as those obtained for *whom*, the risk that even balanced samples may produce skewed results is relatively high. This is the case with *shall* in FLOB.

Another borderline case that calls for supplementary data from CD-ROMs is the question of concord with collective nouns. The press sections yield reliable information only for more frequent words like *government, party* or *public* (Siemund, 1995: 366). Studies based on one newspaper only, however, always risk that the results are not representative of journalistic prose but merely of the house-style of the particular paper. The results obtained from the press sections, in turn, are not necessarily representative of (published) written texts in general. One example would be the spread of the *s*-genitive in BrE. Another case in point is the *going-to* future: The apparent spread (an increase from 30 in LOBpress and Brownpress to 46 in FLOBpress and 67 in Frownpress) would support the hypothesis of a shift towards a more colloquial style in writing; data from the provisional nonfictional subcorpora, however, did not confirm this as a general trend (Hundt, 1997: 143). On closer examination, the increasing use of *going-to* futures in the press sections has to be attributed to a growing use of quotations of direct speech (Mair/Hundt, 1997: 76).

Finally, the studies by Mair (1994, 1995) have shown that the press sections of the standard corpora – in combination with supplementary data from newspapers on CD-ROM – can be used as a source of empirical evidence for grammaticalisation processes. This is a promising field for the application of the completed corpora. Parallel standard corpora are thus expected to go beyond the rather narrow limit of usefulness that Sinclair (1991: 100) ascribes to small, balanced samples: “Presumably, the shorter original corpora did little more than confirm the generally agreed positions on English grammar.”

Notes

1 Ainsworth does not comment on the exact size of her samples, but they are likely to be smaller than the editorial section (Section B) of the standard Brown-type corpus. This assumption is supported by a comparison of her figures for *of*-genitives with those from the editorial section in FLOB (Raab-Fischer, 1995: 131): Ainsworth's corpus yielded 124 *of*-genitives compared with 1,201 in FLOB's editorial section.
2 These figures combine the results of Ainsworth's counts for the categories 'Place' and 'Others' (Ainsworth, 1992: 10).
3 The figures, exclusive of those for the category 'higher animals' (with raw frequencies between 5 and 9), are from Siemund (1995: 362) and Raab-Fischer (1995: 128), respectively.
4 Note that more analytical fine-tuning could be achieved by filtering out those contexts in which *s*-genitive and *of*-genitive are not real equivalents (possible factors restricting the choice would be the length or complexity of the NP). Similar results were obtained by Ljung (1997) from a larger but less stratified newspaper sample.
5 The subcorpora are made up of material from sections D (religion), E (hobbies), F (popular lore) and G (biographical writing and essays). They were tailored in size to fit the press sections. See Hundt (1997) for a list of the texts included in these provisional subcorpora.
6 Very frequent contractions like *don't, can't* and *what's* are also stopwords.
7 I further excluded contractions that were listed by Krug but that did not occur in his spoken data and are therefore even more unlikely to be used in writing (e.g. *mayn't, this's,* or *when'd*). Even though they did not occur in the press sections, it was necessary to exclude these forms. The number of uncontracted strings would have skewed the contraction ratios if they had been included.
8 All forms of *to be* in the present tense (*am, is, are*) are included.
9 A syntactic variable is defined as a set of functionally equivalent forms or variants (see Sankoff, 1988: 152ff. or Jacobson, 1980, for more detailed discussions and alternative definitions).
10 The figures for contracted and uncontracted *not* are from Hundt (1998). The results for individual contractions of auxiliaries are listed in Table 2 of the Appendix.
11 An exception are *had/would*-contractions.
12 Note that Skandera did not include headlines in his analysis. In my analysis of the complete Brownpress, however, I did not get different results. Siemund's and Skandera's results were therefore taken to be comparable.
13 The z-test is a parametric test of significance that, unlike the chi-square test, is applicable to ratios and proportions. Sachs (1997: 440-42) points out that the z-test is applicable whenever the data have been collected from large enough samples, a condition that is met in the case of the press sections. For information on parametric test in general and the z-test in particular, see Butler (1985: 78-97) and Woods/Fletcher/Hughes (1985: 182-84).
14 This table is reproduced from Mair (1997).
15 Other complaints may be indicative of ongoing change (the comments on the *ear-air* merger in NZE would be an example) or persist long after a change has been implemented (an example is the use of *hopefully* as a sentence adverbial which still attracts the wrath of some language purists).

16 The search was based on both the 'spoken demographic sample', i.e. spontaneous conversations (ca. 4.2 million words) and the 'context governed spoken' texts like committee meetings, interviews, TV broadcasts, sermons etc. (ca. 6.1 millions words).

17 Variation between *who* and *whom* with the prepositions *for, of, to* and *with* has been possible since Early Modern English (see Schneider, 1992a: 445).

18 Again, only cases where *who* functions as an object were includ ed.

19 Figures for LOBpress and FLOBpress are from Siemund (1993: 28). All negated forms were included in the search. Contracted *'ll* – for obvious reasons – was not included.

20 Category A consists of 44 samples (ca. 88,000 words), B of 27 (ca. 54,000 words) and C of 17 (ca. 34,000 words).

21 The raw frequencies of *after* were weighted by corpus-size for these tests (a total of 177,053 words in LOBpress, 177,226 in FLOBpress, 178,713 in Brownpress and 177,194 in Frownpress).

22 The figures for LOBpress and FLOBpress are from Siemund (1993: 75).

23 Figures for Brown and Frown include the use of *after* as a non-temporal preposition preceding a NP, as in "[...] he tries to play offense by constantly going after Bush" (Frown A10 55). Siemund does not explicitly comment on this pattern.

24 These include the use of *after* preceding an adverb, a particle or in set phrases like *after all, ever after* and *soon after.*

25 Hundt (1998) discusses three other cases of statistically significant differences between corpora which could not be explained linguistically. The caveat that follows from these case studies is that statistics cannot be used to generate hypotheses. It is only a useful way of summarising complex numerical data and of drawing inferences from them to test existing hypotheses.

Bibliography

Ainsworth, Helen: "The Mark of Possession or Possession's Mark? A Case Study". *New Zealand English Newsletter* 6, 1992, 17-20.

Algeo, John: "Having a Look at the Expanded Predicate." – In Bas Aarts & Charles F. Meyer. (Eds.): *The Verb in Contemporary English. Theory and Description.* Cambridge, 1995, pp. 203-217.

Barber, Charles: *Linguistic Change in Present Day English.* Edinburgh/London, 1964.

Bauer, Laurie: *Watching English Change. An Introduction to the Study of Linguistic Change in Standard Englishes in the Twentieth Century.* London, 1994.

Bell, Alan: *The Language of News Media.* Oxford, 1991.

Butler, Christopher: *Statistics in Linguistics.* Oxford, 1985.

Hundt, Marianne: "Has BrE Been Catching Up with American English Over the Past Thirty Years?" – In Magnus Ljung (Ed.): *Corpus-based Studies in English. Papers from the Seventeenth International Conference on English Language Research on Computerized Corpora (ICAME 17).* Amsterdam, 1997, pp. 135-151.

---: *New Zealand English Grammar – Fact or Fiction? A Corpus-Based Study in Morpho-Syntactic Variation.* Amsterdam/Philadelphia, 1998.

Hundt, Marianne & Christian Mair. "'Agile' and 'Uptight' Genres: The Corpus-Based Approach to Language Change in Progress", forthcoming.

Jacobson, Sven: "Issues in the Study of Syntactic Variation." – In Sven Jacobson (Ed.): *Papers from the Scandinavian Symposium on Syntactic Variation.* Stockholm, 1980, pp. 23-36.

Jahr, Mette Cathrine: "The *S*-Genitive with Non-Personal Nouns in Present-Day British and American English". *ICAME News* 5, 1981, 14-31.

Jucker, Andreas H.: *Social Stylistics. Syntactic Variation in British Newspapers.* Berlin/New York, 1992.

Krug, Manfred: *Contractions in Present-Day English. A Corpus-Based Study of Brachychronic Language Change.* Unpublished M.A. thesis. Exeter, 1994.

---: "Language Change in Progress: Contractions in Journalese in 1961 and 1991/92". *Exeter Working Papers in English Language Studies* 1, 1996, 17-28.

Ljung, Magnus: "The *S*-genitive and the *Of*-construction in Different Types of English Texts." – In Udo Fries, Viviane Müller & Peter Schneider (Eds.): *From Ælfric to the New York Times. Studies in English Corpus Linguistics.* Amsterdam, 1997.

Lovejoy, James: "Prepositions in British and American English – A Computer-Aided Corpus Study". *Arbeiten aus Anglistik und Amerikanistik* 20, 1, 1995, 55-74.

Mair, Christian: "Is *See* Becoming a Conjunction? The Study of Grammaticalisation as a Meeting Ground for Corpus Linguistics and Grammatical Theory." – In Udo Fries, Gunnel Tottie & Peter Schneider (Eds.): *Creating and Using English Language Corpora: Papers from the Fourteenth International Conference on English Language Research and Computerized Corpora. Zürich 1993.* Amsterdam, 1994, pp. 127-137.

---: "Changing Patterns of Complementation, and Concomitant Grammaticalisation, of the Verb *Help* in Present-Day British English." – In Bas Aarts & Charles F. Meyer (Eds.): *The Verb in Contemporary English. Theory and Description.* Cambridge, 1995, pp. 258-272.

---: "Parallel Corpora. A Real-Time Approach to Language Change in Progress." – In Magnus Ljung (Ed.): *Corpus-based Studies in English. Papers from the Seventeenth International Conference on English Language Research on Computerized Corpora (ICAME 17).* Amsterdam, 1997a, pp. 195-209.

---: *Introduction to Diachronic Linguistics.* Unpublished Lecture Script. Freiburg, 1997b.

Mair, Christian & Marianne Hundt: "The Corpus-Based Approach to Language Change in Progress." – In Uwe Böker & Hans Sauer (Eds.): *Anglistentag 1996 Dresden. Proceedings.* Trier, 1997, pp. 71-82.

Peters, Pam & Margaret Fee: "New Configurations: The Balance of British and American English Features in Australian and Canadian English". *Australian Journal of Linguistics* 9, 1989, 135-147.

Quirk, Randolph, Sidney Greenbaum, Geoffrey Leech & Jan Svartvik: *A Comprehensive Grammar of the English Language.* London, 1985.

Raab-Fischer, Roswitha: "Löst der Genitiv die *of*-Phrase ab? Eine korpusgestützte Studie zum Sprachwandel im heutigen Englisch". *Zeitschrift für Anglistik und Amerikanistik. A Quarterly of Language, Literature and Culture* 43, 2, 1995, 123-132.

Sachs, Lothar: *Angewandte Statistik: Anwendung statistischer Methoden.* Berlin/ Heidelberg, [8]1997.

Sand, Andrea & Rainer Siemund: "LOB – 30 Years On… ". *ICAME Journal* 16, 1992, 119-122.

Sankoff, David: "Sociolinguistics and Syntactic Variation." – In Frederick J. Newmeyer (Ed.): *Linguistics: The Cambridge Survey. Vol. 4: Language; the Socio-Cultural Context.* Cambridge, 1988, pp. 140-161.

Sapir, Edward: *Language: An Introduction to the Study of Speech.* New York, 1921.

Schneider, Edgar W.: "Constraints on the Loss of Case-Marking of *Wh*-Pronouns in the English of Shakespeare and Other Poets of the Early Modern English Period." – In Matti Ihaleinen Rissanen, Terttu Nevalainen & Irma Taavitsainen (Eds.): *History of Englishes: New Methods and Interpretations in Historical Linguistics.* Berlin, 1992a, pp. 437-452.

---: "Who(m)? Case-Marking of *Wh*-Pronouns in Written British and American English." – In Gerhard Leitner (Ed.): *New Directions in English Language Corpora. Methodology, Results, Software Developments.* Berlin, 1992b, pp. 231-245.

Siemund, Rainer: *Aspects of Language Change in Progress: A Corpus-Based Study of British Newspaper English in 1961 and 1991.* Unpublished M.A. thesis. Freiburg, 1993.

---: "'For Who the Bell Tolls.' – Or Why Corpus Linguistics Should Carry the Bell in the Study of Language Change in Present-Day English". *Arbeiten aus Anglistik und Amerikanistik* 20, 2, 1995, 351-377.

Sinclair, John: *Corpus, Concordance, Collocation.* Oxford, 1991.

Skandera, Paul: *Computergestützte Korpuslinguistik und Sprachwandelforschung: Grammatische Neuerungen in der amerikanischen Pressesprache seit 1961.* Unpublished M.A. thesis. Freiburg, 1995.

Webster's Dictionary of English Usage. Ed. by E. Ward Gilman. Springfield, Ma., 1989.

Woods, Anthony, Paul Fletcher & Arthur Hughes: *Statistics in Language Studies.* Cambridge, 1986.

Appendix

Table 1: Results of a chi-square test for contraction ratios in the press sections of standard one-million-word corpora. (Italics indicate differences that did not prove significant)

	not-contractions	*be-/has*-contractions	*will/shall*-contractions	*have/had* and *would/should*-contractions
LOB – FLOB	p=0.000	p=0.000	p=0.001	p=0.000
LOB – Brown	p=0.000	p=0.000	p=0.001	p=0.01
Brown – Frown	p=0.000	p=0.000	p=0.002	p=0.000
FLOB – Frown	p=0.000	p=0.000	p=0.001	p=0.01
FLOB – WCNZE	*p=0.387*	p=0.000	*p=1.000*	*p=0.548*
FLOB – ACE	*p=0.225*	p=0.004	*p=1.000*	*p=0.698*
Frown – WCNZE	p=0.000	p=0.000	p=0.001	*p=0.078*
Frown – ACE	p=0.000	p=0.000	p=0.001	p=0.046
WCNZE – ACE	p=0.028	*p=0.328*	*p=1.000*	*p=0.895*

Table 2: Contractions in the press sections of the Wellington Corpus of New Zealand English (WCNZE) and the Australian Corpus (ACE).

	WCNZE		ACE	
	contracted	uncontracted	contracted	uncontracted
I'm	40	25	40	37
you're	19	24	10	23
she's	8	28	13	38
he's	33	117	35	128
it's	162	333	139	317
we're	18	53	15	48
they're	22	102	18	81
who's	7	49	5	53
what's	10	38	8	28
when's	0	0	0	0
why's	0	1	0	4
how's	0	1	0	0
where's	1	0	1	4

Table 2: Contractions in the press sections of the Wellington Corpus of New Zealand English (WCNZE) and the Australian Corpus (ACE). (Continued)

	WCNZE		ACE	
	contracted	uncontracted	contracted	uncontracted
there's	37	133	40	135
here's	4	10	4	3
that's	45	71	34	60
I've	20	38	23	48
you've	11	9	7	15
we've	20	41	15	42
they've	1	29	5	49
who've	0	31	0	19
where've	0	1	0	0
there've	0	8	0	11
that've	0	5	0	4
these've	0	2	0	0
those've	0	0	0	0
I'd	13	33	15	46
you'd	6	2	2	10
she'd	0	14	0	26
he'd	6	94	11	84
it'd	0	78	0	86
we'd	2	28	0	24
they'd	1	56	1	38
who'd	0	26	1	26
why'd	0	0	0	0
how'd	0	1	0	0
where'd	0	0	0	0
there'd	0	18	0	14
that'd	0	20	0	12
I'll	17	6	5	9
you'll	7	7	10	23

Table 2: Contractions in the press sections of the Wellington Corpus of New Zealand English (WCNZE) and the Australian Corpus (ACE). (Continued)

	WCNZE		ACE	
	contracted	uncontracted	contracted	uncontracted
she'll	0	4	0	2
he'll	3	24	4	18
it'll	1	42	2	46
we'll	8	13	10	9
they'll	3	31	4	28
who'll	0	9	2	11
what'll	0	1	0	2
there'll	0	21	3	16
that'll	1	11	0	6
this'll	0	8	0	8
these'll	0	1	0	0
those'll	0	0	0	0

Mike Reynolds and Giovanna Cascio, Sheffield

It's short and it's spreading: the use of Contracted Forms in British Newspapers: a change under way[1]

1. Introduction

> **The fable of the bus conductor**
> You're in your car. It's the morning rush-hour and you're in a hurry. The traffic is heavy. It comes to a halt. A bus ahead is standing still at the bus stop as passengers board, and each one has to show their pass or buy a ticket from the driver. There is no conductor, so this takes two or three minutes since it's busy. The tailback behind the bus jams up the intersections. It's frustrating; you've thought about travelling by bus or train, rather than by car, but the service is not comfortable, not quick and not reliable. It can't be long, you think, before the whole road system collapses into gridlock.

This 'scene-setting' forms the opening paragraph of the third chapter of the little 'taster' edition of Will Hutton's *The State to Come*, a follow-up book to his politico-economic bestseller *The State We're In*, a promotional effort that was given away with a recent edition of *The Observer.* In the paragraph Hutton uses six contracted forms, and could have used four more: 6 actual contractions out of 10 potential ones – a percentage ratio of 60%. In all the rest of the 47-page booklet he uses a contraction on only ten occasions, so there is something marked about their density here. What is it? It is, of course, an indication of a shift in mode, in this instance to narrative from argument. Hutton wishes to illustrate his argument, and to do so he sets a 'scene' and tells a 'story'. To do so and in so doing, he 'relaxes' stylistically. Hence the frequent use of a 'conversational' feature, contractions, or 'contracted forms' (CFs) as we shall label them from now on in this paper.

However, this is to state what we have always up to now believed and been told, namely that CFs are, by definition, "features typical of informal talk" (Leech & Svartvik 1994:11). Roger Fowler places them thus, in his list of features of 'orality' or 'oral mode' in newspapers, under the heading of 'syntax and morphology':

> *Contractions of auxiliaries and negatives.* A standard cue to oral mode, of major importance not only in newspapers but also in, for example,

> academic writing that tries to sound chatty and user-friendly: 'he'll', 'don't', etc. (Fowler 1991: 63)

And R.A. Close, in his grammar for students of English (Close 1975) makes a classically traditional pronouncement that "The contracted forms [...] are commonly used in fluent speech and in informal writing" (Close 1975: 20).

Rivers & Rodriguez (1995), in their guide to journalists on grammar and style have this to say:

> Contractions should not be used in extremely formal writing, but in most writing for newspapers, magazines and broadcast, contractions can be used whenever they would be used in cultivated speech. (Rivers & Rodriguez 1995: 152)

Leaving aside the prescriptive tone of this, appropriate to the purpose of the particular genre of book, it is worth noting that this is up-to-date advice. We shall see how well it squares with current practice.

1.1. Aim and Scope of the study

In this paper we wish to put some of these assumptions about the use of CFs in writing under scrutiny and to suggest that there is a change occurring in their usage. We want to ask whether the use of CFs is increasing and whether their use is spreading from informal to more formal genres. There are both theoretical and practical reasons for undertaking such a study. Theoretically, it is of interest to trace a process of sociolinguistic change, and to ask whether any predictions about the direction of change can be made. Practically, it is useful to be able to provide up-to-date information on a matter of style to those who already have frequent cause to write English, and to those who are learning to do so in many domains; e.g. students in higher education, and people in business and the professions.

In order to do this, we have looked at the use of CFs in three distinct genres in three British newspapers, *The Guardian, The Times* and *The Star* (Sheffield) and compared their current usage with that of 20 years ago. We chose newspapers for our corpus for various reasons. First, as a form of mass media, they reach a large number of people on a frequent basis. Second, they are skilful, professional written products. Third, they are multigeneric in nature and thus allow us to look at a range of discourse types along a scale of formality. As mass media, they are at the edge between formal and informal uses. For all these reasons the press is a good site in which to observe any change in the written language at work. But before describing the data corpus, it is useful to revise what contractions are, how they have come into the language and how they are considered.

1.2. What are CFs?

As is well known, there are two forms of contraction in English, negative contraction (NC) and auxiliary reduction (AR). Negative contraction occurs on modals (e.g. *won't, wouldn't, needn't*) and forms of the verbs *be (isn't, wasn't, weren't, aren't), have (haven't, hasn't, hadn't)* and *do* (*don't, doesn't, didn't*).

Still the major work, to our knowledge, on auxiliary contraction is Zwicky (1970), who, however, investigates the process as a phonological phenomenon. Zwicky lists four classes of auxiliaries undergoing reduction: (i) *is* and *has* (contracting orthographically to *'s*), (ii) *would* and *had* (contracting to *'d*), (iii) *have, will* and *are* (contracting, respectively, to *'ve, 'll* and *'re*) and (iv) *am* (*'m*). With *be*, contraction may occur on its use either as an auxiliary or as a copula verb, as examples (1) and (2) show.

(1) Before you can say 'pregnancy test' *she's wondering* if *he 's* all he seems to be. (John Highfield's 'Tonight's Hit & Miss', *The Star*, 30/12/96)

(2) "The Grant that most of the people in Albert Square know *isn't* the same one that Lorraine has fallen for. *He's* a lot more gentle with her." (John Highfield's 'Tonight's Hit & Miss', *The Star*, 4/3/97)

In addition, there are modal + perfective aspect combined contractions, such as *must've (done), would + have* + past participiple, as in

(3) I'd've loved an ice cream

and many other possible combinations. These combinations, though normal in speech, are not attested in writing. The one exception to this 'rule' is *will ('ll) + have*, but this is still rare. The one example in the data is to be found in (11) below.

1.3. Restrictions on the occurrence of CFs: where they can't occur in writing

In general, for the purposes of this study, we have assumed that if a CF could (or would) occur phonologically, then that constitutes a potential CF-site in writing. Conversely, if it isn't possible phonologically, then it is not counted as a potential CF in the corpus. Apart from the restriction on modal-perfective CFs mentioned above, there are three other circumstances which constrain the occurrence of CFs, one phonological and the other two syntactic. These are the following:

(i). CFs of *be (-'s)* do not occur after the orthographic representation of sibilant sounds, that is after <-s, -ise, -aze, -ize -(t)ch, -(d)ge>. Thus, a contraction is not possible on *this is* or *which is.*

(ii) Contraction does not occur after a parenthesis, e.g.

(4) … but finally even Davies's ingenuity – and McIlwham's versatility – is exhausted (*The Times*, 30/4/97: Barry Millington, concert review [RPO/Maxwell Davies])

(iii) CFs do not occur after a number of types of NP. Some of these have been discussed by Zwicky (1970), who states that restriction of this type "does not depend upon stress considerations" (ibid. p. 334). Basically, he is saying that *preceding* contexts impose *phonological* restrictions, both segmental and prosodic on CFs, whereas with *following* contexts he posits a 'no-deletion' condition which he says works independently of stress restrictions.[1] Zwicky tentatively formulates his 'no-deletion condition' in the following terms:

> It seems that *Auxiliary Reduction* is barred from applying to a form when the constituent following that form has been removed. (Zwicky 1970: 325)

Here are a few examples from the corpus (which have not been counted in the percentage ratios, since they are not counted as representing potential CF-sites.)

(5) … because there was nothing better to watch. Now *there is (*there's)*, we're off. (*The Times*, 24/2/97; Matthew Bond, 'Review' (of previous night's TV))

(6) Sir John Barbirolli was a lover of the game [cricket], but no more than Zubin *Mehta is (*Mehta's)* today. (*The Times*, 30/4/97: Michael Henderson, 'Line and length' [sports column])

(iv) use within subject NPs that contain an embedded clause, with or without *that* expressed – a syntactically conditioned restriction not discussed by Zwicky;[2] e.g.

(7) *Trouble is (*trouble's)*, Watford people are a bit too obliging for the wild world outside. (*The Guardian*, 14/6/97, p. 7 "The scorcher"; [theatre review])

(8) Now the *hope is (*hope's)* that conversely England can sustain their improvement in New Zealand. (*The Guardian*, 14/1/97; p. 21; [cricket report])

(9) ... a fact that fills my heart with joy and exposes this ridiculous series for what *it is (* it's)*- a puffed-up collection of clichéd, state-subsidised Irish whimsy... (*The Times*, 24/2/97; Matthew Bond, sup. cit.)

2. The data

We collected data, as mentioned, from two national broadsheets (*The Times* and *The Guardian*) and one local daily evening paper, the Sheffield *Star.* According to Willings Press Guide (1996 edition, Volume 1: UK), *The Guardian* has a certified sales figure of just below 400,000 (over the period of June to November 1995), which means that it reaches a readership of c. 1.1 million. Of this readership, 80 % belong to social classes ABC1 (professionals and white collar employees), and 42 % are "educated to age 21+" (Willings 1996: 561): i.e. they have received some form of tertiary education. Although Willings gives no information about the readership of *The Times*, this is well known as having a profile similar to *The Guardian*'s. Its circulation is much higher than the latter's, at just over 675,000 (period June-November 1995). *The Star* (Sheffield) is recorded (Willings 1996: 1108) as having a circulation of about 93,000 (or about a fifth of the population of the city) on weekdays, a little lower on Saturdays. Again, no information is given about its readership profile, but John Spencer, Assistant to the Editor on the paper, described how the paper was aimed at a "family audience", and tried to "have a conversation with the reader", reflecting "how ordinary people behave". From this, we infer that it is aimed at a wide cross-section of people in Sheffield, in terms of social class, occupations, ages and lifestyles. It is a popular paper, tabloid in format.

We collected data from three genres within the papers, and from two periods in time. The genres were: (i) the leader articles (editorials), (ii) the 'entertainment pages' – feature articles, previews and reviews, and (iii) the sports pages (reports, feature articles and by-lined columns). We hypothesised that the leaders represented a more formal genre, one in which the paper would be "on its best behaviour", and that the other two genres would be more informal. We collected the current data over the period July 1995 to June 1997, with the vast majority of the data between October 1996 to May 1997. To make the necessary comparisons, we also collected data from *The Guardian* and *The Star* over the period November to December 1976. We analysed a total of 470 articles from the 1996/7 period and 80 articles (from *The Guardian* and *The Star* only) from 1976. A breakdown of this corpus is given in Tables 1 and 2 in Appendix 1.

We contacted the newspapers themselves in order to find out whether they had a policy towards the use of CFs. John Spencer (*The Star)* described CFs as "user-friendly", and that he didn't have "strong views" on their use, "even on weighty topics". Their use in quoting, (i.e. in direct speech) was alright, and in leaders, too, especially the 3rd (and final) leader, which was "always a light one". They would not be forbidden in reviews, nor in reports from a "soft perspective". However, he stated that they would be out of place in a formal type of report, instancing trial court reports as an example of what he had in mind. Altogether, the impression was that CFs were markers of informality, or of conversation rendered in print, as Fowler indicated, and in line with John Spencer's view of the role of a local paper and its desired relationship with its readers.

Victor Keegan, chief leader writer on *The Guardian,* said the CFs were permissible in headlines, where in fact they were sometimes necessary for reasons of column space. Practice varied across news reports: on the whole they were not used, except in direct speech. *Guardian* journalists and leader writers would "go by feel" and "respond to usage" in this matter. This shows an undogmatic attitude towards the use of CFs in the paper. There was no specific guidance on the issue in the in-house style book. In light of this it is worth looking, as we shall below, at actual practice.

Tim Austin, Chief Revise Editor of *The Times*, was more specific. CFs would be kept out of leaders. In general they would only be used in direct speech; they *could* be used in "more relaxed pieces", such as the 'Diary'. He felt that *The Times* had to "keep standards of formal English going." In general, then, senior professional journalists on all three papers reflected back the generally received opinion on the acceptability and meaning of the use of CFs in writing.

3. Hypotheses

These were four, as follows:

1. that the use of CFs has increased over the last 20 years, and can be predicted to increase further. The language is undergoing a change in this aspect of its use;
2. that one of the factors determining the use and spread of CFs is genre; specifically, that, in British newspaper usage, the use of CFs is more frequent on entertainment and sports pages (reports, commentary and feature articles) than in editorials;

3. that, within newspapers, the use of CFs is more widespread in local than in national newspapers, owing to the particular newspapers' perception of their role and readership. Thus, that CFs are more common in the *Star* (Sheffield) than in *The Times* and *The Guardian*. Conversely, their use in the two national broadsheets would be roughly the same;
4. that some CFs are more acceptable than others; and that some are not (yet) acceptable at all; i.e. that there is a 'wave of change' (Downes 1984: 104-12) in progress.

4. Methods

As indicated in the Introduction, the basic measure we took was the percentage ratio of CFs per article. This measure is the number of actual CFs occurring as against the total potential occurrences. We were guided by the following criterion in deciding upon potential sites: would a CF be produced orally at this juncture in the discourse? We excluded from the count examples occurring in the environments listed in §1.3. above. The following article illustrates the method.

(10) EAST ENDERS (BBC1, 7.30pm)
According to actress Jacqueline Leonard, who plays lovelorn Queen Vic barmaid Lorraine, she of the funny accent, the secret of Grant Mitchell's appeal is: "The Grant that most of the people in Albert Square know *isn't* the same one that *Lorraine has fallen* for. *He's* a lot more gentle with her." Well that might be the case but I think *that's* pretty much what estranged wife *Tiffany would have said* until Grant discovered that her soon-to-be-baby probably *isn't* his. In any event, Lorraine has an even bigger problem to cope with than Grant's mood swings – *mum Peggy doesn't like* her and tonight *she's* out to make her least favourite barmaid's life very uncomfortable." (from 'Tonight's Hit and Miss' [TV preview], by John Highfield *The Star*, 4/3/97)

Here there are 6 CFs and two potential CFs ("Lorraine *has fallen*" for *'s fallen*, and "Tiffany *would have said*" for *would've said*), which gives a percentage ratio of 75 %. Two types of CF are present, NC and copula contraction. Auxiliary reduction is not represented here. There is also one non-CF site, i.e. a site where there is no potential CF. In the phrase *"the secret of Grant's appeal is"* it is not permissible to contract the copula . This belongs to type (iv) discussed in §1.3. We may also note how no contraction occurs in the modal perfective construction "*Tiffany would have said*". As stated, this form of CF has not yet been attested.

Having calculated the percentage ratios, we took the means and calculated the standard deviations for CF occurrence for each genre in each of the three newspapers, for the 1996/7 and the 1976 data. With this information we were able to carry out a series of one-tailed 2-sample t-tests to establish the significance in statistical terms of the distribution of CFs in the different discourse sites and comparisons between them. (The tests were one-tailed as we were hypothesising an increase in usage in all cases.) The findings are given in Tables 3 to 14 in Appendix 1, and will be reported on in some detail in the next section.

5. Findings

First we shall compare CF usage across the three newspapers and across the two time-periods in general terms, and then make comparisons by genres. We shall discuss and eliminate the factor of article length as one influencing the density of occurrence. Then we shall report on the distribution of the two types – NC and AR – of CFs, and state what the most and least frequent forms are. This gives some indication of how the change in CF usage is progressing. Then we shall briefly discuss and illustrate variability in CF usage, in terms of actualised and unrealised occurrence in particular cases. Variability is a feature of all linguistic change, and we can see operating in this instance what Aitchison calls 'gradual implementation, gradual spread' (Aitchison 1991: 101).

5.1. Comparisons across the three newspapers

The Star makes a greater use of CFs in all three genres than *The Guardian* and *The Times. The Guardian*, in turn, is more flexible about their use – i.e. uses them more frequently and in a more widespread manner than *The Times.* This confirms the first part of our third hypothesis. This rank order obtains across all three genres in the three newspapers. The rank order of frequency per genre is also the same across the three, namely:

1 – entertainment, 2 – sport, 3 – leaders. The highest mean percentage ratio is 54.46 % for sport in *The Star*, and the lowest (aside from the zero percentages for leaders in *The Times*) is 9.88 % for leaders in *The Guardian.* The mean percentages for all genres for the three newspapers are given below in Figure 1.

When we look at the (incomplete) picture for 1976 and compare it with today, we see that there has been a significant increase in CF usage in all genres where comparison can be made, with the exception of *The Times.* There, as far as leaders are concerned, nothing has changed. No contrac-

	entertainment		*sport*		*leaders*	
	1996/7	*1976*	*1996/7*	*1976*	*1996/7*	*1976*
Star	54.66 %	35.49 %	29.44 %	18.51 %	20.03 %	10.82 %
Guardian	45.25 %	?	14.84 %	?	9.88 %	2.44 %
Times	16.39 %	?	12.42 %	?	0 %	0 %

Figure 1: Mean percentage ratios of CFs across newspapers, genres and periods

tions were used in 1976, and none are used today. *The Times*' policy on this has been given above. This is not to say that CFs are entirely absent in *Times* leaders. There are 5 examples in the corpus, and they are given in Appendix 2. It is to be noted, however, that they are restricted to very special circumstances: use in quotes, from a song in one instance, and a popular saying in another, and in an intertextual reference to a Shakespeare play in a third.

On *The Star*, the increase in CF usage in all genres ranges from the weakly significant in entertainment ($p < 0.1$) (Table 11) to significant ($p < 0.5$) in leaders and sport (Tables 4 and 7 respectively). On *The Guardian*, the increase in CF occurrence in leaders – the only diachronic comparison that we can make – is highly significant ($t = 4.76$, $p < 0.001$; see Table 3).

5.2. Comparisons across genres

5.2.1. Leaders

Tables 3 and 4 show that *The Star* uses more than twice as many CFs in its leaders than does *The Guardian.* The mean percentage ratios are 20.03 and 9.88 respectively. The position since 1976 has not changed in one respect, but changed significantly in another. Twenty years ago *The Star* also used significantly more CFs in its leaders than did *The Guardian*: a mean percentage ratio of 10.82 to *The Guardian's* 2.44. The significant change is in how the mean usage in both newspapers has changed between 20 years ago and today. On *The Star*, this change is significant and on *The Guardian* highly significant.

Table 5 shows a highly significant difference between *Star* and *Guardian* leaders today, in *The Star's* direction, though the difference in this genre was much less significant in 1976 (Table 6).

In most, but not all, cases, there is a greater use of CFs in the 'third leader' than in the other two. This is traditionally thought of as the place for a more light-hearted comment on the newspaper's part, and we can recall John Spencer's comment above about the role of this piece. The example here is a 3rd leader from *The Star*, and has the highest ratio (85.71 %) in all the data sample from this genre. We should note the use of a 'conversational' lexical item referring to television, "the box".

(11) **Showing your age**

It's a little like noticing policemen are getting younger...complaining *they don't* make kids' shows like they used to is proof positive that *you're getting* old.

It's not true, either, that children's TV is failing the quality test – the nominations at Sunday's BAFTA awards were for some of the best drama and documentary material *you'll have seen* on the box in the past 12 months.

The next time you complain about quality, remember that the favourite show of your childhood was probably Help, It's the Hair Bear Bunch, Stop the Pigeon or the Perils of Penelope Pitstop!

(*The Star*, 8/4/97: 3rd leader)[3]

One factor that we wished to eliminate as a cause of the difference between *Star* and *Guardian* leaders was length of article. Although our sample from both papers is roughly the same (83 leaders from *The Guardian* and 79 from *The Star*), there is a very great difference in respective article lengths. For *The Star* leaders (1996/7) the average length is 130 words, and for *The Guardian* (same period) it is just over 500. Accordingly we ran Spearman rank correlation coefficient tests comparing article length with the CF percentage ratios, and these showed that there was no significant correlation in either case.[4] We were thus able to eliminate length as an explanatory factor in the differences between the two newspapers' leaders. This further confirms our hypothesis (the third) that the change in CF usage is more firmly rooted in a local tabloid paper than in a national broadsheet.

5.2.2. Sport

In the sports genre, there has been a significant increase in CF usage over the last 20 years (Table 7), and the differences currently in usages between *The Guardian* and *The Star* (Table 8), and *The Times* and *The Star* (Table 10) are both highly significant ($p < 0.001$). The 2-sample t-test for significance between CFs in sports coverage shows that there is no significant difference between the two broadsheets (see Table 9). This is the only non-significant result in the series. Furthermore, the usage of CFs in this genre is restricted almost exclusively to direct speech quotes. The exception in sports coverage is columns and by-lined feature articles where a limited number of CFs occur outside of direct speech. An example is the following, from the 'Steve McManaman' column (McManaman is a Liverpool F.C. player).

(12) Of course, it will be a chance to relax as well, unwind away from football for a short while, and *it shouldn't be* too bad to be among the cream of the British pop business, but seriously, it is easy to criticise footballers for unwinding; but, done sensibly, it is, surely, a wise thing ...[It] is a certain celebrity of sorts to be recognised like that, to be signing autographs all the time, but *I don't feel* much of a celebrity. I am a professional sportsman. (*The Times*, 24/2/97)

Again, the explanation for this use outside of direct speech may be in the more 'personal' nature of the column as compared with the report.

5.2.3. Entertainment

As already indicated, it is in this genre that CF usage is most widespread. Tables 11 to 14 show *The Guardian* and *The Star* are similar in their density of CF usage – a mean percentage ratio of 45.25 % for the former and 54.46 % (over half) in the latter. The difference between the two newspapers here is only weakly significant at $t = 1.60$, $p < 0.10$. The comparisons between the two broadsheets and between *The Times* and *The Star* are both highly significant – see Tables 13 and 14.

An example of an entertainment article, with a percentage ratio of over 90 % (10 actual CFs and just one potential unrealised CF) is given here, from *The Star*.

(13) A WOMAN OF INDEPENDENT MEANS
C4, 8.30pm
Perhaps it started with Scarlett O'Hara, but Southern belles always seem to come in the indestructible variety – unless *you're* the leading lady of a Tennessee Williams tragedy, in which case *you're* just plain mad. Here *it's* the turn of Sally Field to do her bit for Southern womanhood in a tale of love and loss in Dallas, Texas. The cast also includes Brenda Fricker and Charles Durning. Big mini-series stuff – perfect for watching with a box of chocs and a few Kleenex to mop up the tears *which will* undoubtedly flow. *There's* more to ... [text ends]
ELEMENT OF DOUBT
ITV 9pm.
Gina McKee plays a schoolteacher married to charming – well, *you wouldn't expect* him to be anything else – Nigel Havers. She wants a family but *he isn't* so keen, insisting they wait until *he's clinched* a big business deal. Before you can say 'pregnancy test' *she's wondering* if *he's* all he seems to be. Is he a fraud or is she simply being hysterical?

This is the sort of thing that Alfred Hitchcock did so well with Suspicion and which won Ingrid Bergman an Oscar for Gaslight. Both these films are now over half a century old but still the mad wife/sinister husband plot lumbers on. No ... [text ends]
LES GIRLS C4, 2.20
A lesser Hollywood musical but, with Kay Kendall in the cast, *it can't be* all bad. An amusing tale of a libel case in which every character recalls a different version of events.
(*The Star*, 30/12/96; John Highfield's 'Tonight's Hit & Miss' [TV preview])

5.3. CF occurrence by type and frequency

Table 15 shows that the most frequent CFs are *it's, don't* and *can't.* If all instances of an AR with *be*, and including therein examples of copula and auxiliary reduction, are summed, then these forms account for nearly three quarters of the AR type. In NC, *don't,* taking its imperative and non-imperative uses together, accounts for nearly 28 % of instances, and *can't* for about 15 %. *Won't*, with 15 instances (c. 8 %) is the third most frequent NC.

The general distribution of CFs shows that AR outnumbers NC by approximately 58 % to 42 %. This tendency is replicated in a further check on CF forms in a part of the sports and entertainment samples from *The Times* and *The Guardian* (see note 2 after Table 15). There is, however, an exception to this general tendency: in *Guardian* leaders NCs outnumber ARs by 87 to 37. There is no obvious explanation for this.

	[1]	[2]	[3]
NC (%)	70	41	32
AR (%)	30	59	68
[1] = *Guardian* leaders;	[2] = *Star* leaders;	[3] = *Star* entertainment	

Figure 2: CF forms by type (NC, AR); in percentages; 1996/7 data

Contractions of *will ('ll)* are reasonably frequent, at a little under 10 % of the total. One unusual example is given in (11) – *you'll have seen* – in that it occurs in a modal-perfective combination.

The *'d* form, as a contraction either of *would* or of *had* is still infrequent. For *had*, here are two of the 6 examples counted, both from the entertainment genre ((14) and (15)), and followed by an example of *'d (would)*, from a *Star* leader.

(14) *He'd* met the Duggans during medical training… and they seemed to be the only friends he'd ever had. (*The Guardian*, 6/5/97; Adam Sweeting, 'Last night's TV')

(15) "… but some of the workers there said that once I got home I would probably get flashes in the subsequent months, images of what *I'd* seen coming back at me." (*The Star*, 6/3/97; John Highfield, 'Thursday Movies & Music')

(16) And for your £250 you'll get a pair of trousers made from denim offcuts, stylish but utilitarian, as *they'd say on* the Clothes Show. (*The Star*, 6/3/97; 3rd leader)

5.4. Variability

As Jean Aitchison points out (1991: 89), a feature of all linguistic change is variation. A good place to see this is in the distribution of the commonest CFs, forms with *'s* such as *it's* and *that's.* We have not done any statistics in this area, and so will only present examples of variation in each of these forms. Two are taken from the same *Star* editorial and the other from a *Guardian* leader. In the *Star* examples, the variation is particularly striking in that it occurs within the same sentence.

(17) *It's* perhaps a reminder when *there is* so much cynicism about politics that good, simple ideas like a university for all can still become a reality. (*The Star*, 6/3/97; 2nd leader)

(18) *That's* the kind of politician he is … In an era when the general reputation of politics is low and getting lower, *that is* not an encouraging thought … *That's* a base on which public respect for politics can and must build … Professionalisation may win votes, but it has done little to make people care about politics – and *that is* the real lesson of this election. (*The Guardian*, 1/5/97; 1st leader)

(19) Local authorities spend vast amounts of money and *it's* in everybody's interests that *it is* spent wisely (*The Star*, 6/3/97; 1st leader)

A final observation is that the vast majority of all ARs occur with pronominal subject NPs, though this restriction does not apply to NCs. With ARs, there were only 5 examples counted of non-pronominal subjects, two of which appear in the next example:

(20) *Today's* the day that *Tiffany's* been dreading (*The Star*, 28/4/97; John Highfield 'Tonight's Hit & Miss')

5.5. Rebuttals: a special case of CFs

At present it is barely possible, within the variability of usage, to explain why a CF is chosen on one occasion of use but not on another, even within the same sentence, as we have seen. However, there would appear to be one case that may motivate the use of a CF, and that is when the writer wishes to make a counter-assertion, or rebuttal. We cannot as yet go beyond offering a few examples of this phenomenon, at the same time noting that these examples occur in discourses where the overall use of CFs is not high: this makes them, that is, marked forms. The first example is from outside the corpus, and is given to illustrate that this may be a generalisable use. It is from a book review in an academic journal.

(21) This is not to say that I unreservedly endorse everything that Thomas says. *I don't.*
(Book review in *Language and Literature*, Vol. 5(2), p. 139; 1996)

The same speech act of counter-assertion is involved, we would argue, in the following examples.

(22) Till Death does them part? *It won't*, of course. (*Guardian* leader, 3/12/76)

(23) How on earth has the media failed to report this scandal? *It hasn't.* Contrary to the Home Secretary's assertions, the annual renewal has always been reported. (*The Guardian*, 8/4/97; 2nd leader)

(24) The firm thinks the fine was harsh – *we don't. (The Star*, 19/6/97; 2nd leader)

(25) Certainly, in our view, the reform of the Lords is long overdue. ... *We don't, however,* believe that the Lords should be abolished. *(The Star,* 22/11/76; leader)

(26) The important thing was, however, that until he stepped aside, Harold Wilson was always there to paper over the cracks between the two factions. *Now he isn't* which means the overiding [sic] factor so far as government policy is concerned, is the influence of Roy Jenkins. *(The Star*, 19/11/76; leader)

Is there a hint of emphasis, via the selection of a CF, as a marked form, and so appropriate to the speech act of rebuttal?

5.6. The hypotheses revisited

The first hypothesis, that the use of CFs in newspapers has increased over the past 20 years, has been very clearly confirmed in the case of one of the broadsheets and the local paper. Language use is, then, changing; a process of 'deformalisation' is taking place. We can see this process at work in both editorials and on the entertainments pages, though we should note that the use of CFs was already evident in the latter genre 20 years ago: the trend has firmed up. In part, however, the second hypothesis was disconfirmed. On one of the broadsheets (*The Times*) CFs are still absent from leaders. Further, the increase in the use of CFs, in the one paper (*The Star*) where we can make the comparison, although significant, is not as significant as most of the cross-paper comparisons. The use of CFs is, in general, still restricted to their use in direct speech. It is their selection by a writer as expressing his/her own voice that represents the critical breakthrough.

The third hypothesis is proven to the extent that *The Star* – the local 'family paper' – does use CFs more than either of the broadsheets, with their targeting of an educated, managerial and professional readership. However, the second part of the hypothesis – namely that the two broadsheets would be similar – is not borne out. *The Guardian* and *The Times* differ greatly, as we have seen in their use (or non-use) of CFs in both the more formal leaders and the informal entertainments pages. On entertainments pages, *The Guardian* is much closer to *The Star* than to its competitor newspaper *The Times*. It is only on the sports pages that the two national papers are similar, and both conservative in their usage (cf. Figure 1).

The fourth hypothesis is proven. Section 5.3 showed how certain CFs predominate, in particular CFs with *be*, as copula and as auxiliary, whilst the spread of contraction to modal-perfectives has barely begun.

6. *Conclusions*

This has been a small-scale study, but we are confident that we have managed to gather sufficient evidence to prove our overall hypothesis that the use of contracted forms is spreading. Whether this is evidence of a general social phenomenon, of a relaxation from formality, it is not possible to say; but it is feasible to speculate that this is the case, at least as far as 'linguistic manners' is concerned. It suggests that further work could and should be done in this area. One obvious way to extend this study is to widen it to include other genres. Here, an interesting one would be to look at a selection of academic genres, for instance, the textbook, the academic book and the research article. We have anecdotal evidence so far that the use of CFs is indeed spreading in textbooks; there is little or no evidence that it has spread to the research article. Is that, perhaps, an uptight genre? Anyway, we can further test out what Fowler said, and we quoted at the beginning concerning academic writing, and opine that it is not only a matter of trying "to sound chatty", though it may be a case of trying to be more "user-friendly".

Second, further study is needed on a much larger corpus to see whether any implicational scales on CF usage can be drawn up, such that we can predict that if one particular form exists in a genre, or at least a writer, we can say that others will be present, too. For example, might we be able to say that if a writer uses *'d (would)* we would expect also to find *'ll (will)* at some point?

Tim Austin and *The Times* wish to keep standards going. We ask, persistently, just where are they going? We are confident that they *are* going somewhere, for a language, of course, doesn't stand still.

Notes

1 For listing and discussion of these, see Zwicky 1970, 330-4.

2 However, there may be a relationship once more with phonology here. King (1970) has noted that "the contracted (or weakened or enclitic) form cannot be used at the end of a breath-group" (King 1970, 134). Many of the NPs in this set of examples are lengthy; cf. (9) above.

3 The significance of the exclamation mark at the end here is lost on the authors. Are we, then, showing our age? And if so, how?

4 The results of the Spearman rank correlation coefficient tests were as follows:

- for *The Guardian* leaders (1996/7), $r = -0.063$, $N = 83$, $p > 0.10$. The correlation is not significant;
- for *The Star* leaders (1996/7), $r = -0.096$, $N = 79$, $p > 0.10$; again, no significant correlation.

In both cases the tests were two-tailed.

Bibliography:

Aitchison, Jean: *Language Change: Progress or Decay?* 2nd edition. Cambridge, Cambridge University Press, 1991.

Close, R. A.: *A Reference Grammar for Students of English*. London, Longman, 1975.

Downes, William: *Language and Society.* London, Fontana, 1984.

Fowler, Roger: *Language In The News.* London, Routledge, 1991.

Hutton, Will: *The State To Come.* London, Vintage/*The Observer*, 1997

King, V.: "On blocking the rules for contraction in English." *Linguistic Inquiry*, Vol. I., 1970.

Leech, Geoffrey & Jan Svartvik: *A Communicative Grammar of English.* London, Longman, 1994.

Rivers, W. L. & A.W. Rodriguez: *A Journalist's Guide to Grammar and Style.* Boston, Allyn & Bacon, 1995.

Zwicky, Arnold: "Auxiliary Reduction in English". *Linguistic Inquiry*, Vol. I, 1970, 323-36.

APPENDIX 1 The Data Tables

(a) 1996/7	***Times***	7/10/96-30/4/97	***Guardian***	28/7/95-9/5/97	***Star***	27/7/95-19/6/97
	issues	*articles*	*issues*	*articles*	*issues*	*articles*
Leaders	17	51	30	83	27	79
Sport	6	51	4	51	10	73
Entertainment	6	27	5	19	17	36
(b) 1976				3-14/12/76		2/11-7/12/76
Leaders	–	–	10	30	15	17
Sport	–	–	–	–	11	14
Entertainment	–	–	–	–	10	19

Table 1: Data corpus

Total articles				
	Leaders	*Sport*	*Entertainment*	*Totals*
1996	213	175	82	470
1976	47	14	19	80

Table 2:

2-SAMPLE T-TESTS
(a) Leaders

	1996/7	1976
N	83	30
X (%)	9.88	2.44
SD	12.56	4.75
Range	Ø - 57.14 %	Ø - 22.22 %
t-value: 4.76 (p < 0.001)		

Table 3: Guardian leaders, 1996/7 and 1976

	1996/7	1976
N	79	17
X (%)	20.03	10.82
SD	22.57	10.73
Range	∅ - 85.71 %	∅ - 37.5 %
t-value: 2.52 (p < 0.5)		

Table 4: Star leaders 1996/7 & 1976

	GUARDIAN	*STAR*
N	83	79
X (%)	9.88	20.03
SD	12.56	22.57
t-value: 3.49 (p < 0.001)		

Table 5: Guardian and Star leaders, 1996/7

	GUARDIAN	*STAR*
N	30	17
X (%)	2.44	10.82
SD	4.75	10.73
dfs: 45		
t-value: 3.06 (p < 0.01)		

Table 6: Guardian and Star leaders, 1976
(b) Sport

	1996/7	1976
N	73	14
X (%)	29.44	18.51
SD	29.15	16.23
Range	∅ - 100 %	∅ - 46.66 %
t-value: 1.98 (p < 0.5)		

Table 7: Star sport, 1996/7 & 1976

	GUARDIAN	*STAR*
N	51	73
X (%)	14.84	29.44
SD	18.89	29.15
t-value: 3.35 (p < 0.001)		

Table 8: Guardian and Star sport, 1996/7

	TIMES	GUARDIAN
N	51	51
X (%)	12.42	14.84
SD	14.01	18.89
t-value: 0.73 (*not significant*)		

Table 9: Times and Guardian sport, 1996/7

	STAR	*TIMES*
N	73	51
X (%)	29.44	12.42
SD	29.15	14.01
t-value: 4.28 (p < 0.001)		

Table 10: Star and Times sport, 1996/7
(c) Entertainment

	1996/7	1976
N	36	19
X (%)	54.46	35.49
SD	23.54	26.82
Range	8.33 - 90.1 %	Ø - 80 %
dfs: 53		
t-value: 2.60 (p < 0.01)		

Table 11: Star entertainment, 1996/7 & 1976

	GUARDIAN	STAR
N	19	36
X (%)	45.25	54.46
SD	18.28	23.54
Range	∅ - 78.95 %	8.33 - 100 %
dfs: 53		
t-value: 1.60 (p < 0.10)		

Table 12: Guardian and Star entertainment, 1996/7

TIMES: GUARDIAN 1996/7		
	TIMES	GUARDIAN
N	27	19
X (%)	16.39	45.25
SD	21.17	18.28
Range	∅ - 64 %	∅ - 78.95 %
dfs: 44		
t-value: 4.63 (p < 0.001)		

Table 13: Times and Guardian entertainment, 1996/7

	TIMES	STAR
N	27	36
X (%)	16.39	54.46
SD	21.17	23.54
dfs: 61		
t-value: 6.72 (p < 0.001)		

Table 14: Times and Star entertainment, 1996/7
Guardian [1] Sheffield Star [2] Leaders; Star entertainment [3] 1996/7

Aux. Reduction.				Negative Contraction			
	[1]	[2]	[3]		[1]	[2]	[3]
it's	14	18	34	*don't*	20	8	24
that's	10	5	6	*doesn't*	5	2	5
there's	4	4	12	*can't*	16	6	6
pers.pron. + *'re*	2	4	17	*won't*	11	2	2
pers. pron. + *'d* (*had*)	2	2	2	*isn't*	9	3	9
pers. pron. + *'d* (*would*)	–	–	5				
pers. pron. + *'ll*	1	5	16	*aren't*	2	4	1
what's	3	–	2	*hasn't*	4	–	1
pers.pron./who + *'ve*	1	–	20	*haven't*	–	2	3
pers. pron. +'s (*be* cop.)	–	2	22	*hadn't*	–	–	1
pers. pron. + 's (*be* aux.)	–	–	8	*didn't*	2	1	9
let's	–	4	1	*wouldn't* 2	–	3	
's (has)	–	–	10	*wasn't*	1	–	2
				shouldn't 2	3	–	
				weren't	1	–	–
				couldn't 1	–	2	
				needn't	1	1	–
Totals	37	44	155		77	32	68

Table 15: Distribution of CFs: Negative and Auxiliary reductions

Notes to Table 15

1 Examples of *don't* include its use in both imperative and non-imperative uses. Together, these account for over a quarter (27.8 %) of all NCs.
2 In a partial study of the entertainment and sports articles in *The Times* and *The Guardian*, the totals were 44 NCs to 64 ARs in *The Guardian*, and 49 NCs to 96 ARs in *The Times.*
3 The count was based on the articles in each paper in which there was the greatest concentration of CFs: that is, 12 articles in *The Guardian*, and 15 in *The Times*, in the sports and entertainment genres.
4 Of NCs, *it's* accounts for over a quarter (28.9 %) of all occurrences. Included within this category are cases of *it's* + noun, *it's* + adjective and it's + PP (e.g. *It's out of the way*)

APPENDIX 2

CFs in *Times* leaders – the five examples

1. "If you ever go to Dolgellau / Don't stay at the Lion Hotel / For there's nothing to put in your bellau / and no one to answer the bell." ['Imperfect peace', 24/12/96]: a quote from a ditty, in direct speech.

2. "The old dog is alive. He's bloody alive." ['Heroes of the Deep': 3rd leader], 10/1/97: quote, direct speech.

3. "The play's the thing wherein to catch a new angle on the king" ['Queen Lear': 18/2/97: subtitle to leader; intertextual reference to 'Hamlet'.

4. Labour has thought it prudent since the last election to take as its motto "if you can't beat them, join them" ['Thin Red Line'], 3/3/97: quote; popular saying; direct speech.

Kristina Schneider, Rostock

Exploring the roots of popular English news writing
A preliminary report on a corpus-based project

1. Introduction

It is widely believed that popular English journalism started in the late 19th or early 20th centuries. It can be argued, however, that the roots of this new popular way of writing and designing newspapers go back as far as the 18th century.

The term ‘popular journalism’[1] (or ‘popular press’) can be understood in different ways. A common interpretation is to relate it to a segment of the readership of newspapers, namely the working class and lower middle class (Jucker, 1992: 48ff.). Historically, this view is linked up with studies concerning the growth of the reading public, the increase in literacy, the price of newspapers and the income of the potential readers (e.g. Williams 1961, Hollis 1970).

Yet apart from the definition in terms of readership, the term ‘popular journalism’ is also used to describe the newspaper itself, its content, layout and style. Features commonly attributed to popular journalism in this connection are the inclusion of more soft news (e.g. human interest stories, sensation and crime), the insertion of large headlines and numerous illustrations as well as a more speech-like and emotional use of language. Historical studies have been rare, especially with respect to style, and this, of course, is the motivation behind the proposed project. Since a detailed study of all three areas – content, layout and style – would go beyond the scope of this project, the first two criteria will only be glanced at while the third – and, so far, least examined – feature, the stylistic development, will be analysed more closely in the course of this paper.

Just by looking at the first criterion, namely the content of newspapers and its historical development, it becomes quite clear that there is less novelty in the new, popular content of late 19th century papers than has been claimed. The tendency to use fewer hard news items (e.g. politics and economy) and include more soft news (as described above) did not start in the late 19th century, but can be observed as early as the 18th century. Good candidates for this “lighter” content are the so-called cut-price papers (Harris 1938), illegal, unstamped newspapers that came into existence after the introduction of the First Stamp Act in 1712[2] and had become quite numerous in the 1730s. They were sold at prices well below the standard rate and provided detailed reports on crime, bizarre events, sexual and romantic happenings and the miscellaneous circumstances of low life. This tendency to include more soft news items was then continued in the 19th century, especially in the popular Sunday and evening press (Williams 1977, Lee 1976, Berridge 1978), and probably became most obvious towards the turn of the century.

Similar observations can be made when studying the layout development of newspapers. The main innovations that made papers more attractive are again attributed to the rise of a popular journalism in the late 19th century. Larger headlines, shorter paragraphs and an increasing use of illustrations are commonly viewed as characteristic signs of this new layout (Lee 1976). The development of these features, however, started as early as the 18th century. And again, as in the content development mentioned above, some of these features were introduced by the unstamped cut-price papers of the early 18th century. Since these newspapers were illegal, they depended on street-sale by newspaper hawkers. In order to make these papers more attractive, decorative titles and large pictorial headings with newspaper hawkers as their motif were used. Beside these unstamped cut-price papers, also some of the stamped full-priced newspapers of the 18th century occasionally made use of illustrations. Editions from *The London Evening Post* in 1733, for instance, added pictures to advertisements: a picture of a clock and cover of a book adorned the ads for a clock-maker and a newly published book respectively. In 19th century newspapers, this tendency to use more illustrations was continued. The layout of newspapers was further improved by the use of larger headlines and shorter paragraphs which helped to give the reader periodic relief from eyestrain. Thus, popular layout features that may have become more obvious in the late 19th and early 20th centuries can be traced back as far as the 18th century.

This report concentrates on the study of the third criterion, namely style, and its historical development. To provide a database for the stylistic analysis, a historical newspaper corpus is currently being assembled at Rostock University. The main characteristics of this corpus will be described in the following section.

2. Corpus Design

The Rostock corpus was started in June 1996 and is to be a collection of English newspapers from 1700 to the present in 30-year-intervals.[3] An average span of 30 years was chosen because it can be taken to represent roughly one generation, and newspaper language, as well as language in general, is not likely to change much faster than from one generation to another.

To ensure comparability, all samples are planned to have an equal sample size of 20,000 words. Although there is no such thing as the optimum sample size, the 20,000 word standard was chosen since experience with 20,000 word samples has shown that on the whole these are sufficiently large to provide statistically reliable information about the frequency of occurrence of most syntactic structures (Oostdijk 1988, de Haan 1992). A total corpus size of 600,000 words is to be achieved by the end of 1997.

As far as the content is concerned, only the prototypical news reports – i.e. foreign and home news written by newspaper staff – have been included in this corpus. There are several reasons for not analysing the whole content of these papers. Firstly, news reports as defined above have always been part of newspapers and thus are ideal for diachronic research. Special sections like the sports section were introduced later. Secondly, since different newspaper sections represent different registers by their use of language, concentrating on a certain text type, namely news, ensures the comparability of different samples. The later inclusion of other sections, for instance of sports (Wallace 1977), is likely to distort the overall research results for a newspaper. Last but not least, news reports have been chosen for this corpus because they are usually made up of running text, consisting predominantly of complete sentences; a necessary prerequisite for syntactic studies which will be part of this research. Other text types would not be as suitable for syntactic analysis because of their sketchiness. This, for example, applies to advertisements which – although they have always been part of newspapers and would thus be well-suited for diachronic research – often consist of incomplete sentences and rely largely on visual elements, two facts that are inappropriate for a syntactic analysis.

This corpus design distinguishes the Rostock corpus from another corpus in the field, namely the ZEN (Zurich English Newspaper) corpus collected by Udo Fries. The ZEN corpus is structured in closer ten year intervals and consists of complete newspapers, i.e. it assembles all the texts of a paper. So far, Fries has concentrated on newspapers from the mid-1660s to the end of the 18th century, though an extension up to the 20th century is envisaged (Fries 1994).

Since the aim of the Rostock corpus is to serve as a database for the study of the development of a popular way of news writing, it naturally concentrates on what is regarded as popular papers. For the purpose of comparing the style of popular and quality papers, however, the latter had to be included in the corpus, too. As far as the selection of individual newspapers is concerned, the original intention was to include newspapers that can be characterized as either popular or quality papers and were or have been in existence for a long time. The second criterion was based on the belief that diachronic variation can be best analysed when looking at the steady development of a particular newspaper; as we will see, this original conception had to be modified to a certain extent.

The total corpus is currently made up of three distinct corpus lines, namely two popular lines (down- and mid-market papers) and one quality line (up-market papers) for comparison (see figure 1).

year	corpus-line 1 ('down-market')	corpus-line 2 ('mid-market')	corpus-line 3 ('up-market')
1700	The Post-Man	The Evening Post	The London Gazette
1730	The London Post	The London Evening Post	The London Gazette
1760	Penny London Post	The London Evening Post	The London Gazette
1790/1800	The Sun	The London Evening Post	The Times
1830	The Sun	The Standard	The Times
1860	The Sun	The Evening Standard	The Times
1890/1900	The Daily Mirror	Daily Mail	The Times
1930	The Daily Mirror	Daily Mail	The Times
1960	The Daily Mirror	Daily Mail	The Times
1990/2000	The Daily Mirror	Daily Mail	The Times

Figure 1: A Historical Newspaper Corpus from 1700 to today

The designations 'down-, mid- and up-market' should be approached with some caution and have therefore been put in inverted commas in this figure. A relatively precise distinction between down-market papers (line 1), mid-market papers (line 2), and up-market papers (line 3) can only be applied for the **20th century** with *The Daily Mirror*, *Daily Mail* and *The Times* as typical representatives (e.g. Jucker 1992).

For the 18th and 19th centuries, however, such a classification poses some problems because the literature does not characterize newspapers before 1896 in terms of 'popular' and 'quality' papers, let alone down-, mid- and up-market papers. Thus, criteria like the distinction between official government newspapers and non-official ones, between cut-price and full-priced papers (Harris 1938), their circulation (Sutherland 1935) and a content analysis (percentage of hard and soft news) have been used to fit the older papers into these categories.

As far as the **18th century** is concerned, corpus-line 1 is documented by one of the circulation leaders, the non-official penny paper *The Post-Man*, and two cut-price papers, *The London Post* and *Penny London Post.*

These relatively 'cheap' papers have been chosen because they are likely to have had a more popular content and style than other more official newspapers at that time. Corpus-line 2 for the 18th century is represented by two evening papers, *The Evening Post* (the first evening paper, cf. Linton/Boston 1987) and *The London Evening Post*. The idea behind this choice was that evening papers – like Sunday papers – may have been written in a more popular way. One of the most official newspapers of that time was the full-priced government paper *The London Gazette*, the oldest surviving London paper (Williams 1977), which was regarded as a suitable representative of a quality paper and was thus chosen to represent corpus-line 3.

For the **19th century**, *The Sun* newspaper was selected to represent corpus-line 1. Although it has nothing to do with the modern *Sun* newspaper and very little information on the background of this paper has been available so far, it may probably be regarded as one of the more popular newspapers of that time because of its content. Further investigations into the history of this paper are still ongoing. Corpus-line 2 concentrates again on evening papers, namely *The London Evening Post* and *The (Evening) Standard*, and corpus-line 3 is represented from 1800 onwards by *The Times*.

As far as the collection of newspaper material is concerned, one of the greatest problems is the availability of popular papers. The majority of 18th, 19th and 20th century newspapers preserved as originals, on microfilm or on CD are quality papers. This is not surprising since these are the official papers consisting mainly of hard news and facts which historians consider worth preserving. Thus, only very few of the known illegal, unstamped, cut-price papers of the 18th century are available. Our samples of these papers as well as all the other 18th century newspapers were taken from the Burney Collection of newspapers (British Library). The 19th as well as most of the 20th century papers used in this corpus were taken from the newspaper collection at the Colindale Newspaper Library. For the 1990 texts, original issues of *The Daily Mirror*, *Daily Mail* and *The Times* were used, and preliminary samples of the London *Times* from 1800 to 1960 were taken from *The Times* CD ROM.

The only texts available in computerized form were the *Times* articles on CD ROM as well as three samples from *The London Gazette* kindly provided by Udo Fries (ZEN corpus). All other newspaper material had to be copied from the originals or from microfilm and afterwards be typed into the computer since scanning proved impossible.

All newspaper samples have been given a code number, starting with 10000 and ending with 39000, in intervals of 1000. All codes starting with 1 (i.e. 10000, 11000, 12000, 13000 14000 15000, 16000, 17000, 18000 and 19000) stand for newspapers that belong to corpus-line 1, codes starting with 2 represent newspapers of corpus-line 2, and those starting with 3 belong to corpus-line 3. In addition, the lines of each sample text have been numbered, so that any word can be given a clear reference as to which corpus-line, which newspaper, which year and which line number it belongs to.

The corpus as described above, however, is not the optimal solution yet. It is to be extended and further improved by the addition of other newspapers. First investigations have shown that some newspapers are less suitable than others. In particular, there have been some problems with text samples taken from other collections. This is natural since every collection is guided by certain principles. The texts on the *Times* CD, for instance, have not been selected for linguistic analysis but with regard to their political and historical relevance. Thus, only reports of major events have been included. These texts, however, cannot be regarded as representative samples of the whole newspaper, considering the percentage of home and foreign news and other factors. Moreover, the number of texts available for one year – especially for early samples – is limited. Thus, it was necessary to go back to the original newspapers and type sample texts into the computer as well.

The incorporation of ZEN samples from *The London Gazette* (corpus-line 3, 18th century) did not turn out to be easy either. As mentioned above, the ZEN courpus includes all the texts of the processed newspapers. In contrast, the aim of the Rostock corpus is to concentrate on prototypical editorial texts, i.e. on home and foreign news. The problem with *The London Gazette* is that its content changed in the course of time. While in 1701, it still contained a considerable number of home and foreign news, in 1731 and 1761, almost 90 % of the paper was filled with other text types, mostly government proclamations and addresses. Thus, only a small percentage of the ZEN samples could be used for our purpose. Additional material is being collected.

3. The Changing Style in News Writing – Two Samples

Questions of style and stylistic change are quite difficult to tackle; one reason for this is the proliferation of terms that has accompanied the development of stylistics in the last few decades. There are, no doubt, many very interesting approaches to style, but a great number of them offer definitions that are difficult, if not impossible, to work with. The aim here is to find characteristic stylistic features that can be analyzed computationally or manually and then be compared both synchronically and diachronically.

In this, the present study follows previous empirical investigations into newspaper language or special types of it,[4] for instance sports reporting,[5] all of which have analyzed selected grammatical and/or lexical features. The most comprehensive study with regard to the number of features has probably been Biber/Finnegan's (1992) analysis and comparison of the development of five written and speech-based genres (or registers).[6] It is also one of the few diachronic studies that have been carried out in this field. Their previous analysis (1989) of the development of three written genres – essays, fiction, and personal letters – from the late 17th century to the present had already revealed the following interesting results: With respect to the chronology, all genres tend to follow the same general pattern: 17th-and 18th century texts tend to be moderately or extremely literate, with a transition towards more oral styles in the 19th century, and the development of a distinctly oral characterization in the modern period. With respect to an overall analysis of style, all genres have been drifting towards more "oral" characterizations. That is, across the four centuries, all genres have tended to become more involved, more situated, and less abstract in style.[7]

This proposed study of journalistic style will make use of Biber/Finnegan's parameters as far as possible, in particular regarding their parameters for informational vs. involved production as well as abstract style. The study of these predominantly grammatical features will then be extended by an analysis of lexical features.

Before talking about special aspects of this analysis, however, two samples of newspaper language from the mid 18th and late 20th centuries will be presented to give a first idea of how the style of English news writing has changed in the course of time. Each sample consists of one soft news item (crime/sensation) and one hard news item (politics).

The London Evening-Post.
From TUESDAY, January 2, to THURSDAY, January 4, 1733.

21051 IRELAND.
21052 Dublin, Dec. 26. On Sunday last a most inhuman and barbarous Murder
21053 was committed near Oxmantown-Green on William Dixi, Esq; Lieutenant
21054 in Brigadier Sutton's Regiment of Foot, and Son to Capt. Dixi of
21055 Drogheda. He was shot thro' the Head, stabb'd in the Breast, and had
21056 his Throat cut in a most horrid Manner, and in that Condition found laid
21057 down on the Green near St. Paul's Church, with the Cap of a Woman's
21058 Cloak put under his Head, a charg'd Pistol in his Bosom, and a discharg'd
21059 one in his Hand. He was discover'd first by a Milk Girl, who ran for Mr.
21060 Sharp the Sexton; and he, with the Constable of the Watch, took care of
21061 what Money &c. was found about him, which was so considerable as to
21062 make it believ'd he was not set upon by Robbers; neither was there so
21063 great an Effusion of Blood near him as would have been shed had he
21064 fallen there when he received his Wounds.

From SATURDAY, January 6, to TUESDAY, January 9, 1733.

21325 Venice, Jan. 3. Advices from Constantinople assure us, that Thamas Kan,
21326 General of the Persian Forces, being inform'd that the Sophy inclin'd to
21327 make Peace with the Turks, and had already given private Orders for that
21328 Purpose, march'd to Ispahan at the Head of 80,000 Men, secur'd the
21329 Sophy and having put out his Eyes, proclaim'd his Son (an Infant of a
21330 few Months old) King of Persia. The same Letters add, that the Bashaw
21331 of Babylon having sent for a considerable Succour of Men, Money, and
21332 Provisions, to defend himself against the expected Return of Thamas
21333 Kan, the Ottoman Porte had immediately sent him 3000 Purses, and given
21334 Orders for Troops and Provisions to follow as soon as possible.

The Daily Mirror
May 8, 1996

19650 THE LAW CANNOT STOP HIM
19651 HE IS still free to roam the streets, untouched by the law. He still leers
19652 at his prey several times a day.
19653 So we decided to give him a taste of his own medicine. We stalked the
19654 stalker.
19655 Steward Young is 22. He ought to be enjoying his young life.
19656 Yet he has damned himself to being an object of hatred and fear in his
19657 own town and is driven by an obsession for a married mother 24 years his
19658 senior.
19659 He has been arrested time and time again. He has even tried to take his
19660 own life.
19661 Yet still he cannot keep away. He is driven by the obsession which led
19662 him to smear blood from his own wrists on the front of the woman's shop.
19663 His victim is 46-year-old Jenny Dykes, partner in a wool shop in Essex
19664 town centre.

19225 COMMENT
19226 Giving us work, not welfare
19227 Chris Smith reveals a philosophy which combines common sense with
19228 a bold vision.
19229 He knows it is as important to get away from old Labour ideas as from
19230 current Tory ones.
19231 Under this government we are paying the highest-ever taxes because we
19232 have the worst-ever unemployment record.
19233 Getting people back to work takes them out of state benefits and turns
19234 them into taxpayers. That is the way forward. For Labour and for Britain.
19235 Making the Welfare State truly supportive of those who really need it.

Probably the most striking difference between these 18th and 20th century samples of news writing is the use of very long sentences in the earlier newspaper in contrast to the use of short, sometimes even incomplete sentences in the modern paper (e.g. 19234:[8] *For Labour and for Britain.*).

The **average sentence length** of the two *London Evening-Post* (1733) samples presented is about 56 words, that of the two *Daily Mirror* (1996) samples is about 12 words. These, of course, are extremes, but they represent a general trend in news writing to reduce sentence length. To find out when and in which papers this tendency began is one of the intentions of this study.

The next step will be to look at the historial development of linguistic features that are responsible for creating long sentences. Major features are **sentence complexity** (co- and subordination expressed by conjunctions, e.g. 21060: *and* he ... took care ... , or participles, e.g. 21326: *being* inform'd that ...) and **noun phrase complexity** (extended pre- and postmodifications, e.g. 21053/5: William Dixi, *Esq; Lieutenant in Brigadier Sutton's Regiment of Foot, and Son to Capt. Dixi of Drogheda*).

The comparison of the texts also shows that the number of **passive** verb forms used in the early newspaper exceeds that of the modern paper (21052/3: a ... Murder *was committed*, 21055: He *was shot* ..., 21059: He *was discover'd* first by a Milk Girl, 21062: he *was* not *set* upon by Robbers). Beside the preference of the active voice (19651/2: He *is* still free ... He still *leers* at his prey), modern papers use more **first person pronouns** (19653/4: *we* decided to give him a taste ... *We* stalked the stalker.). The proposed analysis should show how the use of these stylistic features has changed in news writing over the centuries.

Apart from an analysis of the above grammatical features, it will also be worth looking at some lexical features and their development, e.g. **lexical diversity**, word length, the use of core vs. non-core vocabulary, the use of metaphors (19651/2: He still *leers at his prey*, 19653: So we decided to *give him a taste of his own medicine*), the use of superlatives (21052: a *most* inhuman and barbarous Murder, 19231/2: the *highest-ever* taxes ... the *worst-ever* unemployment record), nominalizations, descriptive speech act verbs, creative word play (19653/4: We *stalked* the *stalker*) and collocations.

Last but not least, it will be interesting to study **headlines** in terms of their development; in our two examples they range from mere headings which provide only general information (21051/2: IRELAND. *Dublin, Dec.* 26.) to proper headlines that give a detailed description regarding the content of the following article (19650: THE LAW CANNOT STOP HIM). A further aspect to be investigated is the apparent development from nominal to more verbal headlines, which can also be observed in the above mentioned examples from lines 21051/2 and 19650.

Other striking features of old newspapers, such as different spelling conventions (e.g. 21055: *thro'*, *stabb'd*) and capitalization of nouns (e.g. 21055/6: *H*ead, *B*reast, *Th*roat), will not be pursued further since they are probably less relevant for a characterization of journalistic style.

In the following section, some of the stylistic features chosen for analysis will be discussed in more detail and first findings will be presented and evaluated.

4. *Features of Journalistic Style – Aspects of Analysis*

The first part of this section provides an overview of the stylistic features of sentence length, sentence complexity, noun phrase complexity, passive constructions and personal pronouns, lexical diversity and word length as well as headlines. The rationale behind the selection of these features and the methods planned for their analysis will be explained.

Starting from modern journalistic handbooks and their view of what good news writing is today, the corpus analysis will focus on the historical development of these stylistic features and on finding out when and by which papers stylistic innovations were introduced. The aim is to investigate if characteristics of popular journalism can be found before the end of the 19th century. The second part will present and discuss first results.

4.1. *Overview of Features*

Sentence Length

Sentence length is defined as the average number of words per sentence in a text, which can be determined by computational analysis. In order to get reliable results, however, only the news texts will be analysed; non-sentence material like headlines will be excluded. This, however, does not mean that incomplete sentences within news reports will be left out (cp. 19332: *For Labour and for Britain.*).

Stylistic handbooks advise the use of short sentences in order to make newspaper texts clear, concise and easy to read (e.g. Handel 1962:69), or in William Strunk's words: "Vigorous writing is concise. A sentence should contain no unnecessary words, a paragraph no unnecessary sentences, for the same reason that a drawing should have no unnecessary lines and a machine no unnecessary parts" (Strunk/White 1979: 23).

An average sentence length of about 20 words is recommended (Handel 1962: 85). Readability tests have shown that this is about standard for reading ease. If the average is more than 25 words per sentence, the reader is likely to desert the paper. However, this does not mean that newspapers should never use sentences with more than 20 words.[9] Variation in sentence length keeps writing from becoming boring. Yet in our context, it is the average sentence length which is important for giving us insight as to how sentence length has changed from 1700 to today. Starting from the assumption that there has been a general tendency to reduce sentence length, the study will examine if the more popular papers have always been more radical in this respect.

One explanation for the general tendency to reduce sentence length could be that in the course of time newspaper language – and written communication in general – has moved closer to the spoken word (Biber/Finnegan 1989, Bagnall 1993, Warner 1961).[10] Naturally, it is easier to compose a long and complex sentence in planned written discourse than in speech. Thus, shorter sentences could be taken as a characteristic for the more speech-like style of writing in modern newspapers.

Moreover, the change in the reading public over the last three centuries could be viewed as a factor that has led or even forced journalists to produce texts that are easier to read. A "fairly consistent body of educated readers" in the 18th century (Warner 1961: 155) has developed into a mass readership of all classes in our century. Nowadays, all kinds of different people read newspapers, and the papers have had to adjust their styles to this fact.

In addition, shorter sentences are not only easier but also faster to read. Since the time people can spend on reading newspapers seems to be decreasing whereas the number of pages of newspapers is increasing, the speed of reading becomes another factor to be considered.

Sentence Complexity

Sentence complexity is closely related to sentence length since short sentences will naturally show less complexity than longer ones. Sentence complexity is to be analysed in terms of coordination and subordination expressed by conjunctions and participles. For this syntactic analysis, "problem-oriented tagging" (de Haan 1984) of the corpus is necessary. This term suggests that not all of the language material in the corpus is tagged, but only those parts that are relevant for the project, in this case, conjunctions and participles.

Modern journalistic handbooks recommend, above all, the use of clear, and thus not too complex sentences. "The real movement in the writing", states Hodgson (1993: 34), "comes from sentence construction. [...] Right words allied to fluent construction can give a sense of clarity, pace and commitment that carries the reader with it and makes the best feature writing [...] compulsive reading."

As the sample from *The London Evening Post* (1733) has shown, numerous conjunctions and participles were used in 18th century newspapers to construct very complex sentences. The corpus analysis will be used to show how sentence complexity has changed in news writing from 1700 to today. In addition, the study will investigate when and in which papers the tendency to use simpler sentences started.

Noun Phrase Complexity

Noun phrase complexity is to be analysed in terms of pre- and postmodification of noun phrases (Jucker 1992). For the syntactic analysis of noun phrases, problem-oriented tagging is necessary as well.

Newspaper language in general is characterized by much more complex pre- and post-modification than normally used in written and spoken communication. Previous studies have shown that just over half of all modifiers used in modern newspapers are premodifiers (Jucker 1992). From a diachronic point of view, it can be assumed that a tendency to use post-modification[11] was replaced by a tendency to use more premodifiers.[12] The study will investigate how the percentages of pre- and postmodifications used to specify noun phrases have changed in the course of time and how they differ in popular and quality papers.

Passive Constructions and Personal Pronouns

The percentage of passive sentences in a text can be determined by computational analysis without previous tagging of the corpus.

Journalistic handbooks caution against the overuse of passive constructions. According to Waterhouse (1981: 93), "the place for the passive voice is Whitehall, not Fleet Street". He goes on arguing that the active voice is preferable for newspapers because it answers questions, whereas the passive voice often sounds as if it had something to hide because the agent responsible for a certain action can be omitted. Thus, a tendency to avoid passive sentences goes hand in hand with the tendency to make news writing as clear as possible.

In Biber's study (1988), passives have been taken as one of the most important surface markers of detached style that stereotypically characterizes writing. Since the main purpose of earlier newspapers was to inform rather than to entertain, a detached, objective style of news writing was appropriate. With the quantitative and qualitative change in readership and the appearance of other media as competitors, journalists had to find ways to make their newspapers more attractive and more readable. Thus, the tendency to use fewer passive forms can also be seen in connection with the tendency to use a more lively and more involved style in news writing, a style that shows commitment and carries the reader with it.

The corpus analysis is to reveal how the percentage of passive sentences used in news reports has changed from 1700 to the present and whether popular and quality papers show any differences in this respect.

Another interesting aspect in this context is the use of personal pronouns. It can be assumed that active sentences promote the use of first and second person pronouns, whereas the passive voice is likely to co-occur with third person pronouns. The analysis should show how the use of personal pronouns has changed in time and how it differs depending on the type of newspaper.

Lexical Diversity and Word Length

Lexical diversity can be measured by the type/token ratio, i.e. the relation between the number of 'types' (different lexical items) and the total number of words in a text. This ratio can be determined by computational analysis.

Popular newspapers are sometimes criticised as having "a limited vocabulary" (Lee 1976: 130), i.e. a low degree of lexical diversity. Comparative studies of modern popular and quality papers have shown that popular papers use a relatively small number of stereotypical words, whereas quality papers are characterized by a larger range of vocabulary (Jucker 1992). Thus, it can be assumed that lexical diversity has decreased in the course of time, especially in popular papers.

Another lexical feature attributed to popular journalistic style is the use of shorter words. Thus, word length has also been selected for a diachronic and synchronic analysis of this corpus. There is good reason to assume that 18th century papers use longer words than 19th and 20th century papers, which are more concerned with reading ease.

Word length is defined as the average number of letters per word which can be calculated by the computer. But, perhaps surprisingly, a first analysis showed that the average word length of all texts, no matter from what period or what kind of paper, was almost the same. One explanation for this could be that the number of short function words (prepositions, conjunctions, pronouns, etc.)[13] distorts the average word length. Thus, a second analysis has been started to calculate the word length of lexical words (open classes) only.

Headlines

Last but not least, headlines were chosen for the analysis of this corpus. The underlying hypothesis was that headlines should have become more detailed and specific in the course of time, and that the practice of exclusively using nominal headlines should give way to a tendency to use verbal headlines as well (Simon-Vandenbergen 1981). A first qualitative analysis was carried out manually and will be presented in the following section together with the findings on sentence length.

4.2. First results

Part two of this section is to present and discuss first results. Since a considerable effort has gone into the compilation of the corpus, the analysis has so far been restricted to pilot investigations in some of the fields. Two features of journalistic style, namely the diachronic development of sentence length and headlines have been selected for closer discussion in this paper. Between them they represent the two possibilities of quantitative and qualitative analyses.

Sentence Length

One of the most striking features of 18th century newspapers – as demonstrated in the sample text above – is their use of long sentences. An analysis was carried out to determine how long the average sentence length in earlier newspapers was, and when and in which papers the tendency to reduce sentence length started. First findings are presented in figure 2.

Figure 2 not only indicates that there is an overall trend towards shorter sentence length, but also that this tendency is indeed more pronounced in corpus-line 1.

With the exception of the 1830 sample, corpus-line 1 shows a clear, general tendency to reduce sentence length. From 1800 to 1830, however, there is a slight increase. This may be due to idiosyncracies of the paper representing this period (*The Sun*). A closer examination of the individual sample reveals that two extensive reports have unusually long sentences and thus distort the overall results. This example shows that the principle of choosing one newspaper to represent a corpus-line and a certain period is not altogether convincing and had to be modified. As a consequence, a larger number of newspapers is currently being included in this corpus.

The findings for corpus-line 3 should not be regarded as final results either. This has to do with the fact that all samples from this line (with the exception of the 1996 *Times*) have been taken from other collections of newspaper texts. The samples from *The London Gazette* were provided by Fries' ZEN corpus; samples from *The Times* were taken from the

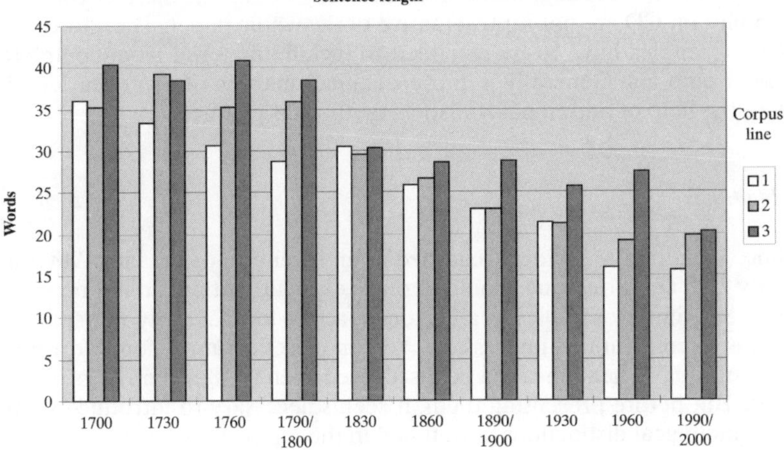

Figure 2:

Times CD. As mentioned before in connection with questions of corpus design, each collection is naturally guided by certain principles, and the principles for text selection in the ZEN and TIMES collections were different from the principles of this corpus.

As for *The London Gazette*, a large part of the content had to be deleted from the original samples since the Rostock corpus concentrates on home and foreign news. Thus, the body of material left for analysis was not large enough for a statistically relevant comparison.[14] A comparative analysis of the average sentence length of all material included in *The London Gazette* proved that different text types are characterized by markedly different averages in sentence length. In 1730, for instance, the average sentence length for home and foreign news in this newspaper was 38.4; the average sentence length of all texts, however, was about 50 words. This difference is caused by the fact that the predominant text types in the *London Gazette* editions from 1730 (and 1760) are proclamations and addresses which are characterized by very long sentences.

As far as *The Times* is concerned, the 1890/1900 and 1960 samples do not show a clear tendency to reduce sentence length. The most obvious reduction of sentence length occurred between 1960 and 1990/2000. This result is especially interesting in comparison with popular papers which show a radical reduction in sentence length much earlier. In general, the average sentence length of the *Times* samples is lower than expected, although it still proves to be higher than in the popular papers of the respective periods.[15] As suggested above, this may be due to the fact that the samples on CD are not representative of the whole paper. Therefore, the *Times* samples have to be extended to include material from complete *Times* editions. Generally, a more detailed analysis of sentence length with the help of additional statistical methods is planned.

Headlines

Since headlines are widely regarded as an invention of the late 19th and early 20th centuries, one should perhaps expect that they do not occur in the 18th century samples at all. Indeed, a first look at early newspapers seems to confirm this impression. Yet, on closer scrutiny, some forerunners of today's headlines can be discovered even in 18th century newspapers. But before presenting them, it seems necessary to introduce some terminological distinctions as outlined in the figure 3.

(A) PORT NEWS (C) Rome, Dec. 21. (D) PART-TIME TORIES MAKE
(B) LONDON OVER £2m ON THE SIDE

Figure 3: Headline Terminology and Examples

The main distinction is between *headings*, a category which Simon-Vandenbergen (1981) and Garst/Bernstein (1982) call "labels", and *headlines. Section headings* describe the general content of a whole section of the newspaper and may refer to several reports either on the same topic (A) or from the same region (B). Their main function is to facilitate orientation for the reader. *Report headings*, on the other hand, give some general information concerning the following report. The earliest report headings consisted of a geographical name and date only (C). In contrast to these general headings, a typical *headline* provides the reader with quite detailed information on the content of the report following (D).

Apart from this classification the pilot study also makes use of accepted terminology to describe the structure of headlines. A *single deck heading/headline* consists of only one deck (or line) (Simon-Vandenbergen 1981), whereas *multi-deck headings/headlines* consist of more than one. Similarly, headings and headlines can occupy one column (*single column headings/headlines*, Hodgson 1993) or can be spread across more than one column (*multi-column headings/headlines*, also called *cross-heads*).

18th century

As already indicated, newspapers in the 18th century contained a limited number of section and report headings. They usually appeared in the simplest form, namely as single deck and single column headings. Sometimes, report headings were not even written in a separate line. Instead, the report started in the same line and was separated from the heading by a full stop only. Compare the following examples:

section headings
(1) LONDON (*The Penny London Post* 1733)
(2) GREAT BRITAIN (*The London Post* 1723)
(3) PORT NEWS (*The Penny London Post* 1733)
(4) Bankrupts since our last List (*The Penny London Post* 1733)
(5) Disasters and Casualties this Week (*The London Evening Post* 1733)

report headings
(6) *Rome, Dec. 21* (*London Gazette* 1700)
(7) *From the* French *Camp near* Legnano, *June 23* (*London Gazette* 1700)

headlines
(8) The Eating Taylor (*The London Post* 1723).
(9) NON-EXPORTATION of WOOL (*The London Evening Post* 1782)

The first real section headings (1-5) consisted of single or extended noun phrases. It is not unlikely that forerunners of these section headings developed out of the first sentence of an article. An example of such a forerunner would be: *Yesterday arrived Two* Holland *Mails, which bring the following Advices* (*The London Post* 1700). Here we still have a complete sentence which is marked off from the following articles by a blank line. This sentence appears in every issue of the paper and always occupies the same spot. The experienced reader expects news from a certain source at this place of the paper and thus, the function of this sentence, namely orientation, is similar to that of the section headings.

The earliest report headings usually consisted of a geographical name and date only. They could appear in very short and simple (6) or longer and more descriptive variants (7).

The most interesting examples in the corpus are, of course, the early instances of headlines, starting with (8) "The Eating Taylor", used in *The London Post* of 1723. The report that followed described how a man called Taylor wagered at a club-feast that after having eaten two large fowls, he could eat another one. Despite his trying hard, he finally gave up and lost the bet. An example from the second half of the 18th century is

(9) NON-EXPORTATION of WOOL (*The London Evening Post* 1782). Both examples are nominal headlines.

A comparison of the early newspapers in this corpus reveals that official papers like *The London Gazette* (corpus-line 3) had the fewest and least specific headings. The number of section headings was very limited; their report headings seldom provided more information than references to place and date. In contrast, more popular papers like *The London Post* and *The Penny London Post* (line 1) and *The London Evening Post* (line 2) show more numerous and more informative section and report headings. Not surprisingly, the first real headlines appear in these papers.

19th century

Newspapers in the 19th century pursued the editorial policies introduced by the more popular 18th century papers: the number of section headings and headlines as well as the amount of information contained in them increased steadily. Their form, however, remained relatively simple: section headings and headlines still appeared in single decks and single columns. Practically all of them were still nominal. Report headings did not occur any longer. Their function was taken over by the more informative headlines. Compare the following examples:

section headings
(10) FOREIGN INTELLIGENCE
(11) POLICE INTELLIGENCE
(12) UNIVERSITY INTELLIGENCE
(13) HUNTING INTELLIGENCE
(14) BIRTHS
(15) MARRIED
(16) DIED (all from *The Sun* 1830)

headlines
(17) CAPTURE OF THE SPANISH FRIGATES AT BARCELONA (*The Sun* 1801)
(18) SATANIC INTERRUPTION OF A ROBBERY (*The Sun* 1830)
(19) DEATH OF MRS. WASHINGTION (*The Sun* 1830)
(20) ATTEMPTED MURDER THROUGH JEALOUSY (*The Evening Standard* 1860)

As the examples (10-16) show, section headings in 19th century newspapers are numerous and informative, thus allowing the readers to find special sections of the newspaper more easily and more quickly.

As far as headlines (17-20) are concerned, they became more elaborate, in particular through the addition of prepositional phrases. A comparison of the different corpus-lines shows that in the 19th century the more popular papers were still ahead of quality papers by using more informative headlines and, consequently, by being more reader-friendly.

20th century

In 20th century newspapers, the importance of section headings decreased markedly. They either disappeared or became reduced to some easily overlooked words on top of the pages. Most attention was and is still given to headlines. At the end of the 19th and beginning of the 20th centuries, popular papers like *The Daily Mirror* introduced a further innovation, namely a new look of headlines which meets today's standards. Compare:

headlines

(21) HOSPITAL ROMANCE
Ward Sister and Dean's Daughter Marries Hospital Porter

(22) **STILL NO REPLY**
Japan completes Her Fortnight's Wait
OMINOUS OUTLOOK
Japanese Squadron May Seize Masampho.
(both from *The Daily Mirror* 1904)

The traditional single deck / single column headings turned into heavier, more striking multi-deck / multi-column headlines. Stories with sizeable headlines were now allowed to cross the page in several 'legs', resulting in a change from 'vertical' to 'horizontal layout' (Hodgson, 1993). With the increased number of decks and columns used by headlines, the amount of information contained in these headlines increased as well.

Another new feature of these headlines is their tendency to become more verbal (Simon-Vandenbergen, 1981) which can be observed in both examples. Compare: (21) "Ward Sister and Dean's Daughter Marries Hospital Porter" as well as (22) "Japan completes Her Fortnight's Wait" and "Japanese Squadron May Seize Masampho".

Again, it is not surprising that popular papers like *The Daily Mirror* took the lead while quality papers lagged behind, preferring to stay with the traditional. In the case of *The Times*, the real changes in the style and design of headlines did not start before the later decades of this century.

5. Conclusion and Outlook

It seems that the corpus-based approach presented here is a feasible way to trace the beginnings of popular journalistic style. The idea of organizing the corpus in three corpus lines, each represented by at least two newspapers, should provide a sound basis for the study. Of the few aspects analyzed in this pilot project, the quantitative study of sentence length has shown that the overall decline in sentence length has always been pioneered by the more popular papers. The qualitative study of headline developments indicates that again the popular papers have always been ahead of the quality papers. Both findings support the assumption that popular and quality papers can be distinguished before the late 19th century and that some roots of popular journalistic style go back to the 18th century.

Notes

1 Another term that has been used to describe the changes affecting newspapers round the turn of the century is 'New Journalism' (Lee 1976: 117ff.). But since this term has been interpreted in very different ways and does not seem to be restricted to the popular press, it will not be used in this study.

2 With the First Stamp Act in 1712, a stamp tax for newspapers was introduced. The loopholes in the act, however, stimulated important developments in cut-price newspaper publication. From 1717 an increasing number of unstamped papers began to appear. Following the dramatic boom that began in the mid 1730s, the number of cut-price papers was reduced by the middle of the following decade (Harris 1938: 21ff.).

3 In some cases, the intervals of 30 years could not be kept exactly because some newspapers were not available for a certain year. In those cases, the closest available newspapers have been chosen, e.g. texts from the 1733 *London Evening Post* were taken for the 1730 period. A more general deviation from the 30-year intervals concerns the turn of the centuries where a larger interval, i.e. up to 40 years, was chosen to facilitate a comparison between the centuries.

4 Crystal/Davy (1969), Rydén (1975), Lüger (1995), Carter (1988), Bell (1991), Diller (1993).

5 Wallace (1977), Ferguson (1983), Ghadessy (1988).

6 In this study, Biber/Finnegan supplemented their previous analysis of three written genres with an analysis of two speech-like genres written for spoken delivery. The term genre is used in the same sense as register (Biber/Finnegan 1992: 688f.).

7 Biber (1988) introduced three dimensions for stylistic analysis: Dimension A (Informational versus Involved Production), Dimension B (Elaborated versus Situation-Dependent Reference) and Dimension C (Abstract Style). Linguistic features relevant for these dimensions include word length, type/token ratio, 1st and 2nd person pronouns (Dimension A) and passives (Dimension C).

8 The original numbering of the corpus was used.

9 Handel (1962: 85) remarks in this context: "Some 60-word sentences are clearer than 'A rose is a rose is a rose'", a statement by the American writer Gertrude Stein (1874-1946).

10 Biber (1988) has used sentence length as a criterion to differentiate written and spoken communication.

11 see sample from *The London Evening Post* (1733) e.g. line 21053/5: William Dixi, *Esq; Lieutenant in Brigadier Sutton's Regiment of Foot, and Son to Capt. Dixi of Drogheda.*

12 see sample from *The Daily Mirror* (1996), e.g. line 19663: *46-year-old* Jenny Dykes.

13 Figures could also be responsible for distorting overall results because the computer counts them as short words.

14 The 1730 and 1760 samples from *The London Gazette* consisted of about 2000 words, whereas all other samples in this analysis contained 10000 words. Additional material will be provided as soon as possible.

15 The only exception is the year 1830, where the samples from *The Sun* and *The Times* have almost the same average sentence length. This, however, was caused by the unusually high average for *The Sun* (see above explanation).

Bibliography

Bagnall, Nicholas: *Newspaper language.* Oxford, 1993.

Bell, Allan: *The Language of News Media.* Oxford, 1991.

Berridge, Virginia: "Popular Sunday papers and mid-Victorian society". – In George Boyce et al. (Eds.): *Newspaper History from the seventeenth century to the present day.* Beverly Hills, California, 1978, pp. 247-264.

Biber, Douglas: *Variation across speech and writing.* Cambridge, 1988.

Biber, Douglas & Edward Finnegan: "Drift in the evolution of English style: A history of three genres", *Language* 65, 1989, 487-517.

---; "The linguistic evolution of five written and speech-based genres from the 17th to the 20th centuries". – In Matti Rissanen et al. (Eds.): *History of Englishes.* Berlin, 1992, pp. 688-704.

Carter, Ronald: "Front pages: lexis, style and newspaper reports". – In Mohsen Ghadessy (Ed.): 1988, pp. 8-16.

Crystal, David & Derek Davy: *Investigating English Style.* London, 1969.

Diller, Hans-Jürgen et al.: *Practical stylistics: British columnists*, (anglistik und englischunterricht 51). Heidelberg, 1993.

Ferguson, C. A.: "Sports announcer talk: syntactic aspects of register variation", *Language in Society* 12, 1983, 153-172.

Fries, Udo: "ZEN – Zurich English Newspaper Corpus". – In Merja Kytö, Matti Rissanen & Susan Wright (Eds.): *Corpora across the centuries – Proceedings of the First International Colloquium on English Diachronic Corpora, St Catharine's College Cambridge, 25-27 March 1993*, Amsterdam/Atlanta, 1994, pp.17-18.

Garst, Robert E. & Theodore Bernstein: *Headlines and deadlines.* New York, 1982.

Ghadessy, Mohsen: "The language of written sports commentary: soccer – a description". – In Mohsen Ghadessy (Ed.): 1988, pp. 17-51.

--- (Ed.): *Registers of Written English. Situational Factors and Linguistic Features*, London, 1988.

de Haan, Pieter: "Problem-oriented tagging of English corpus data". – In Jan Aarts & Willem Meijs (Eds.): *Corpus linguistics. Recent developments in the use of computer corpora in English language research.* Amsterdam, 1984.

---: "The Optimum corpus sample size?". – In Gerhard Leitner (Ed.): *New Directions in English Language Corpora. Methodology, Results, Software Developments.* Berlin/New York, 1992, pp. 3-19.

Handel, Siegfried (Ed.): *Modern Journalism.* New York/Toronto/London, 1962.

Harris, Michael: *London newspapers in the age of Walpole.* London, 1938.

Hodgson, F. W.: *Modern Newspaper Practice. A primer on the press.* 3rd ed., Oxford/London, 1993.

Hollis, Patricia: *The Pauper Press: A Study in Working-Class Radicalism of the 1830s.* Oxford/London, 1970.

Jucker, Andreas H.: *Social Stylistics – Syntactic Variation in British Newspapers.* Berlin, 1992.

Lee, Allan J.: *The Origins of the Popular Press in England: 1855-1914.* London, 1976.

Linton, David & Ray Boston (Eds.): *The newspaper press in Britain – an annotated bibliography.* London/New York, 1987.

Lüger, Heinz-Helmut: *Pressesprache.* 2., neu bearbeitete Auflage, Tübingen, 1995.

Oostdijk, Nelleke: "A corpus linguistic approach to linguistic variation", *Literary and Linguistic Computing* 3,1, 1988, 12-25.

Rydén, Mats: "Noun-name collocations in British English newspaper language", *Studia Neophilologica. A Journal of Germanic and Romance Philology* 47,1, 1975, 14-39.

Simon-Vandenbergen, Annemarie: *The grammar of headlines in The Times.* Brussels, 1981.

Strunk, William & E. B. White: *The Elements of Style.* 3rd ed., Boston/London, 1979.

Sutherland, James R.: "The Circulation of Newspapers and Literary Periodicals, 1700-30", *The Library,* Ser.4, V.15, 1934-35, 110-124.

Wallace, William D.: "How registers register: A study in the language of news and sports", *Studies in Linguisitc Sciences* 7,1, 1977, 46-78.

Warner, Alan: *A Guide to English Style.* London, 1961.

Waterhouse, Keith: *Daily Mirror Style.* London, 1981.

Williams, Keith: *The English Newspaper – an illustrated history to 1900.* London, 1977.

Williams, Raymond: *The Long Revolution.* London, 1961.

Rolf Herwig, Jena

Changing Language in Changing Times

Times are changing. So is The Times?

Despite its ups and downs in a history that by now stretches over two centuries, *The Times* is holding the reputation of being one of the world's greatest newspapers. In public opinion, and this public includes British and overseas readers alike, the latter perhaps even more, its quality is based on its rigorous standards of reporting and writing, its independent and strong editorial principles. For quite a few *The Times* – even today – is more than just a paper, but "rather the very epitome of the British establishment" (*Encyclopaedia Britannica* 1994).[1]

All had started quite differently. Editorial policy was less important for John Walter when in 1784 he announced the birth of a new newspaper, priced ½ penny. Worth a short note in *N.B.* only, editorial principles were placed behind the novelty of the technical experiment. On June 25th 1784, Mr Walter informed the public that a new paper was to be published on January 1st 1785:

> "By His Majesty's Royal Letters Patent.
>
> LONDON, JUNE 25th, 1784.
> MR. WALTER begs leave to inform the public, that, having obtained an assignment of his MAJESTY'S LETTERS PATENT, for the sole privilege of casting, and cementing for use or sale, Types of Words, &c. he has purchased the King's late Printing-House, near Apothecaries-hall, which is now opened for carrying on the printing business in general, upon an approved invention of composing with words entire, their roots, and terminations, instead of single letters, from a system of arrangement, formed with the assistance of the inventor, after a very laborious study and application.
> It must be obvious to the most common understanding, that when an arrangement is formed, from which the Compositor can with facility take up every word he wants, without the space being so far extended as to occasion delay, it must have very superior advantages to the present mode of printing. [...] It may [...] be necessary to suggest, that a neatness and correctness has been experienced, much beyond the common method--it is far less liable to literal errors--there can be no

> wrong spelling, or letters inverted--no dirt can adhere to make the letters at different distances, and the errors of the press are very trifling when a proof is taken. With these advantages, others arise of still greater magnitude; the extraordinary expedition which will attend it, and the short time required for the compositor to learn his business, will tend when the heavy expences already incurred are defrayed, to reduce the charge of printing. [...]
> N.B. Early next winter, A NEW DAILY PAPER will be published, to be named THE UNIVERSAL REGISTER, on a liberal plan, that shall neither be devoted to party invective or fulsome panegyric; and it is hoped the useful and necessary improvements to the method now adopted by most of the present daily publications will meet general approbation."[2]

When on January 1st 1788 the new name *The Times* was adopted, this was above all due to commercial reasons, "both laughable and serious ones".[3] Yet it was still some time before the paper under John Walter III had finally reached the reputation as "Britain's pre-eminent national journal and daily historical record" in 1848 (cf. *Britannica* CD 1994). Independence of editorial views, for example, had been difficult to establish for a pre-Victorian paper. Punitive legal and financial restraints by the government were to ensure that the press served state interests (cf. Negrine 1994, 41). Walter himself spent some time in prison for libelling members of the British royal family. It was during that time that he started organizing a news service from the European continent. Eventually *The Times* achieved its leading position in covering foreign news (cf. *Encyclopaedia Britannica* 1994).

The research interest

The motivation for a linguistic study of (foreign) news report writing is to do with the quasi prototypical role of *The Times* in this special genre. This paper will start from the assumption that the high journalistic quality of the newspaper can be taken as a basis for a study of some of the cultural and language changes that have happened since the birth of *The Times* in the 18th century.

It is generally acknowledged that with the second half of the 18th century the codification of standard English had led to a stage of relative stability of the language (cf. Knowles 1997, 122). Since then, no such tremendous instances of change as those that marked the major stages of the history of English have been recorded. It is equally well acknowledged, and has recently met with increased academic interest, that standard English is far from being something fixed and unchanging (cf. Bauer 1994, 1). The changes that have happened and are happening are less situated in the language system[4] than in language usage. They above all concern meaning changes, words drifting out of use in certain meanings, acquiring new or losing old connotations, appearing in new semantic environments, combining in new collocations etc. Most of these usage changes are subtle and take time before they are recognized as new ways in which the elements of the language can be used to produce meaning. More often than not they are hotly contested.[5] The seemingly never-ending discussions about what is accurate and 'good' English indicate that the change is mainly one of language attitudes rather than codified language forms.

Over 200 years of news reporting in *The Times* should provide ample evidence of how and in which directions this particular kind of written English usage has developed.

The decision to restrict the selection of texts from the news-report genre to reports on war and war-like events has to be justified. For a short study like this, selection and restriction of the subject are always crucial. One overriding principle of corpus selection should be that the texts chosen are comparable to each other in at least some respects. Sadly enough, war, cruelty, hostility have been ever-occurring topics in the news-report columns of *The Times*. Reading the reports on the battles of Gettysburg or the Somme, one intuitively feels that, though they are differently worded, they nevertheless reflect a sad experience shared by generations. It goes beyond a purely academic interest to see how the generations before ours coped with the dramatic events of their time linguistically.

More trivially, but quite important for a study like this, the reports are usually of such a length that makes their inclusion in a text corpus appear appropriate. A more content-orientated reason for the choice was that reports on war events must be a special challenge to a paper that commits itself to true, objective, accurate reporting. Faced with the cruelty and bloodshed of war in general and with the threat to Britain by various enemies in particular, the reporter's language will inevitably mirror different commitments: **to objective information** as an editorial principle on the one hand, and to **emotional**, at times even patriotic **involvement** on the other.

Starting from these preliminary considerations, the following questions will be raised:

1. What changes in style and judgement about what is genre-appropriate can be traced in the war reports from *The Times* for the last 200 years, from roughly 1790 to the present? Can findings that draw on such a relatively limited textual basis reveal anything of a more general nature?

2. Can particular language features be shown to associate with any larger social or cultural dimensions?
3. Which are the linguistic devices that serve the different functional purposes of expressing (a) more distancing objectivity/informativity and (b) moral or emotional involvement/commitment?

The texts

The following texts from *The Times* were chosen for the analysis:

Text 1: *The Times* 16-08-1792 *PARIS, Saturday at Noon*
This is a text on a "war-like" event, the storming of the Palace des Tuileries during the French revolution. Although Britain was not directly involved, *The Times* from the very beginning of the revolution had made it clear that Britain was not just a neutral observer of the events in France. On 30th June 1787 it wrote:

> "This is one of the most awful moments that the French Government has known since the Peace of Utrecht, and as no political event of importance can take place in that kingdom, which is not interesting to Great Britain, we flatter ourselves that the Nation will have every reason to applaud our zeal and industry in procuring the communications which we offer to it."

The Times' "latest intelligence" and "communications" are in fact news reports and commentaries with a double purpose: to provide detailed information on the latest events and to serve the interest of the British state, which seems to have seen any attack on a monarchy as inherently dangerous:

> [...] "it is not now merely the disputes of the NATIONAL ASSEMBLY, and the new modelling of the French Constitution, which claim the attention of our countrymen, in common with all Europe, but the very lives of the ROYAL FAMILY of FRANCE, and the race of a whole monarchy, are at stake." (*The Times* 12-10-1789)

This view of the Paris events as something very close to British interests justifies the inclusion of the text in the series of war reports proper.
A passage of 988 words has been chosen for the analysis. The use of part of a text only is thought to be possible as textual patterns were not included in the list of features to be analysed.

Text **2**: *The Times* 08-04-1854 and June 1854 *Letters from W. H. Russell*

These two letters are reports on the Crimean War (October 1853 – February 1856) by William Howard Russell, the world's first war correspondent. 796 words.

Text **3:** *The Times* 18-08-1863 *The Battles of Gettysburg*
This is a 1112-word passage from a longer description of the first day's battle. Britain again was not directly involved, but due to the "special" Anglo-American relationship, the text shows features both of objective reporting and deeper commitment.

Text **4**: *The Times* 19-03-1917 *Visit to the town* (of Bapaume)
A World War I report (724 words) on the seizure of the French town of Bapaume by the Allied forces.

Text **5:** *The Times* 13-06-1944 *Quick Penetration*
A World War II report covering a day after the successful opening of the second front in Normandy. 919 words.

Text **6**: *The Times* 04-05-1982 *Cruiser torpedoed by Royal Navy sinks*
A report on a decisive event during the Falklands war. 799 words.

The method

The paper applies an approach publicised among others by Biber 1988, Crystal 1991 and Finegan 1992. Diller 1991 describes an application of the approach to text strategies of British columnists.

The basic idea is that particular "linguistic features serve particular communicative functions and that functionally related linguistic features tend to co-occur in particular kinds of texts" (Finegan 1992, 111/112). Therefore varieties can be distinguished according to which linguistic features they (predominantly) utilize. For his study of variation in spoken and written English, Biber counted the frequency of certain linguistic features in various text types and genres and analysed their distribution across these genres (cf. Biber 1988, 63). Similarly, Finegan traced the historical development of three English genres (fiction, essays, letters) by comparing the frequencies of certain linguistic features in texts from each genre and from different centuries. Diller chose six linguistic parameters in order to characterize the strategies of personal and impersonal writing styles of British columnists (1991, 219).

Crystal 1991 describes a stylistic analytical approach he calls "stylistic profiling". It is similar to what Finegan 1992 used for the analysis of the historical development of three English genres. Crystal applied a method that had been developed in speech therapy clinics. A larger number of intuitively or presumably related data are brought together, arranged in such a way that significant patterns emerge and the stylistic identity or 'profile' of a text, a group of texts, a genre etc becomes visible (cf. 222/223).

One of the major problems is the selection of those linguistic features that significantly identify a particular variety of language use. Which features the analyst selects will inevitably shape the 'working model' of the profile. For practical purposes, Crystal proposes to refine the model constantly while it is systematically applied during the analysis.

Interestingly, Crystal's model does not only take "frequency of occurrence" of a specific feature as a grading principle, but also the feature's "overall distinctiveness, in its own right, regardless of frequency" (228). The idea is that some features are salient even if they occur only once or twice, eg. *Amen* as indicater of the text type *prayer.*

Both categories, frequency of occurrence and overall distinctiveness, will be integrated in our approach.

For the exemplification of his method of stylistic profiling, Crystal uses lists of features he considers to be of distinctive value for legal writing (53 features) and newspaper writing (51 features). The features are taken from the areas of language structure and language use, in a similar way as had already been done by Davy/Crystal 1969.

In principle, Finegan has taken the same approach and chosen features he has found to be characteristic of a certain variety and to associate with their constitutive contextual and situational dimensions. As his research interest focuses on orality, the lists of *Purpose Dimension Features* and *Reference Dimension Features* (cf. 1992, 115) naturally overlap only partly with Crystal's. Yet, the method as such is obviously sufficiently elaborate and reliable and has therefore been applied to this study, duly modified according to the requirements of the chosen text type and its particular communicative functions.

Finegan's work is of interest also because his research is fairly closely related to the subject and goals in this paper. For the three English genres he states that

> "English has been shifting to increasingly oral styles over the past few centuries [...] But the eighteenth-century writing clearly bucks the trend. During that century, under the literate norms of the neo-classical philosophy, fiction, essays, and letters became more literate than they had been in the preceding century." (1992, 116)

As the text corpus of this study covers about the same period of time as Finegan's three genres, the answer for question 1 will include a comparison between Finegan's finding and those of this study. Considering the functional proximity of fiction, essay and letter to the news report (text B in fact consists of two letters) one can hypothesize that the reported trend of the increased use of oral styles in English writing also applies to war reports.

Similarly, Diller's categories of "personhood" and "de-personalization" (217) are closely related to both Finegan's categories and those of this paper. His findings underline the validity of the thesis of a general drift of English writing towards orality.

The following linguistic features were finally included in the analysis. They are considered to be capable of shaping the profile of war reports, especially as far as their (more) objective/informative or (more) moral/emotional orientation is concerned. The list is the result of

- intuitive decision after a large number of war reports had been read
- constant refinement during the analysis (Some features, eg. clefting, turned out to be too sparsely used in all the texts. Some others, such as variation in the use of tenses, did not sufficiently discriminate. Narrative passages are written throughout in the past tense.)
- comparison with Finegan's, Crystal's and Diller's lists
- statements in reference books about the expressive potential of lexical and grammatical items

The list certainly should be extended to meet the requirements of a more complex investigation.

List of linguistic features

- connotated lexical items: formal (literary, foreign, archaic, eg. *on the morrow*) – informal (colloquial, eg. *Boche; Fritz*)
- adjectives and adverbs expressing emotion/evaluation[6]
- disjuncts indicating speaker attitude[7]
- unconventional expressive metaphors, eg. *heights which frowned darkly and menacingly*
- technical war vocabulary, eg. *provost companies*
- markers of validity of content, such as
  - disjuncts[8]
  - epistemic modality[9]
  - explicit reference to source of information, eg. *authoritative sources confirmed*
- first and second person reference
- rhetorical questions
- exclamations

- sentence complexity
  - words per sentence[10]
  - subordination-coordination-ratio (as for clauses)
  - finite-nonfinite-ratio (as for clauses)

For the analysis, the occurrences of each of the preceding features were separately registered – and counted. Table 1 presents a summarized version of the findings.

The results

Table 1

1) Features expressing emotion/evaluation	**Text 1 1792**	**Text 2 1854**	**Text 3 1863**	**Text 4 1917**	**Text 5 1944**	**Text 6 1982**
– adj, adv, metaphors per 100 words	1.5	1.3	4.1	3.4	2.5	1.1
connotations						
– formal per 100 words	3.1	0.2	2.7	0.8	0.6	0.3
– informal per 100 words		0.6		0.5		
All features of 1) per 100 words	**4.6**	**2.2**	**6.9**	**4.8**	**3.1**	**1.5**
2) Technical war vocabulary per 100 words	1.0	1.6	1.2	1.5	2.3	2.3
3) Reference to sources; epistemic modality per 100 words	0.3	0.5	0.5	0.2	0.3	3.2
4) Sentence complexity						
– words/sentence	27.0	21.7	43.4	19.2	33.0	19.2
– subordination-coordination ratio in clauses	3.5	2.1	4.1	2.4	2.2	9.6
– finite-nonfinite-ratio in clauses	2.5	2.2	1.7	3.4	3.8	2,5
5) First/second person reference per 100 words	0.4	6.0	0.8	3.1	0.3	0

The comparison of the data reveals contradictory tendencies. Some features show a (more or less) systematic increase or decrease along the time line from 1792 to 1982, others do not.

The figures are to be read as illustrating tendencies. The limited scope of the corpus disallows any claim for statistical significance.

The **increase** of the values for feature **2** (technical war vocabulary) does not surprise. The 200 years from 1792 to 1982 were eagerly used by human kind to produce ever more sophisticated weaponry. This technical development is reflected not only in the frequency with which war terms occur, but even in the more complex word-structure itself:

Text 1:	*Swiss Guards*	Text 6:	*hunter-killer submarine*
	National Guard		*air-craft carrier*
	battalions		task force
	patrole		navy aircraft
	pistol		seacat sea-to-air missile-launchers
	cannons		15 six-inch and eight five-inch guns

The 20th-century texts show a **decrease** in the use of emotional/evaluative means of expression (feature **1**). Whereas text 1 still abounds in expressions such as

> *it makes humanity shudder; my blood freezes with horror; perfidy or stratagem; sealed with blood; a scene of ... ensued; cool, deliberate and premeditated revenge,*

text 6 has considerably lower values in this field. The degree of expressivity or involvement of text 6 items such as

> *largest warship, tremendous battles, absolute necessity, tragic conflict, the task force had every right to ...*

is relatively small compared to the 'strong' potential of the expressions of eg. text 1.

To the modern reader at least, text 3 of 1863 appears as a late representative of neo-classical pomp:

> *Hope reigned triumphant in every Confederate breast; delay was likely to afford the Federals, whose activity with the spade has been repeatedly and marvellously manifested, time and opportunity for intrenching themselves ad libitum.*

The WWI text (text 4) to some extent seems to share the preference for emphatic expression with the 18th- and 19th-century texts (texts 1 and 3 are particularly characteristic), whereas text 2 (W. H. Russell's report from the Crimea) is closer to its modern followers in this respect. It is more factual, less poetic, less formal in style than the other earlier reports.

Differences between texts, though they are close together on the time line, do not come as a surprise, however. We cannot expect every text to 'behave' linguistically similarly just because it dates back to the same period. Any such expectation is ill-founded, especially as long as we cannot exactly describe what the *norm* of a specific text type in a specific period was.

Some of the differences as to emotional commitment can be tentatively explained with the particular situational conditions of text production:

Text 4 is written in the mood of victory. After the murderous battles of the Somme, with 420,000 casualties the most severe losses the British army had ever sustained, the Allied armies had defeated the enemy in that area. Emotion seems to be appropriate. Yet, there is an interesting discrepancy between the *cool* inconsequence of the soldiers and the *elation* felt by the onlooking (!) reporter, a discrepancy that becomes noticeable only if the textual level is included in the analysis. It seems as if what must have been such a sad experience for thousands and thousands of people is meant to appear great and historical by the rich use of inherently expressive adjectives, metaphors or other connotated items in collocations like these:

violent ripping of machine-guns
patient ... energetic ... wonderfully prompt
it was incredible
veritably
(the night was) throbbing with the incendiary fires of the destroyers
profound cavities (for deep holes in the road)

If this argument is accepted as an explanation for the more elevated style of text 4, it could still be argued that text 5 is situated in an almost identical situational context: Bayeux has been taken, the Second Front been opened, the Germans not yet defeated but decisively forced to retreat. The report is, however, clearly different in style to text 4. Emotional envolvement and emphatic evaluation, though not totally absent (*the German locusts; the flood tide of avenging war*) are less salient.

Text 6, though reporting another British victory, clearly also serves the purpose of justifying the losses that were inflicted upon the Argentinian enemy. The neutral, more factual style of reporting may be in accordance with modern language attitudes. It certainly also reflects political attitudes and considerations *The Times* cannot ignore. In the face of a skeptically observing 'world opinion', the report on the killing of hundreds of Argentinians avoids too obvious glorification.

In view of this data it would certainly not be adequate to reduce the phenomenon of decrease of emotionality to nothing more than the writers' stylistic idiosyncracy. The general decrease in expressivity and emotionality is obvious for the majority of texts:

1792	1863	1944	1982
4.6	**6.9**	**3.1**	**1.5**

With due caution, a tendency towards a **less expressive, more factual style of reporting** can be stated. Over the centuries, war reports in *The Times* tend to become less 'literate', less revealing the writer's emotional or moral involvement. The editorial principles of objective information, high informative value of the reports have finally taken over. The Falklands text (6) certainly reports in the least literate manner.

Comparing the results of the analysis so far to Finegan's and Diller's findings, partial agreement can be stated. The decrease in the use of pompous, Latinate words and collocations, which can be reported for the more recent texts, agrees with Finegan's claim: "English has been shifting to increasingly oral styles over the past few centuries" (1992, 116). It is, however, open to dispute if the lack of involvement, the decline in emotionality is compatible with oral expression. As far as war reports are concerned, what is going on seems to be a process of neutralization rather than increased orality.

The interpretation of the style of Russell's report from 1854 still offers some difficulty. Finding a reason why this text is so different in almost every respect (less expressive, more informal, more frequent mention of technical war items, shorter sentences, more coordinated clauses) to texts 1 and 3 can hardly be more than speculation. But the fact that Russell was the first war correspondent who *The Times* had ever sent to a theatre of war speaks in favour of his qualities as a writer and the kind of reporting style the paper obviously expected from its war reports. If his style differed from that of others, it may have been seen even at that time as being better in line with the paper's editorial policy of meticulously accurate reporting.

Feature **5** (first/second person reference) was included in the list because Finegan had raised it to the rank of a distinctive feature of involved discourse (cf. 1992, 155). Also Diller takes this parameter into consideration (1991, 219). The presentation of a war report by an eye-witness in the tradition of a first-person narrative is obviously well-established practice. The data do not throw any light on changing preferences. The occurrence of one text (6) only without any direct reference to the reader or writer would not justify any conclusion that a change in trends is under way.

The total absence of first/second person reference in the most recent war report is however not without interest. Though not characterised by frequency of occurrence, the feature is distinctive **because** of its absence (cf. Crystal/Davy 1969). This characteristic is in accordance with the generally official, distancing stance of text 6. Its profile is characterized by the lack of a linguistically explicit writer-reader-relationship, a large number of technical terms, a complex clause structure, high density of information, constant reference to 'sources'. The latter feature can be interpreted as an indication of changed practices in news reporting. As Bell 1991 and others point out, reports are nowadays often no longer the result of the author's own investigation.

> "[...] many stories contain material selected and reworked from documents generated by newsmakers or other media [...] Some stories are entirely cut-and-paste jobs from such sources." (Bell 1991, 41)

Russell's direct experience of the war can today be replaced by easy and quick access to the electronic resources of news agencies. The byline of text 6 "Nicolas Ashford" possibly just names the compiler of the news.

This has consequences for media language. Different papers can buy the same news from one news agency and publish it in either identical or different formulations. No longer the eye-witness or 'our own correspondent' guarantees the truth of the information, but anonymous sources. To quote Bell once more: "A journalist sanctions the form of language culled from other sources just by adopting it." (1991, 42) Depersonalization seems to be the price that has to be paid for instantaneous, world-wide access to the news. Text 6 has alone 10 references to *authoritative sources, one source, the source, agency reports, a Department spokesman* and three to another reporter. Such practice signals a change in the ethos of reporting, which then can become manifest in its linguistic expression.

The figures for source reference include the use of epistemic modality (feature **3**). Epistemic modal expressions in the context of reporting have the function of relativizing the reliability of the news (*was presumed; was believed; it appeared, I am told, it may now be stated that, it was deemed, apparently* ...). They are not significantly different for any of the periods, apart from text 6 which makes ample use of them. They reflect the traditionally high standard of *The Times* reports in terms of truthfulness and reliability.

The data for sentence complexity (feature **4**) do not allow to hypothesize any systematic tendency although there are widely divergent values for the different texts. The differences have no correlation with the time line. This is true for the words-per-sentence figures as well as clause structure. High and low values can be found for texts from each period. Although one might feel tempted to interpret the saliently high degree of subordination in text 6 as a modern journalistic means of achieving complex sentence meanings together with informational density, this hypothesis is not supported by the only medium degree of non-finiteness of the clauses in this text. The picture is far from being clear.

Texts of all periods can be structurally less complex or more complex. In the texts chosen there is no indication of any preference for more typically oral features of sentence structure such as finiteness of the verb phrase, coordination of clauses and clause elements, reduced noun head modification, or others.

Only text 3 is consistently marked by structural features which are characteristically 'written' and which correspond to its rather pompous lexical means: extremely long sentences (maximum 95 words), the highest share in non-finite clause structures, deeply branched subordinate clauses.

The questions raised at the beginning can now be tentatively answered. For the special genre of war reports, change in style and judgement about what is best suited to meet the requirements of high journalistic quality can indeed be recorded. Less emotionally expressive, morally committed reporting and more distanced and factual styles seem to be gaining ground. This can partly coincide with the general drift of modern English writing towards orality, as reported by other sources. On the other hand, new features of news story writing have come into existence that originate in the social and technological changes in our mass society. Easy and world-wide access to a vast number of electronic resources has reduced the role of the journalist as the originator of the news story. Enumerative references to sources of (prefabricated) news can result in an impersonal, uncommitted style that is largely incompatible with the traditions of oral narration.

Due to the limited scope of the analysis, both as regards the corpus and the features analysed, all statements have to be read as provisional first findings.

As far as the analytical method is concerned, it is crucial which features enter the list. Significantly more experimentation is necessary in order to find out about overt or covert correlations between features. It is equally significant for the interpretation stage that the data are re-contextualized and the textual dimension of language use is not lost sight of.

Notes

1 All references to *Encyclopaedia Britannica* 1994 are to the electronic edition on CD-Rom.
2 All quotations from *The Times* are taken from *Changing Times* CD-Rom.
3 Cf. Letter to the Editor by a certain P.H.S., *The Times* 1-1-1901.

4 Cf. Baugh/Cable 1990 for borrowings and new coinages in the 19th century and after (chapter 19).
5 For a recent and committed description of the complaint tradition in the public's attitude towards language change cf. Aitchison's *Reith lectures* of 1996.
6 Cf. Downing/Locke 1992, 516/517, eg. *outrageous; sheer*. For adjectives and all other 'word' features, a contextual concept of word meaning was applied. Meaning is not seen as inherently or invariably attached to the word, but as determined by the collocational environment of the item.
7 Cf. Downing/Locke 1992, 62, eg. *sadly.*
8 Cf. Downing/Locke 1992, 62, eg. *undoubtedly.*
9 Cf. Downing/Locke 1992, 383, eg. *is believed to ...*
10 As the texts are of different length, all frequences stated are to be read as 'number of instances per 100 words'.

Bibliography

Aitchison, Jean: *The Language Web. 1996 Reith lectures.* Cambridge University Press, 1997.

Baugh, Albert & Thomas Cable: *A History of the English Language.* Routledge, London & New York, 1990.

Bauer, Laurie: *Watching English Change.* Longman, London & New York, 1994.

Bell, Allan: *The Language of News Media.* Blackwell, Oxford UK & Cambridge MA, 1991.

Biber, Douglas: *Variation across Speech and Writing.* Cambridge University Press, 1988.

Changing Times. News Multimedia Ltd, 1996.

Crystal, David: "Stylistic profiling". – In K. Aijmer & B. Altenberg (Eds.): *English Corpus Linguistics.* Longman, London & New York, 1991, pp. 221-238.

Crystal, David & Derek Davy: *Investigating English Style.* Longman, London, 1969.

Diller, Hans-Jürgen: "Text Strategies of British Columnists". – In C. Uhlig & R. Zimmermann (Eds.): *Anglistentag 1990 Marburg. Proceedings.* Niemeyer Verlag Tübingen, 1991, pp. 216-231.

Downing, Angela & Philip Locke: *A University Course in English Grammar.* Phoenix ELT, New York, 1992.

Encyclopaedia Britannica CD (electronic version), 1994.

Finegan, Edward: "Style and Standardization in England: 1700-1900". – In T. W. Machan & C.T. Scott (Eds.): *English in its Social Contexts.* Oxford University Press, 1992, pp. 102-130.

Knowles, Gerry: *A Cultural History of the English Language.* Arnold, London, 1997.

Negrine, Ralph: *Politics and the Mass Media in Britain.* Routledge, London & New York, 1989.

Text 1

The Times 16-08-1792
PARIS,--Saturday at Noon.

IRRUPTION INTO THE PALACE DES TUILLERIES--BATTLE BETWEEN THE SWISS GUARDS AND THE SANS CULOTTES--ESCAPE OF THE KING AND ROYAL FAMILY OUT OF THE HANDS OF THE REGICIDES--MASSACRE OF THE SWISS GUARDS--THE PALACE OF THE TUILLERIES PLUNDERED, AND THE ADJACENT BUILDINGS SET ON FIRE--THE KING AND ROYAL FAMILY SAFE.

(From our regular Correspondent.)

I now sit down to write you a full and distinct account of the most tragical event that ever my eyes witnessed. It is such as makes humanity shudder, and my blood freezes with horror at the very recollection of the massacre and distress to which I was an unwilling spectator. It is with very heartfelt grief that I am obliged to recount to you a scene of bloodshed which will ever remain as a stain on the history of my country, for the outrages were not provoked by any perfidy or stratagem on the part of the Royal Family, but were the result of cool, deliberate, and premeditated revenge.

The event which has just taken place will hardly be believed by posterity. More than a week ago it was everywhere foretold by the numerous incendiaries who are the main springs of the various groups of the Palais Royal, of the Terrace des Feuillans, &c. They had repeatedly declared that it was resolved to massacre the Swiss Guards,--to drive out of the Tuilleries those National Guards who had remained faithful to the King,--and to destroy the Palace, that it might be no longer the abode of Kings. All these particulars were too unfortunately put in execution on Friday. Although all the inhabitants of Paris were fully informed of the dreadful catastrophe which was to take place; although the day and the hour had been fixed upon and known; although the banditti had declared that exactly at midnight on Thursday the generale would begin to beat, and the alarm-bells ring;--yet the Parisians were so infatuated, and in such a state of consternation, that they seemed quietly to bow their necks, and to prepare to be butchered without resistance, if it should be the supreme will of the Mob that they should.

The preparations that were making on Thursday evening threatened some terrible explosion. The streets were illuminated, and the crowds of people in them greater than was ever remembered. It is evident that the decision of the Assembly on the affair of M. de la Fayette had greatly enraged the Jacobin mob, and during the whole day their adherents were busy in exciting such a clamour as might ensure them success on the question for deposing the King.

Scarcely had the clock struck twelve on Thursday night, when all the bells of Paris began to ring the alarm, and the generale was beat in every quarter of the capital. In the Fauxbourgs and in some other places the armed mobs were a long time in collecting together. While the Sans Culottes were assembling in the extremities of the town, the National Guards were joining their respective battalions. Some of them went to the Palace, where already near 600 Swiss had assembled. The remainder of the night was thus passed in the greatest confusion, to the great consternation of the Parisians. The Sans Culottes, joined by a great number of National Guards, did not arrive in force at the Palace, till between six and seven o'clock in the morning of yesterday.

At eight o'clock in the morning a patrole of Swiss Guards was attacked in the Champs Elysees. This patrole was moving towards the castle, and also some courtiers, and some of the King's guards. An alarm was spread, and numbers of armed citizens of the battalion of Marseilles, and of Federates from the different Departments, began to fill the avenues to the Palace and the National Assembly, demanding vengeance on those traitors whom they had seized.--A scene of terrible confusion ensued: The unfortunate victims underwent a sort of mock trial, were convicted, and execution immediately followed. Six of the soldiers had their heads instantly struck off their shoulders, and the mob sat in judgment on the rest, as if they had been coolly guided by real principles of justice, although the sentence was already sealed with blood. It does not appear that there was any ground of accusation against these men, except that there was found on them several cases of pistols loaded. This was a sufficient ground of suspicion, and they were accordingly hung up in the Place de Vendome, and their heads afterwards carried about the town on pikes.

The attack at the Palace began before ten o'clock. It was conducted by a regiment of Cordeliers, some Federates of Marseilles, the Federates of Brest, and a battalion of Guards from the quarter of St. Antoine. A Marseillois Officer appeared at the principal door of the Palace, and demanded entrance for himself and his banditti, from a Swiss officer who commanded there. The Swiss replied that his orders would not permit him to comply. The Marseillois officer instantly applied a pistol to his breast and shot him through the heart. That moment the carnage began, and it lasted the whole day.

During this time, the inhabitants of all the Fauxbourgs were repairing to the Palace and to the National Assembly, accompanied by all the Sections of Paris, armed in the same manner as they were on the 20th of June, and calling out for the dethronement of the King--that he was a Traitor, and had forfeited the Crown. The KING perceiving such a mob of banditti, with fury in their looks began to be alarmed. Just at that moment, he received a message from the Directors of the Department of Paris, warning him of his danger, and advising him to go immediately to the National Assembly, and to take his family with him. He was scarcely out of the Palace before the mob, collected together on the Place du Carousel, insisted on being admitted immediately into the Courts of the Palace. It was impossible for the guards to prevent their irruption. Having rushed in, in vast numbers, they took possession of the cannons which they found in the Courts, and which had been abandoned by the gunners, who had joined the insurgents.

Text 2

Letter: From William Howard Russell in Gallipoli
The Times 08-04-1854 Byline: William Howard Russell
Gallipoli Saturday

My dear Sir

I have only time to tell you that I am so far safe here. The troops marched today at 11 o'clock for the camp distant 8" miles. There is but scanty water and no shelter on the site of the encampment, neither tree nor blade of grass. The management is infamous and contrast offered by our proceedings to the conduct of the French most harmful. Would you believe it?--the sick have not a bed to lie upon. They are landed and thrust into a rickety house without a chair to sit upon or a table in it. The French with their ambulances, excellent Commissariat staff and local surgeries etc, in every respect are immeasurably our superiors. While these things go on, Sir George Brown only seems anxious about the men being clean shaved, their necks well stiffened up and their wastebelts tied. He insists on officers and men being in full fig., no loose coats, jackets etc. His wonderful pack kills the men as the weight is so disposed as to hang from instead of resting on the shoulders. I was not introduced to Sir George by anyone and he took no notice of me the whole time he was on board except one day to take wine with me and to say "Well sir, I'm off now" the day he was going on shore. He offered me no facilities and I did not ask for any and his staff etc of course are afraid of acting when they see the chief so taciturn. I run a good chance of starving if the army takes the field for the company will give me no rations without an order and even if I had one I doubt very much if Sir George Brown would allow me to pitch it within the camp. All my efforts to get a horse have been unsuccessful and I deeply regret I did not bring out one from England. Even at present situated as I am, I cannot get out to the camp, for 17 miles a day with a letter to write would soon knock up a Hercules. I am living in a pig stye--a mud walled room without chair, table, stove or window glass and an old hag of 60 to attend on me who does not understand a word I say. I live on eggs and brown bread, some Tenedos wine and onions and rice. The French have got all the place to themselves. I am told if the army marches I must get a bullock waggon as the commissariat wont allow my things to go on the waggons without an order. Again I was told that they will not allow my things to be taken charge of by the rere (sic) guard and come into the baggage train without an order! I met yesterday Captain Blakely a " pay artillery man who is writing for the Chronicle. He is no better off than myself except in equipments, horses, outfit etc and an excellent servant. I had to discharge mine as he is only good at robbing. I have not heard from the office since I left and I don't know if any letters have got safe. For the present I think my letters should be sent to the "British Camp, Gallipoli" Would you be good enough to acquaint Mr Morris that I have drawn sixty five pounds thro' Mr. Goodenough altogether and that I will write to him by the next opportunity. At present there is only time to subscribe myself.

Your very faithful servant
W H Russell

Dispatch from William Howard Russell in the Crimea
The Times 00-06-1854 Byline: William Howard Russell
(Letter)

My dear Sir

I have just been informed on good authority that Lord Raglan is determined "not to recognise the press in any way" or to give them rations or assistance and worse than all it is but too probable he will forbid our accompanying the troops as soon as he has been written by Starnand. I have only time to say so much and to show you that the promises modern London have not been carried out here. Part of one division--Brigadier Adams--has not got tents. Poor Lord Leveson Gower who is unwell is told by his medical attendant there are no medical suited stores for his complaint. There is no beef for the men for the last three days and they have only mutton which the doctors say will bring on dysentery. Just imagine this. The sappers and miners sent out to Bojuk to survey do so in coatees, worsted, epaulets and shakos full dress in fact, as their undress clothes were not ready when they left. Am I to tell these things or to hold my tongue?

In great haste and much annoyed by what I hear
Yours very truly
W H Russell

Text 3

The Times 18-08-1863 Byline: Francis Lawley

THE BATTLES OF GETTYSBURG
HEADQUARTERS OF GENERAL LONGSTREET, NEAR GETTYSBURG, JULY 1.

After camping near the top of the South Mountain (which, as I have in previous letters explained, is the continuation from Harper's Ferry northwards of the Blue Ridge of Virginia), we proceeded this morning slowly on our road towards Gettysburg. Before us (by "us" I mean the corps of General Longstreet) was the corps of General A.P. Hill; to our left, descending from York towards Gettysburg, was the corps of General Ewell. As we neared the mouth of the mountain gorge, the loud boom of guns between us and the little town of Gettysburg proclaimed that the Federals, who were generally believed to be much nearer to Washington, had advanced thus far to meet us. Undoubtedly, the near proximity of the Federal army to Gettysburg was a surprise to Generals Lee and Longstreet. Before either of these Generals were aware of the fact, General A. P. Hill, coming from the west, and General Ewell descending from the north, were hotly engaged with the enemy, and destined, in the preliminary struggle of the 1st of July, to meet, as it proved, with a triumphant success.

The country in the immediate neighbourhood of Gettysburg, remarkably English in its general aspect, is not unlike many portions of Surrey, especially reminding the spectator of the gently swelling banks densely clothed with trees which are found between the towns of Dorking and Reigate. About four miles west of Gettysburg one of General A. P. Hill's divisions, commanded by General Heth, came upon a strong picket of Federals, thrown out by the 1st corps of their army, under the command of General Reynolds. To the north of the town, the divisions of Generals Rodes and Early, both belonging to General Ewell's corps, found themselves face to face with the 11th corps of the Federal army, which, as the reader will remember, attained at Chancellorsville unenviable notoriety, as comprising within its ranks the "Flying Dutchman," of whose flight it will be long before Carl Schurz, the German orator and Federal General, hears the last. Instinctively, and against the wish of General Lee, between the three Confederate divisions indicated, and the two corps of the Federal army, a hotly contested battle arose. The divisions of Generals Rodes and Early were fortunate in lighting upon the 11th corps and experiencing a resistance which, though it compared favourably with the memories of Chancellorsville, was ill calculated to stem the fiery attack of Stonewall Jackson's veterans. Again the Germans broke and fled, but their swift retreat was not bloodless and unharmed, as it had been through the thickets and copsewood of Chancellorsville. Thickly and heavily shot and shell and musket balls fell with damaging accuracy upon their shrieking ranks, and it is the belief of many that if General Ewell, after driving his enemy for four miles and through the town of Gettysburg, had not, by superior orders, stayed the pursuit within the town itself, his victorious troops would have camped on the night of the 1st of July upon the top of that ridge which upon the two subsequent days all the desperate efforts of the Confederates were inadequate to storm. For the division of General Heth, opposed to General Reynolds and the First Corps of the Federals, a fiercer conflict was in store. Standing firmly on his ground, General Reynolds met the Confederate attack unflinchingly, and it was not until bayonets were on the eve of crossing that several of his regiments, and notably the 24th Michigan and two regiments from New York and Pennsylvania (the latter said never to have been in action before), broke into sullen retreat, leaving about half their number dead and wounded on the ground. The retreat once commenced knew neither pause nor stay until the town of Gettysburg was gained and passed. Among its victims was numbered General Reynolds, one of the most active of the Federal Generals, who yielded his life upon the best contested field which, in the opinion of competent judges, the "Grand Army of the Potomac" had hitherto known. General A. P. Hill, no inexperienced witness, bore willing testimony to the gallantry with which the Federals fought.

If the events of the two following days had not eclipsed the notice taken of the first day's struggle, much more would be said and thought of a Ligny which, though inexpensive to the Confederates, cost the Federals not less than 10,000 in killed, wounded, and missing. The large mass of Yankee prisoners, between 5,000 and 6,000 in number, the headlong retreat to which in the end their troops were driven, the apparently fortuitous occupation by their army of a strong ridge in the rear of Gettysburg, conspired to induce the belief that little more was wanted than a vigorous onslaught on the morrow to drive the Federals from the heights and open the way without let or hinderance to Baltimore or Washington. But even on the night of the triumphant First of July warning voices indicating distrust and apprehension in regard to the strength of the enemy's position were not inaudible. Among others General Longstreet shook his head gravely over the advantages conferred by this position, and thoughts of turning it by flanking were undoubtedly uppermost in his mind and General Lee's. The gallant though premature achievement of the troops of Generals Ewell and Hill, the memories of Bull Run, Manassas, Richmond, Fredericksburg, and Chancellorsville, the impracticability of turning either Federal flank, the impatience of General Hood and his fine division, lightly engaged at Fredericksburg, and absent at Chancellorsville, combined to inspire the leading Confederate Generals with an undue contempt for their enemy, although he was fighting on his own soil, with his back to the wall, and in a position which for strength and eligibility for defence has not been surpassed during 27 months of warfare. It was deemed desirable not even to wait until one of the finest divisions of General Longstreet's corps--the division of General Pickett--had joined the main body. Hope reigned triumphant in every Confederate breast; delay was likely to afford the Federals, whose activity with the spade has been repeatedly and marvellously manifested, time and opportunity for intrenching themselves ad libitum. A cry for immediate battle louder and more peremptory than ever ascended from the Highlanders of Claverhouse or Montrose swelled the gale--timid and hesitating counsels were impatiently discarded; and, as it appeared to me, the mature and cautious wisdom of General Lee had no choice but to float with the current, and to trust the enthusiasm of his troops to carry him triumphantly on the morrow over the heights which frowned darkly and menacingly in our front.

Text 4

The Times 19-03-1917

VISIT TO THE TOWN. "COOL INCONSEQUENCE" OF THE ARMY.
BRITISH HEADQUARTERS, MARCH 18.

Bapaume is ours! The battles of the Somme are won, and the German Army is in retreat. We occupy Le Transloy. Peronne may be in our hands by the time this dispatch reaches London. The whole line of battle north and south of the Ancre and the Somme is in solution; and though I have just returned from Bapaume--this is Sunday morning, though but the first hour after midnight--even in that city it was impossible to learn in the confusion and darkness how far beyond our men had gone. Nor was it advisable to try and find out things being as I found them. The British Army was taking the matter with cool inconsequence. I found it too busy to feel any elation. It had fought hard and long to be there; and there it was. It was going farther, I found dressing-stations and aid posts already established--but, thank goodness, not particularly busy by the wan light of their candles--in ruins and dug-outs which but a few hours before were within German lines.

What in some haste I want you to understand is that our men, with patient skill and labour, energetic and wonderfully--yes, wonder, fully--prompt, are somewhat ahead of time and scarcely anything at all behind the enemy. They are already established and secure where he was this time yesterday, in spite of all his hindrances, and in spite of the ruin their own gunfire has caused. But, the curious fellows, they take it as a matter of course, and showed no more excitement in Bapaume last night--though a little more activity, it is true--than they betray in Albert.

THE SYMBOL OF VICTORY.

But some amount of elation may be pardoned in an onlooker. Here was the symbol of victory for that prolonged series of battles--the fighting from Fricourt to Le Barque, from Gommecourt to Thiepval, to Combles and St. Pierre Vaast, known as the battle of the Somme; and the British Army had won. The French, our good comrades, were delighted. They solemnly shook our hands. They are not niggardly with their praise--they only want to see the Boche well beaten, and they love those who do it.

At the bare word, but a most authentic one, well behind the lines, where I heard with others that we were in Bapaume there was at least a little jubilation. Yet when, several hours later, I found a British soldier, clothed chiefly in a three days' growth of beard and mud, seated among some awful ruins while by candlelight a doctor extracted a little shrapnel from a soft place--he was very chatty and was smoking a cigarette--his chief comment was:--"We went over at ha' past 7 this morning (Saturday) and Fritz beat it. That's all, chum. Fritz got out. He hadn't time to stop."

To get to that dressing station we had had to travel the whole length of that famous field which has been opened by nearly eight months of the most serious fighting of the war.

It was incredible to us when an electric torch showed us an official direction post with the legend, "Baupaume, 2 kilometres." By the wayside was the long wreck of a German ammunition train, caught by our shells. We could see that easily enough, because now the star shells made a radiance as of intermittent arc-lights. They also showed us just in time the profound cavities caused by German mines in the road.

Round a turn of the road, and we were in Bapaume. It was veritably ours. There were the lights of the English in its windows; in a very few of its windows. But round Bapaume the night was crimson and throbbing with the incendiary fires of the destroyer, who had not long since been driven out. His green stars were rising anxiously into the glowing night, looking nervously for his pursuers. What I mean is that if I could tell you what Bapaume looked like, with its wild and improbable lights, and the violent ripping of machine-guns, I would.

But it is not so easy to remember, when one gets out of it at such a time, with bullets whistling past one's ears and shrapnel overhead. One makes good time back, like the galloper who knew more than we did.

Text 5

The Times 13-06-1944

GEN. MONTGOMERY ON OUR GAINS QUICK PENETRATION IN NORMANDY, JUNE 12

The grey old town of Bayeux, which was in the front line when I arrived, is now almost beyond the sound of battle, except for occasional bursts of anti-aircraft fire by night and the boom of naval guns shelling enemy positions in the dense woods to the south. From the Cherbourg peninsula, where the Americans are within 18 miles of Cherbourg itself, to the River Orne, above Caen, the width of the allied lodgement is some 60 miles, and every day it takes longer to drive from the forward areas to the beaches, which, broadly speaking--and there are still one or two unhealthy places--receive no more than a sprinkling of butterfly bombs to interfere with the unceasing task of unloading.

The narrow coastal roads and lateral lanes that curl between high hedgerows, past the mellow walls of Norman farm buildings, or across the open sweep of ripening cornfields, were never built for traffic on the present massive scale. But the provost companies know what they are about; road-signs spring up like the red poppies, and with every journey it becomes easier to get past some atrocious hair-pin bend.

All the concentrated energy that one saw in the marshalling areas in Britain is now released on the flood tide of avenging war. Weapons and vehicles on an unprecedented scale stream up from the sea as they streamed down to it on the other side; under leaden skies some men are moving up to battle as they have always done, on their feet; or they camp in the open fields, or in rare moments of relaxation try their hand at soldier's French with the villagers. Meanwhile, the fair land of Normandy pays part of the price in the destruction of homes and cattle, but it is a price that few people grudge to be free of the German locusts.

TACTICAL SURPRISE

There is the authority of General Montgomery for stating that the landings achieved a large measure of tactical surprise, though there is some evidence in the last-minute stiffening of the coastal screen that the enemy half-expected us in an area which, without being unduly wise after the event, seems to have offered fairly obvious claims for selection.

The Commander-in-Chief, who, as is his wont, has been making informal tours of the whole front in his jeep, yesterday received allied war correspondents at his headquarters, and expressed his complete satisfaction with the success achieved. He was warm in his praise of the fighting qualities of the troops engaged, and of the magnificent support of the allied navies and air forces, without which the operation could not have been undertaken.

The allied landing parties attacked at the selected points with such violence and speed that their initial assault carried them right over the beaches and several miles inland at the first blow. This was in accordance with General Montgomery's directive that the soldiers must be imbued with one idea--to penetrate quickly into enemy territory and peg out claims inland. There were gaps between the landing-beaches and in many instances the concrete emplacements were by-passed with the enemy garrison still remaining in them.

There was the curious but rather nasty situation that these defended localities were still holding out when we were three miles inland. They had to be reduced later on and were held by groups of stout-hearted Germans who fought well and inflicted losses upon us; but it would have been of no avail if we had merely seized a narrow beach-head and dug in. Equally inside the allied lines there were for some days a considerable number of loose Germans and snipers wandering about, and they, too, had to be cleaned up before we could go on with the battle. These snipers included a number of women, married in some instances to German officers, and some of them have been killed.

IN GREAT FORM

A firm lodgement, 60 miles wide, has now been established for use as a base for operations in accordance with the High Command's plan. So far, up to 7,000 prisoners have been taken, among them, curiously enough, several Japanese in German uniform, who are presumably drawn from the large number of Japanese students in Germany. A great many of the enemy, too, have been killed, and from his tour of the front General Montgomery finds our own troops, British and American, in tremendous form.

It may now be stated that among the British assault formations is the 3rd Division, which has been in some of the thickest fighting and has carried itself splendidly. Four years ago it was commanded in France by General Montgomery, who brought it in at Cherbourg and took it out at Dunkirk; and within it is the brigade he previously commanded.

Then no one is more deserving of praise than the British and American airborne divisions or, for that matter, the Commandos who went in, as I have already recorded, at some of the gaps between the beaches--at the fishing village, for example, of Port-en-Bessin, which is cut off from the sands by high cliffs and where a Royal Marine Commando was engaged in extremely fierce fighting.

Now there is a solid front, and such a reassuring air cover that the troops hardly bother to look up at the sound of aircraft. I was out in a forward area yesterday when two fighters streaked low over the tree-tops, and a Welsh sergeant exclaimed in a tone of injured surprise: "They were Messerschmitts!"

Text 6

Cruiser torpedoed by Royal Navy sinks
The Times 04-05-1982 Byline: Nicholas Ashford

Argentina's second largest warship, the 13,645-ton cruiser General Belgrano, was presumed sunk last night after being torpedoed by a British hunter-killer submarine on Sunday night. The news came from Buenos Aires and Washington, but the Ministry of Defence in London declined to confirm or deny it. Conflicting accounts emerged on the number of men feared lost: the Argentine authorities put it as low as 500, while reports from the United States spoke of at least 700. The cruiser was believed to have been just outside Britain's 200-mile exclusion zone around the Falklands when she was hit, but Britain says she was constituting a threat.

As authoritative sources in Washington predicted "tremendous battles" within 24 hours, the Ministry of Defence in London requisitioned the Queen Elizabeth 2 to join the task force.

Mr Francis Pym ended his mission to the United States by telling the United Nations Secretary-General that Britain will not offer any compromise until Argentina withdraws from the Falklands and cedes its sovereignty claim. Mrs Thatcher and her "war Cabinet" will meet today.

Authoritative sources in Washington tonight confirmed that the Argentine cruiser General Belgrano had sunk. It was feared that the loss of life among members of the 1,200 crew was very high. One source said the death toll might have been as high as 700.

There was puzzlement here why the toll appeared to be so heavy, bearing in mind it took the vessel a number of hours to sink after being hit by two torpedoes yesterday afternoon. A number of Argentine vessels were in the vicinity, but it is possible they did not want to approach the stricken vessel for fear of being attacked as well.

It appeared that the British submarine, by firing only two torpedoes had gone out of its way to damage the cruiser and not sink it, in an attempt to reduce loss of life. However, the source added that as the vessel was very old it could have sunk after one hit.

The source said there was now a real possibility of a major battle taking place in the next day or so. Information reaching Washington this evening showed that the Argentines appeared to be preparing for a big attack against the British task force.

"There may be tremendous battles over the next 24 hours," one source said. "My guess is the Argentines may be planning some kind of suicide tactics, such as a mass attack on a British ship."

The sources also said that information reaching Washington indicated that Argentina's single aircraft carrier, Veintianco de Mayo, was suffering technical problems and might not be able to play an effective role in any forthcoming battles.

The torpedoing of the General Belgrano produced a flurry of diplomatic activity here. Sir Nicholas Henderson, the British Ambassador, visited the State Department this afternoon for talks with Mr Alexander Haig, the Secretary of State. The two men were constantly in telephone contact.

A Department spokesman said that if reports of the sinking proved accurate, "we would deeply regret the loss of life. It would point out the absolute necessity of reaching a peaceful settlement to this tragic conflict".

Buenos Aires: Argentina's Joint Chiefs of Staff announced at 5.35 pm local time today (9.35 pm British time) that it had information which suggested that the Cruiser General Belgrano had been sunk (Christopher Thomas writes).

Captain Enrique de Leon Estadas, the official Argentine military spokesman, said that, although the ship had a complement of 1,200, it was operating on a crew which may have been as low as 500 men. He added that he did not know their fate. "We have no idea what is happening. The communications are down", he added.

Tonight, the Argentine Military Command said that a navy aircraft flying over the area spotted lifeboats. Agency reports said that each lifeboat appeared to be carrying between 20 and 25 people.

The Belgrano was launched in March 1938 as the USS Phoenix, and survived the attack on Pearl Harbour in 1941. It had two British Seacat sea-to-air missile-launchers, 15 six-inch and eight five-inch guns. It was bought from the United States in 1951 for $7.8m.

London: Mr John Nott, Secretary of State for Defence, tonight described the General Belgrano as a threat against which the Falklands task force had every right to react in self-defence (Henry Stanhope writes).

Mr Nott said that if Argentina wanted to protect its own troops and avoid the losses of ships and aircraft it had only to withdraw from the area and stop interfering.

He added that Britain's overiding objective was still a lasting peaceful solution negotiated with the Argentine Government, after its troops had withdrawn from the Falklands.

A Ministry of Defence spokesman said tonight: "We are not in a position to confirm or deny Argentine reports".

Tobias Rademann, Bochum

Newspapers on the Internet

I. Introduction

Over the past two years, the Internet – and especially the WWW – has gained an ever broader acceptance not only among the academia but also among everyday users. There is no doubt that the increasing popularity of this info-communications medium and its rapid future development will have a considerable impact on almost every sector of private, corporate, and public life. It is only natural then that this process should also have significant effects on the traditional services provided by the media, and here – among other things – especially on electronic publications.

The present study will investigate these effects by means of referring to the most popular example of electronic periodicals, namely electronic newspapers. Since electronic newspapers differ from their printed counterparts in a number of ways, the following chapter will serve as a brief introduction to this new subgenre by presenting an examination of the various features that tend to characterise it.

Once this overview has been established, a quality analysis will be conducted by taking into account such issues as the general accessibility of the papers' Web sites, their design and appearance, and, of course, the overall content of major electronic newspapers. Although this quality analysis is held on a general level, its perspective mainly stems from the point of view of scientific research projects and higher education.

In a final step, the fourth chapter will centre on the question of how to work with electronic newspaper articles. Thus, details on the various possibilities that exist for downloading and adapting electronic texts will be presented, such as storing the actual files (including additional multimedia elements such as graphics, etc.) on local disks, editing HTML-source codes, and finally converting these into ASCII text files for further linguistic research. The study will conclude with a critical summary of the advantages and disadvantages of electronic newspapers as compared to the traditional printed media, as well as an outlook on the most likely future developments in this field.

The present study will, however, focus on English-language electronic newspapers only, and here the investigation will primarily be concerned with those papers that already offer an acceptable degree of service for scientific research purposes. Where appropriate, selected representatives will be mentioned as well.

II. Feature-Analysis of Online Electronic Newspapers

Over the past three years, electronic newspapers have firmly established themselves as an essential source for retrieving news and information via the WWW, growing in number from 20 in 1993 and 100 by the end of 1994, to a current figure of more than 2,500 world-wide (cf. Tab. 1).[1] However, when looking at these figures, it is of crucial importance to distinguish between high-, average- and low-quality online ENs. Obviously, the number of ENs that offer an acceptable degree of service with respect to both content and form is considerably smaller than the overall number quoted above; and the number of ENs that offer such outstanding features as *USA Today*, *The (Financial) Times*, or *The WSJIE* is smaller still.[2] In this context, there appears to be a trend: As a rule, those online ENs that traditionally belonged to the group of (inter-)national quality dailies in the print sector tend to have sophisticated Web sites – probably mainly because of their financial means and their fear to lose their respective position as "number one information source in [the] region"[3], while most smaller locals (with notable exceptions, of course) only offer very restricted and often highly outdated reports. In order to gain a better understanding of this new subgenre and some of its representatives, the following paragraphs will present a general overview over their most important characteristics such as their formats and distribution methods, the different access restrictions currently in practice, as well as the content and services they offer, and finally their publication frequency.

Updated November 21, 1997 **Total Number of online newspapers currently in the E&P Interactive's Online Newspaper Database: 2560***	
Number of Online Newspapers on the World Wide Web: 2445	
Online Newspapers by (parent company) Type	**Online Newspapers by Region**
Dailies – 1484	Africa – 29
Weeklies – 687	Asia – 120
Business – 112	Canada – 139
Alternative – 71	Caribbean – 22
Publishing Groups – 119	Europe – 414
Specialty Papers – 80	Latin America – 149
News Magazines – 12	Middle East – 33
Online Commercial Services – 37	Oceania – 23
Dial-Ups (BBS) – 33	United States – 1591
Misc – 96	
Copyright © The Editor & Publisher Co. 1997 All Rights Reserved	

Tabelle 1: Total Number of Online Newspapers in the E&P Interactive's Database[4]

Figure 1: A typical screen shot of an electronic newspaper

Although there are numerous formats in which electronic periodicals (EPs) in general and ENs in particular are made available to the consumer, a clear trend can be observed in this field:[5] Primarily resulting from the comparatively low number of overall users connected to the Internet and the basic technical possibilities available at the time, the vast majority of early EPs tended to use the lowest common denominator formats (i.e. ASCII and bitmaps) in order to ensure that the largest number of potential users could access and read their files. The introduction of the WWW, the Internet's most sophisticated navigational shell, and the subsequent exponential growth in the number of users, however, had a significant impact on the design of electronic periodicals / newspapers: The possibility to include multimedia data and hypertext links in any HTML-based document soon resulted in electronic publishers focusing on HTML (Hypertext Markup Language) for their various publications, not least because these documents could be easily displayed by any browser, and could, moreover, be accessed by a large number of amateur users.[6] And although even its latest release, i.e. HTML version 3.2, is far from being perfect for (scientific) publishing (mathematical formulae and chemical symbols cannot be displayed, only to mention two downsides), the vast majority of today's online newspapers is based on this language (approx. 96 %, cf. Tab. 1) and it is foreseeable that this will remain the case in the near future.[7]

As said before, the WWW enables publishers to include multimedia formats within any HTML document. Thus while early ASCII-based ENs contained no more than plain text made up of the 128 unique ASCII symbols, we now frequently find besides text numerous additional elements such as graphics, charts, photographs, as well as animations and sound- and video sequences.[8] Nevertheless, despite its various advantages, there are some considerable disadvantages connected to the use of HTML as well, the two most important of which are the lack of author control with respect to the article's layout (every browser will display a given article differently, among other things depending on the screen size or the preferences the user has entered for features such as font and character size) and the fact that any HTML-file can easily be copied, altered in form and content, and re-distributed by anyone possessing only some basic understanding of HTML programming.

Not least resulting from the above-mentioned downsides to HTML, it is far from being the only format which is used for publishing electronic newspapers and journals: Among others, such formats as Adobe's Portable Document Format (PDF), Postscript, and LaTeX are frequently found in this field as well. While the main problem with these formats lies in the fact that special programs are required for reading them, their most important upside consists in an increased author control over the respective documents with regard to layout and content. It is extremely difficult at present to modify both form and content of files published in any of the three data formats, which makes it easy to include copyright notices within the individual documents.

Very much depending on the different formats electronic newspapers are published in, the means by which they are distributed vary as well. Nonetheless, the two most common ways through which ENs are currently being made available to the consumer are the WWW and eMail. Obviously, all those ENs that are published in HTML have to be made available on the WWW. The numerous links embedded in the individual articles that point not only to additional reports or Web sites, but frequently to graphical elements, photographs, and charts which play an essential role with respect to the article's layout and content make it basically impossible for those files to be viewed other than from the respective paper's Web-site. This implies, however, that everyone who wants to read this paper does not only have to have access to the WWW but moreover that they have to be connected to the Internet at the time of reading – one of the major downsides of this alternative from the perspective of most consumers. On the other hand, fixed-content data formats such as PDF or Postscript but – of course – also plain ASCII text files enable publishers to distribute their ENs via eMail or special agent programs.[9] Provided that the consumer owns the program necessary to display the respective data-format, this is by far the most convenient and most comfortable way for him to read his paper. In contrast to the HTML-alternative, he does not have to be connected to the Internet, but still has full access to the entire paper. However, it is obvious that – at least with ordinary eMails – multimedia elements such as colour photographs, animations or film- and video sequences cannot be included (yet). A summary of the advantages and disadvantages of the various distribution methods is included in Tab. 2 below:

Distribution	Advantages	Disadvantages
via WWW (on-site)	up-to-date, in-depth information on a broad variety of subjects reader may select articles of interest him-/herself articles make full use of multimedia data additional sources for background information may be accessed instantaneously	reader has to be online while reading downloading articles might take some time (esp. in times of network congestion)
via special agent programs	automated delivery no need to be online by the time of reading almost no loading time for an article	fixed content and fixed layout no additional information accessible
via eMail	automated delivery no need to be online by the time of reading almost no loading time for an article	fixed content and fixed layout usu. only plain ASCII texts no additional information accessible

Tabelle 2: Impact of Distribution Methods

B. Access Restrictions

In contrast to printed periodicals where one of the main "access restrictions" lies in their regional availability, we have already seen that indirect access restrictions for online EPs can result from the data format in which they are published, because the format used might make it necessary to have a special program for viewing the paper or may require the user to be connected to the Internet at the time of reading. However, besides these indirect access restrictions, a number of additional – direct – access restrictions have been introduced by the publishers of electronic newspapers. For those papers published on the WWW, it has become common practice nowadays to have the user go through a login-procedure before he can access the data offered (cf. e.g., The *Times* or *The Financial Times [FT.com]*). For accessing the paper's Web-services the user requires a user ID and a password, both of which he will be given in return for filling out a brief questionnaire concerning personal details such as name, sex, address, career, etc. on his first arrival at the site. Upon a later visit, the user will only have to enter ID and password which will then allow him to access all the information available on the respective Web-site. Although, for the time being, most newspaper publishers do not yet bill their customers for their services, there are already companies that do (e.g. *The New York Times* or *The Wall Street Journal Interactive Edition* [*WSJIE*]). Here, subscription forms have to be completed, including details concerning not only one's personal data but also credit card information, etc. Subscription rates for electronic newspapers tend to lie well below those of their printed counterparts (*The WSJIE*, e.g., charges US$ 49.– p.a. for those that do not subscribe to the paper's printed edition); a clear exception is *The New York Times,* the fee of which is extremely high, lying at US$ 35.– per month.[10] However, when comparing the services offered by fee-based quality-online ENs [e.g. *The WSJIE*, *NYT*] and those that are offered free of charge [e.g. *FT.com*, The *Times*], there does not (yet) appear to be so much of a difference in service and article quality.

Nevertheless, it can be expected for the not too distant future that this scenario will change considerably. In today's developing stage, those users that already enjoy the advantages of being connected to the Internet are being taken as test subjects, enabling publishers of ENs to study their reading habits, demands, and needs as well as the amount of work and knowledge required to set up and maintain an electronic newspaper. By granting interested readers free access to their sites, these publishers can gather the experience necessary for later projects to be implemented when the general public is ready for the true onset of the Information Age. It is then that most publishers will probably bill their customers for accessing their pages. In the meantime, the major publishing companies make sure that they "use every weapon [they] can find to establish [their Web-sites] as the [...] first place advertisers think of."[11]

C. Content and Services

Given the definition of printed newspapers, the potential content of their electronic counterparts is basically clear: The reader will, of course, find news, comments, stories, features, columns, letters to the editor, science and technology, sports news, entertainment, education, book reviews, etc. included in any standard-quality electronic newspaper. In addition to these, there are even some papers which feature such issues as classifieds, advertisements, real estate, horoscopes, cartoons, etc. However, it must be said that these will most likely remain exceptions until there is a sufficiently large target audience to justify the expenses necessary for offering comparable services.

As has always been the case with the traditional printed press, the individual content of a given publication very much depends on the kind of newspaper under scrutiny. Although there are no limits to the regional availability of an electronic newspaper on the Internet, constraints are, of course, put on the content as a result of its regional, national, ethical, etc. focus. As paradoxical as this might occur for the Global Village at first sight, but on the Internet, too, there exists a classification of newspapers in international, national, regional, or local papers – mainly resulting from the fact that the vast majority of them stems from a traditional printed background.[12] But the content is also influenced by one other main factor, namely the newspaper's target audience. Here again, the same classification as in the printed press can be applied, leaving us with either quality or popular-press newspapers. However, quite in contrast to the print sector where there tend to be rather few international, quality-press papers and a huge number of regional or local popular-press newspapers, the majority of electronic newspapers offering an acceptable degree of service already are national or even international quality dailies. This is, of course, not too surprising, especially if one bears in mind that access to the Internet is still rather expensive and demands a certain degree of computer literacy which the average consumer (quite in contrast to the international (business) executive, i.e. the target group of quality dailies such as *FT.Com* or *The WSJIE*) does not (yet) possess. Nevertheless, for the not too distant future, it can be expected that this ratio will shift a little in favour of the popular press (not least resulting from the rising Internet awareness of the general public), though high-standard papers giving in-depth information are most likely to remain the popular source demanded on such a medium.

However, what is of primary importance when looking at electronic newspapers is not so much their potential content (basically because it can largely be expected to resemble that of their printed counterparts), but rather their additional services, most of which have so far not been available in printed papers, and thus open up new perspectives as to what can be done with a newspaper. At least from a research point of view, *searchable archives* are unquestionably the most precious additional feature of electronic newspapers. Almost every EN-Web site nowadays includes a hypertext link to a searchable archive of the paper's past editions. These archives typically cover between two weeks to one month (e.g. *The Chicago Tribune* or *the Washington Post*), but – given the current technological developments – it is most likely that archives for entire years can soon be accessed online (the electronic version of The *Times*, for example, already has its entire archive online, comprising every issue from January 1st, 1996).[13] The searchable archives typically feature a keyword-driven search engine that allows for a simple enumeration or combination of keywords which are used to identify the articles of relevance for a given query. The output of such a query usually consists of a hypertext-based list of article headlines / summaries which the user may then browse.

Another feature the value of which must not be underestimated are the countless *hypertext links* to additional online sources. As has been hinted at in the previous paragraphs already, these are highly characteristic for online electronic publications and frequently refer to different reports in the same paper, but also to other Web sites, additional online sources, etc. It is these links that do not only enable the reader to get the often-cited multi-faceted in-depth information on a given subject, but which can furthermore turn the newspaper in the starting point for exploring the Web's resources on a given topic. In this context, interactivity between the paper and its users is frequently supported by means of newsgroups in which participants can discuss not only the various articles and opinions expressed in the paper but also additional questions which might be of interest.[14]

Even today some of the major publishing companies offer services which are likely to belong to the most important future developments in this field: *Personalised Newspapers.* This term describes the possibility of automatically receiving an individualised selection of articles made up of reports, stories, etc. published in the respective paper on that day (see, e.g., The *Times* or *The WSJIE*). To set up such a paper, the only thing a user has to do is define his personal profile by selecting the sections he is interested in (such as national politics, financial news, sports, etc.), and by entering keywords. Once this is done, a CGI script will generate a personalised edition of the newspaper that includes only those articles marked relevant on the basis of the user's personal profile. As time passes, the user may leave his profile unchanged, or he may modify it at any time he wishes to do so. Usually, changes will take effect immediately.[15]

Finally, a number of newspapers offer a *reference library* in which the interested user may find background information on various subjects. These libraries may be fully accessible free of charge (e.g. The *Times'* 'Resource Section')[16], may have to be paid for on a pay-per-use basis, or may allow access to selected articles only. While, obviously, not all papers have such sophisticated services, many offer similar ones, including information on cultural events, etc.

D. Publication Frequency

We have seen already that their being published electronically in combination with the fact that they are made available via the Internet puts hardly any restrictions on the regional availability of EPs / ENs: As long as there is an Internet connection at hand any EP can be accessed and viewed from anywhere in the world. Furthermore, the fact that ENs are distributed electronically means there is no need to "physically" produce and distribute them. Bearing in mind that there are no costs involved and no additional time required for the physical production and distribution of a new issue of any EN, it soon becomes clear that they could (at least theoretically) be published with a higher frequency than their printed counterparts, simply because their production and distribution are much less expensive and time consuming. This tendency is even supported by the possibility of conducting partial updates, which means that publishers may update only certain sections (e.g. to correct mistakes, to bring in additional comments & reactions and last but not least to report about the latest events). Thus it can be summarised that the potential *update frequency* of ENs is considerably higher than the *publication frequency* of their printed counterparts.

Although there is the theoretical possibility to update an EN continuously (i.e. *as the news happens*), this is hardly done at present. There are no obvious reasons behind this artificial restraint, except for the traditional notions of printed newspapers which still tend to very much influence our understanding and treatment of their electronic counterparts. However, while news- and information services such as CNN International, Reuters, or MSNBC already present fine examples of EN-like Web-sites offering continuous sectional updates, it can be expected for the near future that electronic newspapers will follow suit – simply in order to remain competitive.

III. Quality Analysis of Electronic Periodicals

It has sufficiently been portrayed above that electronic newspapers already offer access to a vast amount of multi-faceted up-to-date in-depth information on an almost unlimited variety of subjects and interests. However, in order to be able to avoid the danger of being misled by low-quality information, various attempts have been undertaken in the recent past to create a suitable catalogue of criteria which assist in evaluating a given information resource.[17] And while these criteria are supposed to be applied to individual sources such as working papers, electronic books, etc., they can – in a slightly modified way – also be used to evaluate the quality of ENs in general. On the whole, there are three major issues that determine the overall quality of an electronic newspaper, namely its 'Access', 'Design & Appearance', and 'Content'. The following paragraphs will thus present a brief examination of these issues so that the reader gets an overall idea of the current quality of electronic newspapers and the tasks they may be employed for.

A. Access

The quality of a given EN with respect to its accessibility is largely influenced by both technical and financial access restrictions and by the access quality (cf. Fig. 2 below). While technical access restrictions describe the means by which the EN as such is made available (i.e. WWW, eMail), the financial ones summarise all costs connected with accessing it, such as subscription fees or pay-per-view charges. Finally, the access quality is predominantly affected by the stability of the EN's homepage URL and the available bandwidth which influences both overall loading time of a given article and general accessibility of the site.

With regard to most standard-quality ENs, it can be observed that the vast majority of them are accessible free of charge via the WWW. At least for the time being, they all have comparatively stable URLs which can easily be bookmarked. However, a major problem in the past definitely resulted from the insufficiently low bandwidth at which most of them were made available and the data jams on the Internet as such. As a result, both loading times for individual documents and general access to the papers' Web-sites were far from satisfactory for most of them. However, rather surprisingly for most Internet users, the speed at which data is transferred over the net has increased in real terms over the past few months – in spite of the exponentially risen amount of data traffic.

B. Design & Appearance

Both design and appearance of an electronic newspaper are primarily determined by the clarity with which the information is presented. Here, the organisation of the different sections and articles is important: Is the site clearly structured, i.e. is it easy to navigate and are there instructions included which will help with more difficult tasks? Are the pages concise, or does the reader have to 'scroll forever' until he reaches the end of a WWW-page? In addition, the degree of interactivity and the additional services are equally of importance. Finally, it is, of course, also essential for the design and the appearance of any EN to have a conceptionally exciting layout which invites the reader to go on reading.

As far as current ENs are concerned, it can be determined that hardly any problems exist with respect to this issue: At least the sites of the major newspapers are well organised, with most sections, articles, and tools being intuitive to find. Given the comparative recency of the developments in this field, most publishers pay great attention to the organisation of their sites. Where necessary, they have even introduced major changes in order to ensure that most sections are "only a mouse-click away" (see, e.g.

The London Times which has redesigned its Web-site with the help of frames). The degree of conceptional excitement obviously depends on the tastes of the individual reader, but the vast majority of ENs cannot be said to have a boring layout at all. As far as interactivity and additional services are concerned, it is out of question that ENs tend to have one of their major strengths here. Given the fact that with printed periodicals interactivity is largely restricted to writing letters to the editor and that hardly any additional services are offered whatsoever, there is a huge potential for EPs to exceed their counterparts in this field.

C. Content

Although the two previous points may certainly assist in evaluating the quality of a given information resource (here: electronic newspapers), it is, of course, the content itself which is of utmost interest for anyone who wants to obtain valuable background information. And even though the two features 'accessibility' and 'design & appearance' usually correspond to the overall quality of a given source's content, there may still be ENs around that have a dreadful layout but highly interesting articles or others which have a stunning appearance but no valuable content at all.[18]

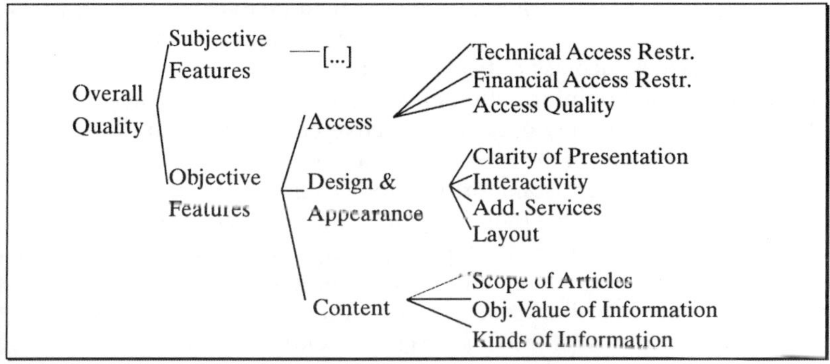

Figure 2: Crucial Factors for Conducting a Quality Analysis

The quality of a paper's overall content is primarily determined by the scope of the articles / the newspaper as such. The scope of a given article can be subdivided into the two features breadth and depth, where breadth refers to the number of aspects covered of the subject in question and depth to the degree of detail the respective article provides (cf. Fig. 2). It has been mentioned before that the primary advantage of electronic periodicals lies in the fact that they can present an in-depth multi-faceted analysis of any subject. This results not only from the possibility of including valuable supplementary links to third-party online sources, but also from the fact that electronic online publications do not have anything like page restrictions. Finally, the amount of graphics included in the individual articles affects the quality of the content as well. Are graphics just included for the sake of 'showing off', or do they give valuable information on the subject?

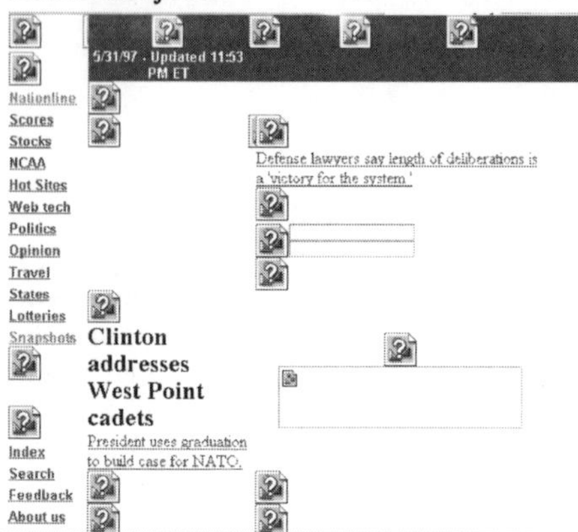

Figure 3: Figure 1 as saved without any editing

The second major characteristic shaping the content quality of any electronic newspaper is the objective value of the information available.[19] The objective value depends on a variety of issues, including the currency of the information and its verifiability. While the value of a piece of information tends to increase with its currency, it is also of utmost importance for the reader to know about its origin, which then enables him to verify its content and to make assumptions about issues such as political colouring, etc.

Finally, the kind of information presented is of interest as well: Do the articles published merely present subjective commentary or do they include objective facts on the latest events and developments?

With respect to the vast majority of today's quality electronic newspapers, there is no doubt that their content quality is satisfactory if not to say above average. The potential scope of an EN is theoretically unlimited, and the major ones available already present good examples for this by including all kinds of background information by offering access to archives, etc. While most of the smaller papers tend to have a highly restricted amount of articles available, it can be expected for the future (i.e. when their target audience grows) that they, too, will make use of the potential technical facilities on the WWW. In addition, the information available tends to be very much up-to-date, and articles include both commentary and factual reporting. Thus the content quality of ENs is hardly anything to be criticised.

As can be inferred from the information presented above, it is indeed possible to evaluate the quality not only of a specific information resource on the basis of the criteria established at the beginning of this section, but also of an entire genre. Of course, there are always exceptions to the rule, but it is important to realise that the overall quality of electronic newspapers already appears to be of a high standard and that there is a huge potential for those ENs that do not yet offer acceptable services. Their most consequential downside, the low bandwidth, can be expected to become less of a problem as a high-capacity Global Information Infrastructure is being implemented.

IV. Working With Electronic Articles

While the paragraphs above were primarily concerned with the overall quality of online electronic newspapers, one important question has so far remained unanswered: What happens when a suitable text is found? Even though this question is particularly important in the context of linguistic research where these articles are frequently used as a basis for further investigation, it is also of relevance for various other kinds of scientific projects, since most texts would have to be archived in one form or other, e.g. in order to be able to re-read them at a later time.[20] Of course, articles could be printed out on any high-quality laser printer and archived in their printed form. While this might be sufficient for most research assignments, it could become necessary to keep an electronic version of the respective text in one's own archive / corpus for one reason or another – and this is where the difficulties tend to come up. It is obviously no major problem to download and store a given HTML file on a local HDD / FDD. Problems arise, however, as soon as multimedia elements such as graphics, photographs or sound- and video sequences are included in the respective article (which is almost always the case, cf. Fig. 3). As these are not part of the HTML file as such but merely embedded as hypertext links in the respective article's source code, the user would have to download each and every single one of them manually (in Figs. 1&3, the cover page of USA Today, the number of graphical elements amounts to 43!). Although this is not too difficult, the user will still have problems when he attempts to view the article later on, since most images, etc. are not stored in the same directory as the HTML file itself. This would make it necessary, however, to edit the HTML source code of the respective article by changing any reference to multimedia elements to the same subdirectory – a task which can be extremely time-consuming and requires a certain degree of experience in HTML programming.[21] In addition, recent developments in Web publishing have made it increasingly difficult to download and store electronic articles, especially for the lay user. Although such problematical commands as e.g. "<BASE HREF="...">" could be changed by hand, it is most of all the increasingly popular JavaScript applets and frames that will make it almost impossible to view the article in its original form once it has been stored on the local HDD.

These issues become even more important when the texts retrieved are to be taken as basis for further linguistic analysis. Here, plain ASCII text is frequently required (e.g. for submitting the articles to taggers or similar research tools, etc.), which will make it necessary to "strip" the source code entirely off the HTML tags. Again, this transformation is fairly easy for HTML-pages with a simple layout, but as soon as tables, multimedia elements, frames, etc. are used, it will require a lot more time and knowledge.[22]

Even though it could be argued that the text itself is the most important element (thus allowing all of the multimedia elements to be neglected), this attitude should become a matter of dispute as the Internet evolves to become one of the leading sources for information. From my own point of view, at least a sub-discipline of linguistics should begin to reflect on the various forms of multimedia elements, since there is certainly much evidence suggesting that these will play an increasingly important role in human communication and that they will act as substitutes for language as we know it (in German, there is an old proverb which goes something like "A picture tells more than a thousand words").

All things considered, it has been demonstrated that handling electronically published articles currently requires a considerable degree of computer literacy and good knowledge of HTML, since the majority of these files will have to be edited before they can be archived or used for further linguistic research. The amount of energy involved in this transformation, however, must not be overestimated. If compared to the fact that printed articles had to be photocopied, scanned or even manually typed in and finally proof-read before anything else could be done with them, the amount of work required for editing HTML-files does not appear to be that exhausting – it is merely completely new for most researchers and thus gives rise to unjustified concerns, unfortunately frequently resulting in its overall rejection. If one bears in mind the effort required for locating and gathering printed information, then this argument becomes even the more invalid.

V. Critical Summary

Even though the term "electronic newspaper" is, strictly speaking, a contradiction in itself, the present study should have demonstrated that this new subgenre has become one of the leading sources for retrieving information over the Internet and that this will remain to be the case for the years to come. It illustrated that although ENs resemble their printed counterparts in many ways, the two differ in various respects, most of which concern issues such as depth of information coverage, recency of articles, degree of interactivity, and finally additional services. However, it is especially in the context of higher education and / or scientific research that the global availability of electronic newspapers is one of their most important upsides. Never before have students and lecturers had access to such a broad pool of up-to-date socio-cultural information from around the world at hardly any cost.[23]

One of the major issues that remains to be discussed, however, is whether consumers (and here particularly lecturers / students) can already access this information. For many, a first major difficulty arises with respect to both technical and financial means required for accessing the information presented on the WWW – and while one might think that this concerns private consumers rather than universities, it is a well-known fact that the number of adequate computer rooms which would enable students and lecturers to take advantage of these new possibilities lies far below what could be called acceptable. But even if these prerequisites were met, there would still be a widespread lack of knowledge among lecturers as far as the handling of these new services is concerned, which frequently results in many avoiding them in the first place, let alone the fact that the vast majority does not even know about their existence or the possibilities they offer.[24]

For many observers, one of the most interesting questions currently is whether or not electronic newspapers can be regarded as full-value substitutes or rather as supplements to their printed counterparts. However, I think the answer to this question is fairly straightforward: It is most likely that the everyday reader will not regard any form of electronic periodical as a substitute for his "beloved" daily newspaper or magazine. The technological and practical restrictions resulting from the necessity of being connected to the Internet are just too big for the time being. Quite in contrast to this target group, electronic newspapers may well serve as good substitutes for groups such as the international business executive, the professional researcher or the student of language, culture, current affairs, etc. Bearing in mind their global availability, the fact that "information is power" and that it is most valuable the more recent it is and the fewer people know about it, electronic newspapers and comparable services have major advantages for these groups – simply because they can present the news *as it happens* and enrich it with various multimedia elements such as text, video- and audio sequences as well as additional links to (third-party) in-depth information resources. For them, high-quality, up-to-date in-depth information on a broad variety of subjects is of primary importance, and this is exactly what the Internet has in store with respect to electronic newspapers. Thus it can be expected that while the academia will continue to exploit the possibilities offered by electronic periodicals in general and by electronic newspapers in particular and will – together with the group of international (business) executives – probably remain its primary target audience for the near future, the everyday user will most likely regard ENs only as supplements to his printed copies, occasionally supplying him with additional information.[25]

To conclude, I personally think that one issue which will be most interesting to watch with respect to electronic newspapers is whether we can free ourselves from the traditional notions connected with their printed counterparts and accept electronic publications which are updated on a continuous basis rather than at fixed intervals, which focus on special interests rather than regional aspects, and which contain various non-printable items such as animations or sound sequences. Finally, it remains to be seen if the rest of the world will manage to catch up on America, as more than half of all online newspapers currently stems from an American background and even more are English-speaking.

Notes

1 E&P Directory of Newspapers (1997). This service claims to be "the most comprehensive reference source of its kind".
2 However, to find out about quite a few high-quality sites, the interested reader might like to consult AJR's "Top 50 News Sites of the Year" to be found at AJR (1997).
3 Associated Press (1996).
4 Table taken from E&P Directory of Newspapers (1997), http://www.mediainfo.com/ephome/npaper/nphtm/stats.htm.
5 For more detailed information on the following see, among others, Wustemann (1997).
6 It has to be mentioned here that it were not so much electronic newspapers, but rather electronic magazines which were the pioneers in this field. The best-known example for a magazine that, from the very beginning, used the new possibilities offered by the Internet was *Playboy Magazine.* To a very high degree, it has been the success of such attempts that later led both newspapers and magazines from different fields of interest to online publishing.
7 Recent attempts have begun to include JavaScript elements as well. Cf., e.g. selected pages at FT.com, as for instance the paper's coverage of this year's British Elections.
8 Although no EN in the traditional sense, the pages at CNN.com are a very good example for this possibility: "CNN demonstrates the possibilities of news delivery on the Internet" (Notess (1996)).
9 A very good example for a PDF-based daily that uses a special agent program to deliver the current copy to the consumer is the eight-page daily news summary *Times Fax* (by *The New York Times*) at http://nytimesfax.com/altfax.html, and one of the most brilliant examples for newspapers / newsletters distributed via eMail is *The Irish Emigrant* (http://ireland.iol.ie/emigrant/ie.html).

10 For a more detailed value-for-money analysis of several individual newspapers see Rademann (1996), pp. 26-41. However, given the costs involved in connecting to the paper's Web-site in addition to the restricted readability (only in front of the PC), rates such as that charged by *The New York Times* do by no means seem justified – even though the *NYT* has won many awards, among others the two top honours in the "World's Best Online Newspaper Awards" (see E&P (1997) for more details) and in the *American Journalism Review's* "Top 50 news sites" (cf. AJR (1997) and Meyer (1997)).

11 Associated Press (1996).

12 It will be one of the most interesting issues to observe over the next few years if the possibilities offered by electronic publishing will lead to the traditional classification scheme of newspapers (i.e. the regional approach) being abandoned in favour of one that is more suitable for an electronic environment (i.e. one where the primary distinctions between newspapers are based on the interests of their target audience rather than their regional availability).

13 It is obvious that accessing such databases will probably not be free of charge as their maintenance tends to be comparatively expensive. There are already quite a few highly sophisticated commercial databases, containing thousands of recently published newspaper articles as well as valuable past files; some outstanding examples are NewsNet, Dow Jones, Lexis-Nexis, and Dialog (for more information see Notess (1996)).

14 See, e.g. *FT.com's* newsgroup "FT.your.views" at news:www.ft.com/.

15 These personalized newspapers must not be confused with personal news and information services / news delivery services which are commercial services offering the possibility of receiving personalized delivery of news of *different* papers / information resources. Examples for these are, among others, PointCast or Newshound. For more information see Quintana (1996) or Rademann (1996), pp. 84-85.

16 See http://www.the-times.co.uk/news/pages/resources/aboutus1.n.html.

17 For more background information on this issue the interested reader might want to check the online 'Bibliography on Evaluating Internet Resources' (one of many), maintained by Auer (1996), or the WWW VL page on 'Evaluation of information resources' (WWW VL (1996)).

18 One of the most outstanding examples for a simple, ASCII-based newsletter featuring highly valuable information is the Irish weekly, *The Irish Emigrant*.

19 Quite in contrast to the objective value of a given piece of information, its subjective quality will always depend on the task and the user's intention.

20 It has to be said here that it is extremely difficult at present – if not to say almost impossible – to order an article from an electronic newspaper that is older than the respective paper's on-site archive through any library. Thus if for any reason one wanted to re-read the article at a later point in time, it is currently the only possibility to keep a copy of it in one's own archives.

21 It will usually not be possible to execute an "edit/replace" command, since not all of the multimedia elements will be located in the same subdirectory on the host computer (advertisements will, e.g., be placed in different locations than navigational bars and photographs).

22 There are various ways in which the text of a given Web page may be saved. One is to save the respective page and strip it with a (commercial) HTML editor; another consists in the possibility to highlight the text on the screen with

the mouse and press "edit/copy" from the browser's menu and insert it in a separate file (e.g. in any normal word processor); a third is to select "save as/ Plain Text (.txt)" from the menu. However, with all of these possibilities, a considerable amount of manual post editing will have to be done.

23 For a more detailed account on how Internet News Services might be employed in (higher) education, the interested reader might refer to Rademann (1997b).

24 See, e.g. Rademann (1997a), section III.

25 For more information on Internet News Services and electronic newspapers cf. Outing (1996), Quintana (1997), and *The Economist* (1996).

Bibliography

AJR: "The Year's Top 50 News Sites." *American Journalism Review AJR Newslink online.* May 6·,1997. [http://www.newslink.org /bestresults.html]

Associated Press: "Newspapers scramble to get online." *The Bakersfield Californian.* Feb. 24, 1996. [http://www.bakersfield.com/tbc/art/TEC/27859@.html]

Auer, Nicole: "Bibliography on Evaluating Internet Resources." University of Wisconsin – Green Bay, 1996. [http://www.uwgb.edu/~auern/crithink.htm (14/11/96)]. Last Modified: 10/07/96.

The Economist: "Newspapers on the Internet still look like interlopers." *The Economist,* 1996.
[http://www.economist.com/review/rev14/rv14/review.html]

E&P Directory: "Editor & Publisher – Directory of Newspapers." 1997.
[http://www.mediainfo.com/ephome/npaper/online.htm, last updated November 21, 1997]

Meyer, Eric K.: "Best of the Web? It Depends on Your Perspective." *American Journalism Review – AJR Newslink online.* May 6, 1997. [http://www.newslink.org/best.html]

Notess, Greg. R.: "News Resources on the World Wide Web." *DATABASE Magazine.* Feb. / March, 1996, pp. 12-20. [http://www.onlineinc.com/database/FebDB/notess2.html]

Outing, Steve: "Online News Services FAQ." *Planetary News.* January 9, 1996.
[http://www.mediainfo.com/e-papers.faq.html]

Quintana, Yuri: "News on the Internet: Technologies and Trends". *OnTheInternet.* Vol. 3, No. 1 (Jan. / Feb.), 1997, 42-46.

Quintana, Yuri: "Design of Internet-Based News Delivery Systems and Its Impact on Society." *INET96*, Annual Conference of the Internet Society. Montreal, Canada. June 26-28, 1996.
[http://balsa.cetp.ipsl.fr/inet96papers/a7/a7_1.htm]

Rademann, Tobias: "Information Unlimited: Employing Internet Resources in Education." *INET97*, Annual Conference of the Internet Society. Kuala Lumpur, Malaysia. June 25-27, 1997. (1997a)
[http://www.ruhr-uni-bochum.de/www-public/rademtbu/private/pubs/inet97.htm]

Rademann, Tobias: "Socio-Cultural Studies Online – Employing Internet News Services in Higher Education." *RUFIS97 – Role of Universities in the Future Information Society,* Conference of the Czech Technical University in Prague. Prague, Czech Republic. September 25-27, 1997. (1997b).

[http://www.ruhr-uni-bochum.de/www-public/rademtbu/private/pubs/rufis.doc]

Rademann, Tobias: *Cultural Studies Online: Information Resources in English-Language Electronic Periodicals.* Ruhr University Bochum: Department for English and American Studies, 1996. [http://www.ruhr-uni-bochum.de/www-public/rademtbu/private/pubs/ep.htm, last updated Dec. 1996]

Wustemann, Judith: "Formats for the Electronic Library." – In *Ariadne – The Web Version.* Issue 8, March 1997. [http://www.ariadne.ac.uk/issue8/electronic-formats/, last updated April 8th,1997]

WWW VL: "Evaluation of Information Sources. The World-Wide Web Virtual Library: Information Quality WWW Virtual Library." [http://www.vuw.ac.nz/~agsmith/evaln/evaln.htm, last updated Oct. 30, 1996]

Online Resources

Cable News Network	http://www.cnn.com
The Chicago Tribune	http://www.chicago.tribune.com/
Dialog	http://www.dialog.com
Dow Jones Information Retrieval	http://bis.dowjones.com/
The Financial Times	http://www.ft.com
The Financial Times Newsgroups	FT.your.views at news:www.ft.com/
Freeloader	http://www.freeloader.com
The Irish Emigrant	http://ireland.iol.ie/emigrant/ie.html
MSNBC	http://www.msnbc.com
NewsNet	http://www.newsnet.com
The New York Times	http://www.nytimes.com
The New York Times' Fax	http://nytimesfax.com/altfax.html
Playboy Magazine	http://www.playboy.com
PointCast	http://www.pointcast.com/whatis.html
Reuters New Media	http//www.reutersnm.com
The *Times*	http://www.the-times.co.uk
The Times Resources	http://www.the-times.co.uk/ news/pages/resources/aboutus1.n.html
Wall Street Journal Interactive Edition	http://www.wsj.com/
The Washington Post	http://www.washingtonpost.com/
WebEx	http://www.travsoft.com/

Helmut Brammerts, Bochum

Autonomous language learning in tandem via the Internet

1. Introduction[1]

An introductory example:

Thomas, 15, has a personal computer at home and has always wanted to have Internet access. However, his parents have always been very reserved about this topic. This all changed when Thomas' English teacher informed the class about the opportunity to work with English, Australian or American students in tandem via the Internet. This way he could prove to his parents that the Internet could be positively useful. Besides, they had long told him that he needed to work more on his English.

Thomas' parents made the following agreement with him: they would buy the modem and pay the DM 6.00 monthly price for Internet access, which would be enough for as many e-mails as he wanted and for several hours of surfing the World Wide Web. Anything above this Thomas would have to pay for out of his pocket money.

During the past months, Thomas has found out that exchanging letters with Jennifer, his American tandem partner, is lots of fun. She is a computer fan just like Thomas, and the things she tells him about her recreational activities in the mountains of Montana (she says that there are actually still grizzly bears there) are often quite exciting. Presently, they write each other twice a week.

Thomas doesn't experience any problems writing about himself and things that interest him. This is because, in the first place, a major portion of every letter needs to be in German so that Jennifer can learn something from him. (His teacher says he has to spend half of the letter to Jennifer writing in German and the other half in English.) He has also noticed that he can use numerous English expressions from Jennifer's letters in his own letters and also uses them sometimes in his English class.

The only thing Thomas hasn't liked about this correspondence has been the many corrections he has to make to Jennifer's letters. However, recently his teacher told the class that they need not correct every single mistake because their partners would not profit from more than 5-10 corrections per letter anyway.[2]

Those who hoped that computers and computer assisted media could essentially facilitate foreign language teaching and especially self-determined language learning have been deceived if they expected too much in terms of the programmability of the computer as a tutor or as a communication partner. However, this is not the case for those who use computer networks, in particular the Internet, to access manifold, current and authentic information in the foreign language and especially as an inexpensive, direct communication medium between foreign language learners and native speakers of the target language.

In this contribution I will present our attempt to utilise the long-known concept of foreign language learning in tandem in combination with the opportunities the Internet provides to benefit schools, universities and adult education.

Autonomous language learning in tandem, whereby two learners with different native languages work together in partnerships to improve their language skills and their knowledge of their partner's culture and background, has steadily gained in importance in the past several years due to the following reasons:

- Learning in tandem calls for and supports transferable qualifications such as the ability to (continue to) learn independently and to communicate and co-operate multilingually and interculturally. Thereby tandem learning meets the need of the economic and political arenas for persons who are able to accept responsibility for their own (life-long) learning and are able to cope with an increasingly global and quickly evolving labour market.
- Improved transportation options and the promotion of mobility in the scope of the European Union along with the general tendency towards globalisation, but in particular the breathtaking technical developments in the area of telecommunication and the computer networking with sinking prices, have made it significantly easier now than in the past for many learners to find tandem partners.
- Learning in tandem is easily adapted to completely different learning conditions, which has been shown by publications of the last few years (Herfurth 1994, J. Wolff 1994, Brammerts & Little 1996). There have been experiences in tandem with learners in different age groups (teenagers and adults), with various types of educational institutions (schools, institutions of higher education, adult education, vocational education), and with different forms of organisation (particularly tandem courses with and without accompanying foreign language courses; with and without learner counselling; between learners in the same place and learners separated by greater distances).

2. The LINGUA and ODL projects

After several successful pilot projects, initially involving the University of Bochum (DE) and the University of Rhode Island (USA) in 1992 and later including the University of Oviedo (ES) and the University of Sheffield (GB), the systematic development of the *International E-Mail Tandem Network* began in 1994 in the European Union LINGUA project of the same name.

The 11 partner universities (Aalborg (DK), Aarhus (DK), Bochum (DE, co-ordination), Coimbra (PT), Trinity College Dublin (IE), Mitthögskolan (SE), Oviedo (ES), ENST Paris (FR), University of Sheffield (GB), HKL Sittard (NL), and Trier (DE)) established an international infrastructure for the promotion of foreign language learning in tandem via the Internet (asynchronous communication per e-mail, synchronous communication in virtual realities such as MOOs,[3] etc.) and developed and published relevant didactic materials.

At the end of the project, over 20 bilingual subnets were in existence, through which approximately 2,000 students from 20 countries had found tandem partners within one year. The services of each subnet include access to the central Tandem Agency in Bochum, to a bilingual e-mail discussion forum as well as didactic materials for learners and learning organisers in the eight partner languages. These materials have been published on the International Tandem Network's World Wide Web server in Bochum.

As part of this project, a number of academic papers were published; a final report in the form of *A Guide for language learning in tandem via the Internet* appeared in all partner languages (e.g. Brammerts/Little 1996 in German, Little/Brammerts 1996 in English).

To solidify these results and to expand tandem learning to educational areas apart from institutions of higher education, particularly to adult education and schools, the same partners with the addition of Torino (IT) started the project *Telematics for Autonomous and Intercultural Tandem Learning* in 1996 within the European programme *Open and Distance Learning (ODL).*
The goals of this two-year project are:

- The development of an open-access database in the Internet (the Tandem Server), in which work materials (aids, activity suggestions and experience reports) on tandem learning for learners, teachers and organisers of tandem learning are available. The Tandem Server now has mirrors in Bochum (DE), Dublin (IE), Oviedo (ES), Paris (FR), Rostov-on-Don (RU), Torino (IT) and Trier (DE).

- The expansion of the International Tandem Network through new language pairs and work materials and the opening of the network to learners of all ages and backgrounds. Presently 29 subnets exist: CAT-DEU (català-deutsch), DAN-DEU (dansk-deutsch), DAN-NED (dansk-Nederlands), DEU-ESP (deutsch-español), RIBO-L (deutsch-English), DEU-FRA (deutsch-français), DEU-HAN (deutsch-hangul (Korean)), DEU-HRV (deutsch-hrvatski (Croatian)), DEU-ITA (deutsch-italiano), DEU-NED (deutsch-Nederlands), DEU-NIH (deutsch-nihongo (Japanese)), DEU-POL (deutsch-polski), DEU-POR (deutsch-português), DEU-RUS (deutsch-russkij), DEU-SUO (deutsch-suomea (Finnish)), DEU-SVE (deutsch-svenska), DEU-ZHO (deutsch-zhongwen (Chinese)), ENG-ESP (English-español), ENG-FRA (English-français), ENG-ITA (English-italiano), ENG-NED (English-Nederlands), ENG-POL (English-polski), ENG-POR (English-português), ENG-SVE (English-svenska), ESP-FRA (español-français), ESP-ITA (español-italiano), FRA-ITA (français-italiano), FRA-NIH (français-nihongo (Japanese)), NED-POR (Nederlands-português).
  At present, approximately 600 to 800 learners find their tandem partners every month through the Tandem Agency. Furthermore, a special Internet tandem work area for pupils called "Language learning in tandem via the Internet" has been installed on the server for education of the German state of North Rhine-Westphalia, *learn:line.*
- Testing and publication of new possibilities for the integration of language learning in tandem in local curricula. Different organisational models for learning in tandem via the Internet are being evaluated in a series of accompanying studies, whereby questions about optimum help for the learner (learner counselling) and possibilities for teachers to integrate tandem in their class work are in the foreground.
- Examination, through pilot projects, of the application of newer technical opportunities in the Internet (virtual realities, Internet phone, video conferencing, etc.) to tandem learning.

The project partners are currently working on a handbook on tandem learning which will contain the most important project results and will be published by the end of 1998 in most partner country languages.

Other universities such as the University of Rhode Island (USA), Matsuyama University (Japan), the University of Rostov-on-Don (Russia) as well as a large number of additional educational institutions, which increasingly include schools and adult educational institutions, have been and are working in the continued development of the network.

3. Learning in tandem

Language learning in tandem is autonomous learning, which as a rule does not replace language courses but rather builds on the knowledge gained in courses and often accompanies them. Tandem learning serves a similar function in the language learning process as does learning outside of class e.g. with newspapers, books, radio, television or videos in the foreign language or as learning through communication with native speakers, for instance on a foreign exchange or in a pen friendship.

Learning in tandem has a great deal in common with the above mentioned forms of learning outside of class: for example, it predominantly concerns learning through communication in the foreign language, and the effectiveness of the learning is dependent on the communication strategies and learning techniques which the learner possesses. However, there are also important differences.

3.1. Definition

Language learning in tandem occurs when two persons with different native languages work together in partnerships to learn the other person's native language, to learn more about the other person and their culture and to exchange knowledge and experiences, for example from work, one's studies or school, or about hobbies.

Language learning in tandem is learning through communication with a native speaker who serves as a model for his[4] partner, provides support in attempts to understand the foreign language and express oneself therein and who can also make corrections. Communication with the tandem partners is always authentic (not simulated) whereby meeting the partner and becoming familiar with his thoughts and world are usually emphasised.

However, the exchange of additional knowledge, particularly in the areas of professional and vocational education, for example between teachers, managers or lawyers who want to become familiar with their partner's field of activity, can also play a more important role in a particular tandem partnership.

3.2. Principle of Reciprocity

Central to language learning in tandem is the principle of reciprocity, which can be summarised as follows:

- Successful learning in tandem is based on the reciprocal dependence and mutual support of both partners. Both partners need to contribute the same amount of effort to their joint learning partnership and to profit to the same extent from their collaboration.

The learners should be willing and prepared to do as much for their partner as they expect from him. Not only do they need to dedicate the same amount of time to each language, but they also need to invest the same amount of energy into preparation, to show the same level of commitment to the learning success of their partner and to be equally attentive to their partner's problems of expression and comprehension. This principle underlines one of the great advantages of tandem learning partnerships as compared to normal communication situations between learners and native speakers, where the learner is usually the only one to profit.

3.3. Principle of Learner Autonomy

The second important principle of learning in tandem is the principle of learner autonomy:

- Each tandem partner is responsible for his own learning process. He also decides *what* he wants to learn, *when* and *how*. Only the support which he has specifically requested can be expected from his partner.

The partners have command of their own language and are knowledgeable of and move freely in the frame of their own culture. In this sense they can help each other as respective experts; however, they are not teachers. They can define neither learning goals nor learning steps and methods for their partner. Not even the preparation of learning material for the partner from specific points of view (e.g. based on knowledge of grammar rules in the native language) can be expected.

This emphasis on each partner's responsibility for their own learning is important since the partners' goals and methods are rarely the same, as each partner generally has had varying learning experiences, is at a different learning level and defines different learning needs. Common tasks for both partners are only useful in exceptional cases, such as at intensive tandem courses, and then still have to accommodate the different starting points and goals of the partners.

The responsibility for one's own learning not only applies to the relationship with the tandem partner, however, but also to learning goals and progressions set from the outside. Learners can concentrate on learning goals and exercises defined in an accompanying foreign language class in their tandem work, and they can also prepare for a standardised language exam with help from their tandem partner. Nevertheless, the great potential of the language learning in tandem context lies in the possibility of combining authentic communication with goal-directed learning. The learning steps arise from communication needs such as the desire to understand or express something.

4. Learning in tandem via the Internet

4.1. Special attributes of Internet tandem

Tandem partners, whose native language is a learner's target language and who also happen to want to learn the learner's native language, usually live far away. However, the Internet helps surmount distances with little cost: even the slowest form of communication in the Internet, namely e-mail, is much faster than regular mail and significantly less expensive than faxing. And even the most expensive Internet forms of communication, which are audio and video conferencing, are cheaper than telephoning. Considering these factors, it makes sense to look for tandem partners who reside in their own country and to communicate with them via the Internet.

In Internet tandem each tandem partner stays in his native living and learning environments, which has both advantages and disadvantages. For example, it is not always easy to recognise and adapt to the circumstances and opportunities that apply to your tandem partner: generally different school and holiday schedules, varying daily demands in school and at home, different kinds of Internet access, etc. On the other hand, it is interesting when the tandem partner remains in his normal environment, as he can then directly relate about himself, his family, friends, school, hobbies and free-time. Also, it is easier for him to answer questions about life in his country and to find authentic information.

4.2. Forms of communication in Internet tandem

Asynchronous and synchronous communication

When a letter or e-mail message is written, direct contact to the tandem partner does not exist. One writes a text, which is usually relatively long, and sends it. The addressee finds the letter when he looks in his mailbox and can then answer the letter. This is referred to as asynchronous communication. However, when two persons carry on a dialogue with one another at a specified time where they can spontaneously and directly react to (generally short) questions as well as ask questions and make comments, the communication is synchronous. Both types of communication are possible via the Internet.

Written and oral communication

Asynchronous communication need not always be written. It has long been possible to send "audio letters" on audio or video tapes. Audio and video documents can be sent via the Internet as attachments to e-mail messages or with the help of special programmes (voice mail). Nor is synchronous communication always oral. Although it is now technically possible to communicate with one another using microphones and loudspeakers as well as cameras and monitors, written synchronous communication continues to be used more frequently: in chat groups, in written virtual realities such as MOOs, etc.

Application to tandem work

All of the following forms of communication can be meaningfully employed for language learning in tandem via the Internet:

- E-mail (written and asynchronous)
- Voice mail (oral and asynchronous)
- MOOs, IRC and chatting (written and synchronous)
- Audio and video conferencing (oral and synchronous)

As a rule, a combination of these forms is advisable for tandem work.

At this time, most tandem partners living in different places use e-mail to work together. Electronic mail is simple to use and does not require, aside from Internet access using a modem, any special computer equipment. The telephone costs are low since the Internet access need only be activated during the actual sending and receiving of e-mail messages; writing and reading the messages can take place without continuous contact to the Internet. If spoken messages are to be sent, the costs rise slightly due to the fact that audio information requires a great deal more memory, meaning that the length of the message multiplies.

In addition, the tandem partners can arrange a specific time to meet in the Internet to carry on a written dialogue via the keyboard and monitor (e.g. in MOOs or on so-called chat channels). The costs are, however, much higher because the Internet connection has to be maintained the entire time. Actual oral conversations require very powerful lines connecting to the Internet (and within the Internet), a condition which is yet only seldom fulfilled.

Previous experience in pilot projects seems to justify advising tandem partners to make use of the possibilities for both asynchronous and synchronous communication in their work with their partner via the Internet. While the work per e-mail appears for the time being to be irreplaceable in the improvement of language skills, synchronous communication presently plays an important role in securing a social relationship between the partners. The partners can get to know each other better through a dialogue, and misunderstandings and problems can be more easily revealed and clarified. Mutual experiences in a virtual reality such as a MOO can certainly be helpful in building a tandem partner relationship.

4.3. How to learn in Internet tandem

Just as in face-to-face tandem, in Internet tandem the partners learn through the authentic exchange of opinions and information. They expand their foreign language knowledge primarily by examining their partner's statements, through their partner's help in understanding and formulating and through his corrections. This results in different opportunities and problems depending on the type of communication.

Characteristic for tandem through asynchronous communication, written in e-mail tandem or oral in spoken letters, is above all the fact that the partners can create and go through their usually long messages, hints and corrections without immediate pressure, able to use customary aids such as dictionaries and grammar books. Since the partners write at least half of each message in their native language, which serves as foreign language input for the partner, this form of communication can be applied after only several months of foreign language classes. Corrections are easily made because the text to be corrected is always available. Some tandem partners who do not understand the function that the correction of mistakes plays in this learning context make the mistake of correcting too much.

Tandem through synchronous written or oral communication is dedicated to dialogue in a narrow sense, allows the partners to be spontaneous in throwing out contextual and linguistic questions and comments and also necessitates quick reactions. The need to quickly convert one's own thoughts into written statements is especially demanding. Pressures of time and of cost connected with this time occasionally make a relaxed learning atmosphere difficult. The partners rarely find time to make corrections.

4.4. Integrating Internet tandem in curricula

The length of time a tandem pair works successfully via the Internet appears to be very dependent on the quality and intensity of the local tandem learner counselling as well as on the extent of recognition that this form of autonomous learning is given at the respective school, university or workplace. Projects covering the following areas are already taking place:

- For professionals who, sponsored by their company, independently work on improving their foreign language skills through Internet tandem and are therein supported by individual learning counsellors.
- For participants of foreign language courses for adults who work in tandem with e-mail tandem partners backed by the support of their teachers.
- For students, who can substitute required courses through individual work in tandem via the Internet.
- For pupils who are encouraged by foreign language teachers to supplement their learning with work outside of class, whereby tandem learning is one possibility along with reading in the foreign language, television, etc. in reaching certain goals.

Internet tandem has, until recently, rarely been used in schools. However, experience with face-to-face tandem in schools as well as with Internet tandem independent of foreign language classes in schools proves encouraging.

A wide range of integration possibilities exist, however. In the minimal integration model, the teacher mentions from time to time the possibilities for continued learning outside of class, including Internet tandem. If some of the pupils in the class work with a tandem partner via the Internet at home or at school, then the teacher can have pupils ask their tandem partners about questions that have come up in class regarding language and culture, discuss letters from the tandem partner, ask pupils to report on their tandem experiences; and he can always practise strategies and skills in class which the pupils can use for learning with their partners: reading strategies, ways of evaluating their tandem partners' letters, etc.

The possibility of systematically integrating Internet tandem into class work also presents itself. The teacher can support individual continued learning by being available for his pupils at set times as a learning counsellor. He can put particular emphasis on individual continued learning by systematically taking it into consideration in the grading process. Yearly folders or portfolios, in which all kinds of learning outside of class is documented, can provide a foundation. He can also systematically address learning strategies and techniques which the pupils need for independent learning. Learning in tandem and other types of learning outside of class then make up the necessary background for practise.

5. *Sources of further information*

The most current and extensive information about language learning in tandem via the Internet will always be found on the Tandem Servers in the World Wide Web. German servers are:

http://www.slf.ruhr-uni-bochum.de/	Tandem Server Bochum
http://tandem.uni-trier.de/	Tandem Server Trier

The pages on "Tandem learning assistance (Help and Tips)" in particular offer learners, however also teachers, valuable help and are continually up-dated and revised.

On the education server of the state of North Rhine-Westphalia the work area "Language learning in tandem via the Internet"

http://www.learn-line.nrw.de/Themen/Tandem

was opened in February 1998 by Helmut Brammerts and Karin Kleppin. It addresses in particular teachers and pupils but also their parents.

The services of the International Tandem Network are currently free of cost for any interested individual or organisation who has access to e-mail. The address of the Tandem Agency is:

tandem@slf.ruhr-uni-bochum.de

To be assigned to an Internet tandem partner, a participant needs to specify – along with first name, last name, native language and target language – if they are a pupil, college student or professional. Teachers can do more than just recommend tandem learning to their classes, they can also try out this type of learning themselves. For example, the collaboration of a German teacher of French with a French colleague teaching German can certainly prove fruitful for both parties. The Tandem Agency tries to accommodate such wishes.

Notes

1 Thank you to Dawn D'Atri for translation and stylistic revision of the English version.
2 This example has been taken and slightly altered from the work area "Language learning in tandem via the Internet" on the server for education of North Rhine-Westphalia, *learn:line* (http://www.slf.ruhr-uni-bochum.de/email/ll/medio-beisp-eng.html).
3 MOO stands for "Multiuser Dungeon, object oriented" and does not mean a lot to non-computer scientists. It denotes textually described virtual realities, which can (virtually) be accessed by users from all over the world.
4 When I use the masculine form of the personal pronoun, I do not intend to exclude women.

Bibliography

Brammerts, H.: Language learning in tandem bibliography. 1996ff. WWW Document: http://www.slf.ruhr-uni-bochum.de/learning/tanbib.html

Brammerts, H. & D. Little (Eds.): *Leitfaden für das Sprachenlernen im Tandem über das Internet*. Bochum: Brockmeyer, 1996. (Manuskripte zur Sprachlehrforschung, 52)

Herfurth, H.-E.: *Möglichkeiten und Grenzen des Fremdsprachenerwerbs in Begegnungssituationen. Zu einer Didaktik des Fremdsprachenlernens im Tandem*. München: iudicium, 1993.

---: "Individualtandem und binationale Begegnungen. Ein Überblick über Verbreitung, Organisation und Konzeptionen des Sprachenlernens in binationalen Kontexten", *Info DaF* 21, 1994, 45-68.

Little, D. & H. Brammerts (Eds.): *A guide to language learning in tandem via the Internet.* Dublin: Centre for Language and Communication Studies, Trinity College, 1996. (CLCS Occasional Paper, 46)

Pelz, M. (Ed.): *Tandem in der Lehrerbildung, Tandem und grenzüberschreitende Projekte. Dokumentation der 5. Internationalen Tandem-Tage 1994 in Freiburg i.Br.* Werkstatt-Berichte, 8. Frankfurt/Main: IKO-Verlag für Interkulturelle Kommunikation, 1995.

Wolff, J.: "Ein TANDEM für jede Gelegenheit? Sprachlernen in verschiedenen Begegnungssitutationen", *Die Neueren Sprachen* 93, 1994, 374-385.

Helmuth Küffner, Hagen

Teaching English for Special Purposes. A Case for Old and New Media

The FernUniversität – Distance Teaching University of Germany

The FernUniversität, the German distance teaching university, was founded in North-Rhine Westphalia in 1974. It is a so-called comprehensive university which means that the possibilities of admission to interdisciplinary and integrated studies are wider than at traditional universities.

For the reader of English not familiar with the German term "fern", meaning "distant", the name of the FernUniversität conjures up pictures of an idyllic campus set in a forest clearing surrounded by trees and ferns. This is in fact the case; but add to this the confusion of terms: distance teaching, distance learning and distance education, it should be explained they are used as synonyms, sometimes, in more recent publications, referred to as "open or autonomous learning".

This contribution describes some distance courses of English offered at the FernUniversität in Hagen, a medium-sized town south-east of Dortmund and the Ruhr area. Face-to-face teaching situations are very rare, although the FernUniversität does not really differ from traditional German universities concerning the contents of the study-programmes. Indeed, teaching English at a distance seems to be a contradiction in itself at first glance. If we agree to a definition of "distance teaching" as "guided self-learning" we have at least two components in the system, which can complement each other's advantages and disadvantages, namely self-learning material and tutorials.

In fact, there is a long tradition of successful language teaching in distance teaching organizations world-wide, both in public and private institutions including secondary as well as higher education. In some ways the experience of already existing distance teaching universities, notably, the Open University in Britain, was made use of and has been further adapted to suit the requirements of the German education system. In particular the use of "new" media has reformed teaching methods through not only specially prepared printed material, but through tapes, video, computers, compact disks as well as tutoring by tutor/computer-marked assignments sent in by post. Thus, distance learning systems combine personal media – tutorials held at study centres – and printed or electronic media.

However, in one aspect the FernUniversität has not been able to follow the trends of the British and Dutch universities in that it is not yet open to everyone without a formal university entrance qualification before enrolling in full degree course programmes.

Although it is always problematic comparing university degrees it can be said the German long-cycle "Diplom" is approximately equivalent to the Anglo-American "Master" degree; the short cycle "Diplom" compares with the "Bachelor" degree.

Initially, the target group for Bridging Courses was for those learners who did not have full university entrance qualifications usually obtained in the final year at secondary grammar school level or senior high school. "Just another form of entrance exams", we may hear sceptics say. Indeed it is a requirement to bridge the gap between school and university to be completed by freshmen during their first year enabling them to start studying their subject, but to do that without going back to school.

The subjects offered in the Bridging Course Programme are: German, Mathematics, Physics, Philosophy, English and French relating directly in language and subject content to the degree course for which the learner has enrolled. Thus, the student of Economics, for example, learns to train not only specialised vocabulary in English in this subject area, but brushes up grammar as well as supplementing what has been lacking in the personal school learning experience of the individual student. Further objectives of the Bridging Courses are to teach background subject matter relating to their degree courses and, in particular, study skills required for studying at a distance such as summary writing, discussion, translation, reading comprehension etc. in a subject context.

Indeed, this is a requirement of the examination regulations laid down by the examination board. It has resulted in teaching skills focusing mainly on reading and writing and not specifically spoken communication skills. However, pronunciation and intonation are trained through the audio-visual additional material, and the presentation of the text material supports discussion and commentary. A network of study centres provides an opportunity, on a voluntary basis, to take part in tutorials. This gives the learner a limited but effective face-to-face learning situation which is strongly recommended before examinations. All courses require the average of approximately five years of school English as a minimum requirement.

Bridging Course "English for Students of Economics"

This Bridging Course enjoys the largest number of enrolments. It aims at providing freshmen with the ability to read, understand and make use of the relevant English literature that s/he is confronted with during his/her studies of Economics. Furthermore, the course material is arranged in such a way to enable the students to competently comment upon economic aspects within his/her professional life or during their course. The student learns to present economic facts adequately, taking into account facts and figures provided.

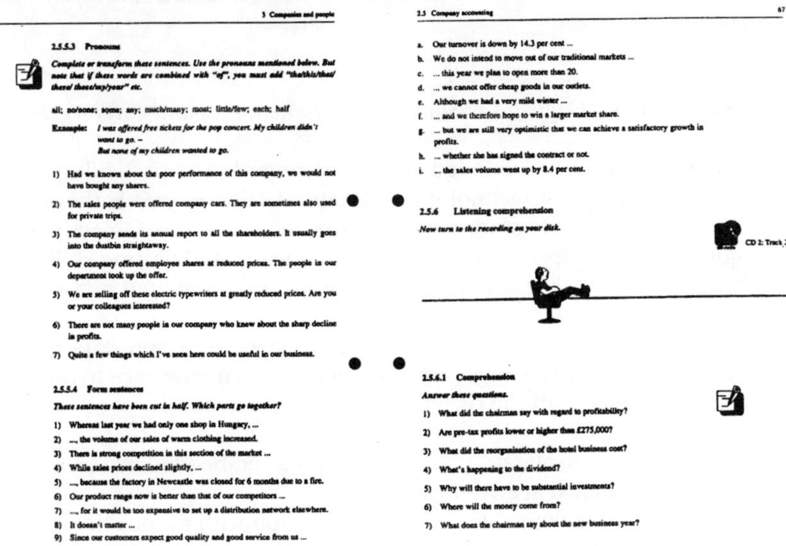

3 Companies and people

2.5.5.3 Pronouns

Complete or transform these sentences. Use the pronouns mentioned below. But note that if these words are combined with "of", you must add "the/this/that/these/those/my/your" etc.

all; no/none; some; any; much/many; most; little/few; each; half

Example: *I was offered free tickets for the pop concert. My children didn't want to go. –*
But none of my children wanted to go.

1) Had we known about the poor performance of this company, we would not have bought any shares.
2) The sales people were offered company cars. They are sometimes also used for private trips.
3) The company sends its annual report to all the shareholders. It usually goes into the dustbin straightaway.
4) Our company offered employee shares at reduced prices. The people in our department took up the offer.
5) We are selling off these electric typewriters at greatly reduced prices. Are you or your colleagues interested?
6) There are not many people in our company who knew about the sharp decline in profits.
7) Quite a few things which I've seen here could be useful in our business.

2.5.5.4 Form sentences

These sentences have been cut in half. Which parts go together?

1) Whereas last year we had only one shop in Hungary, ...
2) ..., the volume of our sales of warm clothing increased.
3) There is strong competition in this section of the market ...
4) While sales prices declined slightly, ...
5) ..., because the factory in Newcastle was closed for 6 months due to a fire.
6) Our product range now is better than that of our competitors ...
7) ..., for it would be too expensive to set up a distribution network elsewhere.
8) It doesn't matter ...
9) Since our customers expect good quality and good service from us ...

2.5 Company accounting 67

a. Our turnover is down by 14.3 per cent ...
b. We do not intend to move out of our traditional markets ...
c. ... this year we plan to open more than 20.
d. ... we cannot offer cheap goods in our outlets.
e. Although we had a very mild winter ...
f. ... and we therefore hope to win a larger market share.
g. ... but we are still very optimistic that we can achieve a satisfactory growth in profits.
h. ... whether she has signed the contract or not.
i. ... the sales volume went up by 8.4 per cent.

2.5.6 Listening comprehension

Now turn to the recording on your disk.

CD 2: Track 2

2.5.6.1 Comprehension

Answer these questions.

1) What did the chairman say with regard to profitability?
2) Are pre-tax profits lower or higher than £275,000?
3) What did the reorganisation of the hotel business cost?
4) What's happening to the dividend?
5) Why will there have to be substantial investments?
6) Where will the money come from?
7) What does the chairman say about the new business year?

Figure 1: "sample page (s) of course material" taken from Bridging Course Engl. for Students of Economics (Course No. 9802, FernUniversität Hagen, 1996)

The written material of the course consists of a refresher unit plus four units with five topics each and a glossary. The texts of the four units deal with the subjects specifically covering a wide range of themes in business practice or economics in general. This includes, for instance, "From raw material to consumer", "Companies and people", "Money and finance" and "The world around us". Each topic comprises a text with extensive bilingual vocabulary, exercises referring to the context, training and improving lingual and lexical abilities, and repeating and intensifying grammatical aspects and exercises. Each unit contains answer keys facilitating reliable self-checking of the learning progress. Additionally there are also special exercises to be sent back to the university. They are corrected by a tutor and returned to the students to give objective feedback on progress in paragraph writing as well as tutorial support.

The complete text material is also available on CD-audio, thus helping the students to improve listening comprehension and to train pronunciation and intonation. The language content is presented intensively thus enabling students to brush up their previous knowledge, to supplement any lacks in it and so to work successfully through the course material. An important objective is training of relevant specialised terminology which is therefore not a requirement before starting the course. Students should have an average knowledge of English (between five and seven years of instruction).

Bridging Course "English for Students of Mathematics and Engineering"

Knowledge of the English language can be regarded as particularly important in the fields of technology and natural sciences and is therefore necessary for university studies and later professional life. Objectives of this course are to improve reading comprehension and writing skills for studying in a distance learning context and to train a limited number of technical terms.

Teaching objectives are facilititated through printed and data-based media as are all the Bridging Courses but with special reference to the following specific needs of the technically oriented learner:

- repetition and consolidation of basic grammar embedded in a technical context of technical articles or texts
- introduction of technical English in connection with prepositions, pronouns or grammatical structures that are relatively common in technical texts
- training of reading and listening comprehension skills through cassettes as well as a lexical trainer on a computer disc
- written analysis and commentary of technical texts
- training of summary and translation skills into German

The programme consists of four units which meet the interests of students of mathematics and engineering. They are comprised of two units with mathematical contents including binary systems, trigonometry, graphs or statistics and two units with contents taken from mainly electrical or mechanical engineering, eg. magnetism, videotext or calculating machines. Every course unit consists of five chapters which deal with a certain subject or theme. These are complemented by exercises and keys to give immediate feedback. Each unit requires the contents and language of the previous one. Students also send in assignments regularly which are marked by tutors giving further feedback and advice during the learning process.

Additional material includes a booklet with further reading comprehension texts, a leaflet on examination skills for the final examination after approximately 80 hours of study, and an English/German glossary.

COACH: Training Software for Specialised Terminology in Modern Languages

In order to provide students of English language courses in "English for Mathematicians and Engineers" or "English for Economics" with supplementary *interactive media*, a survey of vocabulary and foreign language training programmes available on the software market was carried out in 1986. None of them fulfilled our demands for interactivity and flexibility so that we could not adopt an already existing software system. From 1987 to mid-1989 the FernUniversität Hagen, together with a small educational software company (Claudia Röhling Elektronik, Aachen), developed this computer-based vocabulary training programme.

Objectives: The relevance of teaching English vocabulary for special purposes (ESP) to experts in specific fields and students studying in those fields is apparent when the needs of the adult learner are closely examined. A growing number of student exchanges between international universities, and the globalisation of cooperation in various social and economic fields requires more and more sophisticated and specialised language training.

For those communicating in a foreign language the discrepancy between active and passive vocabulary is another important factor. An expert very often knows or can guess the meaning of specialised vocabulary from the context when reading, for instance, an English business journal. However, when it comes to producing a text in the foreign language the active usage of appropriate vocabulary is required, but often lacking. The vocabulary trainer supports the following language learning objectives:

- revision of vocabulary which was once learnt but perhaps over a period of time has been forgotten
- extension of the already existing vocabulary referring to a specific field
- acquiring of vocabulary in a specific context
- correction of typical mistakes made by the German-speaking learner
- repetition of items at random with continual performance feedback
- toleration of slight spelling mistakes to encourage the learner to "keep trying".

This programme cannot, however, (and was never intended to) replace specialised dictionaries.

The *characteristics* of the vocabulary trainer may be outlined as follows: The programme flow follows general findings of the psychology of learning; important decisions are left to the user. The learner can stop practising whenever time or inclination affords and the practice can be taken up again with the former score being stored. The user decides how many words s/he wants to learn in one session. Words which one fails to know remain in the pool and will be repeated again later. The words appear in random order so that the user will not get used to a certain sequence of words. The learner may use an option which presents the correct answer at once if s/he wishes to do so. The learner is not confronted with simple 1:1 translation work, but sees a context in which the word to be learned is marked '≈', leaving an appropriate gap in the sentence to be completed by the learner. If there is more than one correct answer, the system will accept them all. We have tried to anticipate incorrect answers likely to appear (and commented on them) so that if the learner hits one of them s/he learns why his/her translation is not applicable in that very context. If the learner fails to know the correct answer, s/he may call up a clue to help him/her along. In case of failing for a third time to find a right answer the system presents the correct answer(s) together with the phonetic transcription. The phonetic transcription is given with each correct answer.

While developing and improving the COACH-trainer over the past years, we felt that one of the most important media in language learning was missing with CALL-software: the human voice – spoken phrases in a foreign language, with a typical intonation melody, cannot really be replaced by other media.

It is important to stress that only the recorded voice of native speakers, digitizied with the help of A/D converters (sampling) is suitable to be included in a language learning programme. Synthetically produced voice from low cost chips for "talking computers" are known from automobile applications (eg. "Please fasten your seat belt"), but we felt they are not acceptable in a language-learning environment.

The wrong answers entered by the learner are recorded. This has provided the developers with material to anticipate wrong answers to improve the quality of the trainer. The programme-shell of the vocabulary trainer is independent of the language stored in it, therefore being a kind of authoring system. The entry/management system enables general vocabulary as well as items applying to other specialist fields to be stored allowing for flexible implementation and quick revision of old items.

Specialised vocabulary trainers for a number of subjects including Economics, Electrical Engineering, Mathematics, Computer Science, Distance Teaching and Education have been available in different versions.

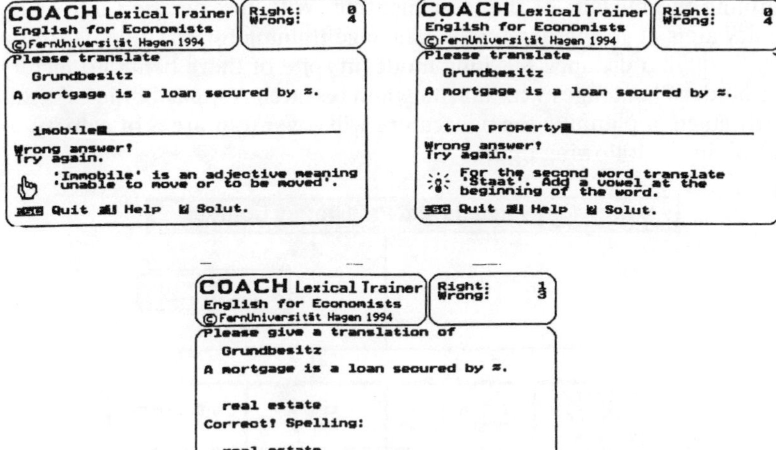

Figure 2: COACH screen display

These have been implemented in different projects in Germany and in different European countries and for various CALL (computer-assisted language learning) projects, including LINGUA- and LEONARDO-supported work.

English for Studying Psychological Texts

Apart from the Bridging Courses, the University of Hagen offers another English option. It is a guide-line in course form to assist students of Social Sciences to study Psychology text books or related literature in the original language.

It has been recognized that school English is not sufficient to cope with specialised terms or abbreviations in this particular subject area. The course consists of two printed course units and a cassette. It requires the same previous knowledge of the language as the Bridging Courses.

The Way Forward

In Spring 1998 the rectorate of the University of Hagen decided to set up a new Centre for Language and Preparatory courses in the faculty for Education and Social Sciences, with the former Unit for Bridging Courses forming the nucleus of this new institute. With this decision university policy aims at strengthening the language training for its students studying through a distance teaching mode, in spite of there being no faculty for modern languages with teaching and research responsibilities. At this early stage of planning the new centre will cover four areas of activity, as shown in the following figure:

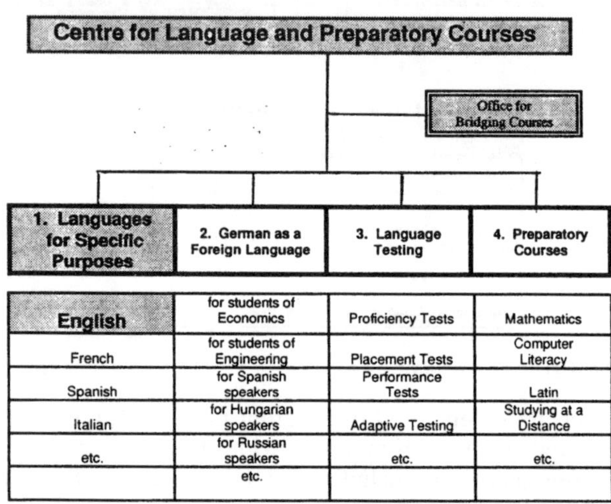

1. Languages for Specific Purposes	2. German as a Foreign Language	3. Language Testing	4. Preparatory Courses
English	for students of Economics	Proficiency Tests	Mathematics
French	for students of Engineering	Placement Tests	Computer Literacy
Spanish	for Spanish speakers	Performance Tests	Latin
Italian	for Hungarian speakers	Adaptive Testing	Studying at a Distance
etc.	for Russian speakers	etc.	etc.
	etc.		

Figure 3: Organisation diagram for the new Centre for languages

For the purpose of this article, only the first box in the first column is of interest: English. Since German students are quite familiar with basic English at an intermediate level because of the German school system, *no* English courses for beginners will be offered. The courses are all English for non-language students, as currently there is no degree programme for modern languages with Bachelor or Master programmes available.

The next generation of distance education courses for *English* teaching purposes will be designed for undergraduate students enrolled in the degree course programmes of the University of Hagen. This includes Electrical Engineering, Economics, Educational and Social Sciences, Law, Mathematics and Computer Science.

The vast majority of students at the University of Hagen are studying Economics. Therefore, it will be necessary to offer an advanced distance education course "English for Students of Economics II" to meet their particular needs. As the European and International market requires German graduates to communicate with international partners about legal matters or within a legal framework, it is intended to have a course in

"English for Law Students" to be placed on the priority list for new courses to be developed. Another subject-oriented course is designed to help students of Social Sciences to have better access to the important English language literature and publications in their study programme. As reading a large amount of literature in the original language is a basic requirement, the reading comprehension strategies of students have to be improved, whereas communication skills are not a priority. Students of Electrical Engineering and Computer Science are required not only to read technical documents from international sources, but have to write technical specifications and descriptions of products and procedures as well as reports in English for their international clientele. Therefore, offering a course in technical writing is currently under review for the near future.

Besides course production development in English there will be a smaller project for developing subject-oriented courses in French (French for Engineering students and Social Sciences). Spanish (for students of Economics) and Italian (for Economics), to meet the needs of priority areas. As in the past authors will be drawn from universities with teaching experience in these subjects and experience as experts in authoring. Native speakers will be included in the course team. Since evaluation with a trial version of the course is a standard procedure for courses developed for distance education purposes, the course completion time will take up to 3 years.

Finally, all new courses will be produced, offered and monitored on platforms ready to be accessed by students world-wide by digital networks (e.g. Internet), sometimes better known under the term "Virtual or Electronic University."

Dieter Wessels, Bochum

Computer-aided Vocabulary Training

Why is vocabulary learning so fraught with problems? Pupils, when asked about problem areas in their foreign language acquisition, always identify vocabulary and grammar in this very generalised form as the two key areas where they encountered serious difficulties. Adults, when called upon to explain their reasons for attending further education classes in foreign languages, invariably give top priority to vocabulary learning and grammar.[1] Quite obviously these two groups of learners diagnose deficiencies which they have encountered in the initial learning process, that is during their time at school and certainly after school, when they have to use foreign languages be it in their private or professional lives. The almost classic goals of foreign language teaching and learning today, that is to say the reading, writing, listening and speaking skills, the skill to communicate sensibly and the skill to move adequately in another cultural and linguistic environment seem to be taking second place. Most learners do not even seem aware of the need to acquire these skills.

What now is the reason for the real or perceived deficiency of foreign language teaching? For the field of vocabulary one will surely have to state that the teaching materials are structured in such a way that students are hardly aware that they are practising the newly acquired lexical patterns. There are often no specific exercises to ensure that the new words and phrases are learned consciously or that their vocabulary is systematically expanded. On the other hand textbooks often do not present or arrange the vocabulary (by topic or communicative situations) to allow for the quick revision of the material without reference to the textbook unit in question. And there is one very obvious reason: as students have to return their books at the end of the school year, these are no longer available for reference and revision purposes.

And we must not forget that in classes 11 to 13, for syllabus reasons, there is no systematic approach to expanding the vocabulary base, which, of course, does not mean to say that teachers do not make any effort to use the reading of texts and discussion in the classroom to broaden the students' vocabulary base. But, and this is probably true, the aspect of vocabulary learning becomes less prominent as students progress to higher levels of achievement.

In addition, it seems to be the generally held opinion among the proponents of foreign language didactics today that in foreign language teaching, where the communicative approach plays a key role, there is no place for exercises taking lexemes out of their situational and linguistic context. The question remains: how do foreign language learners today acquire the words, the collocations, the lexical wherewithal without which communication is virtually impossible? To which must be added the question of how we can ensure that the vocabulary once acquired remains available for active use. And there we broach a more general issue in the discussion about education today: how do we acquire the knowledge, the foundations without which we cannot develop skills?

Nor must we forget the fact that due to non-use a lot of vocabulary tends to fall into oblivion. The volume of words acquired in a period of six or nine years' foreign language training comprises several thousand units if measured in word equations. A considerable part of these will only have been introduced in one unit and not been activated subsequently in the teaching materials. It is quite obvious that such words will quickly be relegated to the passive vocabulary and eventually not be available any more. Take for example the subject fields that feature prominently in school textbooks, such as home, eating and drinking, shopping, town and country. A lot of the related words and phrases acquired at a very early stage are no longer readily available when young students go to Britain on a language course for example, although they are generally considered as being basic vocabulary.

There is consensus then that linguistic communication without the appropriate inventory (availability of a definable base of words and phrases as well as the linguistic structures) is not possible. The problem is how this inventory is acquired and, once acquired, maintained readily available for use.[2] It goes against the grain for most of us to revive the traditional forms of learning new words and phrases (endless copying of vocabulary lists and learning them by covering up one side), and of teachers to check the success of this acquisition process (e.g. through vocabulary tests). That there are more intelligent ways of going about this task is shown by Holtwisch[3] and Beile.[4] A method of learning based on a word data file is difficult to handle for young learners, as it not only requires a lot of organisation and skills for the structuring of the ever growing word material, but also a considerable amount of self-discipline and consistency which is beyond most of us.

It is necessary if we wish to overcome this dilemma to look out for learning aids which can motivate, which will guarantee the long-term success of the efforts invested in the learning process, which give priority to the contextualisation of the lexical item over the word equation and which are suitable to enhance the communicative competence of the learner. These aids must be such that, once a certain vocabulary basis has been acquired, they enable the learner to identify the transfer potential for his/her own learning process (fundamentals of word formation by means of prefixes and suffixes, the meaning of common prefixes and suffixes, compound formation of nouns, and, to a certain extent also, of adjectives and verbs).

Conventional textbooks as a rule have two-language word lists, often supported by foreign language definitions or sample sentences for each textbook unit and, therefore, are quite suitable for the revision of vocabulary in the traditional manner. Often there are alphabetical lists (sometimes with an added reference to allow for the words to be located in the respective texts). But schoolbooks, as we have seen, are only available for a limited period of time and after that cannot be used in the learning process any more.

In this situation help seems to be forthcoming from publishers in the form of long vocabulary lists. But these are mainly targeted at more advanced learners. Almost without exception the words are arranged according to topics. At first sight they may seem a useful tool. But there is no link whatsoever to any textbook series in the respective publisher's list. Apart from listing the words in language pairs and providing the occasional model sentence or reference to related words they do not really offer any advice on what to do with the often comprehensive word material. Nor is there any exercise material to enable the learner to use these words and phrases in context. Such collections are also available for special fields such as economics and law.

At a time when the PC is a tool that people can afford to buy for private use, language work on the PC for many seems to be a distinct possibility to counteract the deficiencies of language work at school. Some of the advantages of language training programs for PC use are blatantly obvious.

- The learner is fully autonomous in determining the time, place and duration of his/her training.
- The medium itself encourages the learner to explore.
- There is instant feedback in contrast to other forms of autonomous learning.
- During the study phase the learner is permanently active. In traditional forms of learning processes there is often the possibility "to switch off" or to hide in the "crowd".
- More recent programs make use of the sound card, thereby integrating the options to listen and to speak in the course work.

Some deficiencies should not go unnoticed, however. Among these there are the spontaneous interactions which are only possible in a group of learners working under the guidance of a tutor: the communication between tutor and student with the vast array of possibilities for action and reaction and commenting which only the classroom situation can provide, the collective work on a problem, group work, the possibility of doing written work and having it looked at and corrected, the complexity and also the individuality of the communication processes between tutor and student and the students amongst themselves. As yet we do not know for certain to what extent the new medium commands the full attention of the learner, thus possibly distracting from the learning process itself. As long as the learner is not fully familiar with the keyboard for example, the input of answers will require a lot of time and concentration. The degree of flexibility of PC programs is limited, answers will only be recognised if they have been anticipated as it were by the authors of the learning material. Other possible answers, which in a classroom situation provide a welcome starting point for comment and semantic expansion, are rejected as false by this medium or not considered at all.

There is probably widespread agreement that teaching or learning materials based on PC-related media can only act as a supportive element of teacher-centred foreign-language tuition. That PC-based teaching materials should fully replace or indeed emulate the tutor in the language learning process is as yet completely unimaginable in view of the complexity of linguistic communication and the diversity of the modes of expression. This does not mean to say that there are stages in the language acquisition process where the systematic training which PC-based materials can provide cannot take place outside the classroom, thereby making time available for demanding communication-related work.

The vocabulary training programs and program elements available today largely fulfil this support function. In view of a lack of generally accepted parameters for the assessment of such programs, it seems sensible to recur to proven criteria and beyond that to consider medium-specific aspects as well. A little brochure published by Cornelsen Software provides some useful criteria for the content and graphic design of learning software (and in this case student-directed software is being referred to). The software should be “adapted to the learning content, the age group and place of learning”. The following guidelines are set out for learning software generally which mutatis mutandis also apply to vocabulary learning programs:

- The work and the exercises are systematically combined with playful elements and phases of relaxation.
- The acquisition of knowledge is supported by acoustic and visual elements.
- Interesting story lines and imaginative artwork enhance the motivation of students.

- Knowledge is imparted in tasks that have some bearing on real life and is applied in simulations that are as realistic as possible.
- Error control is supported by text-related feedback and directions towards a solution of the problem.
- The contents of the learning software have some bearing on the syllabus and on school textbooks.
- Speed, sequencing and the learning path are determined by the student.

Considering the technical possibilities of the hardware and the scope of the software we can postulate that any new development of learning programs for PC-use should aim at the full linkage of audio and visual elements, that is to say, a considerable part of the training material must be available as spoken text allowing interaction, especially if longer passages of text or full sentences are used. But also exercises based on single word solutions provide enough scope for listening and speaking elements to be integrated. The selection of speakers requires great care to ensure articulatory correctness. For the motivation of students there should be a larger number of speakers both female and male. And in view of the role of English as the lingua franca it may be useful to bring in speakers who can demonstrate as it were other varieties of English than the somewhat artificial "received pronunciation" that still dominates much of our teaching in schools. And this does not only mean American English.

Useful hints for the typology of exercises may be gleaned from Birt[5] and Beile,[6] although we must expect that a lot of the exercises that we are familiar with from school books and which have proven their worth will make their reappearance in this new medium. These criteria have largely been applied in the analysis of the vocabulary training programs discussed below.

With one exception all the programs are available as CD-ROMs. The technical requirements generally are a 486 computer – for school- or textbook-oriented programs a 386 computer will often be sufficient – equipped with a soundcard, a CD-ROM drive and a working memory of 4 to 8 MB RAM and a graphics card. The software requirements are Windows 3.1 or higher or Windows '95.

The program most directly aimed at younger learners of English is **Adi-Coktel**. The exercises are accessed via the overall menu from which a variety of topics relating to human activities can be selected. The exercises contain between 4 and 10 tasks presented as right/wrong exercises, selection of the correct answer by mouse click and listening comprehension. Throughout the program the student is supported by audio elements; they can listen to the words and sentences; there is acoustic and visual feedback (positive and negative, but always encouraging). The help button provides useful additional information. During the work phase the set task is always visible on the screen. And cultural aspects are systematically integrated into the exercise material. This program has been created with a considerable input of design, video and audio features. The sound is adapted to the intended juvenile user group, but does not really distract from the established rules of pronunciation. Adi is a useful partner in the learning process, a link between the exercises with many witty comments. The accompanying booklet is mainly directed to parents and very useful in that it facilities the use of the program by giving advice regarding the workplace, setting forth the didactic considerations and the features of the program, explaining the function of Adi as intermediary in the learning process and also describing the functions of the keys for this program.

Easy English is directed to the learner in the first year of English and covers areas such as the alphabet, first words, the topics At Home, At School, Things, Body, Clothes, Food, Public Life and in addition verbs and adjectives and finally the task: Look at the picture and answer. With the exception of the first and the last units the thematic units all have four sets of tasks with an increasing degree of difficulty. Via pictures and words and in a step-by-step approach 24 nouns are learnt in each unit. In the last two sections (verbs and adjectives) and after an introductory phase the words are put into the context of a sentence with between 5 and 10 words. The work with the picture stories at the end are based on yes/no questions and some writing elements. Children's voices are used for the sound sections, a feature that could have been more widely used. Unfortunately, a lot of the drawings feature elements students are familiar with because of their German background; little attempt is made to familiarise them with aspects of British culture. The program also makes little use of feedback and motivational elements. The occasional comment "super" and the disclosed puzzle seem somewhat unimaginative.

In contrast the programs **Alfons 5** and **6** are much more dynamic and richer in ideas. The first menu already, a street scene from which one gets into a multifunctional study by clicking at an appropriate entrance door, provides a motivating start. The vocabulary training sections are set within a window frame, which gradually reveals a full-scale picture as the correct answers are given. The tasks for these two cycles all have the same structure and use numerals, letter chaos for certain word families, similar words and words with double consonants. In the numbers exercises, numbers are to be written as words and vice versa, but although the numbers supposedly range from zero to 999 for year 5 and to 10,000 for year 6, most of the tasks are restricted to two-digit numbers. For the vocabulary work proper the words are arranged in topic areas with a certain amount of overlap. As there are A and B exercises here, there is plenty of practice material available. These exercises, however, are largely based on contrastive English-German word equations. Altogether the presentation of the package is full of ideas and contains a wealth of motivational elements. In case of mistakes reference is made to the lexicon. The role of the tutor as a guide through the program has been given much thought. On the other hand the variety of exercises is somewhat limited. And the spelling system could be improved to allow keying-in mistakes to be used to guide the learner to the correct answer. There are also considerable discrepancies in the volume of material in certain sections which leave the user with the feeling that some parts are unduly difficult. This program does not make sufficient use of the audio function.

In terms of presentation and content **Blacky's Box** is also a program geared to the young learner. The rook Blacky is a well-disposed and sympathetic guide through the program. In contrast, a lot of the explanations seem to be rather complex for the targeted age group. The word list comprises no fewer than 7,300 entries and is available both in English-German and German-English. There is an audio element for each English entry. There is a wealth of vocabulary testing possibilities: testing of the words in alphabetical or indiscriminate order, language, testing of certain word classes only, expressions and verbal phrases. The program has a well-developed spellcheck and also provides statistical feedback. Like some of the other programs it overuses the word equation as a testing mode. Without identifiable context some of the expected solutions are problematical, correct alternatives are not accepted. In addition, there are topic-related vocabulary exercises emphasising activities and objects in the house, music and computer, life on the beach, supermarket and shopping, school and work, London and sightseeing, towns and places and Britain. In these fields the task is to relate activities with word phrases, to click the correct expressions, to write the words for objects, to listen to or read a definition and write the term, to insert words by using the drag-and-drop technique, to spot wrong terms. In spite of this apparent variety the possibilities for PC-exercises have not been exhausted by any means. The number of tasks in the exercises range from 8 to 24 with the tasks mostly concentrating on the single word. In many cases only one exercise is available although the selection menu asks the user to select an exercise. Many exercises would benefit from a model question and answer to give a clear idea of what is expected. The comments to the solutions are very welcome, but should not be so excessively positive when two or three attempts were required to find the correct answer. On the whole Blacky's Box provides a very comprehensive vocabulary training program which in some areas needs revising in terms of linguistic correctness.

The program offered by the big schoolbook publishers Klett and Cornelsen are directly textbook-related. The CD-ROM for **Green Line 6** (similar versions are also available for the other English textbook series) is accompanied by a comprehensive booklet and is extremely useful for revising the new vocabulary for each of the units in the book. The word material is presented in word equations, although the directions English-German or German-English are optional. The words are used in the context of the sentences as found in the texts and also accompanied by short explanations to facilitate the solution. The program also has a useful spellcheck. If correct, the answer is confirmed by the speaker. Otherwise the item is presented several times to ensure the equation is learned. The contextualisation requires a considerable degree of familiarity with the original text. The spelling and grammar must be correct for an answer to be acceptable. The program is sufficiently "intelligent" to recognise correct alternative answers, but they are ultimately rejected because they do not fit into the context. The program is very attractive in the presentation (screen layout, colours, print type, structuring of the screen) and altogether covers about 1,300 vocabulary items. It is a pity that the close link to the textbook does not allow for a larger variety of answers which would have opened up tremendous transfer potentials. Also the scope of the exercises could have been more imaginative.

With **English Coach Multimedia** Cornelsen offers a very comprehensive software package for its textbook series English G and contains exercise materials for reading and listening comprehension, grammar and vocabulary relating to the textbook units of the respective age group. The exercises can be accessed via a landscape menu (the icons are not immediately obvious). In the vocabulary training section there is the choice of training, memorising and test mode. The training phase contains exercises for the allocation of words to a subject area, for the integration of the words into tree structures, whereas in the memo mode you listen to the words and then fill them into a sentence pattern and in the test mode ultimately the words are presented in German or English, and the answer has to be keyed in. Here again, as in so many other programs, the lack of imagination in providing motivating exercises becomes obvious. Because of the close link of textbook and CD-ROM training material the scope for correct answers is very limited. Linguistically the program is very sound. The program is accompanied by a comprehensive booklet and also extensive explanations on the CD-ROM itself. More work could be done on the screen and here in particular the print type needs to be more legible against a greyish background which does not give sufficient contrast.

English One and Two is a full-scale general language learning program using American speakers in a British setting on two CD-ROMs. It is clearly targeted at adult learners and based on dialogues covering everyday situations of young people, a program in which vocabulary training is only a by-product. The full word list for the first CD-ROM has approx.

1,300 lexical items and for no obvious reason only 300 to 350 on the second. In the exercise mode the words are to be learned in lists and by covering up one side, whereas in the writing mode the learner is asked to find the English or German equivalent of the given term. The items are presented in exactly the same order in which they appear in the original vocabulary list. In the vocabulary section of this program there are certain deficiencies. Thus the spelling differences between British and American English are referred to as "special forms". And whether words like "crazy" or "ball-point pen" are uncommon in British English is at least open to doubt. "On the weekend" is certainly not an English phrase as maintained. The fact that for English "ambulance" there is only the wrongly spelt German translation "Ambulance" demonstrates that this program has received only a minimum of editorial attention. The testing modes are utterly unimaginative and dated. The letter type and the screen background in this particular section is certainly not user-friendly.

For adult learners one can find a range of very comprehensive programs on the market. While for the teenage and school markets the level of achievement to aim a program at can be gauged with a high degree of reliability, this is not possible for the adult market where skill levels and expectations of prospective users are likely to differ widely. Of course, program authors and marketers have that in mind when they label their programs as suitable for beginners or advanced students. Thus the Hueber Viva program **Aktiv Wortschatz** is divided into these two sections. The program offers very comprehensive training material with no fewer than 2,000 sentences and 4,000 exercise items. For both beginners and advanced students there are the following types of exercises: multiple choice, What fits where?, write correctly, word pairs, differences in meaning and arranging words. For the advanced students there are further exercises such as letter puzzles, right and wrong and translations. The number of tasks per group varies considerably, thus making some groups very demanding but also time-intensive, and 108 items in one section is certainly overtaxing the learner and makes for a very tedious and repetitive exercise. Apart from the vocabulary exercises all the words are gathered in a glossary which can be activated at any time either in English-German or in German-English. A very large number of the sentences are recorded for listening, The material is meant to serve as preparation for popular language tests such as the VHS certificate, the Cambridge First Certificate or the TOEFL-test. As in so many cases before there is a distinct lack of variety in the exercises, and some tasks are not clearly phrased: under the heading "word pairs" learners are asked to form compounds, and the request to "write correctly" does not seem to imply anything else but to find antonyms. The criteria for allocating points for the exercises can only be seen as half-hearted attempts to introduce statistical and motivational elements and are haphazard. On the other hand the material covers a lot of ground and is often presented with great linguistic competence. This in itself is a considerable achievement. Important aspects of formal presentation (screen layout, colours, contrast) have again been badly neglected. And also the wrapping is rather unassuming. Considering the scope of the material this program is more than priceworthy.

As the title indicates the programs **Spotlight Games** and **Spotlight "Sprach"spiele Wirtschaftsenglisch** make extensive use of playful elements. There are five different types of games as well as a marathon session, i.e. a mixture of these five game elements: 1. allocation of words to topics by means of the drag-and-drop technique after topic preselection; 2. slot machine requiring the linkup of definitions and words; 3. scoreboard with multiple-choice tasks of different levels of difficulty; 4. right/wrong exercises (combination of knowledge and linguistic tasks); 5. homophones. This structural element of games, where speed also plays a role, is highly motivating, but may at times distract from the language work which it is supposed to serve. Some of the tasks require some explanations and often can only be performed properly after some items have been missed. The soundcard is not used for language recordings, instead it helps to enhance the game structure. What is also badly lacking is a complete list of all the vocabulary items covered in this program. Some exercises (slot machine) seem quite difficult, as they include a good range of admittedly useful phrases which the average learner will not have readily available. Also the fact that there is usually only one correct solution may lead to some irritations among certain learners. The size of the lettering is a problem here and there (scoreboard). Material which is identical in the typology and layout of exercises but different in content is available for learners of general English and learners of business English.

The program **English Vokabeltrainer** leaves the learner very much on his own. The startup menu offers a large variety of options, which are difficult to understand as there is no immediate explanation unless one turns to the help function. Nor is there any accompanying booklet to explain the functions of the program. It is true that extensive information can be obtained via the help function, but then it is difficult to find out immediately which of the large number of headings can provide the most urgently needed explanation. And although the options in the startup menu may be plentiful, the variety of exercises is rather limited and, in view of the large number of vocabulary items covered here (no fewer than 5,300), work with this program soon leads to a certain degree of boredom, because there is such an obvious lack of variety and motivational input. Good use is made of the sound feature. The word dictation serves the purpose of both a listening and writing exercise, the other exercises are drag-and-drop, multiple-choice and gaps to be filled in. The principle behind most of the exercises is word equations and utterly demotivating in this frequency. An amazing lack of expertise can be noted in the multiple-choice exercises in which very often two of the distractors are so obvious that the exercises provide no real challenge. The glossary contains many irrelevant items, such as first names; but words for countries are missing. Further there is an obvious similarity in the layout of the screen and the structure of certain exercises in Aktiv Wortschatz.

The **Bertelsmann Language Trainer** is a complete English learning program and consists of four levels: basic, intermediate, advanced and business. My comments only refer to the vocabulary sections. In each section (in the basic package there are four, in the intermediate and advanced sections there are three each and in the business package there are two sections) ten topics can be selected for vocabulary training. In each section 25 to 35 vocabulary items are introduced, so that the course as a whole contains no fewer than 3,500 items and in addition 450 training items in the business section. In the training mode "Explore" the items can be studied in detail. There is a sound recording for all the words. By clicking the translation, comments regarding grammar, derivations and usage in a sentence context can be activated, a very useful addition to the overall course material. In the exercise mode illustrations are used as well as drag-and-drop and multiple choice-based tasks and combination exercises. At the more advanced stage there is also a phase of relaxation in which the learner can do crosswords with the new word material. In the final test mode all these elements are combined. In the intermediate, advanced and business packages there is also a CD for revision purposes, but the revision exercises in the vocabulary sections are identical in all three packages. Type and size of the lettering as well as the screen background (lack of contrast) could be further improved. For learners used to British English the American pronunciation might prove a little difficult at first. Again, as in so many other programs before, the lack of variety in the vocabulary exercises is a problem. The drag-and-drop exercises are increasingly replaced by multiple-choice exercises. And in spite of the often unusually high number of distractors work with these exercises becomes tedious after a while. There is no communication to speak of with the learner. On the other hand it must be said that the vocabulary exercises which, after all, constitute only one element in a much more comprehensive course, offer considerable scope for practice. For each topic there are forty or more tasks. The words are mostly presented in full sentences or little situations. The level of difficulty has been well gauged. The audio and speaking functions are systematically integrated into the program.

With more than 9,000 entries **TMX English** is by far the most encompassing of the vocabulary training programs discussed here. The very comprehensive accompanying booklet, also a rare feature in the programs for the adult market, provides a systematic introduction to all the functions of the program. There are possibilities to add to the general vocabulary list and also to the thematic lists. The following features are available for vocabulary training: in the verb training mode there is a given time limit to deal with a selection of words (adding other verb forms, translation into German). The fill-in exercises require the appropriate selection from a list of terms provided. The language laboratory mode is the only opportunity for interactive work in the program and allows the learner to listen to and repeat more than 800 sentences. The core element of the TMX-program is the vocabulary trainer. It is up to the learner to determine the language sequence (English-German or German-English), the area in the alphabet, the level of difficulty, the ratio of multiple-choice and fill-in exercises, the possible exclusion of phrases or context-related items. Some of these tasks can be integrated into sets of exercises: Word equations are to be formed with six options to choose from, or by keying in the English or German equivalent. Items where there were problems are presented again. The exercise material is comprehensive and clearly geared to the adult learner. It requires at least a full year of foreign language tuition.

And finally a small textbook-related vocabulary trainer should be mentioned which was developed for use in conjunction with the Cornelsen-Oxford textbook **Englisch in Wirtschaft und Handel**. This trainer is made up of 16 training units (based on the textbook units) with 30 to 50 of the most important words of the respective unit which are shown in a sentence context. There are two stages of the help function to assist the learner in finding the solution. The program allows up to five correct solutions which can be established by activating the scroll function. For all the correct answers the learner also has access to the phonetic transcription. In case of wrong answers the learners are given some explanation and help to find the correct solution. This program is available under DOS. Students enrolled at the Fern-Universität Hagen can obtain a vocabulary trainer which is structured in very much the same way, but for which audio and speaking functions are also available (**Fachwortschatztrainer Englisch für Wirtschaftswissenschaftler**).

This is only a cursory survey of a large diversity of vocabulary trainers or of vocabulary trainer elements in more comprehensive language learning packages. The most satisfactory programs from the point of view of learner integration and communication with the user, selection of material and their presentation are without doubt all those programs which are clearly designed to support textbook work, possibly because the target group is very clearly defined, but very likely also because there is more long-term experience with the development of language learning materials in the respective publishing houses.

It is disappointing to note that the variety of exercises used for vocabulary training falls considerably behind what we have come to accept as standard in textbooks. This seems to indicate that the technical problems to be solved in connection with the animated presentation of language learning materials on the computer screen are so complex as to leave little room for the authors to draft imaginative and motivating exercises. This applies in particular to the programs for the adult market where the enormous wealth of material stands in stark contrast to the lack of diversity in the exercises. There are very few exercises involving word formation patterns, synonyms, antonyms and homonyms, exercises on the borderline between vocabulary and grammar (transformation of nominal into verb structures), exercises involving more complex structures than single words or compounds to name but a few very traditional types. Very little progress has been made so far with the networking of audio and visual elements with interactive features. It is simply not enough to keep the interactive elements at the listen-and-repeat levels which are all too familiar from the bygone days of the language laboratory. If the new medium of the audio-CD-ROM is not to suffer the same fate as the language lab programs, then authors, publishers, program designers will have to pick their brains to explore and hopefully exhaust the tremendous potential that this new tool provides for the language learning process.

Notes

1 Holtwisch, p. 175
2 Weis, p. 174; Didaktilus, p. 102
3 Holtwisch, pp. 175/176
4 Beile, p. 65ff
5 Birt, "Structure and Vocabulary – Parts 2 – 3"
6 Beile, pp. 66 – 84

Bibliography

Bach, Gerhard: "Computergestützte Materialentwicklungen für den Fremdsprachenunterricht: Wortschatzanalyse und Textannotation", *Neusprachliche Mitteilungen aus Wissenschaft und Praxis* 42, 1989, 171-176.

Bahns, Jens: "Word Partnerships – Kollokationsübungen für die Wortschatzarbeit", *Zielsprache Englisch* 23, 1993, 7-12.

Beile, Werner: "Wortschatzübungen in englischen Lehrwerken der Sekundarstufe I", *anglistik und englischunterricht* 32, 1987, 61-86.

Birt, David: "Structure and Vocabulary – Parts 1-3", *Zielsprache Englisch* 21 (Heft 1), 1991, 4-5; (Heft 2) 1991, 12-15; (Heft 3) 1991, 17-22.

Didaktilus: "Wortschatzarbeit = Vokabellernen", *Neusprachliche Mitteilungen aus Wissenschaft und Praxis* 43, 1990, 101-103.
Glaap, Albert-Rainer: "Der Stellenwert der Wortschatzarbeit in den Richtlinien", *anglistik und englischunterricht* 32, 1987, 7-17.
Gude, Kathy: "Thirteen tips for vocabulary exercises", *Zielsprache Englisch* 23 (Heft 1), 1993, 6-11.
Hohmann, Heinz-Otto: "Sprachkompetenz und lexikalische Lernarbeit", *anglistik und englischunterricht* 32, 1987, 17-32.
Holtwisch, Herbert: "Kreative Wortschatzarbeit in der Sekundarstufe I", *Neusprachliche Mitteilungen aus Wissenschaft und Praxis* 46, 1993, 175-185.
Kielhöfer, Bernd: "Wörter lernen, behalten und erinnern", *Neusprachliche Mitteilungen aus Wissenschaft und Praxis* 47, 1994, 211-220.
Küffner, Helmuth: "Das Programm COACH: Interaktives Vokabeltraining mit akustischer Sprachausgabe", *Empirische Pädagogik* 5, 1991, 249-260.
---: "Entwicklung und Erprobung eines Fachsprachenvokabeltrainers mit akustischer Sprachausgabe". – In Jürgen Fechner (Ed.): *Neue Wege im computergestützten Fremdpsrachenunterricht*, Berlin & München, 1994, pp. 165-183.
Schmidt-Schönbein, Gisela: "Der Computer im Frendsprachenunterricht – ein neuer Nürnberger Trichter für Wortschatzarbeit und Kontextverständnis", *anglistik und englischunterricht* 32, 1987, 123-129.
Voss, Bernd: "Call: Programme – Probleme – Perspektiven", *Neusprachliche Mitteilungen aus Wissenschaft und Praxis* 44, 1991, 248-255.
Weiss, Dieter: "Untersuchungen zur langfristigen Verfügbarkeit von Wortschatz im Leistungsfach Englisch", *Neusprachliche Mitteilungen aus Wissenschaft und Praxis* 39, 1986, 174-180.

Selected material for computer-aided vocabulary training

Alfons Lernsoftware Englisch 5 und 6, Schroedel Verlag GmbH
Blacky's Byte Box (7. Schuljahr), Schroedel Verlag GmbH
Easy English. An Educational Game, Westermann Lernspielverlag
Coktel English, First Steps (Klasse 3 & 4), Sierra Coktel (Deutschland)
Englisch I. Multimedia Sprachtrainer (Kommunikationstrainer, Sprachkurs, Vokabeltrainer), Digital Publishing
English Coach Multimedia, (Vokabeln-Grammatik-Action), Cornelsen Software GmbH
Englisch in Wirtschaft und Handel, Cornelsen & Oxford
Green Line 6. Vokabeltrainer, Heureka Klett Verlag
Hueber Viva. Aktiv Wortschatz Englisch, Max Hueber Verlag
Kreisel, Uwe und Tabbert, Pamela Ann, English One & Two, Rowohlt-Systhema
Langenscheidt's Language Explorer, Langenscheidt
Language Trainer English (Basic, Intermediate, Advanced, Business), Bertelsmann
PC Sprachtraining Englisch, Klett
Spotlight games, Englisch lernen, Systhema Verlag GmbH & Spotlight Verlag GmbH

Spotlight "sprach"spiele, Wirtschaftsenglisch, Spotlight Verlag GmbH & Systhema Verlag GmbH
TMX Englisch, Sunflowers GmbH

This is only a summary outline. There are constantly new materials on offer, very often in cheap versions.

Andrea Sand, Freiburg

Machine-readable corpora in research and teaching: A survey

Machine-readable corpora provide a valuable tool for linguistic data collection, especially for non-native speakers of English, who cannot rely on introspection and rarely have the means to conduct extended fieldwork and informant testing (which in turn is likely to be biased by the presence of a non-native interviewer). The following survey is intended as a brief introduction for those who have never used computer corpora, describing different types of corpora available and pointing out possible applications in English language research and teaching. For reasons of space, I will only discuss corpora for off-line use, i.e. which are available on diskette and CD-ROM and do not require access to the Internet.[1] Details about the availability of a corpus or further reading are given in the notes.[2]

What is a corpus?

A corpus is basically any collection of authentic, naturally[3] occurring speech, written or spoken. Machine-readable corpora, referred to as "corpora" from now on, present the material in a format that allows computer-aided analysis of larger amounts of text. However, it is useful to distinguish between text collections for archiving purposes and corpora compiled according to certain research-oriented principles. The major principles of corpus compilation are balance, representativeness and size. A corpus solely consisting of articles from one single British newspaper could not be regarded as representative of "British English" as a whole, and even for a balanced representation of British press language, it would have to contain articles from many different British newspapers, national and regional.[4] On the other hand, the complete collection of a whole year of, for instance, *The Guardian*, can be a useful research tool as well. I will refer to such collections as "full-text databases" to distinguish them from corpora compiled for linguistic purposes. Full-text databases and corpora usually also differ with regard to size: the number of words contained in a corpus as well as in every individual text is always identifiable in a linguistic corpus to allow comparative and statistical analyses. This is not the case for full-text databases compiled for content-oriented storage, which, however, are generally much larger than linguistic corpora.

Major types of corpora

Over the last three decades, a large number of corpora designed for linguistic analysis have been compiled and made available to researchers.[5] They can be classified roughly into three groups:

1. "classic" 1,000 000-word corpora
2. modern "mega-size" corpora
3. specialized corpora.

Since they are used for different research purposes, I will briefly describe typical representatives of each group, including information on availability, hardware and software requirements for their use and some examples of their application in English linguistics.

The "classic corpora" – old and new

The first corpus later to become a "classic" was compiled at Brown University (Providence, Rhode Island) between 1963 and 1964 under the direction of W. Nelson Francis and Henry Kučera. It consists of roughly 1,000 000 words of written American English published in 1961, divided into 500 texts of 2,000 words each. Like most other classic corpora, the Brown corpus can be obtained from the International Computer Archive of Modern English (ICAME) in Norway. It is available on diskette and microfiche, but also as part of a CD-ROM distributed by ICAME. Contact ICAME at the Norwegian Computing Centre for the Humanities, Harald Hårfagresgt. 31, N-5007 Bergen, Norway or via e-mail at icame@hd.uib.no.

The Brown corpus comprises a number of genres, including press reportage, religion, science, government documents and fiction. In the late 1970s, this pioneering compilation was matched by a corpus of written British English published in 1961, assembled in cooperation by teams at the universities of Lancaster, Oslo and Bergen – hence its name Lancaster/Oslo-Bergen corpus, commonly abbreviated as LOB. It also contains 500 texts of approximately 2,000 words, and the distribution into text categories is almost identical to that of the Brown corpus. For the first time linguists were able to perform comparative analyses of British and American English without having to rely on incidental observation, basing their hypotheses on a matching sample of 1,000 000 words from each variety.[6] This breakthrough in intervariety-research led to a number of follow-up projects, for example the Kolhapur Corpus of Indian English, which was compiled between 1980 and 1986 at Shivaji University, Kolhapur, using material from

1978 along the same categories as the Brown corpus. Another corpus compiled according to the Brown guidelines is the Macquarie University Corpus of Australian English, which contains material published in 1986. In addition to the 2,000-word text units required, it also contains all complete texts to facilitate text-linguistic research. Other countries took up the challenge as well (though their corpora are slightly different in structure from LOB and Brown), for example New Zealand with the Wellington Corpus of New Zealand English (1986-1990) or Canada with the Corpus of English-Canadian Writing (on-going compilation since 1984).[7]

More recently, another dimension has been added to intervariety research based on 1,000 000-word corpora: diachronic change over 30 years, or one generation of speakers. The Freiburg Update of the Lancaster/Oslo-Bergen Corpus of Written British English (FLOB) and the Freiburg Update of the Brown University Corpus of Written American English (Frown) contain material published in 1991 (FLOB) and 1992 (Frown). Claims about on-going change in the two major varieties of English can thus be tested with the help of matching text corpora.[8]

The limitation of the corpora modelled on Brown is their restriction to published written material. For the longest time, the only available corpus of spoken standard British English was the London-Lund Corpus (LLC), which was compiled at Lund University using material from the Survey of English Usage collected mainly in the 1960s.[9] The corpus consists of about 500,000 words of recorded and broadcast speech, which have been prosodically transcribed. This method provides the analyst with an abundance of information on stress patterns, intonation and other features that are lost in purely orthographic transcription, but leads to difficulties in comparing word frequencies, because rising and falling intonation of the same item are treated as two different forms by many retrieval programs. But the major disadvantage was the fact that no comparable corpora were compiled for other varieties of English – the LLC remained a singular project.

The International Corpus of English (ICE) project is aimed to remedying this situation by taking up the "classic" 500 x 2,000-word format, but combining private and public spoken material, as well as published and unpublished written texts for a large number of varieties. The corpus will include 18 subcorpora from countries where English is the first language (e.g. UK, USA, Canada, Australia, New Zealand, Ireland) or a major (second) language with official status (e.g. East Africa, Jamaica, Nigeria, Hong Kong, South Africa, India, Philippines). Once completed, the ICE core-corpora will allow extensive intervariety research, while a number of more specific text types or collections of complete texts will enable linguists to extend their analysis into further areas of interest, such as text-linguistics or pragmatics.[10]

With regard to hardware requirements, the "classic corpora" are relatively easy to manage. The most basic equipment needed would be a PC with a version of MS-DOS 3.x or above, a large hard disk and a 386 or faster processor. A faster processor and a CD-ROM drive are useful, since many corpora are available on CD-ROM and the handling is more convenient than with floppy disks. But in addition to the necessary hardware, the "classic corpora" require some kind of research software before you can put them to use, because the corpora themselves simply consist of ASCII-textfiles. Without the right software tools, you could read them like a book, but you could not do any computer-based research. There are a number of retrieval software options, and I will only mention a few widely available programs.[11] A good option for beginners in corpus linguistics would be the *TACT* program, an easy-to-use freeware package,[12] which allows the user to compute frequency lists and rankings, statistical distributions and collocations and to conduct searches of user-defined categories. A wildcard option allows searches for beginnings (e.g. prefixes) or endings of words, as well as the base form of a lexeme including all derivatives and inflected forms. For example, all adjectives ending in *-ish* can be looked up by typing .* *ish*, while all words containing the new prefix h*yper-* are tracked down with the formula *hyper.**. A popular commercial program is *Wordcruncher*,[13] which has the advantage that several "classic corpora" are available on a CD-ROM distributed by ICAME as ready-to-use *Wordcruncher* files. The functions of *TACT* and *Wordcruncher* are comparable.[14] An example for a more sophisticated, but also more expensive, software option would be *Wordsmith*,[15] which can process larger amounts of texts and perform more statistical and concordancing functions.

Thus equipped with at least one corpus and suitable retrieval software, you are ready to tackle linguistic problems. The "classic corpora" with their limited size and text extracts rather than full texts are most suited to morpho-syntactic research. Such core-grammar phenomena are usually frequent enough to yield a sufficient amount of data for analysis. It often comes as a surprise to the corpus novice how rare most lexical words are. Thus, common English words such as *helicopter, booklet, disgust* and *goodwill* occur only once each in Brown.

But one corpus can be used to find out more about phenomena like the use of the Saxon *-s* genitive as opposed to the construction with *of* by helping to identify possible contexts for each variant.[16] A comparison of LOB and Brown or FLOB and Frown can reveal grammatical differences between British and American English, for example the different use of conjunctions and prepositions, differences in infinitival complementation, use of tenses or the subjunctive or the choice of wh-pronouns.[17] All the often-quoted differences between American and British English, such as use of *will* versus *shall*, *holiday* versus *vacation*, *dreamt* versus *dreamed* – to name a few – can be tested on real data. The comparison of LOB and Brown with their respective updates can also be used to test the hypothesis that British English is becoming more and more Americanized. Some linguists use annotated (or tagged) versions of these corpora for very sophisticated stylistic research combining a large number of features to address the question of the linguistic differences between various text genres.[18] Most commonly corpora are tagged for parts of speech, i.e. each word receives a computer-readable code specifying the part of speech, e.g. <mass noun> or <transitive verb>. This procedure renders the corpus more difficult to read, but allows the easy distinction of English homographs, e.g. the relative pronoun *who* and the interrogative pronoun *who* or the word *cut* as noun or verb. But partial tagging for specific research interests or semantic tagging are also possible. Of the corpora discussed so far, LOB and Brown are available in wordclass tagged versions.[19]

Modern "mega-size corpora": The British National Corpus

I have chosen the British National Corpus (BNC) as an example of the multimillion-word corpora that came into being after the development of more advanced computer technology. Generally speaking, these corpora are not for use at your home PC. In most cases, they were compiled by the publishers of English language dictionaries, who need a very large sample to determine meaning and usage of lexemes. Naturally, these companies are not too eager to share the results of their cost-intensive work with the general academic public. For example, the Bank of English Corpus, which is being continuously compiled for the Collins COBUILD dictionary and contains about 8,5 million words of spoken language and several hundred million words of written text, is only accessible by arrangement at the place of compilation.[20] The BNC was compiled by Oxford University Press, and due to its hardware requirements (UNIX workstation/server) and price (ca. 150£) it is also not a feasible option for individual students or teachers. However, the BNC is accesible at a number of German universities,[21] and the discussion of its merits and possibilities may well prompt some readers to explore it themselves.

The BNC consists of roughly 100 million words of contemporary British English, with 90 % written material, both published and unpublished from 10 different topic domains (e.g. arts, commerce, world affairs) and 10 % spoken material in orthographic transcription. The most interesting component of the spoken part are the approximately 4 million words of the spoken demographic sample, which consists of spontaneous speech recorded over 24-hour periods by individuals selected to represent the regional and social variation in British English. The whole corpus is tagged for parts of speech and each text also contains a header with information about the text, the speakers, the location and time of the recording and the speech event among others.[22]

Working with the BNC

The corpus comes with its own retrieval software, a program called *SARA*, which works in MS-Windows and is therefore quite comfortable to use. *SARA* allows searches not only for lexemes, strings of or parts of lexemes, but also for any type of tag (part of speech, text information, speaker information etc.) and complex queries consisting of a combination of elements, e.g. the occurrences of laughter in spontaneous speech. However, due to increased complexity (as compared to *TACT* and others) and the huge corpus size, a search may take very long.

The BNC contains not only more text than other corpora, but also more extra-linguistic information, which is accessible through the retrieval program. This is a definite advantage over the "classic corpora". Apart from its merits in the field of lexicography, it is thus more suited for pragmatics and discourse-oriented research. It was also intended as a tool for sociolinguistic and dialectological research, but only a very small part of the corpus is tagged for dialect or social class of the speakers. For example, only about 2 million words of the spoken demographic sample are consistently tagged for social class. In general, the BNC is more suited for investigations into regional or non-regional urban non-standard speech than into traditional rural dialects.

The huge amount of data also made it necessary to use automatic transcription and tagging systems, which have a number of weaknesses: non-standard forms are often not transcribed consistently, homophones are transcribed wrongly, part-of-speech tags in spoken text are wrongly assigned due to "incomplete" syntactic environments and other "hazards" of spoken language. When working with the spoken component, it is therefore necessary to double-check all results and thin out the "misses".

The large variety of spoken and written text types make the BNC especially attractive for those who want to identify the linguistic and extra-linguistic contexts of a specific form or construction. Especially in language teaching, it is often overly simplistic to tell students that a form "doesn't exist" or "is never written". Working with a large corpus like the BNC will help students to become aware of the more complex linguistic reality, namely that most forms are possible in certain contexts. For example, even though style-manuals keep telling their readers that contractions are not permissible in written English, corpus research shows that in recent newspaper texts *don't* is chosen over *do not* in about 3 out of 4 cases. We have to acknowledge that some contractions, like *don't*, have reached more or less norm status, while others, like *gotta*, are still reserved for markedly informal writing.[23] It can also be rewarding to compare the linguistic behaviour of different age groups, social groups or sexes to test existing stereotypes, e.g. to see if men really use more swearwords than women.

Despite its shortcomings, the BNC is the largest collection of authentic British English that is widely available, and it complements the "classic corpora" by stressing a large number and great diversity of text types instead of a rigid corpus design and comparability with other varieties.

Specialized corpora

Specialized corpora were compiled with a very specific research interest in mind. They are usually relatively small (often less than the 1 million words of the "classics") and it would not be feasible to discuss them all within the scope of this survey. For example, the Guangzhou Petroleum English Corpus, consisting of ca. 400,000 words taken from British and American texts on petroleum processing, is only of limited interest to the average linguist.[24] I will therefore concentrate on two areas, which are more central in English linguistics: the history of the English language and the speech behaviour of certain social groups.

Historical corpora

The most well-known historical corpus is the diachronic part of the Helsinki Corpus, compiled at the University of Helsinki.[25] It comprises roughly 1.6 million words, covering a variety of written genres between the years 850 and 1720, which is basically the development from Old English to modern English. This means, however, that the number of words available for each individual period is not very large. A project designed to remedy this point at least for the Early Modern English period is the Lampeter Corpus of Early Modern English Tracts, compiled at the University of Technology Chemnitz-Zwickau.[26] It concentrates on one very common genre of the period, the pamphlet or tract, and combines two texts each from six different domains for each decade between 1640 and 1740, yielding a total of ca. 1.1 million words. The texts are accompanied by headers containing information about the author and characteristics of the text to allow sociolinguistic or textlinguistic research. Another recent project covering the span between 1650 and 1990 is the ARCHER Corpus, which stands for "A Representative Corpus of Historical English Registers".[27] It consists of British and American texts from seven written (including diaries, letters, fiction, expository and scientific writing) and three written-to-be-spoken (drama, fiction dialogue and sermons) registers or genres. The corpus will contain 10 texts for each genre per 50-year period, amounting to a total of over 1 million words; however, in some areas the American variety is underrepresented due to a lack of material. The entire corpus will be tagged for grammatical categories. These three corpora allow interested linguists to trace the entire history of the English language with the help of computer-readable texts. It will be possible to analyze and illustrate processes of grammaticalisation or of semantic change. A certain form or construction, such as the progressive, can be studied beginning with its first attestation, followed as it becomes more frequent and finally obligatory in certain contexts. The only difficulty in corpus-based diachronic linguistics arises from the great degree of variation with regard to the spelling of a lexeme. The researcher has to keep all variants in mind and combine a number of searches in each case.

Groupspecific corpora

Sometimes, linguists are interested in the linguistic behaviour of certain social groups and even "mega-size" corpora like the BNC do not contain enough material spoken or written by this specific target group. In many cases, a corpus tailored to the research interest will be compiled. The advantage of computer-readable corpora in this kind of sociolinguistic research lies not only in the easy access to the data collected, but also in the fact that other linguists can then use the corpus for their own research. Their results are more transparent and comparable than if they had each compiled a smaller database of their own. For example, those interested in studying the language of youngsters can resort to the Polytechnic of Wales Corpus (PoW), which records the speech of 120 children between 6 and 12 years of age in orthographic transcription.[28] Teenager talk can be studied with the help of the Bergen Corpus of London Teenage Language (COLT),[29] which consists of roughly 500,000 words of spontaneous conversation between London teenagers (13-17 years of age). A first transcription of the corpus became part of the spoken demographic sample of the BNC, but the compilers in Bergen have since re-edited the transcription, identifying speakers and filling in gaps previously coded "unclear". In addition to the orthographic transcription, part of the corpus is also transcribed prosodically and will be published on a CD-ROM together with sound files of the actual recordings. This kind of processing is the most advanced and more or less ideal form of data storage: every user can check suprasegmental features or actual phonetic realisation by listening to the recordings. Since every transcription is in itself an interpretation, this method ensures absolute transparency of the analytic process.

Another social group of potential interest for students and teachers of English are other learners of English. The International Corpus of Learner English (ICLE) is being compiled for the contrastive analysis of the linguistic behaviour of foreign-language learners of English. It will eventually contain 11 parallel subcorpora (with 200,000 words each) of essays written by advanced learners with mother tongues as diverse as French, Finnish or Chinese.[30] File headers provide information on the social and linguistic background of each student. Although the individual corpora are quite small, the ICLE project as a whole will enable researchers and instructors to uncover "non-native" features in the syntax, lexis and stylistics of advanced learners, as well as to distinguish "universal" learner features from L1-specific interferences. The contrastive approach can help to identify those areas where learners would profit most from authentic native-language teaching tools.

Working with Specialised Corpora

The specialised corpora, of which there are many more than I have had space to discuss, are a very heterogenous group. Generally speaking, the hardware and software requirements for their use are like those for the "classic" corpora. They are meant to supplement the two other types by providing data that does not appear in those corpora aiming to represent the contemporary standard of the language.

Conclusions

After having introduced different types of corpora and commented on some of their potential uses in linguistic research, I want to end with a few general remarks on corpus-based studies of English. The major caveat for all those who plan to use computer-readable corpora for their future work is the right match of research interest and corpus or corpora. It is as useless to hunt for rare or specialized lexemes in a smaller "classic" corpus as to look up all occurrences of a common function word in a large corpus like the BNC. Corpora containing written material only are not suitable for dialectal or sociolectal research, just as corpora containing only one genre do not provide a good basis for generalizations about the state of the language in general.

If these restrictions are kept in mind, corpora are very useful research tools, since they provide large amounts of authentic data, which are statistically analysable. The automatic retrieval puts impressionistic observation into perspective – a very striking feature may be overestimated unless its frequency in relation to alternative forms is considered.

In language teaching, corpora are part of a movement away from formalised prescriptive grammar to a more context-sensitive approach to language use. Corpus-based dictionaries (like the *Collins COBUILD English Language Dictionary*) or grammars (like Quirk, Greenbaum et al.'s *A Comprehensive Grammar of the English Language*) are already widely used in language teaching. But the best reference works are – by nature – not up-to-date. It is very revealing for advanced students to be able to check on their grammars or dictionaries, and to find out that *help somebody do something* is not only more common in American English than *help somebody to do something*, but also in British English as represented by the spoken demographic sample of the BNC. Historical corpora and – for the micro-perspective – full-text databases of English language newspapers[31] enable students to trace the development of new words or formatives into the language, e.g. how *cyber-* moved from specialized high-tech jargon into everyday usage. Advanced students can also increase their language awareness by complementing a discussion of environmental policies by looking up all occurrences of *eco-* or *bio-* in a newspaper on CD-ROM or a larger corpus like the BNC. The usually vague notion of "environment" will become more specific by a comparison of the yielded terminology, and additionally, students will find out more about productive word formation patterns.

If teaching a good command of idiomatic and pragmatically adequate English is the aim, computer-readable corpora are the easiest way to obtain authentic working material. In advanced foreign-language teaching they make easy the step from what is grammatical to what is natural, common and stylistically appropriate usage.

Notes

1 Information about the on-line use of the Internet for linguistic purposes can be found in a number of recent publications. Cf. Doris Feldman, Fritz Wilhelm Neumann and Thomas Rommel (Eds.): *Anglistik im Internet.* Heidelberg, 1996 or Elisabeth Cölfen, Hermann Cölfen and Ulrich Schmitz (Eds.): *Linguistik im Internet: Das Buch zum Netz – mit CD-ROM*. Opladen/Wiesbaden, 1996, especially Josef Schmied: "Networking corpora", pp. 113-128. The University of Freiburg also provides a learner's program for students of English using the Internet called *Startrampe.* It is accessible under *http://www.uni-freiburg.de/philfak3/eng/rampe/index.htm* in the *WorldWideWeb.*

2 A note auf caution is necessary, however: In no other area is information outdated faster than in the area of computers. Some of the information given about websites or e-mail addresses may be no longer valid by the time this article is published. In that case, you can use a search engine in the Internet to find out what you need.

3 By "natural" data, I understand unself-consciously produced discourse, recorded in the context of a typical situation (not under lab test conditions) and produced with a real communicative purpose. On the importance of natural data for many types of linguistic investigation, see Wallace Chafe: "The importance of corpus linguistics to the understanding of the nature of language". – In Jan Svartvik (Ed.): *Directions in Corpus Linguistics*. Berlin/New York, 1992, pp. 82-89.

4 See for instance Jeremy H. Clear: "The British National Corpus". – In George P. Landow and Paul Delany (Eds.): *The Digital Word: Text-Based Computing in the Humanities*. Cambridge, MA, 1993, pp. 167ff.

5 For a more complete overview see Appendix A in Tony McEnery and Andrew Wilson: *Corpus Linguistics*. Edinburgh, 1996, pp. 181-187 or Lita Taylor, Geoffrey Leech and Steven Fligelstone: "A survey of English machine-readable corpora". – In Stig Johansson and Anna-Brita Stenström (Eds.): *English Computer Corpora*. Berlin, 1991, pp. 319-354, which is not as recent, but contains more details on format and availability. For those with access to the Internet, an up-dated list of corpora is available on the fileserver of the International Computer Archive of Modern English (ICAME) at FAFSRV@NORBERGEN.

6 LOB is also available through ICAME. For an account of the kind of comparative research made possible by LOB and Brown, see Bengt Altenberg's bibliography in Stig Johansson and Anna-Brita Stenström (Eds.): *English Computer Corpora*. Berlin, 1991, pp. 355-396.

7 Availability: **Kolhapur Corpus** (on diskette) via ICAME; **Macquarie Corpus** through The School of English and Linguistics, Macquarie University, 2109 N.S.W., Australia; **Wellington Corpus** through the Department of Linguistics, Victoria University of Wellington, PO Box 600, Wellington, New Zealand; **Canadian Corpus** (on floppy disks and Tallgrass streaming tape) through Margery Fee, Director, Strathy Language Unit, 207 Stuart Street, Room 316, Rideau Building, Queen's University, Kingston, Ontario K7L 3N6, Canada. For further reference see S. V. Shastri: "The Kolhapur Corpus of Written Indian English and work done on its basis", *ICAME Journal* 12, 1988, 15-26; Peter Collins and Pam Peters: "The Australian Corpus Project". – In M. Kytö, O. Ihalainen and M. Rissanen (Eds.): *Corpus Linguistics, Hard and Soft*. Amsterdam, 1988, pp. 103-120; Laurie Bauer: "Progress with a corpus of New Zealand English and some early results". – In C. Souter and E. Atwell (Eds.): *Corpus-Based Computational Analysis*. Amsterdam, 1993, pp. 1-10 or Laurie Bauer: *Manual of Information to Accompany the Wellington Corpus of Written New Zealand English*. Wellington: Dept. of Linguistics, Victoria University.

8 FLOB and FROWN are available directly on diskette or via ftp from Lehrstuhl Prof. Christian Mair, Englisches Seminar I, Albert-Ludwigs-Universität, Postfach, D-79085 Freiburg im Breisgau and will appear on the next corpus CD-ROM distributed by ICAME early in 1998. FLOB and Frown were designed to mirror their predecessors as closely as possible. However, due to changes in the world of publishing, some minor adjustments had to be made in the selection of individual texts. Cf. Andrea Sand and Rainer Siemund: "LOB – 30 years on...". – In *ICAME Journal* 16, 1992, pp. 119-122.

9 The London-Lund Corpus is available through ICAME. 34 of the conversations have also been published in book form by Jan Svartvik and Randolph Quirk (Eds.): *A Corpus of English Conversation*. Lund, 1980. For further reference see also Jan Svartvik (Ed.): *The London-Lund Corpus of Spoken English*. Lund, 1990.

10 So far, only the subcorpus for Great Britain has been completed. For all subcorpora, contact Gerald Nelson at the Survey of English Usage, University College London, Gower Street, London WC1E 6BT, Great Britain. E-mail: uclegen@ucl.ac.uk. A CD-ROM with recordings and transcriptions of 20 texts per variety will be released in 1999. For more detailed information on ICE corpus design, see Sidney Greenbaum: "Introducing ICE" and Gerald Nelson: "The Design of the Corpus". – In S. Greenbaum (Ed.): *Comparing English Worldwide: The International Corpus of English*. Oxford, 1996, pp. 3-12; 27-35.

11 A longer list of software including a brief description of each program and where it can be obtained can be found in Appendix B of Tony McEnery and Andrew Wilson: *Corpus Linguistics*. Edinburgh 1996, pp. 189-192.

12 Freeware (or shareware) means that the program can be obtained without a charge from the Centre for Computing in the Humanities, Robarts Library, Room 14297A, University of Toronto, Toronto, Ontario M5S 1A5, Canada or via the Internet by anonymous ftp from their server (epas.utoronto.ca) or the ICAME server (nora.hd.uib.no).

13 Contact Johnston and Co., PO Box 446, American Fork, UT 84003, USA for the distribution of *Wordcruncher*.

14 Cf. Hermann Walter: "Results and problems of text retrieval – a comparison of TACT and WORD CRUNCHER", *CCE Newsletter* 5 (1+2), 1991, 57-65.

15 For more information about *Wordsmith*, contact Oxford University Press, Walton Street, Oxford, OX2 6DP, GB or visit their homepage at http://www1.OUP.co.uk/oup/elt/software/wsmith, where you can also test the program.

16 Cf. Roswitha Raab-Fischer: "Löst der Genitiv die *Of*-Phrase ab? Eine korpusgestützte Studie zum Sprachwandel im heutigen Englisch", *Zeitschrift für Anglistik und Amerikanistik* 43, 1995, 123-132, which is based on the comparison of several corpora.

17 Cf. for example John Algeo: "British and American grammatical differences ", *International Journal of Lexicography* 1, 1988, 1-31 or Edgar Schneider: "Who(m)? Case marking of wh-pronouns in written British and American English." – In G. Leitner (Ed.) *New Directions in English Language Corpora*. Berlin, 1992, pp. 231-245, both based on a comparison of LOB and Brown.

18 Cf. Douglas Biber: *Variation Across Speech and Writing*. Cambridge 1988 or Douglas Biber: "A typoloy of English texts", *Linguistics* 27, 1989, 3-43.

19 Numerous tagging programs are available for individual tagging purposes. You could try the AMALGAM-tagger developed at the University of Leeds, which works via e-mail and allows you to use eight different sets of tags. E-mail: amalgam-tagger@scs.leeds.ac.uk.

20 If your research project would benefit from using the massive amount of data contained in the Bank of English Corpus, contact The Bank of English, Westmere, 50 Edgbaston Park Road, Birmingham, B15 2RX. If you should fail to get access, you could also try the Longman Dictionary corpus, which contains about 30 million words. Contact Longman Publishing for the Longman/Lancaster English Language Corpus.

21 For example, at the University of Freiburg the BNC is accessible for students and researchers in the English department and the university's CIP-Pool. I am aware of 26 German universities that hold a license for the BNC. For one near you, enquire via e-mail at natcorp@oucs.ox.ac.uk.

22 For more information see Lou Burnard (Ed.): *User Reference Guide for the British National Corpus.* Oxford, 1995, or contact the BNC-website of the Oxford Text Archive, http://info.ox.ac.uk/bnc.

23 Cf. Manfred Krug: *Contractions in Present-Day English. A Corpus-Based Study of Brachychronic Language Change.* Unpublished MA thesis. University of Exeter, 1994.

24 If you are nevertheless interested, contact the Guangzhou Training College of the Chinese Petroleum University for details.

25 The corpus is available via ICAME. The University of Helsinki has also compiled smaller corpora of Early American English (17th and 18th century) and Older Scots (between 1450 and 1700). Please contact the Department of English, University of Helsinki, Porthania 311, 00100 Helsinki, Finland or e-mail Prof. Matti Rissanen at mrissanen@cc.helsinki.fi.

26 The corpus is available through ICAME or the Oxford Text Archive, Oxford University Computing Services, 13 Banbury 13, Oxford OX2 6NN, UK (http://sable.ox.ac.uk/ota/). See Josef Schmied: "The Lampeter Corpus of Early Modern English Tracts". – In M. Kytö, M. Rissanen and S. Wright (Eds.): *Corpora Across the Centuries.* Amsterdam, 1994 , pp. 81-89, for further reference.

27 See Douglas Biber et al.: "The design and analysis of the ARCHER Corpus – A progress report." – In M. Kytö, M. Rissanen and S. Wright (Eds.): *Corpora Across the Centuries.* Amsterdam, 1994 , pp. 3-7, for further reference. Unfortunately, the first version of ARCHER to be released will contain mostly pre-1900 texts. This "draft version" will be available via ICAME. For further details or in-house use of the complete corpus, contact Douglas Biber, Department of English, Northern Arizona University, Flagstaff, AZ 86011-6032, USA or e-mail biber@nauvax.ucc.nau.edu.

28 The computer-readable parsed version is available through ICAME. For the original tapes and hardcopy of a prosodic transcription contact Dr. Robin P. Fawcett, Department of Behavioral and Communication Studies, Polytechnic of Wales, Treforest, Cardiff CF37 1DL, UK.

29 The corpus is available through the English Department, University of Bergen, Sydnesplassen 7, N-5007 Bergen, Norway or e-mail hannc.aas@eng.uib.no. It can also be used via the Internet: a pilot version of 151 texts can be accessed with the help of a web-version of *TACT* at the COLT homepage (http:// www.hd.uib.no/colt) or contact Hanne Aas for a user-ID to access the complete corpus on-line. A CD-ROM with the orthographic transcriptions and wordclass-tagging will be circulated by ICAME in 1999.

30 For the already completed subcorpora of ICLE contact the coordinator Sylviane Granger, Department of English, Université de Louvain, Place Blaise Pascal 1, B-1348 Louvain-la-Neuve, Belgium (e-mail granger@etan.ucl.ac.be) or the ICE headquarters in London (cf. note 10). For further details about the corpus see Sylviane Granger: "Learner English around the world." – In S. Greenbaum (Ed.): *Comparing English Worldwide. The International Corpus of English.* Oxford, 1996, pp. 13-24.

31 Many British and American newspapers are available on CD-ROM (e.g. GB: *The Guardian, The Times,* or *The Economist*, US: *The Washington Post, USA Today,* or *The New York Times*). The disadvantage in using these CD-ROM for linguistic research is their retrieval software, which is geared toward content-oriented searches. Grammatical function words generally cannot be retrieved, and instead of presenting the results in a short keyword-in-context (KWIC) format, the software forces the user often to download a complete article for each "hit".

Bibliography

Algeo, John: "British and American grammatical differences", *International Journal of Lexicography* 1, 1988, 1-31.

Altenberg, Bengt: "A bibliography of publications relating to English computer corpora". – In Stig Johansson & Anna-Brita Stenström (Eds.): *English Computer Corpora*, Berlin, 1991, pp. 355-396.

Biber, Douglas: *Variation Across Speech and Writing*, Cambridge, 1988.

---: "A typology of English texts", *Linguistics* 27, 1989, 3-43.

Biber, Douglas et al.: "The design and analysis of the ARCHER Corpus". – In Merja Kytö, Matti Rissanen & Susan Wright (Eds.): *Corpora Across the Centuries*, Amsterdam, 1994, pp. 3-7.

Bauer, Laurie: "Progress with a corpus of New Zealand English and some early results". – In Clive Souter & Eric Atwell (Eds.): *Corpus-Based Computational Analysis*, Amsterdam, 1993, pp. 1-10.

---: *Manual of Information to Accompany the Wellington Corpus of Written New Zealand English*, Wellington: Dept. of Linguistics, Victoria University.

Burnard, Lou: *User Reference Guide for the British National Corpus*, Oxford, 1995.

Chafe, Wallace: "The importance of corpus linguistics to the understanding of the nature of language". – In Jan Svartvik (Ed.): *Directions in Corpus Linguistics*, Berlin/New York, 1992, pp. 82-89.

Clear, Jeremy: "The British National Corpus". – In George P. Landow & Paul Delaney (Eds.): *The Digital Word: Text-Based Computing in the Humanities,* Cambridge, MA, 1993, pp. 167-169.

Collins, Peter & Pam Peters: "The Australian Corpus Project". – In Merja Kytö, Ossi Ihalainen & Matti Rissanen (Eds.): *Corpus Linguistics, Hard and Soft*, Amsterdam, 1988, pp. 103-120.

Cölfen, Elisabeth, Hermann Cölfen & Ulrich Schmitz (Eds.): *Linguistik im Internet: Das Buch zum Netz – mit CD-ROM*, Opladen/Wiesbaden, 1996.

Feldman, Doris, Fritz Wilhelm Neumann & Thomas Rommel (Eds.): *Anglistik im Internet*, Heidelberg, 1996.

Granger, Sylviane: "Learner English around the world". – In Sidney Greenbaum (Ed.): *Comparing English Worldwide: The International Corpus of English*, Oxford, 1996, pp. 13-24.

Greenbaum, Sidney: "Introducing ICE". – In Sidney Greenbaum (Ed.): *Comparing English Worldwide: The International Corpus of English*, Oxford, 1996, pp. 3-12.

Krug, Manfred: *Contractions in Present-Day English. A Corpus-Based Study of Brachychronic Language Change*, Exeter, 1994 (unpublished MA thesis, University of Exeter).

McEnery, Tony & Andrew Wilson: *Corpus Linguistics*, Edinburgh, 1996.

Nelson, Gerald: "The design of the corpus". – In Sidney Greenbaum (Ed.): *Comparing English Worldwide: The International Corpus of English*, Oxford, 1996, pp. 27-35.

Raab-Fischer, Roswitha: "Löst der Genitiv die *Of*-Phrase ab? Eine korpusgestützte Studie zum Sprachwandel im heutigen Englisch", *Zeitschrift für Anglistik und Amerikanistik* 43, 1995, 123-132.

Sand, Andrea & Rainer Siemund: "LOB – 30 years on...", *ICAME Journal* 16, 1992, 119-122.

Schmied, Josef: "The Lampeter Corpus of Early Modern English Tracts". – In Merja Kytö, Matti Rissanen & Susan Wright (Eds.): *Corpora Across the Centuries*, Amsterdam, 1994, pp. 81-89.

Schneider, Edgar: "Who(m)? Case marking of wh-pronouns in written British and American English". – In Gerhard Leitner (Ed.): *New Directions in English Language Corpora*, Berlin, 1992, pp. 231-245.

Shastri, S.V.: "The Kolhapur Corpus of Written Indian English and work done on its basis", *ICAME Journal* 12, 1988, 15-26.

Svartvik, Jan (Ed.): *The London-Lund Corpus of Spoken English*, Lund, 1990.

Svartvik, Jan & Randolph Quirk (Eds.): *A Corpus of English Conversation*, Lund, 1980.

Taylor, Lita, Geoffrey Leech & Steven Fligelstone: "A survey of English machine-readable corpora". – In Stig Johansson & Anna-Brita Stenström (Eds.): *English Computer Corpora*, Berlin, 1991, pp. 319-354.

Walter, Herrmann: "Results and problems of text retrieval – A comparison of TACT and WORD-CRUNCHER", *CCE Newsletter* 5 (1+2), 1991, 57-65.

Fritz-Wilhelm Neumann, Erfurt

The Full-Text Database: principles of searching and pattern-matching in the machine-readable corpus of English poetry

The Cambridge publishers, Chadwyck-Healey, herald the coming of a new age of scholarship. They have established themselves as the most powerful providers of full-text databases in English literature, and their enterprise seems to be gaining momentum. Their programme is comprehensive: apart from the English poetry full-text database, English verse drama, Shakespeare, early English novels, and the variants of the English Bible, extensions of magnitude have been announced for 1998: 20th century English poetry, the Swift supplement to the poetry corpus, American poetry and so on.[1] Unfortunately, speaking from the purely academic point of view,[2] this is a well-endowed commercial initiative. Academic providers of electronic texts such as the Oxford Text Archive, the English Server of Carnegie Mellon, or the Gutenberg Project will presumably not be able to match their strength for very long. Sometimes, I have a nightmarish feeling that Chadwyck-Healey will dispose of the academic providers of Internet services in the same ruthless and efficient way as Bill Gates was able to push the less successful aside. As Microsoft obviously intend to monopolize the global software market, Chadwyck-Healey will similarly make their database pay off in the near future. If we take into account the release of ABELL (*The Annual Bibliography of English Language and Literature*), which seems to be more reliable than the MLA Bibliogaphy, even the impartial observer will readily come to the conclusion that LION (Chadwyck-Healey's on-line database) could allow the humanities scholar to forget the qualities of the Internet as a whole.

Anyway, Chadwyck-Healey's electronic texts are the most reliable ones, even if they are not based on the most recent critical editions of the poets' works. At our own university we decided to acquire the poetry database because a similar collection of material bought from antiquarian booksellers or in the form of modern critical editions would have cost far more. The Cambridge publishers have thus made available a collection of poetry to a broader public which the reader will hardly come across outside Great Britain and the U.S. In addition, as Susanne Schmid has argued in this volume, Chadwyck-Healey has created a user-friendly interface for their databases, which is, however, no longer state of the art.[3] When the publishers extracted a subset of love poems from the English Poetry database and granted free access to the public, there were over 300,000 searches for poems over a period of three weeks.[4] Most web users searched for words like 'darling', 'love' and 'kiss', there were also some people interested in the 'kinky' side of love: 'loathsome', 'frog' and 'shoe' seemed to be equally important. Popular as the World Wide Web is, what does the machine-readable corpus contribute to serious scholarship and to classroom work alike? New avenues are to be explored.

The purpose of this essay is to familiarize the reader and potential user with the new tool, thus facilitating access to the electronic full-text database. As a first step, I shall discuss the nature of the corpus. Secondly, the rules of string operations and pattern matching which underlie any form of searching and probing into the corpus will be explained. To conclude, as an alternative, an elaborate search engine for cluster reading will be sketched out. The problem is really twofold: The interface keeps the user within limits which may discourage scholars from using the database, whereas more elaborate search engines require sophisticated programming which will scare off even more people.

The Nature of the Corpus

So, let's assume that within a very short period of time, the current canon of English literature will be available on the net in machine-readable form and that academic servers will only provide texts for more special purposes, as is the case with the various women writers' projects which are filling in the gaps left by Chadwyck-Healey, who had relied on the predominantly male canon recognized by the *New Cambridge Bibliography* as poets of English. At the same time as we are discussing the nature of the corpus, the canon of English literature has once again come under revision. This is mainly due to feminist critics such as Anne Mellor, the co-editor with Richard Matlack of the new anthology of *British Literature 1780-1830* intended for classroom use, and such as Ina Schabert, whose literary history on feminist lines has caused quite a stir.[5] Whether or not their decision to follow the entries in the NCBEL which notoriously omitted women authors may be seen to be arguable, the Chadwyck-Healey corpus simply presents English poetry as such. Understandably, the scholars in charge of the NCBEL had notions of awarding the status of 'minor' contributions to English literature which differed from late 20th century views. But whatever the possible objection against the limitations of the Chadwyck-Healey full-text database of English poetry, the main point is that their corpus constitutes a comprehensive academic library in machine-readable form. My favourite Chadwyck-Healey CD holds 38,000 English poems of the period dating from 1700 to

1800, which in itself is one of the many incredible feats of modern information technology.

While corpora compiled by linguists are mainly random collections,[6] which equally holds true for the items of English and American literature on the Internet, the organization of a comprehensive database is, however, significant in another respect. The masterpiece will be retrieved side by side with the garbage of literary history. Since we have trained our students to appreciate the individual achievement, namely a unique combination of conventional and innovative elements of poetry, Shelley is considered more important than Erasmus Darwin, and Byron will always be remembered as a great satirist more often than William Combe, the author of *Dr Syntax in Search of the Picturesque*. But a corpus should clearly transcend the limits imposed by any canon, which is rather crystallized in the anthology and is taken up in the curriculum of the departments of English. In extending our scope beyond the canon, the corpus will change our views of the system of literature as such.

Reading a corpus means searching for a cross-section presented not by coherent texts but by bits and pieces connected on pre-defined lines. This differs from the traditional approach to studying literature in many ways. The point is that we need new categories for piecing corpus information together. That Shakespeare coined a phrase like "my love is like a fever" in one of his darker sonnets might be an invaluable find, if one has a predilection for associating love with an ailment. In the age of machine-readable sources, this sort of investigation has become sheer fun. In the same way the first occurrence of a word in printed poetry can be traced beyond the sources quoted by the Oxford English Dictionary. Did Wordsworth like pets? Just have a look at the full-text database. When our university acquired the Chadwyck-Healey database of English poetry, it was priced at £ 24,000, which should rule out the more facetious inquiries into the corpus. If, however, you prepare a lecture on the representations of the city in English poetry or on the image of women in English romanticism, you immediately see how helpful a machine-readable corpus proves by the abundance of material it can produce.

Chadwyck-Healey are obviously building their hopes on the fact that new schools of criticism will emerge and render their databases indispensable to the humanities. One day, computing will be in the grasp of the average humanities scholar. The machine-readable corpus will doubtless enable advances to be made into new areas of literary criticism, providing that the critic acquires a workable knowledge of handling the new tools. New perspectives, which can easily be derived from existing theory, are to be put into practice in order to carry out research into new dimensions of intertextuality in the system-like character of literature in general and poetry in particular. Accordingly, this essay will first of all expand on the concept of the search, which, incidentally, is an utterly un-English notion of grappling with a new situation. If taken seriously, however, concept-oriented research into comprehensive corpora of literature requires hardware with an unprecedented storage capacity, just imagine the amount of storage space and memory which are required for processing 1,000 English novels, which one can easily download from various Web sites, in addition to the material offered by Chadwyck-Healey.

Apart from search tools, the first generation of computers produced thick volumes of concordances of the major writers in English without ever changing our notion of literary criticism. Endless word lists stand in stark contrast to the intricacies of critical reasoning when scholars set pen to paper. So far, computing has failed to make any serious impact on literary criticism. But, hopefully, times will change.

The Nature of the Machine

An obvious problem is that the computer scientists who design the most sophisticated software tools and the humanities scholars who are trying to improve their own professional performance are hardly able to communicate with each other, because they ignore the needs and habits of their new partners. The present state of the art which has filtered through to the humanities departments can be described as a user-friendly combination of search and concordance routines, which are doubtless powerful tools considering the amount of materials they so swiftly process. Tens of thousands of users who, as mentioned above, are obviously interested in the appearance of frogs in love poems, will be duly reassured, in spite of the frogs failing to turn into princes or princesses when kissed by the user's mouse.

Objectivity is the first advantageous side-effect of computing.[7] When we use search tools or write retrieval programmes, we have to submit to the rules of formal computer logic. Any string meeting the conditions defined in the search will be retrieved for further examination, which could be any line in a poem with the string '*ing,' (= any word terminating with 'ing' plus comma) or with any other string. If we inquire how Petrarchan conceits swept through the ages of English poetry, any combination of 'ey*' (wildcard for eyes, eying etc.) with 'love' or 'beaut*' (truncation for beauty, beauties, beautiful etc.) should do a good job. However vague the terms of this query are, however exhaustive the material presented by the computer, the large number of diffuse quotations obtained just might prove again and again that it is useful to reconsider material one would have liked to exclude from the original query. Due to the 'stupidity' of the machine, the frame of searching has to be defined with formal rigour but allowance has also to be made for the extensive covering of the field of inquiry. There will even be surprises you would never have dreamt of from just perusing the text. Most often, the critic will not have the feeling of having overlooked anything of importance, but there will also be samples which make one revise what one had in mind when initially setting the filter. Formal objectivity thus tends to counterbalance any too narrowly preconceived notions of one's research aim.

Literary criticism has to be translated into string operations, which are also necessary, because a full-text database normally implies that the corpus is not 'tagged', meaning not annotated.[8] It is also the case that no database structure can be relied on when we start our search. Apart from the fact that all the words are indexed, 'full-text' means that the material has not been sifted and put into the appropriate field or slot of the database, which would accelerate searching. The Chadwyck-Healey team used tags, which are visible in the source code, only for the purpose of formatting the text in order to reproduce it fairly reliably on the screen and in print. For more detailed information, database builders either resort to hypertext links[9] or to parallel storage devices, i.e. different files which are used to store the original version of the text, the record number of each word, the tags containing syntactic or semantic information tied to each word, and index files for administering the whole system.[10] However simple the keying in of a single word might appear, the architecture of a large database poses a number of technical questions. But don't let us worry about what is going on behind the interface of a comprehensive database which is supposed to be user-friendly.

Pattern matching

The most complex flow-chart cannot conceal the fact that the machine operates by simple steps. Any complex concept to be processed by the machine must be cut down to the string level and be matched with other strings. Thus, corpus reading is in reality string processing, which is commonly named pattern matching, as the strings of characters form patterns. The machine does not know that these are meant to be words. There are the tailor-made search routines implemented by the producer of the database, which are normally a combination of different algorithms such as a very flexible Boolean search programme combined with concordancing and indexing for full-text data and information drawn from database entries. The deficiency of Boolean search, which permits complete matches only, is compensated for by permitting truncation, wildcards, and logical operators (AND, OR, AND NOT) to specify the conditions of the query and to perform a parallel search for a second item in relation to the first one.[11] The ready-made search interface is to be distinguished from what I would like to call free corpus investigation, the programmes of which match thesaurus-like lists of key elements. This method has the advantage of including as many different elements as possible in the search: the phraseology of poetic diction and of a specific discourse, a set of poetic motifs and themes, or a catalogue of standard imagery. A strategy for complex pattern matching will be suggested at the end of my paper.

There is an important caveat against the so-called automatic analysis of texts: the researcher should never relinquish control of what the machine is doing at the semantic level. In areas of learning and research other than the humanities, there are many fields where linguistic standardization is practiced, whereas in literary history language is hardly suitable for surface operations such as automatic indexing. Recently, information scientists have proposed to chop up the text into trigrams to improve retrieval. This means that the machine will not match the string "frog", but instead will process a finite calculable representation of the text consisting of the elements "#fr", "fro", "rog", "og#" whilst including the boundary markers of the word. This statistically-based method may be helpful to spot related entries in encyclopaedias or databases or it may help running Internet research engines, but I am not so sure about its usefulness if applied to Dickens and Joyce, for example, in order to 'measure' intertextuality in terms of general similarity of diction or subject matter.[12]

Literary critics devote their attention more to the uniqueness of the existing work of art than to the probability of how often an item (such as, e.g., verbs denoting sensual perception in the late nineteenth and early twentieth-century English novel) will occur in a particular period or in a corpus. Filtering is intended for the specific detail, which, as an electronic replica of the work of art, is a verifiable 'event' in history as well. However popular statistics may be in a number of departments which are doing research in computational linguistics, the ideographic approach of the humanities differs radically from calculations of probability. From the point of view of the humanities scholar, who is out of his depth in statistics, mathematicians are skating on thin ice,[13] as the unique detail, which must be explained historically, is beyond their scope.

With this in mind, we can tailor pattern matching queries on one word or on one simple concept (first use, borrowing, evolution in different contexts, obsoleteness), which is to be distinguished from those investigations which presuppose more complex semantic fields and related ideas. In the following areas, one-dimensional queries are suggested:

- 'Arrowy' was introduced by George Chapman into English poetic diction when he translated Homer.[14]

- Wordsworth borrowed the word ‘arrowy’ from Erasmus Darwin and Charlotte Smith, which, as a simple case of intertextuality, is source hunting without any form of generalization or elucidation whatsoever.[15]
- The evolution of the word ‘arrowy’ is a case of intertextuality and a mark of shifting paradigms from starting off as an analogy to becoming poetic diction. It was made popular owing to the success of Pope and subsequent translators of Homer, but it definitely acquired an existence of its own in mid-18th-century descriptions of meteorological phenomena.[16] Tracing the history of one word through different contexts and collocations can throw new light on the interaction between the stock of knowledge available in a culture and the semantics of poetry. It may be highly rewarding to investigate the ways poets rework their system of poetic expression to keep up with intellectual changes and the revolutions in society.
- Strangely enough, speeding trains were not treated as ‘arrowy’ by Victorian or twentieth-century poets. This is the word I particularly miss in Stephen Spender’s poem “The Express”.[17] Bonitos, however, did speed ‘arrowily’ in Southey’s poem on Puritan emigration.[18] With more than 330 hits, ‘arrowy’ continues, however, to be quite a popular metaphor throughout nineteenth century poetry.[19]
- When did technology become food fit for poets? This operation would require a long sequence of keywords, which could not be processed by the Chadwyck-Healey interface in reasonable time. But the question remains: How have English poets reacted to the machine throughout the centuries? An important chapter in cultural history can be written on the transformation of technology into poetic language. If we commence with the image of the railways in nineteenth-century English poetry, we can find widespread concern expressed in the material about the new technology.[20]

If the search is aimed at far-reaching abstractions and concepts of literary history, a network of related ideas must be fitted into a limited number of keywords. This is a major heuristic operation that must be sketched out in advance by the critic. Sometimes he or she should be very cautious in forming an opinion from consideration of the evidence produced from the corpus. However tightly-knit the net of phraseology appears today, the critic should keep in mind that the conclusion arrived at by inference might be based on an investigation which is not very systematic. The more complex the abstractions you are devising are, the higher the risk that the evidence will be thoroughly misleading. Notwithstanding the possible deficiencies in the retrieval system under discussion, the following examples will suggest different aspects of multi-dimensional searching which appear to be rewarding:

- Conclusions such as "Coleridge disliked pets" summarize the results of a number of queries which are necessary to produce sufficient evidence for this. The filter must be set for a list of all the pets favoured by the English of the age together with the collocating verbs expressing like and dislike.
- A concept such as late 18th-century sentimentalism requires a more complex combination of queries which are based on a long list of keywords used for describing sensations, feelings and the appropriate environment in which they are then projected.
- Transcendance in romantic poetry or the concept of time are conveyed through the language of philosophy and a range of metaphorical settings. Problems of metaphysics must be boiled down to a meta-level of phraseology imposed by the machine.
- A long-range abstraction based on multiple queries from different stylistic and thematic angles summarizes the collective achievement which is represented by the corpus ("English romanticism is less artificial than classicism").

Query concept:	love and the supernatural
Keyword level:	love AND (frog* OR witch* OR dwar*...)
Recall:	frog*, witch*, dwar*...

References to the supernatural left unmarked: ???	

Consequently, there are two essentials one should be aware of: List processing based on a thesaurus is designed to detect all the relevant items of the phraseology and to concurrently handle a number of conditions such as a minimum number of occurrences within a given range before adding the matches to the recall. Secondly, in human language, repetition, variation and amplification occur, especially when important information is to be conveyed. Emphasis is one of the fundamental laws of rhetoric. Anyway, you will easily get most of the best hits. As a rule, matches form clusters whenever the author of the text wants to make sure that the reader gets the message. Since there are hardly any hardware restrictions left as to the comprehensiveness of the thesaurus, complex pattern matching has become fairly reliable.

Clusters and Adjacency

The COBUILD *Bank of English*[21] has shown that adjacency is a very important field of inquiry in corpus research. The property of adjacency covers all the hidden rules that human language habitually obeys in combining words and parts of speech. The thing is that these habits of collocation exceed the scope of any grammar or lexicography imaginable, whereas a concordance programme will easily highlight the principles of what one might call 'elegant or suitable association'. Adjacency may partly be explained by the history of the language, partly by the existence of discourse patterns and a definite phraseology. The literary critic will investigate the latter, the linguist the former.

But any more ambitious study will be forestalled by the Chadwyck-Healey interface, or it will take far too long to carry on the operation. Their search routine will handle quite an impressive number of alternatives connected to the initial string ("love") by the logical operators: love AND (frog* OR witch* OR bird* OR hors* OR beast* OR ...).[22] If the aim of the search, however, is to identify the phraseology of love throughout the decades, the adjacent strings cannot be determined beforehand. In the interface, there is no concordance-like command for the output of "any word within a range of 20 before and after LOVE". Copying all the poems where LOVE occurs would not be helpful. More sophisticated software such as *TACT, WordCruncher* or the *Oxford Concordance Programme* are prerequisite for any systematic study of collocations. What is declared to be a search for adjacent words by the Chadwyck-Healey manual (e.g. "paradise lost") is a combination of two strings; and there were, of course, good reasons for implementing a more flexible routine to check the less immediate cases of adjacency, which can be equally significant. Just key in "frogs within 12 words before/after love" and you see how often frogs and other creepy things really invade the tender feelings of love in English poetry.[23]

The procedures described in the first part of this paper are based on deduction from an abstract level ('sentimentalism') down to the terms of search at keyword level. Adjacency surveys, however, operate the other way round. The machine produces a sorted list of collocations, which has to be submitted to further analysis including searches for analogues in order to confirm the first inferences. Content analysis and automatic reading procedures, which are used by information scientists, will not really be helpful.[24] Material produced by opinion researchers can be evaluated automatically, but the variants of poetic diction are too complex. The scholar's aim is to ask new questions: Why is love so often associated with images of anorganic matter or with creepy things? The next step would be to zoom in on the context of the terms which appear so interesting at first glance. Sometimes the critic gets the impression that he has discovered new byways of English literature no colleague has yet paid attention to. But the most fascinating effect of corpus reading is the sensation of control which it creates in the critic's mind, when he or she is sweeping through the endless 'shelves' of the database, coming across minor poets who were, surprisingly, able to create beautiful lines although they have been unable to sustain this level for the whole poem. Adjacency surveys are the best method for scouting out the corpus.

Database reading thus consists of various strategies. For the sake of precision, it would be wiser to perform the search for complex clusters and adjacency with one's own routines in a subset drawn from the Chadwyck-Healey material. One of the major inconveniences of their corpus, however, is the fact that it will take quite a time to draw a sub-corpus from it. But once the material is on one's own hard disk, it will, at least, save a lot of time, and furthermore, the corpus subset can be improved by other material downloaded from various Internet sites.[25] At this level, programming skills are required, which will be a problem in many humanities departments. There is no recommendation for a particular language, but it should include powerful functions for string operations.

Algorithms and Modules

The computer and the electronic corpus are the instrument and the medium to redescribe the broad river of literary history. Augustan poetic diction may, perhaps, be too erudite an example to start with and to introduce the idea that many areas in human communication can be described by patterns of phraseology, but due to its restrictions, it easily lends itself to string operations.

The corner-stone of one of my retrieval projects was Wordsworth's early poem "Lines written under a Yew-tree", which was published in the *Lyrical Ballads* of 1798. This poem is obviously a cross-section of three layers of phraseology:

- Augustan ("fleecy flock"; "verdant herb")[26]
- Sentimental/churchyard school ("mossy sod")
- Wordsworthian ("true knowledge")[27]

The evolution of English poetry can be described as a process of moving away from the artificial to the details of everyday life. But a survey of the evolution will show how formative Augustan poetic diction really was. Pre-romantic and romantic poetry were thus checked against a thesaurus consisting of three areas: (1) Augustan poetic diction, (2) analogous patterns, which were popular in the description of nature since the mid-century, and (3) elements of Wordsworthian moral philosophy. This would have taken weeks using the Chadwyck-Healey interface, as the most fundamental list of words we had compiled consisted of more than one hundred items. Additionally, words with the suffixes which are typical of derivations from poetic diction were to be marked.

In the first study, some 30,000 poems of the era were checked by a sequence of pattern-matching routines. This study thus focussed not only on different layers of a phraseology which originated in Augustan poetic diction but more specifically on the modifications issuing from it since the mid-century. Under the influence of science, middle-class sentimentalism, Keatsean richness, Shelleyan idealism and Byronic satire, and finally under the pressure from middle-class moral philosophy, the patterns of Augustan diction were extended. A sophisticated search engine should be programmed on modular lines. Accordingly, in the processing of the materials, three modules were applied: the first one to identify the different layers of poetic diction by lists which each consisted of some 100 items. The second module measured the distance between the occurrences of poetic phraseology and filtered out those clusters where three or more items occurred within the distance defined. In this way, some 5,000 clusters were extracted from the corpus, which is still within the scope of readability, and, as a subcorpus, submitted to further analysis by the scholar. In this way, practicing the new computer positivism will show that good judgement is supported by the hard evidence of computing.

Is there any theory of literary criticism which is more amenable to corpus reading than 'positivism'? Intertextual relations and other forms of system continuity may support an evolutionary view of literature. As the variants of poetic diction really are at the heart of romantic poetry, the study can now be directed to the phraseologies competing with each other and forming a 'palimpsest' of romantic, pre-romantic and Augustan languages. Concurrently, significant deviations from the established patterns and the extension of the original pattern come to the fore. Extension, deviation and innovation may be due to a shift in the cognitive mechanism evident in the use of descriptive language. Formal generalization was replaced by realistic detail. This is the process which changed the character of poetic language during the 18th century. The devices used in pattern matching can easily be adapted to the more specific moments of displacement. Following the definitions of linguistic frame theory, the patterns of poetic phraseology can thus be defined as conceptual frames with stereotyped aspect options.[28]

Accordingly, the computer will recognize the connection between generalization, (as far as it occurred in Augustan poetic diction), its basic object and its related properties. The programme module for retrieving the patterns of poetic diction and its descendants or replacements is thus enabled to take into account the relation between the Augustan item, the conceptual frame and its major aspect(s): verdant [+ grass + green]; fleecy flock [+ sheep + wool]. The extended algorithm identifies formal displacement and content continuity (from "verdant herb" to "green grass") as well as the new elements without any precedent in poetic diction. This distinction is very helpful for discerning the subtle shifts in late 18th-century poetry. An obvious problem, however, is where to draw a line, as the dictionary to be used by the machine rapidly grows, the total number of operations to be performed by the machine increases even more rapidly.

In this study different retrieval devices provided a basis for further enquiries on traditional lines. In contrast to statistical evidence, retrieval engines scan the corpus in order to throw new light on materials with which we are, principally, sufficiently familiar just by arranging the evidence in a new way or, which is more obvious with regard to an extensive corpus, we add new materials to what we already know.

Results

Due to the existence of large corpora, literary historians are now able to comprehend the system of literature as a larger entity and not as the individual achievement of a few prominent poets. Many writers have contributed to it. But for the computer-addicts in our profession, there is one golden rule to be obeyed in order to overcome the deadlock which is caused mainly by the disregard of computing brought about by statistics and a number of similarly inconclusive studies. I wonder if the following result of computer reading will ever be sufficient to make an inroad into mainstream criticism, but it is typical of what ends up on your desk for close reading and further analysis, and it may restart the whole process of searching on a new modified basis. The new insight, which was gained by retrieval algorithms, must be demonstrated as relevant to the reading of a particular work of literature. Let's have a look at the first lines of Southey's poem "Oliver Newman: A New England Tale":

I. FUNERAL AT SEA.
The summer sun is riding high
Amid a bright and cloudless sky;
Beneath whose deep o'er-arching blue
The circle of the Atlantic sea,
Reflecting back a deeper hue,
Is heaving peacefully.
The winds are still, the ship with idle motion
Rocks gently on the gentle ocean;
Loose hang her sails, awaiting when the breeze
Again shall wake to waft her on her way.
Glancing beside, the dolphins, as they play,

Their gorgeous tints suffused with gold display;
And gay bonitos in their beauty glide:
With arrowy speed, in close pursuit,
They through the azure waters shoot;
A feebler shoal before them in affright
Spring from the wave, and in short flight,
On wet and plumeless wing essay
The aërial element:
The greedy followers, on the chase intent,
Dart forward still with keen and upturn'd sight,
And, to their proper danger blind the while,
Heed not the sharks, which have for many a day
Hover'd behind the ship, presentient of their prey.
[...]
Upon the deck assembled, old and young,
Bareheaded all in reverence, see them there;
Behold where, hoisted half-mast high,
The English flag hangs mournfully;
And hark! what solemn sounds are these
Heard in the silence of the seas?
"Man that is born of woman, short his time,
And full of woe! he springeth like a flower,
Or like the grass, that, green at morning prime,
Is cut and withereth ere the evening hour;
Never doth he continue in one stay,
But like a shadow doth he pass away."[29]

The machine marked these lines, because it matched "hue" (5), "gentl*" (9), "gold" (12), "gay" (14), "arrowy" (15), "azure" (16), "plumeless wing" (19), and "aërial element" (19). This cross-section throws new light on the continuity and function of elevated style in nineteenth-century poetry: "Green grass" and "azure", one of the favourite words of Augustan diction, are used side by side. In the unfinished epic on Quaker emigrants meeting Indians in the forests of America, which is otherwise ponderous and boring,[30] Southey beautifies the Atlantic. Even by their name "Bonitos" are more beautiful than the common tuna. Thus, Southey creates the pathos appropriate for the sea funeral by means of an almost obsolete phraseology.

Conclusion: Purposeful Searching

Apart from checking details such as the question of how often Wordsworth referred to frogs, which he did just once, corpus reading will focus on the overall properties of a given period, or subgenre, or poet even. This will produce a shift of emphasis away from the individual achievement. For the first time in the writing of literary history, critics will really be able to analyse the systems of literature and the continuities and currents and cross-currents of intertextuality. One of the deficiencies of the Chadwyck-Healey is the chronology of the particular text. This field of scholarly editing is missing from the database, as the bibliographical information provided by the database is restricted to the editions they had used for keying in, which, understandably, was an early version of the collected works free of copyright. Purposeful searching should aim at an intermediate corpus of samples of the phraseology under investigation. The corpus yields a sub-corpus, which requires further processing. The concept of phraseology comprises any stereotyped form of expression in rhetoric as well as in literature. It is the surface likeness of what can be expressend in a blunt as well as in a subtle way. There are keywords of culture, themes and motifs. Any further probing into a subset of the corpus will yield continuities and discrepancies, but it will throw further light on the evolution of cultural stereotypes and habits persistent in human communication.

Nevertheless, the heuristic impact of the retrieval strategies cannot be under-estimated. Mainly due to Chadwyck-Healey databases and their tailor-made search engines, new avenues of research in literary history are opened up even to the 'computer illiterate'. The queries and programmes filtering the corpus will produce new configurations of motifs, new sequences in the history of semantics and new insight into the sources which made the evolution of English poetry possible. "Arrowy" would be a case in point. It derives from the popularity of the various translations of Homer during the 18th century, but it equally proves how influential Erasmus Darwin really was and thirdly that beside the artfulness of poetic diction there was the precision of meteorological observation rendered in the language of poetry. This confirms the view that throughout its history English poetry has always been a tightly-knit system.

Information Retrieval has established itself as a branch of science in its own right. This reminds one of the fact that one of the aims pursued by information science is to provide the user-friendly interface. If the user of the Chadwyck-Healey corpus is the average client probing into the holdings of a library with a vague idea of what he really needs, probabilistic approaches might help him to make up his mind.[31] Approximative searching will be helpful irrespective of the number of hits. At a first glance, this sort of guesswork, supported by statistical devices, appears as fascinating as the weighting procedures developed by the so-called search engines on the Internet. Nevertheless, it is always up to the scholar himself/herself to distinguish between significance and irrelevance and the machine will always remain what it is: a mere tool, however sophisticated it appears. But after the extravagances of pure theory and sophisticated statistics, computing promises a return to the sound principles of positivism. The Chadwyck-Healey database is a good platform to start from.

Notes

1 See Ewald Mengel's paper in this volume.

2 See, for instance, electronic journals and databases such as EMLS (*Early Modern Literary Studies*,Toronto) and EESE (*Erfurt Electronic Studies in English*). Their respective URLs (Internet addresses) are
http://users.ox.ac.uk/~emls/emlshome.html
http://webdoc.sub.gwdg.de/edoc/ia/eese/eese.html.

3 See, for instance, the *Deutsche Literatur von Lessing bis Kafka* CD released by Directmedia (1997); their search engine is far more flexible, as it permits the search for themes on long lists of keywords.

4 *LION update* May 1997.

5 Anne K. Mellor/Richard E. Matlak (Eds.): *British Literature 1780-1830*, New York, 1996; Ina Schabert: *Englische Literaturgeschichte aus der Sicht der Geschlechterforschung*, Stuttgart, 1997.

6 See, for instance, the 'early' approach to sampling by Milic; Louis T. Milic: "The Century of Prose Corpus", *Literary and Linguistic Computing* 5, 1990, 203-208; ders.: "The Century of Prose Corpus: A Half-Million Word Historical Data Base", *Computers and the Humanities*, 29, 1995, 327-337.

7 Rommel confirms Fortier's view, see *"And trace it in this poem every line": Methoden und Verfahren computergestützter Textanalyse von Lord Byrons* Don Juan, Tübingen, 1995, *passim*.

8 See The Victorian Women Writers Project (http://www.indiana.edu/~letrs/vwwp/), The Women's Resources Project (Women's Studies/Women and Literature;
http://sunsite.unc.edu/cheryb/women/wshome.html), Nineteenth Century Women Writers
(http://clever.net/19cwww/), and The Women Writers Project
(http://twine.stg.brown.edu/projects/wwp/wwp_home.html); Kathryn Sutherland: "Challenging Assumptions: Women Writers and New Technology". – In Warren Chernaik, Caroline Davis, and Marilyn Deegan (Eds.): *The Politics of the Electronic Text*, London, 1993, pp. 53-67.

9 Cf. Josef Schmied: "Networking on Corpora". – In Doris Feldmann et al.: *Anglistik im Internet. Proceedings of the 1996 Erfurt Conference on Computing in the Humanities*, Heidelberg 1997, pp. 113-128.

10 This system is used by the Institut für Maschinelle Sprachverarbeitung of Stuttgart University.

11 See, for instance, Robert Sedgwick: *Algorithms*, Reading, Mass., 1983; George W. Smith: *Computers and the Human Language*, New York, 1991.

12 Recent approaches are discussed by Roland Brünken: *Automatische Rekonstruktion von Inhaltsbeziehungen zwischen Dokumenten. Benutzeradaptives Information-Retrieval in Wissensbasen.* Phil. Diss. Erfurt, 1998, pp. 51-66; in this chapter, Brünken refers to J. D. Cohen: "Highlights: Language- and Do-

main-independent Automatic Indexing Terms for Abstracting", *Information Science* 46, 1995, 162-174.

13 Paul A. Fortier and K. J. Keen: "Change Points: Ageing and Content Words in a Large Database", *Literary and Linguistic Computing* 12, 1997, 15-22; Rosanne G. Potter: "Literary Criticism and Literary Computing: The Difficulties of a Synthesis", *Computers and the Humanities* 22, 1988, 91-98.

14 In *The Odysses of Homer* (1616), George Chapman uses "arrowy quiver". Pope's translations were very popular and commercially successful. Pope, however, did not take up "arrowy", which shows how restricted was the notion of correctness which reigned in the poetry of the Augustan age.

15 Wordsworth used "arrowy" just once ("XXXII. Composed on the Banks of a Rocky Stream"). The most likely sources or analogues are Erasmus Darwin and, more probably, Charlotte Smith.

16 Mid-century poets like Thompson and Gray used "arrowy" in connection with "sleet" and "frost". The latter combination is to be found in Dyer's didactic poem *The Fleece* (1757).

17 Stephen Spender uses "jazzy madness" and "like trajectories from guns" instead. The shift from an antiquated to a modern military technology is obvious. "Jazzy", which mirrors the culture of the 'roaring twenties', would be a suitable bi-syllabic analogue for 18th-century poetic adjectives.

18 Robert A. Southey, "Oliver Newman: A New England Tale" (1845): I. Funeral at Sea.

19 According to Chadwyck-Healey.

20 The database invites the user to draw a subset of nineteenth-century railway poetry from it.

21 The COBUILD database is accessible via telnet, but, unfortunately, subscription fees are somewhat forebidding. There is, however, free access to a demo version on their Web site; see http://titania.cobuild.collins.co.uk/.

22 To treat Chadwyck-Healey in a proper way: Under current hardware equipment (166-mhz CPU; 32 MB RAM), the search engine can decently cope with about 20 alternatives in one search, e.g. love AND (bird* OR frog* OR creepy OR witch* OR dwar* ...) limited to one poet, which is quite good.

23 There is virtually no maximum distance.

24 See, for a good survey on content analysis studies, Robert Hogenraad, Dean P. McKenzie and Colin Martindale: "The Enemy Within: Autocorrelation Bias in Content Analysis of Narratives", *Computers and the Humanities* 30, 1997, 433-439.

25 See for the Internet addresses (URLs) of the major Web sites holding electronic texts the *Erfurt Electronic Studies in English* jump page: http://webdoc.sub.gwdg.de/edoc/ia/eese/urls.html#literature.

26 See, for a comprehensive list of Augustan poetic diction, John Arthos: *The Language of Natural Description in 18th Century Poetry*, London, 1966 [1949].

27 The starting point was Wordsworth's early poem "Lines Left upon a seat in a yew-tree which stands near the lake of Esthwaite, on a desolate part of the shore, yet commanding a beautiful prospect", which displays a cross-section of the different layers of phraseology. The poem was published in the "Lyrical Ballads" (1798).

28 See Lawrence Barsalou's survey of "Frames, Concepts, and Conceptual Fields". – In *Cognitive Psychology: An Overview for Cognitive Scientists*, Hillsdale, N.J., 1992. Another promising approach has been suggested by G. Lakoff, *Women, Fire, and Dangerous Things,* Chicago, 1987.

29 Reproduced from the English Poetry Full-Text Database published by Chadwyck-Healey Ltd.

30 The poem was begun in 1815 and posthumously published in 1845. See, for the background in romantic imperialism, Friedrich Brie: *Imperialistische Strömungen in der englischen Literatur.* Halle, 1928, pp. 85-90; Jean Raimond: *Robert Southey.* Paris, 1968, *passim*. The point may be that certain features of Augustan diction are used in 18th-century imperialistic poetry.

31 See, for instance, Norbert Fuhr and Thorsten Hoffmann, "A Prototype for Integrating Probabilistic Fact and Text Retrieval". – In Harald Killenberg, Rainer Kuhlen & Hans-Jürgen Manecke (Eds.): *Wissensbasierte Informationssysteme und Informationsmanagement.* Konstanz, 1991, pp. 94-103; Rainer Kuhlen (Ed.): *Experimentelles und praktisches Information Retrieval. Festschrift für Gerhard Lustig.* Konstanz, 1992. One of the classical sources is, of course, G. Salton and M. J. McGill: *Introduction to Modern Information Retrieval.* New York, 1983; Conrad F. Sabourin: *Computational Linguistics in Information Science*, 2 vols. Montreal, 1994.

Bibliography

Atkins, S., J. Clear & N. Ostler: "Corpus Design Criteria", *Literary and Linguistic Computing* 7, 1992, 1-16.

Arthos, John: *The Language of Natural Description in 18th Century Poetry*, London, 1966 (1949).

Barsalou, Lawrence W.: *Cognitive Psychology: An Overview for Cognitive Scientists*, Hillsdale, N.J., 1992.

Blacklog, P.: *Computer Programming*, Manchester and Oxford, 1991.

Brie, Friedrich: *Imperialistische Strömungen in der englischen Literatur*, Halle, 1928.

Brünken, Roland: *Automatische Rekonstruktion von Inhaltsbeziehungen zwischen Dokumenten. Benutzeradaptives Information-Retrieval in Wissensbasen.* Phil. Diss. Erfurt, 1998.

Cohen, J. D.: "Highlights: Language- and Domain-Independent Automatic Indexing Terms for Abstracting", *Information Science* 46, 1995, 162-174.

Dendien, Jacques: "Access to Information in a Textual Database: Access Functions and Optimal Indexes". – In Ian Lancashire (Ed.): *Research in Humanities Computing*, Oxford, 1991, pp. 308-24.

Feldmann, Doris, Fritz-Wilhelm Neumann & Thomas Rommel (Eds.): *Anglistik im Internet. Proceedings of the 1966 Erfurt Conference on Computing in the Humanities*, Heidelberg, 1997.

Fortier, P. A., K. J. Keen & J. Fortier: "Change Points: Ageing and Content Words in a Large Database", *Literary and Linguistic Computing* 12, 1997, 15-22.

Friedman, Edward A., James E. McClellan III and Arthur Shapiro: "Introducing Undergraduate Students to Automated Text Retrieval in Humanities Courses". – In David S. Miall (Ed.): *Humanities and the Computer*, Oxford, 1990, pp. 103-112.

Fuhr, Norbert and Thorsten Hoffmann: "A Prototype for Integrating Probabilistic Fact and Text Retrieval". – In Harald Killenberg, Rainer Kuhlen & Hans-Jürgen Manecke (Eds.): *Wissensbasierte Informationssysteme und Informationsmanagement*, Konstanz, 1991, pp. 94-103.

Greco, Gina L. & Peter Shoemaker: "Intertextuality and Large Corpora: A Medievalist Approach", *Computers and the Humanities* 27, 1993-94, 349-356.

Hogenraad, Robert, Dean P. McKenzie & Colin Martindale: "The Enemy Within: Autocorrelation Bias in Content Analysis of Narratives", *Computers and the Humanities* 30, 1997, 433-439.

Irizarry, Estelle: "Stylistic Analysis of a Corpus of Twentieth-Century Spanish Narrative", *Computers and the Humanities* 24, 1990, 265-274.

Kuhlen, Rainer (Ed.): *Experimentelles und praktisches Information Retrieval. Festschrift für Gerhard Lustig*, Konstanz, 1992.

Lakoff, G.: *Women, Fire, and Dangerous Things*, Chicago, 1987.

Lancashire, Ian: *The Humanities Computing Yearbook 1989-90*, Oxford, 1991.

LION update 1 (May 1997).

McKinnon, A.: "Mapping the Dimensions of a Literary Corpus", *Literary and Linguistic Computing* 4, 1989, 73-84.

Milic, Louis T.: "The Century of Prose Corpus", *Literary and Linguistic Computing* 5, 1990, 203-208.

---: "The Century of Prose Corpus: A Half-Million Word Historical Data Base", *Computers and the Humanities* 29, 1995, 327-337.

Potter, Rosanne G.: "Literary Criticism and Literary Computing: The Difficulties of a Synthesis", *Computers and the Humanities* 22, 1988, 91-98.

Raimond, Jean: *Robert Southey. L'homme et son temps. L'oeuvre – Le rôle*, Paris, 1986.

Rommel, Thomas: *"And trace it in this poem every line": Methoden und Verfahren computergestützter Textanalyse von Lord Byrons* Don Juan, Tübingen, 1995.

Sabourin, Conrad F.: *Computational Linguistics in Information Science*, 2 vols., Montreal, 1994.

Salton, G. & M. J. McGill: *Introduction to Modern Information Retrieval*, New York, 1983.

Sedgewick, Robert: *Algorithms*, Reading, Mass., 1983.

Sinclair, John: "Basic Computer Processing of Long Texts". – In Geoffrey Leech & Christopher N. Candlin (Eds.): *Computers in English Language Teaching and Research*, London, 1986, pp. 185-203.

Smith, George W.: *Computers and the Human Language*. New York, 1991.

Sutherland, Kathryn: "Challenging Assumptions: Women Writers and New Technology". – In Warren Chernaik, Caroline Davis, & Marilyn Deegan (Eds.): *The Politics of the Electronic Text*, London, 1993, pp. 53-67.

Ewald Mengel / Carmen Müller, Bayreuth

LION (Literature Online) – A Virtuous Beast in the Electronic Jungle

1. Situation Report: Electronic Literature on the Internet

Only a few months ago, a number of German newspapers repeatedly printed an expensive half-page advertisement by the *Bundesverband Druck,* intended to draw the attention of the German reading public to electronic texts and, so it seems, confirm their prejudices against this new medium. "Grimm's fairy-tales on the screen?" the advert asks [my translation]. "A mere push of a button and the fairy-tale books are gone. Now a synthetic voice tells of 'Snow White and the Seven Dwarfs.' 'Puss in Boots' is a computer animation. 'Hansel and Gretel' – just a flicker on the screen. And 'The Frog Prince'? Megabyte will not turn him into a prince when he is thrown at the wall. A creepy tale? We shall continue to print on paper to make sure that the fantasy of our children is not absorbed by the realm of electronics. Your Printers' Guild".

Advertisements of this kind reveal that the printing business is suffering from a severe shock caused by the arrival of new electronic media. The polemical form of the advert, which does not enlighten the readers but throws sand in their eyes, is a clear sign of the running retreat in which the printers are presently involved. Of course they should know that electronic texts are not intended to replace books, and that their virtual form of existence necessarily implies that they have different functions.

A variety of approaches and methods have been developed in the field of computer applications in the humanities, including stylometry and statistical methods of determining authorship, on the one hand, and thematic methods and approaches, on the other.[1] However, the number of scholars doing research with the help of a computer is still relatively small. In Germany, only a handful of people seem to be interested in the new medium. Especially the older generation refuse to have anything to do with computers. It is not only the fact that computers, in their opinion, are too difficult to handle and speak a foreign language. It is rather a question of principle. For them, the ditch between the humanities and the world of modern science and technology is simply too deep, and 'apartheid' seems to be the best policy.

Moreover, some of their arguments against the employment of computers in literary scholarship seem only too well-founded. Occasionally, interpretations produced by computer-aided text analysis resemble excursions into the field of mathematical statistics; more often than not, there is a discrepancy between the huge efforts invested and the meagre and disappointing results; last but not least, one sometimes gets the impression that the tool of the computer seems to limit rather than extend one's insights into the nature of literature.

While computers have been used for quite a while in literary text analysis, electronic texts on the internet are a fairly recent achievement.[2] Here, too, one encounters problems which are created by the new medium. 'Traffic jams' on the internet are a fairly common phenomenon, and the number of scholars who have access to it is still comparatively small. The most important problem, however, consists in the fact that the majority of the texts which can be loaded on the screen are unreliable from a philological point of view. In his article "History and Philosophy of the Project Gutenberg", Michael Hart, for example, points out: "We do not write for the reader who cares whether a certain phrase in Shakespeare has a ':' or a ';' between its clauses. We put our sights on a goal to release etexts [!] that are 99.9% correct in the eyes of the general reader."[3] Since philologists hold that it is important to find out whether Shakespeare's sentences have a colon or a semicolon in them, *Project Gutenberg* texts as yet do not seem to be a scholarly hunting ground.[4]

Another reason for the hesitancy with which philologists meet electronic texts may lie in the restrictions imposed upon research by the medium itself. At first sight, it seems fascinating to be able to sift comprehensive corpora of electronic texts with the help of search engines for characteristic key terms or stylistic peculiarities. More often than not, however, the initial enthusiasm disappears while the awareness is growing that word counts or stylometric analysis offer only limited insights into the nature of literary texts.

2. *LION*

LION, Chadwyck-Healey's commercially available collection of literary texts on the world wide web, is a virtuous beast in the electronic jungle.[5] It is the most comprehensive, philologically reliable database of electronic texts which the internet presently has to offer. In marked contrast to many other electronic text archives, its target group is not the general reader but academic scholars, teachers and students of literature. It contains more than 210,000 electronic texts of poems, plays and novels in English, but it also offers various other services such as reference works (bibliographies and dictionaries), a master index, a poet's corner, and an internet bookshop. As such, it promises to be an electronic paradise for the academic scholar and critic.

In the following, we shall first give a short overview of this unique source of literary information, starting with a detailed summary and a description of its contents. In a second step, two examples are given to illustrate how this new tool may be put to good use in literary scholarship. In conclusion, we shall point out a few problems and perspectives.

The homepage of LION offers a well-structured table of contents containing links which lead to the different areas of the service. The most important aspect of LION is its range of full-text **Literary Databases**: *African-American Poetry* from 1750-1900 (nearly 3,000 poems); *American Poetry* from 1600-1900 (more than 40,000 poems); twenty versions of the *Bible in English* from the tenth to the twentieth century; over 200 complete works of *Early English Prose Fiction* from 1500-1700; a database of *Editions and Adaptations of Shakespeare* with eleven major editions from the First Folio to the Cambridge edition of 1863-6, twenty-four separate printings of individual plays, selected apocrypha and related works and over one hundred adaptations, sequels and burlesques from the seventeenth, eighteenth and nineteenth centuries; *Eighteenth Century Fiction* (77 complete works from the period 1700-1780); *English Drama* from 1280-1915 (4,000 plays by 1,200 authors); the *English Poetry* database (containing more than 165,000 poems by over 1,250 poets from 1100-1900); and, last but not least, *Modern Poetry* from 1972-1997 (with the works of 54 Carcanet poets and 15 Oxford poets comprising 122 volumes of poetry. Altogether, these databases contain more than 210,000 individual works. They can be accessed either under the genre headings used above or by the so-called **Master-Index,** in which they are listed a second time by author and by title. Additionally, the Master-Index, which is continuously expanded, includes authors and works freely available on the Internet.

Next to this extensive collection of literary databases, LION offers selected **Reference Works**. The *Annual Bibliography of English Language and Literature* (*ABELL*) provides the user with over 100,000 entries of scholarly articles, doctoral dissertations, books and reviews published from 1920 onwards; the *Bibliography of American Literature* with references to nearly 400,000 works by American writers from the period of the Revolution to 1930; the *Cambridge Biographical Encyclopedia* with 13,200 biographical articles; the *Cambridge Encyclopedia* with more than 26,000 entries and 60,000 cross-references; the *King James – 'Authorized Version'* (complete text with prefatory matter, notes and glossaries); the *Periodicals Contents Index: Literature* which offers an index to over 800,000 periodical articles. Additionally, LION provides its users with *Webster's Third New International Dictionary, Unabridged*. Finally, and as a special service, LION can also be used as a gateway to other websites on the internet: the **Web Resources** page allows access to approximately

500 other websites that might be of interest for the literary scholar. These sites contain, for example, discussion lists and groups, author pages, research resources and journals.

Literary Databases, Reference Works, Web Resources and the Master Index form the 'heart' of LION. In order to explore them effectively, LION's search engines enable the user to define specific and application-oriented search routines in each of these sections.

Generally speaking, LION's search engines can search for single or combined words or word stems, employing truncation search or using Boolean and proximity operators. The possibility to browse indexes for authors' names facilitates making the right finds.

The full-text **Literary Databases** can be searched individually or across the genre and period boundaries. It is possible to restrict the search to genres (depending on the database), periods, authors, gender, or to particular works. Each search result is displayed by a Summary of Matches page which also allows access to the work in question. The Full Text page identifies the author, the title of the work, and the edition used to produce the electronic version, successively displaying the full text. The exact location of the match within the context of the work is highlighted by an icon. It is especially helpful that all the supporting Reference Works are accessible from any point in LION, but they can also be searched individually. The *Bibliography of American Literature,* for example, can be searched for authors, titles, publishers, or dates and places of publication. The same applies to the *Annual Bibliography of English Language and Literature.* Looking up *Wuthering Heights* in the Title Keyword Index, for example, produces 131 matches which are listed in the Summary of Matches Page. Browsing indexes support the search for all the items mentioned.

An equally useful tool are the further **Web Resources** selected by Chadwyck-Healey from the innumerable offerings of the net. Firstly, the user is asked to select the period in which he or she is interested, choosing from *Classical*, *Medieval*, *Renaissance*, *Restoration/18th Century*, *Romanticism*, *19th Century*, *20th Century* or *General*. Secondly, LION then proposes to specify the research area: *Discussion Lists and Groups* lead to literary discussion groups and listservers; *Author Pages* connect to the works of an author or to an individual work; *Research Resources* contain general sites, literary homepages and library catalogues; *Journals* display a list of electronic journals or their indexes. Selecting "Restoration/18th Century – Research Resources", for example, offers a *Dictionary of Sensibility*, an *Eighteenth Century English Novel Research Guide*, a *Restoration Drama Homepage*, or a *Tristram Shandy Bibliography.*

The **Master Index,** which includes both the commercially distributed Chadwyck-Healey databases and other freely available literary works on the internet, can be searched by Author and Title Keyword, both of which are browsable. The results of a search are shown in a Summary of Matches page which displays the number of hits found, the exact name of the author, the short title of the work, the size of the work in kilobytes and its location. A single click will then lead to the full-text wherever it is located on the internet.

There can be no doubt that the various and manifold possibilities of LION described so far are impressive. However, for the philological analysis of literary texts, the scholarly reliability of the available material is of utmost importance. From an editorial point of view, Chadwyck-Healey has taken special care to ensure that this demand is fulfilled, knowing that only the careful electronic reproduction of reliable editions can guarantee world-wide academic acceptance. Generally speaking, Chadwyck-Healey has made special efforts to secure the copyright for first-choice editions wherever they were available. In those cases in which the copyright could not be obtained, other – though not greatly inferior – choices became necessary. Every once in a while, the user may find an occasional typing error, resulting from the simple fact that all the material had to be keyed in manually. However, occasional typing errors may also be found in first-class editions and do not affect the work with the databases in a serious way. In comparison to the printed version, moreover, electronic texts on the internet have the great advantage that they can be continuously revised and re-edited.

According to the editors, the Master Index and the Web Resources of LION are updated weekly. Thus LION proves to be a dynamic instrument. Under the supervision of an academic editorial board, existing databases are revised regularly, new databases and services added. Special pages in LION keep the users informed about changes, additions and plans to develop the service.

Around the databases described above, Chadwyck-Healey has built additional sources of information which complement the literary texts in a remarkable way. For the teacher and student of literature, the **Writer in Residence** Page (**WIRE**), for example, is a noteworthy addition. Alternately, contemporary poets hold the position of 'writer in residence' for a certain period of time and present one of their works, the text of which is printed on this page weekly. In order to be able to listen to the poet himself reading from his/her work, LION lets the user download RealAudio, provided the PC is equipped with a sound card. WIRE has various subdivisions. *Masterclass* is intended to be a kind of creative writing workshop offering new lectures about writing poetry every two weeks. *Poetry Surgery* allows users to submit their poems for critical analysis and appreciation and gives professional advice. *Discussion Groups* encourage the users to send in their comments about the works presented and to discuss literary topics. Finally, the *Biography* section gives detailed information about the life and the works of the respective Writer in Residence. With WIRE, then, Chadwyck-Healey attempts to develop LION as a teaching resource and add a multi-media-based dimension.

Another useful tool is the **Services** section. Modern editions of the works which users are allowed to download through LION may also be ordered in book form from the *Internet Bookshop*. The *Webmaster's* page encourages users to make comments about any aspect concerning *Literature Online,* whether this be queries, criticism or suggestions for new additions or changes.

It remains to be stated that a commercially-oriented service like LION has its price. LION shows great flexibility regarding the subscription options for interested clients. Annual subscription prices for the individual corpora depend on the number of concurrent users and range from £ 250 for *The Bible in English* via £ 450 for *Eighteenth-Century Fiction* to £ 2,000 for *English Poetry* (one user only). The whole package is to be had for ca. £ 12,000 a year. There are special arrangements for universities and schools, and it is possible to subscribe to any single element of LION or to combine different elements according to the needs of its users. Licencees of the CD-ROM versions of the same corpora previously edited by Chadwyck-Healey are granted a 90% discount on the regular subscription prices. Still, the charges are so considerable that individual or private persons will hesitate to subscribe, but LION makes sense for institutions, schools, universities or research groups. For reasons of promotion and distribution, Chadwyck-Healey offers free trial runs for a limited period of time to any university, school, or institution with access to the internet and considering subscription.

Regarding the software requirements, Chadwyck-Healey prefers to stick to the basics. LION runs with Netscape Navigator 2.0 and Microsoft Internet Explorer 3.0; however, the *Bible in English* and *Editions and Adaptations of Shakespeare* demand Netscape Navigator 3.0 if the user intends to synchronize different versions of the full text. If not, Netscape Navigator 2.0 works perfectly fine.

3. Two Examples

In the following section of our article, we should like to give two examples in order to illustrate in which ways LION can be used in literary scholarship. In our first example, we propose to analyze the fictionalization of female self-confidence in the English novel of the eighteenth century.

Literary scholars generally agree that female self-confidence can be found in English novels of the nineteenth century. With regard to the eighteenth-century novel, however, especially the canonized works of male authors such as Defoe, Fielding, or Sterne, it is generally assumed that women are portrayed according to the conventional roles which are ascribed to them in eighteenth-century society. Here, Richardson, perhaps, is an exception to the rule – unless one would take the view that Pamela's resistance to Squire B.'s attempts to seduce her is a confirmation rather than an undermining of ascribed gender roles. What about the other, less well-known novelists, though? What about the numerous women writers that lead a shadowy existence among their better-known male colleagues?

Chadwyck-Healey's machine-readable electronic database consists of 77 complete novels written by major and minor (male and female) authors. Because of the technical requirements of the search engine, our investigation has to be based on words and word combinations. On the one hand, this is rather restrictive because a normal reading of the novels would enable one to find whole passages and maybe even chapters in which female self-confidence is thematized. On the other hand, nobody would possibly take the trouble to read through all of these novels. LION's search engine allows us to search the whole corpus for important key words and terms within only a few seconds, which adds to the attraction of this new instrument. This does not mean, however, that LION saves us the trouble of reading the texts. Once found, the respective passages, chapters, and novels must be read more closely.

Our first attempt to find passages relating to female self-confidence produces disappointing results. The word 'self-confidence' does not turn up at all, although a look into the *Oxford English Dictionary* reveals that it was used as early as 1653.

What does this mean, then? Is it possible that female self-confidence does not exist before, say, the novels of Jane Austen early in the nineteenth century? In order to find an answer to this question we now search for opposite terms such as 'bashfulness' or 'shyness'. Here our search is more successful, and the machine comes up with a number of hits which seems to confirm the established conventional picture of women in eighteenth-century society.

If we are unwilling to give up our search at this point, it is due to the realization that there is an obvious explanation for the non-occurrence of 'self-confidence' in our texts. 'Self-confidence' is a term which 'conceptualizes' and interprets the signified on the level of linguistic reflection. Female self-confidence in the novels, however, may take a variety of non-conceptualized, more concrete forms since it has to be narratively realized or 'staged'. On the diegetic level, it may be reflected by the language of female characters, by their gestures, or, to use an eighteenth-century term, by their manners in general. It may also be encountered extra-diegetically in the narrators' comments and descriptions.

Two conclusions can be drawn from this insight. First, the conventional social discourse about women in the eighteenth century should be used as a foil or background against which female self-confidence can gain relief. The conduct books are especially helpful in this context because they establish the female norm and construct the female gender from a male point of view. Secondly, we have to set up a whole catalogue of search words relating to female self-confidence. What we are searching for are deviations from or negations of the norm which could be understood as expressions of female self-confidence. They narrativize the first stirrings of an as yet unshaped female identity, a confirmation of 'difference' or, alternatively, a claim for equality which is accompanied by the rejection of male projections and role models.

'Normal' female behaviour, i.e., one that conforms to the established social norms and conventions, can be met more frequently, however. Women are usually portrayed as shy and demure creatures. The cover of Chadwyck-Healey's prospectus for Eighteenth-Century Fiction, for example, bears an illustration by Joseph Highmore for Richardson's novel *Pamela.* The illustration shows Pamela and Mr. B. in Mr. B.'s summer residence. What interests us in this connection is their body language. The squire has put his arm around her shoulder. With his left hand he clasps her left hand, and it seems that he wants to draw her closer. Pamela's right hand, however, indicates resistance. While he is looking directly at her, her eyes are directed to the ground. The male look takes possession of her while she becomes the passive object of his gaze.

The input 'cast-down eyes', 'eyes fby [i.e., 'followed by'] cast down' or 'she look* fby down' produces a list of hits taken from various novels. Equally successful is the input 'she looked him in the eye', 'bold-face', (from Richardson's *Pamela*), or similar expressions. In order to throw light on the situational and semantic field in which the phrase 'cast-down eyes' is used in English literature in general, we now dare to cross the genre boundaries and search the English Poetry Database for the same combination of words. Our investigation generates a list of examples in which 'cast-down eyes' are filled with different meanings. In the presence of royal authority, for example, it is fitting for both men and women to look down to the ground. As far as men are concerned, this gesture is usually related to thoughtfulness or melancholy. In contrast to this, the cast-down eyes of women in their encounter with men are expressive of shyness and humility. In one poem from the nineteenth century, 'the cast-down eyes' are related to a mother looking down upon the cradle of her child, a gesture which has nothing to do with female self-confidence but which adds the aspect of 'motherliness' to the cast-down eyes of the woman.

Which conclusions can be drawn from these examples? First, the electronic corpora of texts might be used in developing a grammar of the body language of female self-confidence (or the lack of it) in novels from the eighteenth century. The same is imaginable for the English novel of the nineteenth century, which is, by the way, soon to be included in LION's corpora of electronic texts. Imaginable is also a contribution to the grammar of male body language. Since LION allows us to differentiate between male and female authors, a comparative analysis of the different narrative representations of men and women seems promising. An investigation such as this one, which compares the fictionalization of female self-confidence by male and female novelists and demonstrates how the respective gender is seen with 'other eyes', also opens the new medium to feminist approaches.

But let us come back to our analysis of female self-confidence in the eighteenth-century novel. From the conduct books we can gain a set of terms which provides the foil against which female self-confidence can be measured. Concepts such as 'weakness', 'dependence', 'respect', 'blushing', 'bashfulness', 'modesty', 'delicacy', 'sensibility', 'meekness', 'feebleness', etc. constitute what is 'normal' and construct the female as the weaker sex. Opposite concepts such as 'strength', 'independence', 'forwardness', 'boldness', 'confidence', 'fortitude', 'prudence', 'intelligence', 'firmness', 'sagacity', however, point in the direction of female self-confidence. The task of finding relevant passages becomes easier with the aid of truncation search, by which all possible forms of a lexeme (including adjectives, verb forms, continuous forms, etc.) can be discovered. Thus the input 'depend*' produces 'dependance' along with 'dependent', 'depended', or 'depending'. The lexeme 'oblig*' shows up as noun, verb (in different tenses), adjective, or adverb. With the help of proximity search, the search instrument can be further refined. Proximity search allows one to find two related words following immediately upon each other or within a certain distance, which has to be indicated. The formula 'female near 4 manners', for example, allows one to find phrases in which the word 'manners' turns up within a distance of 4 words after 'female'. Especially useful for our purposes prove node/collocate pairs such as 'female fby bashfulness' or 'her fby boldness'. If the nodes 'female' or 'her' in this string, which are neutral in character, are replaced by the term 'womanish', we get a list of stereotypical qualifications which are ascribed to the female sex from a male point of view. It is interesting to note in this context that female authors also resort to this stereotypical qualification because they have obviously internalized and appropriated the male value system.

Searching for female self-confidence in this way finally produces a list of passages from various novels which can then be analyzed more closely. Since the hits which LION comes up with show the search terms only within a very limited context of about 10 words, it is necessary to read through whole chapters and even novels to interpret the selected texts correctly. The fact that the texts exist in machine-readable form does not imply that the act of reading becomes superfluous. Also, the interpretation of the text still remains to be done. All the computer can do is make the search for relevant passages much easier and quicker; we can include greater numbers of texts into our analysis; we can also consider hitherto obscure or unknown texts that have been reproduced in electronic form. In this way, the new medium may be said to influence our approaches and methods of research, since it allows us to ask questions which have not been asked before and which probably would not be asked if the texts did not exist in a machine-readable form.

The results of our search for female self-confidence in the English novel of the eighteenth century may be summarized in the following way: all in all, the representation of women in the eighteenth-century novel is a reflection of the conservative and traditional views characteristic of society in general. There are no revolutionary attempts to redefine the female role, and more often than not women are confined to their roles as lovers, housewives and mothers.

If female self-confidence can be found, it is in little actions and gestures. Especially female authors discuss the subordination of women and seek to improve their social status. There is no direct and outspoken social criticism, however, but they express their opinion in an indirect way, through images, metaphors and symbolic events. If a woman is represented as an especially 'forward' or 'bold' creature, this is done with the intention of criticizing and punishing her unorthodox and immoderate behaviour. In this way, even female authors confirm the established social norm. It should not be overlooked, though, that the question of female emancipation is thus introduced into the novel, and sometimes one gets the impression that this form of representing female self-confidence amounts to a 'probing' or 'stretching' of established social norms or boundaries. Another convention of representing female self-confidence makes use of a male character who is a model of moral excellence and who takes the side of the female whom he applauds for her self-confident ways. Last but not least, the authors create positive female stereotypes in which traditional female attributes such as beauty and modesty are combined with qualities like intelligence and education. These new stereotypes are meant to repudiate the conventional prejudice that too much education and intelligence are unbecoming in a woman and bring out her 'male' qualities.

In comparison to female writers, men are more conservative and traditional in their portrayal of female characters. Although they know about the existing injustices and are aware that many prejudices are untenable, they cling to the established opinions and are afraid that female emancipation could impinge upon their own rights and threaten their dominance. Their novels bear witness to the fact that we are in a phase of transition. There is a conflict between the individual realization that things have to change and a more conservative tendency towards the preservation of the status quo. Still, their novels, too, show the tendency to draw a more subtle and differentiated picture of the situation of women in society. This picture is not to be understood as a mimetic reflection of the current situation, however, for reality proves to be less advanced. But if the reflected changes cannot yet be put into practice, they can at least be toyed with in fiction, and the novel has a social function in so far as it is turned into a forum of discussion.

Our second example is taken from nineteenth-century poetry. We already know that the arrival of the natural sciences such as biology, geology, or astronomy left an indelible impression on the Victorian age and resulted in a paradigm shift in the Victorians' outlook on life. Lord Alfred Tennyson's *In Memoriam*, a longer poem from the middle of the nineteenth century, may serve as an example. Here Tennyson calls the natural sciences his 'terrible muses'.[6] Due to the influence of biology, astronomy and geology, all the traditional assumptions about creation and man's position at the centre of it were shattered, and the idea of a dynamic and ever-changing cosmos replaced that of a definitive and final act of divine creation. Tennyson's poem bears witness to this conflict and tries to come to terms with the new facts of life. As far as Tennyson is concerned, then, the relation of science and poetry seems a worthwile object of investigation.

What about the many other poems of the Victorian age, though? Do they also deal with the natural sciences? If yes, which role do the latter play in nineteenth-century poetry? When does the term 'science' in the modern sense appear in a poem for the first time? What are the attitudes of the poets to science in general? Working with LION allows one to answer these questions.

We select the *English Poetry Database* and restrict the search to the nineteenth century. The input 'science' produces 2,275 hits in 498 entries. In order to refine our search, we select the option 'title or first line'. The search engine now comes up with 61 hits in 41 entries in which the term 'science' turns up in the titles of the poems or in their first lines. Since LION allows us to differentiate between 'Early 19th century (1800 – 1835)', 'Mid-19th century (1835 – 1870)' and 'Late 19th century (1870 – 1900)', we can refine our search even further. The greatest number of hits (30 hits in 16 entries) can be found between 1835 and 1870, whereas there are only 15 hits (14 entries) between 1800 and 1835 and 16 hits (11 entries) between 1870 and 1900.

Many interesting observations can be made with regard to the contents of these poems. The poets' attitudes toward science range from downright hatred or animosity[7] to enthusiastic welcome and celebration[8]. On the one hand, we have poets such as Frederick W. O. Ward, George Barlow, Charles Tennyson, James Rhoades, Charles Mackay, or Henry Ellison, who reject the "Cancer research"[9] or "Wisdom's new and ghastly college"[10] and point out that there is another form of wisdom or knowledge that cannot be found by vivisection or through the "missing link"[11]. On the other hand, we register attempts to reconcile 'the old gospel and the new'[12] and prove that they are not mutually exclusive. The most important attempt stems from Francis William Newman, who tries to overcome the conflict or gap between science and religion, experience and faith, and proves that they support each other: "For as the sailor's eye learns by practice to evade illusions, /and his observations become sensitive, and his judgement sagacious;/ So does the eye of the soul and its sagacity improve by culture:/ And Experience strengthens Faith, until Faith grows confident,/ Discerning God's Goodness and Presence, as overruling and eternal."[13] All in all, the English Poetry of the nineteenth century bears witness to how deeply the Victorians' trust in mankind's position at the centre of the universe was shaken and how desperately they tried to come to terms with the new facts of life.

4. Summary and Conclusions

A recurring objection against the employment of computers in literary analysis is the claim that computers are just tools or instruments which make the life of the scholar a bit easier but do not allow fresh insights or produce new results. This objection is correct in so far as the scholar still has to do the thinking and that the machine cannot tell him which questions he/she should ask. However, LION allows one to search large corpora of electronic texts in only a few seconds. It is possible to search across the boundaries of genres and centuries or to restrict the search to a definite period or to either male or female authors. The scholar working with electronic corpora should take this into account. Admittedly, it is not always easy to come up with the right questions. The reason for this is that one has to learn how to apply the new tool and adapt one's approaches to the electronic medium. This necessity can both restrict and extend one's scope of research. On the one hand, the application of the computer in literary scholarship is restricting because the object of research is determined by the tool one employs and the more common tasks of interpretation may not be carried out by the help of the machine. On the other hand, computers can extend one's scope of questions. The larger the corpora become, the less likely it will be that an individual scholar takes the trouble to search all the texts in a conventional way. He will gladly delegate this task to the computer, which does not tire out and produces a list of relevant passages within a few seconds. The most fascinating searches are those which cross the boundaries of genres and centuries and include a great amount of different texts. But here it is also most difficult to develop sensible projects that make use of the opportunities which the computer has to offer. Working with LION gives one the feeling, however, that there are many 'unplumped seas' out there which are waiting to be discovered and mapped, and that it is worthwile to put some effort into it.

Notes

1 Cf. Thomas Rommel, *'And trace it in this poem every line': Methoden und Verfahren computerunterstützter Textanalyse am Beispiel von Lord Byrons Don Juan,* Tübingen: Narr, 1995, especially pp. 26-67.
2 Cf. also *Anglistik im Internet: Proceedings of the 1996 Erfurt Conference on Computing in the Humanities*, ed. Doris Feldmann, Fritz-Wilhelm Neumann and Thomas Rommel, Heidelberg: Winter, 1997.
3 Article published in electronic form. See home page of *Project Gutenberg* http://promo.net/pg/history.html#beginningphil.
4 *Project Gutenberg*, too, promises philologically reliable texts from the year 2001 onward. Cf. the article by Michael Hart.
5 URL: http://lion.chadwyck.co.uk.
6 See also my essay "Tennysons Verrat an den 'schrecklichen Musen': *In Memoriam* im Leistungskurs Englisch der gymnasialen Oberstufe", *Literatur in Wissenschaft und Unterricht*, 20, 1987, 409-425.
7 Cf., for example, William Allingham: "The Eyes of Modern Science do not grow/ In the head, but hind-parts, and still gaze below." Source text: *Blackberries,* London: Reeves and Turner, 1890, p. 23.
8 Cf. George Dyer: "Ode on Science": "Now see her rise serenely great,/Dispensing golden blessings from on high,/ A sun, in more than royal state, /Supreme she rules, amidst a cloudless sky:/ See Dulness close her eye of lead!/ See Superstition's reptiles dead!/ Sloth drag along her slimy way,/ And Ignorance retire from the day!" Source text: *Poems,* 2 vols., London: Longman & Rees, 1802, vol. 1, p. 49ff.
9 George Barlow, Sonnet XV: "The Sons of Science". Source text: *The Poetical Works,* 11 vols., London: Glaisher 1902-1914, vol. 10, p. 248.
10 Frederick William Orde Ward: "The Old Gospel and the New". Source text: *'Twixt Kiss and Lip, or Under the Sword*, Vol. *Ballads, &c. The Old Gospel and the New,* 3rd ed., London: Garner & Co, 1890, p. 44.
11 Henry Ellison, "Science and Faith". Source text: *Stones from the Quarry; or Moods of Mind,* London: Provost and Co, 1875.
12 See footnote 10.
13 Francis William Newman, "Intuition and Verification". Source text: *Theism, Doctrinal and Practical, or, Didactic Religious Utterances,* London: Chapman, 1858, First Book: *The Theory of Religion,* p. 22ff.

Susanne Schmid, Berlin

"Alps Piled on Alps" – the Romantic Sublime and the Keyword Search Function in Chadwyck-Healey's *English Poetry Full-Text Database*. A Case Study

The Sublimity of Reading – Reading the Sublime

The concept of the sublime, evoking the individual experiences of terror, awe and joy in the face of the vast and incomprehensible, seems hardly compatible with the idea of a rational and efficient computer programme. And the mere prospect of reading a poem – particularly a sublime poem such as "Tintern Abbey" or "Mont Blanc" – on a computer screen must needs insult the Romantic seeker of solitude. Here is Wordsworth's view on how to enjoy reading:

> [...] Whereupon I told,
> That once in the stillness of a summer's noon,
> While I was seated in a rocky cave
> By the sea-side, perusing, so it chanced,
> The famous history of the errant knight
> Recorded by Cervantes, these same thoughts
> Beset me, and to height unusual rose,
> While listlessly I sate, and, having closed
> The book, had turned my eyes toward the wide sea.[1]

If we took this mode of solitary reading in a sublime environment as the only valid and rewarding way of doing so, we would have to repent and resign from all literary criticism. Yet if we move beyond the authority of the Romantic poet's voice we will just bear his certain displeasure at our procedure.

As our readings take place in a far less than sublime environment, we can only resort to the option of reading up on the sublime at a distance from the actual experience. Where do we start? In truly academic fashion we will turn to literary criticism first: Monk's and Weiskel's seminal studies plus a number of more recent articles[2] will take us to some Romantic poets of the sublime – mainly to Blake, Wordsworth and Shelley. Most criticism concerned with the Romantic sublime deals with this section of the "visionary company" (Bloom) and rarely with any other well-known Romantic poets, let alone with any lesser known ones. Considering the importance of pre-Romantic aesthetic theories on the sublime (e.g. John

Baillie, Edmund Burke) and the huge amount of travel writing raving enthusiastically about uncivilized nature, one should assume that sublimity in poetry cannot be restricted to a handful of canonized men. The traditional way of finding more poems would be to read through a pile of anthologies. A more recent guide to a virtually overwhelming amount of material is Chadwyck-Healey's *English Poetry Full-Text Database* that can be used to search through a large corpus of poems for sublime moments. This search outline enables users to retrieve a list of authors and texts containing one or several specific keywords. In that sense, the programme functions as a mega-concordance and is particularly useful for conducting research on so-called 'minor', i.e. less canonized poets, for whose works no such research tool exists. The search can also be narrowed down to specific periods or to one or several authors. Unfortunately, it is not possible to conduct a search semantically – e.g. to type in "sublime" and obtain all those poems on the sublime that do not contain the actual word in their texts or titles. As Romantic poems, no matter how much they focus on the sublime, rarely contain this word, suitable keywords have to be found. In any search, the usefulness of the material offered by the database largely depends on a careful working out of relevant search terms. Therefore, before running the actual search, we have to map out some concepts of the sublime.

No universally accepted definition exists. The aesthetic concept goes back to Longinus, a first-century Greek author, whose treatise "Peri Hupsous" was translated into French by Boileau in 1674. Only then did the term "sublime" gain currency in aesthetic discussions. It was mainly used to describe the appearance and effect of anything of vast dimensions, especially landscape features. In the eighteenth century, the cult of the sublime reached a climax. The fascination with both ordered and disordered, civilised and uncivilised nature is reflected in various aesthetic theories. One of the best-known and most far-reaching tracts was Burke's *Philosophical Enquiry into the Origin of our Ideas of the Sublime and Beautiful* (1757), which builds up a contrast between the sublime and the beautiful. Whereas the latter causes pleasure, the former evokes terror to the point of obliterating the self:

> Whatever is fitted in any sort to excite the ideas of pain, and danger, that is to say, whatever is in any sort terrible, or is conversant about terrible objects, or operates in a manner analogous to terror, is a source of the *sublime*; that is, it is productive of the strongest emotion which the mind is capable of feeling [...][3]

Burke strictly separates the sublime from the beautiful, assigning prettiness and weakness to the latter and thereby feminizing it. The sublime, in contrast, carries connotations of masculinity. Certainly not all theoreticians and poets have followed Burke's dichotomy of pain and pleasure. Wordsworth and Coleridge associated the sublime not with terror but with awe and joy. Others separated the emotions of terror and joy less strictly. Another frequently used term describing landscapes is "picturesque". The semantic boundaries are not always clear and sometimes the use of "picturesque" resembles that of Burke's "sublime".

The varying approaches all locate the sublime on three levels:

(1) Themes: Longinus remarks that sublimity is caused by physical vastness, hugeness. Therefore, wild and inaccessible mountain ranges or wide oceans were regarded as sublime.
(2) Style: Often elevated style is used in order to describe sublime moments. Whereas to many late twentieth-century beholders, the sublime has become grotesque and can therefore be only talked about in an ironic manner, the eighteenth century treats it in a serious way.
(3) Effect: Profound emotions (terror, awe, joy) are evoked.

Literary Criticism has established that the melting of subject and object, of self and other is one distinctive feature of the Romantic sublime. In this transcendent sublime, the ego leaves the boundaries of self. The material and the ideal melt into one another.[4] A "transubstantiation" of identities takes place.[5] When explaining the Romantic sublime, critics frequently refer to Wordsworth, especially to the *Prelude*, where the speaker describes a fusion of his imagination and the surrounding nature into the "one mind".[6] Also Shelley's "Mont Blanc" is often quoted as embodying the Romantic sublime. It starts:

The everlasting universe of things
Flows through the mind, and rolls its rapid waves,
Now dark – glittering – now reflecting gloom –
Now lending splendour, where from secret springs
The source of human thought its tribute brings
Of waters, – with a sound but half its own,
Such as a feeble brook will oft assume
In the wild woods, among the mountains lone,
Where waterfalls around it leap for ever,
Where woods and winds contend, and a vast river
Over its rocks ceaselessly bursts and raves. (l. 1-11)

The dynamics of human thought and the flowing water overlap. Speaker and scenery are intricately interwoven, becoming separate entities only in the course of the poem. "Mont Blanc" is a notoriously difficult text, eluding the grasp of interpretation. Charles H. Vivian argues that Shelley uses the surrounding landscape in order to show the workings of the mind[7] – a mind that is anything but self-contained, rather struggling violently but finally overpowering the scenery.

These texts have been read in a new light by feminist critics. Anne Mellor argues that this melting of subject and object into one another is a typical feature of masculine Romanticism. Nature, which is usually feminized, is appropriated by the male poet, who then, like Wordsworth, claims her as a "Brother".[8] Although Mellor does not explicitly postulate a feminine vs. a masculine sublime, her readings of Burke, Wordsworth, Radcliffe and others imply the existence of two distinct and gender-specific uses of the sublime. In the melting of subject and object as in Wordsworth's "one mind" she points out a struggle for domination that results in an act of male empowerment over female nature, a process that another feminist critic, Patricia Yaeger, finds at work in Shelley's "Mont Blanc", where the speaker is at first overpowered by the landscape but eventually masters it.[9] Yaeger explains the male longing for the sublime as a typically masculine attitude motivated by an Oedipal longing for a union with the mother.[10] Unlike men, women express their awareness of this desire and therefore manage to draw clear boundaries between subject and object. Also, Mellor argues that women writers of the Romantic period have distanced themselves from the melting of self and other and have used the sublime in different ways.

To return to *English Poetry*; the programme is an excellent tool for finding more material on the gender-specific use of the sublime. Our keyword search must aim at finding a number of sublime poems in order to compare poems by male and female writers.

The Search for the Sublime

The programme offers the following search possibilities:

- Poem keyword
- First line/Title keyword
- Poet name
- Period

The data are stored on five CDs, which follow a chronological order: disc 1 600 – 1603, disc 2 1603 – 1700, disc 3 1700 – 1800, disc 4 1800 – 1900 (A – K) and disc 5 1800 – 1900 (L – Z). The overall time span from 600 – 1900 falls into 16 subdivisions. As the category "Romanticism" is not offered by *English Poetry*, the search periods chosen have to be "1750 – 1800" (disc 3) and

"1800 – 1835" (discs 4 and 5), which roughly cover pre-Romanticism and Romanticism proper. The most important search function for our purposes is the "poem keyword" function that can be used for one or several keywords. What are suitable keywords? As "sublime" is rather useless, some typical elements of the sublime have to be used instead. Burke and others frequently refer to landscape features that evoke a strong emotional response through their greatness of dimension. As the keywords "mountain(s)," "crag(s)," "rock(s)" etc. are too vague and also occur far too frequently in poetry, our search will be restricted to one geographical area. The epitome of the sublime are the Alps, constantly featuring in eighteenth-century travel descriptions as in the following letter written by Thomas Gray in 1739. Here is the way up to the Grande Chartreuse:

> It is six miles to the top; the road runs winding up it, commonly not six feet broad; on one hand is the rock, with woods of pine-trees hanging over head; on the other, a monstrous precipice, almost perpendicular, at the bottom of which rolls a torrent, that sometimes tumbling among the fragments of stone that have fallen from on high, and sometimes precipitating itself down vast descents with a noise like thunder, which is still made greater by the echo from the mountains on each side, concurs to form one of the most solemn, the most romantic, and the most astonishing scenes I ever beheld: Add to this the strange views made by the craggs and cliffs on the other hand; the cascades that in many places throw themselves from the very summit down into the vale, and the river below [...][11]

Gray's description must have hit the popular taste. He skillfully blends the ingredients of the Alpine sublime – the vastness of the scenery, a narrow road, pine-trees, a precipice, loud noises – thus building up an atmosphere of danger and allurement. Similar stock elements are to be found in the paintings of Salvator Rosa, who contributed enormously to the popularization of the Alps. His landscapes influenced a whole generation of English painters and poets, who then went to find the sublime in parts of the British Isles, especially the Lake District and the Welsh and Scottish mountain ranges.

What are the exact search terms that have to be typed in? Our keywords are "Alp," "Alps" and "Alpine". Unfortunately, not all Alpine poems contain the morpheme "Alp-". Shelley's famous "Mont Blanc" does not and would therefore not show up in our list. Yet all Alpine poems posses a local marker, the name of a mountain, pass, river, town or lake. "Mont Blanc," one of the best-known Alpine locations, can therefore be used as an additional keyword. As Coleridge's "Hymn Before Sun-Rise, in the Vale of Chamouni" refers to this mountain as "Blanc," "Blanc" can serve as yet another keyword. We can also use "Chamouni"/"Chamonix," simply to see whether the programme comes up with any Alpine poems in which location is determined through that village alone. This village opens up a frequent problem with placenames in pre-twentieth-century texts because of the variety of spellings in which it appears: "Chamouni" in Coleridge and Shelley, "Chamouny" in Wordsworth and later in the nineteenth century it becomes "Chamonix," the present spelling.[12] We now have the following keywords: Alp, Alps, Alpine, Mont Blanc, Blanc and Chamo*n*. The possibility remains that some well-known Alpine poem is left out, but the keyword search function gives us a huge and awe-inspiring amount of material:

disc 3	period 1750-1800	213 references
disc 4	period 1800-1835, letters A-K	348 references
disc 5	period 1800-1835, letters L-Z	260 references

Disc 1 (600-1603) offers only 42 references. Disc 2 (1603-1700) lists 189 for practically one century – hardly surprising, the Alps were no tourist attraction before the eighteenth century. Disc 3 gives 158 references for the period 1700-1750, less than for the following fifty years, thus showing the gradual increase in interest. Discs 4 and 5 give 507/502, i.e. an overall 1009 references for the years between 1835 and 1900, thus bearing witness to the continuing attractiveness of the Alps.

Here is the list of poets including Alpine heights in their poems (1750-1835):

Disc 3: Anna Laetitia Aikin, Mark Aikenside, Christopher Anstey, James Beattie, Thomas Blacklock, William Blake, Samuel Bowden, William Lisle Bowles, Michael Bruce, Sir James Bland Burges, Richard Owen Cambridge, George Canning, James Cawthorn, Robert Colvill, William Combe, William Cowper, John Cunningham, Erasmus Darwin, William Dodd, John Duncombe, William Falconer, Francis Fawkes, Robert Fergusson, John Hookham Frere, William Gifford, Oliver Goldsmith, James Grahame, James Grainger, Anne Grant, William Hayley, George Huddesford, James Hurdis, Richard Jago, Edward Jerningham, Henry Jones, George Keate, John Langhorne, George Lyttleton, Hector MacNeill, William Mason, Thomas James Mathias, Robert Merry, William Julius Mickle, Richard Polwhele, Samuel Jackson Pratt, Henry James Pye, Mary Robinson, John Scott, Anna Seward, Christopher Smart, Charlotte Smith, John Hall Stevenson, Percival Stockdale, Joseph Warton, Isaac Watts, Thomas Sedgwick Whalley, Helen Maria Williams, John Williams, Alexander Wilson, John Wolcot, James Woodhouse, Ann Yearsley.

Disc 4: John Anster, Edwin Atherstone, Joanna Baillie, Bernard Barton, Nathaniel Thomas Haynes Bayly, Robert Bloomfield, Henry Boyd, Sir Samuel Egerton Brydges, Charles Bucke, Alfred Bunn, George Gordon Noel Byron, Jeremiah Joseph Callanan, Thomas Campbell, John

Clare, Hartley Coleridge, Samuel Taylor Coleridge, Joseph Cottle, George Croly, Robert Charles Dallas, George Daniel, George Darley, Thomas Dermody, Sir Aubrey De Vere, Charles Isaac Mugo Dibdin, Isaac D'Israeli, George Dyer, Ebenezer Elliott, Thomas Erskine, John Galt, Robert Gilfillan, William Glen, Janet Hamilton, Felicia Dorothea Hemans, John Abraham Heraud, William Herbert, James Hogg, Thomas Hood, Mary Howitt, James Henry Leigh Hunt, Samuel William Henry Ireland, John Keats, John Kenyon.

Disc 5: Walter Savage Landor, John Leyden, Samuel Lover, Henry Francis Lyte, William Maginn, James Clarence Mangan, Richard Mant, Richard Alfred Milliken, Henry Hart Milman, John Mitford, David Macbeth Moir, James Montgomery, Thomas Moore, John Moultrie, John Nicholson, Sydney Owenson, Thomas Love Peacock, Robert Pollok, Thomas Pringle, Bryan Waller Procter, Edward Quillinan, Ann Radcliffe, John Hamilton Reynolds, Samuel Rogers, Percy Bysshe Shelley, Horatio Smith, James Smith, Robert Southey, Charles Strong, Thomas Noon Talfourd, John Thelwall, William Thomas Thomas, Mary Tighe, Alaric Alexander Watts, Jeremiah Holmes Wiffen, William Wordsworth, Francis Wrangham.[13]

This makes 127 men and 15 women. Whereas *English Poetry +*, another database by Chadwyck-Healey that contains far fewer poems (5080), offers the possibility of a gender-based search, our version does not. And where are the women, anyway? The comparatively small number of women poets writing about the Alps is partly due to the fact that women travelled less frequently, and if they did they would not go on a Grand Tour that was reserved to male travellers. On the other hand, seeing the Alps was no necessary precondition for writing about them, as Radcliffe's novels show. They contain compelling descriptions of Alpine scenery, although Radcliffe had never seen the Alps at a close range.[14] When she travelled to the continent in 1794, she could not enter Switzerland because of passport difficulties at the border. For her observation of the sublime, she had to do with the Rhine valley and the Lake District instead.

Travel restrictions are not the only reason for the meagre turnout of women poets in *English Poetry*. Its basis is the *NCBEL* (*New Cambridge Bibliography of English Literature*, 1969-72) and therefore any problems inherent in this latter publication are being perpetuated. Because the *NCBEL* dates from pre-women's studies days, a variety of women writers who have been rediscovered by feminist critics are not included. Only 18 out of the 34 women poets found in Ashfield's recent anthology *Romantic Women Poets 1770-1838* are listed in Chadwyck-Healey's book-bound bibliography (based on the *NCBEL*) that comes with the package. Missing are: Mary Hays, Hannah More, Eliza Knipe (later Clarke, later Cobbold), Anne Hunter, Mary Hunt, Mary O'Brian, Anna Maria Jones (née Shipley), Jane West (née Iliffe), Anna Maria Porter, Jane Taylor, Maria

Jane Jewsbury (later Fletcher), Maria Abdy (née Smith), Mary Browne (later Gray), Catherine Grace Godwin (née Garnett), Emma Roberts, Charlotte Brontë. Of course, Charlotte Brontë is listed in the *NCBEL*, but as a novelist. Six other 'missing' women poets are also mentioned in the *NCBEL*, but not under the section "poets" either.[15] If poets who were mainly concerned with other genres have been left out or have only been included sporadically, the data are not as comprehensive as one might wish. Yet one has to concede that the database contains a huge amount of names that even a specialist in a certain period might not know. So it both perpetuates and breaks up certain aspects of canonization, surprisingly in the most canonical of literary genres, poetry.

We now have enough poems to explore the Alpine sublime. The first discovery is that most poems we are given are not set in the Alps. Many of them only use the Alps for the purpose of poetic diction.

"Thy neck is fairer than the Alpine snows" – the Alps in Poetic Diction

When women and the Alps came together in poems of the Romantic period, the poet was often male. Literary conventions prescribed certain elements for the praise of female beauty, and the comparison between a woman's white skin (of course pointing to more than skin-deep moral purity) and Alpine snow is not infrequent: "a bosom white as Alpine snow" in Francis Fawkes's "Bramham Park", or more extended in Mary Russell Mitford's "Beauty: An Ode":

> Her neck of such a dazzling whiteness,
> As swans the rude stream breasting;
> Whilst her fair cheek's effulgent blush
> Seems like the evening's rosy flush,
> On Alpine snows reflected. (l. 57-61)

Male beauty can also be compared to Alpine snow:

> As on the painted turf the shepherd lies,
> Sleep's downy curtain shades his lovely eyes;
> And now a sporting breeze his bosom shews,
> As marble smooth, and white as Alpine snows.
> (John Cunningham, "Love and Chastity: A Cantata", l. 57-60)

Yet the fascination evoked by the snow's brilliant whiteness is also associated with coldness: "Within whose bosom, cold as Alpine snow,/No heav'ns kindled, and no seraphs glow" (Edward Jerningham, "Lines on

'The Baviad' and 'The Pursuits of Literature'", l. 103/4). Another set of imagery is based on the solidity and strength of the rocks: "Fear not, for like an Alpine rock,/I will sustain the trying shock" William Combe writes in his satire, "The Tour in Search of Consolation" (l. 535). James Hurdis also makes use of Alpine imagery in order to demonstrate the steadfastness of "the noble soul" (l. 1598): "It stands above weak insult, like an Alp" ("Adriano, or the First of June", l. 1601).

The Alps also serve as a point of reference for British landscape: "Scotia's Alps" (Anne Grant, "The Highlanders", l. 63) or "Alpine rocks of Cumberland" (John Nicholson, "On Returning from London", l. 20). In his long poem, "British Months; A Poem in Twelve Parts" Richard Mant uses the Alps as a foil in order to criticize the vogue that regards British landscapes as second-rate in comparison with the distant Alps:

> But homelier scenes and milder sights
> From Ocean waves and Alpine heights
> Recall the Muse's wandering wing,
> To ponder nearer views; and sing
> The fruits, which yet unsung remain,
> Of fleeting April's fertile reign.
> ("April", l. 879-884)

Also, the huge waves of maritime tempests are occasionally likened to the Alps: "By tempests lash'd, the billowy Alps arise" (Henry James Pye, "Naucratia; or Naval Dominion", l. 36). In spite of their sublimity, the Alps do not escape being domesticated:

> Here, ladies, here are grapes, (spread out your arms!)
> Purple as evenings; figs, and cakes, whose tops
> Make the dull whiteness of our frosted Alps.

Thus Nephilia in Bryan Waller Procter's "The Florentine Party" invites her guests (l. 195-197). This is the only instance of domestic use of the sublime, surprisingly written by a man. Yet the overall response evoked by the Alps is, quite in accordance with pre-Romantic and Romantic aesthetic theories, a mixture of terror and joy, stock responses to a poetic standard topic. So far, no gender-specific use of the Alps has become visible.

The Feminine Sublime

Turning to poems with Alpine settings, we can now see if Mellor's claim of the gendered nature of the sublime is valid. Although Mellor argues in

Romanticism and Gender that the fusion of subject and object is a characteristic of masculine Romanticism, she concedes that female writers such as Helen Maria Williams, who grew up in the vicinity of mountain ranges, give proof of a "heightened sensibility"[16] in the face of the sublime.

Williams's "A Hymn Written among the Alps" presents a speaker, an "I," approaching a "thee" (God) in dialogue. These partners stay apart as separate entities throughout the text. Williams's poem stands in the Protestant tradition of the Book of Nature. There is none of Wordsworth's melting into "one mind". The surrounding stock elements of Alpine description (storm, avalanche, glacier, pines, eagles) are all fixed in their specific localities, and so is the speaker. The alluring dangers of the sublime open themselves up to the beholder but she does not threaten to stumble or fall. In the middle of the poem, her mind aspires to transcend the world:

Where midst some vast expanse the mind,
Which swelling virtue fires,
Forgets that earth it leaves behind,
And to it's heaven aspires. (l. 33-36)

Yet the empowerment conveyed in Shelley's "Mont Blanc" cannot be felt in Williams's poem. By naming the process of transcendence, Williams's speaker avoids the absorption into the other. Right to the end of her poem, they stay separate entities:

In every scene, where every hour
Sheds some terrific grace,
In Nature's vast o'erwhelming Power,
Thee, Thee my **God**, I trace. (l. 77-80)

Unlike Shelley's speaker in "Mont Blanc," Williams's does not attempt a union with the surrounding landscape, or – in Yaeger's terminology – the subject does not attempt to achieve a return to the mother. Williams's poem contains no violent struggle, no (male) desire for oneness, which, in Freudian terms, is ultimately a desire for death.

Radcliffe's "Storied Sonnet," in which a man meets his death in the Alps, can be read as a comment or even a parody of the masculine sublime. Here is the story of her hapless traveller:

The weary traveller, who, all night long,
Has climb'd among the Alps' tremendous steeps,
Skirting the pathless precipice, where throng

Wild forms of danger; as he onward creeps
If, chance, his anxious eye at distance sees
The mountain-shepherd's solitary home,
Peeping from forth the moon-illumin'd trees,
What sudden transports to his bosom come!
But, if between some hideous chasm yawn,
Where the cleft pine a doubtful bridge displays,
In dreadful silence, on the brink, forlorn
He stands, and views in luna's dubious rays
Far, far below, the torrent's rising surge,
And listens to the wild impetuous roar;
Still eyes the depth, still shudders on the verge,
Fears to return, nor dares to venture o'er.
Desperate, at length the tottering plank he tries,
His weak steps slide, he shrieks, he sinks – he dies![17]

Radcliffe's interest in Burke is well-documented. The sonnet's adjectives ("tremendous", "wild", "anxious") point back to Burke's repertoire. Her protagonist closes the gap between subject and object in the most direct manner imaginable: "He shrieks, he sinks – he dies!" Death is preceded by the loss of control over body ("his weak steps slide," "he sinks") and language ("he shrieks"), indicating a regression to infantile patterns of movement and utterance. Our late twentieth-century perception turns these Gothic horrors into a mock sublime that can only be read as a grotesque encounter of the "I" and its projected fears. For us, the traveller's death is to be experienced from the distance created through laughter. Radcliffe does not use the sublime with a satiric intention but, unlike the sonnet's male traveller, she does not seem to be taken in by the transcendent sublime of the Shelley and Wordsworth variant. By describing the fusion of subject and object to its last possible consequence, Radcliffe and her speaker remain outside the actual process of melting. The poem is composed by Emily, the heroine of *The Mysteries of Udolpho*, who exorcises her fears by loading them onto a scapegoat. In Mellor's view, Radcliffe equates the masculine sublime with patriarchal tyranny.[18] Yet in this poem it is a man who becomes the victim of his own prejudices.

Other women's Alpine poems also avoid fusion. Charlotte Smith's verse narrative, "The Peasant of the Alps," a tale of a hermit's love and suicide, contains a reference to the poet at the end of the text by which she draws a parallel between herself and the hermit – like him, she has lost her felicity. In fact, Charlotte Smith was highly successful in stylizing and marketing the unhappy circumstances of her life.[19] Again, the threat of death/suicide is banned by being projected onto a man. Yet for the speaker/poet herself, the Shelleyan fusion of mind and nature is not feasible.

In Felicia Hemans's "Evening Among the Alps", the eighteenth-century responses to the sublime can no longer be traced. The Romantic fascination with uncivilised nature has given way to a pastoral description that excludes any passionate emotions. Her Alps are far from evoking any overwhelming feelings at all – they are just pretty:

Where awful summits crown'd with snow,
In soft and varied colours glow;
There, in some grassy shelter'd spot,
The Alpine shepherd forms his cot;
And there, beside his peaceful home,
The fairest mountain-flowerets bloom;
("The Alpine Shepherd", l. 3-8)

The fusion of self and other is no issue for Hemans, who cannot be allured into expressing any passionate feelings. The examples show three different approaches to the sublime: Williams's religious aspiration, Radcliffe's Burkean terror and Hemans's construction of pastoral prettiness. The Wordsworthian and Shelleyan variant of the sublime is not promoted in these women's poems. Clearly, different degrees of proximity exist: Williams is emotionally much closer to the landscape than Hemans is. Although the mountain mirrors her emotions, she does not transcend the boundaries between the material and the immaterial the way Shelley does.

The Masculine Sublime: "the thundering mass unflinching heard"

So far, we seem to have proved Mellor's claim as to the difference between the feminine and the masculine sublime – but only if we accept that Shelley and Wordsworth (and the rest of the visionary company) constitute male Romanticism as such. Yet a look at other male poets' accounts of the Alps provides a modified picture. The stock elements (pines, eagles, glaciers, avalanches, storms) abound everywhere. John Mitford, Samuel Rogers, Alaric Alexander Watts, William Lisle Bowles, George Keate and Thomas Sedgwick Whalley also make use of them in their Alpine poems. But like the women poets, they shrink from letting their speakers' and beholders' individualities merge into the "one mind," although, again, different degrees of proximity can be observed. Here is one male traveller, who refuses altogether to be drawn in:

Steel were his nerves, his sinews brass,
Who first with vaulting footsteps rose

Sublime; and from the virgin-pass
Look'd down upon eternal snows:
Who, by the raving storm unscared,
'Mid *Alpine* precipices strode;
The thundering mass unflinching heard.
(Francis Wrangham, "To the Post-Chariot of a Friend, Going Abroad", l. 9-15)

Nature, feminized as a virgin, sets the process of male empowerment ("strode") into motion. But the traveller's soldierly stoicism, anticipating later constructions of the imperial aloofness of British men, keeps him from projecting himself and his inner life onto the landscape. His act of domination does not entail the breaking down of boundaries between the material and the immaterial. Weiskel's "transubstantiation" does not occur. Neither does it in Watt's "Chamouni," a description of the nightly silence of the Alps which is interrupted by a powerful and noisy avalanche. The Alps function again as a realm of danger and allurement uniting opposites: peace and danger, loudness and stillness, etc. Robert Merry's traveller, looking back at a journey through the Alps, also expresses repulsion and attraction:

So the poor traveller from some Alpine height
Looks backward on his journey with affright,
For still past dangers past his thoughts confound,
And other dangers threaten still around;
The headlong precipice, the icy pass,
The whelming Avalanche's monstrous mass [...]
These all in dread confusion strike his heart
He fears to stay, not ventures to depart.
("The Pains of Memory", l. 75-80, 85-86)

No melting between subject and object occurs.

On the basis of the material provided by the database, we can conclude that the 'transcendent sublime' of the Shelleyan and Wordsworthian variant, regarded as typical of the Romantic period, constitutes in fact an exceptional way of writing about the sublime. Most male and female poets deal with the sublime without taking the ultimate step of breaking down the boundaries between self and other. True, different degrees of proximity between the speaker and his or her environment can be observed. Maybe research had better concentrate on different approaches or on poses like Wrangham's. This does not suggest that the sublime is not referred to in a gendered fashion – Wrangham's "virgin-pass" and Wordsworth's 'Brother' Nature bear witness to that. Yet a simple dichotomy of a masculine vs. a feminine sublime seems problematic.[20] Of course, the fusion of subject and object is by far not the only one of Mellor's criteria to establish a gendered use of the sublime. Some of the positive traits of the feminine sublime she lists are the establishing of mutual relationships and the taking of the sublime into the home.

The question remains why scholars and literary critics have concentrated for so long on this one representation of the sublime. It is surprising that scholarship has drawn its theories from very few texts written exclusively by male authors. This construction of the sublime has obviously served the needs of a general and academic readership with a desire for transcending the mundane world. Moreover, the interpretative community that has established the rules for our readings of the Romantics was and still is predominantly male. One can only assume that the notion of male power over female nature must be very alluring indeed. Yet feminist critics have also fallen into the trap of canonization, taking two well-known male exponents of the Romantic period to be representative of all masculinity of that period, although most male writers' poems of that age make use of the sublime in a different way from Wordsworth and Shelley. So this article also constitutes a plea for the preservation of minor male poets. Feminist criticism has revised and extended the canon, but this process has to continue and take account of male writers as well – if only to contradict male academic opinion.

Limitations and Prospects for New Quests

So far, so good. *English Poetry* has led to some insights into the Alpine sublime that would be hard to achieve without the textual basis offered. Yet the approach has its limitations. What is lost if one only considers the texts offered by *English Poetry* is the prose context – the large number of novels and philosophical tracts dealing with the sublime. And how representative are our findings? And how valid is an approach that, for practical reasons, translates the sublime into the Alps alone? Some uneasiness arises from pinning a discursive formation down to a specific object or location. If one wants to identify a discourse, one ought to look at specific collocations – as far as wild and inaccessible landscapes are concerned, "crag," "torrent" etc. might be useful. Here, however, we reach the limits of *English Poetry* as a research tool. If already the keywords "Alp" etc. give us a large amount of poems with no Alpine settings, the number of non-sublime texts dug up with the mentioned search terms would be even greater. What no amount of keywords can supply is a complete list of sublime poems. "Tintern Abbey," epitomizing the melting used as a criterion, does not show up in our search because it is set in pastoral nature. Moreover, the sublime does not even have to be tied up with nature. In Keats's "On First Looking into Chapman's Homer" the discovery of Homer becomes a sublime experience, which is expressed in the speaker's silence.

Can we still justify the use of *English Poetry* for the discovery of the sublime? The database has provided valuable material. Yet no research project can organize its collection of material through *English Poetry* alone. The database is useful at an early stage for the compilation of texts but needs to be complemented. It can also be valuable in the later stages of a project when one wants to find out quickly in which contexts a specific term appears. Generally, it is easier to search for materially concrete items. Anyone interested in how many nightingales apart from Keats's decorate Romantic poetry will find Chadwyck-Healey's search routine extremely valuable. Similarly, contexts for the use of mythical figures can be established. Or someone doing research into the literary discourses of industrialization may type in specific industrial objects, names of machines or inventions, and then go off with hundreds of poems by hitherto unknown writers.

English Poetry uncovers new angles simply by providing texts of 'minor' poets which are often difficult to get hold of, especially if they exist only in rare and expensive early editions.[21] The editorial policy of *English Poetry* is to use collected editions that are no longer subject to copyright restrictions. Consequently, they contain no critical apparatus and very few footnotes. Besides, *English Poetry* is based on the notion of a single stable text. Variants are rarely admitted – they are in the case of Wordsworth's *Prelude.* The two-book *Prelude* of 1799 and the two versions of 1805 and 1850 are included. Minor textual variants in most authors, however, are ignored. The advantage of having access to a large number of poems that the departmental library might not stock is reduced by the constant necessity of having to walk to that very library in order to consult the Oxford Companion to English Literature or the OED. The information given on the lives of the poets and the few footnotes are too scanty to be useful. Maybe a later on-line version could integrate works of reference. Because many of the poems are little-known, the bibliographical information should also stretch to more than the publication date of the volume. Unfortunately, the year in which a poem was written is not given. As many of the poems, especially collected editions, were edited posthumously, one cannot even determine the decade in which a particular poem was produced. Also some technical aspects need to be improved. In the present version, one can only browse through the poem with the use of the "page down" button. No "go to line ..." command exists. Since one cannot easily skip part of the poem, moving around an 800-line text can be rather tedious. Finally, copying the texts into a word processing programme is rather difficult and time-consuming. It is in fact easier to print out the poem and then to type it into the text of a handout manually than to retrieve it from *English Poetry.*

In spite of its shortcomings, *English Poetry* is still superior to other similar search routines offered on the Internet. The Gutenberg project that aims at making large amounts of literary texts electronically available also offers a search routine,[22] which, when confronted with the same keywords as above, gives the cryptic answer: "No Items or Too Many Items Found". Another Search Routine, "Representative Poetry On-Line. Version 2.0"[23] only gives 24 references (*English Poetry*: over 2000), all of them from the texts of male poets, who seem to be the sole representatives of EngLit. In spite of its democratic claim, the Internet prepetuates gender stereotypes, not only on pornographic websites but also in the formation of an electronic canon. In comparison to various projects that are largely devoid of women writers, *English Poetry* appears rather progressive.

The *English Poetry Full-Text Database* definitely provides a useful research tool. Although the computer has been accused of being instrumental in destroying the culture of reading, this programme rather contributes to the discovery and perusal of literary texts. Even though the material reality of Wordsworth's surroundings (the cave, the sea) has quite an alluring potential, it has found a serious rival in the virtual reality of having English Poetry on five CDs, accessible in one room, even though this room may be a neon-lit office. But, quoting Shelley: "Poetry turns all things to loveliness."[24]

Notes

1 Wordsworth, *Prelude* (1850) V, 56-64. All quotations of poems are taken from *Chadwyck-Healey's English Poetry Full-Text Database.*
2 Cf. bibliography.
3 Burke, 39.
4 Bode, 299.
5 Weiskel, 58.
6 Wordsworth, *Prelude* (1805) VI, 568.
7 Vivian, 55ff.
8 Wordsworth, *Prelude* (1805) XIII, 89. Cf. also Mellor, 90.
9 Yaeger, 197.
10 Yaeger, 204.
11 Gray, I, 122 f.
12 *English Poetry* offers the possibility of using an asterisk (*) to indicate that any number of letters may follow. "Chamo*n*" leaves open a number of varieties: Chamonix, Chamounix, Chamouni. This use of the asterisk is not feasible in the case of "Alps" because the keyword "Alp*" also allows for "alphabet", "Alpheus" etc.

13 The length of the texts varies from 14-line sonnets to Samuel Egerton Brydges' *The Lake of Geneva, a poem, moral and descriptive, in seven books.* London 1832.

14 Ware, 19-22.

15 These include Mary Hays, Hannah More, Anne Hunter, Jane West, Anna Maria Porter and Jane Taylor. Another omitted eighteenth-century poet is Mary Leapor, well-known during her lifetime. Cf. Mandell's criticism of Chadwyck-Healey (Mandell, 1995) and the website with Leapor's poetry (Mandell, 1997).

16 Mellor, 97.

17 Radcliffe, "Storied Sonnet", I, 169. The poem also appears in *The Mysteries of Udolpho*, I, 169. Unfortunately, *English Poetry* only refers to an edition of Radcliffe's poems as the source but does not mention the actual novel.

18 Mellor, 91.

19 Labbe, 68.

20 Mellor herself problematizes dichotomies of that sort in her introduction, 11.

21 McGann.

22 http://www.promo.net/pg/query.cgi

23 http://www.utel/rp/intro.html

24 Shelley, 505.

Bibliography

Ashfield, Andrew (Ed.): *Romantic Women Poets 1770-1838. An Anthology.* Manchester, 1995.

Bloom, Harold: *The Visionary Company. A Reading of English Romantic Poetry.* London, 1961.

Bode, Christoph: "Shelley's 'Mont Blanc': The Aesthetic 'Aufhebung' of a Philosophical Antinomy". – In Horst Höhne (Ed.): *Romantic Discourses. Papers delivered at the Symposium on the Bicentenary of the Birth of Percy Bysshe Shelley, Ahrenshoop, October 2-5, 1992*, Studien zur Englischen Romantik 7. Essen, 1994, pp. 286-299.

Burke, Edmund: *A Philosophical Enquiry into the Origin of our Ideas of the Sublime and Beautiful*, ed. James T. Boulton. London, 1987.

Chadwyck-Healey: *English Poetry. The English Poetry Full-Text Database.* 5 CDs.

English Poetry. A Bibliography of the English Poetry Full-Text Database, ed. Chadwyck-Healey. Cambridge, 1995.

Easthope, Antony: *Wordsworth Now and Then.* Buckingham, 1993.

Ferguson, Frances: "The Sublime of Edmund Burke, or the Bathos of Experience", *Glyph* 8, 1981, 62-78.

Gray, Thomas: *The Correspondence*, 3 vol.s, ed. Paget Toynbee/Leonard Whibley. Oxford, 1935, repr. 1971.

Labbe, Jacqueline M.: "Selling One's Sorrows: Charlotte Smith, Mary Robinson and the Marketing of Poetry", *The Wordsworth Circle* 25, 1994, 68-71.

Mandell, Laura: "New Romantic Canons in the Same Old Classroom. Update#1 – A Newsletter", 1995 (http://miavx1.muohio.edu/~mandellc/update/update1.htm).

Mandell, Laura (Ed.): "The Poetry of Mary Leapor", 1997 (http://miavx1.muohio.edu/~mandellc/ leapor/leapor.htm).

McGann, Jerome: "Radiant Textuality", 1996 (http://jefferson.village.virginia.edu/public/jjm2f /radiant.html).
Mellor, Anne K.: *Romanticism and Gender*. New York, 1993.
Monk, Samuel H.: *The Sublime. A Study of Critical Theories in XVIII-Century England*. Ann Arbor, 1960.
Project Gutenberg (http://promo.net/pg).
Radcliffe, Ann: *The Mysteries of Udolpho*, 2 vol.s, London, 1959.
Representative Poetry On-Line: Version 2.0, ed. W.H. Clawson et al. (http://www.utel/rp/ intro.html).
Shelley, Percy Bysshe: "A Defence of Poetry". – In Donald H. Reiman & Sharon B. Powers (Eds.): *Shelley's Poetry and Prose*. New York, 1977, pp. 478-508.
Vivian, Charles H.: "The One 'Mont Blanc'", *Keats-Shelley-Journal* IV, 1955, 55-65.
Ware, Malcolm: *Sublimity in the Novels of Ann Radcliffe. A Study of the Influence Upon her Craft of Edmund Burke's* Enquiry into the Origin of our Ideas of the Sublime and the Beautiful, Essays and Studies on English Language and Literature XXV. Lund, 1963.
Weiskel, Thomas: *The Romantic Sublime: Studies in the Structure and Psychology of Transcendence*. Baltimore, 1976.
Yaeger, Patricia: "Toward a Female Sublime". – In Linda Kauffman (Ed.): *Gender and Theory. Dialogues on Feminist Criticism*. Oxford, 1989, pp. 191-212.

Tobias Rademann, Bochum

Special investigator Kenneth W. Starr, a weak tendency, and transboundary shipment of waste: Practical examples in electronic translation for high-school and university students.

I. Introduction

The recent developments in the field of computing and information technology have opened up interesting new perspectives with respect to computer-aided translation (CAT). While most essays published so far on this topic primarily centre on how computers can be employed in professional translation, though, this paper aims at providing some practical advice for *learners* of English, i.e. primarily pupils, students and – at least to some extent also – semi-professionals. For this purpose, several examples will be discussed in the following paragraphs, detailing in how far new approaches can be made to improve the quality of translations (here from German into English). The report is divided into three major sections, the first of which will provide some information on how one can improve one's translation by "getting acquainted with the topic", while the second will centre on the basics of corpus-based translation, and the third will briefly portray the value of EU databases for translators.

II. Getting acquainted with the topic – Electronic Newspapers in Translation

As Kornelius et al. have partly illustrated (Kornelius 1997), the Internet offers a rich pool of sources providing (linguistic) information of various kinds. However, one of the most difficult issues for language learners in this context is that they have to assess the quality of these sources before being able to employ them for their purposes. If this step is not taken (and, as experience tells us, in the majority of cases it is not, for lack of time or knowledge), serious problems may arise with respect to the quality of their own translation, most of all resulting from the fact that they did not take into account the possibility of having accessed low-quality or even false information. If, for instance, students want to find the correct translation for the job title of "Nordirland-Ministerin Mowlam" and do not realise that the source they found via a search engine like AltaVista or Yahoo was written by a non-native speaker, e.g. a learner of English in his second year who published his term paper on the Web, they run the risk of using an expression which is far from correct, since the title used by the student in his essay must not necessarily have been "Secretary of State for Northern Ireland", but one that *he thought* was appropriate, such as "Northern Ireland Minister" (a typical *German* translation). Thus one of the principal questions in this context is *which sources* students can use without needing to spend (too much) time trying to assess their quality.

Bearing in mind the kinds of texts used for translation purposes in schools and universities, three fields appear to be of principal interest: Literary texts, current (political) affairs, and special-purpose texts (e.g. economics, law). Although it will be rather difficult to find sources on the Internet that help with translating texts taken from the first category, there are numerous sources which can be referred to when translating texts belonging to the latter two. However, given the statement made above that the quality of Internet references currently presents one of the main problems, especially for learners who will frequently not be able to judge upon the overall phraseology used, there appears to be one genre which is almost ideally suited for students of English interested in improving the quality of their translations: Electronic Newspapers.

While the broad number of linguistically distinctive varieties inherent in any average-quality *printed* newspaper has made them a playground for translation purposes over many years, the immediate global availability of their electronic counterparts and the fact that most of them are available free-of-charge has added to their popularity (see Rademann's (1998) report on *Newspapers on the Internet* in this issue). Obviously, any of the major quality dailies such as The *Times* (London), *USA Today*, or the *Wall Street Journal* (the most widely-read US daily!) will be of immense value for students translating texts on current (political) affairs and even special-purpose reports.

But in how far exactly are electronic (quality) papers of value in this context? Take, for example, a headline in the *FAZ*: "Meineid, Zeugenbeeinflussung, Amtsmißbrauch – Anschuldigungen gegen Clinton" (*FAZ*, Saturday, September 12, 1998). When translating this headline, there are several problems which may arise. First of all, the grammar and wording of newspaper headlines often differs considerably from 'normal' sentences, a fact which is responsible for their frequent omission from translation tasks. However, a quick glance in an electronic newspaper, and the problem is solved: Almost any Saturday paper from the states uses almost exactly the same words, for instance *USA Today*: "Witness Tampering, Abuse of Power, and Perjury", while the *Washington Post*'s headline reads "Clinton Accused" – thus we easily manage to get an idiomatic translation.

When reading through some of the articles on this topic, students will soon come up with a considerable amount of idiomatic vocabulary used in this context:[1]

Repräsentantenhaus	- Congress
Starr-Dokument	- Starr Report (NOT Document!)
Amtsenthebungsverfahren	- impeachment
Sonderermittler (Starr)	- not used as title; instead: Kenneth (W.) Starr
Gründe (für Amtsenthebungsverf.)	- grounds (NOT reasons!)
Fraktionsvorsitzende	- Minority Leader[...]

There can thus be no doubt that simply by reading a few newspaper reports published in the language into which the document is to be translated, the students' translation will be much more idiomatic than it would have been had they referred to a conventional dictionary only.[2] A good proof for this assertion is the translation of another phrase taken from the article quoted above: "Gründe für ein Amtsenthebungsverfahren". While most smaller dictionaries do not even list "grounds", Langenscheidt's Muret-Sanders gives us a pool of different terms such as "reason", "basis", "foundation", "cause", while it is only in the 15th position (more than 1 ds" with the comment that it is used "bes. zur Beweisführung, Rechtfertigung, Verteidigung, etc)". Evidently, there is a good chance that students overlook this definition and use another one instead; but even if they do not, it would take much longer than with any electronic text. In addition it could be argued that it will be much easier to remember "grounds" if it was read several times in the context of "impeachment" than looked up at an isolated position in a dictionary. Finally, the translation for "Fraktionsvorsitzender" is not listed at all; all that can be found is "Fraktionsführer" which is translated by

> leader (*od.* chairman) of the parliamentary group (*od.* party), Parliamentary Party Leader, *Br.* chief whip, *Am.* floor leader, (Der kleine Muret-Sanders (1995))

making "den Fraktionsvorsitzenden der Demokraten, Gephardt" (*FAZ*) to "the floor leader of the democrats, Gephardt", while a more idiomatic translation would have been "Minority Leader Richard A. Gephardt" (*Washington Post*, Saturday, September 12, 1998; Page A14).

Furthermore, students will realise that certain phrases and expressions are used differently or not at all in English. A title such as that of "Sonderermittler", which is frequently used in any German-language publication on this topic, can hardly ever be found in an English-language newspaper report. Here, the title is omitted and the Christian name is used instead, making "Kenneth (W.) Starr" the idiomatic translation for "Sonderermittler Starr". Where the title is used, it is used on its own, without the name, and is not translated as "special investigator", but rather as "independent prosecutor" (The *Times* (London), September 12, 1998, frontpage).

If we come back to the example of the "Secretary of State for Northern Ireland" quoted in the introductory passage above, another interesting observation can be made in this context. While the Internet in general – and electronic newspapers in particular – can be of help for those students who do not know how a given word or phrase (here the title of "Nordirland-Ministerin") is to be translated (provided that they chose high-quality reference sources), it can also be of great value for those who already have a certain 'nose' for problems, i.e. more advanced learners of English. Let me illustrate what I mean with a case which recently arose in a Staatsexamen translation.[3] Students had to translate a newspaper report referring to "Nordirland-Ministerin Mowlam". When translating such phrases or titles, advanced learners will remember from their Landeskunde classes that some members of the British government are called "Minister", while others are called "Secretary of State" or "Secretary" for short. But who is called what, or, more precisely, what is Ms Mowlam's correct title? Here, too, the answer can be found quickly with the help of Internet sources: If her name is entered in the search engine of any quality electronic newspaper, one will soon find a reference to either "Secretary of State [for Northern Ireland]" or "Northern Ireland Secretary", thus, without actually having read any text in full, you have found two correct titles for the lady in question, and you KNOW that the "Nordirland-Ministerin" is NOT a "Minister".[4]

The fact that students are able to compare texts taken from different countries will even help to make them aware of the differences in spelling and vocabulary used, such as "center" vs. "centre", etc.[5] Names of institutions are yet another interesting issue in this context. As the example of "Minority Leader" quoted above has demonstrated, here, too, newspaper articles will prove to provide much more idiomatic translations than dictionaries ever can.

Finally, it can be argued that students can be made aware of differences in style, since more and more popular-press newspapers have been released on the Internet over the past few years as well. The *Online Mirror*, for instance, has the following headline and introduction on its frontpage of 12 September:

> CLINTON'S SEX FILES
> SHAMED President Clinton
> had oral sex with Monica
> Lewinsky NINE times and

took part in a further sex
act, the explosive Starr
report claims.

In the rest of the article, words such as "disgraced Clinton" and phrases as "a few days later the lovers were back together" or "Lewinsky unbuttoned her jacket – and they got down to business" clearly mark a different style from any of the articles quoted so far.

III. Introduction to Corpus-aided Translation

While anyone with access to the Internet and only a basic knowledge of the technical aspects involved can benefit from the examples quoted in the previous section (thus especially pupils and students), the following paragraphs are concerned with what may be called the very basics of corpus-aided translation. A corpus is "A collection of linguistic data, either written texts or a transcription of recorded speech, which can be used as a starting-point of linguistic description or as a means of verifying hypotheses about a language", Crystal (1991) (see also Sand's paper on *Corpus Linguistics* in this issue). Thus in order to work with a corpus in translation, two prerequisites have to be met: First of all, the user needs to have access to a corpus, and secondly, (s)he needs to know how it works. Consequently, this possibility is primarily of advantage for advanced language students (the popularity of corpus linguistics has increased considerably over the past few years at universities) and for (semi) professionals.

There is a considerable number of corpora around at present, with its number increasing almost daily.[6] However, one of the most elaborate corpora currently available is the 100m word-comprising British National Corpus (BNC).[7] The Internet has also had a considerable impact in this field, since it has now become possible for anyone connected to this infocommunications medium to access corpora which have been made available throughout the world or to download them and store them on one's local harddisk.

To which extent may such corpora now be used to assist students in translation? All things considered, there are about three major tasks for which they are of interest, namely (a) to find out about the collocations of a given word, (b) to establish word fields, and (c) to get some information on the word classes.

As far as the collocations of a given word are concerned, I would like to refer to an example taken from the second kind of texts that students are most likely to be confronted with, namely that of special-purpose reports. Students who have chosen economics as their field of interest in

English language studies *(Wirtschaftsenglisch als Fachsprachenvertiefungsgebiet)*, could, for instance, be required to work on a stock exchange report. If now asked to translate expressions such as "heftige Kursschwankungen", "kräftige Kapitalzuflüsse", "der XXX Index brach ein", "sinkende Aktienkurse", "sehr hektisches Geschäft", or "mäßige Umsätze", it will be one of the most difficult things for them to choose an idiomatic adjective-noun / adverb-verb combination. It can hardly be disputed that most of the ordinary dictionaries will be of little value here, since they will usually not include any of these two-word combinations.

Having read some English-language stock exchange reports, though, it soon becomes clear that this field is marked by a highly restricted number of terms and expressions (see Rademann (1996); for an older account on the subject using printed papers cf. Wessels (1983)), and that there is thus only a limited number of idiomatic two-word combinations that can be regarded as correct translations. The headline "Der Nikkei-225-Index ist eingebrochen" (*FAZ*, Saturday September 12, 1998) could never be translated as "The Nikkei-225-Index collapsed", since this would imply there was a crash; it would rather have to be translated as "Nikkei tumbles" (*FT.com* (*Financial Times* online edition) Saturday, September 12, 1998), meaning there was a sharp drop in share prices. Likewise, it would be absolutely wrong to translate the German "In Sydney war die Tendenz ebenfalls schwach" (*FAZ*) by anything like "In Sydney, the tendency / trend was also weak" – one will never find words such as "tendency" or "trend" in this context in an English-language newspaper article, but rather "Sydney fell sharply" or something comparable. However, both "collapsed" and "tendency" were the only terms included in the dictionary (Muret-Sanders (1995)) that appeared to be suitable translations here.

If students now have access to a corpus of stock exchange reports (they could either construct their own ones by collecting texts taken from the respective sections of electronic newspapers and storing them on their local harddisk, or they could use any of the well-known corpora that include comparable sections), they can use the various tools that come along with them (such as the BNC's SARA) or any of the commercial ones (such as Mike Scott's WordSmith (published by OUP))[8] to build a concordance showing the collocations of words. Without doubt, they would quickly get a list of terms and phrases denoting, among other things, falling and rising share prices or indices. This list would include such expressions as "falling prices", "sharp drop", "heavy turnover", "dips below xxx level", "sharply down", "shares fell", etc.; when translating texts now, students can use the lists obtained in order to produce more idiomatic translations.

In order to illustrate the value of corpora with respect to the collocations of a given word, let me come back to this year's Staatsexamen once again: In one paragraph, students had to translate the sentence "Sie erinnerte an den letzten Mord in Nord Irland". Most of them translated it as "She reminded of the last murder in Northern Ireland", not taking into account the fact that 'to remind' always needs an object in English. Given the number of cases in which this translation occurred, I wanted to make sure I was not wrong myself, thus I used the BNC's SARA query interface to look up all instances of 'to remind' in this corpus. When investigating roughly 300 samples, the only exception I found was the one below, confirming my initial assumption:

> The jokes are like, like that, those Yeah can you see that better there? Let's have a look What? Have you read it? No what he took the sewing machine I haven't read it yet I'll turn this down oh remind over in the cold, do business last winter with matching jean and shorts I told my with, they must get hold of a new windscreen before going home Oh look Just Good Friends. Who?

The second major advantage of employing corpora for translation purposes can be seen from the fact that they enable users to create word lists, containing the (most frequent) words used in the respective corpus (section). Even a very simple analysis of stock exchange reports, for instance, clearly showed that words such as "broker(s), "company(s), "down", "fell" or "gains" were among the most frequently used words of articles belonging to this field (see Rademann (1996)). These lists, too, can easily be created using any of the programs described above, and can then be used to assist students with their translations. They could use these lists of "common words" for their preparation or during the translation process, which would again help them to come up with a more idiomatic translation in the end.

Finally, more advanced translators might want to check on the quality of their translations by comparing the relative frequency of word classes their report contains as compared to that of the respective section in the corpus. Especially with respect to a comparison between English and German texts, it has often been said that English is a more verbal language, and that we would thus have to take care of verbalising our translations. However, while statements such as this would, of course, have to be verified for individual genres first, a professional translator might be interested in seeing whether his English matches that of native speakers with respect to such grammatical aspects. In order to judge on the quality of his translation, he could thus send his text through a tagger[9] and compare its outcome with that of the corpus. Should he find that the relative frequency of nouns in his text is markedly higher (lower) than the average relative frequency of nouns in the corpus, he might re-check his translation on this aspect.

IV. Additional Internet Sources

On the background of the need to verify the quality of a given Internet source before using it for translation purposes (be it to search for a given word or phrase or to build a small special-purpose corpus from it) in connection with the fact that most pupils and students will or cannot adequately cope with this task for various reasons at present, only one additional online source for translations will be briefly discussed here – after all, the danger resulting from the use of inadequate material of which so much can currently be accessed on the net is far too high and should not be underestimated by teachers.

The last kind of online sources to be mentioned here are the databases provided by the EU, such as SCAD*Plus*, Celex, Cordis, etc (see EU (1998)). And although it is primarily (semi) professionals who should benefit most from these databases, students may also employ them for their purposes. The fact that most EU documents have to be translated into several languages, such as English, German, French, Spanish, etc. and that each of them carries a unique identification number, allows us to easily match any two of these documents in order to find out how certain terms and phrases have been translated. The quality of these documents is supposed to be very high, not least because they are translated by highly-trained professionals. Given the immense amount of information included in these databases, they are certainly far more valuable than any kind of dictionary, especially since they often contain the latest technical terms which will not be found in any other reference work. Thus, their principal field of application is obviously also the translation of special-purpose reports, e.g. on environmental or law issues. Let me again illustrate this with a personal example: A few weeks ago, I was asked by two of my colleagues from the Faculty of Economics whether I could translate an article they had written on "Grenzüberschreitende Abfallverbringung in der EU" which was to appear in the English-language edition of *Wirtschaftsdienst*, a journal called *Intereconomics*. The report analysed economic and legal issues that have to be taken into account when considering the pros and cons of transfrontier shipment of waste within the EU and third countries (see Werbeck / Hecht (1998)). As the thoughts presented in their paper dealt with the latest findings in this area, and because the subject as such can be considered a very young one, no (special-purpose) dictionary I found was of great assistance in translating such terms as "gefährlicher Abfall" (hazardous waste), "Abfallrahmenrichtlinie" (framework directive on waste), or "grenzüberschreitende Abfallverbringung" (transfrontier disposal of waste). However, when looking on the Internet for some of these phrases, I came across the EU databases mentioned above. I logged in to the most promising one, and, having found a German document (such as a *Richtlinie* or a *Verordnung*) that contained the phrase or term in question, I simply looked it up in the respective English-language *directive* or *council regulation*, thus ensuring I always used the correct translation. In the end, I ended up not only with a considerable amount of printed paper lying on my desk, but also with an idiomatic translation of a text on a highly specialised topic in which my knowledge of English had been rudimentary at the most.

V. Conclusion and Critical Summary

It was the intention of the present paper to demonstrate in how far learners of a foreign language (here: English) such as high school and university students can benefit from some of the new means that have become available for translators in an ever more computer-centred environment. For this purpose, the discussion focused on three major issues, namely the value of electronic newspapers for translation, the basics of corpus-aided approaches, and last but not least the numerous databases made available by the EU.

Although printed newspapers, some of the major corpora, and obviously a vast pool of EU documents had been available for years prior to the introduction of the Internet, it was argued that this info-communications medium made it possible to distribute the electronic versions of these documents without any time lags and additional costs, resulting in a much broader audience being able to access and use them, especially at schools (well, hopefully) and universities. Furthermore, the electronic versions have another important advantage over their printed predecessors, since they can be searched and their content can be analysed automatically (with respect to vocabulary, etc.).

It was common to all these measures that they aimed at assisting students in making their translations *more idiomatic*: Electronic newspapers allowed them to find out about idiomatic vocabulary used in texts on a certain topic, from a certain region, or a given social class, while corpora enabled translators to establish collocations, the most commonly used words of a genre, and also the relative frequencies of word classes, while finally EU databases were said to be another (high) quality example for looking up and comparing words (especially technical terminology) in context in a broad variety of different languages.

In addition, it must not be forgotten that these approaches can also be of great value in another context, namely with respect to self-assessment. Especially when students need to prepare themselves for their exams and finals, the sources discussed in this essay can be employed for checking on the quality of one's own translations. Students could, for instance, translate a German newspaper article on a topic that is in the news, and could then compare their translation with two or three articles taken from English-language quality-press electronic newspapers. By doing so, at least advanced learners of a foreign language would thus be able to get an (objective) impression of the quality of their translations and would at the same time learn new idiomatic vocabulary and grammar, since they would necessarily work on these texts.

What a brave new world! Just give students access to the Internet, and within days the quality of their translations will improve in ways never seen before!

The sarcasm inherent in the last sentence obviously focuses on one of the most important delusions currently entertained when talking about topics similar to that of the present paper. Most people are excited about the enormous potential the Internet offers. We can readily access thousands of documents and sources we dared not hope for some years ago, and we can communicate with anyone in the world at (hardly any) cost. But while the Internet may be a medium that *facilitates access* to a vast pool of information sources of all kinds, it has *considerably increased* the need to be able to judge on the quality and value of these sources at the same time.

The problems humans have in finding and selecting the kind of information they need from the vast pool of information available on this new medium MUST NOT be underestimated. And the younger – and thus also less experienced and less educated – users are, the higher is the risk of accessing low-quality sources on this network, and by doing so retrieving wrong (and with respect to the content in some instances even psychologically harmful (see the Starr report, for instance)) information.

There can be no doubt that the means portrayed in the passages above do by no means replace common dictionaries or grammar books, especially for beginners. It is only once students have gained a well-founded knowledge of the respective language that they are ready to employ these sources in their work and benefit from their usage. And the sources quoted above are only of value if they are used as supplements to what has so far been employed in foreign language learning.

On the background of what has just been said, it should have become clear that translation has NOT become easier in the information age; the various means available for translators on the Internet present *yet another* group of tools the appropriate handling of which has to be learned *before* they can be employed in everyday translation. But when – and only when – their handling is learned, they have the potential of enabling students and professionals to improve the quality of their work considerably.

Notes

1 Vocabulary taken from texts published on CNN.com, *USA Today*, The *Times* (London), and *The Washington Post* (weekend of September 11th-12th, 1998).
2 Obviously, there can be no question that the same is true for printed newspapers. However, their electronic counterparts are of advantage in at least three respects: First of all, they are available at the same time that any German paper is published or that a given topic is in the news – which is especially true for papers from countries such as Canada or Australia (in addition, they can even be accessed later, since most have electronic archives), secondly, most of them are free-of-charge, and finally, students can search reports for certain expressions without having to read the full text of the article.
3 Obviously, none of the searches advocated here is possible in the exam situation itself; nevertheless, they can be conducted when students prepare themselves for the exams or when they are doing their homework.
4 Clearly, one could also enter this query in any general-purpose search engine such as AltaVista or Yahoo. However, bearing in mind the remarks made above on the importance of the quality of a source found on the Internet, students would have to verify the quality of the respective source first before using it in their translations, a step which is not necessary with ENs.
5 In addition, it must not be forgotten that by reading texts from newspapers published in different nations students will also learn about how the respective topic is viewed in different countries; however, this will only indirectly help them with their translations.
6 Given the definition of Crystal (1991) quoted in the introductory passage to this section, any electronic archive of newspaper texts could also be regarded as a mini-corpus. However, since most major corpora offer many linguistically sophisticated research tools, the present study will primarily focus on them.
7 For some more background information on this project cf. BNC (1996) and Burnard/Aston (1998).
8 See Mike Scott's (author) homepage at: http://www.liv.ac.uk/~ms2928/index.htm or OUP's website at http://www.oup.co.uk, sections 'Electronic Publishing' and 'English Language Teaching' for more information.
9 A tagger is a computer program that attempts to automatically assign the word class and grammatical category (adjective, noun, verb in the past, etc.) to a given word. Usually, some manual post-editing needs to be done once a given text is sent through a tagger, since no output of those available at present is 100% correct.

Bibliography

Burnard, Lou & Guy Aston: *The BNC Handbook. Exploring the British National Corpus with SARA*. Edinburgh Textbooks in Empirical Linguistics, Edinburgh University Press, 1998.

BNC: The BNC's homepage (1998) can be found at: http://info.ox.ac.uk/bnc/

Crystal, David: "Corpus", – In *A Dictionary of Linguistics and Phonetics*, 3rd ed., Blackwell, 1991.

EU (1998): Index page of EU databases can be found at: http://europa.eu.int/gen-info/info-de.htm

Hecht, Dieter & Nicola Werbeck: "Waste without frontiers". *Intereconomics*. No. 3, Vol. 33 (May/June), 1998, 137-145.

Kornelius, Joachim & Frank Austermühl: "Neue Formen der fachlexikographischen und übersetzungsbezogenen Recherche: Bericht über eine wissenschaftliche Weiterbildungsmaßnahme unter besonderer Berücksichtigung (meta-)lexikographischer Aspekte". *Lexicographica*. Vol. 13., 1997, 264-279.

Der Kleine Muret-Sanders: *Langenscheidts Großwörterbuch der Englischen und Deutschen Sprache*. 6th edition. Langenscheidt KG: Berlin, Munich, 1995.

Rademann, Tobias: Characteristic Features of Stock-Exchange Reports. Working Paper. Ruhr-University Bochum, 1996.

Wessels, Dieter: "'Markets strong on revived interest rate optimism. Gilts active – equity index up 11.1' – Das Börsengeschehen im Spiegel der englischen und amerikanischen Wirtschaftspresse." *A&E (Anglistik und Englischunterricht)*. Vol. 21., 1983, 61-86.

Jens P. Becker, Kiel

The Go-Between: Vom Roman zum Film

Programm

"My sagacious readers will not need to be told that a film of a novel is to be judged on its merits as a film and not on fidelity to its original", schrieb Dilys Powell 1943 in ihrer Kritik zu *Jane Eyre.* Diese *en passant* gemachte Bemerkung (Powell, 330) ist sicher auch ein Programm der Filmkritikerin gewesen, die in ihrer 50jährigen Tätigkeit für die *Sunday Times* (1939-1989) der Filmkritik eine neue Dimension gegeben hat, und die nicht müde wurde, den Status der neuen Kunstform Film gegenüber der alten Kunstform Literatur zu verteidigen. Ich möchte mir Powells Zitat als Programm borgen und dem Leser damit auch eine endlose und unfruchtbare allgemeine Abhandlung zum Thema Literatur/Film ersparen. Seit Lester Asheims Dissertation (1949) und George Bluestones Klassiker *Novels into Film* (1957) ist hier eine kaum noch überschaubare Literatur entstanden, die selbst von einer so ausführlichen Bibliographie wie der von Harris Ross (1987) kaum vollständig wiedergegeben wird. Als konziseste Einführung in die Problematik kann Franz-Josef Albersmeiers Einleitung zu dem interdisziplinären Suhrkamp-Band *Literaturverfilmungen* (1989) empfohlen werden (und sicher ist auch Joachim Paechs Buch in der Sammlung Metzler hilfreich). Ohne theoretische Arbeiten wie z.B. Irmela Schneiders *Der verwandelte Text: Wege zu einer Theorie der Literaturverfilmung* (1981) herabwürdigen zu wollen, kann man mit Albersmeier konstatieren: "So sinnvoll solche Typologien sind, so schwer tun wir uns mit ihnen, wenn es gilt, eine konkrete Literaturverfilmung einzuordnen" (Albersmeier, 22). Praktikable Wege zur Vermeidung der Theorie-Falle scheinen Bücher wie z.B. Brian McFarlanes *Novel to Film: An Introduction to the Theory of Adaptation* (1996) zu bieten, in dem anstelle der Theoriediskussion eine Anzahl von "case studies" die Mechanismen der Adaption verdeutlichen, wenn man so will, eine Rückkehr zu Bluestone.

Eine objektive Diskussion zum Thema Literatur/Film wird durch einige insinuierte oder ausgesprochene Grundannahmen, die immer wieder vorgebracht werden, erschwert. Immer und immer wieder ist von "Werktreue" die Rede, immer wieder wird die Literaturvorlage als künstlerisch überlegen und der Film als inferior dargestellt (oder in den Augen von Cineasten vice versa). Und immer wieder scheinen die Theoretiker im alleinigen Besitz der Wahrheit zu sein. Nur sie wissen, wie das jeweilige Werk zu lesen ist und wie es verfilmt werden soll. Vielleicht wären diese Theoretiker mit dem glücklich, was James Agee einmal beiläufig und ironisch als "a good faithful adaption of *Adam Bede* in sepia, with the entire text read offscreen by Herbert Marshall" (Agee, 216) bezeichnet hat. Ich möchte im folgenden die Verfilmung von L.P. Hartleys *The Go-Between* unter ausgesuchten Aspekten nachzeichnen, um die Probleme einer Romanverfilmung zu verdeutlichen. Ich habe *The Go-Between* als Beispiel gewählt, weil hier der Weg vom Buch zum Film ungewöhnlich und einmalig ist ("an unusually close transcription of a novel in cinematic terms" [*Oxford Companion to Film*, 292]), und ich habe mit der Auswahl auch im Auge, daß man Roman, Drehbuch und Film durchaus im Unterricht behandeln kann.

Text

L.P. Hartleys Roman *The Go-Between* (1953 [hier zitiert nach der Penguin-Ausgabe von 1987]) erhielt 1954 den Heinemann Foundation Prize der Royal Society of Literature, und der Roman ist (woran die Verfilmung vielleicht nicht ganz unschuldig ist) beim Lesepublikum der beliebteste Roman eines heute leider ein wenig unterschätzten Autors geblieben. Der Roman entführt uns in das Jahr 1900, eine "recherche du temps perdu". Nicht nur die für eine Epoche symbolische Jahreszahl markiert das Thema "Zeit", ein Thema, das Hartley mit Proust und Powell (*A Dance to the Music of Time*) gemein hat. Mit an Henry James geschulter psychologisch feiner Charakter- und Detailschilderung entwirft Hartley das Bild des dreizehnjährigen Leo Colston, der im heißen Sommer des Jahres 1900 von Marian, der Schwester seines Schulfreundes Marcus Maudsley, zu einem *postillon d'amour*, einem "go-between" zwischen dem Landsitz der Maudsleys und dem Farmer Ted Burgess gemacht wird. Klassengegensätze der edwardianischen Gesellschaft, Landschafts- und Naturbeschreibungen, die Schilderung eines Cricketspiels zwischen Brandham Hall und den Dorfbewohnern: der Roman vereint alle Klischees der edwardianischen "Englishness", die uns heute von Merchant/Ivory auf Celluloid präsentiert werden. Der Entwicklungsroman hat mit dem Jahr 1952 eine zweite Zeitebene, hier öffnet der Erzähler zum ersten Mal sein Tagebuch des schicksalhaften Sommers, hier wird der 65jährige Lionel Colston bei einem Besuch in Brandham zum letzten Mal zu einem "go-between", um zwischen Marian und ihrem Enkel zu vermitteln (die Inhaltsangabe von *Kindlers Literatur Lexikon* ist an diesem Punkt leider irreführend). Kritiker wie John Betjeman und Walter Allen haben den komplexen Roman gelobt und ihn in der "great tradition" englischer Romankunst gesehen.

Filmgeschichte

Dank der Bemühungen der BBC und des Gespannes Merchant/Ivory werden Bildschirm und Leinwand seit Jahren mit "Kostümfilmen" überflutet, die uns mehr oder weniger akkurat eine spezifische Epoche wiedergeben, und die in den meisten Fällen Literaturverfilmungen sind (die auch dafür sorgen, daß Autoren wie Jane Austen oder E.M. Forster neue Leser finden). Häufig täuschen die Ausstattungsorgien darüber hinweg, daß die Bilder leer bleiben, die Literaturverfilmung wird, wie z.B. bei Russells *Lady Chatterley's Lover,* auf eine Art Photoroman reduziert. Als Joseph Losey *The Go-Between* dreht, befindet er sich in direkter Konkurrenz zu Visconti: *Tod in Venedig* erscheint gleichzeitig mit *The Go-Between* in den Kinos. Visconti hatte schon 1963 mit *Il Gattopardo* eine maßstabsetzende Literaturverfilmung vorgelegt und damit eine Art Retro-Kino begründet, gleichzeitig war in England *Tom Jones* erschienen. Bo Widerbergs *Elvira Madigan* (1967) wurde zu einem Welterfolg, der das Publikum nach schön photographierten vergangenen Epochen geradezu lechzen ließ. Literaturverfilmungen wie *Far from the Madding Crowd* (Schlesinger 1967), *Women in Love* (Russell 1969), *The Virgin and the Gypsy* (Miles 1970), *The Devils* (Russell 1971), *The Hireling* (Bridges 1973) und *Barry Lyndon* (Kubrick 1975) entstanden in rascher Folge. *The Go-Between* kann als ein Teil einer neuen Retro-Bewegung des englischen Kinos verstanden werden, die über *The French Lieutenant's Woman* (Reisz 1981), *Chariots of Fire* (Hudson 1981), *Amadeus* (Forman 1984) und *The Shooting Party* (Miles 1984) direkt zu Merchant und Ivory führt. Allerdings haben nicht alle Filme die kritische Distanz, die Losey zu seinem Gegenstand entwickelt (Pauline Kael spricht hier von "Losey's need to condemn the decadence that attracts him" [Kael, 320]). In Frankreich wird Bertrand Tavernier, der zu Loseys frühesten und wortgewaltigsten Bewunderern zählt, den Stil von Loseys intellektuellem "period piece" mit *Un dimanche à la campagne* (1984) weiterführen. Bei diesem Film könnte man filmhistorisch auch den Einfluß von Renoir annehmen, muß aber hinzufügen, daß Renoir auch als Einfluß für Losey (und vielleicht auch für Hartley) gesehen werden kann. Die Kritik hat immer wieder auf den Zusammenhang von *La règle du jeu* (1939) und *The Go-Between* hingewiesen.

Autor

Beinahe alle Spielfilme sind in irgendeiner Weise "Literatur"-Verfilmungen, da sie, wenn sie nicht die Klassiker der Weltliteratur verfilmen, eine irgendwie geartete literarische Basis haben, eine Kurzgeschichte eines unbekannten Autors, ein Theaterstück von Amateurschriftstellern (*Cas-*

ablanca), ein Motiv aus einer literarischen Vorlage. Seit der Entstehung des Films als neuer Kunstform blicken Autoren auf Hollywood, machen sich filmische Techniken zu eigen (John Fowles hat das in seinen Notizen zur Entstehung von *The French Lieutenant's Woman* ausgeführt) oder schreiben Romane so, daß die einkalkulierte Verfilmung keine großen Schwierigkeiten bereitet (*Publisher's Weekly* sprach schon 1917 von "cinema novels"). Albert Van Nostrand, der 1960 mit *The Denatured Novel* den Niedergang des Romans beklagte, hat hier mit "Hollywood Pay-Off" ein lesenswertes Kapitel über das Verhältnis der Schriftsteller zur Filmindustrie. Autoren können versuchen, in ihren Verlagsverträgen die Filmrechte an ihre Zustimmung und beratende Mitwirkung zu binden (je berühmter sie sind, desto besser werden die vertraglichen Konditionen sein). Die Mitarbeit des Autors an einer Literaturverfilmung kann zu einer gelungenen Verfilmung führen, man denke an Fowles' Rolle bei der Verfilmung von *The French Lieutenant's Woman* (Volker Behrens hat in seiner Dissertation über die Verfilmung diesen Aspekt sorgfältig dokumentiert). Joseph Losey suchte, wie bei all seinen Filmen, schon früh den Kontakt zu dem Autor ("getting relevant additional material from L.P. Hartley" [Ciment, 241]), und Hartley hatte ihm in einem Brief die autobiographische Basis des Sommers in Norfolk im Jahre 1911 erläutert:

> The house where I actually stayed as a boy was Bradenham Hall in Norfolk, somewhere between Wendling and East Dereham... It belonged to the Rider Haggard family, who had let it to some well-known coal merchants called Moxey: their son was my school friend, who asked me to stay... All I can remember of the house was a double staircase, the cedar tree in the garden, and the Deadly Nightshade in an outhouse. (Caute, 253)

Informationen dieser Art sind sicherlich reizvoll, aber ist das "relevant additional material" wirklich so relevant? Ohne mit New Critics et al. den Tod des Autors apostrophieren zu wollen, könnten wir bei Literaturverfilmungen, die wie bei *The Go-Between* einen extrem der Werktreue verpflichteten Drehbuchautor und Regisseur (Kritiker haben Losey immer wieder vorgeworfen, daß er sich infolge seiner engen Zusammenarbeit mit den Autoren geradezu abhängig von ihnen machte) haben, sicher auf den Autor verzichten. Die groß publizierte Anwesenheit des Autors bei den Dreharbeiten dient häufig nur Werbezwecken. Hartley konnte einer Aufführung von Pinters *The Dumb Waiter* und *The Room*, zu der man ihn eingeladen hatte, damit er das Werk des Drehbuchautors kennenlernte, nichts abgewinnen. Er war aber später von Pinters erstem Drehbuchentwurf (1964) sehr beeindruckt und verfolgte die Dreharbeiten mit lebhaftem Interesse.

Kommerz

Literaturverfilmungen sind kommerzielle Unternehmungen, ein Aspekt, der von den Theoretikern der Literaturverfilmung gerne ausgeklammert wird. Selbst wenn Regisseur, Drehbuchautor und Kameramann sich nur der reinen Werktreue-Vision des Philologen verschrieben haben (und *The Go-Between* wäre eins dieser seltenen Beispiele), muß doch das Vorhaben finanziert werden. Studio, Produzent, Literaturagenten etc. bringen ihre eigenen Forderungen mit – und plötzlich haben wir in der Stummfilmfassung von *Moby-Dick* eine Liebeshandlung, die wir in Melvilles Text nicht entdecken können. Die amerikanische *New Yorker*-Autorin Lillian Ross hat mit ihrem Buch *Picture* (1952) die Entstehung von John Hustons Literaturverfilmung *The Red Badge of Courage* in allen Details verfolgt und nachgezeichnet. Die Lektüre dieses Buches kann immer wieder empfohlen werden, um die Dimensionen des Einflusses zu verdeutlichen, die der Kommerz auf die Werktreue-Vision hat. Für Losey war *The Go-Between* ein acht Jahre langer Kampf gegen Literaturagenten, Besitzer von Anteilsrechten, Produzenten und Studiobosse. Ursprünglich hatte Alexander Korda die Rechte gekauft, aber wie Hartley vermutete: "he never meant to make a film of the book[...] I was so annoyed when I learned this that I put a curse on him, and he died almost the next morning" (Caute, 254) – offensichtlich besaß Hartley ähnliche Fähigkeiten im Bereich der Magie, die seinen jugendlichen Helden im Roman auszeichnen. Losey war schon bevor *The Servant* in die Kinos kam an Pinter herangetreten und hatte ihm Hartleys Roman ans Herz gelegt. Pinter antwortete damals: "I think *The Go-Between* is superb... it's wonderful. But I can't write a film script of it. I can't touch it. It's too painful, too perfect, if you know what I mean" (Caute, 254). Pinter begann einen ersten Entwurf, aber im Sommer 1964 kam das Projekt zum Stillstand, da sich (ähnlich wie bei der Visconti-Verfilmung von *Tod in Venedig*) ein neuer Besitzer der Rechte meldete. Der Prozeß um die Filmrechte wurde erst 1968 beendet. Ein Jahr der schwierigsten Finanzierungsverhandlungen sollte folgen, bevor die Dreharbeiten beginnen konnten. Der Drehbuchautor Pinter verdiente an dem Film mit 75.000 Pfund mehr als der Regisseur (20.000) und alle Nebendarsteller (30.000) zusammen. Wir haben hier den für Literaturverfilmungen seltenen Fall, daß die Posten "story rights" und "writers" mit 145.000 Pfund den größten Teil des Filmbudgets ausmachen. Der Darsteller des kleinen Leo Colston, Dominic Guard, erhielt lediglich 1.000 Pfund. L.P. Hartley war zwar mit seinem Gewinn nicht zufrieden, mußte sich aber von Losey zurechtweisen lassen, daß Regisseur und eine großer Teil der Schauspieler für "no cash at all" gearbeitet hätten und daß Hartley ja noch mit Neuauflagen und Neuübersetzungen rechnen könne. Losey hatte 1964 Julie Christie für die Rolle der Marian haben wollen, 1970 erschien sie ihm trotz "a kind of freshness that might work" (Ciment, 240) zu alt. Aber der Financier des Filmes, der spätere Lord Delfont, bestand auf dem Weltstar Julie Christie, die nun mit dreißig eine Zwanzigjährige spielen mußte. Wenn wir Julie Christie in diesem Film mit der Rolle der Marian Maudsley identifizieren, dann ist das sicher ein Glücksfall. Was hätte passieren können, wenn der EMI-Chef Delfont eine andere Schauspielerin favorisiert hätte? Unzählige Literaturverfilmungen sind dadurch ruiniert worden, daß Produzenten ihre Freundinnen im Film unterbrachten. Aber auch der 75jährige Hartley, der seine Beteiligung an den Filmarbeiten sichtlich genoß, wurde nicht müde, alle möglichen Blondinen aus seinem Bekanntenkreis für die Rolle der Marian zu empfehlen. Der wunderbare Name Bernard Delfont kann nicht über den etwas zweifelhaften Charakter des Mannes hinwegtäuschen, dessen eigentlicher Name Boris Winogradsky war und der neben seinem Bruder Lew Grade (dem späteren Lord Grade of Elstree) der mächtigste Mann in der englischen Filmindustrie war. Im Gegensatz zu seinem Bruder, der große Verdienste als Financier des englischen Films der 70er Jahre hatte, war Delfont kaum an künstlerischen Dingen interessiert. Losey hat Delfont immer gehaßt (der Fairness halber sollte man sagen, daß Lew Grade in seiner Autobiographie *Still Dancing* das Bild eines liebenswerten Lord Delfont zeichnet). Eine kleine Episode am Ende der Dreharbeiten mag Delfonts Geiz beleuchten: er organisierte eine "Royal Premiere" in Norwich mit der Anwesenheit der Königinmutter, Hartleys und Pinters, stellte dann aber die Kosten der Mitorganisatorin Lady Harrod vom Council for the Protection of Rural England in Rechnung.

Actors

Theaterstücke erleben vielfältige Realisationen, jede Inszenierung ist eine eigene Interpretation des Textes, jede Inszenierung hat andere Darsteller, die unserer Vorstellung von der idealen Rollenbesetzung entgegenkommen oder nicht. Romane werden meist nur ein einziges Mal verfilmt, selten können wir aus mehreren Verfilmungen eine ideale Verfilmung auswählen. Opernfreunde haben die Wahl aus einer Vielzahl von Inszenierungen auf CD, bei Romanen müssen wir mit einer Verfilmung vorliebnehmen, auch wenn sie uns als eine Ansammlung von Fehlbesetzungen erscheint. Spätestens seit Wolfgang Iser wissen wir, daß:

> Die Eigenart des Vorstellungsbildes [...] sich dort besonders fassen [läßt], wo man die Verfilmung eines gelesenen Romans sieht. Denn hier habe ich eine optische Wahrnehmung, die vor dem Hintergrund

meiner Erinnerung an Vorstellungsbilder steht. Der spontane Eindruck, der sich bei der Verfilmung von *Tom Jones* einstellt, beinhaltet eine gewisse Enttäuschung über die relative Armut der Figur im Vergleich zu jenem Bild, das man sich von ihr bei der Lektüre gemacht hatte. (Iser, 222-223)

Chandler stellte sich Philip Marlowe eher wie Cary Grant vor, wir kennen ihn als Humphrey Bogart. James Bond ist bei Fleming sicherlich ein anderer als Sean Connery, aber an den haben wir uns so gewöhnt, daß wir Moore, Lazenby, Dalton und Brosnan als schlechte Kopien empfinden. Basil Rathbone erscheint uns als Sherlock Holmes akzeptabel, Heinz Rühmann als Maigret nicht. Robert Redford könnte Jay Gatsby sein, aber ist Tim Roth Conrads Marlow? Wir haben feste Vorstellungen von unseren Romancharakteren, allerdings hat jeder Leser seine eigenen Vorstellungen. Im Gegensatz zur Oper, wo uns "the willing suspension of disbelief" unsäglich dicke Primadonnen als Susanna nur wegen der Stimme ertragen läßt, sind wir bei Romanverfilmungen nicht zu Kompromissen bereit, ein Punkt, den viele Adaptionstheorien aussparen. Es kann lehrreich sein, bei der Behandlung im Unterricht eine ideale Besetzungliste zu erstellen und zu diskutieren, warum (oder warum nicht) der betreffende Schauspieler die ideale Verkörperung eines Romancharakters ist. Für Leo/Lionel Colston bietet *The Go-Between* mit dem 16jährigen Dominic Guard und dem 62jährigen Michael Redgrave in beiden Fällen eine gute Wahl. Wir können akzeptieren, daß der Film das Alter von Leo von 13 auf 16 ändert, die Ebene der Initiationsgeschichte wird durch das Pubertätsalter (auch Hartley war in jenem Sommer in Norfolk sechzehn) noch akzentuiert. Michael Redgraves abweisende Körpersprache, seine regungslose Mimik, illustrieren den "foreigner in the world of emotions" (280). Nebenrollen in Literaturverfilmungen sind häufig besser besetzt als die Hauptrollen, hier kann der Regisseur noch auswählen, die Hauptrollen schreibt ihm das Studio vor. Die Nebenrollen von *The Go-Between* sind ohne Zweifel hervorragend besetzt: Margaret Leighton als Mrs. Maudsley (die eine Oscar-Nominierung erhielt und zu Recht Deborah Kerr vorgezogen wurde), Michael Gough als Mr. Maudsley und Edward Fox als Lord Trimingham. Der Sohn von Loseys Agenten Robin Fox – sein Bruder spielte die Hauptrolle in *The Servant* – ist von nun an für den Rest seiner Karriere die Inkarnation des aristokratischen Engländers, auch wenn die Narben des Maskenbildners die Entstellung durch die Verletzung im Burenkrieg (61) von Viscount Trimingham schönen (Caute, 258). Der Schauspieler Alan Bates ist einer der wenigen, denen der Übergang von Bühne zum Film jederzeit gelungen ist, sein Ted Burgess wurde von allen Kritikern gelobt. Bates kam mit Losey, der wahrlich kein Regisseur war, der gut mit Schauspielern umgehen konnte, sehr gut zurecht, er empfand auch Loseys und Pinters Rollenvorgaben als hilfreich. Das einzige Problem bei der Besetzung stellte Julie Christie dar (die schon mit Bates in einer anderen viktorianischen Liebesgeschichte, *Far from the Madding Crowd*, gespielt hatte), denn sie war inzwischen für die Rolle zu alt und lehnte aus diesem Grund den Part der Marian zunächst ab (1964 war sie bereit gewesen, die Rolle zu spielen). Sie hatte 1965 schon einen Oscar für ihre Rolle in *Darling* erhalten, die Verfilmung von *Doctor Zhivago* (1965) machte sie zum Weltstar. Losey hat sich in Interviews herablassend über ihre Schauspielkunst geäußert (Dirk Bogarde war da anderer Meinung [Bogarde, 243-245]), aber es gibt kaum Schauspielerinnen, über die sich Losey nicht negativ geäußert hätte. Julie Christie erhielt mit 50.000 Pfund Gage mehr als alle anderen Schauspieler zusammen. Aber auch noch ein Vierteljahrhundert nach der Premiere kann man sagen, daß sie das Geld wert war, da sie die Schönheit und sexuelle Berechnung (Ciment, 308-309) sicherlich besser zum Ausdruck bringt als Mia Farrow, eine von Loseys Wunschkandidatinnen, es gekonnt hätte. Es ehrt Losey, daß er vom Starsystem der Studios wegwollte und den Film mit gänzlich unbekannten Schauspielern drehen wollte (Ciment, 240), aber er hat in *The Go-Between* wie schon zuvor in *The Servant* eine ideale Kombination von Stars und Neulingen gefunden.

Regie

Der Amerikaner Joseph Losey (1909-1984) wurde nach dem Erfolg von *The Servant* (1963) und *Accident* (1967) in Europa zu einem Kultregisseur. Zu diesem Zeitpunkt konnte er schon auf eine lange Karriere als Schauspieler, Theaterregisseur (man denke an seine *Galileo Galilei*-Inszenierung mit Charles Laughton im Jahre 1947), Hollywoodregisseur und Opfer der McCarthy-Hexenjagd zurückblicken. England als selbstgewähltes Exil brachte für die Filme des Gesellschaftskritikers eine Thematisierung des englischen Klassensystems. Und der Zusammenarbeit mit Harold Pinter, für den die absurden Nuancen der englischen Gesellschaft ein ständiges Thema sind, verdanken wir neben *The Go-Between* zwei weitere hervorragende Literaturverfilmungen, *The Servant* und *Accident.* Joseph Losey ist als Regisseur für Literaturverfilmungen sicherlich ein Glücksfall, ein vielseitig begabter und belesener Intellektueller, der schon im Todesjahr von Proust *Du cotê de chez Swann* las, der den ganzen Conrad gelesen hatte (viele Kritiker fühlten sich bei Losey-Filmen an Conrad erinnert) und davon träumte, *Nostromo* zu verfilmen. Der davon träumte, das Unmögliche zu versuchen und Prousts *A la recherche du temps perdu* zu verfilmen. Joseph Losey ist niemals "an actor's director" gewesen, jemand, der auf die Sorgen und Nöte der Schauspieler einging. Von all seinen Darstellern ist wahrscheinlich Dirk Bogarde sein einziger Freund geblieben. Losey war ein Regisseur, der abstrakt in Bildern denken konnte. Er brauchte für seine Filme kein "story board" als Vermittlungsinstanz zwischen Text und Bild wie viele seiner Kollegen (die Funktion des "story board" wird bei Theorien der Literaturverfilmung viel zu wenig beachtet). Losey wußte als Regisseur auch genau, was die Kamera konnte (Ciment, 156-157), und die Zusammenarbeit mit seinen Kameraleuten wie Douglas Slocombe (*The Servant*) und Gerry Fisher (*Accident*, *The Go-Between*, *M. Klein*) ist ihm sehr wichtig gewesen. Losey zeigt in den 60er Jahren die Handschrift eines *auteur* (Caute, 328-336), der die vollständige Kontrolle über alle Bereiche des Films hat, sein Kontrollieren der kleinsten technischen Details konnte seine Crew zur Verzweiflung bringen. Er wird zum Liebling der französischen Filmkritik, insbesonders der junge Tavernier propagierte den Ruhm seines Idols und ist später als Regisseur nicht unbeeinflußt von Losey geblieben (man vergleiche *The Go-Between* mit *Un dimanche à la campagne,* und vielleicht ist *Daddy Nostalgie* mit Loseys Lieblingsschauspieler Dirk Bogarde auch eine Hommage an Losey). In Deutschland galt man 1968 in cineastischen Zirkeln nichts, wenn man nicht mindestens dreimal *Accident* gesehen hatte. Die deutsche Begeisterung für Losey ist von Georg Alexander, Peter W. Jansen und Wolfram Schütte in dem *Joseph Losey*-Band der Reihe Hanser liebevoll dokumentiert. Losey hat Tom Milne (1967), Wolfram Schütte (1976) und Michel Ciment (1979) in langen Interviews als Interpret seines Werkes zur Verfügung gestanden. Die umfang- und detailreichste Biographie, *Joseph Losey: A Revenge on Life*, von David Caute ist 1994 bei Faber erschienen.

Drehbuch

Drehbuchautoren genießen kein großes Ansehen, ein gescheiterter Drehbuchautor, F. Scott Fitzgerald, hat das mit seiner literarischen Figur Pat Hobby deutlich gemacht. Manchmal können Romanciers Drehbücher schreiben, Faulkner wäre ein Beispiel. Häufig fällt es Dramatikern leichter, Ben Hecht und Charles MacArthur haben das gezeigt. Aber es gibt auch berühmte Drehbuchautoren wie Dalton Trumbo, die zuvor nicht literarisch hervorgetreten sind. Und sicherlich gibt es auch Filmregisseure, die ihre eigenen Drehbücher schreiben, was Losey selbst als ein Unding empfand (Caute, 333). Drehbücher gehörten lange Zeit schon deshalb nicht zu einer literarischen Gattung, weil sie nicht veröffentlicht wurden; die französische Reihe *l'Avant-Scène* war viele Jahre lang das einzige, auf das Cineasten zurückgreifen konnten. In den letzten 25 Jahren hat hier eine radikale Umwälzung stattgefunden, man kann sich beinahe vor publizierten Drehbüchern nicht mehr retten (sogar das Internet enthält ganze Skripts wie z.B. Tarrantinos *Pulp Fiction*). Das Drehbuch hat als “Lesefilm” literarischen Rang bekommen, und Harold Pinter, dessen erste fünf Drehbücher im gleichen Jahr wie *The Go-Between* erschienen, steht wegbereitend am Anfang der Neubewertung einer unterbewerteten Literaturform (Behrens, 166-179). Pinters Zusammenarbeit mit Losey von *The Servant* bis zu dem nicht realisierten Proust-Projekt, von dem wir allerdings Pinters Drehbuch besitzen (*The Proust Screenplay*, 1977), ist eine erstaunliche künstlerische Symbiose zweier grundverschiedener Charaktere. Pinter entdeckte in dieser Zusammenarbeit, daß seine Art Theaterstücke zu schreiben, ihn für bestimmte Literaturverfilmungen prädestinierte. Insbesonders Schauspieler waren von seinen Drehbüchern angetan. So schreibt Dirk Bogarde:

> Pinter doesn’t give you instructions like a packet of instant minestrone. The instructions are implicit in the words he offers so sparingly for his characters to speak. There is a popular and far too widely-held belief among many actors, and directors too (not to mention critics) that Pinter writes pauses. I don’t think that he does. But I do think that he is one of the few writers who are brilliant in the text they *don’t* write. His pauses are merely the time-phases which he gives you so that you may develop the thought behind the line he has written, and to alert your mind itself to the dangerous simplicities of the lines to come… (Bogarde, 235).

Allerdings mußte Pinter auch mitansehen, daß seine hochpolierten literarischen Kunstwerke, wie sie uns in der gedruckten Form begegnen, nicht immer vom Regisseur (oder Produzenten) honoriert wurden. Die Geschichte der Zusammenarbeit von Pinter und Losey ist auch eine Geschichte von heftigen künstlerischen Auseinandersetzungen. Für die Wiedergabe der beiden Zeitebenen des Romans hatte Pinter ein komplexes System ersonnen, das die Handlung der 50er Jahre durch Bilder oder Ton im Off in den Film interpolierte (Caute, 261) – bei dem Drehbuch zu *The French Lieutenant’s Woman* sollte er ähnlich vorgehen. Studio und Geldgeber wollten diese Stellen bis zuletzt aus dem Film streichen (Caute, 261-261), einige Passagen, die durchaus sinnkonstituierend waren (Caute, 262-263), wurden geopfert. Dieses irritierende Sich-Einmengen eines “zweiten Films” in die Filmhandlung des ersten (Jansen, 144-146) geht weit über eine konventionelle Rahmenerzählung hinaus, ist aber durch den Text, der ja Erinnerung thematisiert, gerechtfertigt (Caute, 306). Es spricht für Losey und seinen Respekt gegenüber Pinters Drehbuch, daß er von Pinters Konzeption, die dem Zuschauer einiges abverlangt, so viel wie möglich gegen den Widerstand des Studios gerettet hat (Caute, 264-

265). Aber Losey wußte auch, was er an Pinter hatte, selbst wenn der mittlerweile weltberühmte Dramatiker als Drehbuchautor noch ein Novize war (Walker, 215-216). Losey hat immer wieder betont, daß die Drehbücher, die Pinter für ihn geschrieben habe, besser als seine übrigen Drehbücher seien (Ciment, 242). Und obgleich er Pinter visuelles Denken absprach ("I don't think he has any visual sense at all" [Ciment 242]), betonte er: "his writing is always visually evocative, but at the same time it gives me a great deal of room" (Ciment, 242). Offensichtlich enthält der Text nicht nur kreative Pausen für den Schauspieler, sondern auch jene Leerstellen, die den visuell denkenden Regisseur herausfordern. Kino ist neben den Bildern eine Welt der Emotionen, Kafka hat im Kino geweint ("Im Kino gewesen. Geweint", Güttinger, 162), Thomas Mann hat im Kino geweint ("Sagen Sie mir doch, warum man im Cinema jeden Augenblick weint oder vielmehr heult wie ein Dienstmädchen", Güttinger, 264). Pinters scheinbar objektiv-kühler Text täuscht über die Emotionen des Schriftstellers hinweg. Pinter hat bei der ersten Lektüre von *The Go-Between* geweint (Caute, 254) und hatte sich vor dem Drehbuch gefürchtet, weil er dann über Monate hinaus dauernd in Tränen aufgelöst wäre (Jansen, 141).

Film

Die erste Phase der Filmforschung der deutschen Anglistik hatte sich auf die Edition von Drehbüchern und Filmskripts (es sei an die Reihe des Gunter Narr-Verlags erinnert) konzentriert. Hierbei ging es um die Etablierung einer zitierbaren Basis für die Filmanalyse. An dieser Stelle kann aus Platzgründen weder eine Filmtranskription noch eine Sequenzanalyse geleistet werden (dennoch könnte man im Unterricht mit ausgewählten Filmstellen so vorgehen). Sequenzanalysen, die wie ein "close reading" eines literarischen Textes sehr ergiebig sein können, liegen für einzelne Filme vor, als Beispiel sei auf Band 36 dieser Zeitschrift (*a&e* 36, 147-169) und Behrens (Behrens, 104-151) verwiesen. David Caute hat in seiner Losey-Biographie einen "running commentary" zu dem Film (Caute, 266-273), der auch als Basis einer Analyse dienen kann. Mittlerweile ist (ähnlich wie in der Erzählforschung) das filmische Erzählen in den Mittelpunkt des Interesses gerückt, David Bordwell hat hier mit *Narration in the Fiction Film* Pionierarbeit geleistet. Man kann in *The Go-Between* verfolgen, wie stark sich die Kamera an der Perspektive des kleinen Leo orientiert und geradezu voyeurhaft Gesellschaft und Raum erkundet (Ciment, 308). Die erste Begegnung Leos mit Marian zeigt in komplizierten Einstellungen ein schüchternes Annähern. Das Bild Marians taucht später, unvermittelt in den Film montiert, als bleibende Erinnerung Leos wieder auf (und es wird am Filmende ebenso verwendet werden). Losey ist ein Regisseur, der mehr auf das Stilmittel der "mise-en-scène" als das der Montage vertraut, was an manchen Stellen sehr komplizierte Kombinationen von "crane shots" und Zoom-Einstellungen verlangte (Ciment, 310-311). Lange Kameraeinstellungen geben ein Gefühl von Ruhe, lediglich die "nervöse Sensibilität" (Jansen, 142) des Zooms zeigt die trügerische Ruhe, in der sich die selbstgefällige edwardianische Gesellschaft bewegt. Die Kamera präsentiert, wie die Perspektive des Romans das Außen, das der Außenseiter Leo sieht. Dieses "Außen" wird derart enervierend perfekt dargeboten, daß der Zuschauer für die Welt dahinter sensibilisiert wird: "because all these sensual details are so physically realized you end up hearing the unsaid, seeing the unseen" (Walker, 439). Komplizierte Erzählperspektiven wie bei Henry James, Joseph Conrad oder William Faulkner empfand Losey als Herausforderung für das Kino: "But it's the kind of thing the cinema can do, and the cinema is rarely used for the things it's cut out to do. And that's what interests me (Ciment, 306). Losey war sich darüber im klaren, daß sein persönlicher Erzählstil mit langen Kamerafahrten, "mise-en-scène" und dem Verweilen auf Räumen, die die Personen längst verlassen haben, ein Publikum überfordern könne. Aber als ein selbstloser Diener der literarischen Vorlage bestand er gleichzeitig auf der Ausschöpfung der Möglichkeiten der Sprache des Films, und glaubte auch daran, durch den Einsatz von experimentellen Mitteln innerhalb einer traditionellen Struktur das Publikum erziehen zu können (Ciment, 306). Loseys Stilmittel (am besten dargestellt bei Caute, 328-336) haben ihm nicht nur positive Kritiken beschert. Manche Kritiker empfanden seine filmischen Mittel als manieriert, wobei sie verkennen, daß Losey immer nur auf der Suche nach einer kinematographisch-visuellen Wahrheit war: "I think more and more the film medium is [...] not a novel, not the conventional Hollywood screenwriter's form, it is a visual form [...] In other words a form in which images take the place of words [...] And you never use a word when you can use an image" (Caute, 334-335).

Camera

Kameraleute haben (ähnlich wie Drehbuchautoren) lange Zeit im Verborgenen leben müssen, sie waren kein Teil von Hollywoods Starsystem. Aber ohne Gregg Toland wären *Wuthering Heights* und *Citizen Kane* nicht die Kunstwerke, die sie sind. Ohne Eugen Schüfftan gäbe es den "poetischen Realismus" von Marcel Carné nicht: die Liste der Kameraleute, die Filme stärker als der Regisseur geprägt haben, ist lang. Dem versierten Techniker Losey ist immer bewußt gewesen, welche Leistung seine Kameraleute (sowohl der "director of photography" als der "camera operator") erbrachten, und er hat sich in den Interviews mit Milne, Schütte und Ciment sehr ausführlich und detailversessen über die technisch-handwerklichen und künstlerischen Qualitäten seiner Kameraleute ausgelassen. Dem Kameramann von *The Go-Between*, Gerry Fisher, schrieb Losey nach den Dreharbeiten: "In fact I think it is the best photographic work of its kind that I have ever seen" (Caute, 260). Losey hatte in seinen Arbeitsnotizen für den Film folgende Vorgabe:

> The picture should look hot and like a slighty faded Renoir or Constable – the colours mostly gold and brown, the green minimized as much as possible under the circumstances. The skies and their clouds and the peculiar light of Norfolk [...] also the chiaroscuro of the corridors and secret passages [...] the present day sequences should stand out photographically. Whether this is done by filter or optically or with a change of raw stock [...] They should all at least be in dull weather [...] cold in tone [...] as against the dream-like quality of the 1900 story. (Caute, 259-260)

Gerry Fisher fühlte sich bei den Dreharbeiten an seine Kindheit auf dem Lande erinnert (Caute, 260), und sicherlich ist ihm die Evokation einer pastoralen "temps perdu" technisch hervorragend gelungen. Für den Film ließ Losey Fisher viele Freiheiten, und bei der engen Zusammenarbeit von Regisseur und Kameramann läßt es sich schwer entscheiden, ob die Stilelemente des Films wie "mise-en-scène", Einsatz des Zoom, lange Kamerafahrten und innere Montage auf Losey oder Fisher zurückgehen. Wenn das Kunstmittel des Zoom-Einsatzes – man kann hier beinahe von einem "foregrounding" sprechen – wohl auf Fishers Rechnung geht (Jansen, 141-142), so hat Losey dies Stilmittel (das er für nicht unbedenklich hielt [Caute, 260]) doch ästhetisch verteidigt (Ciment, 310-311).

Soundtrack

Manche Romane enthalten Musik, Prousts *A la recherche du temps perdu* lebt von der wiederkehrenden Sonate von Vinteuil. Viele Romane enthalten keinerlei Musik, aber alle Literaturverfilmungen enthalten einen musikalischen Soundtrack. Filmmusik ist ein Relikt aus der Zeit des Stummfilms, als noch Orchester beschäftigt wurden, um die Verbindung zwischen den Bildern zu verdeutlichen und die dargestellten Emotionen zu unterstreichen (Güttinger, 280-282; Pauli, 179-230) – und vielleicht auch um das laute Geräusch des Filmvorführungsgeräts zu übertönen. Obwohl Filmmusik ein Wesensmerkmal des Spielfilms zu sein scheint, tun sich Theoretiker des Films mit ihr schwer (Dadek, 23-24), Theoretiker der Literaturverfilmungen gehen so gut wie nie auf das Phänomen ein. Losey hätte die Musik von Elgar nehmen können (Visconti nimmt Mahler für *Tod in Venedig*), aber er will keine Musik aus der Zeit der Jahrhundertwende, er will etwas Modernes, Verfremdendes. Die Filmmusik von Richard Rodney Bennett, der die Musik für *Far from the Madding Crowd* und zwei Losey-Filme geschrieben hatte, wird verworfen. Losey schwebt abstrakte Jazzmusik vor, als er Michel Legrand (der die Musik zu Loseys *Eva* geschrieben hatte) mit der Komposition beauftragt. Regisseure brauchen nichts von Musik zu verstehen, Losey verstand etwas davon. 1936 hatte er das erste Jazzkonzert in der Carnegie Hall organisiert, durch seine Vermittlung erhielt Hanns Eisler ein Rockefeller-Stipendium, um sein Standardwerk über Filmmusik schreiben zu können. Am Ende von Loseys Schaffen steht eine vieldiskutierte *Don Giovanni*-Inszenierung. Legrands Variationen für zwei Klaviere und Orchester, die nicht nur Losey später an Legrands Musik für *The Thomas Crown Affair* erinnern sollte, funktioniert im Film niemals wie konventionelle Filmmusik. Die Musik, die beinahe autonom von der Handlung existiert, sogar gegen sie existiert, distanziert den Betrachter (Jansen, 142) im gleichen Maße, wie sie die Gefühle von Leo verdeutlicht (Ciment, 310; Schütte, 41). Aber der Soundtrack enthält noch mehr. Neben der akustischen Markierung der Szenen des "zweiten" Films der 50er Jahre (die durch eine andere Aussteuerung zusätzlich zu der Bildebene den Zeitsprung markiert), präsentiert uns der Film dank der Leistung des Toningenieurs Peter Handford eine erstaunliche Geräuschkulisse. Man kann hier eine Erbschaft der Radiozeit von Losey sehen (Ciment, 98). Der Zuschauer wird neue Verfremdungseffekte entdecken (wie die Eisenbahngeräusche, die die pastorale Landschaft in Frage stellen): die Trennung von Bild und Dialog wird zu einem Stilmittel der späten Losey-Filme. Das Endprodukt (Musik, Dialog der 1900-Ebene "on" oder "off", Dialog der 1952-Ebene "on" oder "off", Außengeräusche der 1900- und 1952-Ebene) erreicht vielleicht nicht die Dichte der kontrapunktischen Stimmkollagen, die Glenn Gould für den kanadischen Rundfunk produzierte, hat aber ansatzweise deren Komplexizität.

Costumes

Für die Kunsthistorikerin Anne Hollander, Autorin der Standardwerke *Seeing Through Clothes* und *Sex and Suits*, ist es keine Schwierigkeit, "costume blunders" im Film zu entdecken (Hollander, 54-62). Viele Zuschauer können das auch, ohne Kostümhistoriker zu sein. Plötzlich entdecken wir Armbanduhren an römischen Senatoren, tragen englische

Seeoffiziere im 18. Jahrhundert Uniformen, die es nur in der Phantasie von Hollywooddesignern gibt (von den Phantasieuniformen der bösen Deutschen in Hollywoodproduktionen ganz zu schweigen). Greta Garbos Krönungsornat in *Queen Christine* ähnelt mehr einem Abendkleid der 30er Jahre, und von der Kleidung Robert Taylors in der *Kameliendame* kann man kaum auf die historische Epoche schließen. Im 19. Jahrhundert widmen Schriftsteller dem Thema Kleidung als Zeichen von Rang, Status und Stil viel Raum, und L.P. Hartley tut das als ein legitimer Nachfolger von Henry James und Proust auch. Der Roman ist durchzogen von Bemerkungen, die sich auf die codifizierte, ritualisierte Bedeutung der Kleidung für die edwardianische Gesellschaft beziehen. "Only cads wear their school clothes in the holidays. It isn't done" (41) belehrt Marcus seinen Gast und fährt fort: "And, Leo, you mustn't come down to breakfast in your slippers. It's the sort of thing bank clerks do". Und Leo erfährt weiter: "... there's another thing you mustn't do. When you undress you wrap your things up and put them on a chair. Well, you mustn't. You must leave them lying wherever they happen to fall – the servants will pick them up – that's what they're there for". (41) Für Leo, den sein Norfolk-Jackett als gesellschaftlichen Außenseiter kennzeichnet, ist Marcus "the arbiter of elegance and fashion" (41). Aber auch ohne Marcus erkennt er beim Cricketmatch die Klassenunterschiede: "All our side were in white flannels. The village team [...] distressed me by their nondescript appearance; some wore their working clothes, some had already taken their coats off, revealing that they wore braces" (127). Wenig später wird Leo Ted Burgess kaum wiedererkennen, weil auch der weiße Flanellhosen, die Insignien der "upper middle class", trägt. Diese sozialen Feinheiten des Textes, die vestimentären Zeichen eines hochcodifizierten kulturellen Textes, sind bei Pinter in guten Händen. Und wenn der Amerikaner Losey auch ein Außenseiter (wie Leo) der englischen Gesellschaft sein mag, so konnte er in diesem Punkt Pinter und seinen Beratern, insbesonders Carmen Dillon und John Furness, vertrauen. Das Ergebnis ist makellos, selbst kleinste Details (z.B haben die Fräcke um 1900 noch keine Brusttaschen) wurden berücksichtigt. Losey hatte viel Wert darauf gelegt, die Kleidung natürlich wirken zu lassen:

> I think we had to make it appear as if the characters aren't wearing 'costumes' but the clothes of the day, which is *today* for the time you are watching the film [...] Most of the costumes were genuine; we made very few others. And we all lived in the house. They wore the clothes all the time and they ate as well as acted in their costumes [...] We got everything right. That's how it has to be, for once you've got the exact house, accessoires, costumes, something then springs to life (Ciment, 311-312).

Cricket

In der Mitte des Romans steht ein Cricketspiel, in dem Leo Colston als Ersatzmann das Match entscheidet. Die Beschreibung des Spiels mag das Herz des englischen Lesers (wie das siebte Kapitel von A.G. Macdonells *England, Their England*) erfreuen, für nicht-englische Leser kann es unverständlich wirken. Aber das Cricketspiel ist auch (ähnlich wie in Ian Burumas *Playing the Game*) eine perfekte Metapher für die edwardianische Gesellschaft, und es akzentuiert die Personen und Handlungsebenen des Romans: Leo bleibt der Außenseiter (trotz seiner spielentscheidenden Leistung wird er auf dem Spielbogen nicht erwähnt, da er kein "player" sondern nur ein "substitute" ist). Lord Trimingham zeigt auch im Spiel die Überlegenheit und Eleganz des edwardianischen Gentleman, die Illustration dessen, daß das Empire "on the playing fields of Eton" entstanden ist (Girouard, 232-248; Dobbs, 118-148). Mr. Maudsley beweist auch im Spiel seinen Charakter ("The qualities that had enabled Mr. Maudsley to get on in the world stood by him in the cricket field", 130). Ted Burgess' Spiel ist eine Illustration und Extension seines Charakters, es ist sicherlich symbolisch, daß er von Trimingham und Leo besiegt wird. "But there was something else, something to do with Marian, sitting on the pavillion steps watching us" (138), heißt es im Text, eine nicht zu übersehende sexuelle Komponente. Pinter hat diese Szene liebevoll (wie schon die Cricket-Szene in *Accident*) gestaltet. Viele seiner Theaterstücke enthalten ja einen Verweis auf den englischen Nationalsport (und Pinter spielte in den 70er Jahren zusammen mit Tom Stoppard in einer Cricketmannschaft der englischen Dramatiker). Obgleich Losey Cricket haßte und die Geldgeber die Szene streichen wollten ("The distributors wanted me to cut it: 'Americans don't understand cricket. You've already had cricket in *Accident* [...] Who wants to see a cricket match?'" [Ciment, 315]), behielt er die Szene nach langen Diskussionen mit Kürzungen ("...Harold had included too much detail [he plays cricket], and it wasn't necessary" [Ciment, 315]) im Film. Instinktiv erkannte Losey, daß Pinter hier Hartleys Vorgabe noch pointiert hatte:

> ...the important thing in the cricket match was to build up the antagonism, jealousy and fears of the different characters, players and spectators, the mother, the father, the friend, the friend's brother, Ted, Marian, the villagers on the one side, the people from the manor on the other (Ciment, 315).

Pinter hatte die Cricketszene noch zusätzlich durch die Off-Stimmen von Marian und Lionel Colston (Pinter, 330) mit dem Ende des Films in

Verbindung bringen wollen, aber diese komplexe Verknüpfung fiel, wie viele von Pinters Akzentuierungen, dem "editing" zum Opfer.

Raum

England als Drehort für *heritage films* bietet sich geradezu an, Landschaft und Architektur sind in vielen Gegenden seit Jahrhunderten unverändert. Dank freundschaftlicher Kontakte zu den Adelskreisen Norfolks (der Klasse, die der Marxist Losey im Film zum Gegenstand seiner Kritik macht), konnte Losey den gesamten Film "on location" drehen. Ein leerstehender Adelssitz, Merton Hall, aus dem Jahre 1660 wurde für den Film renoviert und von Carmen Dillon neu dekoriert, die Cricketszenen und die "outhouses" mit dem "Deadly Nightshade" wurden in der Nachbarschaft gefilmt (der Plan, den Film am Originalschauplatz von Hartleys autobiographischer Geschichte, Bradenham Hall, zu drehen, konnte nicht realisiert werden). Auch bei der Wahl des Drehortes finden wir wieder Loseys Detailtreue, die, wie uns Dirk Bogarde versichert (Bogarde, 235-236), bis zur Oberflächentextur aller gefilmten Gegenstände innerhalb des Raumes ging (Caute, 329). Aber nur so erreicht er das an Caravaggio gemahnende "chiaroscuro of the corridors and secret passages" (Caute, 260). In Loseys und Pinters Filmen werden die Innenräume zu "handelnden Personen", Wolfram Schütte sieht die Personen "durch das Etui der 'Behausungen'" definiert und konstatiert eine "Treppenmanie" Loseys (Schütte, 46). In der Tat könnte man über *The Servant* und *The Go-Between* sagen, daß die Treppe zu einer Art Hauptdarsteller des Films wird. Ein Stilmittel, das Losey mit Antonioni teilt, ist der "vacated space" (Caute, 330). Wenn Leo von Marians Verlobung erfährt, bleibt die Kamera noch Sekunden auf dem Weg, den Leo und Marcus längst verlassen haben. Dieses Verharren auf Bildern des unbelebten Raumes gibt dem Zuschauer wie eine Pintersche Pause einen Augenblick Zeit zum Nachsinnen, betont aber die Bedeutung des Raumes, in dem die Personen manchmal Fremde sind, um so mehr. Georges Poulet hat mit seinem Buch *L'Espace Proustien* 1963 gezeigt, daß Prousts Roman nicht nur eine Suche nach der verlorenen Zeit, sondern auch eine Suche nach dem verlorenen Raum ist. Mit dieser Proustschen Dimension interpretiert der Film Hartleys Roman und kann so als Vorstudie zu Loseys Proust-Projekt verstanden werden.

Lexikon

GO-BETWEEN, The, GB 1971 [...] An unusally close transcription of a novel in cinematic terms, *The Go-Between* maintains the dislocated time structure of L.P. Hartley's book as well as describing the action entirely through the experiences of the narrator. LOSEY reveals his own favourite themes in the text – intrusion, initiation, class differences – and expresses them with subtlety and elegance: The nuances indicated in his Hollywood work, operating through physical gesture as much as through dialogue, here reach a remarkable degree of accomplishment. The film was awarded a richly-deserved Grand Prix at CANNES. (*Oxford Companion to Film*, 292)

Literaturverzeichnis

Agee, James: *Agee on Film. Vol. I.* New York, 1969.

Albersmeier, Franz-Josef & Volker Roloff (Eds.): *Literaturverfilmungen.* Frankfurt, 1989.

Armes, Roy: *A Critical History of British Cinema.* London, 1978.

Asheim, Lester Eugene: "From Book to Film: A comparative analysis of the content of selected novels and the motion pictures based upon them". Unpublished doctoral dissertation, Chicago, 1949.

Behrens, Volker: *Das Spiel mit der Illusion in 'The French Lieutenant's Woman': Ein Vergleich von Roman, Film und Drehbuch.* Würzburg, 1994.

Bluestone, George: *Novels into Film.* Berkeley, 1957.

Bogarde, Dirk: *Snakes and Ladders.* London, 1978.

Bordwell, David: *Narration in the fiction film.* London, 1985.

Caute, David: *Joseph Losey: A Revenge on Life.* London, 1994.

Ciment, Michel: *Conversations with Losey.* London, 1985.

Dadek, Walter: *Das Filmmedium: Zur Begründung einer Allgemeinen Filmtheorie.* München, 1968.

Dobbs, Brian: *Edwardians at Play.* London, 1973.

Girouard, Mark: *The Return to Camelot: Chivalry and the English Gentleman.* New Haven, 1981.

Grade, Lew: *Still Dancing.* London, 1988.

Güttinger, Fritz: *Ein Stall Voll Steckenpferde.* Zürich, 1966.

Hartley, L.P.: *The Go-Between.* Harmondsworth, 1987.

Hollander, Anne: "The 'Gatsby Look' and Other Costume Movies Blunders", *New York*, May 27, 1975, 54-62.

Iser, Wolfgang: *Der Akt des Lesens.* München, 1976.

Jansen, Peter W.: "The Go-Between". – In *Joseph Losey.* (mit Beiträgen von Georg Alexander u.a.), München, 1977, S. 139-146.

Kael, Pauline: *Reeling.* New York, 1977.

McFarlane, Brian: *Novel to Film: An Introduction to the Theory of Adaptation.* Oxford, 1996.

Milne, Tom: *Losey on Losey.* London, 1967.

Oxford Companion to Film. Ed. Liz-Anne Bawden. Oxford, 1976.

Paech, Joachim: *Literatur und Film.* Stuttgart, 1988.

Pauli, Hansjörg: *Filmmusik: Stummfilm.* Stuttgart, 1981.

Pinter, Harold: *Five Screenplays.* London, 1971.

Poulet, Georges: *L'Espace Proustien*. Paris, 1963.
Powell, Dilys: *The Dilys Powell Film Reader*. Oxford, 1992.
Ross, Harris: *Film as Literature, Literature as Film: An introduction to and bibliography of film's relation to literature*. Westport (CT), 1987.
Ross, Lillian: *Picture*. New York, 1952.
Schneider, Irmela: *Der verwandelte Text: Wege zu einer Theorie der Literaturverfilmung*. Tübingen, 1981.
Schütte, Wolfram: "Interview". – In *Joseph Losey*. München, 1977, S. 21-48.
Van Nostrand, Albert: *The Denatured Novel*. Indianapolis, 1960.
Walker, Alexander: *Hollywood England: The British Film Industry in the Sixties*. London, 1974.

Ingo Neubert, Reutlingen

Sichtweisen des Fremden: Der amerikanische Dokumentarfilm und das Lernziel interkultureller Kompetenz; dargestellt an der *Direct-Cinema*-Produktion *The Chair* zur Situation der Todesstrafe in den USA.

1. Problemstellung und Zielsetzung

Die Geisteswissenschaften, allen voran die philologischen Disziplinen, sehen sich gegenwärtig einem bisher nicht gekannten Legitimationsdruck ausgesetzt. Ihre Funktionen und Gegenstandsbereiche müssen sich verstärkt an Faktoren eines tiefgreifenden gesellschaftlichen Wandels messen lassen. Zu nennen sind hier primär die europäische Integration und die Globalisierung der Märkte und Kommunikationsprozesse, die Staaten und Länder enger zusammenrücken lassen. Der Wissensaustausch zwischen unterschiedlichen Kulturen nimmt rapide zu, gleichzeitig treten kulturelle Differenzen vermehrt ins öffentliche Bewußtsein. Die audiovisuellen Medien sorgen für einen permanenten Informationsfluß, der Zeit und Raum immer rascher schrumpfen läßt. Ein globaler Nachrichtenmarkt beliefert die Welt mit Reportagen, Photos und Fernsehbildern rund um die Uhr, erzeugt die Illusion der "Überallverfügbarkeit" jedes Geschehens. Parallel dazu steigt das Orientierungs- und Sinngebungsbedürfnis des einzelnen.

Der Erwerb kulturspezifischen Wissens wird angesichts dieser Entwicklung zu einem vorrangigen Lernziel. Die Auseinandersetzung mit sozialen, politischen, wirtschaftlichen und historischen Aspekten eines fremden Landes unter kritischem Rückbezug auf die eigene Kultur steht dabei gleichrangig neben der Erforschung der Kommunikationsformen und -wege, die uns – oft in vielfältiger Brechung – Bilder des Fremden vermitteln, in scheinbar Vertrautes verwandeln und unsere Vorstellungsmuster beeinflussen. Neben der Annäherung an die fremde Kultur in ihren unterschiedlichen Ausprägungen ist deshalb die Analyse von Fremdwahrnehmungsprozessen und die Einsicht in die Bedingtheiten von visuell vermittelter Information eine wichtige didaktische Aufgabe. Sie kann nicht hoch genug eingeschätzt werden in einer Zeitphase, in der Schülergenerationen mit dem Fernsehen aufwachsen und "Wirklichkeit" mehr und mehr über die Bildschirmmedien erlebt wird.

Für den Erwerb der hier skizzierten Form von interkultureller Kompetenz bietet der amerikanische Dokumentarfilm im Rahmen des Englisch-unterrichts und des Anglistik-/Amerikanistikstudiums ein reichhaltiges didaktisches Übungsfeld. Doch während ganze Schulklassen bereits im Internet surfen, wird der Dokumentarfilm in Seminaren und Klassenzimmern bislang nur zögerlich eingesetzt. Immer noch gilt es, Vorbehalte gegenüber dem Medium abzubauen. Mißverstanden als ein 'Spiegel der Wirklichkeit', als Abbild von Gegebenem, das ohne viel eigene Gedankenarbeit rezipiert werden kann, wird ihm von der einen Seite allenfalls der Status eines Hilfsmittels zuerkannt, das die Funktion der Illustrierung oder des Belegs eines Sachverhalts übernehmen kann, der schriftlichen Quelle jedoch an Vielschichtigkeit und Informationsreichtum unterlegen bleiben muß. Die andere Seite betont den Konstruktionscharakter von Filmbildern und sieht ihr primäres Ziel in der Offenlegung von Manipulationsmechanismen und Lenkungsstrategien filmischer Codes. Auf ein bloßes rhetorisches Mittel reduziert, das "Wirklichkeit erfindet", wird dem Dokumentarfilm von dieser Position aus letztlich jeder Erkenntnisanspruch verweigert.

Beide Extrempositionen der Objektivismus-Relativismus-Debatte[1] werden ihrem Untersuchungsgegenstand kaum gerecht. Herauszuarbeiten ist vielmehr sein Stellenwert als historisches Dokument, das in der unmittelbaren Aufzeichnung authentischer Ereignisse eine besondere Form der Geschichtsschreibung bietet, die gegenüber dem geschriebenen Text eine eigene Qualität und Aussagekraft besitzt. Was leistet nun der Dokumentarfilm als Zeugnis einer anderen Kultur? Wie fördert eine kritische Auseinandersetzung mit ihm das Lernziel interkultureller Kompetenz? Am Beispiel des amerikanischen Dokumentarfilms *The Chair* sollen im Hinblick auf diese Fragestellungen Prämissen und Funktionen des Mediums skizziert werden.

2. The Chair *und das* Direct Cinema*: Der Blick auf fremde Erfahrungswelten*

Der 1962 produzierte *Direct-Cinema*-Film *The Chair* führt in einen Extrembereich amerikanischen Strafvollzugs – fernab von der Lebenswirklichkeit der Mehrheit der US-Bevölkerung. Geschildert wird das Gnadenverfahren eines zum Tode Verurteilten, dem bis zur anberaumten Hinrichtung auf dem elektrischen Stuhl nur wenige Tage verbleiben. Im Mittelpunkt stehen die Bemühungen des Chicagoer Rechtsanwalts Donald Moore, mit der Beweisführung einer Rehabilitation seines Mandanten, des wegen Raubmordes verurteilten Schwarzen Paul Crump, die Umwandlung der Todesstrafe in eine lebenslange Haftstrafe zu erwirken.

Mit dem Crump-Fall enthüllt *The Chair* einen Konfliktherd, der bis in die jüngste Gegenwart heranreicht und in der westlichen Welt als isoliertes, uramerikanisches Phänomen gelten kann: Die legale Tötung Straffälliger als Mittel der Justiz. Fällt der Begnadigungsfall noch in eine Zeit, in der ernste Zweifel an der Verfassungskonformität der Todesstrafe aufkommen,[2] so hat die Kehrtwende im Rechtsempfinden Amerikas längst stattgefunden. Mit derzeit weit über 3000 Inhaftierten, darunter 49 Frauen, erreicht die Zahl der Todestraktinsassen einen Rekordstand.[3] Trotz internationaler Proteste und zahlreicher Appelle – etwa des Europäischen Parlaments und des Europäischen Gerichtshofs für Menschenrechte – werden vor allem in den südlichen Bundesstaaten der USA immer mehr Todesurteile verhängt und vollstreckt, Berufungsverfahren zunehmend eingeschränkt.[4] *The Chair* ist in seiner Thematik somit beklemmende Aktualität beschieden.

Wenn unter dem weiträumigen Begriff "Kultur" Ordnungsmuster des Lebens zu verstehen sind, die entwickelt werden durch

> [...] Sitten, Gebräuche, Rituale, Gewohnheiten, Normen und Werte sowie andere Formen des Wissens und Glaubens, die auf vielfältige Weise im täglichen Leben zwischen Menschen und ihren Lebensbedingungen 'vermitteln' [...],[5]

so geraten in *The Chair* elementare Funktionsweisen und Glaubenssätze der amerikanischen Kultur auf den Prüfstand. Der Überlebenskampf eines einzelnen gegen die Strafjustiz des Staates stellt jene Regeln zur Diskussion, die den gesellschaftlichen Konsens, das Zusammenleben der Individuen innerhalb der Gemeinschaft garantieren wollen: von den Leitgedanken unveräußerlicher Persönlichkeitsrechte in der US-Verfassung über konkurriende Auffassungen von 'moderner' und 'archaischer' Strafe[6] im Rechtsempfinden von Bevölkerung und Staatsorganen bis hin zum prinzipiellen Verständnis von Rechtsstaat und Demokratie. Mit der Frage nach der Wirkung des Films in seiner Eigenschaft eines für den amerikanischen Fernsehmarkt konzipierten Unterhaltungsprodukts rückt das prekäre Beziehungsgefüge zwischen Justiz, Medien und Öffentlichkeit in den Blickpunkt.

The Chair setzt vier Tage vor Crumps Exekutionstermin, am Sonntag, dem 29. Juli 1962, mit der Dokumentation ein und schildert den Verlauf der Ereignisse als ein Drama in fünf Akten, die jeweils einen Tag im chronologischen Ablauf umfassen. Die Kamera beobachtet Staatsanwalt und Verteidiger bei der Verfahrensvorbereitung, dokumentiert minutiös die Mechanismen des Gefängnisapparats, der sich für den Tötungsakt rüstet, und führt den Zuschauer in die Anhörung vor dem Gnadenausschuß, in der über das Schicksal des Verurteilten verhandelt wird. Hauptklimax des Films ist die Bekanntgabe von Gouverneur Kerners Gnadenerlaß am Mittwoch, dem 1. August.

Der Grad der Anschaulichkeit und Unmittelbarkeit der im Film präsentierten Ereignisse übertrifft Methoden der herkömmlichen narrativen Fernsehberichterstattung ebenso wie Darstellungsmöglichkeiten schriftlicher Texte. *The Chair* verdankt dies den Gestaltungsmitteln des *Direct Cinema*, als dessen Pionier Richard Leacock gelten kann. In Verbindung mit den *Time-Life*-Korrespondenten Robert Drew und Gregory Shuker sowie dem Kameramann Donn Alan Pennebaker zeichnet er für *The Chair* und zahlreiche andere *Direct-Cinema*-Filme verantwortlich.[7] Prägend für die neue Strömung im Dokumentarfilm-Genre zu Beginn der 60er Jahre sind technische Neuerungen wie eine leichte, handgehaltene Kamera und tragbare Tonaufnahmegeräte, die erstmals eine weitgehend problemlose Aufzeichnung von szenischem Ton ermöglichen. Sie verleihen dem Filmemacher eine bislang ungekannte Mobilität und eröffnen ihm völlig neue Zugangsmöglichkeiten zu den Ereignissen. Die auf ein Minimum beschränkte Filmausrüstung gestattet eine relativ unauffällige Drehweise, die Leacocks Ziel des "Unkontrollierten Filmens" einzulösen verspricht: Das Geschehen soll sich möglichst frei und ungehindert vor der Kamera entfalten, weitgehend unbeeinflußt von der Drehsituation und ohne Einmischung des Filmemachers.[8]

Eindrucksvolles Beispiel spezifischer Artikulationsmöglichkeiten des *Direct Cinema* liefert *The Chair* mit einem zweieinhalbminütigen *Tracking Shot*[9], der den Scharfrichter des Cook County Jail entlang der weitläufigen Korridore der Strafanstalt in den Exekutionsraum begleitet und die Inspektion des elektrischen Stuhls beobachtet. Ausschlaggebend für die dramatische Wirkung der Sequenz ist der Eindruck des Zuschauers, er bewege sich mit der Person im Bild physisch in die Szene hinein. Die Identifikation mit dem variablen Kamerastandpunkt vermittelt dem Betrachter das Gefühl, selbst in Bewegung zu sein. Damit wird er zu einem Mitagierenden, Mitbetroffenen der gefilmten Situation. Das virtuelle Eintauchen in den Raum ist kein erregendes Erlebnis von Dynamik und Mobilität, wie in anderen *Tracking-Shot*-Sequenzen des Drehteams, sondern ruft im Rezipienten eher den Affekt der Furcht hervor. Die Kamera versetzt den Zuschauer in den Blickwinkel des Delinquenten, der sich in den finsteren Gängen des Gefängnisses auf seinem 'letzten Weg' befindet. Von den Bildern geht eine sogartige Wirkung aus, die den Betrachter in die Thematik des Films 'hineinzieht'. Hier soll unmittelbar durchlebt werden, was dem Verurteilten Paul Crump bei einer Ablehnung des Gnadengesuchs bevorstünde. Dies ist eine zentrale Argumentationsstrategie in dem Plädoyer gegen die Todesstrafe, das *The Chair* vor dem Zuschauer ausbreitet. Nur im Medium des Films ist eine solche auf Empathie gegründete Darstellung möglich, und kein anderes Kommunikationsmittel vermag eine derartige Involvierung des Zuschauers zu erzielen. Mit dem Gang in die Todeskammer und der eingehenden Betrachtung des elektrischen Stuhls enthüllt die Kamera einen Tabubereich des amerikanischen Strafvollzugs. Denn Exekutionsstätten und -instrumente, wie auch der Hinrichtungsvorgang selbst, werden vom Blick der Öffentlichkeit streng abgeschirmt. *The Chair* dringt somit nicht nur hinter die Mauern der Strafanstalt, sondern auch hinter die Fassaden, die in der US-Gesellschaft um die Todesstrafe errichtet werden.

Der Authentizitätsanspruch dieser Sequenz ergibt sich aus der extrem langen, 'unzerschnittenen' Einstellung: Bildfolge und Bildinhalt erscheinen kongruent mit dem zeitlichen und thematischen Ablauf der originalen Ereignisse.[10] Dennoch gilt auch hier Peters prinzipielle Beobachtung zur "Struktur der Filmsprache":

> Das Bild besitzt einen gewissen Abstraktionsgrad, und es besteht immer eine Distanz zwischen Bild und Abgebildetem. Das Bild ist kein Duplikat des Abgebildeten, sondern ein Zeichen, in dem das Abgebildete *verstanden* wird. [...] Zudem macht ein Bild eine Sache immer sichtbar unter einem bestimmten Gesichtspunkt. Dieser spezifiziert die Mitteilung, macht das Bild zu einer Formulierung eines bestimmten Gedankens oder Gefühls.[11]

Das Filmbild ist damit stets – in Richard Leacocks Worten – "an aspect of the filmmaker's perception of what took place in the presence of the camera."[12] Dementsprechend transportieren die Bilder des Films eine Fülle an Datenmaterial, das entschlüsselt werden muß, um die Sehweise des Filmers sichtbar zu machen. Hierbei ergeben sich für den Dokumentarfilm eine Reihe von übergreifenden Fragestellungen: Läßt die Sehweise des Kamerateams Rückschlüsse darauf zu, wie Amerikaner sich selbst wahrnehmen? Mit welchen Mitteln wird Kritik an der eigenen Kultur geübt? Welche Geschichtsauffassung liegt der filmischen Aufzeichnung authentischer Ereignisse zugrunde? Ein Blick auf Personendarstellung und Handlungsführung des Films kann hier interessante Aufschlüsse bieten.

3. Anwalt Moore: Die Fallvorbereitung als "inneres Drama"

Mittelpunkt der Filmhandlung ist die Person des Anwalts, Don Moore. Ein Hauptteil der Drehaufnahmen – rund 30 bis 35 Stunden an 'Rohmaterial' – wird für die Aufzeichnung von Telefonaten verwendet, die Moore im Zeitraum von zwei Tagen führt.[13] Die Kamera beobachtet ihn bei seinen Bemühungen, Vertreter von Presse und Kirche für den Fall zu mobilisieren und verzeichnet seine Reaktion auf entsprechende Zu- und Absagen, die für Crumps Schicksal entscheidend sein können. Durch den besonderen Blickwinkel – Moores Gesprächspartner sind weder sicht-noch hörbar – erlebt der Zuschauer den Handlungsverlauf nicht 'objektiv' mit, sondern ausschließlich in der Wirkung auf Moore: 'Schauplatz' der Handlung wird das Mienenspiel des Protagonisten. Die Szenen geben Einblick in die mühevolle Kleinarbeit der Fallvorbereitung, spüren jedoch zugleich einem klassischen Motiv des *Courtroom Drama* nach: der Anwalt in der Rolle des Initiationshelden, den die Aufgabenlast und Verantwortung des Falles vor eine berufliche und persönliche Bewährungsprobe stellen.

Höhepunkte in diesem Psychogramm sind Moores Zusammenbrüche vor laufender Kamera: Zweimal ist der Anwalt zu Tränen gerührt, als ihm Unterstützung für seinen Mandanten zugesichert wird. Entsprechend dem Ziel, ein "inneres Drama" sichtbar werden zu lassen,[14] folgt die Gliederung der Einstellungen einer dramatischen Struktur. Die Ankündigung eines wichtigen Telefonats und Moores atemloses Lauschen am Hörer erzeugen den steigenden Spannungsbogen; der Gefühlsausbruch, in dem sich die psychische Anspannung entlädt, bildet die Klimax des Segments; Moores dunkle Vorahnung, die Zusage könne "im letzten Augenblick" wieder zurückgezogen werden, leitet die Wende zur fallenden Handlung ein; eine heitere Dialogpassage zwischen Anwalt und Sekretärin sorgt für das retardierende Moment, bis sich schließlich mit einem erneuten Anruf die 'Katastrophe' vollzieht: Die Zusage wird wieder zurückgenommen, Moore erleidet in seinem "Kampf, Paul Crump zu retten",[15] eine Niederlage. Mit der Hervorhebung der psychischen Belastung des Anwalts in der Rolle des 'Lebensretters' lenkt *The Chair* den kritischen Blick auf ein Staats- und Rechtssystem, in dem es offenbar den taktischen Bemühungen eines einzelnen überlassen bleibt, ob ein anderer dem Tod preisgegeben oder weiterleben wird.[16]

Der jähe Wechsel von 'positiven' und 'negativen' Erzählschritten wird für die Montage des Films – die Selektion, Beschneidung und Komposition des Rohmaterials – zu einem rezeptionsästhetischen Prinzip. Antizipationen werden geweckt und bis zu einem Grad vorangetrieben, an dem diese sich ganz zu erfüllen scheinen; anschließend jedoch vollzieht sich ein Schritt zurück, das Denouement wird verschleppt. Mit dieser Form von "dramatic discontinuity" in der Handlungsführung lehnt sich der Dokumentarfilm an Erzählweisen des klassischen Melodrams an, bei dem das Aufwallen entgegengesetzter Empfindungswelten stets neu entfacht, ihre Kollision aber bis zum größtmöglichen Effekt hinausgezögert wird.[17]

Was Robert Rosenstone mit Blick auf den historischen Dokumentarfilm feststellt, kann auch für *The Chair* gelten: "Verfilmung von Geschichte" bedeutet die "sinnstiftende Anordnung des Materials in Form einer Erzählung".[18] Anhand der von Peripetien geprägten 'Schreibweise' verweist *The Chair* auf den Aspekt der Unkontrollierbarkeit, der nach Meinung vieler Kritiker das Todesstrafensystem in Amerika kennzeichnet: angefangen von einer uneinheitlichen Urteilspraxis im Strafverfahren bis hin zu unkalkulierbaren Mechanismen in Berufungs- und Gnadenverfahren. Die Entscheidung über Crumps Schicksal, so implizieren die Stimmungsumstürze, wird primär von Zufall und Willkür beherrscht. Aus diesem Blickwinkel widerspricht die Handhabung der Todesstrafe den Prinzipien einer gerechten, rationalen Rechtspflege.

Sieht sich Crumps Anwalt auch phasenweise dem Kräftespiel eines Verfahrens ausgeliefert, das ihn von Tatkraft und Zuversicht stets erneut in Tiefen der Erschöpfung und bangen Ungewißheit zurückstößt, so dominieren gemäß einer schematischen Figurenkonzeption unbeugsamer Kampfgeist und Siegeswille. Die Szenen sind so montiert, daß Moore in vertraulichen *asides* zur Kamera seine Schwachpunkte und momentanen Niederlagen unmittelbar kommentiert – nach einem Rückschlag richtet er sich gleich wieder auf und schöpft neue Vitalität und Energie.[19] Mit der Hervorhebung von Moores Selbstbeherrschung und Durchsetzungskraft betont Leacock in der Personendarstellung des Anwalts einen klassischen Wesenszug des amerikanischen Helden – ein Schema, das auch in anderen Filmen der Drew Associates zu finden ist.[20]

4. Fremdwahrnehmungsmuster des Drehteams: Die Darstellung des Verurteilten

In seiner Zugehörigkeit zur afroamerikanischen Bevölkerung und in seiner Situation des Todeskandidaten ist der Verurteilte in zweifacher Weise zur sozialen Peripherie zu rechnen. Der Blick der Kamera auf Crump als Angehöriger einer extremen Minderheit der US-Gesellschaft gibt Aufschluß über die Fremdwahrnehmungsmuster des Drehteams. Diese, so zeigt sich, sind von reduktionistischen Formen geprägt. Bereits die Vorstellung von Crump als Romanautor in der Exposition des Films bemüht ein klassisches *death row cliché*, das in Mediendarstellungen häufig gebraucht wird; ein weiteres Zeichen für eine stereotype Wahrnehmung ist die Form der Bildkomposition, die als Leitmotiv dient. Bei dem wiederholten Blick in Crumps Zelle ist der Kamerastandpunkt so gewählt, daß ein von Gitterstäben gebildetes Rechteck im Bildvordergrund Crumps gesenkten Kopf im Bildmittelgrund umrahmt. Bildvorder- und Bildhintergrund sind 'kongruent': Die Gitter der Zellentür finden ihre Entsprechung in den Gittern des Zellenfensters. In dieser auffallend symmetrischen Komposition scheint Crump jeglichen Bewegungsspielraums beraubt. Dieser Eindruck wird durch den Mangel an Tiefendimension[21] noch verstärkt – das Zelleninnere schrumpft auf eine schmale Fläche. Gegenlicht und Unterbelichtung lassen die Person im Bild nur als Silhouette sichtbar werden. Die so erzeugte düstere Aura will Crumps Todesbedrohung visualisieren und zeichnet ihn in der Situation des Wartens auf den Gouverneursentscheid einsam und niedergeschlagen.

Hier läßt sich in der Personendarstellung ein Muster erkennen, das auch auf andere Filme der Drew Associates, wie etwa *Crisis: Behind a Presidential Commitment*, übertragbar ist. Danach werden Schwarze überwiegend als passive Gestalten gezeichnet, als Erleidende, denen von tatkräftigen, fortschrittlichen Weißen der Weg in eine bessere Zukunft geebnet wird. Die Schwarzen – heißen sie nun Paul Crump oder James Hood und Vivian Malone, wie die beiden Studenten in *Crisis* – fungieren in der Welt von Produzent Robert Drew nurmehr als Katalysator für die Aktionen der Weißen. Und letztere sind es auch, die dem Zuschauer als Identifikationsfiguren präsentiert werden. Hieraus erklärt sich, daß der zum Tode Verurteilte in den wenigen Segmenten, die ihm gewidmet sind, als *flat character* erscheint, der kaum durch spezifische Charaktereigenschaften individualisiert wird und somit in der Typisierung verharrt.

5. Zwischen "Thrill-Killing" und Aufklärungsintention: Die Ambivalenz der Medienberichterstattung in Todesstrafenfällen

Todesstrafenfälle üben auf die Medien stets große Faszination aus. Die der Grundsituation inhärenten Motive von Trübsal und Leid, Gewalt und Furcht, *suspense* und Hoffnung auf 'glückhafte Errettung' sind Ingredienzien klassischer Melodramen, geeignet, die Gemüter eines breiten Zielpublikums zu bewegen. Jüngstes Beispiel ist das von den Medien zelebrierte Gnadenverfahren der 38jährigen Karla Faye Tucker im Staat Texas. Trotz zahlreicher Proteste im In- und Ausland wird Tucker im Februar 1998 mittels der Giftspritze hingerichtet. Die Urteilsvollstreckung setzt ein Signal für die Freigabe der Todesstrafe auch für Frauen – bislang ein Tabu in der Todesstrafenpraxis Amerikas in diesem Jahrhundert.[22] Im Vorfeld der anberaumten Exekution berichten amerikanische TV-Sender, allen voran *CNN*, in abendfüllenden Live-Sendungen über Tuckers Schicksal. Bilder von Schaulustigen und Demonstranten vor den Toren der Hinrichtungsstätte wechseln mit Erfolgsprognosen von Sachverständigen zum Einspruchsverfahren der Verurteilten, Studio-Diskussionen thematisieren die gesellschaftliche Akzeptanz der Hinrichtung einer Frau. Angesichts dieser Form von Direktsendungen "vor Ort" gewinnt die Frage nach einer Medienethik, nach Aufgaben, Publikumswirkung und Grenzen der Live-Berichterstattung, besondere Dringlichkeit.

The Chair liefert zu diesem Problemkreis wichtiges Anschauungs- und Diskussionsmaterial: Auch der Dokumentarfilm zielt auf den Absatz im US-Fernsehmarkt.[23] Bewertet man die hohe Medienresonanz, die Crumps Gnadengesuch verursacht,[24] so ist zu berücksichtigen, daß in Todesstrafenverfahren ein berechtigtes öffentliches Interesse besteht, weil hier Menschenleben auf dem Spiel stehen und gesetzgeberische und richterliche Entscheidungen ins kritische Blickfeld geraten. Die Medien sehen ihre Aufgabe darin, die von der Verfassung ausdrücklich geforderte "Öffentlichkeit der Gerichtsbarkeit" herzustellen. Deshalb beanspruchen sie ungehinderten Zugang zu allen Phasen eines Verfahrens und berufen sich auf den ersten Zusatzartikel der Verfassung, der Rede- und Pressefreiheit garantiert. In ihrer begleitenden Berichterstattung streben sie ideell eine Wächterrolle an und verfolgen das Ziel, Urteilsfindungen transparent und auf ihre Gesetzmäßigkeit hin nachprüfbar zu machen.[25] Diesem Ziel stehen jedoch festgefügte Marktgesetze gegenüber. Ein verschärfter Wettbewerb fordert die Exklusivmeldung, die rasche, unverzügliche Veröffentlichung, die die Aufmerksamkeit eines Massenpublikums auf sich zieht. Die Verletzung von Privatsphäre und Menschenwürde der gefilmten Personen wird dabei billigend in Kauf genommen.

The Chair setzt sich diesem Vorwurf mit einer Serie von Kreuzschnitten aus, die Großaufnahmen von Crump unmittelbar mit Großaufnahmen des elektrischen Stuhls kollidieren lassen. Auf diese Weise soll Crumps Todesbedrohung drastisch 'ins Bild' gesetzt werden. Verschiedene Mittel dienen der dramatischen Emphase. Wird zunächst ein Photo aus der Zeit seiner Verhaftung mit einer Aufnahme des Stuhls montiert, so werden bald Filmbilder des Crump der 'Jetztzeit' mit Aufnahmen der Tötungsmaschine kontrastiert. Ein *Match Cut*[26], ein *Insert Shot*[27] und eine *Standkopierung*[28] sollen zur Eindrücklichkeit der Bilder beitragen, die in der Kollision gegensätzlicher Inhalte – hier der lebende Mensch, dort die Vorrichtung, die ihn zu Tode bringen soll – auf eine schockartige Wirkung abzielen. Die Montage steuert mit diesen Stilmitteln die Erwartung des Zuschauers auf das Kommende, indem sie eine der beiden 'Lösungsmöglichkeiten' des Konflikts durchspielt und uns vor Augen führt, was geschehen wird, wenn Crump nicht begnadigt wird. Durch den wiederholten Vorgriff auf mögliches Zukünftiges entsteht die 'Finalspannung' des Films, der jedes einzelne Segment untergeordnet wird. Hier erhebt sich die dringliche Frage, ob und inwieweit die Todesbedrohung eines Menschen zu handlungsdramatischen und rezeptionsästhetischen Wirkungen benützt werden darf. Das Ziel der Aufklärung, das 'Sichtbarmachen' des drohenden Konflikts, konkurriert dabei mit dem Ziel der spannenden Unterhaltung.

Der Vorwurf des "Thrill Killing", der medialen Zubereitung einer Urteilsvollstreckung als spannende Fernsehunterhaltung, ist jüngst im Hinblick auf die aggressive TV-Vermarktung des Karla-Tucker-Falles von verschiedener Seite erhoben worden.[29] Auch *The Chair* läßt sich von dem 'Tatbestand' nicht freisprechen, die existentielle Situation des zum Tode Verurteilten zu Spannungszwecken und Momenten des Nervenkitzels auszunützen. Die Hervorhebung einer lebensbedrohlichen Gefahrensituation, die kurzfristig in der Vorwegnahme von Crumps Tod gipfelt, soll den Zuschauer kontinuierlich in Angst und Schrecken versetzen. Der Dokumentarfilm bedient sich hier ausgiebig der Erzählkonventionen des Spielfilm-Thrillers. Aufnahmen des Scharfrichters in der Todeskammmer und Wiederholungen des *Tracking Shot* entlang der Gefängniskorridore werden in die Filmhandlung eingestreut als wiederkehrende Konfrontation mit einer scheinbar unabwendbaren Bedrohung, die im Betrachter den für das Genre charakteristischen "thrill" bewirken soll, eine über die Angst erzeugte physische Reaktion, den "Schauder der Erregung".[30] *The Chair* läuft hier Gefahr, dem Diktat der Publikumswirksamkeit zu erliegen, das die Todesstrafenproblematik in Form eines delektablen Unterhaltungsthrillers verpackt, der Konsumenten eine 'Lust an der Angst' verspricht.

Als Hauptklimax des Films führt die Kamera in der 73. Filmminute Crumps Reaktion auf die Begnadigung vor Augen. Die Großaufnahme konzentriert sich auf die Mimik der Person, die deutliche Zeichen großer Anspannung erkennen läßt. Knapp dem Tode entronnen, zeigt sich Crump angesichts der geballten Medienpräsenz irritiert und formuliert stockend Worte des Dankes, nur um nach kurzer Zeit, von Gefühlen überwältigt, abzubrechen. Die Einstellung führt deutlich vor Augen, daß *The Chair* – gemäß Robert Drews Konzept einer Charakterenthüllung unter nervlicher Belastung[31] – ganz auf jene persönlichen Krisenmomente ausgerichtet ist, in denen die betreffende Person die Kontrolle über ihre Gefühle verliert. Weil *The Chair* diese Krisenpunkte so ausschließlich zur Handlungsklimax erhebt und als Spannungsmomente aneinanderreiht, scheint der Vorwurf berechtigt, daß der Film sich gerade mit jenen Kräften verbündet, denen Anwalt und Mandant ausgesetzt sind. Ganz im Sinne des Leistungsdenkens, das *The Chair* in der Personendarstellung von Anwalt Moore propagiert, will die Kamera in jenen *breakdowns* ausgiebig studieren, ob und wie die Situation 'bewältigt' wird. Damit aber begibt sich der Dokumentarfilm in die Nähe eines Voyeurismus, der seiner gesellschaftskritischen Intention zuwiderläuft.

6. Historische Fallstudie oder Courtroom Drama? Die Dokumentation der Gnadenanhörung

Die Anwesenheit der Kameras vor dem *Illinois State Pardon and Parole Board*[32] eröffnet in *The Chair* die Möglichkeit zu einer historischen Fallstudie, die für Rechtswissenschaftler und Soziologen authentisches Quellenmaterial bereitstellt. Denn hier sind die gegnerischen Parteien des Verfahrens erstmals in eine gemeinsame rhetorische Situation gestellt, hier werden die Argumente unterschiedlicher Strafauffassungen elaboriert und kontrastiert. Das Wechselspiel von Zeugenaussagen, Plädoyer und Erwiderung bietet Gelegenheit, Auffassungen von Reue und Sühne, Strafe und Vergeltung auf reflexiv-analytischer Ebene greifbar werden zu lassen. So wird Anwalt Louis Nizer, der Moore im Verfahren unterstützt, auf dem Höhepunkt seines Plädoyers zum Sprachrohr einer reformierten Strafauffassung, die den Sühnegedanken und das Vergeltungsprinzip der Todesstrafe ablehnt und stattdessen als Ziel des modernen Strafvollzugs die Besserung und Wiedereingliederung des Straftäters in die soziale Gemeinschaft propagiert. Nizers Ausführungen sind die 'Glaubenssätze' des Films, der thematische Kernpunkt, um den sich alle Bilder gruppieren.

Dem historisch-dokumentarischen Gehalt der Aufnahmen, die auf der Tonebene auch zu einer Analyse des Soziolekts der Sprechenden herausfordern, steht jedoch der subjektive Blickwinkel des Films gegenüber. So geht der überwiegende Teil der Kürzungen, die die ursprünglich sechseinhalbstündige Sitzung auf 28 Minuten kondensieren, auf Kosten der Anklage: Das Plädoyer von Staatsanwalt Thompson weist allein sechs Kürzungen auf; insgesamt räumt der Film der Anklage sieben Minuten, der Verteidigung knapp 18 Minuten an Redezeit ein.

Eine entscheidende Phase in der Auseinandersetzung zwischen Anklage und Verteidigung markiert das Rededuell zwischen Anwalt Nizer und dem Zeugen der Staatsanwaltschaft, Bundesrichter Richard B. Austin – 1953 einer jener Ankläger, die für Paul Crump das Todesurteil forderten. Austin vermißt bei Crump ein öffentliches Bedauern der Tat und deklariert deshalb eine behauptete Läuterung als Heuchelei. Die Bestätigung des Todesurteils durch zwei Gerichtshöfe im Berufungsverfahren sieht er als Beweis für die Rechtmäßigkeit der anberaumten Exekution. Crumps Anwälte beschuldigt er, mit dem Gnadengesuch diese "einhellige Rechtsprechung umgehen" zu wollen.

Die Wirkungskraft von Austins energisch geführter Aussage wird durch verschiedene Strategien von Kamera und Montage entscheidend abgeschwächt. So ist seine Rede überwiegend mit *Reaction Shots* der Verteidiger montiert; die Aufmerksamkeit des Zuschauers wird von der 'gegnerischen' Argumentationslinie auf die Reaktion der Anwälte gelenkt, die bereits intensiv den 'Gegenangriff' vorbereiten. Während Nizers scharfem Verhör wird Austin nur noch ganze 18 Sekunden ins Bild gesetzt. Die durchgängige Kameraperspektive der Aufsicht weist ihm den Part des Unterlegenen zu. Nizer hingegen verleiht die Kamera durch die Perspektive der Untersicht eine überhöhte physische Größe. Sie charakterisiert ihn als eine Person von Macht und Gewicht und verleiht seiner Argumentation Geltung und 'Wahrheit'. Auf *Reaction Shots* wird bei seiner Rede fast ganz verzichtet. Rhythmisch verändert sich durch den

Zoom die Aufnahmedistanz, so daß Nizers strenge, maßregelnde Mimik in der Großaufnahme ebenso zur Geltung gelangt wie seine resolute Gestik in dem vergrößerten Bildausschnitt der Halbnahaufnahme; eine Hand ist autoritär in die Hüfte gestemmt, die andere pocht im Rhythmus der Intonation energisch auf den Tisch. Optisch wie auch verbal geht der Anwalt als Sieger aus der Befragung des Zeugen hervor.

Den Wortwechsel zwischen Nizer und Crumps ehemaligem Ankläger gestaltet *The Chair* zu einem Schlagabtausch mit verteilten Rollen. Indirekt weist Nizer in seinen Ausführungen Austins Position den primitiven Rachegedanken zu, Kameraführung und Montage unterstützen diese Argumentation in ihrer einseitigen Sympathielenkung. Die Gnadenanhörung wird auf diese Weise nach den klassischen Regeln eines *Courtroom Drama* des Hollywood-Stils gestaltet, bei dem der spannende Wettstreit gegnerischer Parteien im Zentrum steht. Einblicke in Verfahrensmechanismen der Anhörung stellt *The Chair* in einen Interpretationsrahmen, der von Erzählkonventionen des Spielfilms geprägt ist.

7. Die Filmaufzeichnung als ein Stück Rechtsgeschichte

Der Dokumentarfilm will den Zuschauer in den privilegierten Blickpunkt eines Augenzeugen versetzen, der miterlebt, wie sich ein Stück Rechtsgeschichte vollzieht. Die von Crumps Anwälten ausgearbeitete Argumentation schildert der Film als einen Schritt in bislang unerschlossenes Rechtsterrain mit Präzedenzwirkung.[33] Folgt man den Ansätzen der Narratologie-Forschung, dann besteht 'Geschichte' aus einer Vielzahl von Diskursen, aus "[...] Darstellungen und Interpretationen, deren Bedeutungen auf der kommunikativen Ebene immer unsicher [...]" und vorläufig sind.[34] Auch die filmische Erzählung von *The Chair* muß deshalb bei einer eingehenden Untersuchung von Relativierung und Ergänzung begleitet sein. Bezugsrahmen und Beziehungsfelder sind hier schriftliche Quellen zum Crump-Fall, wie etwa die Berichterstattung in der Tages- und Wochenpresse, oder die jährlichen Berichte und Statistiken zur Todesstrafensituation in den USA von *Amnesty International*.[35] Zweifel an einer Präzedenzwirkung des Crump-Falles erweisen sich als berechtigt, blickt man auf eine *AI*-Studie, die für die Situation von Todestraktinsassen in Illinois, Mississippi und Louisiana noch 20 Jahre *nach* dem Crump-Fall feststellt:

> Die Insassen der Todestrakte verbüßen keine Freiheitsstrafe wie andere Gefangene; sie werden in ihren Zellen bis zur Hinrichtung "verwahrt". Die Rehabilitation dieser Menschen ist nach Auffassung staatlicher Behörden völlig irrelevant.[36]

Die Beobachtung rührt an einen der größten Streitpunkte in der Debatte um die Todesstrafe. In den Brennpunkt der Diskussion gerät die Dauer der Berufungsverfahren. Weil langjährige "Verzögerungen" zwischen Verkündung und Vollstreckung des Todesurteils vom Gesetzgeber nicht beabsichtigt seien, so das Argument des Staates, schließe die Todesstrafe die Möglichkeit einer Rehabilitation des Verurteilten von vornherein aus. Deshalb dürfe eine Läuterung – ob real oder frei erfunden – auch nicht als Revisionsgrund anerkannt werden.[37]

Auf dem langen Weg zur *Furman*-Entscheidung im Jahr 1972, mit der der Gerichtshof die Todesstrafe – so wie sie bislang gehandhabt worden war – außer Kraft setzt,[38] ist Crumps Begnadigungsfall sicherlich als wichtiger Mosaikstein zu werten, der die Aufmerksamkeit der Öffentlichkeit auf die Todesstrafenproblematik gelenkt und zur Sensibilisierung der staatlichen Behörden beigetragen hat. Der Dokumentarfilm beschönigt jedoch die Sachlage, indem er den Eindruck erweckt, der erfolgreiche Abschluß des Falles sei nun *unmittelbar bindend* für geltendes Recht und damit ein entscheidender Reformschritt in der Todesstrafen*gesetzgebung*. Damit macht der Film nicht deutlich, daß das Begnadigungsverfahren und der Gnadenakt des Gouverneurs keinen feststehenden, gesetzlich fixierten Rechtsmaßstäben und keiner gerichtlichen Kontrolle unterliegt. Vielmehr handelt es sich um eine Entscheidung, die nach pflichtgemäßem Ermessen erfolgt. Die Argumentationsführung von Anklage und Verteidigung vor der Kommission ist kein Rechtsstreit und der Erlaß des Gouverneurs kein richterliches Urteil, das als Orientierungspunkt für ähnlich gelagerte Fälle in der Zukunft *zwingend* heranzuziehen wäre.

Bei einer Bewertung des Films ist jedoch der zeitliche Abstand zu berücksichtigen, aus dem wir heute, 35 Jahre nach der Produktion von *The Chair*, von einem privilegierten Blickpunkt aus urteilen. Daß die Gegner der Todesstrafe am Ende der 60er Jahre nur eine Schlacht, nicht aber den Kampf gewinnen und die Todesstrafe bereits zu Beginn der 70er Jahre eine Renaissance erlebt, ließ sich aus der Perspektive des Drehteams sicherlich nicht erspüren. Sie ist nicht rückwärtsgewandt auf Vergangenes, sondern geschehensbegleitend auf unmittelbar Gegenwärtiges gerichtet. *The Chair* ist getragen von einer Aufbruchstimmung, von einem optimistischen, hoffnungsvollen Ausblick, der die progressiven innenpolitischen Strömungen der Dekade widerspiegelt. Mit der Stilisierung des Crump-Falles zu einem unmittelbaren Umkehrpunkt im Rechtsempfinden Amerikas will der Film seinem Reformappell an Strafvollzug und Rechtsprechung Nachdruck verleihen. Gerade weil er dem Geist seiner Entstehungszeit verhaftet ist, wird *The Chair* zu einem rechtshistorisch aufschlußreichen Untersuchungsgegenstand.

Mit der ausführlichen Aufzeichnung der Anhörung vor der Gnadenkommission rückt *The Chair* in die Nähe einer Gerichtsreportage. Damit steht der Film im Produktionsjahr 1962 am Anfangspunkt einer brisanten Entwicklung, in deren Verlauf immer mehr Gerichtsverhandlungen in den USA von den Medien beobachtet und schließlich auch live der Nation am Fernsehschirm übermittelt werden. Seinen vorläufigen Höhepunkt findet dieses *Courtroom TV* in dem "most publicized murder trial in history"[39], dem Doppelmord-Prozeß gegen den afroamerikanischen Ex-Footballstar James Orenthal Simpson, der 1995 in Los Angeles stattfindet. Der Simpson-Fall offenbart sich als gigantisches Medienspektakel, das die überwältigende Mehrheit der amerikanischen Bevölkerung in den Bann schlägt.[40] Unzählige TV-Stationen übertragen den neun Monate währenden Marathon-Prozeß, der in einem aufsehenerregenden Freispruch mündet, live aus dem Gerichtssaal[41] und erheben ihn zum Top-Nachrichtenereignis, dem alle anderen Themen untergeordnet sind. Die weltweite Ausstrahlung aus der laufenden Hauptverhandlung entfacht auch in Deutschland eine Diskussion über die Möglichkeiten eines Gerichtsfernsehens auf deutschen Kanälen.[42]

Die Anwesenheit von Kameras im Gerichtssaal birgt stets die Gefahr des Präjudizes. Unausgewogene, voreilige Berichterstattungen, die bereits im Vorfeld von Beweisaufnahme und Zeugenvernehmung eine Schuld oder Unschuld des Angeklagten implizieren, können dem noch ausstehenden Urteil unzulässig vorausgreifen und Geschworene, Zeugen und Richter in Urteilsfindung und eidesstattlichen Aussagen beeinflussen.[43] Wie stellt sich das Problem von *free press versus fair trial* für den Dokumentarfilm? Eine Einwirkung auf den Verlauf des Gnadenverfahrens über eine begleitende Berichterstattung, bei der das gedrehte Filmmaterial unmittelbar im Fernsehen ausgestrahlt wird, ist den Filmemachern nicht möglich, da *The Chair* erst zehn Wochen nach Drehbeginn als fertiges Produkt vorlag.[44] In deutlicher Weise grenzt Richard Leacock sich hier zur Herangehensweise der Fernsehteams ab:

> In our case the issue was that we not interfere with the judicial process. I would have been against running out from the hearing and putting what we had on to a TV news show because I think that this kind of action can create havoc with the judicial system. [...] in general I shudder to think of a world where documentary filmmakers decide who gets the AX![45]

Dennoch ist zu fragen, ob nicht allein die *Präsenz* des Drehteams im Vorfeld und während der Anhörung einen Einfluß auf die Entscheidungsfindung im Crump-Verfahren ausgeübt hat. Leacock sieht diese Gefahr als ein potentielles Problem von *The Chair*, wenn er betont:

> To me, the more difficult point is that of the filmmaking *process* effecting the outcome of the case, or even becoming part of a punishment.[46]

Daß die Anwesenheit des Filmteams zu der großen Publizität des Crump-Falles und indirekt zu einer Lenkung des Verfahrens beigetragen haben mag, läßt sich an Leacocks Auskünften zur Drehsituation ablesen.[47] So steht mit der *Time-Life*-Gruppe als Sponsor ein einflußreicher Medienkonzern hinter dem Drehteam; Leacock verweist ausdrücklich auf das hohe Prestige von *Time-Life*, das der Kamera den außergewöhnlichen Zugang zu allen Phasen des Geschehens ermöglicht habe. Daß dies dem Fall auch zu einer großen Öffentlichkeitswirkung verhilft, liegt nahe. Die Annahme wird gestützt durch Leacocks Hinweis auf das erklärte Ziel der Anwälte Crumps, mit den Filmaufnahmen eine möglichst hohe Publicity des Falles zu erzielen. Wenn es die Strategie der Verteidigung ist, zu Crumps Läuterung so viele Zeugenaussagen wie möglich zu gewinnen, dann ist offensichtlich, daß die Anwälte die Stimmungslage der Öffentlichkeit für ihre Sache zu instrumentalisieren suchen. Moores Fallvorbereitung konzentriert sich deshalb in erster Linie auf 'Öffentlichkeitsarbeit': Bereits Wochen vor dem Anhörungstermin geben Anwalt und Delinquent zahlreiche Interviews und suchen die Medien auf das Argument der Rehabilitation einzustimmen.[48]

Inwiefern wählerprogrammatisches Kalkül für Crumps Begnadigung ausschlaggebend gewesen ist, läßt sich nicht eindeutig ausloten. Die Mutmaßung ist jedoch legitim, daß ein massiver öffentlicher Druck – mit herbeigeführt durch die Drehsituation von *The Chair* – Gouverneur Kerner letztlich zum Gnadenerweis bewegt. Unter rechtsstaatlichen Gesichtspunkten und dem Aspekt der Unabhängigkeit der Entscheidungsinstanzen ist diese Einflußnahme prinzipiell als bedenklich einzustufen.

Die mit *The Chair* aufgeworfene Streitfrage um die Zulassung von Fernsehkameras bei Gerichtsverhandlungen ist angesichts der Zunahme der Medienmacht in den USA und in Europa aktueller denn je. Zwei Entscheidungen des Supreme Court markieren in den USA den Ausgangs- und vorläufigen Endpunkt der Trendwende zum "TV-Zeitalter der totalen Zugänglichkeit".[49] Noch im Bemühen, dem Medienansturm im Gerichtssaal Schranken zuzuweisen, bescheinigt der Oberste Gerichtshof 1965 in der *Billie-Sol-Estes*-Entscheidung einem Angeklagten in Texas, die hohe Medienpräsenz während der Verhandlung habe sein Recht auf ein ordnungsgemäßes Verfahren beeinträchtigt. Die Obersten Richter schreiben der hohen Publicity des Falles eine präjudizierende

Wirkung zu und heben hervor, eine hohe Medienpräsenz in einer Verhandlung übe auf Zeugen, Richter und Geschworene eine hemmende und konzentrationsmindernde, vom Verfahren ablenkende Wirkung aus, führe gar unter Umständen zu Unterbrechungen der Verhandlung und beeinträchtige damit das Ziel der Wahrheitsfindung erheblich. Für den Angeklagten sei die Präsenz von Fernsehkameras eine ständige Belästigung; von Richtern, die in ihr Amt gewählt werden, könne das Verfahren vor den Augen der Medien zudem als politische Waffe und als Selbstdarstellung mißbraucht werden.[50] 16 Jahre später jedoch stärkt ein Urteil des Supreme Court nachhaltig die Position der Medien im zähen Kampf um Lockerung der Restriktionen. In seinem Urteil vom 26. Januar 1981 entscheidet das höchste Gericht im Fall *Chandler versus Florida* ausdrücklich,

> [...] daß ein Bundesstaat berechtigt ist, Kriminalprozesse durch Radio und Fernsehen live aufnehmen und senden zu lassen. [...] Der *Angeklagte* habe im Einzelfall nachzuweisen, daß die Unparteilichkeit der Jury oder die einzelner Beteiligter durch die Medien (ob im Print- oder im elektronischen Bereich) beeinträchtigt worden sei. Es sei inzwischen möglich durch eine weiterentwickelte Technik, Gerichtsverhandlungen ohne jede Störung ihres Ablaufs unauffällig aufzunehmen. Das Fernsehen habe sich in der Bevölkerung als Medium durchgesetzt. Es bestünde daher ein erhöhtes Interesse an seiner Berichterstattung.[51]

Die negativen Ausmaße dieses *Court-TV* führt der oben erwähnte Simpson-Prozeß beispielhaft vor Augen. Er droht zum *mistrial*, zum Fehlprozeß zu werden, der das gesamte Prinzip der amerikanischen Geschworenengerichtsbarkeit in Frage stellt. So zeigt sich, daß eine die Unparteilichkeit der Jury garantierende Abschirmung der Geschworenen vor dem allumfassenden Informationsfluß der Medien nicht mehr praktikabel ist; Zeugen geben Fernsehinterviews, bevor sie ihre Aussage vor Gericht abgeben und bahnen Verträge für Talk-Shows und Werbeauftritte an; Zeugen drohen ihre Aussage im Verfahren zu verweigern, weil sie sich dem durch die hohe Medienpräsenz erzeugten psychischen Druck nicht mehr gewachsen fühlen; Zusammenbrüche von Befragten während eines Kreuzverhörs werden von der Kamera ebenso öffentlich zur Schau gestellt wie Aussagen zu Details aus der Intimsphäre des Beschuldigten; dessen mimische Reaktionsweisen auf den Argumentationsgang der Anklage werden der Nation am Fernseher vorgeführt und geben immer neuen Anlaß zu Mutmaßungen und Spekulationen; Staatsanwälte und Verteidiger richten die Dramaturgie ihrer Plädoyers – unterstützt von *High-Tech* im Gerichtssaal – nach der Wirksamkeit auf ein Millionenpublikum aus; die Ingredienzien des Falles selbst werden in zahllosen TV-

Kommentaren nach dem Muster einer *soap opera*, mit *back story*, *supporting actors*, *subtext* und *plot points*[52] zubereitet.

Die Vereinnahmung der Jurisprudenz durch die Unterhaltungsindustrie scheint perfekt und gebiert eine neue Form des Entertainment, das "Jurotainment".[53] Die amerikanische Nation wird auf diese Weise zur Fernseh-Jury, die am Bildschirm über den zu verhandelnden Fall zu Gericht sitzt. Diese Situation rückt in gefährliche Nähe eines Volksgerichts, bei dem die Rechtsprechung sich einem beispiellosen öffentlichen Druck der Masse ausgesetzt sieht, der einer objektiven Wahrheitsfindung entgegensteht. Die Berichterstattung zum "Jahrhundertprozeß" um O.J. Simpson markiert damit einen Endpunkt, an dem das von *The Chair* zu Beginn der 60er Jahre propagierte Streben nach mehr Transparenz und Überprüfbarkeit der staatlichen Organe seine Pervertierung erfährt und zu einer Unterminierung nicht nur des Rechtssystems, sondern auch der Menschenwürde des Beschuldigten führt.

9. Die Geschichtsauffassung des Dokumentarfilms – The Chair *als zeithistorisches Dokument*

Von einem amerikanischen Drehteam ursprünglich für ein amerikanisches Zielpublikum produziert, kann *The Chair* dennoch in ethnographischer Weise[54] rezipiert werden. Zuschauern anderer Sprach- und Kulturräume, in diesem Fall dem deutschen Publikum, erschließt der Dokumentarfilm ein kontextorientiertes Problembewußtsein für eine Gesellschaft, von der zwar bereits eine Vielzahl medienvermittelter Bilder existiert, deren Teilaspekte aber dennoch, oder gerade deshalb, außerhalb unseres eigenen, unmittelbaren Erfahrungsbereichs liegen. Eine kritische Auseinandersetzung mit *The Chair* vermag Amerikabilder zu korrigieren, zu relativieren und zu ergänzen.

Bei der Begegnung mit *The Chair* muß die Gefahr einer ethnozentrischen Rezeption berücksichtigt werden. Die vehemente Sozialkritik des Films kann bei Zuschauern zu einer Sehweise führen, die die eigene Position erhöht und die andere Kultur vorschnell abwertet; viele Bildsignale können sich von der Außenperspektive als "typisch" für die amerikanische Gesellschaft darstellen. Weil 'Verstehen' stets "durch das eigene Welt- und Selbstverständnis vermittelt" wird,[55] prägen Wahrnehmungsmuster sowohl des Drehteams wie auch des jeweiligen Rezipienten den Kommunikationsprozeß, den der Film auslöst. Diese doppelte Brechung dem Lernenden erfahrbar zu machen, ist eine wesentliche Aufgabe bei der Vermittlung interkultureller Kompetenz. Vorrangiges Lernziel ist es, Sinnbildungsprozesse und Lenkungsmechanismen des Filmtextes zu entschlüsseln und kritisch zu hinterfragen. Das dadurch gewonnene Bild von

Vorstellungsstrukturen und Bedeutungszusammenhängen der anderen Kultur muß stets in Relation zur eigenen Kultur gesetzt werden, um Differenzen und Gemeinsamkeiten herauszuarbeiten. Mit der Diskussion um Ausmaß und Verfügungsbereich staatlicher Gewalt gelingt dem Dokumentarfilm dieser Rückbezug: Er sensibilisiert den Rezipienten für das Spannungsverhältnis von Staat und Individuum auch im eigenen Land. Die Auseinandersetzung mit der Thematik des Films und mit der Form ihrer Vermittlung kann bei Schülern und Studenten engagierte Identifikations- und Abgrenzungsprozesse in Gang setzen, die wiederum ein wesentliches Ziel interkultureller Kompetenz befördern: die Orientierungsfindung in einer pluralistischen Gesellschaft und die Formung der eigenen Identität.[56]

Die Impulse hierzu liefert *The Chair* nicht aus dem distanzierten Blickwinkel eines Lehrfilms, der eine didaktisch aufbereitete Erörterung von Fakten, Zahlen und Rechtsauffassungen bietet, sondern durch eine Sicht "von unten", auf unmittelbar Betroffene. Mit der Hervorhebung und Betonung der Stimmungslagen von Anwalt und Delinquent schildert *The Chair* die Krisensituation des Crump-Falles aus einer subjektiven Erfahrung, in einem personengebundenen, emotionalen Kontext. Für Sozial- und Rechtshistoriker wird er zu einem lohnenden Untersuchungsgegenstand, denn er bietet eine dezidierte Gegenperspektive zu den automatisierten Verfahrensmechanismen, die der Staat in Todesstrafenfällen in Gang setzt. Nicht das menschliche Einzelschicksal, sondern ein Regelwerk an juristischen Bestimmungen steht dabei gemeinhin im Vordergrund.

Doch der Film *kommentiert* nicht nur kritisch die soziale Realität seiner Zeit, er ist in seiner spezifischen Machart auch ein *Produkt* soziokultureller Faktoren, die sich in den Erzählformen der Filmbilder manifestieren. So reduziert *The Chair* die Diskussion um die Todesstrafe auf ein Konfliktmuster, das an frühe Melodramen erinnert. Anwalt Moore verleiht der Film Züge des empfindsamen, tugendhaften Helden, der als Repräsentant eines fortschrittlich-emanzipierten Bürgertums für Freiheits- und Menschenrechte streitet und im wechselvollen Auf und Ab des Verfahrens dem Spiel eines launischen Machtapparats ausgesetzt scheint. Staatsanwalt Thompson, der für den Vollzug des Todesurteils plädiert, rückt *The Chair* in die Nähe des *evildoer* aristokratischer Provenienz, der klassische Eigenschaften wie Hybris, Eitelkeit, korrumpierte Moral und Kaltherzigkeit verkörpert.[57] Vor diesem Hintergrund wird der Crump-Fall zu einer Machtprobe zwischen den Rudimenten des Mittelalters und den Schwungkräften der Aufklärung, personifiziert in den Handlungsträgern des Films.

Mit dieser an historischen Erzählkonventionen orientierten Interpretation zeitgenössischer Ereignisse verfolgt *The Chair* eine besondere

Form der 'Geschichtsschreibung'. In ihr wird die aufrüttelnde Botschaft verkündet, daß elektrische Stühle – ebenso wie Galgen und Gaskammern – als Relikte des Mittelalters auf den Schrotthaufen der Geschichte gehören. Die Todesstrafe wird zu einem Anachronismus stigmatisiert, dessen sich ein fortschrittlich-demokratisches Amerika ebenso entledigen werde wie den Zeiten absolutistischer Herrschaft der 'Alten Welt'.

Die Sensibilisierung des Zuschauers für Reformen in Strafjustiz und -vollzug will *The Chair* über die Konsolidierung bürgerlich-konservativer Normen und Werte herbeiführen. Dies führt zu dem ambivalenten Charakter des Films. So glorifiziert *The Chair* mit dem Leitmotiv des Wettstreits, bei dem der Stärkere den Sieg davonträgt, ein Leistungsdenken, das auf eher systemkonforme Weise das Prinzip von Kampf und Macht propagiert. Besonders deutlich wird dies im Finale des Films. Nach erfolgreichem Abschluß des Falles begleitet die Kamera Anwalt Moore zu einem Pferderennen und erhebt ihn auf der sonnenbeschienenen Zuschauertribüne zum Sieger: Der tosende Applaus auf den Rängen scheint Moore selbst entgegenzubranden. Die Weitaufnahme zweier Kopf an Kopf galoppierenden Pferde ist unschwer als metaphorisches Bild auszumachen. Es verweist auf den knappen Ausgang des Falles, bei dem die gegnerischen Parteien sich einen dramatischen Wettkampf lieferten. 'Zu siegen' ist der dominierende Antriebsmechanismus, der alle Helden der Drew-Produktionen beherrscht.[58] Moore, so sagt uns Leacocks Kamera, hat nicht nur die berufliche, sondern auch die persönliche Bewährungsprobe, vor die ihn der Crump-Fall stellte, bravourös gemeistert, einen doppelten Entwicklungsprozeß erfolgreich vollendet. Der individuellen Selbstbehauptung der Person verleiht *The Chair* zugleich historische Größe. Bedeutet das Gnadenverfahren "a turning point in legal history", so ist Anwalt Moore der Pionier, der – gemäß berühmter Vorfahren wie der von der Kamera zu Beginn des Films zitierte Abraham Lincoln – die *Frontier* zum Wohl der Menschheit weiter voranschiebt und den Horizont erweitert. Hier offenbart sich das zutiefst optimistische Weltbild der Drew Associates, die auch mit *The Chair* einen letztlich ungebrochenen Fortschrittsglauben in Szene setzen und die Auffassung vertreten, daß Geschichte von tatkräftigen und aktionsreichen Menschen 'gemacht' wird.

Mit dieser durch Themenwahl, Kameraführung und Montage erzielten "Schreibweise", die die Sehgewohnheiten eines Massenpublikums erfüllen will, gibt *The Chair* Aufschluß über die in der US-Gesellschaft verankerten Mythen, Ideale und Wertvorstellungen. Zugleich zielt der Film mit dem Plädoyer für die Resozialisierung von Schwerkriminellen auf eine Bewußtseinsveränderung des Publikums und stellt eine Form der Gegenöffentlichkeit zur herrschenden Meinung seiner Zeit her. Im Stil eines *muckraking journalism* dringt die Kamera in tabuisierte Bereiche, um

Mißstände in Gesetzgebung und Strafvollzug Amerikas anzuprangern. Im Zusammenspiel dieser unterschiedlichen Facetten wird der Film zu einem faszinierenden Stück Kultur- und Rechtsgeschichte Amerikas. In seiner Doppelfunktion von aufklärerischem Instrument und gesellschaftskonformem Unterhaltungsprodukt steht er exemplarisch für die sozialen Spannungen und Verwerfungen einer ereignisreichen Dekade amerikanischer Geschichte.

*

The Chair ist Bestandteil einer repräsentativen Sammlung von weit über hundert amerikanischen Dokumentarfilmen von den zwanziger Jahren bis zur Gegenwart. Sie sind im *Deutschen Filmarchiv für Nordamerikastudien* zusammengefaßt, das am *Göttinger Institut für den Wissenschaftlichen Film (IWF)* eingerichtet wurde. Für den Unterricht an Schule und Universität können die Filme als Video vom *IWF* entliehen werden.[59] Benutzern dieser in Europa wohl einmaligen Filmsammlung stellt die Buchreihe *Studien zum Amerikanischen Dokumentarfilm*[60] Arbeitsmaterialien bereit, die für den Einsatz der Filme in sozialwissenschaftlichen, amerikahistorischen, landeskundlichen und filmwissenschaftlichen Lehrveranstaltungen Anregungen und Verständnishilfen geben.[61] Die interdisziplinäre Ausrichtung und der experimentelle Spielraum der Untersuchungsfelder spiegelt die Komplexität und Vielschichtigkeit des Mediums Dokumentarfilm.

Anmerkungen:

1 Vgl. Lothar Bredella: "Der amerikanische Dokumentarfilm: Zugang zur amerikanischen Wirklichkeit?". – In Lothar Bredella & Günther H. Lenz (Eds.): *Der amerikanische Dokumentarfilm: Herausforderungen für die Didaktik*, Giessener Beiträge zur Fremdsprachendidaktik, Tübingen, 1994, S. 87-89.

2 William J. Bowers: *Legal Homicide: Death as Punishment in America, 1864-1982*, Boston, 1988, S. 25-27.

3 Hugo Adam Bedau (Ed.): *The Death Penalty in America: Current Controversies*, New York, Oxford, 1997, S. 14. Amnesty International: *Todesstrafe in den USA*, Frankfurt/Main, 1989, S. 11; Ernst Schmiederer: "Live aus der Todeszelle", *Die Zeit*, 33 (11. August 1995), S. 50; Carola Kaps: "Internationale Proteste konnten Karla Faye Tucker nicht retten", *Frankfurter Allgemeine Zeitung*, 30 (5. Februar 1998), S. 3.

4 Vgl. Ulrich Schiller: "Die Mehrheit verlangt den Tod", *Die Zeit*, 23 (29. Mai 1992), S. 10.

5 Jürgen Kramer: *British Cultural Studies*, München, 1997, S. 9. Zur Definition des Begriffs "Kultur" siehe auch: Klaus P. Hansen: *Kultur und Kulturwissenschaft: Eine Einführung*, Tübingen, Basel, 1995, S. 14-15.

6 Das von der Staatsanwaltschaft verfochtene Todesurteil basiert auf dem Strafrechtsgrundsatz der *Talion*, der klassischen alttestamentarischen Vergeltungsforderung. Sie zielt auf eine der Tat qualitativ und quantitativ entsprechenden Strafe und sieht das Ideal der Gerechtigkeit nur durch die Vergeltung von Gleichem mit Gleichem erfüllt. Dem steht in *The Chair* eine durch Crumps Anwälte vertretene reformierte Auffassung von Strafe gegenüber, die als Ziel die Resozialisierung des Straftäters vorsieht. Vgl. hierzu: Karl Bruno Leder: *Todesstrafe: Ursprung, Geschichte, Opfer,* München, [2]1987, S. 250.

7 Als Direktor der Broadcast Division der *Time-Life* Verlagsgesellschaft sichert Robert Drew die finanziellen Mittel für die Entwicklung neuer Aufnahmegeräte und die Produktion der Filme. In den Jahren von 1960 bis 1963 sind die Drew Associates – eine zuweilen bis zu 75 Mitarbeiter umfassende Gruppe von Bildphotographen, Journalisten, Filmtechnikern und Dokumentarfilmern – die Hauptvertreter des *Direct Cinema*. Seinen Anfang nahm das Pionierprojekt 1954 im Zusammentreffen von Drew und Leacock. Vgl. Stephen Mamber: *Cinema Verite in America: Studies in Uncontrolled Documentary,* Cambridge, Mass., 1974, S. 62, 116.

8 Ulrich Gregor: "Leacock oder das Kino der Physiker", *Film* 4, 1966, S. 18; Gideon Bachmann: "The Frontiers of Realist Cinema: The Work of Ricky Leacock", *Film Culture* 22/23, 1961, S. 12-33.

9 Eine besondere Form der 'Fahraufnahme', bei der der Filmer mit handgehaltener Kamera einer Person zu einem Zielort folgt.

10 Entgegen dem Prinzip, keine Ereignisse nachzustellen, wird die Sequenz jedoch erst einen Monat nach Abschluß des Falles gedreht, um den elektrischen Stuhl in Ausschluß der Presse- und Fernsehreporter vor die Kamera zu bekommen. Leacocks *Tracking Shot* vermittelt dennoch wesentliche Merkmale des *Direct Cinema.*

11 Jan-Marie-Lambert Peters: "Die Struktur der Filmsprache". – In Franz Josef Albersmeier (Ed.): *Texte zur Theorie des Films*, Stuttgart, 1979, S. 375, 376.

12 Richard Leacock, Brief an den Verfasser vom 29.12.1989, S. 4.

13 Gregor, "Leacock oder das Kino der Physiker", S. 18.

14 Vgl. Mark Shivas: "Interviews: Richard Leacock", *Movie* 8, April 1963, S. 17.

15 So das *voice-over* in der Exposition des Films.

16 Der Erzähler in *The Chair* betont, Moore arbeite ohne Entlohnung und evoziert das Bild des selbstlosen Anwalts, der für die gute Sache kämpft. Angeklagte, die sich einen privaten Anwalt leisten können, haben in den USA erfahrungsgemäß weitaus größere Chancen, einem Todesurteil zu entgehen als jene, die sich durch Pflichtverteidiger vertreten lassen müssen. Deren materielle Mittel und juristische Kompetenz zur Vorbereitung und Durchführung von Todesstrafenprozessen reichen oft nicht aus. Kritische Stimmen sehen deshalb in der Todesstrafe ein Strafinstrumentarium, das der Staat 'exklusiv' nur für die ärmsten Schichten der US-Gesellschaft 'reserviert'. Vgl. Clinton Duffy und Al Hirshberg: *Exekution*. Übers. v. Ursula Albrecht, Köln, 1964, S. 253 und Amnesty International: *Todesstrafe*, S. 55-60.

17 Thomas Elsaesser: "Tales of Sound and Fury: Observations on the Family Melodrama". – In Bill Nichols (Ed.): *Movies and Methods*, II, Berkeley, 1985, S. 181.

18 Robert A. Rosenstone: "Geschichte in Bildern / Geschichte in Worten: Über die Möglichkeit, Geschichte zu verfilmen". – In Rainer Rother (Ed.): *Bilder schreiben Geschichte: Der Historiker im Kino*, Berlin, 1991, S. 73.

19 Nach der Absage des Kardinals von Chicago, Crumps Gnadengesuch offiziell zu unterstützen, tröstet sich Moore mit einer stillen Freude an den Unwägbarkeiten der Verfahrensvorbereitung und resümiert schließlich: "That's what makes trial work interesting!". Moores "asides" – ein von Leacock geprägter Terminus – können bedingt gleichgesetzt werden mit der klassischen Form des Reflexionsmonologs im Theater "[...] zur Analyse der Situation und der eigenen Gefühle [...]." Elke Platz-Waury: *Drama und Theater: Eine Einführung*, Literaturwissenschaft im Grundstudium, 2, Tübingen, 1978, S. 58. Nicht zuletzt deshalb erscheint der Anwalt in *The Chair* als dramatischer Held.

20 Mamber: *Cinema Verite*, S. 129.

21 Für die Aufnahme wird ein Objektiv mit relativ großer Brennweite benützt: Der Blickwinkel ist eingeschränkt, die Schärfe flach.

22 *Frankfurter Allgemeine Zeitung*, 30 (5. Februar 1998), S. 3.

23 Im Juli 1962 gedreht, wird *The Chair* erst zwei Jahre später, im Oktober 1964, als Schlußlicht der *Living Camera*-Serie ausgestrahlt, zu der 12 der seit 1962 produzierten Drew-Associates-Filme zusammengestellt sind. Vgl. Mamber: *Cinema Verite*, S. 96.

24 Die *New York Times* vergleicht das öffentliche Aufsehen um das Crump-Verfahren mit der Publizität des Caryl-Chessman-Falles, der 1960 in Kalifornien zum Politikum wird und eine weltweite Diskussion um die Abschaffung der Todesstrafe auslöst. N.N.: "Governor Spares Condemned Slayer in Illinois", *New York Times*, 2. August 1962, S. 53. Vgl. Leder: *Todesstrafe*, S. 215.

25 Vgl. J. Edward Gerald: *News of Crime: Courts and Press in Conflict*, Westport, Conn., London, 1983, S. 4, 5, 155, 166.

26 Ein Zoom nach vorn lenkt die Aufmerksamkeit auf Crumps Nase, im folgenden Bild ist die Nasenöffnung der Kopfmaske des elektrischen Stuhls zu sehen.

27 Eine Aufnahme von Crump wird in die Bildfolge eingeschnitten, die den Gefängnisdirektor im Exekutionsraum beobachtet.

28 Die Bilder werden 'eingefroren' und sollen sich so dem Zuschauer umso nachhaltiger einprägen.

29 Stewart O'Nan: "Für tot erklärt", *Frankfurter Allgemeine Zeitung*, 30 (5. Februar 1998), S. 41. Stefan Kornelius: "Tod zur Prime Time", *Süddeutsche Zeitung*, 29 (5. Februar 1998), S. 3.

30 Wolfram Tichy (Ed.): "Thriller". – In *Buchers Enzyklopädie des Films*, Frankfurt/Main, Luzern, 1977, S. 773. Vgl. Georg Seeßlen und Bernhard Roloff (Eds.): *Kino der Angst: Geschichte und Mythologie des Film-Thrillers*, Grundlagen des populären Films, 5, Hamburg, 1980, S. 20-21.

31 "What makes us different from other reporting, and from other documentary film-making, is that in each of the stories there is a time when a man comes against moments of tension, and pressure, and revelation, and decision. It's these moments that interest us most. Where we differ from TV and press is that we are predicated on being there when things are happening to people that count." Bachmann: "The Frontiers of Realist Cinema", S. 118.

32 Ein vom Gouverneur einberufener fünfköpfiger Gnadenausschuß, der nach Anhörung der Zeugenaussagen und Plädoyers von Staatsanwalt und Verteidigung dem Gouverneur einen nichtbindenden Empfehlungsspruch übermitteln wird.

33 So betont der den Bildern unterlegte Kommentar, der von Moore und Nizer begründete Standpunkt sei "unprecedented in American law" und verkündet

wenig später: "If Louis Nizer and Don Moore argue successfully, this case would make a turning point in legal history."

34 Kramer: *British Cultural Studies*, S. 67.

35 Amnesty International: *Jahresbericht 1997*, Frankfurt/Main, 1997.

36 Amnesty International: *Todesstrafe*, S. 161.

37 Clay Gowran: "Crump Stakes His Last Hope on a Unique Appeal", *Chicago Tribune* (22. Juli 1962), S. 1, Kol. 1. 1953 zum Tode verurteilt, verbringt Paul Crump bereits neun Jahre im Todestrakt.

38 Bowers: *Legal Homicide*, S. 18-19.

39 In *Newsweek*, zitiert nach: Gerhard Mauz: "Unverkennbar – Ronald Reagan: Zum Beginn des Prozesses gegen O.J. Simpson in Los Angeles", *Der Spiegel*, 4/1995 (23.1.1995), S. 136. Simpson wurde zur Last gelegt, seine geschiedene Frau und deren Bekannten erstochen zu haben.

40 Presseberichten zufolge verbuchte der amerikanische Nachrichtensender *CNN* während seiner Gerichtsberichterstattung eine 700prozentige Steigerung der Zuschauerzahlen. Ingrid Kölle: "Die Anwälte sind zu Stars geworden", *Stuttgarter Zeitung* (11.10.1995), S. 24.

41 Aufnahmen im Gerichtssaal erfolgen über eine fest installierte, ferngesteuerte Kamera, auf die der Vorsitzende Richter restriktiv einwirken kann.

42 Angeführt von dem Nachrichtensender *N-TV* fordern Privatsender wie *RTL*, *SAT 1* und *PRO 7*, entsprechend dem amerikanischen Muster deutsche Gerichtssäle für Fernsehkameras zu öffnen. Die Vorsitzende des Bundesverfassungsgerichts, Jutta Limbach, sowie die damalige Bundesjustizministerin, Sabine Leutheusser-Schnarrenberger, sprechen sich in der öffentlichen Debatte entschieden gegen eine Änderung des Gerichtsverfahrensgesetzes aus, das Ton- und Fernsehaufnahmen während der Verhandlung verbietet. TV-Diskussionsrunde "Talk im Turm", *SAT 1*, 1995.

43 Deshalb werden vielerorts in den Vereinigten Staaten die Geschworenen für die Dauer des Verfahrens unter oftmals größtem Aufwand von der Öffentlichkeit und der Medienberichterstattung abgeschirmt. Diese "Quarantäne" zur Vermeidung jeglicher Beeinflussung von außen kann jedoch nur unzureichend funktionieren und wird vor allem bei mehrmonatigen Prozessen zu einem ernsten Problem. Vgl. Gerald: *News of Crime*, S. 163.

44 Brief Richard Leacocks vom 29.12.1989, S. 5.

45 Brief Richard Leacocks vom 5.2.1990, S. 2.

46 *Ibid.*, S. 1. Meine Hervorhebung.

47 Brief Richard Leacocks vom 29.12.1998, S. 1-2.

48 *Chicago Tribune*, 22. Juli 1962, S. 1, Kol. 1.

49 *Der Spiegel*, 23.1.1995, S. 145.

50 Michael Kronenwetter: *Free Press versus Fair Trial: Television and other Media in the Courtroom*, New York, London, Toronto, Sydney, 1986, S. 47-59.

51 *Der Spiegel*, 23.1.1995, S. 144. Vgl. J. Edward Gerald: *News of Crime*, S. 159-161.

52 Michael Schwelien: "Die letzte große Rolle des O.J. Simpson", *Die Zeit*, 42 (14.10.1994), S. 96.

53 Leo Wieland: "Die seltsame Geschichte eines 'perfekten' Mordes", *Frankfurter Allgemeine Zeitung*, 231 (5.10.1995), S. 13.

54 David MacDougall: "Prospects of Ethnographic Film". – In Bill Nichols (Ed.): *Movies and Methods*, I, Berkeley, 1976, S. 135-150.

55 Lothar Bredella & Günther H. Lenz (Eds.): *Der amerikanische Dokumentarfilm*, S. 84.

56 Kramer: *British Cultural Studies*, S. 66, 67.

57 Zu den Frühformen des Melodrams vgl. Bill Nichols: *Movies and Methods*, II, S. 168, 169; Georg Seeßlen & Bernhard Roloff (Eds.): *Das Kino der Gefühle: Geschichte und Mythologie des Film-Melodrams*, Grundlagen des populären Films, 6, Hamburg, 1980, S. 16, 19.

58 Jean Claude Bringuier: "Libres propos sur le cinéma-vérité", *Cahiers du Cinema*, 25, Juli 1963, S. 14-17. Louis Marcorelles: "L'Epérience Leacock" *Cahiers du Cinema*, 140, Februar 1963, S. 11-17.

59 *Institut für den Wissenschaftlichen Film*, Nonnenstieg 72, Postfach 2315, 37013 Göttingen. Tel. (0551) 5024-0, Fax (0551) 5024-400.

60 Die Buchreihe *Studien zum Amerikanischen Dokumentarfilm* wird herausgegeben von Hans Borchers, Stephan Dolezel, Jürgen Heideking, Peter Lösche und Alfred Weber und erscheint im *Wissenschaftlichen Verlag Trier*.

61 Ausgangspunkt der Einzelstudien ist jeweils ein detailliertes, bebildertes Transkript des behandelten Films, das neben der Beschreibung der Kamerasprache auch den Wortlaut der Filmhandlung wiedergibt.

Bärbel Mosner, Bochum

Book in one hand, pencil in the other. How we can exploit the still unchallenged advantages of our most traditional medium.

The dichotomy between the bookworm and the computer freak, also known as the PC potato, is non-existent. Why, then, should the teaching profession worry about youngsters' reading habits and concern itself with fresh approaches to the teaching of reading? Print literacy, as current research suggests, remains the driving force behind success in our modern multi-media society. That is why various steps are being taken in our educational system to encourage the younger generation to read books. In this paper I should also like to reflect on a new practice which promises to promote literacy and textual competence amongst advanced learners and to help them benefit from the specific advantages of reading books.

1. Of bookworms, PC potatoes and the role of reading in modern media education

Although the mass media have been circulating the alarming news that reading is in drastic decline, recent research on reading has revealed that the looming picture of a largely illiterate society is more of a sensationalist distortion than an accurate representation of facts.[1] It is true: teachers, education experts and researchers worry about those young people who do not read and about a potential increase in those who will ignore books and newspapers in future. At present, roughly one third of young people do not read, although they are not illiterate in the strict sense of the word. Secondary illiteracy is related to factors in children's homes, mainly to a lack of role models in reading, for boys especially, and restricted access to books and newspapers and to an attitude of passive consumerism.

It seems, however, that for a majority of the population the status of the book as a medium of information and entertainment has remained unchanged despite the advent of audiovisual and electronic media. A surprisingly large number of young Germans, two thirds by current reckoning, enjoy reading books and newspapers and rank the book as the third most important medium in their lives, with television taking first place and audio media second.[2] The major incentive to read books in one's leisure time lies in the scope for imagination and full immersion in a fictitious world. What goes on during reading, picturing the setting, seeing the characters in one's mind's eye, filling in details, for example, has a stimulating effect on readers and rewards them for their efforts. Once young people have discovered the satisfaction they can gain from reading, they are unlikely to give up the habit. Baacke's 1990 media study reveals that reading habits are not threatened by the use of other media. This view has recently been confirmed by researchers who reject the notion of rivalry between the different media. It even looks as if the use of one medium, the book, makes the use of the other media more rewarding: computer freaks read handbooks and devour magazines to keep up-to-date; punk rockers collect books and articles about their favourite musicians; radio hams find their most relevant information in specialist literature. Therefore we have to abandon the obsolete dichotomies of "the book versus the other media" or "the bright bookworm versus the unhealthy PC potato, the chronic computer user". Still, we are right to give reading priority among the different literacies because it provides the indispensable basis for private and professional success. In reading we foster and enhance complex abilities which relate to problem-solving skills. The book with its pages of printed text works on the non-iconic symbol system of written language, the understanding of which calls for a great variety of mental actions and commands the use of cognitive strategies. Findings about avid readers suggest that there is a strong link between print literacy and other literacies, that youngsters with highly developed reading skills benefit from these skills in many other contexts. Young habitual readers have been found to understand TV programmes even better than habitual viewers.[3] Their success is put down to receptive skills which they have learned to use in a sophisticated and active manner. Young habitual readers seem to lead socially satisfying lives: they make films and do not just watch, they produce their own tapes and do not just listen to music, they take an interest in social activities.[4] With print literacy young people acquire the prerequisite of a socially and academically advantageous education. Therefore we may conclude that efficient reading instruction provides the most effective media education. The greatest challenge lies in our ability to stimulate mental activity in the younger generation.

2. The book: the most learner-friendly medium

When we consider the learner's needs and abilities, we discover a number of reasons why the book lends itself to educational purposes. It is an easily accessible and easily handled medium. Readers do not need to purchase any extra equipment such as batteries, cables or an interface. Once they hold it in their hands it is ready for use. The book is an object they can take possession of, buy, own, write their names on, carry around, read on the bus or in bed. The medium allows for a physical closeness that may eventually lead to a personal closeness, to readers regarding their copy of *Romeo and Juliet* as "my Shakespeare". That is not a trivial matter, reading researchers tell us: they have observed that keen readers develop personal relationships with books and that they enjoy reading most when they can immerse themselves in gripping stories that invite identification.[5]

Of course reading for pleasure differs from reading for instruction, for instance insofar as set texts and reading lists are often less entertaining than the titles chosen for private reading. What is more, learners are expected to stretch themselves and accept books as food for thought and not just for pleasure. Therefore they have to cope with recalcitrant texts, too. It is interesting to note that in learning environments young people themselves prefer printed texts to other media, reading the book to watching the film or listening to the audio tape. What is it that makes the book the learner's medium of choice? In foreign language classes at school as well as at university teachers have repeatedly had the experience that learners are most afraid of "not understanding", be it something e.g. in English, French or Polish. To overcome this fear the book has proved to be an extremely learner-friendly medium. The printed text gives readers more time to think than a spoken text on audio tape, film or video. With the printed text readers can process the information in their own time and set their own pace, and this proves to be particularly reassuring to foreign language learners. In our mother tongue we perceive speech as a string of words, although that is an illusion because "one word runs into the next seamlessly [...]. We simply hallucinate word boundaries".[6] The foreign language learner does not possess the same amount of experience and knowledge, of phonological rules and the likelihood of combinations, of lexical items and their collocations, to hallucinate successfully. The increased risk of incomprehension always presents a source of immense stress in a learning environment. Take Irvine Welsh's *Trainspotting*[7], a book and a film which have acquired a cult-like status among youngsters also in countries outside the UK. If German foreign language learners saw the film in the original version they would be unable to enjoy it as much as the dubbed version even if the visual information still added to a basic understanding of what is going on. If they listened to the audio cassette, they would not understand anything at all. To follow *Trainspotting* on tape is far beyond the average German learner especially since acoustics make listening a strenuous task with sound effects and the distinct rattle of trains in the background. Another enormous difficulty of the "talking book" arises from the local vernacular spoken by the main characters. Since the film as well as the audio cassette force viewers and listeners to adapt themselves quickly to the strict pace of the presentation and to an unfamiliar sound image, they cannot take a break to work out what is being said. Readers, however, have much more power over the reception process than listeners or viewers. They can take several measures to avoid the frustrating experience of being unable to catch up. Rather than break off the reading process they can slow it down, which is the normal form of adjustment even skilled readers resort to when they switch from texts in their mother tongue to those in a foreign language. Readers can decide upon their need for pauses and sever the eye-contact whenever they want to, e.g. to reflect upon a phrase, to consult a dictionary, to translate the unfamiliar graphophonetic spelling into the English they know or to indulge in associations and images. When they come back to the page in the book, the printed text is waiting for them where they left off. Another distinct advantage of reading books is that readers are allowed and encouraged to turn back the pages to look for a vaguely remembered clue, the proper understanding of which makes a great difference to the comprehension of the entire book. Thus the book presents learners with an ideal medium to foster major reading skills and metacognitive strategies, e.g. selecting specific repair mechanisms to cope with difficulties and assessing their own performance, their comprehension.[8]

3. "Book in one hand...": Measures taken to encourage young people to read

Public education may not exert as decisive an influence on children's reading habits as reading experiences in the family and in the reading environment at home, but it bears a clear responsibility: outside schools and universities young people do not get much chance to develop textual competence and critical reading. Therefore they need systematic instruction from professional teachers who, firstly, nurture the basic skills, secondly, arouse and sustain motivation to read and, thirdly, stimulate reflective knowledge and critical thought. Only readers can become autonomous learners because they can select and consult books of their own choice to promote their own learning. That is why a wide variety of steps can be taken to form a positive attitude towards reading and to strengthen the learner's emotional relationship with books:

- Creating a stimulating reading environment: to tempt youngsters to pick up a book, schools and local authorities invest large sums of money in school libraries and cosy reading corners. Primary school classrooms are equipped with shelves and rugs to provide an area to which children can retire with their books for a while. In such a sheltered reading corner within the classroom pupils learn to respect their classmates' need for peace and quiet.

- Initiating activities and projects: some schools organize book clubs, debating societies, book cafés where pupils meet to discuss books, where they are read to by a teacher or fellow pupil or where they can participate in reading competitions. Supported by nationwide foundations such as *Stiftung Lesen*, schools invite pupils to attend public readings by well-known authors, to visit exhibitions, for example, about children's literature that deals with the experience of Jewish boys and girls in Nazi Germany.
- Pursuing a reader-oriented approach in the classroom: following findings in reading research, more emphasis is being placed on reading techniques and skills, for example in official syllabuses.[9] Awareness-raising lessons about the reading process are often included in German and English classes to assist pupils to acquire metacognitive strategies to control their own reading. In teaching units focusing on literary texts, teachers involve pupils and students in selecting books for classroom reading by supplying them with extracts, blurbs, reviews and summaries before a final decision is taken. In addition, advanced learners read and review books of their own choice for brief oral presentations. It is hoped that recommendations provided by their peers may motivate young people to turn to the book that has been reviewed for their private reading. Concerning the classroom approach in EFL (English as a foreign language) classes, Nünning advocates continuing reforms in three major areas: giving the literary canon greater variety by adding, for example, contemporary novels by female writers and authors from outside the UK and the US; emphasizing educational goals such as social and intercultural learning through the reading of foreign language literature; developing learner- and reader-oriented teaching methods.[10]
- New methods in the literature classroom: extracts from syllabuses and publications for teachers show that the view that a text is a self-contained object and that readers need only extract its meaning has long been abandoned. Teachers have started to experiment with forms of *empathetic* and *creative* writing to involve learners in pre- and post-reading activities (e.g. writing additional chapters or scenes, making diary entries for a character in a book) and with forms of *exploratory* writing to engage readers in while-reading activities (e.g. gap filling, rearranging jumbled sentences or paragraphs, annotating, logging, drawing response charts).[11] In the attempt to engage readers in a dynamic, creative and personal process, teachers have to be careful not to throw out, as it were, the baby with the bathwater. They are right in reassuring learners that their own thoughts and readings are superior to regurgi-

tated interpretations. However, a witty and creative but inconclusive reading is not an alternative to a bland or standardized performance, it is rather the opposite and equally undesirable extreme. At present the challenge in teaching literature to the foreign language class lies in the pursuit of an integrated approach, in reconciling the demands of learner-oriented principles with a text-based concept that safeguards against the "anything-goes" mentality.

4. "...pencil in the other": What young readers can gain from working with books

To the experienced reader certain habits come almost naturally: we pick up a new book, seize a pencil, and, while our eyes are darting across the pages, circle a word here, underline a phrase there, scribble a couple of remarks between the lines or in the margin, or jot down a concise comment in an extra note-book. Young learners who have not yet become accustomed to those habits, read and, to their own dismay and frustration, forget. They need to be shown how they can train effective while-reading skills which will not only boost their mnemonic power but by sharpening their sense of perception will also enable them to use other media competently and intelligently. The point that is being made here is that the basic skills which constitute media competence can best be acquired from working with books and printed texts before they can be applied to other media.

4.1. Underlining and annotating – a case for traditional practices

Underlining and circling words or phrases may look like a very basic while-reading activity. Yet, it is one which young readers are unable to perform efficiently, as they tend to use it indiscriminately. When they are set the task of underlining significant words, most of them get carried away and end up highlighting entire pages in yellow, pink and green. The intended effect of marking for meaning is lost and the enthusiasm for colour turns orientation into confusion. Therefore inexperienced readers are best provided with scanning tasks, which can be surprisingly demanding and very useful in developing sensitivity to language (e.g. "Read through the newspaper report about a football match and underline all those words that are associated with battle and war."). With more open tasks (e.g. "Underline the main ideas.") learners need to be reminded of the simple rule "Read first, mark later": they must have finished reading the entire paragraph or page before they can put highlighter to paper. Following this guideline their selection process will become more conscious and they will automatically underline only few phrases, confining themselves to those that are meaningful to them. Scanning and highlighting tasks are ideal introductory activities for foreign language learners since they can display their reading comprehension in a semi-verbal way. They need not express their ideas in the target language, yet their response is *not* non-verbal because they underline selected words and sentences in the foreign language.

The printed text is by far the most appropriate medium to introduce learners to another traditional technique the educational value of which cannot be overestimated: the use of *annotations*. Readers can record their spontaneous ideas almost literally while reading because they need not take their eyes off the page. No other medium can achieve a comparable closeness and immediacy. When texts are presented through audio or video material, the learners have to cope with at least two practical difficulties. 1. Unless they are in a position to stop the cassette or video recorder, they are always in danger of getting left behind and missing essential points. The stressful experience of constantly having to catch up on what has been said is intensified by the need to make extensive notes. 2. If listeners or viewers registered their responses and nothing else, they would later on find their own notes too cryptic to be of any use. Before they can make even the briefest comment ("!" or "Too true") or jot down a question mark to express their doubts, they need to make notes of or even summarize the scene or episode that their comment refers to. Marginal notes in books, however, are specific to a particular word or line which is already printed. When readers pick up their books a month or even a year after their first reading, they are still able to clearly relate their responses to the referent.

Although the electronic text, just like the printed text, allows readers to process the information in their own time, it cannot compete with the unique convenience offered by the book. To be able to write something in the margin of an electronic text readers have to use a format that is different from the one used for viewing and reading. And, what is more, they have to take measures to ensure that their annotations are clearly recognizable as such, since these notes must not be confused with authorial insertions in the primary text. Thus, more time and careful preparation are needed to exploit the electronic medium.

Finally, pages in a book provide space between the lines and the paragraphs. To help learners make efficient use of their marginals teachers can encourage them to occasionally *write* between the lines what they *have read* between the lines. What young readers can gain from this technique is an increase in their mental activity and intellectual involvement which will contribute to a deeper understanding of the text.

4.2. The reading log – sketches of a new practice

Amongst the wide range of new methods which are entering the literature classroom, the reading log deserves greater attention, because it is a promising way of putting the integrated approach into practice. The concept of the reading log is modelled on the personal diary which is kept as an ongoing record of day-to-day affairs and the diarist's response to them.[12] Confiding one's uncensored and most intimate thoughts to a diary as if to a *close* friend enables the diarist to read and review entries later from a *distance* – a distance also in time which allows insights into patterns of response and reflection on blind spots that are not acknowledged in the heat of the moment. The main purpose of a reading log is to support readers' mental participation, to encourage guessing and anticipating, re-evaluating and questioning. It raises learners' awareness of their own understanding of a novel or a play or a story *before* pre-set tasks, teacher questions and student answers can channel and manipulate their own reading. In making vague impressions and thoughts explicit in writing, readers take the minutes of their own reception process while reading, recording ideas *before* they forget them. To introduce classes to the use of the reading log, teachers need not make drastic changes in their teaching methods. What is needed, however, is a fundamental respect for the individual student's experience of reading.[13]

At present, the majority of German students in schools, colleges and universities are not familiar with keeping a reading log. My practical experience with beginners and advanced students shows that they benefit most from a concise handout in combinaton with an induction session in which they can talk about the basic principles, discuss practical issues and negotiate the later use of the log in the classroom and in further assignments.[14] After a brief introduction the reading log should be completed individually before classroom work on a literary text begins.

4.2.1. Selected results from work in progress

In April 1996 a log study was begun at the Ruhr-Universität Bochum which is based upon the reading logs kept by advanced learners of English while they were reading through Shakespeare's *Romeo and Juliet*[15] in preparing for a seminar. The study aims to explore the educational potential of the reading log, its strengths and its limitations. This paper will consider only those results that shed some light on the effects which the keeping of a log may have on the reading of books.

What evidence is there to suggest that the reading log may strengthen the relationship between the book and the reader?

The practice of writing one's guesses and predictions down has a *motivating effect*. Even though their entries commit readers to nothing, even though they can change their opinions in the solitary activity of writing their logs whenever they like, an explicit prediction provokes a competitive spirit. Readers are eager to find out whether they were right or not, for example in anticipating that someone would spy on Romeo and Juliet's secret rendezvous in the balcony scene. Their entry motivates them to carry on reading to confirm or correct their prediciton, and, in the case of a false guess, to trace back the signs they misread or overlooked.

The practice of writing while reading establishes strong *intellectual ties* between the reader and the book. My study shows that learners not only spend more time working with one book but also that they automatically resort to close reading. They are not content to skim a scene or grasp the main idea, as they need to deepen their understanding to be able to articulate their ideas. Thus they spend more time reflecting about unfamiliar words and difficult passages, looking up expressions in a dictionary or in the notes, trying to pinpoint where specific complications lie. The strong cognitive links between the readers and the play are mirrored in the frequent use of quotations in the log. There seem to be different reasons why they copy words, phrases and, occasionally, an entire passage, for example, to:

- add authenticity to a sentence which summarizes or paraphrases the scene ("Two friends are talking about Romeo who is 'blind in [sic] his love'..." II, i, 32),
- emphasize a specific reading or judgement (" 'I wonder at this haste' is a bit ridiculous. Her [Juliet's] marriage with Romeo was more than hasty." III, v, 118),
- identify the exact phrase that has triggered an emotional response ("I like the verse 'A pair of star-crossed lovers take their life'. It implies fate, longing and something that is out of somebody's reach." Prologue, 6).

The reading log constitutes an *emotional link* between the reader and the book, mainly because it documents the reader's growing confidence in his or her ability to cope with a Renaissance text in a foreign language. Apprehensive remarks in the first entries contrast with the relief with which readers later write "I have really got used to the language by now". They also gain confidence in their own judgement about the text, and they appreciate the sheltered space where they can praise and criticize the play, express agreement as well as irritation or lack of understanding. Responding emotionally in writing, readers can get rid of nervous tension. As the log is an ideal place to make notes of things they do not understand, of words and phrases that are not yet clear, they need not panic, because they know they can always come back to their notes, should a specific point not be clarified in the next few pages. The log can put their minds at rest because it contains all those things they understand plus those that still puzzle them, about which they will want to talk to their fellow students or teachers or consult a reference book.

Some logs illustrate an almost *personal* relationship as readers directly address characters in the play, e.g. to warn Romeo not to go to Capulet's ball where he might be discovered as a Montague. Some readers comment explicitly on how they used to stand in awe of Shakespeare, the cultural icon, from whom they kept their distance because they found his plays too complicated, his language too remote. In their logs they emphasize their surprise at finding so many bawdy scenes, funny scenes, obscenities and vulgarisms in *Romeo and Juliet.* They observe that they had formerly associated a Shakespearean play with an educational experience rather than an enjoyable one. The reading log helps to close the gap between a contemporary reader and a famous but remote text from the traditional canon. And that may eventually encourage learners to read more books by the same author.

What evidence is there to suggest that the reading log assists learners in benefiting from the specific advantages of reading books?

Keeping a reading log is time-consuming. It slows down the reading process, though at the readers' own pace and to their own advantage, but it does not slow them up. Bearing in mind that reading is a problem-solving activity, we can now say that the log makes the process of problem-solving visible and accessible. Some readers are not aware of their own strategies and only notice them when they reflect upon them to make their entries. In the long run, *the awareness-raising effect* of the log can contribute to learners' discovering metacognitive strategies, to their realizing when it is useful to note something down in their mother tongue, how best to make use of diagrams and drawings, why to consult which book of reference and how to assess the efficiency of these strategies. What looks like a disruption of the reading process gives readers a break in which valuable mental activity increases. Keeping a log stimulates precisely those activities that are characteristic of reading: picturing, anticipating, gap-filling, to name just a few.

4.2.2. Prospects for the new practice

At present all the signs are that in teaching environments the popularity of the reading log will continue to increase. One of the biggest UK-based publishers for instance, Longman Group UK Limited, provides young readers with educational editions of novels and plays that have one page of suggestions on how to keep a reading log included at the front of the book. In Germany, too, more and more teachers, lecturers and researchers are becoming aware of the advantages of the reading log.[16] In the federal state of Brandenburg, no less an authority than the official ministerial syllabus for English even recommends the use of *Lesetagebücher*, reader diaries, to help learners develop effective receptive strategies.[17] Three major trends in the teaching of literature will sustain interest in the reading log:

1. The impact of post-structuralist theory upon teaching has led to renewed emphasis on students' text production.

> The response to a text is itself always a text. Our knowledge is itself only a dim text that brightens as we express it. This is why expression, the making of new texts by students, must play a major role in the kind of course [English literature for first year college students. B.M.] we are discussing.[18]

The reading log is of special interest because it expresses and integrates fragments of the mental text.

2. The learner-oriented approach calls for the development of new methods that allow students to explore their own thoughts on works of literature. So far reader-oriented concepts have largely ignored the fact that the reader considered in literary theory is the implied reader.[19] Numerous publications about the reading process insinuate that the hypothetical reader and the empirical reader are identical, whereas practical teaching experience makes it unmistakably clear that this is not so.[20] Reading logs are documents produced by authentic readers whose response may at times differ considerably from the implied reader the author had in mind at the time of writing the book. Like other exploratory techniques the reading log represents practices that signal recognition of the active reader and the autonomous learner.

3. Reading researchers have drawn attention to cognitive and metacognitive strategies that seem to be responsible for successful reading experience. They recommend that these strategies be further explored in empirical studies and targeted in literature classes.[21] Due to the staying power of responses preserved by writing, reading logs can be used as a resource to study one's own reading strategies.

Weighing up my own and my students' experiences with logs and the major results of the log study, I can strongly recommend the use of the reading log with advanced learners and advise teachers to experiment with it. But I should also like to call attention to some problematic issues. Overtaxing the strengths of a new practice can easily backfire, no matter how learner-friendly it is meant to be. As early as 1992 Anderson reports a student complaining: "We have been journaled to death".[22] Gilbert's scepticism must also be taken seriously. She observes that the reading log can be corrupted by marking and grading the "personal voice" in it, which eventually leads to students feigning something that they have perceived as their teacher's tastes.[23] I would therefore advise teachers to use the reading log sparingly, if discerningly, in order to capitalize on its advantages and to motivate learners to accept it as a new form of working with books. It prepares the ground for rich textual analysis because it enables learners to bring first reading impressions, questions, misunderstandings and their own interests to bear in the discussion and in the written work. As we anticipate a great "diversity of opinion in the class" and "integrity of response"[24], the reading log will improve the quality of the reading experience and increase the chance that learners will discover the gratification which reading books can bring. It may not be a universal cure-all and it cannot work miracles, but it makes working with books in the foreign language literature class an exciting and refreshing experience for both: learners and teachers.

5. Conclusion: quality not quantity

In May 1997 a well-known German weekly published the results of an opinion poll about the perennial problem of a literary canon.[25] Authors, critics, entrepreneurs and public figures had been asked to name three to five literary titles which school-leavers, *Abiturienten*, should have read in their German class. Beside some thought-provoking answers and intriguing recommendations several replies betrayed their writers' indignation: how could they be expected to restrict their choice to less than half a dozen books, when school-leavers should have read twenty, thirty or fifty or as many as one hundred as some suggested! Members of the teaching profession, who had oddly enough been excluded from this survey except for one "pedagogue", will surely shake their heads in a mixture of amusement and amazement at the hopelessly unrealistic suggestion that 17-to-19-year olds slog through a long list of set books in their German classes, in addition to only slightly shorter ones in their other subjects such as English, French or philosophy. I could not help thinking of the anecdote about Woody Allen's experience with speed reading: in reply to the question about what he remembered of Tolstoy's *War and Peace*, which he had read in two and a half hours, Allen is said to have answered, "It was about some Russians". Regardless of how we view the issue of a literary canon, teachers must object to proposals which accentuate *quantity* and which lead students to tick off books like items on a shopping list. To provide learners in schools and universities with effective reading instruction, one that stimulates mental activity and personal involvement, we should insist on *quality.* It is not the quality of the books I am concerned about, but the quality of the reading experience, which makes it necessary to employ different approaches for different purposes.

To round off this article, I would like to recapitulate three steps teachers can take to make the reading of books more attractive: 1. Reading out loud and reciting in class, a long neglected practice, is worth considering because it improves meaningful reading and involves the entire group of learners in an enjoyable activity which can sensitize them to enjoy poetic language. 2. There must be room for extensive reading which does not entail textual analysis and interpretation. Students select books of their own choice and share their experiences in a monthly "review lesson". 3. Many learners will find intensive or close reading a demanding task especially if they have difficulty concentrating. Rather than abandoning reasonable expectations altogether, their teachers can help them acquire textual competence through reading, interpreting and reflecting critically upon a small number of selected books. Instructing learners on how to use annotations and logs provides teachers with the opportunity of motivating and supporting learners in summoning up the discipline which is required for demanding tasks.

Learners who have been shown how to read books efficiently receive the best possible preparation for the challenges other media will confront them with. Rather than letting waves of sounds and images and an unstoppable flow of information wash over them they can follow spoken, visual and electronic texts actively and analytically. Thus the call for sophisticated reading instruction based on the use of the book should not be confused with nostalgic longing for late 19th century teaching methods. On the contrary, by insisting on the use of books in reading instruction we acknowledge the importance of media literacy in contributing to the development of its principal components: the active and the analytical handling of information. It is a literacy of this quality which young people need to be able to face the 21st century independently and intelligently.

Notes:

1 Among the many publications about reading habits, some of the more recent are Heinz Bonfadelli: "Lesen und Fernsehen – Lesen oder Fernsehen?" – In Bodo Franzmann et al. (Eds.): *Auf den Schultern von Gutenberg. Medienökologische Perspektiven der Fernsehgesellschaft.* Berlin & München, 1995, pp. 229-240; Günter Burger: "Fremdsprachlicher Literaturunterricht und die Erkenntnisse der Leseverhaltensforschung", *Praxis des neusprachlichen Unterrichts* 1, 1996, 3-8; Aimée Dorr & Craig Brannon: "Media Education in American Schools at the End of the Twentieth Century". – In *Medienkompetenz als Herausforderung an Schule und Bildung.* Ein deutsch-amerikanischer Dialog. Kompendium zu einer Konferenz der Bertelsmann Stiftung vom 18. bis 20. März 1992 in Gütersloh. Gütersloh, 1992, pp. 69-103; Bettina Hurrelmann: "Lesen als Schlüssel zur Medienkultur". – In *Medienkompetenz als Herausforderung an Schule und Bildung.* pp. 249-265; Ulrich Saxer: "Medien als Gesellschaftsgestalter". – In *Medienkompetenz als Herausforderung an Schule und Bildung,* pp. 21-31; Ulrich Saxer: "Lesen als Problemlösung. Sieben Thesen". – In Franzmann: *Auf den Schultern von Gutenberg,* pp. 264-268; Spiegel-Verlag & Stiftung Lesen (Ed.): *Jahrbuch Lesen '95.* Fakten und Trends. Hamburg / Mainz, 1995; Stiftung Lesen (Ed.): *Lesen zum Erlebnis machen.* Hinweise, Tips und Informationen zur Leseförderung. Mainz, 1994.

2 Cf. Spiegel-Verlag & Stiftung Lesen (Eds.): *Jahrbuch Lesen '95*, pp. 55-87; Dieter Baacke, Uwe Sander & Ralf Vollbrecht: *Lebenswelten sind Medienwelten.* Opladen, 1990, pp. 246-248.

3 Cf. Bonfadelli: "Lesen und Fernsehen...", p. 230; Saxer: "Medien als Gesellschaftsgestalter", p. 80.

4 Cf. Baacke, Sander & Vollbrecht: *Lebenswelten sind Medienwelten*, p. 248.

5 Cf. Günter Burger: "Fremdsprachlicher Literaturunterricht und die Erkenntnisse der Leseverhaltensforschung", *Praxis des neusprachlichen Unterrichts* 1, 1996, 5.

6 Steven Pinker: *The Language Instinct.* The New Science of Language and Mind. London, 1995, p. 159.

7 Irvine Welsh: *Trainspotting*, London, 1993.

8 For a detailed discussion of learning and reading strategies see Anita Wenden & Joan Rubin (Eds.): *Learner Strategies in Language Learning.* Englewood Cliffs, 1987; Jürgen Donnerstag: "Anmerkungen zu einem integrativen Modell fremdsprachlichen literarischen Lesens". – In Wilfried Gienow & Karlheinz Hellwig (Eds.): *Prozeßorientierte Mediendidaktik im Fremdsprachenunterricht.* Frankfurt am Main, 1993, pp. 59-71; media specific effects on the reception process are discussed e.g. in Gert Rickheit: "Verstehen und Verständlichkeit von Sprache". – In Bernd Spillner (Ed.): *Sprache: Verstehen und Verständlichkeit.* Kongreßbeiträge zur 25. Jahrestagung der Gesellschaft für Angewandte Linguistik GAL e.v., Frankfurt am Main, 1995, p. 17.

9 Cf. e.g. Kultusministerium des Landes Nordrhein-Westfalen (Ed.): *Richtlinien und Lehrpläne für das Gymnasium – Sekundarstufe I – in Nordrhein-Westfalen. Englisch.* Frechen, 1993, pp. 149-153; Ministerium für Bildung, Jugend und Sport des Landes Brandenburg (Ed.): *Vorläufiger Rahmenplan. Englisch. Gymnasiale Oberstufe. Sekundarstufe II.* Potsdam, 1992, pp. 26-28.

10 Cf. Ansgar Nünning: "Literatur ist, wenn das Lesen wieder Spaß macht!", *Der Fremdsprachliche Unterricht. Englisch* 27, 1997, 4-12.

11 Cf. e.g. Lothar Bredella & Werner Delanoy (Ed.): *Challenges of Literary Texts in the Foreign Language Classroom*. Tübingen, 1996; Daniela Caspari: *Kreativität im Umgang mit literarischen Texten im Fremdsprachenunterricht: theoretische Studien und unterrichtspraktische Erfahrungen*. Frankfurt, 1994; Susan Hackman: *Responding in Writing*. The use of exploratory writing in the literature classroom. Sheffield, 31995.

12 Cf. Gustav René Hocke: *Das europäische Tagebuch*. Wiesbaden & München, 1978; Helga Levend: "Mein liebes Tagebuch", *Psychologie Heute*, Juni 1996, 52-55.

13 Cf. Hackman, op.cit., p. 3.

14 Cf. Bärbel Mosner: "Das literarische Leser-Lerner-Tagebuch. Ein Lernverfahren für den handlungsorientierten Englischunterricht", *Praxis des neusprachlichen Unterrichts* 2, 1997, 154-164.

15 Herbert Geisen (Ed.): *William Shakespeare. Romeo and Juliet & Romeo und Julia*. Stuttgart, 1994.

16 Cf. e.g. Liesel Hermes: "Learning Logs als Instrumente der Selbstkontrolle und als Evaluation in literaturwissenschaftlichen Proseminaren". – In Wolfgang Börner & Klaus Vogel (Eds.): *Der Text im Fremdsprachenunterricht*. Bochum, 1995, pp. 85-98.

17 Ministerium für Bildung, Jugend und Sport des Landes Brandenburg (Ed.), op.cit., p. 35.

18 Robert Scholes: *Textual Power*. Literary Theory and the Teaching of English. New Haven and London, 1985, p. 20. Cf. also Michael Wendt: *Konstruktivistische Fremdsprachendidaktik*. Lerner- und handlungsorientierter Fremdsprachenunterricht aus neuer Sicht. Tübingen, 1996, pp. 72-84.

19 Cf. Wolfgang Iser: *Der Akt des Lesens*. Theorie ästhetischer Wirkung. München, 41994, pp. 50f.

20 Freese makes a clear distinction between the two types of readers; cf. Peter Freese: "Textanalyse oder Rezeptionsgespräch? Zu einer Kontroverse der gegenwärtigen Literaturdidaktik", *Englisch Amerikanische Studien*. Zeitschrift für Unterricht, Wissenschaft und Politik 1, 1986, 53.

21 Cf. Christiane Kallenbach: "Das Konzept der subjektiven Theorien aus fremdsprachendidaktischer Sicht". – In Lothar Bredella & Herbert Christ (Eds.): *Didaktik des Fremdverstehens*. Tübingen, 1995, pp. 81-96; Irene Oftering: "Wie begegnen Schülerinnen und Schüler einem fremden Text?" – In Bredella & Christ (Eds.): op. cit., pp. 97-111; cf. also Lothar Bredella & Werner Delanoy (Eds.): *Challenges of Literary Texts in the Foreign Language Classroom*. Tübingen, 1996.

22 As quoted from Hermes: "Learning Logs...". op. cit., p. 91.

23 Pam Gilbert: *Writing, Schooling and Deconstruction. From Voice to Text in the Classroom*. London, 1989.

24 Hackman, op.cit., p. 72.

25 "Der deutsche Literatur-Kanon. Was sollen Schüler lesen? DIE ZEIT-Umfrage (1)", DIE ZEIT Nr. 21, 16. März 1997, pp. 50,51.

Bibliography:

Baacke, Dieter, Uwe Sander & Ralf Vollbrecht: *Lebenswelten sind Medienwelten*. Opladen, 1990.

Bonfadelli, Heinz: "Lesen und Fernsehen – Lesen oder Fernsehen?" – In Bodo Franzmann et al. (Eds.): *Auf den Schultern von Gutenberg*. Medienökologische Perspektiven der Fernsehgesellschaft, Berlin / München, 1995, pp. 229-240.

Bredella, Lothar & Werner Delanoy (Eds.): *Challenges of Literary Texts in the Foreign Language Classroom*. Tübingen, 1996.

Burger, Günter: "Fremdsprachlicher Literaturunterricht und die Erkenntnisse der Leseverhaltensforschung", *Praxis des neusprachlichen Unterrichts* 1, 1996, 3-8.

Caspari, Daniela: *Kreativität im Umgang mit literarischen Texten im Fremdsprachenunterricht: theoretische Studien und unterrichtspraktische Erfahrungen*. Frankfurt, 1994.

Donnerstag, Jürgen: "Anmerkungen zu einem integrativen Modell fremdsprachlichen literarischen Lesens". – In Wilfried Gienow & Karlheinz Hellwig (Eds.): *Prozeßorientierte Mediendidaktik im Fremdsprachenunterricht.* Frankfurt am Main, 1993, pp. 59-71.

---: "Kognitive Strategien literarischen Lesens in der Fremdsprache". – In Uwe Multhaup & Dieter Wolff (Eds.): *Prozeßorientierung in der Fremdsprachendidaktik*. Frankfurt am Main, 1992, pp. 142-156.

Dorr, Aimée & Craig Brannon: "Media Education in American Schools at the End of the Twentieth Century". – In *Medienkompetenz als Herausforderung an Schule und Bildung*. Ein deutsch-amerikanischer Dialog. Kompendium zu einer Konferenz der Bertelsmann Stiftung vom 18. bis 20. März 1992 in Gütersloh. Gütersloh, 1992, pp. 69-103.

Freese, Peter: "Textanalyse oder Rezeptionsgespräch? Zu einer Kontroverse der gegenwärtigen Literaturdidaktik", *Englisch Amerikanische Studien*. Zeitschrift für Unterricht, Wissenschaft und Politik 1, 1986, 50-65.

Geisen, Herbert (Ed.): *William Shakespeare. Romeo and Juliet & Romeo und Julia.* Stuttgart, 1994.

Gilbert, Pam: *Writing, Schooling and Deconstruction. From Voice to Text in the Classroom.* London, 1989.

Hackman, Susan: *Responding in Writing.* The use of exploratory writing in the literature classroom. Sheffield, [3]1995.

Hermes, Liesel: "Learning Logs als Instrumente der Selbstevaluation in literaturwissenschaftlichen Proseminaren". – In Wolfgang Börner & Klaus Vogel (Eds.): *Der Text im Fremdsprachenunterricht.* Bochum, 1995, pp. 85-98.

Hocke, Gustav René: *Das europäische Tagebuch.* Wiesbaden / München, 1978.

Hurrelmann, Bettina: "Lesen als Schlüssel zur Medienkultur". – In *Medienkompetenz als Herausforderung an Schule und Bildung.* Ein deutsch-amerikanischer Dialog. Kompendium zu einer Konferenz der Bertelsmann Stiftung vom 18. bis 20. März 1992 in Gütersloh. Gütersloh, 1992, pp. 249-265.

Iser, Wolfgang: *Der Akt des Lesens.* Theorie ästhetischer Wirkung. München, [4]1994.

Kallenbach, Christiane: "Das Konzept der subjektiven Theorien aus fremdsprachendidaktischer Sicht". – In Lothar Bredella & Herbert Christ (Eds.): *Didaktik des Fremdverstehens.* Tübingen, 1995, pp. 81-96.

Kultusministerium des Landes Nordrhein-Westfalen (Ed.): *Richtlinien und Lehrpläne für das Gymnasium – Sekundarstufe I – in Nordrhein-Westfalen. Englisch.* Frechen, 1993.

Levend, Helga: "Mein liebes Tagebuch", *Psychologie Heute*, Juni 1996, 52-55.

Ministerium für Bildung, Jugend und Sport des Landes Brandenburg (Ed.): *Vorläufiger Rahmenplan. Englisch. Gymnasiale Oberstufe. Sekundarstufe II.* Potsdam, 1992.

Mosner, Bärbel: "Das literarische Leser-Lerner-Tagebuch. Ein Lernverfahren für den handlungsorientierten Englischunterricht", *Praxis des neusprachlichen Unterrichts* 2, 1997, 154-164.

Nünning, Ansgar: "Literatur ist, wenn das Lesen wieder Spaß macht!", *Der Fremdsprachliche Unterricht. Englisch* 27, 1997, 4-12.

Oftering, Irene: "Wie begegnen Schülerinnen und Schüler einem fremden Text?" – In Lothar Bredella & Herbert Christ (Eds.): *Didaktik des Fremdverstehens.* Tübingen, 1995, pp. 97-111.

Pinker, Steven: *The Language Instinct.* The New Science of Language and Mind. London, 1995.

Rickheit, Gert: "Verstehen und Vertsändlichkeit von Sprache". – In Bernd Spillner (Ed.): *Sprache: Verstehen und Verständlichkeit.* Kongreßbeiträge zur 25. Jahrestagung der Gesellschaft für Angewandte Linguistik GAL e.V., Frankfurt am Main, 1995, pp. 15-30.

Saxer, Ulrich: "Lesen als Problemlösung. Sieben Thesen". – In Bodo Franzmann et al. (Eds.): *Auf den Schultern von Gutenberg.* Medienökologische Perspektiven der Fernsehgesellschaft. Berlin / München, 1995, pp. 264-268.

---: "Medien als Gesellschaftsgestalter". – In *Medienkompetenz als Herausforderung an Schule und Bildung.* Ein deutsch-amerikanischer Dialog. Kompendium zu einer Konferenz der Bertelsmann Stiftung vom 18. bis 20. März 1992 in Gütersloh. Gütersloh, 1992, pp. 21-31.

Scholes, Robert: *Textual Power.* Literary Theory and the Teaching of English. New Haven / London, 1985.

Spiegel-Verlag & Stiftung Lesen (Ed.): *Jahrbuch Lesen 1995. Fakten und Trends.* Hamburg / Mainz, 1995.

Stiftung Lesen (Ed.): *Lesen zum Erlebnis machen.* Hinweise, Tips und Informationen zur Leseförderung. Mainz, 1994.

Welsh, Irvine: *Trainspotting.* London, 1993.

Wenden, Anita & Joan Rubin (Eds.): *Learner Strategies in Language Learning.* Englewood Cliffs, 1987.

Wendt, Michael: *Konstruktivistische Fremdsprachendidaktik.* Lerner- und handlungsorientierter Fremdsprachenunterricht aus neuer Sicht. Tübingen, 1996.

Publications Received

Thiessen, Rudi: *Urbane Sprachen – Proust, Poe, Punks, Baudelaire und der Park. Vier Studien über Blasiertheit und Intelligenz. Eine Theorie der Moderne.* Berlin: Vorwerk 8, 1997. 239 S., DM 48,- (ISBN 3-930916-09-6)

"Oft hat man sie blasiert genannt. Diese lieben, verwöhnten, verwünschten Kinder, diese Süchtigen des Mondes. Aufforderungen (doch anders zu sein), Beschimpfungen (wenn die Aufforderungen nicht fruchteten). Sie blieben blasiert und sie wußten warum. Früh schon hatten sie den Verdacht der Dummheit der Gefühle, und früh schon wollten sie damit sich nicht abfinden. Früh schon hegten sie einen Verdacht gegen die Wirklichkeit einer Welt als Phantom und Konserve. Und so ließen sie sich nicht täuschen durch die vermeintliche Sicherheit des eigenen Gefühls und ahnten, daß keine der Inszenierungen, die sie sich wählten, ihre eigene Kreation war. Also blieb nur Geschwindigkeit, und so wurden sie schnell. Wunder an Geschwindigkeit."

Keiper, Hugo & Christoph Bode, Richard J. Utz (Hrsg.): *Nominalism and Literary Discourse. New Perspectives.* Amsterdam und Atlanta, GA: Rodopi, 1997. (Critical Studies 10) 370 S., ca. DM 60,- (ISBN 90-420-0278-6)

Influential accounts of European cultural history variously suggest that the rise of nominalism and its ultimate victory over realist orientations were highly important factors in the formation of Modern Europe since the later Middle Ages, but particularly the Reformation. Quite probably, this is a simplification of a state of affairs that is in fact more complex, indeed ambiguous. However, if there is any truth in such propositions – which have, after all, been made by many prominent commentators – one may no doubt assume that literary texts will have responded and in turn contributed, in a variety of ways, to these processes of cultural transformation. It seems of considerable interest, therefore, to take a close look at the complex, precarious position which literature, as basically a symbolic mode of signification, held in the perennial struggles and discursive negotiations between the semiotic 'twin paradigms' of nominalism and realism.
This collection of essays (many of them by leading scholars in the field) is a first comprehensive attempt to tackle such issues – by analyzing representative literary texts in terms of their underlying semiotic orientations, specifically of nominalism, but also by studying pertinent historical, theoretical and discursive co(n)texts of such developments in their relation to literary discourse. At the same time, since 'literary nominalism' and 'realism' are conceived as fundamentally aesthetic phenomena provoking a genuinely 'literary' debate over universals', consistent emphasis is placed on the discursive dimension of the texts scrunitized, in an endeavour to re-orient and consolidate an emergent research paradigm which promises to open up entirely new perspectives for the study of literary semiotics, as well as of aesthetics in general. Historical focus is provided by concentrating on the English

situation in the era of transition from late medieval to early modern (c. 1350-1650), but readers will also find contributions on Chrétien de Troyes and Rabelais, as well as on the 'aftermath' of the earlier debates – as exemplified in studies of Locke and (post)modern critical alterations, respectively, which serve to point up the continuing relevance of the issues involved. A substantial introductory essay seeks to develop an overarching theoretical framework for the study of nominalism and literary discourse, in addition to offering an in-depth exploration of the 'nominalism/realism-complex in its relation to literature. An extensive bibliography and index are further features of interest to both specialists and general readers.

Detobel, Robert & Uwe Laugwitz (Hrsg.): *Neues Shakespeare Journal. Bd. 2 Entdeckungen und Fälschungen.* Buchholz in der Nordheide: Verlag Uwe Laugwitz, 1998. 180 S., ca. DM 24,- (ISBN 3-933077-01-X)

"Eine meiner stärksten Überzeugungen ist, daß es völlig falsch und vergeblich ist, in der Lebensgeschichte eines Autors nach dem Zugang zu seinen Werken zu forschen" – diese Worte Tolkiens zitieren die Herausgeber, ebenso wie Alan Poseners Behauptung, es sei "[g]rundsätzlich [...] unmöglich, vom Werk direkt auf den Autor zu schließen". Die Herausgeber hingegen halten dies für *grundsätzlich falsch*, was sie unter anderem anhand eines Aspekts aus Tolkiens Werk begründen. Sie sind der Meinung, "daß von jedem annähernd umfangreichen *Werk* jeden Autors [...] auf das *Leben* dieses Autors geschlossen werden kann". Für einen solchen Schluß müssen zwei Grundvoraussetzungen erfüllt sein: *Verständnis* des Werkes, d.h. eine gewisse Bereitschaft, sich mit etwas Fremdem wie dem Geschriebenen eines anderen Menschen auseinanderzusetzen, ohne dieses vorschnell zu kategorisieren. Die zweite Voraussetzung ist das *Wissen* um die Biographie der Autoren, wovon diese vieles zu Lebzeiten nur ungern preisgeben.
Es geht also um die Verknüpfung von biographischen Realien mit dem Verständnis des Werkes, wenn man das *Rätsel* Shakespeare lösen will – zumindest ansatzweise, denn vieles wird nicht mehr in Erfahrung gebracht werden können. Die Quellen sind aber ungleich vielfältiger als etwa die zur Antike, von deren Literatur ja nur etwa 10% erhalten ist. Wenn man also nicht wird entscheiden können, ob Terenz ein Strohmann für Scipio oder Laelius war, so wird sich doch klären lassen, ob William Shakspeare oder Edward de Vere Shakespeares Werke verfaßten?

Aarts, Jan, Inge de Mönnink & Herman Wekker (Eds.): *Studies in English Language and Teaching. In honour of Flor Arts.* Amsterdam and Atlanta, GA: Rodopi, 1997. 308 S., US-$ 63,- (ISBN 90-420-0304-9)

The present volume is dedicated to Flor Aarts, one of the leading scholars in anglicist linguistics in the Netherlands, a lecturer and professor of English language (Old, Middle and contemporary English) for more than thirty years. He has always been a typical representative of the Dutch, or, perhaps more correctly, the northwest European school in English linguistics. His academic career bridged the period between the late fifties, when philology or historical linguistics were cur-

rent issues of discussion, the sixties and the seventies, focusing on English Transformational Grammar, and the eighties and nineties, with attention centering around language use and corpus data. Another feature characterising Aarts's work is the concern for the pedagogical application of the knowledge accumulated in linguistic research, a topic of unbroken interest in Dutch anglicist studies.
Therefore, as the editors claim, it almost goes without saying that a book dedicated to Flor Aarts does not only contain papers on English language research, but also papers on English language teaching. Correspondingly, it consists of two parts, entitled 'Language' and 'Teaching', respectively. But, likewise appropriately, the line of division between the papers in the two parts is said to be sometimes rather thin, because the interaction between the two themes is so strong – as, indeed, it should be.

Power, Mary & Ulrich Schneider (Eds.): *New Perspectives on Dubliners.* Amsterdam and Atlanta, GA, Rodopi, 1997. (European Joyce Studies 7) 298 S., Paper US-$ 23.50, Bound US-$ 78.50

When *Dubliners* first appeared in 1914, the stories were regarded as something unmistakably new, though not always understood, as they failed to fit into established narratological patterns. But in the course of time, as readers began to realise that *Dubliners* were not merely the early work of the author of outstanding novels but that it was as distinguished as Joyce's later fiction, literature accounted for this fact in the form of books about *Dubliners* from various critical vantage points, scholarly journals, annotated editions, and translations. All these developments prompted the production of the present volume.
It offers pluralism of interpretation in keeping with recent critical developments. The various essays are hoped to extend the readers' knowledge of the stories and to lead to further discussion and debate. The contributors invoke Lacan, Cixous, Deleuze, Girard, Derrida, Jameson, Paul De Man, Hartmann, Lyotard, Foucault and others. The approaches vary from the hermeneutics and supreme good sense of Fritz Senn to the work of Margot Norris and John Gordon in reading *Dubliners* stories through Joyce's later fiction. What is also offered is Marie Dominique Garnier's Feminist Theory, the New Historicism of Carol Schloss, the Discourse Analysis of Ulrich Schneider, the Structuralism of Wolfgang Karrer and Post-Structuralism of Laurent Milesi. Jana Giles, a young creative writer, provides a view of Joyce's editing. If there is any special emphasis in this collection, it lies in corresponding arguments for the cyclical structure of *Dubliners* advanced by Karrer and Power. Karrer makes a strong, reasoned case for the cohesiveness of the first three stories – those of childhood – and Power argues that the stories of public life are more tightly connected than has previously been shown.
Many of the stories in *Dubliners* are discussed, though no special effort is made to be inclusive. "Grace" is the subject of two essays since it is unexpectedly rich and interesting, and has often been overlooked.

Osinski, Jutta: *Einführung in die feministische Literaturwissenschaft.* Berlin/Bielefeld/München: Erich Schmidt Verlag, 1998. 216 S., DM 29,80 (ISBN 3-503-03710-1)

Die feministische Literaturwissenschaft ist ein umstrittenes Fachgebiet, dessen kurze Geschichte geprägt ist von Selbstbehauptungsstrategien gegen Angriffe von außen und internen Flügelkämpfen. Die Positionen sind nicht nur verschieden, sondern zum Teil unvereinbar.

Der Band bietet einen problemgeschichtlichen und systematischen Überblick über Entwicklungen und Tendenzen von den 70er Jahren bis heute. Er stellt sozialhistorische und ideologiekritische Ansätze, *die écriture féminine*, den *French Feminism*, die *Gender Studies* und die Adaption der Diskursanalyse vor.

Die Einführung will nicht feministischer Selbstbestätigung dienen. Sie unterzieht Postulate, Modelle und Interpretationen einer kritischen Überprüfung und versucht, Denkweisen verständlich zu machen, ohne Zustimmungszwang auszuüben.

Brodersen, Kai: *Das römische Britannien: Spuren seiner Geschichte.* Darmstadt: Primus Verlag, 1998. 260 S., DM 42,- (ISBN 3-89678-080-8)

Britannien war seit dem ersten nachchristlichen Jahrhundert fast 400 Jahre lang eine römische Provinz. In diesem Buch läßt der Autor ein lebendiges Bild dieser bedeutenden Epoche der römischen Herrschaft entstehen. Er stellt literarische Quellen wie Caesar's *Commentarii de bello Gallico* vor, übersetzt sie mit vielen hilfreichen Zusätzen und erklärt ausführlich, wie wir diese Texte heute zu verstehen haben. Auch Münzen, Bauwerke und Inschriften präsentiert er in dem vorliegenden Band. Er zeigt, was diese Quellen verraten, wenn man sie richtig zu deuten weiß.

Klaus, H. Gustav & Stephen Knight (Hrsg.): *The Art of Murder: New Essays on Detective Fiction.* Tübingen: Stauffenberg Verlag, 1998. (ZAA Studies 3) 204 S., DM 78,- (ISBN 3-86057-732-8)

Crime fiction has been a major element of Western culture for the last two centuries, but only recently have cultural critics analysed how the many forms of crime fiction reveal the changing anxieties of audiences over time and the manifold ways in which psychic consolation can be offered in the form of a detective. This collection of essays by international scholars focuses on aspects of the development of the genre through to its most recent reformations in the feminist thriller. Expert light is cast on such elusive but important topics as Agatha Christie's linguistic patterns, the style employed by Dashiell Hammett, Raymond Chandler and their followers and the use of chess as a focal motif. *The Art of Murder* thus provides a sense of the range and variation of the crime fiction genre over two hundred years, and also a carefully selected series of penetrating insights into the nature, causes and effects of murderous writing from its origins to the present.

Freiburg, Rudolf & Arno Löffler, Wolfgang Zach (Hrsg.): *Swift: The Enigmatic Dean. Festschrift for Hermann Josef Real.* Tübingen: Stauffenberg Verlag, 1998. (Studies in English and Comparative Literature 12) 324 S., DM 128,- (ISBN 3-86057-312-8)

For more than thirty years Hermann Josef Real has dedicated both his time and energy to the study of the Anglo-Irish satirist Jonathan Swift. As an inspired university teacher Real has filled generations of students with enthusiasm for the Dean of St. Patrick's. As a passionate scholar he enjoys an international reputation of great distinction and has set standards in modern Swift studies with his edition of *The Battle of the Books*, with his monographs and critical commentaries, with his translations and with more than fifty scholarly articles. As the director of the "Ehrenpreis Institute for Swift Studies" he has managed to turn the university of Münster into a stronghold for Swiftian scholarship. *Swift Studies*, the scholarly paper, founded by Real ten years ago has developed into a prestigious forum under his aegis, and has meanwhile become an invaluable instrument for the learned discussion of all questions concerning Swift's life and work. The present Festschrift *Swift: The Enigmatic Dean* honours the academic achievements of Hermann Josef Real. It contains new contributions from friends, colleagues and fellow Swiftians from all over the world.

Gohrband, Detlev & Bruno von Lutz (Hrsg.): *Seeing and Saying: Self-referentiality in British and American Literature.* Frankfurt am Main/Berlin/Bern/New York/Paris/Wien: Peter Lang Verlag, 1998. 215 S., DM 65,- (ISBN 3-631-32236-4)

The perception of the world and the (illusionary) attempts at representing it have been a long-standing concern of self-referential writing. *Seeing and Saying*, the follow-up volume to *Self-Referentiality in 20th Century British and American Poetry*, presents a range of essays dealing with the awareness in literature of the perceptional and representational hazards of saying the world of experience, sight and memory. The writers discussed range from the Renaissance to Post-Modernism, fom Lady Mary Wroth to John Fowles.
Contents: Self-referentiality in historical perspective. Visuality, gender and critical language. Post-modern versions of self-referentiality. Painting, photography and poetry. The politics of evaluation. Images of gods laughing.

Fink, Hermann: *Von* Kuh-Look *bis* Fit for Fun*: Anglizismen in der heutigen deutschen Allgemein- und Werbesprache.* Frankfurt am Main/Berlin/Bern/New York/Paris/Wien: Peter Lang Verlag, 1998. 228 S., DM 69,- (ISBN 3-631-30838-8)

Seit dem Zweiten Weltkrieg hat Amerika einen immensen Einfluß auf die deutsche Sprache und Kultur genommen, der in einer Reihe von Erhebungen quantitativ an Einzelbeispielen untersucht worden ist. Der Band analysiert breitgefächert das tausendfache Anglizismenaufkommen in der illustrierten Zeitschrift, der überregionalen Presse, der Boulevard-Zeitung, der Jugend-Presse und den Werbeschriften. Besonderes Augenmerk gilt dabei auch der sprachlichen Kreativität der entlehnten englischen Wörter am Beispiel des Modeanglizismus *Look* sowie der in der deutschen Werbung verwendeten Angloamerikanismen vielfältigster Prägung und kommentiert deren Sinn und Unsinn.

Achilles, Jochen & Carmen Birkle (Hrsg.): *(Trans)Formations of Cultural Identity in the English-Speaking World*. Heidelberg: Universitätsverlag C. Winter, 1998. (Anglistische Forschung 251) 324 S., DM 98,- (ISBN 3-8253-0565-1)

The obvious interethnic and intercultural problems in the Americas, Asia, Africa, and Europe have generated a renewed and widespread interest in the developments, theories, and expressions of cultural identities. The different perspectives of the contributions to this volume converge in three thematic clusters: political patterns and constellations, gender role definitions, and representational modes, all of which shape and influence the generation and transformation of cultural identities. The essays which deal with the political dimension of cultural identities address the conflict between unitary essentialism and multicultural hybridity. They agree on both the untenability of essentialist positions and on the danger of confusion, shapelessness, and loss, inherent in identities which are based on multiplicity alone. They also show the centrality of linguistic and textual structures for a resolution of these dialectics. Common to the essays which focus on gender is the interest in an ethics which allows for women's emancipation but does not lose touch with reality. Concepts such as gift and love, advocacy, and the coexistence of tradition and progress are tentative suggestions of such ethical norms. The essays which primarily deal with modes of the representation and mediation of cultural identities deepen and expand the emphasis on textuality which is also noticeable in the other contributions.

Dölvers, Horst: *Fables Less and Less Fabulous*. London: Golden Cokkerel Press, 1997. 208 S., £ 29,- (ISBN 0-87413-584-2)

This study examines more than one hundred fables in prose and verse, most of them original in content, some highly original in form. Horst Dölvers refutes the assumption that the fable declined in popularity after 1800 and the days of La Fontaine, Swift, Gay, and Lessing. According to Dölvers, the "Fox of Fable", as Lord Lytton called him, stayed very much alive in emblematic fables with verbal pictures, in parables and fanciful reveries.

Most of the texts studied in this book are taken from Victorian collections and poetry anthologies, and are presumably unknown. An extensive documentation presents verse fables according to the different functions they served – in humor, satire, and education, religious and philosophical speculation, and as drawing-room entertainment full of erotic innuendo. Emblematic fables in verse were at first clearly typological in their Christian reading of worldly things. Then, mirroring the intellectual history of the times, they evolved in the course of the century toward religious and philosophical scepticism, until they turned into a plain denial of life as meaningful.

This book's second part focuses on three Victorian books, applying semiotics (including theories of discourse). A review essay of Lord Lytton's *Fables in Song* (1874) by Robert Louis Stevenson contains perceptive remarks on the "post-Darwinian fable", a newly developing variant turning away from "old stories of wise animals or foolish men" to confront "truths that are a matter of bitter concern". Lytton's reveries deserve rediscovery as narratives that skilfully manipulate their readers by a hierarchical ordering of discourses – nudging them into ideological positions that, to many readers, must have appeared commonsensical. At the same time, they tend to sap the complacencies of common sense.

A picture book by Walter Cane, an *Aesop* in limericks (1887), shows the illustrator's art as no less Houdinian. For Crane's plates seem designed to escape, by subtle subversion, from mere "picturing" into "picturally pointing", a technique of multiplying signifiers to make them available for social and political interpretations. Finally, Anna Sewell's children's classic *Black Beauty*, if simple, should be read as anything but plain: its speaking silences makes the reader feel that man and beast are divided rather than united by their ability to communicate. The horses, shown as capable of speaking like humans, do not share man's multiplicity of discourses – nor consequently, the duplicity resulting from their use.

Kroner, Bernd & Ulrike Schauer: *Be Prepared: Kopiervorlagen für Vertretungs- und Freiarbeitsstunden im Englischunterricht. Band 1: Klasse 5/6* und *Band 2: Klasse 7/8.* Köln: Aulis Verlag Deubner & Co. KG, 1998. 132 bzw. 152 S., DM je 38,-

Be Prepared bietet fertige Kopiervorlagen für Übungen zu zentralen Inhalten des englischen Sprachunterrichts in den Klassenstufen 5/6 und 7/8 aller Schulformen. Die Einheiten sind so gestaltet, daß sie in Anlehnung etwa an die Grundidee der Freiarbeit von den Schülern in selbständiger Arbeit bewältigt werden können. Grundlegende didaktische Felder wie beispielsweise Wortschatz oder Landeskunde, in besonderem Maße aber der übungsintensive Pflichtbereich der Grammatik, sind in kopierfertigen Arbeitsblättern lehrwerkunabhängig aufbereitet. Somit entfällt für den Lehrer die mühevolle Einarbeitung in die geschlossene Konzeption eines eingeführten Lehrwerkes. Beide Bände gliedern sich jeweils nach didaktischen Schwerpunkten in zahlreichen Übungseinheiten.

Langenscheidt's Power Dictionary. Berlin/München/Wien/Zürich/New York: Langenscheidt-Verlag, 1998. 888 S., DM 29,90 (ISBN 3-468-13112-7)

Das neue Langenscheidt *Power Dictionary* ist ein innovatives Englisch-Wörterbuch, das sich hauptsächlich an jugendliche Lerner mit deutscher Muttersprache richtet. Diese Zielgruppe wird auf vielfältige Weise angesprochen: Das Wörterbuch enthält ca. 66.000 Stichwörter in beiden Sprachrichtungen (Deutsch-Englisch/Englisch-Deutsch), wobei der Aufbau – dem jugendlichen Benutzer angemessen – unterschiedlich ist: der englisch-deutsche Teil enthält vor allem Stichwörter aus alltags- und schulrelevanten Bereichen mit knappen Erläuterungen und Hinweisen zur Fehlervermeidung. Im deutsch-englischen Teil besteht eine gezielte Stichwortauswahl, die sich auf das Vokabular des jungen Lerners konzentriert. Wissenswertes zu idiomatischen Übersetzungen, Anwendungsbeispiele, Warnungen vor Stolpersteinen und andere Zusatzinformationen werden gegeben. Verständliche Erklärungen, benutzerfreundliche Lautschriftangaben sowie eine deutliche Hervorhebung aller Stichwörter schafft für den Lerner große Übersichtlichkeit. Der Verzicht auf Abkürzungen, Sonderzeichen und für den Schüler irrelevante Informationen erleichtert dem jugendlichen Lerner den Umgang mit dem Wörterbuch. Glossen mit sprachlichen, aussprachebezogenen und landeskundlichen Informationen, Farbillustriationen und ein Anhang runden das Bild ab.

Anschriften der AutorInnen

Dr. Jens P. Becker, Englisches Seminar, Christian-Albrechts-Universität, Olshausenstr. 40, 24098 Kiel (Germany)

Dr. Helmut Brammerts, Seminar für Sprachlehrforschung, Ruhr-Universität Bochum, Universitätsstr. 150, 44780 Bochum (Germany)

Giovanna Cascio, Dept. of English Language and Linguistics, University of Sheffield, 5 Shearwood Road, Sheffield S10 2TD (United Kingdom)

Prof. Dr. Hans-Jürgen Diller, Englisches Seminar, Ruhr-Universität Bochum, Universitätsstr. 150, 44780 Bochum (Germany)

Dr. Evelina Graur, 1 University Street, Faculty of Letters and Sciences, RO-5800 Suceava (Rumania)

Prof. Dr. Rolf Herwig, Friedrich-Schiller-Universität, Ernst-Abbe-Platz 4, 07740 Jena (Germany)

Dr. Marianne Hundt, Englisches Seminar I und II, Albert-Ludwigs-Universität, Rempartstr. 15, 79085 Freiburg im Breisgau (Germany)

Dr. Geert Jacobs, UFSIA – University of Antwerp, ICTL, Prinsstraat 13, B-2000 Antwerp (Belgium)

Dr. Helmuth Küffner, Fern-Universität Hagen, In der Krone 17, 58084 Hagen (Germany)

Prof. Dr. Ewald Mengel, Universität Bayreuth, Englische Literaturwissenschaft, Postfach 101251, 95440 Bayreuth (Germany)

Bärbel Mosner, Englisches Seminar, Ruhr-Universität Bochum, Universitätsstr. 150, 44780 Bochum (Germany)

Carmen Müller, Universität Bayreuth, Englische Literaturwissenschaft, Postfach 101251, 95440 Bayreuth (Germany)

Ingo Neubert, Humboldtstr. 30/62, 72766 Reutlingen (Germany)

Prof. Dr. Fritz W. Neumann, Universität Erfurt, Institut für Anglistik, Philologische Fakultät, Nordhäuserstr. 63, 99089 Erfurt (Germany)

Karsten Pedersen, Ph.D., Asgårdsvej 96, 4100 Ringsted, (Denmark)

Tobias Rademann, MA, Englisches Seminar, Ruhr-Universität Bochum, Universitätsstr. 150,44780 Bochum (Germany)

Dr. Mike Reynolds, Dept. of English Language and Linguistics, University of Sheffield, 5 Shearwood Road, Sheffield S 10 2TD (United Kingdom)

Dr. Andrea Sand, Albert-Ludwigs-Universität, Englisches Seminar I und II, Rempartstr. 15, 79085 Freiburg im Breisgau (Germany)

Dr. Susanne Schmid, Freie Universität Berlin, FB Neuphilologie, WE 1, Gosslerstr. 2-4, 14195 Berlin (Germany)

Kristina Schneider, MA, Institut flir Anglistik/Amerikanistik, Universität Rostock, August-Bebel-Str. 28, 18051 Rostock (Germany)

Dr. Elena Semino, Dept. of Linguistics and Modern English Language, University of Lancaster, Bailrigg, Lancaster, LAI 4YT (United Kingdom)

Prof. Dr. Mick Short, Dept. of Linguistics and Modern English Language, University of Lancaster, Bailrigg, Lancaster, LAI 4YT (United Kingdom)

Prof. Dr. Anne-Marie Simon-Vandenbergen, Universiteit Gent, Vakgroep Engels, Rozier 44, B-9000 Gent (Belgium)

Prof. Dr. Friedrich Ungerer, Institut ftir Anglistik/Amerikanistik, Universität Rostock, August-Bebel-Str. 28, 18051 Rostock (Germany)

Prof. Dr. Torben Vestergaard, Dept. of Languages and Intercultural Studies, Aalborg University, Kroghsstraede 3, DK-9220 Aalborg 0 (Denmark)

Dr. Dieter Wessels, Englisches Seminar, Ruhr-Universität Bochum, Universitätsstr. 150, 44780 Bochum (Germany)

Dr. Michael White, Escuela Universitaria de Ciencias Empresariales, Universidad Complutense de Madrid, Calle Islas Felipinas 3, E-28003 Madrid (Spain)

Martin Wynne, Dept. of Linguistics and Modern English Language, University of Lancaster, Bailrigg, Lancaster, LAI 4YT (United Kingdom)